DARING TO DREAM

Law and the Humanities
for Elementary Schools

DARING TO DREAM

Law and the Humanities for Elementary Schools

Compiled and edited by
LYNDA CARL FALKENSTEIN
and
CHARLOTTE C. ANDERSON

ABA Special Committee on Youth Education for Citizenship

Supported by a grant from the National Endowment for the Humanities

Printed in the United States of America
Produced by the ABA Press

Standard Book Number: 0-89707-028-3
Library of Congress Catalog Card Number: 80–67087

The American Bar Association
1155 East 60th Street, Chicago, Illinois 60637

Why "Daring to Dream"? Because children do and we must. We must have the vision to imagine a world far more equitable, just, and humane than the one we know. We must have the courage to develop and implement ways of creating that world—both for ourselves and for our children. We must dare to dream of a better world. It is the premise of this book and the project out of which it grows that creative law and humanities programs in elementary schools are one possible means of realizing that dream.

ABOUT THE BOOK

The majority of the articles in this book were written for a symposium held in May 1978. Others were specially commissioned to round out the final compilation. Readers will discover that much of the material found here is applicable to secondary as well as elementary schools. It also should be noted that the ideas expressed here—like all worthwhile ideas—are evolving.

ABOUT THE EDITORS

Lynda Carl Falkenstein is Associate Professor and Director, Law-related Education, at Portland State University, Portland, Oregon. She served as Coordinator of the American Bar Association's project, Law and the Humanities: Designs for Elementary Education, during the project's initial 2 years of development. She received her Ph.D. degree from Stanford University, where she focused on factors affecting implementation of innovations in curriculum. At present, Ms. Falkenstein's efforts are directed toward research and program and curriculum development as they relate to teaching about law in an international context.

Charlotte C. Anderson is currently Coordinator of the American Bar Association's project, Law and the Humanities: Designs for Elementary Education. Prior to this appointment she was on the faculty of the School of Education, Northwestern University, where she directed the undergraduate teacher education program. She received her Ph.D. degree from Northwestern University, focusing on elementary social studies curriculum development and teacher education. She is a major consultant and author of the K–6 social studies program *Windows on Our World*, published by Houghton Mifflin Co.

CONTENTS

FOREWORD

R. Freeman Butts

We are just emerging from a decade which Sydney E. Ahlstrom, Yale historian, has aptly called the "Traumatic Years," when "the nation's sense of purpose fell to its lowest ebb" (1978). He refers to issues of race and racism, war and imperialism, sex and sexism, exploitation and environmentalism, and government and the misuse of power. Robert Lekachman, City University economist, says, "The public mood is sour, cynical, and self-serving" (1978). In November 1978 John Herbers of the *New York Times,* after surveying a large number of political leaders and scholars, found that they went well beyond what the opinion polls have been telling us for several years. Not only has the public's confidence in government become eroded and subordinated by self-seeking and privatism, but the government itself is being fragmented and Balkanized. Single-issue politics are weakening the political parties, the lobbying by special-interest groups far outweighs that of public-interest groups, and the moral authority of the presidency and government at all levels has reached a low point: "There is a consensus that no coalition of interests is strong enough to set priorities for the overall public good . . . to root out inefficiency and corruption in government programs, and to inspire confidence in political leadership."

President Carter himself echoed these findings in the summer of 1979. Faced with the sudden crunch of the gasoline crisis, President Carter focused on this "crisis of confidence" in his energy address to the nation just before the shake-up of his cabinet.

The end-of-the-decade mood in the field of education is no less gloomy. The educational graphs all seem to point downward: decline in school budgets, decline in teaching jobs, decline in teachers' morale, decline in student test scores, decline of confidence in public schools, and decline of innovation in the face of "back to the basics," minimal-competence testing, and accountability. Some things do seem to be rising among students: violence, crime, vandalism, teen-age pregnancies, drugs, and indiscipline.

Also rising are a mood of pessimism about the value of public education, on one hand, and a preoccupation with all sorts of educational "alternatives," on the other. Proponents of Proposition 13 in California gave little thought to what sudden and drastic tax cuts would do to public schools. Advocates of a rash of other proposals, however, have given considerable thought to the advantages of strengthening private schools with public money through tuition credits or through voucher systems.

R. Freeman Butts is Professor Emeritus of Teachers College, Columbia University, and recently Professor of Education at San Jose State University. He is author of *The Revival of Civic Learning,* to be published by the Phi Delta Kappa Education Foundation.

Again, California seems to be taking the lead by an initiative to amend its state constitution to legitimize what I have called the "private pursuit of the public purse" by embedding a full-scale voucher system in the state constitution. I believe the movement represents a particularly formidable alliance between privatism in politics and excessive pluralism in education. Curiously, the voucher idea also seems to be a popular solution in the eyes not only of conservative politicians and neoconservative scholars in the academic world, but also of radical-left revisionist historians and critics in the educational profession itself.

Without belaboring further the malaise of the 1970s about education or lengthening the litany of examples of pessimism, let me turn to the challenge of the 1980s. I believe that one of the most helpful means of combatting privatism in politics and excessive pluralism in education is what I have called a "revival of the civic learning." There are many signs of a revival of the original civic goal of education which the founders of the Republic proposed 200 years ago as one means of meeting the "Critical Period" of the 1780s. Then, as now, the founders believed that their era was marked by a drastic decline in the sense of obligation for the common good and by an accelerating rise in aggressive self-interest. Their sense of crisis led them to frame the Constitution as the basic instrument of a new and more unified political community devoted to institutionalizing the Revolutionary ideals of liberty, equality, justice, and personal obligation for the public good.

As for education, the predominant institutions of 200 years ago were private schools, religious schools, proprietary schools, and a host of "alternatives" in education designed to appeal to a diversity of religions, communities, and social classes. The founders believed, however, that in the long run the cohesive civic goal of education should be given the highest priority, over literacy for its own sake, or preparation for a job, or entrance to college, or individual self-development. They expressed the faith that public schools would become a major force in forging *Unum* out of *Pluribus* in education, as the Constitution would do in politics.

Now we face the decade of the 1980s, which surely promises to be not just another "critical period" to be viewed with alarm by ivory-tower scholars. A public deeply wounded by the impacts of the "traumatic years" of the 1960s and 1970s is now being belabored by the twin hammer blows of rampant inflation and disappearing energy resources. This combination poses a historic turning point for American education, a genuine crisis. It may lead to a crescendo of attacks upon public education in favor of fragmentation of the political community. Or it may very well induce the public to support genuine wide-scale attempts to enable the schools to provide children and youth with a much better common preparation for coping with the threats to the historic ideals and values of our democratic political community. One sign of this willingness is the rapidly expanding growth of law-related education in secondary schools, amply documented in the volumes sponsored by the American Bar Association's Special Committee on Youth Education for Citizenship and elsewhere.

The genius of *this* book is that it represents a major effort to focus on improving civic learning in the elementary schools, long before children reach high school. And, best of all, it signalizes an attempt to draw upon two great cultural traditions in such a way as to make this revival not just another fad to be "added on" to an overburdened curriculum. The goal of the project which the papers in this book helped launch in 1978 is to call upon the humanities as well as the law to revivify civic learning in elementary schools.

The humanities are precious repositories of a wide range of written expressions dealing with the quality of human experience as it has been embodied in the ideas, values, aspirations, achievements, and failures of humankind over long periods of time. The law is the result of a historical and continuing process whereby rules are deliberately formulated for living in and governing an ordered society. At its best, the law seeks to establish an operational framework within which humane ideas and values may be achieved. In its most general sense, then, this project will try to design a variety of curricula for the schools which will provide a sequence of experiences selected and organized to enable children of elementary school age to live morally, creatively, and effectively as persons who are becoming citizens of a democratically ordered society.

This undertaking is enormously sensitive and complicated. It requires the best efforts of those trained in the scholarship of the humanities and of the law, along with those expert in knowledge about the growth and development of young children and in curriculum building. This is why I speak of a "revival of civic learning." I wish to call to mind the multiple connotations of "learning."

Historians have long written about the "revival of learning" of the twelfth and thirteenth centuries as a time when the discovery of the Greek and Latin classics helped initiate a remarkable intellectual and creative renaissance in western Europe. "Learning" thus brings to mind the corpus of knowledge and scholarship associated with the humanities and the law which can inform and challenge the intellectual and creative talents as well as the moral and legal pursuits of humankind. Ideas, concepts, and values of justice, freedom, equality, authority, morality, obligation, due process, privacy, participation, loyalty, pluralism, human rights, and the common good are dealt with in both traditions. The humanities and the law may have differences of approach to such ideas and values, but they also have commonalities which should be sought and reenforced where appropriate.

But "learning" also connotes educators' concern for the ways children grow, develop, and learn at different stages of their cognitive, affective, moral development. Vast resources of recent research in the social and behavioral sciences are available to illuminate the ways in which learning takes place among different individuals and in different group settings. The task is thus to draw upon such psychological and behavioral research as well as upon studies in the humanities and the law in order to design experiences for children that will (1) motivate and involve them in their own learning experiences in such a way as to (2) develop the values, knowledge, judgments, and skills required for coping with and contributing to an increasingly complex society devoted to a democratic ethos.

In December 1977, Charles Frankel, an eloquent spokesman and leader in the humanities and a longtime colleague and friend of mine at Columbia University, wrote: "In every generation in which the humanities have shown vitality, they . . . have performed an essential *public, civic, educational* function: the criticism and reintegration of the ideas and the values of cultures dislocated from their traditions and needing a new sense of meaning. This is what humanistic scholars did in fifth- and fourth-century Athens, in the thirteenth century . . . in the Renaissance, and in the nineteenth century. Can they perform this function now?"

I hope that this volume and the project it represents will indeed be able to mobilize resources from the humanities and the law to enable elementary schools to perform their "essential public, civic, educational function" and thus to give a new sense of meaning to the democratic ideas and values which have been dislocated from our traditional civic community. I hope that we can signalize here a revival of civic learning for the 1980s as a symbol of our determination to give an affirmative answer to the question posed by a distinguished humanities scholar who with his wife was the victim of a brutal and wanton homicide in the privacy of their home in the spring of 1979. I hope that such a tragic violation of the deepest values of both the humanities and the law will heighten our urgent resolve to strengthen the ties that could bind up the wounds of the 1970s by drawing upon the best of the humanities, the law, and education on behalf of a more just and free political community during the 1980s.

REFERENCES

Ahlstrom, S. E. National trauma and changing religious values. *Daedalus,* 1978 (Winter), p. 20.
Frankel, C. The academy enshrouded. *Change,* 1977 (December), p. 64.
Herbers, J. Governing America. *New York Times,* November 12, 1978.
Lekachman, R. Proposition 13 and the new conservatism. *Change,* 1978 (September), p. 27.

NEH PROGRAMS IN EDUCATION AND THE LAW

John Hale

Emerson wrote in the essay *Self-Reliance* that "an institution is the lengthened shadow of one man"—a statement steeped in humanistic sentiment. More recently institutions, especially federal ones, have been described in naturalistic or mechanistic terms. The movement from humanistic to nonhumanistic descriptive models would seem to be symptomatic of an alienation from larger institutions, even those of which one is a part. This distance may be a function of a lack of understanding of how institutions begin, grow, and change, and how human intelligence and initiative affect the course of institutional evolution. Explaining the "ways" of an institution is, at times, a task requiring Miltonic talents. In most instances, however, an examination of the background and purposes of the institution straightforwardly reveals its inner dynamics.

In the case of one federal agency, the National Endowment for the Humanities (NEH), the processes of development and decision making seem to be both rational and humanistic. This makes the task of explaining future directions in one particular area—law-related education—a relatively simple matter. It seems appropriate in an examination of institutional operations and law-related education to trace broadly the NEH's pertinent legislative history in order to illumine prospects for future work in this field.

The NEH was created in 1965 by an act of Congress which stemmed from a concern that the United States' position of world leadership be based on achievement "in the realm of ideas and of the spirit," as well as on "superior power, wealth, and technology." Congressional action in authorizing the NEH was directly responsive to the findings of the Commission on the Humanities, created in a joint effort by the American Council of Learned Societies, the Council of Graduate Schools in the United States, and the United Chapters of Phi Beta Kappa. The 20-person commission was headed by Barnaby Keeney, then president of Brown University; it began work in early 1963 and its final report was dated April 30, 1964. The report was brief (its statement and recommendations totaled only 15 pages) and pointed. It argued for the establishment of a National Humanities Foundation and made recommendations as to its scope and functions.

The first proposed legislation designed to carry out the commission's recommendations was introduced in August 1964 by Congressman William S. Moorhead of Pennsylvania. His bill followed the report of the commission closely, although it also

John H. Hale is a Program Officer for Elementary and Secondary Education of the National Endowment for the Humanities. He is a graduate of Duke University in English and classical studies and, prior to coming to the Endowment in 1976, was a free-lance writer.

drew upon certain provisions of the National Science Foundation Act of 1950; this bill largely provided the prototype for subsequent legislative proposals in Congress.

In a speech at Brown University in September 1964, President Johnson in effect endorsed the commission's proposals. Subsequently, in the first week of the Eighty-ninth Congress, 76 bills were introduced to establish a National Humanities Foundation, the number of cosponsors eventually growing to 105 members of the House and 40 members of the Senate. On September 29, 1965, the National Foundation on the Arts and the Humanities Act was signed into law by the president. The legislation created coequal endowments for the arts and the humanities, which operated autonomously from the beginning.

In the authorizing act, Congress set forth a declaration of purposes. Insofar as it relates to the humanities, it states that:

The encouragement and support of national progress and scholarship in the humanities, while primarily a matter for private and local initiative, is also an appropriate matter for Federal concern.

A high civilization must give full value and support to man's scholarly and cultural activity, in addition to science and technology.

It is necessary and appropriate for the Federal Government to assist humanities programs conducted by local and state organizations and by private agencies.

It is appropriate for the Federal Government to sustain a climate encouraging freedom of thought and the material conditions facilitating the release of creative talent in the humanities.

The world leadership which has come to the United States must be founded upon world-wide respect for this nation's high qualities as a leader in the realm of ideas and of the spirit.

In order to implement these findings it is desirable to establish the National Endowment for the Humanities.

The act then provides this definition:

The term "humanities" includes, but is not limited to, the study of the following: language, both modern and classical; linguistics; literature; history; jurisprudence; philosophy; archaeology; comparative religion; ethics; the history, criticism, theory, and practice of the arts; those aspects of the social sciences which have humanistic content and employ humanistic methods; and the study and application of the humanities to the human environment with particular attention to the relevance of the humanities to the current conditions of national life.

Specifically, the NEH has received legal authorization to:

1) develop and encourage the pursuit of a national policy for the promotion of progress and scholarship in the humanities;
2) initiate and support research and programs to strengthen the teaching potential of the United States in the humanities by making arrangements (including contracts, grants, loans, and other forms of assistance) with individuals or groups to support such activities;
3) award fellowships and grants to institutions or individuals for training and workshops in the humanities;
4) foster the interchange of information in the humanities;
5) foster, through grants or other arrangements with groups, education in and public understanding and appreciation of the humanities;
6) support the publication of scholarly works in the humanities; and
7) insure that the benefit of its programs will also be available to (American) citizens where such programs would otherwise be unavailable due to geographic or economic reasons.

The first item on this list of authorized activities was the subject of some discussion during the past year. After an assessment of the operations, policies, and procedures of the NEH, the Surveys and Investigations Staff of the House Appropriations Committee produced a report critical of the NEH's resistance to the "development and pursuit of a national policy for the humanities." The NEH responded to this criticism by noting the failure of the investigators to recognize the precision of language with which the Congress approached this sensitive area in drafting the initial authorizing legislation. The investigators failed to note the critical difference between what they called a "national humanities policy" and the legislative references to a "national policy of support" and "national policy for the promotion of progress and scholarship." The distinction here is more than semantic; the difference is crucial to the philosophy of government and the concepts of cultural pluralism and academic freedom so precious to our national traditions. The operation of the NEH revolves around the cyclical review by ad hoc peer review panels of applications for grants which compete for the limited funds at hand. This system reflects the proper concern that federal agencies not effect a cultural authoritarianism through their funding mechanisms. As private foundations erode in the face of inflation and other pressures, and the federal government assumes an increasingly large proportion of discretionary cultural support, this concern becomes even more cogent. (Apparently the Appropriations Committee agreed with the NEH's response to this question, as no action was taken to implement the report's recommendations.)

The concept of pluralism implicit in the rich diversity of applicants and reviewers extends beyond provision of NEH support for a broad spectrum of applications to the process of determining appropriate areas of support among federal agencies. Once again, quotation of the authorizing legislation is useful. The NEH is directed to "correlate programs, insofar as is practicable, with existing Federal programs, designated State humanities agencies and with those undertaken by other public agencies or private groups, and shall develop the programs of the Endowment with due regard to the contribution to the objectives of the Act which can be made by other Federal agencies under existing programs."

As a result, policy deliberations involve and take into account the programs and guidelines of other federal agencies and departments. Interagency consultation and planning have been established between NEH and: the National Endowment for the Arts, the Office of Education, the Institute of Museum Services, the Smithsonian Institution, the National Science Foundation, the International Communications Agency, and the Department of Energy. Because this planning deals with sensitive areas of government involvement, the agencies concerned have proceeded with caution. Care has been taken to ensure that the efforts to eliminate program overlap and duplication do not impair the government's traditional flexibility in offering an appropriate range and level of support to educational and cultural institutions and organizations.

By definition, the competing principles of economy ("overlap") and service ("flexibility") create omnipresent tensions in the decision-making processes at both the individual-program level and the broader level of interagency cooperation. The nature of the NEH mandate exacerbates those tensions. Activities in the humanities can conceivably be encompassed within the purviews of many agencies. Responses to "social action" goals, particularly in education, very often are realized in projects emphasizing work in the humanities. The result of the tension is a process of constant realignment of interests within NEH programs in reaction to other federal initiatives in order to avoid unnecessary duplication of effort. Those efforts have always been most strenuously pursued at precollegiate levels where traditional interpretations of the disciplines of the humanities have been least applicable.

The foci of NEH programs are influenced, as well, by information garnered from nonfederal sources. The structure and content of projects funded by the Elementary and Secondary Education Program, for instance, reflect the contributions of humanities educators in the field and of the public at large. Whether because of the dubious merits of large federal curriculum projects of recent decades or a general appreciation of the need to tighten belts in recessionary times, review panels have tended of late to support proposals of moderate size with very specific plans for activities clearly within the scope of the humanities disciplines. The result, of course, is that projects without traditional humanities content but with generally humanistic goals (in areas such as global education, moral education, expository writing, and citizenship education) have been less enthusiastically promoted. The Elementary and Secondary Education Program's flexibility has been further reduced by an ever-increasing number of applications—spurred by budget cuts for staff and curriculum development in local school districts—competing for grant funds whose real value is not keeping pace with inflation.

In the interests of making optimal use of limited funds and of furthering programs in education in the humanities, the NEH cooperates with the Office of Education and other agencies in order to create, whenever possible, a continuum of funding possibilities. An example of that spirit of common purpose is the relationship between the NEH's Elementary and Secondary Education Program and the Office of Education's Law-related Education Program. Projects of national visibility supported by the NEH (such as the Law in a Free Society Project of the State Bar of California and the American Bar Association's recent work with law and the humanities at the elementary level) can, in fact, lay legitimate claim to having helped set the stage for the creation of the Law-related Education Program. In the face of continuing student apathy, those projects have provided substantial models of successful work in an area of education lacking the guidance of an individual intellectual discipline. Not surprisingly, the Commissioner of Education took advantage of this experience by including NEH representation in the Study Group for Law-related Education.

Since the Law-related Education Program has not begun to disburse funds, the programmatic interpretations of appropriate purview inherent in the review of proposals have not yet been completely settled. This issue boils down to an effort to keep one's colleagues in other agencies informed of proposals which may pose difficulties in this regard. Given the inclusion of jurisprudence in the NEH's legislative mandate and the maintenance of support for teacher training, curriculum development, and other activities related to the improvement of teaching and learning in the humanities, it is reasonable to expect that investigations into the relationships between law and history, literature, and philosophy will continue to be explored with NEH support. The title of a recent curriculum development grant to the Institute for Research in History—"Perspectives on Women in America's Legal Development"—suggests the variety of potential explorations in the humanities and the law.

The salient characteristics of the NEH and other agencies, therefore, seem to be neither obduracy nor ignorance. While these agencies may not be Emersonian in concept, they are governed by a collective process which retains both human attributes and humanistic perspectives.

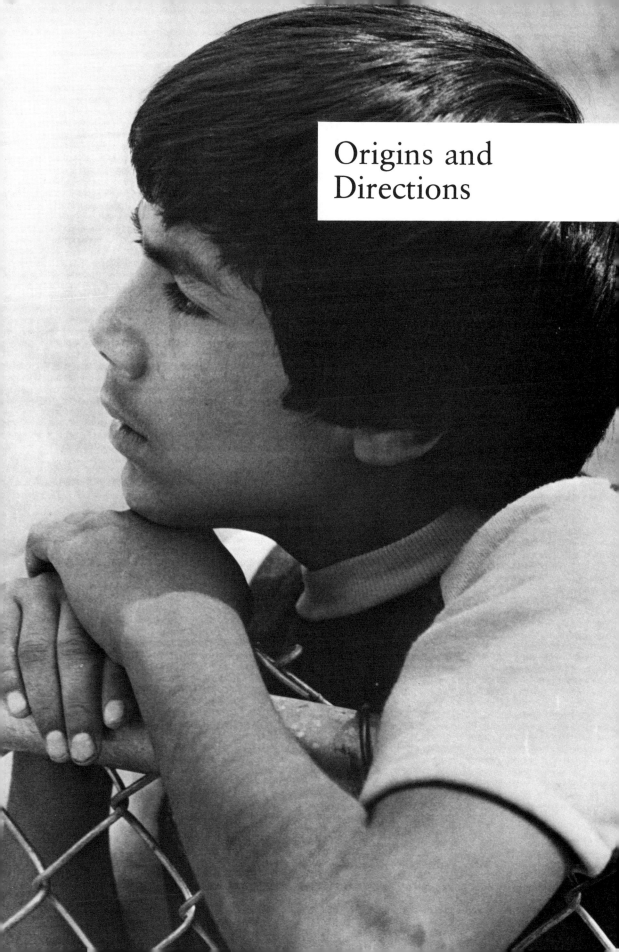

Origins and
Directions

The ABA/NEH Elementary Project: Background and Overview

Norman Gross

The elementary project that is the impetus and context for this volume is reviewed here. It is appropriate that Norman Gross is the author of this review, for his concern and vision were responsible for the birth of this project. Together with Charles White of the YEFC staff, he developed the proposal that was funded by the National Endowment for the Humanities. We, the past and current project coordinators (including, now, Mabel McKinney-Browning), owe a special debt to both these people. For, once the project was born, they delivered it into our hands to nurture and shape—an act of both good faith and courage we salute.

A recognition of the critical links among law, the humanities, and elementary education lies at the heart of this book and the ABA/NEH project. For it is during children's formative years that they begin to explore, develop, and internalize the essential capacities upon which our system of jurisprudence and vision of effective citizenship are based—reaching fair decisions, exercising critical judgment, balancing individual freedoms with the social good, and so on.

The kindred spirit and shared objectives of law and humanities were powerfully stated at the 1954 Harvard Conference on the Teaching of Law in the Liberal Arts Curriculum. There, the following reasons were advanced for utilizing the study of law in achieving traditional liberal arts objectives:

That an understanding of law is essential to an understanding of the political values of American society and of the international community; and that it illuminates not only political science but also other disciplines such as philosophy, history, economics, sociology, and anthropology;

That the study of law is an important means of developing the student's sense of justice and his capacity for responsible judgment; and

That the study of law is an important foundation in the training of students for the responsibilities of social, economic, and political activity.

Norman Gross is Staff Director of the Special Committee on Youth Education for Citizenship of the American Bar Association. A lawyer and educator, he is author and editor of many law-related education materials.

The Challenge and the Opportunity

Since its inception in 1971, the ABA's Special Committee on Youth Education for Citizenship has been committed to translating the vision and potential expressed at the 1954 Harvard conference into effective instructional programs in our nation's schools. The development of law-related education (LRE) during the early seventies, however, primarily emphasized secondary education, with few creative and pioneering efforts devoted to the elementary grades. Despite repeated efforts—through publications, workshops, and special-emphasis programs—elementary LRE remained an ignored and forgotten stepchild.

Various factors contributed to this neglect. First, law and humanities were generally viewed as disciplines best suited for advanced studies, as areas too sophisticated and complex for the elementary curriculum. Second, pressures for reemphasizing the "basics" discouraged and impeded the development of innovative programs in elementary education. A YEFC survey conducted in 1974, for example, revealed that many elementary educators who sought to institute LRE programs found support systems to be minimal or nonexistent.

Moreover, the limited time, funds, and energies in the burgeoning LRE movement were being devoted to the more obvious and accessible part of the school curriculum—secondary social studies. There was, thus, a paucity of established materials and programs that elementary educators could replicate or adapt to their needs.

In light of these obstacles, it was obvious to those of us in law-related education that programs

3

in elementary law and humanities could be instituted only through an intensive and comprehensive effort. In 1977, the National Endowment for the Humanities provided such an opportunity through its award to the ABA Special Committee of a 3-year grant to revitalize citizenship instruction and other aspects of the elementary curriculum through programs in law and the humanities.

The program has four major objectives: (1) identifying a philosophical and programmatic framework for elementary law-related education; (2) involving a cadre of law and humanities programs in developing a rich variety of models and materials; (3) providing extensive assistance to these and other law and humanities programs; and (4) promoting widespread awareness and dissemination of exemplary programs in the field. The classical disciplines of law and the humanities were to provide the operational framework for the program and, as distinguished constitutional scholar Paul Freund noted in his essay "Law in the Schools," the challenge was to adapt these disciplines to the educational level of young children and the practical realities of elementary education.

The First Two Years

The initial efforts of the ABA/NEH project have encompassed two major goals—to develop a variety of effective models and approaches in elementary LRE, and to assemble the best current thinking on all facets of elementary LRE program development and implementation. To accomplish the former, we solicited program proposals from all parts of the country and ultimately selected seven projects, each of which is concentrating on a distinct aspect of elementary LRE. At the same time, we have sought to ensure continual coordination and cooperation among these projects so that their respective efforts would emerge as viable and complementary components of a comprehensive and broadly structured elementary LRE program.

The projects and their particular areas of concentration are as follows: Bank Street College and Cottage Lane School (New York)—teaching law and humanities through a student self-governance program for grades K–6; Center for City Building Educational Programs (California)—infusing law and humanities into a cross-curriculum program in which children construct a model city in the classroom; Institute for Political/Legal Education (New Jersey)—teaching children about law and humanities through active participation in play groups, classrooms, families, and neighborhoods; Law in a Free Society (California)—developing dissemination strategies for LRE programs, including a program designed by Law in a Free

Society; Maryland Law-related Education Program—designing curriculum modules, grades K–4, and an in-service course for teachers to promote citizenship/law-related education through the informal curriculum; Tri-County Law-related Education Project (Oregon)—infusing law and humanities into a school district's scope and sequence design; Wyoming LEGIS (Law in the Elementary Grades Infusion System) Program—infusing law and humanities into published basal social studies texts.

Tremendous credit must be given to the pioneering work of the people involved in these projects. Over a remarkably short period of time, their commitment, creativity, and unbounded energy have been the central factors in the early success of this project. It is important to emphasize that, beyond their involvement in several summer institutes, team leader meetings, and regional conferences—all supported under the NEH grant—they have received no financial support from the NEH or the ABA. Rather, their developmental efforts have been underwritten by their respective projects and have usually entailed time and energies far beyond regular working hours. This dedication to their individual program areas and the overall project objectives has produced a special spirit of concern, purpose, and direction in our efforts.

The second major focus of the initial grant period was the Symposium on Elementary Law and the Humanities. Held in May 1978, it brought together scholars and practitioners from law, education, and the humanities to explore the multifaceted topics covered in this publication. While it is our hope that this publication will generate increased awareness of elementary law and humanities and serve as a catalyst for wide-ranging program development, the value of the symposium extends far beyond what is readily apparent on these pages. For the intensive deliberations, debates, and early drafts produced by the symposium provided critical insights into the diverse and complex dimensions of elementary LRE.

Without such enlightened and incisive input at this initial phase of the project, it is doubtful whether we would have avoided the many pitfalls inherent in such an ambitious undertaking or realized the accomplishments that have thus far taken place.

The Third Year and Beyond

While the first several years of the project have been devoted to developmental activities, the third year is concentrating on dissemination. Through various conferences, publications, and clearinghouse services, we intend to raise awareness of the many excellent elementary LRE programs already in existence and stimulate widespread replication and developmental activities.

Among the events scheduled for the third year are presentations at the National Council for the Social Studies annual meeting, the inaugural Elementary LRE Regional Conference in Dallas (involving the states of Kansas, Oklahoma, and Texas), a K–12 summer institute in San Antonio, publication of an elementary LRE brochure, a special elementary LRE section in *Social Education,* and publication of this symposium book. In addition, YEFC staff and elementary project leaders are involved in a wide range of consulting and clearinghouse activities designed to establish elementary LRE as a coequal partner in LRE development throughout the country.

Upon completion of this 3-year cycle of activities, what lies ahead for the NEH project and elementary LRE? Guidance for future activities is provided by the Rand report on implementing and sustaining innovations (Berman & McLaughlin, 1978) and the NSF study on the status of precollege social studies education (Shaver et al., 1978). The Rand report, which examined the impact of four federal programs on educational change, indicates that most projects that fail to become part of the school curriculum have underestimated the time needed to effect change in educational practice. In addition, they have not carefully laid the foundation for institutionalization, that is, the process by which innovations become an integral part of the school district's curricular program and regular budget. The study points out that, in order for this to occur, a broad base of support for the program must be established early in its implementation. This means that community and school decision makers must be behind the program, and teachers must be comfortable with it and feel that it contributes to their effectiveness in the classroom. The report highlights the special role of the school principal, who is described as the "gatekeeper of change."

The NSF study reinforces many of the Rand findings. It emphasizes that unless the classroom teachers and other district personnel, especially school principals, are committed to a program, it simply will not endure. Teacher and administrator commitment is achieved when these individuals understand and concur with the basic goals of the program, recognize how to implement it in their schools or classrooms, and acknowledge its contributions to their professional responsibilities.

These and the other critical findings of these studies suggest the need for careful and comprehensive follow-up and training if we are to realize the lofty objectives of the NEH project.

While it is clear that a strong foundation for program development has been established, a reduction in the intensive, coordinated elementary emphasis established during this initial 3-year period would regrettably result in minimal long-term impact of the program. It would simply become another of the many worthwhile innovations with great potential but unrealized goals.

We are therefore seeking additional support from NEH and other foundations and agencies to maintain, strengthen, and expand the accomplishments of this elementary project. Already, YEFC has received grants from the M. D. Anderson Foundation and the American Bar Endowment for this purpose. It is hoped that NEH will also provide supplementary funding in support of institutes, publications, and clearinghouse services that reflect the best research available in educational innovation.

Within the general YEFC program as well as the activities of national, state, and local LRE projects throughout the country, law-related education is truly becoming a K–12 effort, reflecting a systematic, developmental approach to citizenship and social studies instruction. If we compare the state of the art today with LRE development just 3 short years ago, it is clear that we are dealing with a desirable, effective, and practical area of curriculum innovation. We intend to build upon this solid foundation in the years ahead, and we encourage the readers of this symposium book and those concerned with the forgotten "basic" of citizenship education to join with us in creatively addressing this important area of school instruction.

The Product of Many Contributions

In closing, I would be remiss if I did not acknowledge the special contributions that various individuals and organizations have made to this NEH project. Of course, our deepest appreciation is extended to the National Endowment for the Humanities for their strong support and pioneering efforts in this area. Of particular note is the continued guidance and support we have received from NEH program officers William Russell and John Hale. Subsequent funding from the M. D. Anderson Foundation and the American Bar Endowment has been instrumental in enabling us to carry forward the wide-ranging activities that have marked the initial years of this effort. We appreciate their strong support and commitment to elementary education.

Within the field of law-related education, there have been many active and dedicated contributors. The team leaders of the seven participating projects and their colleagues have provided strong, constant, and spirited input to all facets of our project activities. Throughout, other LRE leaders from the national, state, and local levels have provided vital guidance and support to these activities.

Within the ABA, special acknowledgment must be given to Lynda Falkenstein, Charlotte Anderson, and Mabel McKinney-Browning. They have tackled what many have described as an almost impossible task with tremendous competence, commitment, and creativity. I also want to acknowledge the dedicated efforts of our elementary subcommittee—R. Freeman Butts, C. Thomas Ross, Judith V. Torney, Margaret Bush Wilson, and ex-officio member Isidore Starr—whose continued guidance and counsel have contributed immeasurably to the project. My thanks also to the other members of the Special Committee, Advisory Commission, and staff, whose contributions may not be as visible as those mentioned above but have certainly been most important.

A Closing Thought

In his presidential address at the Forty-fourth Annual Meeting of the National Council for the Social Studies in 1964, Isidore Starr described his conception of the humanities:

For me, the humanities represents a mood, a method, and a commitment. The mood is one of optimism concerning the destiny of man tempered with realism. In contemplating the great equations of life, the spirit of the humanities sees more good in man than evil, more justice than injustice, more beauty than ugliness, more truth than falsehood, more triumph than tragedy. The method is one of honest and scrupulous inquiry into the human condition, the ways of man, tempered with intellectual humility concerning the answers to the big questions—the cosmological questions. This mood, this method and this commitment can flourish only where there is full, free, and frank communication and cooperation among those who profess to teach and practice the humanities.

If we are able to establish the mood, the method, and the commitment described by Dr. Starr, we will have no difficulty in effecting the objective of meaningful elementary LRE in our nation's schools.

REFERENCES

Berman, P., & McLaughlin, M. W. *Implementing and sustaining innovations* (Federal programs supporting educational change, vol. 8). Santa Monica, Calif.: Rand, May 1978. R-1159/8-HEW

Shaver, J. P.; Davis, O. L., Jr.; & Helburn, S. W. *An interpretive report on the status of pre-college social studies education based on three NSF-funded studies.* Washington, D.C.: National Council for the Social Studies, 1978. Available from ERIC/CHESS

Elementary Law-related Education: The State of the Art, 1978

Susan Davison Archer

Any sound plan for future action must rest securely on a clear perspective of what has come before. Susan Archer has been in an especially advantageous position to observe the law-related education movement over the past several years and, thus, is well qualified to sketch such an overview of elementary law-related education. In addition, her background as a primary teacher and her work with other elementary educators give her special insight into the prospects and potential for development at this level. Others similarly committed to good elementary law-related education will appreciate the author's frustration with the lack of extensive elementary development so far and her obvious excitement over potential development represented by the law and humanities project.

In this historical overview, the author identifies a few quality programs, beginning with the work of Law in American Society, which are evidence that law-related education is applicable to young children's needs and the elementary school curriculum. The author describes some of the major problems she and others faced over the past several years and notes areas where progress has been made and where more work must be done. She closes her remarks by making a strong plea that this work not be haphazard. Rather, she calls for the development and application of carefully thought-out directions and goals for elementary law-related education. These papers and the Symposium discussions represent the beginning of our ongoing efforts to develop and apply such sound guidelines for law and humanities.

Beginnings

The year 1973 was an exciting one for me! That was the year I was first introduced to the idea of law-related citizenship education. The implications of this type of education seemed to me to be far reaching, especially at the elementary level, where citizenship attitudes and social reasoning patterns are being formed. Law as a discipline might help us find many relevant ways to teach our young children about the process of conflict resolution and to help them develop critical-thinking abilities. Law as a reflection of values might give teachers an important tool for helping children examine their own daily experiences relating to justice, equality, and freedom. Law as an institution pervades the lives of all of us at all ages, so why hadn't many of us been teaching about it?

I accepted a position on the staff of the American Bar Association Special Committee on

Youth Education for Citizenship (YEFC) and enthusiastically joined with others who were actively promoting efforts in the field. Once I was actually involved in that day-by-day process, my idealistic enthusiasm was somewhat tempered by the realities. An awful lot of work had to be done if this movement was to make any impact at the elementary level.

At that time it was possible to be quite optimistic about the direction of the movement for junior and senior high schools. There were already several major high-quality curriculum development and teacher training projects with a secondary focus. YEFC's *Directory of Law-related Educational Activities* (Working Notes No. 2) (Gross, 1974) described many of them. Even though much more had to be done at the secondary level, it was clear that support—from administrators, classroom teachers, community leaders, parents, and students—was mounting.

The story at the elementary level was unfortunately a little different. Most elementary educators had never heard of law-related education, and those who had certainly did not believe that it had anything to do with teaching in the elementary grades. There were significantly fewer elementary efforts under way, and, among those projects which did include elementary compo-

Susan Davison Archer is a former teacher in private and public schools and former Assistant Staff Director of the American Bar Association's Special Committee on Youth Education for Citizenship. She is currently writing curriculum and consulting in elementary law-related education.

7

nents, almost none concentrated exclusively on that level. There were even fewer which included the primary grades in their "elementary" programs.

As the YEFC staff searched for existing efforts, most reports of activity at the elementary level included programs which only presented factual information about specific laws; stressed the punitive consequences of breaking laws; centered around an "Officer Friendly" approach, featuring stereotyped presentations of the helpful police officer; or conducted court tours. While certain of these programs served useful functions in specific situations, they did not encompass what I felt to be the many exciting possibilities of a good elementary law-related education.

One of the most promising routes was being traveled by Law in a Free Society, a project initiated by the state bar of California in 1970. This project had already begun work on a K–12 curriculum to be used in teacher in-service training programs. Activities and materials for all grade levels focused on eight basic concepts: authority, diversity, freedom, justice, participation, privacy, property, and responsibility. This approach caused much excitement among many of us who were seeking ways to use a law-related curriculum at the elementary level.

Another approach came from the Law in American Society Foundation, which had been working since the mid-1960s on a law program for grades 4–12. The project, initially conceived through the Chicago Bar Foundation, included both curriculum development and the coordination of teacher training institutes. Its elementary materials, *Law in a New Land* (Ratcliffe, 1972), were among the first in the field and emphasized the development of law in America. This historical approach helped make the materials especially useful in many intermediate classrooms which were already emphasizing U.S. history as the social studies curriculum.

The Law in a Free Society project and the Law in American Society Foundation seemed to be the only major national projects making significant contributions to the elementary field. Some intermediate-level materials and training programs had also come out of the Lincoln Filene Center for Citizenship and Public Affairs at Tufts University in Boston. In addition, there were a few major state and local programs, which included the Law for Public School Use program in Oklahoma, the Children and the Law project of the Minnesota Bar Association, the Law in a Changing Society Project in Dallas, the Cincinnati Center for Law-related Education, and the Law Education in Atlanta Schools program. Most of these projects and a few others were then in germinal phases, and some have since made significant contributions to the field.

Despite the limited number of quality elementary projects which existed in 1973, it seemed at that time that some of the "new" techniques and educational theories might assist in our efforts. Inquiry, one of the basic tools at all levels of law-related education, was "hot." Values clarification à la Sid Simon was creeping into many teacher inservice programs, and it was becoming clear that some understanding of values had to be a component of law-related units. Kohlberg's theories on moral reasoning development were being published and had even been translated into a few materials for elementary-level children (for example, Guidance Associates' First Things: Values filmstrip series). Efforts to construct relevant guidelines for elementary political education were also being undertaken by the Citizenship Development Program at the Mershon Center of Ohio State University under the encouragement of the American Political Science Association. All these efforts, we hoped, might in some way assist the direction of elementary law-related education.

Early Problems

Unfortunately, even with some of these "kindred spirit" efforts, it was quite clear that much more groundwork had to be laid before elementary law-related education could begin to grow. At least five major problems faced us.

Looking back 5 years, it seems to me that then the major problem—and the one least identified—was the absence of formal efforts to define in any organized way some of the goals possible for elementary programs. Those of us with solid understanding of the interests and learning patterns of young children needed to discuss thoughtfully what we wanted to be doing, at what grade levels, to what degree, and by what means. Research on political socialization and on moral development was helpful, but it seemed that no one was trying to synthesize, to integrate, or to propose in concrete or theoretical terms how all this could relate to elementary law-related education. We had a lot of good hunches and strong instincts that what we were trying to do would be significant for the education of the elementary child, but in-depth exploration of why, where, when, and how to go was still needed.

A second problem, which was more immediately obvious, was a lack of major institutional support. While many state departments of education and local educational systems were nibbling at the possibility of making commitments to secondary law-related education, few were ready to explore the implications for elementary programs. The reasons for this varied somewhat from place to place, but there were several common elements. One often was the heavy pressure to emphasize basic reading and math skills to the exclusion of "extra" or innovative programs. It was also difficult for some to accept that a subject as "sophisticated" as law truly had a place in the elementary classroom. In addition, the easily generated enthusiasm for secondary law-related education often overshadowed the possibilities for programs at the elementary level.

Besides the problems of developing theoretical frameworks and getting institutional support, there was the difficulty in providing quality training for elementary teachers. To their credit, a few law-related teaching training programs did try to include an elementary component. Unfortunately, it was not always easy for those programs to identify or respond to the special needs of elementary teachers. They were often grouped into sections geared to deal with content and process most appropriate for the secondary level. This problem was further complicated by the low numbers of elementary teachers who had heard about law-related education and were seeking some training. Those of us engaged in teacher training were disappointed time and time again as we worked with two or three elementary teachers in a room adjacent to a secondary session filled with 20 or 40 people. Those of us especially interested in working with primary teachers had to redirect our enthusiasm toward the upper elementary grades—at least temporarily.

Scarcity of usable curriculum materials was also an immediate problem. Teachers attending institutes and in-service meetings were encouraged to develop their own lessons, and, through generous sharing, mimeographed collections of homegrown ideas for classroom activities were often put together. While this sometimes uncovered a great deal of creativity, it rarely led to a well-integrated curriculum. YEFC and other groups tried to identify various types of supplementary commercial materials which could be adapted to law-related lessons, but it was clear that these were not enough. I had the fortune to lead many workshops to introduce educators to law-related education. I cannot express the extent of my discomfort at the disappointment shown by participants, enthusiastic about carrying programs back to their schools, when they asked the inevitable question: Where do we get the materials? There was no satisfactory answer.

Finally, in 1973 a formidable problem was evaluation. Evaluation of elementary law-related educational programs was almost nonexistent. Few were even trying to grapple with the question of how to approach an evaluation procedure of this kind. Obviously, a concomitant problem was the scarcity of evaluative evidence supporting elementary law-related education, which affected both general credibility and funding. Part of the difficulty, of course, was due to the lack of theoretical definition, as I have already discussed.

Another part of the difficulty was how to collect evidence when the most appropriate evidence might be measured by long-term effects. The programs which existed were only newly born!

On the Way

Although the problems seemed formidable, slowly some progress began. It is to the credit of places like Rochester, New Hampshire, a small community which sought and received monies to develop a K–6 law-related curriculum guide especially geared for its system, and the state of North Carolina, which piloted some elementary law-related programs integrating some of Kohlberg's thinking, and a handful of other projects, that they could make a commitment to pioneer in such a new field. These were tiny efforts compared to what was needed nationwide, but they were important beginnings. Some of the most encouraging efforts came from K–12 projects which recognized programs for elementary children as foundations for secondary programs, and not as watered-down versions of more sophisticated upper-grade programs. Statewide projects in Maryland, New York, Pennsylvania, Texas, and many other states have made strong commitments to elementary law-related education since 1973, as have such local projects as the Cincinnati Center for Law-related Education and the Salt Lake City Schools Law in a Free Society Project.

Many of these projects have had to develop a large part of their own curriculum materials at the elementary level. While materials for junior and senior high schools mushroomed in both quantity and quality, law-related materials designed specifically for young children are still sparse, especially at the primary level. Law in a Free Society developed K–12 instructional kits using the same conceptual framework built into their inservice materials. The Law in Action Series (West Publishing Company), originally designed for junior high students but quite adaptable for use with intermediates, stresses particular themes—the justice system, juvenile law, lawmaking, consumerism, and the police—which are related to both legal concepts and legal knowledge. These then are added to Law in American Society Foundation's *Law in a New Land,* which, as discussed earlier, uses a historical framework to emphasize to intermediate students how law works in our society.

Supplementary materials are much more numerous, and many of them are fairly good when used to emphasize particular themes or concepts. Some audiovisual materials which are intentionally law-related include *Foundations of Justice* (Law in American Society Foundation, 1975) and *Law and Justice for the Intermediate*

Grades (Pathescope Educational Films, 1974), both designed for upper elementary children.

In addition, some relevant materials fall under the more general categories of citizenship, values, guidance, moral development, and similar areas. These include materials such as the Basic Concepts Series (16-mm films from Learning Corporation of America, for grades K–3); The Citizenship Adventures of the Lollipop Dragon (filmstrip kit from Society for Visual Education, for grades K–3); and First Things: Values and First Things: Social Reasoning (filmstrip kits from Guidance Associates, for grades K–3).

Children's literature is yet another source of materials for the elementary teacher. Many of Dr. Seuss's stories are examples of the numerous books that can be used as springboards for discussions of such issues as fairness, equality, authority, responsibility, etc. Slowly some of this literature is being identified. There is still a great need to make teachers aware of it and to give them some ideas about how to use it.

One of the most promising developments at the elementary level has been in the promotion of teacher training programs. In 1973, to my knowledge, there were only three or four summer training programs which included K–6 components. *None* that I know of was designed specifically for K–6. Slowly this has changed. Each summer a few more 7–12 programs have been extended to include elementary teachers. Here and there a program just for elementary teachers has popped up. The 1977 YEFC compilation of summer teacher training workshops and institutes listed 49 entries. Over half of them included spaces for elementary teachers, and most of those specified primary-grade teachers in their invitations. Three were designed specifically and exclusively for the elementary teacher, and many others included separate sections in which elementary teachers could explore their own particular needs. In addition, numerous in-service programs and one-day workshops are now being offered. And after my initial experiences in presenting workshops to nearly empty rooms, I am delighted to say that elementary teachers' attendance at workshops and institutes has increased dramatically and often matches attendance by secondary teachers.

I am encouraged not only by the increasing number of training programs for elementary teachers, but also by the increasing quality of many of these programs. The special needs of elementary teachers and their particular situation are beginning to be recognized. Quality programs still include law content, but they help teachers develop methods and units through which children can learn law-related concepts. In the best programs time is being set aside to help the already overburdened elementary teacher find ways to integrate the teaching of law into an existing curriculum. Some programs are also trying to give teachers time to consider how school life generally teaches our children about law and citizenship. I and many others have a special appreciation of Nancy Wyner's efforts to help us see the importance of this last aspect of law-related education.

The problem of evaluation has not been so significantly addressed. Those who are faced with the challenge of designing "competency-based" education perhaps have found one handle to use. That framework, however, may only leave educators with more difficult questions, such as how to test reliably competencies which do not show up well on objective tests. In a society which demands accountability, much more serious thought needs to be given to this area. In my heart, I have a nagging suspicion that this problem may never be completely resolved. The real proof of law-related pudding may be in the quality of citizenship exhibited not only now but 20 and even 50 years from now. The more subtle effects on personality and social relationships may never be measured. Realistically, however, I know that even if the total of all learning that results can never be measured, other more objective and limited methods must be used now in order to give this movement legitimacy and monetary support.

In connection with this problem of evaluation, something must be said about the effect of the art on the lives of individual children and on the collective lives of the groups they belong to. I have no statistical evidence to present to you. However, I have yet to talk to a teacher who has used some aspect of law-related education who has not been delighted with the children's enthusiasm and by observable changes in behavior and/or thinking processes. In the face of imperfect curriculum materials, training programs, and other obstacles, I cannot help but believe that we are onto something significant.

The Challenges to Be Met

Where do you go from here? I feel sure that the participants at this symposium are full of brilliant ideas about what we should be doing. I am sure that many of those ideas are fairly specific and address problems in a way that the broad scope of this paper prevents me from even attempting.

However, since I am rarely given such a fine opportunity to express my opinion in public, I would like to emphasize one concern about the direction in which I hope we can go.

I have a strong hope that we can begin seriously to address the problem of more concretely establishing possible directions and goals for law-related education in the elementary classroom. Perhaps this symposium is a first step. Some may say that with all the practical work left to be done, energy spent in this way will be of little real help. However, I strongly feel that much of our thinking is still too fuzzy. This is not to say that we should strive for *one* definitive structure through which we all must work or one set of goals to which we all must adhere. Obviously, in our society such a structure would be suicidal and would certainly stifle our creative juices. But we need to be doing careful thinking and research about how children really do learn about the law, which concepts and skills can be dealt with at what age levels and in what order, and other similar and related questions. Many alternative models need to be developed and options proposed.

I am aware that some formal thinking is beginning to be applied to these questions. I am also aware that informally every teacher using a law-related focus is probably thinking about them. But these thoughts need to be brought together, raised in dialogues, and collected for those seriously interested in approaching the subject. The body of literature needs to be expanded. This might, as a side effect, legitimize the subject for school systems and teacher training institutions. It would also provide more direction to curriculum developers. But, more important, it would help practitioners explore and make use of some of the more subtle and less easily measured—and per-

haps most significant—possible educational outcomes for our children. Included in this thinking would have to be more emphasis on finding out how the school environment affects children's learning about law-related values and institutions and their acquiring of law-related skills. I am sure many other important areas will be identified.

In conclusion, I believe that the state of the art of elementary law-related education is unclear. We are at a turning point. Up to now we have just been beginning to get our feet wet. Now the time has come to take the plunge and begin to address each of the questions that has been surfacing in the past decade. Unless we do that, I fear that much of what has thus far been attempted will fade into the background with so many other half-begun educational movements.

REFERENCES

Gross, N. (Ed.). *Directory of law-related educational activities* (2nd ed.). Chicago: American Bar Association, Special Committee on Youth Education for Citizenship, 1974.

Law in American Society Foundation (Gallagher, A. F., & Ratcliffe, R. H., Producers). *Foundations of justice.* Columbus, Ohio: Merrill, 1975. [Filmstrips]

Pathescope Educational Films, Inc. *Law and justice for the intermediate grades: Making value decisions.* New Rochelle, N.Y.: Pathescope Educational Films, 1974. [Filmstrips]

Ratcliffe, R. H. (Ed.). *Law in a new land.* Boston: Houghton Mifflin, 1972.

Law and the Humanities for Elementary Schools: The Coordinators' Perspectives

Charlotte C. Anderson and Lynda Carl Falkenstein

This article can probably best be characterized as an emergent synthesis. It represents some of the perspectives on law and the humanities for elementary schools that we, the editors, have gained from the collective wisdom of this text and from our development work over the past few years. Tapping into these resources has been both challenging and rewarding, and we anticipate further challenges and rewards as development and dissemination continue. As has been our past experience, we also anticipate that each new day, week, and month will shed new light on past conclusions, and our perspectives will be refined, sharpened, and often altered.

We thought it would be so simple. Agree upon a definition of law, make reasonable connections to the humanities, and the rest would follow naturally. With wonderful idealism (and a share of naiveté) we began our search for the "right" description of law. Fortunately, from the beginning the search suggested that any single definition of law would be not only elusive but unsatisfactory. This extraordinary phenomenon defied consensus among experts. Some defined law in "black letter" or case-law terms. Others viewed it conceptually, while still others described it as a discipline characterized by an identifiable body of knowledge. And others with equally firm conviction pronounced law to be a kind of ordering differing from society to society.

The impossibility of confining law to a single or narrow definition is perhaps one of its most salient and powerful features. It is a multidimensional, complex, and, hence, rich phenomenon. Roger Fisher, professor of law at Harvard University, metaphorically suggests that, in our search to understand law, we should consult not a dictionary but, rather, an atlas. An atlas, he implies, would expose the many facets of law, portray its diverse manifestations, explore the relationship of law to the broad range of human endeavor. A comprehensive atlas of law reveals it as a vital thread woven not only throughout our own society but throughout societies dotting the globe.

This perspective emphasizes the power of law in virtually every aspect of human life. Students learn that it is a central organizer of society, or, as

Paul Freund, professor of constitutional law at Harvard, characterizes it, "the glue or stiffening agent in the fabric of society." Most important, law takes on an alterable quality. That is, students understand that it is not struck immutably in concrete but rather is shaped by values and traditions, reflecting the desires of society at any given time in history. If it is not immutable, an individual can affect its tone, quality, and implementation. The student's responsibility and role as a citizen surface with exciting potential, for here is a concept of law in which human beings have the final say.

Not surprisingly, our effort to pin down a definition of the humanities took us over much the same course as the one we traveled in trying to define law. As with law, we concluded that any single definition would do injustice to the richness, scope, and variety of the humanities, which are noteworthy for examining the broad scope of human experience through space and time. The real power of the humanities rests not in any single discipline but rather in their collective wisdom and spirit. The collective concerns of the humanities have a basic theme, for in one way or another each explores and seeks to understand more fully the eternal questions about the nature of being human—and, as Jerome Bruner has reminded us, "how to become more so."

The relevance of the humanities to law-related education is that they seek to understand human experience from their own unique perspectives, to give meaning to universal questions, to improve the quality of life, to provide expression by and communication among peoples. By explicitly linking law and the humanities in designing education programs, we can harness a vital force. Oliver

For information about the authors of this article, see About the Editors (p. vi).

Wendell Holmes might well have had our task in mind when he delivered the admonition, "Connect your subject with the universe and catch an echo of the infinite, a glimpse of the fathomable process, a hint of the universal law."

By consciously linking law and the humanities, we stretch our own perspectives so that we do not view law and law-related issues from the limited and, perhaps, ethnocentric stance of our own societal experience. Rather, we consider the broad range of human experience as it has been affected by and has affected law. At the same time, linking law and the humanities ensures that we become more aware of the personal, human concerns of individuals whose lives are touched by law. The humanities remind us that we are a thinking, feeling, creating species whose individual heritages and experiences influence how we relate to one another and to institutions, such as the law.

Implications for Curriculum

The implications for any curriculum (formal or informal) of focusing on the nexus between law and humanities are considerable and exciting. First and perhaps foremost, a law and humanities curriculum greatly lessens the likelihood that law may be taught as an end in itself. Instead, students learn that its value is as a tool to further human values and societal goals. This perspective suggests a broad range of activities which can be undertaken by students themselves to better understand and promote laws which are more just and responsive to societal needs.

Such a curriculum is as much a "perspective" or a view of education as it is a substantive content area. That perspective guides us to draw upon the full spectrum of human experience and be alert to the individual needs of the developing child. Such a view reminds us that the children in our schools represent a broad array of cultural heritages, and we must be sensitive to the different views of law and law-related issues growing out of this diversity. For example, a child from a Chinese-American household might well perceive authority and privacy—central law-related concepts—quite differently than would a child from a Spanish-American household.

This perspective also reminds us to be continually attuned to and demonstrate respect for the individual. Constant vigilance is needed because the many metamorphoses of a growing child are relentless and often subtle. As seasoned teachers are well aware, it is not unusual for a child who in September cannot resist breaking every classroom rule to become the most trustworthy classroom citizen of all by April. And the teacher who is not alert to this shifting response may continue to treat the child as a recalcitrant.

A perspective that respects the individual also recognizes the legitimacy of varying learning styles as well as the intrinsic need to create and to express oneself. A law and humanities program might, for example, include opportunities for children to experience the many aspects of freedom—another basic law-related concept—through various art forms such as dance, music, and painting. Other learning experiences might be organized around a piece of literature.

Most important, this point of view encourages a global perspective of law. The context for law-related education is greatly expanded—from the student's own experiences to the experiences and conditions of peoples around the planet. Law, after all, is not the exclusive domain of any people or culture. To understand its true dimensions, students must see it operating across and affecting human beings throughout the world.

In considering the educational implications of linking law and the humanities in this project, it is important to keep in mind that we are talking about young children—children of ages 5 to 11 or 12. This fact has special implications. For one thing, considerable translation and adaptation are required. John Dewey called this process "psychologizing the subject matter." By this he meant that teachers need to have a sound foundation both in the discipline (art, social science, English, law, etc.) and in child development and learning theory, so they can make the material meaningful for children. The challenge for elementary law and humanities programs, then, is considerable.

In regard to law, this means that we must carefully consider what aspects of law *can* have meaning for children. The police officer on the corner, the squad car, the police station, the judges in their black robes, prison bars, the courthouse, the courtroom, and similar objects and people bring the law to the child. So do such processes as rule making, deciding between right and wrong, and exercising and responding to authority. How children perceive each of these will in some degree shape how they perceive "law."

It is important that children have basic information about the structures and processes of the legal system—what police officers do; what happens in a courtroom; how laws and rules are made and changed. But it is even more important that children understand the basic principles on which these structures and processes rest—principles such as justice, freedom, due process, equity. If they are taught by an insightful teacher, these principles can have meaning for children and significantly enrich their lives. The challenge for elementary educators, then, is: (1) to identify those aspects of the legal system that children can understand; (2) to strip away the exterior trappings of the political/legal system to reveal the underlying principles on which the institutions are based; and (3) to impart this information and convey these principles and associated processes through a developmentally sound curriculum. And this is indeed a challenge. Centuries of jurisprudential scholarship have been devoted to analyzing legal principles, and many more promise to be. The next step—translating these findings and applying them to the curriculum—is an equally engaging task for educators.

In one sense the challenge is every bit as great when we confront the humanities. The use of the term itself is a hurdle that has to be overcome. That hurdle is the baggage that we educators carry with us from our own educations. It is a fairly safe bet that the first time we ever consciously confronted something called "the humanities" was in "Humanities 101" in college or high school. The musty text for that course—which still sits on many of our bookshelves—was/is a mammoth tome full of Greek plays and pictures of Grecian urns and Roman arches. Humanities 101 for 6-year-olds? Hardly! And when we look beyond this personal encounter, we come face to face with a cataloging of "the humanities" such as that supplied by the National Endowment for the Humanities. (See John Hale's article in this book.) Again, on the face of it, the humanities as delineated here appear suited for upper-level students only. Philosophy in the kindergarten? Never. But what if we take Dewey's approach and do with the humanities what we have advocated doing with the law? What do we find, for example, when we strip away the accouterments of the discipline of philosophy? We find people asking and seeking answers to such questions as "Who am I?" "What does it mean to be human?" "What is the nature of good? of evil? of right? of wrong?"—questions, of course, that all children ask in their own ways and for which they often desperately seek answers. The same possibilities hold for all the disciplines within the humanities.

A first step in developing law and humanities programs for young children is to identify those aspects of the humanities which relate to law. Philosophical issues, for example, which most immediately relate to law are moral and ethical questions. Some literary works are especially potent vehicles for examining legal and moral issues. Notable among these are classics such as *Antigone, A Man for All Seasons,* and *Huckleberry Finn.* Another way of looking at this nexus of law and the humanities is to examine how law shapes human creation and expression, and, conversely, how the humanities shape the structure and function of the law. If a single goal could be identified as the desired outcome of such a "mix," it would be the creation and maintenance of societies in

which every individual achieves fulfillment.

Once we have identified those aspects of the humanities which are law-related, we must approach them as we approach the law in designing curricula. That is, we first need to strip away the exterior, formal trappings the humanities have accumulated and get down to the core principles and issues they are addressing. Then we must convey these principles, these issues, through developmentally sound curricula.

When we go through this process of "psychologizing the subject matter" with both law and the humanities and mix the two, we have a vitally rich and relevant curriculum for young children. Such a curriculum provides children with the knowledge, skills, and attitudes they need to be fulfilled as individuals and to contribute to the common good. In other words, a good law and humanities curriculum is effective citizenship education.

As we have worked with various elementary law-related projects over the past few years, we have come to recognize that there is a broad range of legitimate educational goals of such programs. But as we examined those goals and contemplated what others might be considered, a basic set of outcomes emerged which characterize good elementary law-related programs generally and law and humanities programs more specifically. These learning outcomes can be characterized as movement along a set of continua which have at one end characteristics inimicable to effective, responsible citizenship and at the other end characteristics needed by citizens of a pluralistic, democratic society. Seen in these terms, the major goal of law-related education is to move children away from negative characteristics and toward characteristics more in keeping with the demands of democratic stewardship. Hence, law-related education is congruent with good social studies in general and is a means of fostering the goals of citizenship education.

The set of continua shown in Table 1 represent some of the most critical learning outcomes sought by elementary law-related programs. A basic premise of this project is that by drawing upon both law and the humanities in the ways discussed, we can design learning experiences which will facilitate significant movement along each of the continua (Wheeler, Anderson, McKinney-Browning, & Falkenstein, 1980).

Critical Concerns

This collection of essays raises a broad range of vital issues which must be addressed if successful programs in law and the humanities are to be undertaken. Recognizing in advance that every conceivable question could not be discussed (or even surface) in any collection of articles with

Table 1

Children moved away from:	Children moved toward:
Perceiving law as restrictive, punitive, immutable, and beyond the control and understanding of the people affected	→ Perceiving law as promotive, facilitative, comprehensible, and alterable
Perceiving people as powerless before the law and other sociocivic institutions	→ Perceiving people as having potential to control and contribute to the social order
Perceiving issues of right and wrong as incomprehensible to ordinary people	→ Perceiving right and wrong as issues all citizens can and should address
Perceiving social issues as unproblematic	→ Perceiving the dilemmas inherent in social issues
Being impulsive decision makers and problem solvers who make unreflective commitments	→ Being reflective decision makers and problem solvers who make grounded commitments
Being inarticulate about commitments made or positions taken	→ Being able to give reasoned explanations about commitments made and positions taken
Being unable to manage conflict in other than a coercive or destructive manner	→ Being socially responsible conflict managers
Being uncritically defiant of authority	→ Being critically responsive to legitimate authority
Being illiterate about legal issues and the legal system	→ Being knowledgeable about law, the legal system, and related issues
Being egocentric and indifferent to others	→ Being empathic, socially responsible, and considerate of others
Being morally immature in responding to ethical problems	→ Being able to make mature judgments in dealing with ethical and moral problems

SOURCE: Anderson, 1980.

space limitations, we wish to stress a few issues or concerns which may not receive the emphasis they deserve in the articles which follow. We believe these points are relevant to successful innovation in law and humanities and to curriculum innovation more generally. These issues may serve as a context for the ideas, questions, and encouragements in the subsequent articles.

The first question that needs to be raised concerns a fundamental assumption underlying the title of this book and the elementary education effort with which it is associated. That is the assumption that a law and humanities effort in elementary schools is indeed a good thing! That it is a positive step seems obvious to some of us. But how many supporters can we count? One hundred? A thousand? A few thousand? The question is much more than academic, for no major curriculum reform can take place—whether it concerns the new math or new science or, in this case, a major direction in civic education—without the massive support of the citizenry.

Two additional questions emerge here. The first is much easier to deal with than the second. It has to do with the process of conveying information to the general public. We must ask just how much knowledge people have about the articulated goals of this new curriculum effort. This

should not be an after-the-fact question, because citizens must have an active role in defining and refining those goals and processes. Here we are really talking about the nebulous area of community education. In her paper in this volume, Frances Link urges us to consider inventing a new concept of community education—one which does not just deliver data and after-the-fact decisions, but which involves citizens in a kind of curriculum "negotiation." Whatever model(s) communities select—and surely there must be myriad designs—we believe the need for effective community/citizen education is urgent. It must happen concurrent with, not subsequent to, curriculum development. It is not a supplemental but an integral part of effective curriculum innovation, regardless of focus.

The second question is more difficult, for it goes to the heart of what citizens believe and feel, not just what they know. We must ask ourselves to what extent the majority of people—regardless of how much data they have about a law and humanities program—really do support the concept. The bottom-line question thus becomes, To what extent are the humanities valued in our society?

Probably most of us would rather not explore that question too much because a positive response does not appear to be likely. There is little indication from the society at large that the humanities rank high on our list of national priorities. Quite the contrary. Too often they are explicitly attacked under the rubric of "educational frills" and other abusive descriptions. If, in fact, our untested conclusion is correct—that the humanities are not highly valued in this society—what direction do we then take? Quit? Move ahead with eyes closed hoping for the best?

We hope that we will answer the above questions, "Of course not!" We must move ahead, but thoughtfully, fully recognizing the social context in which our curriculum innovation takes place, for that social context is going to have an impact on the innovation again and again. If the general society does not presently support the overall principles of the curriculum effort, an effective community education program is absolutely essential.

We recognize that these questions and issues may cast a pall over our effort, but we also feel that the long-term stakes are too high to avoid such questions. Only by looking at the world as it *really* is, do we see any hope of changing it.

Another issue which is unpleasant to confront concerns both the numbers of children and the nature of the audience such a curriculum might reach. The basic issue here is the need to avoid any semblance of elitism. Probably no curriculum effort can less afford, in fact or perceived reality, to be clouded with an "elitist" aura. We are not so naive as to think any curriculum reform will revolutionize public education; that is not even our goal. We are concerned, though, that the goals of programs in law and humanities have significance for all children—not just those destined to be successful by accident of birth and family background. Such programs must reach out to touch the thousands—perhaps millions—of young people who are not in traditional school environments or who are in environments usually considered "lost" by increasing numbers of educators, social workers, parents, and others who care. We must avoid a curriculum serving the privileged few. We cannot count ourselves successful until children living in neighborhoods such as the South Side of Chicago, South Boston, and other inner cities, as well as depressed rural areas, experience and contribute to the richness of a law and humanities elementary school curriculum.

And, finally, we must remind ourselves that law-related concerns stretch well beyond American political boundaries. Carlos Cortés (1980) makes this point: "Perceptions of law, of justice, of equity, of discrimination, of crime and punishment, of legal processes and of law-related institutions do exist in other nations and they vary enormously from nation to nation, from culture to culture, and even among ethnic and other groups within any country. If we are to cope successfully with the challenges of the 1980's and beyond, we all need greater insight into the patterns and significance of this law-related diversity."

A genuine law and humanities curriculum must reflect the international context in which it exists. The study of law and the humanities should contribute to improving students' effectiveness as citizens of their own nation and of the world.

REFERENCES

Anderson, C. C. Promoting responsible citizenship through elementary law-related education. *Social Education,* 1980, *44,* 383–386.

Cortés, Carlos. Media in the internationalizing of law-related education. *Synergy,* 1980 (Spring), in press.

Wheeler, R., Ed. Social studies and the elementary teacher. Anderson, C. C.; McKinney-Browning, M.; & Falkenstein, L. C., Guest Eds. Law-related education. *Social Education,* 1980, *44,* 381–397.

A Framework for Viewing Law and the Humanities in the Elementary School

Isidore Starr

A fundamental assumption of this book and its collection of articles is that *an important relationship between law and humanities already exists*. The assumption proceeds a step more by suggesting that the nexus between these two areas is especially significant at the elementary grades. Stating that the nexus exists and that it probably is a very important one is a considerably easier task than articulating the specifics inherent in that generalization. In this paper, however, Isidore Starr takes on that task by describing an environment rich in constant transactions between law and humanities.

One of the most important contributions of this paper is the framework it provides for implementing curricular and programmatic designs which themselves reflect the intersection of law and humanities. The author develops this framework around five widely known concepts: liberty, justice, power, property, and equality. The framework underscores a theme running throughout this collection of essays; that is, anything less than a *systematic effort* toward integration of law and humanities will most likely prove—at the very least—ineffective. A directionless approach will produce fragmented, unimportant, and perhaps even counterproductive results.

This essay initiates a process of dialogue and probing which is continued throughout this book. It is somewhat ironic—but altogether fitting—that the author should lead us to this process by focusing our perspective on a specific framework and at the same time reminding us of the breadth of our legitimate concern if we are to draw from the humanities. Quoting Terence, he teases and stretches our perception of the context for law-related education: "I am a human being, and nothing human is alien to me."

The world of the law is landscaped with rules and regulations, police and bureaucrats, judges and legislators. It is a world that seems cluttered with many commandments—"thou shalt" and "thou shalt not's," ritualistic proceedings, obscure language, and omnipresent penalties. The world of the humanities is landscaped by roads heading toward such horizons as beauty, truth, justice, liberty, and equality. It is a world of inspiring ideals, exalted language, spiritual values, moral insights, and aesthetic standards. Although, at first glance, these two worlds seem separate, in reality they intersect at various points. The quest for the citizen of virtue, prudence, and wisdom, the righteous individual, and the good society finds its way into the world of law with its concern for the inalienable rights of life, liberty, and the pursuit of happiness, for due process of law, equal justice under law, and peaceful resolution of value conflicts.

The late Edmund Cahn, one of our most distinguished legal philosophers of the century, in commenting on this relationship between law and the humanities, observed:

In every mature society, there is considerable overlap between legal questions and moral questions. A man who violates the law against murder likewise violates a moral precept against killing; fraud and theft are condemned not only by courts but also by consciences; in short, law and morals frequently do their work with the very same item of human behavior. In a democratic society like ours where the law reflects many of the people's basic values, this overlap becomes all the more extensive and important. Under the official appearance of deciding the legal issues presented to them, American judges are often required to assess moral interests and resolve problems of right and wrong. It is realistic to look at the law not merely as a technical institution performing various political and economic functions but also as a rich repository of moral knowledge which is continually reworked, revised, and refined. [1956, p. 3]

Isidore Starr is Professor Emeritus of the City University of New York and past president of the National Council for the Social Studies. His most recent publications include *The Idea of Liberty* and *Justice: Due Process of Law,* both published by West Publishing Co.

17

As we traverse the worlds of the humanities and the law, we are—to invoke a famous Platonic metaphor—like chariots drawn by the twin steeds of reason and emotion. Confronted by a maze of conflicting value positions, the arguments of adversaries, differing interpretations of the law, majority and dissenting opinions, and contrasting philosophies of law and of life, one is tempted to give free rein to the steed of emotion and proclaim: "A plague on all your houses!"

The steed of reason, however, is generally there, champing at the bit and serving as a constant reminder that the world has no intention of stopping to let us get off. There is no easy escape for most of us. The journey must go on, and eventually thought and feeling in tandem may move most of us through the maze of life with a better appreciation of direction, detours, and destination.

Children, like adults, live in a network of legal relationships. Their names, food, clothing, and shelter are law-related, as are the streets they walk on, the bikes they ride, the buses they take, and the schools in which they learn. The very word "child" connotes legal rights and responsibilities.

Children also live in the world of the humanities. Their universe of do's and don'ts and rights and wrongs is reflected in thoughts and feelings about good and bad, fair and unfair. They respect and resent; they yield and rebel; they cry and they plead; and they live and endure in a world of "buzzing confusion" and imposed patterns of conduct.

What really goes on in the minds of children? There is no dearth of studies. Recent researchers in the field of moral judgment have drawn up typologies of responses arranged under such rubrics as preconventional, conventional, and postconventional. These attempts to connect ages with stages categorize the responses of children to moral and ethical dilemmas as moving from the amoral, premoral, or instinctive through the opportunistic to the principled autonomous position. John Rawls in *A Theory of Justice* (1971) places the psychological categories within the philosophical framework of the morality of authority, the morality of association, and the morality of principle. The research and the reflections on the moral judgment of children are relevant to the enterprise of joining the law and the humanities in a curricular design for the elementary school.

How does one structure a strategy for moving intelligently and without fear through the intersecting worlds of the law and the humanities? This, of course, is a critical question. For the teacher of children in the elementary school, the challenge is a crucial one. Without a frame of reference for introducing elementary school students into the worlds of the law and the humanities, the pattern of instruction becomes fragmented and directionless.

What follows is a suggested framework for viewing law and the humanities in the elementary school. In preparing it, I have drawn on the ideas which I developed in an essay on a "Rationale for a New Emphasis on Citizenship Education," which was prepared for the National Task Force on Citizenship Education (Starr, 1977). The framework is built around five major or landmark ideas in the law and the humanities: power, justice, liberty, property, and equality. These are words found in the Declaration of Independence, the United States Constitution and the constitutions of the states, the United States Bill of Rights and the state bills of rights, and other important documents. In addition, words such as "liberty" and "justice" are mouthed, more often than understood and appreciated, when the Pledge of Allegiance is proclaimed. The time has come for us to move out of ritual and into a realistic assessment of the meaning of these ideas as they affect our lives.

In examining the dimensions of each of the five ideas, I refer to the case-study approach. The advantage of this method has been described by Cahn in vivid terms:

...it is only in the concrete case that rational speculation can draw to it the flesh and blood of imaginative projection, and an abstract personal subject can be converted into a vibrant personality. The concrete case alone offers a stage suitable for projected drama, where it prompts the emotions, the glands, and the viscera to join with the faculty of reason in the experiences of a moral evaluation. In a concrete case, the sense of wrong is informed with some general personal commitment; in other words, there is real water in the cup and its presence there has put real lives at stake...human wisdom is on the mettle only where there is a practical risk, which imports responsibility and the felt burden of a personal involvement. [1956, p. 19]

This emphasis on the case method does not negate the importance of other strategies, such as moral dilemmas, hypotheticals, role-playing continuums, collages, mock trials, and field visits to courts and other governmental agencies. The case study, if done skillfully, is one of the most effective ways of getting the steeds of reason and emotion into a trot, at the very least, and into a gallop, at best.

The framework which I shall describe represents a perspective on the subject of the law and humanities. In a field as vast and challenging as elementary education, the more frameworks we have, the more certain we are of appealing to the minds and emotions of teachers and students.

The Idea of Power

Children are confronted with the idea of power in the concrete form of brute force and in the abstract form of legitimate authority. Like adults, children live in an atmosphere or nexus of power relationships. We could say that children are over-powered—physically, morally, and legally—by adults, in general, and by parents, teachers, preachers, and police, in particular. Commands and mandates come from the family unit, the teacher's instructions, the police officer's badge, and the pulpit. Sanctions take the form of censure, censorship, a ruler, a paddle, or ultimately a confrontation with the juvenile justice system.

Children live in a world of symbols and signs. The flag, the police officer's badge, the Capitol, the White House, the police station, and the courthouse signify aspects of the law. The signs are omnipresent: Stop, Yield, Keep Off the Grass, Do Not Touch, No Trespassing, Private Property, and No Loitering, among many others. Each carries a legal message buttressed by a threat of punishment.

How does one explain to children the difference between the exercise of legitimate authority by parent, teacher, government official, and police officer, and the unlawful power of the bully, the gangster, and the mob? Why is some authority legitimate and other authority illegitimate?

In his interviews with children relating to the game of marbles, Piaget (1962) discovered that children are aware of the jurisprudential aspect of marbles which relates to the origin of rules. For some the marble rules have mystic origins, while for others the rules are handed down by God or parent.

The mystic-theistic explanation has ancient roots. The Greek myth of Zeus and Athena is perhaps too risqué for the average elementary school. Any attempt to clean it up would do grave injustice to the orgiastic and capricious behavior of the gods. Perhaps the Mesopotamian myth of the gods Anu and Enlil is more appropriate. The former was the god of the storm and of coercion. Dennis Lloyd explains this godly connection in this way:

> The myths of Anu and Enlil reveal the deeply felt human need for order and the concomitant belief that such order . . . demands the combination of two essential elements, authority and coercion. Without the recognition of some authority whose decrees and sentences determine the structure of order in the world there can be no organized society and therefore the authority of divine rule makes possible the functioning of the universe as a social whole. But without the element of force to ensure obedience to the divine decree the universe could never attain the role of statehood. [1964, pp. 26–27]

There are other myths and stories which seek to trace the origins of power and the nature of legitimate authority. One could juxtapose the religious interpretation of one Supreme Being or several gods with secular explanations. William Golding's *Lord of the Flies* is on the surface an adventure story of English choirboys plane-wrecked on a tropical island. The thin veneer of civilization is quickly cut away to disclose the classic conflict of good and evil, brute force and reasonable authority, the nature of law and the meaning of justice.

Creative teachers have translated this story into an exercise entitled "The Island Game," in which, in imagination, students are placed for a period of time on an island without adult supervision. A leisurely paced exercise under the guidance of a nonintrusive instructor can lead to illuminating developments. Some classes will probably arrive at Aristotle's typology of governmental power: rule by one, rule by a few, and rule by the many. Given time, the activities may even confirm Aristotle's prediction of cyclical patterns. They may also reflect Max Weber's categories of authority: charismatic, traditional, and legal. Actually, it is too much to ask the elementary school child to mirror the sophistication of distinguished thinkers. It would not be unusual, however, to find these students reflecting some of the traditional questions relating to power and authority within this context.

Robinson Crusoe and other well-known (as well as teacher-created) stories and exercises can serve as lead-ins to the quest for an understanding of the origins of power and power relationships. Dilemma situations such as "Classroom without Rules" or "The Lawless Town" (a town without law-enforcement agencies) have been used successfully to pose the classic questions: Is might right? Why are rules and laws necessary? What is the source of power which legitimates laws and rules?

History and literature are depositories of case studies of legal authority, charismatic leadership, and unlawful domination. Hammurabi and his Code of Laws, Moses and his Ten Commandments, medieval kings and popes, the chiefs of Indian tribes, the leaders of primitive societies, and modern and contemporary dictators and democratic leaders offer opportunities for intellectual adventures in exploring the idea of power. These episodes of personal and impersonal authority open the door for a costs-and-benefits analysis of power in society as it affects each of us. (Two relevant anthropological studies exploring the relationship between law and primitive societies are Hoebel, 1954, and Gluckman, 1965.)

Lurking behind this inquiry is the omnipresent

issue of the nature of human nature. Do we really need rules and laws to regulate our conduct? Or are we so inherently evil that our conduct must be regulated by informal rules and formal legislation? This historic and philosophical debate between Rousseau et al. and Hobbes et al. can be translated for classroom study. It holds great promise for the law and humanities approach to understanding the role of law in American society and in the world community. A discussion of this humanities-centered issue of the law may even touch the hearts and minds of young students in ways in which traditional materials regularly fail to do.

There comes a time inevitably when the idea of the social compact as a source of power makes its appearance in the curriculum. Our Declaration of Independence states categorically that government derives its power from the consent of the governed. This principle is reflected in the United States Constitution, with its ringing Preamble: "We, the people of the United States, in order to form a more perfect union." This, in turn, can become the prologue for the study of the Founding Fathers' views on the desirability of decentralization of powers under a federal system with separation of powers and checks and balances. The corrupting influence of power, so feared by the framers of the Constitution, was reflected in the principle of limited power, which was eventually incorporated in a bill of rights.

Power transformed into legitimate authority by the social impact of the Constitution is wielded by men and women. There are those who use the power of the vote—the ballot—to elect leaders. This raises the perennial question of how to choose for positions of power those individuals who meet the moral and ethical standards demanded by a democratic republic. Meshing the major components of the idea of power with courses of study and a curriculum for the elementary grades is a formidable assignment for innovators and creative teachers.

The Idea of Justice

The idea of power is inevitably connected with the idea of justice. Adolf Berle has commented that there is a love-hate relationship between the two, while Cahn has noted that justice is "a word of magic evocation," which troubles our thoughts, arouses our emotions, and stimulates our glands. The Holocaust, torture of the innocent, execution of an innocent man or woman, or the incarceration of political prisoners in insane asylums generally evokes either silent anguish or cries of "Unfair!" and "Unjust!" It is our sense of injustice, says Cahn, which forces us to try to define the idea of justice, and it is this sense of justice and in-

justice which coalesces us into programmatic crusades for reform.

Children are confronted with the idea of justice in the concrete form of fairness in treatment and in the abstract form of due process of law in the school and community. Our contemporary views of justice as due process of law can have little meaning to the young unless they are introduced to those customs of the past which were designed to separate the innocent from the guilty. The medieval ordeals by fire, water, and battle, as well as the ingenious instruments of torture which have bloodied the soil of history down to the present day, offer opportunities for comparing what was with what is and with what ought to be.

There are episodes in ancient, medieval, and modern history which are useful in examining with students the relationship between power, justice, and law. For example, what can we learn about the values of Babylonian society and the nature of justice from a study of some of the provisions of Hammurabi's Code of Laws? What does a reading of the Ten Commandments tell us about the values of ancient Hebrew society? In early colonial Massachusetts, "a stubborn and rebellious son of sufficient understanding, sixteen years of age" who was disobedient to his parents could be put to death. This, too, tells us a great deal about moral values and legal enactments and the sense of justice in some societies. Each episode or example calls for inquiry about explanations, as well as supported critical judgment.

The comparative study of punishments carries with it value systems relating to human dignity. Socrates drinking hemlock, a witch burned at the stake or hanged, branding and mutilation, pillory, stocks, the dunking stool, prisons, and capital punishment by electricity, shooting, or drugs may be too gruesome for some elementary students, but instructive for many.

Turning to contemporary society, the Pledge of Allegiance and the Preamble to the Constitution mention justice, but the term is not defined with any degree of precision. It is reasonable to infer that the Fourth, Fifth, Sixth, and Eighth Amendments of the Bill of Rights convert abstract justice to procedural justice. The judicial process or procedure that is the due of any person accused of a crime is converted to a series of principles designated as due process of law. To avoid laundry-listing these great rights, I offer a schema for presenting due process of law. If we conceive of the courtroom as a theater, then we can involve students in the quest for the script, the props, the title of the drama, the starring roles, the subordinate players, the audience, and the press. If the dramatis personae do not assume the roles mandated by legal tradition, the morality play can easily become an immorality farce. The corrupt or prejudiced judge, the bribed juror, the perjured witness, or the incompetent counsel or prosecutor tilts the scales toward injustice.

The symbol of justice, the goddess with the scales and the sword or book, has had an interesting history. Originally without blindfold, she was free to observe the human comedy and to sift the guilty from the innocent. Corrupt justice in the Middle Ages led some jesters to blindfold her to show to all the world that the goddess was blind to justice. In later centuries the blindfold was interpreted to mean that justice was impartial because the goddess was not interested in the color, religion, or wealth of the accused (Simmonds, 1977). With the racial revolution the blindfold has been removed so that the poor and the disadvantaged in our society can stand before the goddess and demand her intervention through the balancing of the scales.

Since the adversary system is our way of seeking the truth in the forum of justice, it is desirable that the scales be equalized. Recent landmark rulings of the court in this area can be translated as evidence of sensitivity to the need for counsel for the poor, protection against unreasonable searches and seizures, and insistence that police refrain from coercing confessions. Such famous English maxims as "A man's house is his castle" and "A person is innocent until proven guilty beyond a reasonable doubt" can serve as entry points to study of the nature of criminal justice in this country.

The mock trial offers teachers and students the opportunity to apply previously acquired knowledge about due process of law to a historic or contemporary issue. The witchcraft trials and the famous cases of Roger Williams, Anne Hutchinson, or Peter Zenger offer scripts for student involvement in the judicial process. The meshing of skills and knowledge often results in appreciation of the strengths and weaknesses of our system.

Our system of due process of law can be evaluated on various levels by comparison with other methods designed to settle disputes. The blood feud, the duel, "the law of the jungle," retaliation, and the Eskimo song duel (Hoebel, 1954, pp. 93 ff.) have been used to achieve justice in some societies. Each has its rationale, and each has played a role in the clarification of procedural justice.

The evolution of the idea of juvenile justice from harsh codes to the juvenile courts today is an important part of the story of justice. Certainly, the young ought to be introduced to the due process of juvenile hearings and the alternative ways of disposing of such cases. Combining this subject with that of the mushrooming wave of juvenile crime offers ways of exploring the causes of crime and procedures for confronting this serious contemporary development both in the schools and in society at large.

For students, as well as for adults, the police represent power, authority, and justice. Meetings with police, role playing of problems confronting police, and trips to police stations and police academies can give students a realistic picture of the nature of the police officers' responsibilities. Such experiences may result in empathy, instead of vilification or apotheosis, and may bring each of the parties closer to an understanding of the other in the quest to clarify the meaning of justice on the streets, as well as in the courts.

The Idea of Liberty

The idea of liberty is symbolized by the Liberty Bell and the Statue of Liberty. We sing of our "sweet land of liberty" and "let freedom ring." Liberty is enshrined in such challenging slogans as "Give me liberty or give me death!" The Declaration of Independence refers to it as an inalienable right, the Preamble to our Constitution designates it as "blessings," and the Pledge of Allegiance promises liberty and justice for all. What does all of this mean in the mind of a child required to mouth it at the command of a teacher in a daily ritual or confronted by it in a living American document, such as the Bill of Rights?

Liberty is not an easy term to define. Abraham Lincoln put it very well when he said, in an address in Baltimore, April 18, 1864:

The world has never had a good definition of the word liberty, and the American people, just now are much in want of one. We all declare for liberty, but in using the same word we do not all mean the same thing. With some the word liberty may mean for each man to do as he pleases with himself, and the product of his labor; while with others the same word may mean for some men to do as they please with other men, and the product of other men's labor. Here are two, not only different, but incompatible things, called by the same name, liberty. And it follows that each of the things is, by the respective parties, called by two different and incompatible names—liberty and tyranny. [Quoted in Bohle, 1967, p. 228]

To avoid for the moment detours into definitions, I would like to suggest that for teaching purposes the First Amendment in the Bill of Rights is an excellent operating definition of liberty. It encompasses six significant principles: separation of church and state, religious freedom, freedom of speech, freedom of the press, the right to assemble peaceably, and the right to petition the government for redress of grievances.

Each of these six dimensions offers opportunities to dig into the past and to discover how these principles came to be incorporated in this unique document. In the study of colonial America, the role of the established church is crucial to an understanding of morals, ethics, and the law. Theocractic government made a sin a crime and a crime a sin. The long and tortuous road from colonial religious intolerance as a way of life to contemporary religious freedom as a constitutional right must be walked by students because it is the road to understanding that monumental metaphor—the wall of separation.

For elementary school students the walk can be leisurely, with periodic pauses before the statues of those who had a vision of liberty of conscience: Roger Williams, Anne Hutchinson, Lord Baltimore, William Penn, James Madison, and Thomas Jefferson, among others. Their thoughts are reflected in courageous stands, in memorable quotes, and in such great documents as the Maryland Act of Toleration, the colonial charters of Rhode Island and Pennsylvania, the Virginia Statute of Religious Liberty, the Constitution, the Bill of Rights, and the Northwest Ordinance.

Of course, elementary school children have been and continue to be exposed to this material, but have they and are they studying these great episodes and documents with a view to analyzing why some dissenters and leaders of change, the "bad guys and gals" of yesteryear, have become heroes and heroines in our history books? Is it possible that the dissenters of today may become the inspirational leaders of tomorrow?

Separation of church and state is a most important, but highly sensitive and controversial issue. The biographical approach is probably the simplest entry point to this complex problem. The extent to which teachers can move into the topics of financial assistance to parochial schools, released time, and compulsory prayers and Bible reading in the public schools will depend on the maturity of the students, the skill of the teacher, and the intellectual climate of the community.

As in separation of church and state, teaching religious freedom is relatively simple when one focuses on general principles. The rub comes when we move into particular cases: conscientious objectors to war, required flag salute, and the refusal of the Amish to send their children to public high schools. Here once again the professional skill of the teacher and maturity of the students are not enough. The community must be receptive to sophisticated discourse in the place of simplistic and safe clichés.

Do we have the right to say anything, anywhere, and anytime? Is the First Amendment absolute in its protection of freedom of expression? It is certainly worthwhile to explore with students in a general way the various interpretations of the First Amendment: the absolute position, the preferred position, the clear-and-present-danger rule, and the balancing principle.

The real test of the First Amendment's free speech provision is in the concrete case. Why is free speech prohibited or limited in the library and in the classroom? Why is certain language regarded as improper? When does speech become slander? When does speech become conduct? The story of Socrates, the case of the Tinker children and their black armbands, the use of "fighting words," and the case of Irving Feiner, an unpopular speaker confronted by a hostile audience, force our students to face significant value conflicts demanding resolution. The latter case has important implications for classroom decorum (*Feiner* v. *New York*, 340 U.S. 315 [1951]). Does an individual or a group have the right to interrupt and to disrupt the right of a speaker to address an audience in the street or in an auditorium? Does the American Nazi party have the constitutional right to march in Skokie, Illinois, a Chicago suburb heavily populated with Jews, many of whom survived the Holocaust?

The great American name in the history of the press is John Peter Zenger, a printer. Covered wherever American history is taught, this important case is rarely given the attention it deserves. The issue of seditious libel, truth as a defense, and Andrew Hamilton's eloquent speech to the jury can be meshed into a dramatic, memorable, and authentic episode. Its colonial theme has been reflected in recent cases upholding the right of the press to print falsehoods about public officials, provided there is no malice.

Although reviled by the Federalist press, Thomas Jefferson championed it in these words: "The basis of our governments being the opinion of the people, the very first object should be to keep that right and were it left to me to decide whether we should have a government without newspapers, or newspapers without a government, I should not hesitate a moment to prefer the latter" (from Padover, 1953, p. 93).

The press, in which we include the popular media of television and radio, has been prominent in significant episodes in our history: Watergate, the Pentagon Papers, and the free press–fair trial dilemma. Each of these cases evoked emotional attacks on the press and spirited defenses. In simplified versions, these case studies can evoke the constitutional as well as the moral arguments which inhere in censorship and freedom. Where issues of freedom of the press are relevant in the school environment, the classroom becomes a forum for the dissemination of ideas. The time to begin wrestling with these dilemmas is at the elementary school level, when children should be encouraged to take a stand on the continuum from state censorship to complete freedom of the press, and on variants of this perplexing theme.

The right to assemble peaceably and the right to

petition the government for redress of grievances are generally overshadowed by the foregoing rights. It is a mistake to bypass these rights because each is helpful in explaining an aspect of the idea of liberty. The reluctance to sign one's name to a petition or join an organization, especially if it is involved in reform, is widespread. Are these rights really a part of the world of political reality, or are they merely glittering generalities to be worshipped from afar? Are they "parchment barriers" or sturdy bulwarks against the capricious and arbitrary thrusts of public officials?

Eternal vigilance may be the price of liberty, but only a program of education in the dimensions of the idea of liberty can inform the people of why they ought to be vigilant.

The Idea of Property

Like the air, property surrounds us on all sides. We plant in it, build on it, walk and ride on it, produce and consume it, and save it. The three fundamental necessities of life—food, clothing, and shelter—are property. We protect it, worship it, steal it, and give it away. Nations claim it as air space and water shorelines, and wage wars over it. Political ideologies and economic systems grapple with its uses and distribution.

Accumulation of wealth is a part of the American dream. Children reflect this drive in a variety of ways. Anyone who has seen schoolchildren fight over seats, books, pencils, paper, and other articles is familiar with the cry, "It's mine!"

Children, like adults, move in a world of property relationships. They have their private possessions which they have bought or had purchased for them. They learn at an early age the difference between mine and thine. Some get allowances; others earn money; and some even save. Daily they are informed by television advertisers that they are disadvantaged if they do not possess more of a never-ending line of products of dubious merit.

Even before children enter school, the mine and thine relationship is expanded to include the more abstract distinction between private and public property. Traffic regulations for riding, biking, speeding, and playing in the streets are law-related examples of restriction on property rights. That which belongs to the school and to the community belongs to all of us, and, therefore, the uses of private property may be restricted as to time and place.

Our daily property transactions take place against a backdrop of history and political theory. Our Declaration of Independence speaks of life, liberty, and the pursuit of happiness, while our Bill of Rights protects life, liberty, and property. Is the pursuit of happiness to be equated with the acquisition of property? John Locke, who exerted a significant influence on colonial leaders, concluded; "The great and chief end, therefore, of men's uniting into commonwealth and putting themselves under government is the preservation of their property" (*Second Treatise on Civil Government,* chap. 8, sec. 95). Locke also defined property as including life, liberty, and estates. For him, as for many others, property is an all-embracing idea which is basic to the dignity and integrity of the individual as well as to the viability of a democratic republic. One of the assumptions on which this position is based is that property makes available options and alternatives and ways of effectuating change.

For the drafters of the Constitution and the Bill of Rights, property was a paramount consideration. For example, our law of the land protects patents and copyrights; it prohibits the taking of property for public use without just compensation; it permits taxing and borrowing; it proscribes unreasonable searches and seizures and the forced quartering of soldiers in homes on the principle that "a man's house is his castle"; it provides for bankruptcy; and it prevents states from impairing the obligations of contract.

With these observations as background, let us focus on the practical question of teaching the idea of property in the elementary schools. A starting point might be the world of the child as it relates to real and personal property. Land, money, and things represent webs of legal and social relationships. Legal rights and legal obligations flow from possession or ownership or both. Such signs as Private Property, No Trespassing, Do Not Enter, and Public Property invite analysis of property rights. The home, the school, the public park, the family car, the public bus, the street, and the private yard can all be used as case studies of mine and thine, private and public.

Children engage in barter and trading, giving and lending, and such transactions can be used as entry points to examining the idea of property. Taking property without the permission or against the will of the owner opens the door for a discussion of laws relating to burglary, robbery, and theft, as well as plagiarism.

As consumer, the child is the beneficiary, as well as the victim, of advertisers. The study of advertising and the analysis of its messages are essential to an appreciation of the use and abuse of property. The sooner children learn to differentiate the misleading from the instructive media messages, the better it will be for the individual and the community.

As consumers, children are always entering contractual relationships, either through the intervention of adults or on their own initiative. Purchases are contracts; the loan of school books or equipment is a contract; library books are borrowed; and money may be loaned or borrowed. It is not difficult to illustrate the rights-responsibilities-remedies nexus of contractual relationships by designing an actual contract. Such a document covering the loan of school books or equipment or school lockers could detail in simple language the precise conditions relating to the care of school property, as well as the penalties for failure to live up to the terms. From this elementary step the students can be moved to an edited version of the installment agreement and the landlord-tenant lease. When students are able to confront these awesome documents in edited language, they will better understand the never-ending legal relationships which will mark their lives.

There is an aspect to property law which puzzles students. As a rule, merchants will not contract with minors because the law protects children against the enforcement of most contracts. Faculty advisors are necessary as the cosigners of contracts made by students on behalf of their organizations. The reasons for this precedent deserve classroom discussion, since at first glance this seems to be a case of discriminatory treatment.

The study of American history, as well as other cultures, offers insights into the changing nature of property relationships. Slaves, serfs, indentured servants, and women as human property were accepted by intelligent people in the past as a natural component of the human condition. The study of economics raises issues of the distribution of wealth, the prevalence of poverty, and the role of the government in relation to each. The nature of the private enterprise system, as well as that of contrasting systems, can be presented in a variety of ways to young children.

The confrontation between the supporters of the quality of environmental life and the defenders of the right to use property for economic expansion or economic progress has produced such appealing slogans as "Pollution and Progress," "Save the Environment," "Protect the Wilderness," and "Protect Our Jobs." The complex nature of the controversy, however, compels the search for a hierarchy of values in contemporary society.

In the classic confrontation between property rights and human rights, we move from rules, tools, and institutions of the law to the law as humanity. In seeking legal solutions to these troubling questions, we might heed the advice of Justice Oliver Wendell Holmes: "To know what you want and why you think that such a measure will help it is the first but by no means the last step toward intelligent legal reform. The other and more difficult one is to realize what you must give

up to get it, and to consider whether you are ready to pay the price" (1960a, p. 209).

The Idea of Equality

Our Declaration of Independence proclaimed for all the world to hear that "all men are created equal," and most of our history since that time has focused on the meaning of equality. The Declaration reflected the temper of the times. Slaves and women were excluded from consideration. One was regarded as a chattel; the other, an appendage. Untaxed Indians were not regarded as part of the population for representation.

The Civil War did not free the slaves. The legal status of property had to be changed by constitutional amendments to overrule the Dred Scott case. The Thirteenth Amendment freed the slaves, the Fourteenth Amendment made the freed slave a citizen, while the Fifteenth Amendment prohibited denying the right to vote on account of "race, color, or previous condition of servitude."

In his memorable "I Have a Dream" speech, Martin Luther King, Jr., declared that, when the architects of the Constitution and the Declaration wrote their magnificent words, "they were signing a promissory note to which every American was to fall heir." That note was defaulted on for so many years. The lawlessness which characterized evasions of the three Civil War amendments is found in most history books, and the moral dilemmas raised by these practices—the supreme law of the land versus the folkways of a community—can be translated into resources suitable for the maturity levels of children.

The march of the equalitarian amendments takes us to the Nineteenth, dealing with woman suffrage. As in the case of the black man and woman, there were many participants in the march toward equality. Abigail Adams kept reminding John that, "whilst you are proclaiming peace and good will to men, emancipating all nations, you insist upon retaining an absolute power over wives." She goes on to warn that "notwithstanding all your wise laws and maxims, we have it in our power, not only to free ourselves, but to subdue our masters, and without violence, throw both your natural and legal authority at our feet" (Smith, 1962, vol. 1, pp. 255–226).

The Seneca Falls Declaration and Resolution on Woman's Rights rewrote the Declaration of Independence, 130 years ago, to read: "That all men and women are created equal." These words were finally heard in the Congress in the second decade of the twentieth century.

Gradually and inevitably, the Twenty-third, Twenty-fourth, and Twenty-sixth rectified inequalities in the election of public officials. One enfranchised District of Columbia voters in the election of the president and the vice president, another abolished the poll tax in federal elections, and the third extended the right to vote to 18-year-olds. Since the Constitution is the supreme law of the land, the march of the equalitarian crusade should be part of the education of our young people. Its subject matter raises serious questions about the morality of discrimination and the persistent gap between our principles and our practices.

Children are sensitive to unequal or unfair treatment in their homes, in their classrooms, and in their schools. They know when they are treated as inferior to some or superior to others. With this realization as a starting point, the juxtaposition of past and present can be useful in clarifying the nature of the idea of equality and the events and the personalities that have contributed to a change in attitude toward the victims of prejudice, discrimination, and hate.

In the past, the status of indentured servants, Indians, slaves, women, and children represented legal relationships which permitted victimization. In recent years the crusade against inequality in education, housing, employment, and accommodations seems to have lost some of its momentum. Progress is painfully slow, and that is discouraging for many. But there is no escape from this American dilemma.

Affirmative action, with its programs for assisting minorities in joining the mainstream of American life, has aroused the backlash of protest. How to resolve this clash of interests will try the patience of a saint and the wisdom of a Solomon. This especially difficult dilemma of goals or quotas does not excuse an escape from history. Teachers owe it to their students to initiate discourse in this area so that issues can be clarified and the options analyzed.

The clash between the constitutional mandate for equality and the conscientious plea to right the wrongs of the past can be translated into role-playing situations in which the issues get under the skin of the students. Among the possible episodes are Rosa Park refusing to move to the back of the bus; a black couple trying to buy a house in an all-white neighborhood; a Chicano applying for a job in an all-white firm; a school setting up an honors class and reserving several places for black, Indian, and Chicano students; or white students being bused into an all-black elementary school. The situations are many, and the only prerequisites are the teacher's creativity and courage to try something important.

The frame of reference for dealing with the idea of equality was suggested by the late Senator Everett M. Dirksen, when he paraphrased John Donne, in urging his colleagues to pass the Civil Rights Act of 1964: "Every denial of freedom, every denial of equal opportunity for a livelihood, for an education, for the right to participate in representative government diminishes me. There, is the moral basis for our cause" (quoted in Bohle, 1967, p. 141).

The Law and the Humanities: An Intermix

In teaching the law from a humanities perspective, the elementary school teacher can reach out to such sources as art, architecture, sculpture, music, and the rich depository of literature, as well as law. Each of these sources, in turn, can motivate students to create their own works of art and literature.

There are paintings, prints, and drawings depicting justice and injustice. For example, *The Indignant Eye* (Shikes, 1969) is a unique collection of satiric prints and drawings from the fifteenth century to Picasso, which bears on the themes we have discussed. I mention this to evoke thoughts of similar works useful for our deliberation.

There is an obvious architecture of the law. Many courthouses resemble Greek temples. Why? What is the psychology of this type of building? Is it a holy place? A special place? A different type of place? The Supreme Court building in Washington is the best example of this architecture, with its famous architrave announcing Equal Justice under Law.

The interior of a courthouse has a distinctive arrangement. The judge sits on a high bench and looks down on the proceedings. Why? Some courthouses have jury boxes, while others do not. What can we infer from this arrangement.

We find a sculpture of the law outside courthouses. The traditional figure of justice is a woman with scales, book, or sword. With an eye to equality, the United States Supreme Court entrance is graced by both a male and a female figure. One depicts the Guardian or Authority of the Law; the other, Contemplation of Justice. The impressive bronze entrance doors have eight sculpted relief panels which take us back in history to Achilles, Julian, the Justinian Code, Coke, the Magna Carta, and Marshall. Within the building itself are sculpted panels depicting historic law-givers before and after the Christian era. In fine, the Supreme Court building, as well as other courthouses, can be used as the core of a unit on landmarks in the history of the law (see *The Supreme Court,* n.d.; Mason, 1977).

There is much in music and song about the law. Contemporary ballads such as "Alice's Restaurant" and "Convoy," among others, offer insights into how some of us regard the law when it impinges on our lives. Gilbert and Sullivan's *Trial by Jury* and the "Policeman's Lot" from *Pirates of*

Penzance are additional examples of the law in musical comedy.

A number of plays have examined aspects of the law. Arthur Miller's *The Crucible,* the Japanese drama *Rashomon, Inherit the Wind,* and *The Andersonville Trial* portray the conflict of values which inheres in the drama of the trial.

I mention these with full realization that they may be much too difficult for the elementary school child. There must be significant plays for that age group. If there are not, then we must write them.

Some Concluding Thoughts

The spirit of the humanities has been captured, in my judgment, in Terence's famous observation: "I am a human being, and nothing human is alien to me." In a similar spirit, Justice Oliver Wendell Holmes, Jr., urged: "Connect your subject with the universe and catch an echo of the infinite, a glimpse of its unfathomable process, a hint of the universal law" (1960b, p. 57).

It is in this spirit that the law as a humanity should be approached. It should embrace the literature of autobiography, biography, tales, poems, and stories; the art and architecture of the law; the music and poetry of protest against injustices, as well as the songs of triumph; the thoughts of historians and social scientists; and the landmark rulings in the law. Anything that helps illuminate the relationship between law, on the one hand, and liberty, justice, equality, property, and power, on the other, is competent, relevant, and material to the study of the law within the context of the humanities.

In the short run, we face two great bicentennials. In 1987 we shall be celebrating the bicentennial of the drafting of our Constitution, the oldest living constitution in the world. In 1991 we shall be commemorating the bicentennial of the ratification of the Bill of Rights.

How shall we prepare for these milestones? What should be the agenda for the schools and for communities throughout the land?

Our symposium offers us a historic opportunity to mesh our thoughts on ways and means of fusing the law and the humanities into viable resources for elementary school instruction. Perhaps out of our deliberations will come materials and methods which will lead children to

focus on ways of transforming injustice into justice, license into liberty, inequality into equality, poverty into economic security, and political powerlessness into civic dignity and constructive activity in the political, economic, and social arenas.

There is an especially exciting flavor to the law-humanities nexus. It will improve instruction in the schools; it will arouse students' interest in serious dilemmas and landmark decisions; it will, we hope, democratize the atmosphere in the classroom and in the school; and it will enable each of us to cope more effectively with the demands of a law-saturated society. At the same time, it will hold up before us Jefferson's dream of life, liberty, and the pursuit of happiness—a dream that continues to urge us to reach just beyond the horizon.

REFERENCES

Bohle, B. *The home book of American quotations.* New York: Dodd, Mead, 1967.

Cahn, E. *The moral decision: Right and wrong in the light of American law.* Bloomington: Indiana University Press, 1956.

Gluckman, M. *Politics, law, and ritual in tribal society.* Chicago: Aldine, 1965.

Hoebel, E. A. *The law of primitive man.* Cambridge, Mass.: Harvard University Press, 1954.

Holmes, O. W. Ideals and doubts. In R. D. Henson (Ed.), *Landmarks of law.* Boston: Beacon, 1960. (a)

Holmes, O. W. The path of the law. In R. D. Henson (Ed.), *Landmarks of law.* Boston: Beacon, 1960. (b)

Lloyd, D. *The idea of law.* Harmondsworth, Middlesex: Penguin, 1964.

Mason, D. The Supreme Court's bronze doors. *American Bar Association Journal,* 1977, *63,* 1395–1399.

Padover, S. K. (Ed.) *Thomas Jefferson on democracy.* New York: New American Library, 1953.

Piaget, J. *The moral judgment of the child.* New York Collier, 1962.

Rawls, J. *A theory of justice.* Cambridge, Mass.: Harvard University Press, 1971.

Shikes, R. E. *The indignant eye.* Boston: Beacon, 1969.

Simmonds, A. The blindfold of justice. *American Bar Association Journal,* 1977, *63,* 1163.

Smith, P. *John Adams.* New York: Doubleday, 1962.

Starr, I. Rationale for a new emphasis on citizenship education. In *Education for responsible citizenship: The report of the National Task Force on Citizenship Education.* New York: McGraw-Hill, 1977.

The Supreme Court of the United States. Washington, D.C.: Supreme Court, n.d. Available from the Supreme Court.

A Framework for Viewing Law and the Humanities in the Elementary School

Paul F-Brandwein

One of the most challenging (indeed provocative) aspects of defining the nexus between law and humanities is the a priori task of defining these areas of concern. What in fact are the legitimate concerns of law and humanities? In this article Paul F-Brandwein presents readers with a broadened vision of the humanities and their potential for enriching the lives of all people.

While Brandwein's article discusses the several concepts outlined by Isidore Starr and concurs that they are valuable as a framework for teaching about law and humanities, his own paper focuses on yet another key aspect of the subject, the climate of education. Presented in this paper are what the author terms metavalues—those values which, in turn, according to Brandwein, should provide the framework for deriving other values and curriculum goals. Those metavalues—truth, beauty, justice, love, and faith—are at once the rubrics and the necessary elements of a humane environment.

The author agrees with Starr that the vehicles of the humanities, such as art, literature, dance, philosophy, history, are rich in their capacity to convey the metavalues he describes. Most of all, these vehicles and their intersection with law illuminate what appears to be a fundamental and valuable message of this article: Brandwein reminds us that "the essence of humanity is at the same time the essence of the humanities as curriculum."

Americans continue to believe that initial social and intellectual inadequacies can be ameliorated by altering the environment, and most continue to assume that altering the school's social and intellectual environment means altering teaching policy and practice. To alter teaching is to alter the plans (curriculum) and modes (methods) of instruction; and this, in turn, means altering the manner by which we conserve, transmit, rectify, and expand our knowledge and skills, our concepts and values, so that they are widely accepted and generously shared. And we are urged to do this for the entire spectrum of social and intellectual capacity. Clearly our social purpose is to spread self-esteem, power, and privilege over the entire range of ability and to reduce disability in any sector, and this through the modes of education. And, now, we are met to consider whether the law, within the framework of the humanities, might add the antecedents necessary to the full life

Paul F-Brandwein is Director of Research at Harcourt Brace Jovanovich, Inc. He is currently synthesizing his research of over 25 years in a work to be titled *Essentials in the Transformation of the Schools.*

of a citizen in an open society—a society where social action is to be gained by balanced opinion, votes without coercion. We would have people with a discipline of responsible consent, or dissent, who between impulse and action interpose evidence, reason, judgment, and compassion.

I have assumed the privilege of these introductory remarks precisely because Isidore Starr's paper is one informed by evidence, reason, judgment, and compassion. Moreover, if I read him correctly, he advocates the concordance of reasonable and compassionate minds; and I am persuaded that, in him, is the love of the defenseless—in this case, the child. If I read him correctly, he considers curriculum to be, in effect, a "compact delivery system of the culture" and defends, with clarity and conciseness, the proud heritage of our culture in its practices, in its systems of beliefs, and in its systematic assertions—its documents and its laws. Starr would distill those elements of the culture which he considers relevant into five conceptual schemes, "major or landmark ideas" in the law and the humanities: *power, justice, liberty, property,* and *equality.* He tells us that the time has come to "move out of ritual and into a realistic assessment of these ideas as they affect our lives."

Although it is sporting, in the academic world, to disagree, to warm up with the calisthenics of urbane argument with which the university equips us, to hone the fine point or reinterpret this point or that, or argue whether this or that bit of evidence is germane, I shall gratify myself with neither the calisthenics nor the quibble. It is abundantly clear that schooling is a science of practice, not of the laboratory—and certainly this is true of education and, I suspect, of the law. It is further clear to me, as one who has spent his life in orchestrating *compact delivery systems of the culture* (shorthand: curriculum), that what Starr proposes is feasible and, further, that *strategies and tactics of instructed learning* (instruction) can be married to the curriculum of the five conceptual schemes he proposes. We should consider *instructed learning,* as Bruner (1966) calls it, as a surrogate definition for instruction. We need to remind ourselves that we are not primarily concerned with learning in the random sense, but with instructed learning, which is nonrandom and usually takes place in a constructed environment—a classroom, a community, or a society. We do not, for example, teach children to pick pockets, to steal, to kill. Indeed, the school is an agent of society passing on its concepts, values, and skills—its epistemology, ethics, aesthetics, and axiologies—to its children. Education (as compared with schooling) is, to my mind, a far broader concept; it is the lifelong search for personhood—and it is the search for personhood which undergirds Starr's purposes, it is the warp and woof of his proposal.

In a word, from my perspective as a curriculum designer and as a researcher, Dr. Starr's framework is sound, feasible, practical. It can and should form one of the frameworks upon which the law and the humanities should be considered in the light of Starr's own proposal: "In a field as vast and challenging as elementary education, the more frameworks we have, the more certain we are of appealing to the minds and emotions of teachers and students." The question then becomes, What kind of design for the framework he suggests? Let me recommend for purposes of reference only a design of a framework for instructed learning in the law and the humanities.

Reflect, if you will, that I speak of teachers, not instructors: a teacher is as large as life, and the instructor, only as large as his or her subject matter. And there's the rub: to teach the humanities, which must deal with the humane use of human beings, demands teachers. And children, who are of supreme moral worth, deserve teachers. And the kind of society we advocate here requires teachers.

A Design for a Framework

The kind of design I recommend for your consideration is offered in papers presented at Harvard University, at Colorado College, and at the University of the Pacific (see Brandwein, 1969, 1971, 1977). These are curriculum grids (curricular forms) developed on a conceptual base, with five major conceptual schemes forming the base; each conceptual scheme is defined in a statement which is intended to limit its range.

As we examine a curricular grid based on concepts, we note an ascending order of concepts—each one having more intellectual power, requiring more cognitive and affective skills, and demanding more experience; we are not to do damage to maturation. We go—where we can and where we really "know" what to do—from the familiar to the unfamiliar, from the concrete to the abstract, from the simple to the complex. (This is *not* obeisance to Piaget or Kohlberg, who—to my mind—have exceeded the wisdom of their data).

Having done the insupportable to Starr by having placed his indomitable ideas in a curricular vise, I now avail myself of Charlotte Anderson's charge to bring to bear on his thesis certain aspects of schooling which might be obstacles to the realization of his excellent proposal. Indeed, in his paper, Starr explicates the origins of the problems I press upon you. He states, "The very word 'child' connotes legal rights and responsibilities," and again, "They respect and resent; they yield and rebel; they cry and they plead; and they live and endure in a world of 'buzzing confusion' and imposed patterns of conduct." Perhaps I might state these as paradoxes within the context of schooling, which, for discussion, I arbitrarily call the "paradox of equal treatment," the "paradox of fair or just treatment," and the "paradox of psychological freedom." I shall deal with these briefly, and then proceed to argue that Starr's curriculum is indeed a humanities curriculum but deserves a matrix of a larger scope.

The "Necessary" Antecedents

We seem to have a cranky vision of schooling, of children and teachers at odds. No matter what we do, no matter how excellent our practice, someone, some pupil insists on *not* being successful. This is surely perverse. One wonders at the perversity of the population which "will not" succeed—by our measures. Does not the perversity lie in us? Does it not stem from our eternal assumption that somehow schooling frees capacity, neutralizes flawed personality, corrects the impress of genetics and the habituation of childhood, ennobles motivation, and frees special talent? Nevertheless, one who confronts schooling—schooling in any country—knows that the essential purpose of schooling is not to free the individual, but to modify behavior in the interests of society. (This is not to say that society will not eventually learn that freeing the child to find his or her full potential is freeing him or her for full participation in society—always with appropriate guidance.) To many schooling means that through appropriate curriculum and instruction or the perfect methodology of trained adults (notably teachers) *everyone* can be taught to read, to write, to number, to think freely and to inquire freely with the competence prescribed for adults. Not so.

Naturally, equal access to opportunity must become fact as well as policy. Nevertheless, we do recognize the astonishing variability of the human population—particularly its young; we recognize (when we wish to) that this remarkable variability is not only our strengh, but the guarantee of our freedom. To treat everyone as "same" or "similar" is to set aside the facts of variability. Herein lies the "paradox of equal treatment"; in curriculum and instruction (in schooling) there is nothing so unequal as the equal treatment of unequals.

Within any segment of schooling—curriculum, instruction, classrooms, playing field, textbooks, music, art, social studies, mathematics, science, etc., etc.—the gifted, disadvantaged, handicapped, and so-called normal must be given *equal opportunity* and *equal access* to a variety of opportunities (say courses, extracurricular activities, sports, compassionate guidance); but once this is afforded, the facts of variability and the necessity for a teacher to meet the needs of the children require that they be given *differential treatment*. This differential treatment is at all times to be afforded all with "constructive affection" (Margaret Mead's term). Otherwise, how can girls and boys fulfill themselves as they seek their individual excellence in pursuit of their powers? To achieve self-esteem and worthwhileness, as Coopersmith (1967) defines them, is for children to achieve "power"—the power coming out of self-esteem, an increase in capacity, and a sense of worthwhileness.

That is to say, we cannot develop a curriculum enveloping the law and the humanities which enables children to probe the nature of equality and power without attending to a situation in schooling which denies them the equality coming from the equal opportunity to make the most of their gifts, talents, powers—and so, in turn, denies the power coming out of the fulfillment of these gifts. That is the "paradox of equal treatment."

Second, if we examine the records of students in our schools (the major cities are the best examples), we find that 30%–40% of children and youth are in possession of 75% of all the "failing marks." Sometimes these "failing grades" are entered into the record, sometimes the boy or girl is merely passed on and then leaves school without adequate competence to face a rapidly burgeoning postindustrial society. A simplistic statement this, but almost at the point of "truth": in affording all equal (the "same") treatment, we use the methods and materials which are successful with 60%–70% to "teach" all the students. There are enough data to show that the methods of instruction (see paradox of psychological freedom below) which are useful for the successful 60%–70% are not useful for the other 30%–40%. And these methods and materials are detrimental for the gifted. So—at present—we produce a "failed" segment of youth year in year out. How will they function as adults? What will they contribute to society? Who is "unsuccessful" in our industrial society? Who goes to jail—and returns to jail? This, then, is the "paradox of fair or just treatment."

By law we require children and youth to attend school; the teachers of the institution which they attend (who are employed by the city, county, or state and are therefore legally *in loco parentis*) regularly fail 30%–40% of those forced by law to attend. Now it is clear that there are methods of instruction, choices in curriculum, and methods of administration which fit this "failing" group and would, it seems to me, make schooling successful or at least tolerable for the group. We are ready, it seems, to ask these young to serve in the armed forces and, if necessary, to lay down their lives for their society. But we have not as yet come to the point where we will meet their needs during their compulsory years of schooling. If we build a curriculum based on the concept of justice, must we not provide the young with just treatment? Can they honorably participate in the work of the institutions in which they feel unjustly treated? (Some 2 million children and youth are not now in our schools; some drop out; some never go.)

And then there is that special variety of research called "educational research." It is almost always statistical, seldom engaged in the careful, patient observation of individual children. Almost always the *individual—the individual child*—who is, as individual, of supreme moral worth, is lost in the arms of the larger statistic. If we would listen we would hear the child's cry—"Alone and afraid/in a world I never made."

We recognize that in the paradoxes of "the quest for equal treatment" and "the quest for fair and just treatment" I have been dealing with two faces of the dilemma. It is not a *di*lemma, however, but a *tri*lemma.

We think we know that there are many ways of

learning, that the most efficient ways of instructed learning make use of multisensory approaches, varieties, or procedures—procedures which appeal not only to the processes of linear sequencing but also to simultaneous processing (so-called left and right brain lateralities). What do we find, however, in the classroom? We find a "paradox of psychological freedom." Starr presses for case studies, field trips, music, art, plays, and many other ways of getting into the nervous system, all of which offer the child means to exercise his or her idiosyncratic ways of learning. But what transpires in the classroom? My research relentlessly demonstrates that by the sixth grade teachers talk 50%–70% of the time; by the ninth, 60%–80% of the time; by the tenth or eleventh, 70%–90% of the time; and in the senior year, 90% of the time or more. The lecture is as omnipresent in the high school as in the college. But picture the youngster who in 6 hours of schooling will spend as much as 4–6 hours in the passive state—listening and trying to retain what is "lectured" in memory or notebook. The fact is, with present modes of administration (which in turn depend on community approval and support) teachers are simply overloaded with subject matter and numbers of students, and lecturing seems to be a useful economy. But lecturing will eventually be seen as aversive; it is a mode of presentation, not a mode of teaching. When one lectures one cannot know whether one is teaching; teaching implies an overt response of the learner to demonstrate understanding or, at least, participation.

Thus we speak of a magnificent curriculum in the law and the humanities, based on equality, justice, and liberty—and by our very methods of instruction (curriculum) we deny equality, justice, and liberty to certain citizens at possibly the most sensitive period of their participation as citizens—namely, as learners. Certainly the denial is not because of ill will or indifference but because, in the public mind, schooling is not yet valued. Yet it is the way in which society conserves and transmits its concepts, values, and skills—and failing to do so, places itself in peril. And, of course, as was said earlier, schooling should be the way in which society not only conserves and transmits its concepts, values, and skills, but rectifies and expands them. In my view, based on considerable observation, most teachers are ready to advance the causes of education, but we in the United States consider schooling as not of the first priority. Yet it is the reservoir of our major resource.

At this time, in our classrooms sit a future president, a future discoverer of the field theory, of a cure for cancer, of a new way of securing energy, of ways of "curing" our environment of its pestilence and pollution, someone who will discover how children learn, and someone who will invent a school for all children. I am thus compelled to turn to a certain *climate* of schooling which is essential for the kind of work in which the law will be embraced by the humanities.

The Climate of the School

Why are we gathered here? Who—or what—are our enemies? Are they not ignorance, stupidity (defined as being wanting in understanding; it has nothing to do with IQ), inhumanity, meaninglessness? In these terrible times, when we face such countless terrors, are there any alternatives to securing equality, justice, liberty to each of us?

I am persuaded that nothing less than a change in the climate of schooling is essential. I am persuaded that without a change in climate—without a direct stance, an honest strike at the inhumanity and meaninglessness which now pervade our schools, curricular thrusts such as are proposed here may not succeed. I am persuaded with Jerome Kagan that what we need to restore are "faith, honesty, and humanity." It seems clear to me that honesty and humanity and faith can be found in the compact delivery system of the culture we know as the humanities. And, of course, the law is central to the humanities.

Humanities Curriculum as Basic to a Sanative Climate

Gandhi said, "My life is my message." And Socrates' eloquent statement, "The unexamined life is not worth living," was true, and truer still in light of his death. He died when his death could be counted as more worthy than life. To be truly human is to measure one's life against the ideals prized by humankind.

The humanities deal precisely with the ideals prized by humankind—our need first to create a meaningful life, then to impart the knowledge of what that means—to give to the world a template of thought and deed. The humanities in general fulfill a purpose that Northrop Frye ascribed to literature in particular. Literature, Frye tells us, enables humankind to imagine not only the kind of life it would like to live, but also the life it would not seek.

The essence of humanity is thus at the same time the essence of the humanities as curriculum. This seems a play on words, but it is not.

No one who has human aspirations emulates those who honor the killer, the sadist. Killing and cruelty are considered inhuman—and inhumane. We honor truth, beauty, love, faith, justice; we call them human virtues and attributes. To possess them is to be humane. In effect, and in fact, the humanities as curriculum comprise the essential values of humanity: *truth, beauty, love, faith, justice*. Humankind measures the quality of its existence against these values. They are the superordinate goals of humankind, its metavalues.

Are they not also very near the kinds of superordinate goals and metavalues we should put before children? Are they not the superordinate goals and ideals of teachers, and their needs, as well? Are they not the superordinate goals and ideals of education, the measures by which we determine whether we are human, and not brute?

Examine any curriculum—which is, after all, a tool of those who would civilize—in order to discover its underlying philosophy. Do we find it proclaiming that its just and true ends are falsehood, ugliness, tyranny, hatred, and cynical disbelief? We always find as its basis the universal metavalues: truth, beauty, justice, love, and faith. And the curriculum, particularly in the humanities, seeks ways to realize them.

The humanities are concerned with the symbolic—expressed in the imagery of literature, music, art, drama, and dance. The precious forms of the civilized, the documents, the books, the monuments: this symbolism reflects the deepest aspirations of humankind and the need to understand the meaning and nature of the human condition, to penetrate the mystery of human destiny.

The prime purpose of planning a curriculum is the reduction of complexity. In the chaos of experience, we all try to edit and interpret experience in a search for meaning. It is not the world we see that we encompass in experience. We sort out what we see; we reduce experience to meaning. It is not the world we see that is, in the end, important. What is significant is the world we build out of what we see. Schooling is experience in search of meaning. A school (a place for schooling) is a design for the search for meaning. And in its search for meaning it seeks to help the child reduce the complexities of his or her experience to wholes—to meanings. The world that children come upon should not remain an alien and confusing environment, but must become a place that they understand. The world must become their home.

The school is the environment that reduces random encounters and complexity. It reduces complexity through the constructs (the concepts and values) it assembles into a curriculum. The curriculum, in turn, having reduced the complexity of experience, reduces complexity in instruction and yields stability. But this conceptual structure also promotes the accommodation to variety necessary for teaching the humanities to children.

Sadly, these enduring measures of humankind, which are central to the humanities, have been left to chance encounter in the past. Truth, beauty, love, justice, and faith are as important as matter, energy, interaction, interdependence, and the like. The ideals have endured because they are of highest moral worth. They are not only important to the well-being and mental health of men and women, but are the means by which they gain life and build on it. We need not only physicists, linguists, artists, sociologists, and psychologists, but also ethicists.

Individuals live and die. But the human endures, or, at least, has endured until now. The purpose of this symposium—or at least one of its purposes—is to press forward with a humane act: the building of a curriculum informed by humaneness—by justice, equality, liberty—in a word, by humanity. The human endures perhaps because the ideals of truth, beauty, justice, love, and faith endure.

Humankind is at a turning point in its civilization. Our schools are facing the first true generalizing of education: all children will come to school and stay there. They will have equal access not only to opportunity, but also to a variety of opportunities. This is a goal of education. We are about to realize that there is nothing so unequal as the equal treatment of unequals—unequals in experience, history, and previous opportunity. In the coming years—no matter how long it takes—we will give each individual his or her due: as child, as human. We base this resolve on the belief that every child is of supreme moral worth.

The humanities, like all disciplines, have concepts that are particular to the discipline. Atom, ion, gene, magnetism establish the environment of science. Property, vote, government, nation, group, race, region, economy seem to be associated with social science, which is, depending on the school of thought, either an integral part, or not, of the humanities. Poem, symphony, color, line, choreography, sonnet, ballet, song, picture, drama indicate a departure from science, social science, or mathematics. They belong to the world of the humanities.

Thus, while Starr suggests a law-related social-studies-centered curriculum based on the concepts of equality, liberty, freedom, property, power, I would suggest that these are but subconcepts of the larger world of the humanities. That is, they are subconcepts of the great foothold metavalues and conceptual schemes: truth, beauty, justice, love, and faith.

In my studies of curriculum, I find bits here and there of the law, but no consistent effort, although there have been some probes. I know of the Legal Education Project, its publication lists, its tentative and limited successes, and its general malaise. So I endorse the need to relate the law to elements of the curriculum, but I urge a more careful consideration of what is meant by the humanities. Certainly there is a tendency to take a part of the humanities, the social sciences, and equate that portion with the whole. First, we should not be put off by any mutterings such as "lowered standards," "the kids won't work," "the parents don't care," "back to the basics," and the like. These are symptoms of discontent which always emerge between "wars" of any kind, whether they involve military or social combat; they are the empty-headed phrases of those who are relieved of guilt and anxiety when they invoke these phrases. Friedenburg (1966) and Goodlad (1964) have probed the malaise and suggest that the school's climate does not help a child develop a "core of one's own," and Goodlad notes that although the school's ends are good, teachers do not have the time or perhaps the inclination to search for "what lies beneath" the surface of a child's behavior.

Perhaps Kagan has put it in a way close to our purpose:

I want to see schools begin to serve the needs of society. Ancient Sparta needed warriors, Athens needed a sense of the hero, the ancient Hebrews needed knowledge of the Testament, nineteenth-century Americans needed managers and technicians—*and the schools responded beautifully in each case by providing the kind of people that society needed.* What do we need now? I believe that we need to restore faith, honesty, humanity.

Every society must sort its children according to the traits it values. We will never get away from that. A society needs a set of people whom it can trust in and give responsibility to for the health of its people, the legal prerogatives of its people, wars of its people. The function of the school system is in fact to prepare this class. [1973]

A climate in the schools in which law can flourish requires a climate in which children can flourish. And teachers as well. For if the teachers' needs are not met, neither will those of the children be met.

A Permanent Agenda for Humankind

We value others as we wish to be valued. If we learn compassion, we value the worth of others despite their limitations. Compassion teaches us to recognize that even a person's shortcomings are part of his or her uniqueness. Identity is achieved in an environment where this uniqueness, which results in variety, is prized. In our society we would have each child become compassionate as well as competent. Our studies show that all curricula embody this ethic in one form or another. Being a proud people, and only in our more courageous moments willing to admit that we are also people of deep feelings, we do not use terms that would label us as "soft." Yet it takes great courage

to be compassionate and to admit that compassion is equal to or as necessary as competence. Teaching, after all, is more than just a profession; it is a mercy.

If we would but use what we know, there would be no need for pollution, pestilence, or poverty. We could control overpopulation and disease; we could eliminate shortage; we could conserve our environment, making it sanative and beautiful. If we lived by the ethics and aesthetics we know, man's inhumanity to man would cease. Our science has made us capable; it could help make us human. Children would come to believe in humankind as heroic. But first, in the words of Albert Schweitzer, we need to be "finished with ourselves." Schweitzer achieved this. He took on a life of service to others, using his gifts and fulfilling his destiny in pursuit of a special excellence.

Modern men and women can also be heroic if, between impulse and action, they interpose evidence, reason, and judgment, compassion side by side with competence.

Once we measure ourselves against the only ideals worthy of aspiration—truth, beauty, justice, love, and faith—we will be on the road to completion of our agenda. And if we live according to this agenda, we will become, in the words of Dag Hammerskjöld, "truer, stronger, kinder, warmer, simpler, and gentler." It is time.

It is time that the permanent agenda of school and society, of parent and child, of teacher and pupil come to be this: to become truer, kinder, gentler, warmer, simpler, quieter, humbler, and so to become firmer, stronger, and wiser.

REFERENCES

Bruner, J. S. *Toward a theory of instruction.* Cambridge, Mass.: Belknap, Harvard University Press, 1966.

Brandwein, P. F-. *Toward a discipline of responsible consent: Elements in a strategy for teaching the social sciences in the elementary school.* New York: Harcourt Brace Jovanovich, 1969.

Brandwein, P. F-. *The permanent agenda of man: The humanities (a tactic and strategy for teaching the humanities in the elementary school).* New York: Harcourt Brace Jovanovich, 1971.

Brandwein, P. F-. *The reduction of complexity: Substance, structure, and style in curriculum.* New York: Harcourt Brace Jovanovich, 1977.

Coopersmith, S. *Antecedents of self-esteem.* San Francisco: Freeman, 1967.

Friedenberg, E. Z. *The vanishing adolescent.* New York: Dell, 1966.

Goodlad, J. S. *Education and the idea of mankind.* New York: Harcourt Brace Jovanovich, 1964.

Kagan, J. A conversation with Jerome Kagan. *Saturday Review of Education,* 1973 (April), pp. 41–43.

Children's
Learning

An Introduction

"I have often wondered, when I was representing a child in a delinquency or neglect proceeding," a children's advocate has mused, "what it meant for me to go up to a nine- or ten-year-old and say, 'I'm your lawyer. Here I am; tell me what to do. What do you want me to do in representing you?' What do the children think of me? What do legal rights mean to them? What are the long-term consequences for a child of being told you have a lawyer, you have rights, and we are going to defend you in court?" (Ward, 1976).

Implicit in this attorney's reflection is the recognition that such experiences teach. Or, to put it another way, children learn from these experiences, and what they learn in turn affects the kinds of citizens they can be and will be in the future. Fortunately for the welfare of the children and of society in general, we are beginning to understand better the nature of political/legal socialization and to isolate childhood antecedents to competent, responsible adulthood. We are discovering the critical variables which influence how children perceive events and how they respond to them. We are discovering, also, something about the character of events or experiences which are relevant for certain types of learning. We know, for example, that the experience of going to court teaches children about our justice system.

But we also know that children don't have to encounter the justice system directly or experience such overtly "legal" settings as courts and police stations to gain basic law-related knowledge and competencies. A multitude of other experiences accessible to all children can either facilitate or hinder this development. Childhood games, for example, teach about the nature of rules. The methods teachers use to assign classroom housekeeping tasks teach about responsibility and equity. Family decision-making processes teach about authority. Disputes on the playground develop skills in conflict management. History lessons convey messages about the values society condones or condemns.

Children respond to and interpret these kinds of experiences in various ways. Each of the papers in this section discusses particular factors affecting children's learning and makes assertions about desired learning outcomes as both relate to law and humanities. Each author stresses different aspects of childhood, of schools, and of society that are relevant to the topic. Each has preferences for given approaches. All, however, agree that *every* child has the right to both self-esteem and social competency. And all agree that the elementary school years offer special opportunities for sociocivic development. Finally, all recognize the tremendous opportunity and responsibility this implies.

REFERENCE

Ward, M. S. Legal policies affecting children: A lawyer's request for aid. *Child Development,* 1976, *47,* 1–5.

Social and Political Thinking in Children: Implications for Law and Humanities Education

Nancy B. Wyner

Children's social and political thinking is a complex, multidimensional process which has received a great deal of attention from researchers and theoreticians over the last two decades. Concomitantly, the curricular and instructional implications of such research findings and theoretical constructs have been explored and hotly argued. Nancy Wyner courageously enters this fray by discussing in this paper some of the theories and research she feels to be particularly relevant to education in general and to a law and humanities program in particular. She draws heavily on Piaget's work in noting that developmental as well as interactive forces shape children's sociopolitical learning. Among the interactive forces she cites are adult-child relationships. She notes that the studies show that adults who treat children with respect instead of using arbitrary authority lay the foundation for group social responsibility which carries over into adulthood. The paper concludes with a set of competencies for law and humanities which the author draws from the research reviewed.

Prologue

Episode 1. A few weeks ago I was at the local supermarket to replenish the family food supply. Ours had been exhausted during The Great Storm. Two little guys skimmed around the corner of the aisle and positioned themselves behind the Ritz Cracker display carton. Their motions were attuned to each other, knowing the game, yet sharing in its creation. From the corner of my eye I watched as they leveled their finger-guns at this basic citizen. I resisted a counteroffense and remained poised. An argument erupted between them: "No! There needs to be more robbers before you need more cops. So you be the robber and then we'll both be cops!" I moved on, pleased by the durability of this familiar game, admiring the logic and negotiating skill of these two supermarket ruffians.

The episode is wonderfully commonplace, simple at the surface. As the action is repeated each player will learn the sequences of his part and of the other player. They may negotiate for roles and argue over strategies, but they do not overtly teach each other the actions. They interact, perceive, and experience in each other's actions their part and the part of the other player.

In this supermarket intrigue there are other fascinating dimensions. The response ·itself demonstrates interest and a scant bit of information that one of the youngsters has gathered about the meaning of, need for, and role of law enforcement. The location for the scene is not a school but my local supermarket, quite an unremarkable, arbitrary setting in community life. As a seasoned observer of children, I also discover a high degree of involvement, interpersonal competence, and some pretty skillful tactics for managing conflict.

The little episode introduces us to children's thinking, their social skills and perceptions. It also provokes us to consider settings in which children travel about as learners.

Episode 2.

"In the third grade I got an American Legion citizenship award. They were awarded every semester in each grade. One to a boy and one to a girl. I thought then that this was a special thing—even at that age I was overly attached to public, preferably in written recognitions of merit. I never knew exactly why I got this reward, and as I grew older, I felt it was because I was an orderly, neat, nonagitative, approval-seeking child. I seemed to express these qualities that said I would fit in, accept authority and obey rules. The dilemma of citizenship now is that the most useful, creative, important citizens don't always obey the rules and, in fact, they work to change them, so why did they give me an award for obeying rules? I'm still trying to learn to have enough courage and strength not to when I think I shouldn't."[Wyner, Note 1, p. 33]

Nancy B. Wyner is Assistant Professor at Wheelock College, Boston, Massachusetts. She has written many articles on the development of civic competency in young children.

In this anecdote, a producer of a children's television show recalls a memorable citizenship experience. Her reflections inform us of the enduring impact of early experiences and the influence of an award system for conveying values and instructing behavior. Here the school is the location, but who are the teachers? And what should the learner be learning?

Episode 3.

"I picked up two kids one night who were sitting in the schoolyard at 12:10 a.m., ages eight and nine, from two different families. They were both high off some type of pill. They told me where they received them. I spent 15 months trying to arrest a 15-year-old pill-pusher and when I did, the court system put him back in the street before I left the courthouse." [Wyner, Note 1, p. 34]

What about the environment in which children are becoming citizens? What about the experiences of these minors? What are their thoughts in this encounter with the law? What about the police detective who reports this anecdote, a man who is caring, trying to help children?

These last two anecdotes were collected during a research project I recently conducted at the Education Development Center. This descriptive study documents a community-based participatory approach involving citizens in defining citizenship education for children. The data generated a stunning perspective on the complexity of citizenship education and the compelling social forces that are involved in educating children for citizenship (Wyner, Note 1).

The episodes move from the charming and benign to the disordered reality that children and adults face in their everyday lives. Each story is threaded with law-related elements—rules, scraps of information about law enforcement, meanings and values of citizenship, and children's encounters with adult authority.

The law resonates throughout our experiences. We cannot avoid teaching and learning about law. Nor can we overlook the power of these personal experiences to influence our behaviors and attitudes or the perceptions and behaviors of children. Imprudently, we have looked to the schools as the major institution, along with families, for preparing children for citizenship. But children are thinking, active learners in and out of school, and we must be clear about the limitations of our impact as educators, all the while searching for effective ways to carry out the work of schooling for citizenship. It is my intention in this paper to examine changing orientations in research in order to cultivate our own intuitive and rationally conceived understandings of law-related education for elementary programs. One thing is certain. Teaching about the law is by no means limited to schools and families, nor is it a new idea. Its philosophy, content, and processes preoccupied distinguished curriculum workers like Socrates and Plato in ancient times, as well as the admirable textbook writers of the Bible, the Torah, and the Koran.

Introduction

This paper discusses salient themes and viewpoints drawn from emerging research in the social and political development of children. There was no attempt to be definitive. Such an effort would have altered my course considerably, limiting discussion of implications and prospects for curricular work. Besides, others have already prepared comprehensive and useful reviews (Bryan, 1975; Roedell, Slaby, & Robinson, 1976; Shantz, 1975).

My scan of the literature is selective, guided by two interests. Awareness of patterns and orientations in current research in social and political development is an important knowledge base, and so it served as a first priority. The information will help us chart the terrain of social and political development. Second, I searched for guiding perspectives that can apply to curriculum development in law-related education.

The discussion will focus on key ideas in social and political development for early and middle childhood, ages 5–12, approximately. Implications for curriculum and teaching will be considered.

Backgrounding

Information about the child's understanding of the social and political world is remarkably scarce. The body of information we do have is work of the last decade. What we have accumulated hardly compares with the research that helps us understand the child's thinking processes and ways of understanding the physical world. That is rather curious; as adults, we are so inextricably linked to the child's social and political experiences, one would think that we would know much more. Nevertheless, there are large gaps in our information.

The fifties and sixties were periods for extensive research in political socialization and moral development. The study of social development emerged in the last 10 years. These research traditions overlap and have a deep Piagetian imprint. Piaget helped us view the natural development of children's conceptions as a structured series of invariant stages. Some orientation about these stages of cognitive development, the egocentrism of childhood, and "decentering" are important to grasp as part of the curriculum-building process. To know something of these key ideas frees one to understand notions of development applied to political, social, and moral domains.

Conceptions of thinking in children are partly determined by our understanding of adult thinking. Yet Piaget theorizes that we continue to reorganize our world view as we progress through natural states and that therefore the thinking of children is qualitatively different from that of adults. A brief sketch of developmental stage characteristics clarifies some of these distinctions. For a more thorough grounding in Piaget, curriculum planners should consider an intensive in-service component and readings.

At the *preoperational stage* (approximately 2 to 6 years of age), the child moves beyond the sensory stage of infancy to use symbolic language and mental imagery. He/she relates to the observable, the near at hand. Thinking is intuitive, personalized, egocentric. During this phase (heteronomous) rules and authority are external and authoritarian based.

At the *concrete operational stage* (approximately 6 to 12 years of age), the child develops the capacity for logical-deductive thought and relates to an ordered set of events, grasps history. There is a major shift during this period to a more democratic peer culture.

Social thinking. Most popular accounts of Piaget focus on his interests in logical-deductive thought and overlook the extent to which he acknowledges the contingency of human development on the environment. His view of self-discipline, reciprocity, and the emergence of the moral personality is indicative of his interactionist orientation and his interest in social cognition.

In "The Right to Education in the Present World"(1973), an essay of major importance, Piaget discusses the role of authority in the child's development. He theorizes that the child has three spontaneous emotional tendencies. The first two are a need for love and a feeling of fear of those who are bigger and stronger. Unilateral, authoritarian adult behavior is an interplay between these two tendencies—stressing the child's needs and fears, enforcing dependency. Piaget suggests that when the adult expresses respect for the young child, the child merges the first two emotions into a third, the feeling of obligation—an inner acceptance of rules engendered by the child's response to the person whom he/she respects, "one who is the object of both affection and fear at the same time and not only one of these two emotional states." Through these interactions the child moves beyond dependence and the concomitant rebellion it inspires to independence and reciprocal relationships characterized by mutual respect, cooperation, and growing self-discipline.

According to Piaget: "Education, founded on authority and only unilateral respect, has the same handicaps from the ethical standpoint as from the intellectual standpoint. Instead of leading the individual to work out the rules and the discipline that will obligate him or to work with others to alter them, it imposes a system of ready-made and immediately categorical imperatives on him" (1973, p. 119).

The educational significance of mutual respect and methods based on the spontaneous social organization of children "is precisely to permit them [children] to work out a discipline where the necessity is discovered in action itself, instead of being received ready-made before being able to be understood. . . . to lead the child to construct for himself the tools that will transform him from the inside—that is, in a real sense and not only on the surface" (Piaget, 1973, pp. 118–121).

By resorting to mutual respect instead of authority, to reciprocity and obligation, and not external obedience and conformism, we help the child build a sense of inner confidence "which encourages the development of the moral personality more than any restriction or external punishment" (Piaget, 1973, p. 120).

Are there methods we can develop in the classrooms that will enhance mutual respect and promote reciprocity and obligation to support that sense of confidence and consequent social order? What can we teach children within the context of their social world that will help them develop social and political understanding?

Developmental psychologists interested in the social relations children invent for themselves have discovered a Piaget-oriented sequence of stages for social development. Within this context, Robert Selman's work in social perspectivism and interpersonal awareness stands out as a pioneering effort to discover and describe issues of interpersonal awareness and the process of social reasoning that prods and nudges social cognition to higher levels of adequacy (Selman, 1975; Selman, Jaquette, & Lavin, 1977). Social perspective-taking abilities, according to Selman, are based on the assumption that a child who can undertake another point of view can understand and share the feelings of others by coordinating the viewpoints of self and others through reasoning.

In reviewing research in legal socialization, Tapp lends support to this approach. She observes that "socializing experiences that encourage tolerance for others and incorporate tolerance from others would effectuate greater acceptance of rights in real-life contexts" (Tapp & Levine, 1974, p. 380), indicating that law and politically centered issues readily yield to examination through perspective taking and reasoning strategies, and that mutuality and reciprocal thinking evolve through this process.

Selman proposes five levels of perspective taking, as outlined in Table 1. Perspective-taking levels are intended to describe at given stages the

Table 1. Levels of Perspective Taking

	Level	Description
Ages 4–6	0	Egocentric perspective taking Although the child can identify superficial emotions in other people, he often confuses others' perspective with his own. He does not realize others may see a social situation differently from the way he does. He recognizes there is more than one perspective on a situation, but assumes they are identical.
	1	Subjective perspective taking Child begins to understand that other people's thoughts and feelings may be the same as or different from his. He realizes that people feel differently or think differently because they are in different situations or have different information.
	2	Self-reflective perspective taking The child is able to reflect on his own thoughts and feelings. He can anticipate others' perspective on his own thoughts and feelings and realize that this influences his perspective on others. Recognizes reciprocal influences rather than objective assessments.
	3	Mutual perspective taking The child can assume a third-person point of view. He realizes that in a two-person interaction each can put himself in the other's place and view himself from that vantage point before deciding how to react.
Emerges after 8 years	4	Qualitative-system perspective taking The adolescent conceptualizes subjective perspectives of persons toward one another to exist not only on the level of mutual expectations, but also on deeper levels. Perspectives between persons are seen as forming a network or system. There are multiple levels of perspective taking and multiple systems of perspectives.
	5	Symbolic interaction perspective taking Perspective taking is seen as a method for the analysis of interpersonal and social relations. Due to the nature of human subjectivity itself, one does not necessarily "know" the other's perspective as content. Mutual understanding occurs through the use of similar processes of social reasoning.

SOURCE: Selman, 1975, pp. 130–132.

way a child understands social relationships. The paradigm suggests that development occurs through the "exercise" of the child's reasoning and "exposure" to the reasoning of peers. The school setting is regarded as an appropriate place to do these "exercises." Interpersonal and moral reasoning discussion within a group becomes the basis for change and growth in reasoning, since one has to rethink one's own ideas when presented with diverse viewpoints. Guided peer discussions about social and political concepts such as fairness, trust, sharing, the need for rules and laws, and diversity are areas of applicability.

Selman might be thought of as a cartographer whose work in mapping out the contours of interpersonal awareness through perspective taking and reasoning provides a nonrelativistic set of educational goals oriented toward greater adequacy in children's relationships within their social world. In his most recent work, he identifies four domains of relationships—the child's conceptions of persons, friendships, peer groups, and parental/child relationships. He persistently asks how the developmental level within each of these areas relates to the experiences the child has had in a particular area. For example, he attempts to clarify whether a child's experience of leadership, as either leader or follower, influences his developing conception of leadership. Table 2 offers a useful analysis of the issues and dynamics of social relationship. The information can be viewed as organizing elements around which we might construct learning experiences (Selman, Jaquette, & Lavin, 1977, p. 267).

Selman would like youngsters to become "friendship philosophers" and engage in peer

Table 2. Issues of Interpersonal Awareness Related to Conceptions of the Individual, Close Friendships, Peer Group Organization

Individual	Friendship	Peer Group
1. *Subjectivity:* covert properties of persons (thoughts, feelings, motives); conflicts between thoughts or feelings within the person	1. *Formation:* why (motives) and how (mechanisms) friendships are made; the ideal friend	1. *Formation:* why (motives) and how (mechanisms) groups are formed; the ideal member
2. *Self-reflection:* awarenss of the self's ability to observe its own thoughts and actions	2. *Closeness:* types of friendship, ideal friendship, intimacy	2. *Cohesion/loyalty:* group unity
3. *Personality:* stable or predictive character traits (a shy person, etc.)	3. *Trust:* doing things for friends; reciprocity	3. *Conformity:* range and rationale
4. *Personality change:* how and why people change (growing up, etc.)	4. *Jealousy:* feelings about intrusions into new or established friendships	4. *Rules/norms:* types of rules and reasons for them
	5. *Conflicts:* how friends resolve problems	5. *Decision making:* setting goals, resolving problems, working together
	6. *Termination:* how friendships break up	6. *Leadership:* qualities, and function to the group
		7. *Termination:* why groups break up or members are excluded

SOURCE: Selman, Jaquette, & Lavin, 1977.

discussions to discover the dimensions and issues of friendship, or reason together about why groups get formed, the types of rules groups need, ways of resolving problems by working together, and so forth. The approach requires that students develop communication skills and learn how to function cooperatively in groups. The setting might be class meetings, peer group discussions, or planned action-oriented activities, but the intention is to stimulate higher levels of social reasoning.

Though still in an early phase of research, Blasi's search for stage-characteristic rules of responsibility bears attention (1976). He has conducted structured interviews to determine growth toward independent responsibility. In his research the term "responsibility" is used to define "that relation of necessity that an individual establishes or recognizes between himself and his own action, before the action takes place as well as after it has been performed." In an initial formulation the following developmental sequence is suggested:

1. A move away from literal interpretation of the rules
   (a) Seeing laws in terms of purpose rather than form
   (b) Identifying with the authority's mind and understanding the impossibility of foreseeing every eventuality

(c) Comparing the relative importance of the purpose in the letter of the law. [Loevinger, 1976, p. 34]

Blasi's research may provide important new insights that link responsibility to development, suggesting educational goals that might foster growth in this area.

The developmental theme has also been applied to examining ways in which children form prosocial conceptions and behaviors such as helping, caring, sharing, and cooperation (Mussen & Eisenberg, 1977). As we give thought to preparing children to participate in the democratic political process, these behaviors seem implicit and fundamental. How do we foster prosocial development? Bryan (1975) reports on a number of laboratory investigations concerning practices particularly regarding children's understanding of helping and cooperation. He indicates that "modeling of helping, both verbally and motorically, expressions of affect, group-based rewards, and consistency between moral preachings and practices, to name a few, are probably important antecedents of children's helping and cooperation" (p. 42).

Hess and Torney (1967) discuss models that help explain the political socialization process, for example, the Identification Model, which "focuses on the way a child copies the behavior of an authority (like a parent)," and the Role Transfer Model, which focuses on the way a child takes a role with which he is familiar (as a child in his home, a pupil in his school) and transfers role-appropriate behavior to the political system (as a citizen). The importance of these interactions in the schools and classrooms cannot be overemphasized, since what is proposed is that the child is actively learning from the informal messages of and cues about the political environment from the informal messages and cues that others model.

Perhaps the most problematic aspect of the modeling process in law and citizenship education is an out-of-focus view of ourselves as socializing agents, adults who are actively modeling, influencing, and contributing to students' perceptions about the political/legal system. In this crucial interaction of teaching and learning, educators often do not think about children's perceptions of authority, the use of power, the management of conflict, etc. Indeed, instead of recognizing our influence, we emphasize *differences* between adults and children and among the children. We seem to have developed an advanced technology for categorizing people, further distancing them from each other—those who have power and those who do not, those who are adult and those who are young, those who are white and those who are nonwhite—*categories based on essential differences.* Commonalities are obscured—the search for a sense of belonging, of mutuality; the need to feel effective and competent; the fear of loss and separation; the meaningfulness of trust; the sharing of common values. A greater emphasis on social interactions, stressing at least initially the commonalities of human experience, would put students in touch with a more relevant, more dynamic understanding of the nature of group life as it relates to underlying values of political and legal structures.

The interplay between how children develop social and political conceptions, values, and behaviors through identification and how adults as socializing agents help children acquire this understanding through modeling is indeed worthy of reflection. Can we help educators become more conscious of their modeling role? Is modeling an appropriate strategy for teaching basic democratic concepts such as participation and responsibility? What can we learn about children's perceptions of adult roles in the social/political environment? Interest in the power of modeling should lead us to examine carefully the time children have in situations in which they actually observe prosocial, contributing adult citizens. Can we plan law-related learning in which the quality and the quantity of time children spend with real role

models—not fictitious people or story-land animals, but citizens who are modeling citizenship—is of central importance?

Infusion of the development trend in areas of social and political learning is increasingly evident. Although there are many arguments about structuralism, stage sequences, and issues of methodology and bias, the credibility of sequential development is growing. International studies provide especially impressive documentation supporting the major effect of age on changing social and political conceptions. In this context, Connell's (1971) and Torney's (Torney, Note 2; Torney, Oppenheim & Farnen, 1975) studies are of particular interest.

Political thinking. An articulated developmental perspective for children's political thinking might well begin with ideas generated by Connell, an Australian psychologist. Working in the late sixties, Connell was interested in how the child builds an interpretive structure about the political world. He conducted Piagetian-type interviews with Australian children and concluded that "children learn about politicians and political events through other people, their contact with politics is indirect . . . they build their attitudes and ideas on adult sources on information already interpreted by adults, rather than by directly manipulating or acting on the physical world" (1971, pp. 17–18).

According to Connell's research, construction of a political view goes on with continuity from childhood to adolescence. He proposes a sequential process (1971):

- To age 7, *political prologue:* The child's capabilities are characterized by: (*a*) intuitive thinking, (*b*) a lack of synthesizing power, (*c*) reality blended with fantasy and misconceptions, (*d*) an emerging political consciousness.
- Age 7–8, *development of political thought beyond intuition:* Through mastery of factual information the child: (*a*) distinguishes political and governmental world from other areas of life, (*b*) begins to conceptualize about political roles, (*c*) develops a highly generalized conception of government with little grasp of political structure or boundaries of political activity, (*d*) has rudimentary perceptions of power relationships and awareness of an external world with "special and important" people.

A more cohesive and fully realized interpretation is drawn from a cross-cultural study of civic education in 10 democratic countries by Torney et al. (1975). They describe changes from the "sheltered" view in childhood to a "sophisticated" or realistic view of society in adolescence. These ideas are proposed in a stage-sequenced scheme that the authors indicate is somewhat speculative.

Although the cross-cultural study that serves as the data base for shaping the stages was not intended to demonstrate growth from one stage to the next, one hopes that a long-term developmental follow-up will be initiated to reduce cause for speculation. The various patterns that seem evident are organized into *five stages of political socialization:*

Stage 1: Very vague, inarticulate notions, with emergent images of one or two institutions, e.g., the police.

Stage 2: What may be called the "sheltered" view, in which primarily the harmonizing values and processes become established.

Stage 3: An intermediate stage of growing awareness of social conflict, of economic forces, of the UN, of multiple institutional roles, etc. but essentially still with a sheltered orientation.

Stage 4: What has been called the sophisticated or realistic view above, with less stress on fair-mindedness and understanding, clear awareness of both the cohesive and divisive functions of many institutions, of overlap between institutional functions, of social bias, low participation, oppressive potential, etc.

Stage 5: Scepticism, a general contempt for institutions and lack of belief in their efficiacy [*sic*], an emphasis on discordant functions, unfairness and class bias, denial of participation and of improved understanding. [Torney et al., p. 318–319]

According to the researchers:

The *sheltered view* includes firmly established patterns of authority and obedience, public safety and crime prevention, freedom of expression, fair shares, improved understanding, and a lack of awareness of social conflict and trials of strength; the *sophisticated view* of society includes both cohesive and divisive functions of institutions, economic conflict and class bias, less fairness and understanding, low participation, and low general efficacy of institutions. In between these two stages children gradually learn to distinguish and articulate the role of institutions more sharply and with greater subtlety, and to tolerate multiple functions; above all, they become aware of broad conflicts and opposing forces in society, and the need to institutionalize these processes. [Torney et al., 1975, p. 318]

These patterns of political socialization tend to overlap with suggested sequences for interpersonal awareness. Generally, they express an application of Piaget's description of the logic of children's thought. Direct experience and reasoning "exercises" related to the social/political concepts clustered in the proposed sequences provide some of the dynamics that stimulate the child's thinking processes.

Reasoning is also an important aspect of legal socialization. As defined by Tapp and Levine (1974), legal reasoning "is characterized by a changing conception of rights and roles vis-à-vis authoritative rule systems." They argue that the goal of legal education is "to attain a basic comprehension of substantive law and legal process," and that the role of legal socializers as protagonists in legal education is to "encourage expression and independence rather than repression and dependence, so that ultimately the individual can develop reasoning principles well-suited to analyzing complex problems and integrating diverse viewpoints" (p. 4).

The reader might be reasonably distressed by the proliferation of viewpoints that propose stages of development. In social cognition we have referred to interpersonal, political, and legal territories, and one can point to stages in representational ability, and so forth. How can we conduct our teaching responsibilities through this complex terrain if developmental levels are varied and yet interrelated within an individual child and among children? Do these fixed schemes or stages grasp the shifting, dynamic, and unique aspects of human behavior? Since children's work and their thinking capabilities are different from adults' they must be viewed in a developmental context. However, the principles that govern analysis of developmental sequences must be broadly based, recognizing the interactive nature of learning and the *processes* that lead the child to self-awareness and adult behavior.

Implications for Curriculum and Teaching

The developmental perspective. A strong developmental perspective characterizes emerging research on children's social and political thinking. The ideas are shaped, in large part, by a cognitive-developmental typology that charts out sequential stages and the interactive nature of learning. The child is seen as actively struggling to make sense of his/her own social/political world in accordance with a logic that is qualitatively different from that of adults. The paradigms discussed suggest that we can more reasonably estimate the age at which socially/politically oriented instructional strategies can effectively mediate growth tasks. The role of the educator, then, in promoting social and political thinking is to stimulate the natural course of development by helping organize and construct meaningful, appropriate growth tasks. Principles in design and planning should include:

■ Approaches that acknowledge that the "social" and "political" worlds of children and the relationships and issues within these natural groups are the medium for children's thinking and learning about the needs, values, and underlying structures of people coexisting as community and society. Selman's work suggests that curricular attention should focus on the sociopolitical issues of friendships, peer group organizations, and family groups and the inherent issues of these social units (conflict, decision making, etc.). These approaches must recognize that children's thinking is extended and nourished by situations in which they are directly involved, that they are cognitively stimulated by real-life experiences. Fictional, dilemma-type situations, simulations, and readings in children's literature are extremely important sources for information, and often provide a chance for students to exercise their growing capabilities. But these activities cannot replace the significance of "real life" as a context for learning.

■ Techniques that can help children gain more generalized conceptions of group life. Guided peer-group discussions that encourage reasoning seem to have the potential for stimulating interpersonal and political awareness. Communication and participation skills are developed in these peer-group experiences as part of the reasoning process—involving children in expressing viewpoints, listening to each other, etc. These competencies are identified more specifically in a later section of this article. Peer-group discussions emerge as a *central* instructional technique.

■ Opportunities for children to interact and identify with adult models who can influence the child's self-esteem and social values. We tend to underestimate the potent influence teachers and other adult socializers have on children's perceptions of authority, cooperative behaviors, and social values. We also tend to overlook the child's need to share in the positive emotional states of models whom they believe possess strengths and competencies which they struggle to achieve. Because of the interactive nature of learning, ways of relating to children are ways of teaching.

Teachers, however, are only one group of educators in the child's social/political world. Learning must include opportunities for children to talk with and observe other adult socializers engaged in citizen roles—rule makers, law enforcers, community people helping to create a working community. Children need direct experience in the political settings of community life and with those adults who value their roles as citizens. Reenactment and reconstruction of these experiences through role play, gaming, simulation, creative drama, and reading in children's literature are important instructional strategies that enrich and clarify these experiences, helping the child toward a more competent, "sophisticated," and conceptual grasp of society.

Teachers and the mini-legal system of the classroom. People who describe the complex process of American children's political development argue that the political/legal dynamics of the classroom have an important impact on the child's perceptions of the adult political world. There is also increasing interest in processes and interactions that educate. The implication we might draw, then, is that we should consciously examine the issues and interactions of the classroom perceived as a mini-legal system. Potentially our purpose is to uncover some of the political/legal characteristics of the classroom for curriculum planning, striving toward more deliberate, conscious use of the classroom setting for politically centered learning. We might consider our strategy as an informal extension of Selman's conceptions of issues relating to friendships, peer-group organizations, etc. This approach is concerned with increasing political awareness in the context of the mini-legal system of the classroom.

When teachers decide what classroom resources are communal property, they teach about sharing, ownership, and property rights; when teachers select pictures with faces of white and nonwhite children and display them on classroom bulletin boards, they are teaching about diversity. When principals and teachers make all the school rules and impose collective punishment or otherwise unfair restrictions on students, they teach about a political process and control.

In Table 3 I propose an analytic framework that draws on highly generalized characteristics of our legal/political environment. Discussions involving reasoning about the mini-legal systems of schools and classrooms can stimulate a more expanded view of the political nature of the schooling environment.

As I used this model in law-related education workshops to encourage reasoning and discussion about political processes in classrooms, I found that teachers and administrators often referred to the enforcing, punishing, and controlling nature of legal systems, even though participants could later point to many instances in which laws were perceived as protective safeguards! Reasoning can bring about a more diverse view of the legal process, especially if one begins this approach by actively investigating all of the responses people have observed within their own experience. Underlying this model is the assumption that adult socializers—especially teachers—need to recognize the school as a political environment before they can comfortably discuss these issues with children.

Children thinking about authority and power. Authority and the use of power are important components in political, social learning. We tend to think of power as an adult issue, an evil theme;

Table 3. Mini-legal Systems of Schools and Classrooms—Analytic Framework

Characteristics	Some Possible Responses
People—active, thinking, feeling people in- and outside the system	Learning, changing, influencing others, developing expectations
	Alienated, creating conflict
	Controlling, enforcing
	Creating new ideas, resolving social problems
	Protecting
Structures	In terms of space and human behaviors: (*a*) boundaries (i.e., classrooms, schools, neighborhoods, courtrooms, nation); (*b*) mechanisms or procedures—the constitutional framework: discussion, decision making, due process, appeal or repression, authoritarian control
Potential issues	An evolving interpretation of the constitutional framework
	Continuing search to uncover and support group values
	Stimulation of rights consciousness and legal/political/social competence including coexistence and independent responsibility
	Challenges and threats to constitutional rights of members, i.e.: (*a*) group punishment for behavior of individuals and unfair punishment of individuals; (*b*) misuse of authority/power; (*c*) racism, sexism, inequities that limit full participation

yet it is the essence and the dynamic underpinning of group life. Indeed, supportive authority is an essential ingredient in the experience of children becoming citizens, moving them, as Piaget indicates, toward self-discipline, mutual respect, and feelings of obligation.

Is the topic of authority and power unsuitable for children to discuss and reason about? Only if we assume that they know nothing about power. Ask them. They know about presidents and police, they know about bullies and bosses. Can we teach children that power is a way of contributing to group life? Can we teach them that what you need to be a competent learner and a responsible person is power? That using your powers in coexisting and getting along is what we value more than battling and bullying; that racism and sexism are ways of using power but so is learning to live with diversity?

Issues of national civic identity. Law-related education is a keystone of citizen development, and its focus on understanding laws, political processes, and values is a basis on which we build a sense of national civic identity—a collective conception of national history and the knowledge and appreciation of shared values, principles, and national symbols. Though there is remarkably little attention to issues of national civic identity, it is appropriately within the realm of political/social thinking and the socialization process. Our practices here remain obscure and inconsistent.

Perhaps one of the most stressful and complex issues in this context is our approach to teaching children about the flag of the United States and the rituals and rules that surround related classroom activities of the pledge of allegiance. Within the context of law-related education there are objective, sound, rational alternatives that can help students and educators evolve a suitable contemporary instructional plan for teaching about national symbols of civic identity. President Woodrow Wilson set forth the problem: "This flag which we honor and under which we serve, is the emblem of our unity, our power, our thought and purpose as a nation. It has no other character than that which we give it from generation to generation. The choices are ours."

In classrooms throughout the country children are required by law to state the pledge of allegiance and salute the flag. And yet many of these youngsters haven't the vaguest notion of the meaning of the words they mouth. Nor do they have the opportunities to discuss the historical significance of the United States flag as a truly national flag representing all of our citizens.

A conceptual approach to the study of flags, the concept of "flagness," would help children balance their symbolic experiences with cognitive learning. In studying about "flagness," children might: (1) reason about why people use flags; (2) discuss chief characteristics in the design of the United States flag and other flags; (3) study the changing history of the symbols and what they represent in the design of the U.S. flag and others;

(4) develop understanding of the hugely complex vocabulary of "flagness," like salute, pledge, etc.; (5) develop a reasoned understanding of the meaningfulness of flags in our history and in the history of the world community; and (6) learn about laws that determine the care and use of the U.S. flag. We are engaged in a good deal of "hidden" teaching when we avoid discussion of this important symbol of our national civic culture and need, I believe, to acknowledge that the colorful variety of flags and symbols often presented to children at public occasions are testimony to the diversity of our cultural heritage and the freedom of expression within our political system.

An initial set of competencies suggested by the research and teaching practice. Throughout, we have talked about stages of development, levels of adequacy, and the importance of using group interaction processes for nudging and stimulating growth in social and political thinking. Guided by the research discussed in this paper and earlier writings, I have identified a preliminary set of competencies, outlined in Table 4, that are perhaps best thought of as guideposts for curricular planning. They should be rigorously discussed and argued about. Perhaps we might call that process curricular reasoning.

Conclusion

Summarizing an international study in civic education, Torney et al. (1975) observe:

The ideal goal may be a well informed citizenry, supportive of democratic values, basically supportive of and capable of influencing government policy, and interested in participating in civic activities. Our data show that these four aspects of good citizenship not only are independent but are influenced by different practices or in some cases are influenced in different directions by the same practice. The recognition of the interdependence of these systems of socialization is critical to our understanding of the process. Tinkering with a new course here or setting up a new educational requirement for teachers there is unlikely to produce significant movement toward an ideal citizenry in any country. [Pp. 336–337]

I share the concern for "tinkering" and know the comfort that would come from defining a specific set of practices, a "basic" kit, a discrete listing of strategies to achieve our goals. But perhaps the vitality and growing energy of the law and citizenship education movement is indicative of a commitment to a broadly conceived response to complex educational issues and an awareness of the challenging, difficult task ahead.

REFERENCES

Blasi, A. Personal responsibility and ego development. In R. de Charms (Ed.), *They need not be pawns: Toward self-direction in urban classrooms.* New York: Irvington, 1976.

Bryan, J. H. *Children's cooperation and helping behaviors.* Chicago: University of Chicago Press, 1975.

Connell, R. W. *The child's construction of politics.* Melbourne: Melbourne University Press, 1971.

Hess, R. D., & Torney, J. V. *The development of political attitudes in children.* Chicago: Aldine, 1967.

Kohlberg, L. Stage and sequence: The cognitive-developmental approach to socialization. In D. A. Goslin (Ed.), *Handbook of socialization theory and research.* Chicago: Rand McNally, 1969.

Loevinger, J. *Ego development.* San Francisco: Jossey-Bass, 1976.

Mussen, P. & Eisenberg, B. *Roots of caring, sharing, and helping: The development of prosocial behavior in children.* San Francisco: Freeman, 1977.

Piaget, J. The right to education in the present world. In *To understand is to invent: The future of education.* New York: Grossman, 1973.

Roedell, W. C.; Slaby, R. G.; & Robinson, H. B. *Social development in young children—a report for teachers.* Washington, D.C.: National Institute of Education, Department of Health, Education, and Welfare, January 1976.

Selman, R. L. A developmental approach to interpersonal and moral awareness in young children: Some theoretical and educational implications of levels of social perspective taking. In J. Meyer, B. Burnham, & J. Cholvat (Eds.), *Values education.* Waterloo, Ont.: Wilfrid Laurier University Press, 1975.

Selman, R. L.; Jaquette, D.; & Lavin, D. R. Interpersonal awareness in children: Toward an integration of developmental and clinical child psychology. *American Journal of Orthopsychiatry, 1977, 47(2).*

Shantz, C. U. The development of social cognition. Chicago: University of Chicago Press, 1975.

Tapp, J. L. & Levine, F. J. Legal socialization: Strategies for an ethical legality. *Stanford Law Review,* 1974, 27 (November).

Torney, J. V.; Oppenheim, A. N.; & Farnen, R. F. *Civic education in ten countries: An empirical study.* New York: Wiley, 1975.

Wyner, N. B. Children becoming citizens. In A. Pagano (Ed.), *Social studies in early childhood education* (Bulletin 58). Washington, D.C.: National Council for the Social Studies, 1979.

REFERENCE NOTES

1. Wyner, N. B. The Cambridge Study: Involving citizens in defining citizenship education for children (Research Report, Grant No. PO-0770549). Washington, D.C.: Office of Citizen Education, Office of Education, February 1978.

2. Torney, J. Child development, socialization and elementary political education (Commissioned Paper No. 11). Washington, D.C.: Elementary Political Education Project, National Science Foundation, April 1973.

Table 4. Competencies in Social and Political Thinking

Citizen competencies develop as the child:

Engages in thinking and reasoning and interacts with adults and peers and:

Early childhood:
Begins to identify emotions in other people
Actively listens to what another person thinks, feels, intends
Collects accurate information, begins to organize it systematically
Communicates own viewpoint to another person and in a group context
Learns to take turns talking and listening, sharing, and helping
Shares ideas, feelings through language and symbolic representation
Clarifies misconceptions through questioning, observing, comparing with accurate information
Recognizes there is more than one point of view than his/her own, though they are assumed to be identical (a basic stage of perspective building and role taking)
Develops personal sense of helping, cooperation, participation, interdependence

Middle childhood:
Communicates reasons for his/her ideas, feelings to others in a group context, or in one-to-one relationships
Understands the importance of having accurate information
Begins to understand other people's thoughts and feelings are different from his/her own
Recognizes that different people have different experiences, information, interests, needs, yet acknowledges commonalities as well
Reflects on his/her own thoughts, feelings, behavior
Recognizes reciprocal influences people have on each other's thoughts, feelings, and behavior
Can assume a viewpoint other than his/her own and views self from that vantage point, "putting oneself in someone else's shoes," gaining a sense of the mutuality of roles
Demonstrates increasing awareness of the rights, needs, feelings of self and others and takes responsibility for promoting these rights, etc.
Participates cooperatively as a result of productive, satisfying group experiences and social collaboration
Can alter behavior to achieve and promote more effective interpersonal relationships

Engages in social/political interactions and:

Early childhood:
Becomes aware of rules of establishing boundaries, insuring personal safety, protecting group life
Begins to understand the need for rules, laws and the processes for democratically making and changing rules/laws in the group life of the classroom, local settings
Develops an increasing degree of personal freedom and self-discipline based on a reasoned approach to making choices, determining personal values, learning limits set by supportive authority
Is knowledgeable about symbols of national civic identity (i.e., flag, anthem, pledge) and is aware of national symbols of other world communities
Demonstrates increasing awareness and understanding of basic concepts of citizenship, for example, cooperation, fairness, authority, participation, pluralism, freedom, governance, social responsibility, equity, and interdependence

Table 4. Competencies in Social and Political Thinking

Citizen competencies develop as the child:

Engages in social/political interactions and:

Early childhood:	Participates in groups discussing social-political issues, developing a sense of competence about oneself as a member of groups
	Is knowledgeable about roles and responsibilities of leaders and authorities (a president, mayor, police officer, teacher, principal, parent)
	Demonstrates competencies in leadership roles among peers, increasingly knowledgeable about and able to use democratic processes, i.e., open-group discussion, due process, deci-making strategies (consensus, voting)
	Demonstrates increasingly responsibility for achieving one's own rights and the rights and needs of others through the active application of knowledge, competencies, personal values
Middle childhood:	Distinguishes the political and governmental world from other areas of life and has knowledge of the general purpose and functions of government
	Is conversant with major documents of our constitutional democracy (Bill of Rights, Constitution) and begins to compare their principles with the political orientation of other nations in the world—building toward a global perspective
	Understands the facts and principles of our two-party political system and its importance in the growth of democracy
	Is increasingly knowledgeable about citizen-oriented subject matter, e.g., poverty, racism, environmental protection, scarcity of resources, conflict, global interdependence, and can apply due process for conflict and resolution
	Demonstrates a reasoned approach to conflict situations and can apply due process for conflict management, planning and advocacy techniques for constructive change
	Shows ability to postpone immediate solutions in view of long-range consequences

Another view . . .

Social and Political Thinking in Children: Implications for Law and Humanities Education

Calvin M. Miller

The author of the previous paper acknowledged the limited scope of her analysis of children's sociopolitical learning. In this paper, Calvin Miller seizes the opportunity to identify some of the critical factors not discussed or fully developed by Wyner. Among these is the utility of the work of theorists who take quite divergent perspectives for understanding how children acquire political knowledge and competencies. Another factor stressed here is that the models for citizenship provided by teachers and schools may fall far short of a democratic ideal. The paper goes on to highlight what the author terms a "fundamental dichotomy between the socialization of white and minority and poor children." These are but a few examples of how the author prods us to recognize the complexities inherent in the task of preparing citizens for effective, ethical participation in a pluralistic democratic society.

Significantly, Nancy Wyner's paper concerns itself with (1) developmental learning theories (Piaget), (2) political learning (political socialization), and (3) a law education model for elementary schools (teachers and the mini-legal system of the classroom). In her introduction, the author states that "there was no attempt to be definitive. Such an effort would have altered our course considerably." Her paper, then, becomes a highly suggestive general piece which has no specific message beyond the proposed model. (I.e., is the trend in socialization research to follow the Piagetian developmental model? If yes, can we then say that in political socialization of the child, applicable concepts of law or law education or citizenship are deposited at each age level?)

Even so, the major suggestion of the paper is item 3 above: teachers and the mini-legal system of the classroom as a model for law-related education in elementary schools. This idea demands critical scrutiny.

On the surface the model sounds like a good one. But when we acknowledge that schools and teachers are protagonists for a traditional establishmentarian notion of law, order, respect—in fact, the maintenance of an unquestioning status quo—we must reflect. Massialas maintains that "in the political socialization of children and youth the school maintained an attitude of passiv-

ity and compliance" (1972, p. 258). He further notes: "The school generally took its directives from the power groups in the community and traditionally sanctioned or promoted an education that was racist in content. It also enforced certain conditions that negated individual initiative and freedom. The schools aiming at 'training for citizenship' introduced strict discipline and unquestionable respect for authority" (1972, p. 258). Very interestingly, Wyner states that "when principals and teachers make all the school rules and impose collective punishment or otherwise unfair restrictions on students, they teach about a *political process of control*" (italics added). This statement is indicative of the polite approach. The "political process of control" is outright authoritarianism.

These ideas suggest that schools and teachers are the poorest models for reflecting a beneficial ideal for "law-related education." In a desegregating society most schools are struggling to avoid the most profound law of the land: "Racial segregation is unconstitutional." The Boston schools are under court receivership, and the majority of other schools throughout the nation either are operating under a court-approved plan or are in the process of developing a plan for approval. There has been very little voluntary desegregation of schools in support of *Brown* v. *Board of Education.* What kind of model is this? How is this explained? Or better, in terms of political socialization, what attitudes are resulting: efficacy, cynicism, activism, submissiveness, or what? We must know the answers to these questions.

Calvin M. Miller is Professor of Political Science and Dean of the School of Humanities and Social Sciences, Virginia State College. He was co-director of RAPS (Research in Afro-American Political Socialization).

47

Finally, the model idea cannot be taken absolutely. Jaros concludes that the overall impact of research on the school as a socializer is at once "disappointing and stimulating" (1973, p. 112). In the Petersburg study, the authors assumed that "beliefs about the social and physical environment affect personal outlook and behavior" (Hicks, Miller, Miller, & Stone, Note 1). To this extent, this outlook (perception) would block an image/model (head of household/parent) from becoming a direct agent of socialization. The study supported this assumption by its finding that "submissive children are less likely to be politically acquiescent. They are more likely to see the Petersburg government as fair, the head as cynical and themselves as politically active. Children who perceive local political inequity tend to come from relatively low socio-economic backgrounds where the head is politically cynical" (Hicks et al., Note 1, p. 13).

Other general problem areas of Wyner's paper are (1) definitions, (2) use of political socialization indexes, (3) other learning theories, (4) the dichotomous nature of the desegregated classroom, and (5) other teaching methodologies.

What is law-related education? What is its purpose? Is it to provide inputs into citizenship or into "good citizenship?" Should a good citizen obey an unjust law which contradicts the constitution? Are we talking about order, stability, constitutional law, statutory law, or the entire criminal justice system? ("In an effective law-related program the focus is on how the American legal and criminal justice system personally affects the lives of the students within the classroom or school" [Banks & Cleggs, 1977, p. 357]).

Therefore some basic definitions should have been stated for the readers' general direction. Also, whereas Piagetian thought implicit in Selman, Bryan, Connell, and Torney and her associates is well taken, this approach overlooks the works of Jerome Bruner, Jacob Getzels, Phillip Jackson, and Herbert Thelen, who point out the enormous capacity of children and adolescents to understand and initially analyse the world around them (Massialas, 1972, p. 245). "Political Socialization is generally the process of acquiring and changing the culture of one's own political environment. Political socialization may be measured through the use of indexes, the most important of which are (1) political efficacy; (2) political trust; (3) citizenship duty; (4) expectations for political participation; (5) political knowledge and (6) other nation or world concept" (Massialas, 1972, pp. 3–4). (Note the inclusion of a change of process in the definition. Also, in Hicks et al. [Note 1, p. 6] some special indexes were designed for political cynicism, acquiescence, activism, fairness, and socioeconomic

condition.) These indexes are important because they relate to the results of socialization. The Wyner paper does not deal with these indexes in respect to law-related education. If the author was concerned only with the "process of acquiring" (learning), without a concern for the results (efficacy, etc.), then we have been presented with only one side of political socialization. I feel very strongly that "efficacy and cynicism" in children are as important as the Piagetian typology, and both have implications for curricula development in the elementary school.

Another very important issue in children's political socialization is glossed over. There is a fundamental dichotomy between the socialization of white children and that of minority and poor children (see *Changes in Political Knowledge*, 1978; Hirsch, 1971; Ramsey, Note 2). Also, numerous studies concerned with socialization to political participation point out that, compared to whites, during the first 17 years of life, blacks are less politically efficacious, more cynical, more knowledgeable about politics sooner, more partisan, more disaffected from the political system, and more disposed to political discussion (Greenberg, 1969, 1970a, 1970b, 1970c; Lyons, 1970; Orum & Cohen, 1973).

These particular findings have grave implications for the teaching of law-related matters in a desegregating environment. It seems to me that a resocialization is implied in order to bridge this dichotomy within the classroom. And this resocialization would have to deal with "not law and order, power, authority and pluralism" (political science concepts) but the more normative matters of "right, good and justice" (Wolin, 1960). Bridging this gap of political socialization within the classroom moves us away from status-quo models within the desegregating society using the pedagogic method of inquiry and participation for societal good (Gillespie & Mehlinger, 1972; Massialas, 1972).

In order to add other dimensions to Nancy Wyner's paper, I recommend that:

1. Learning theories other than Piagetian typology be considered.
2. Curricular strategies be developed which will bridge the gap between the white middle class and the black and poor within the desegregated classroom.
3. A positive program be established which would impel all schools and all teachers to teach and reflect a concern for the good, the right, and the just. I do not accept the placid construct of the status-quo school and teachers as passive models.
4. Law-related education should include the entire criminal justice system.

5. Citizenship should be defined as "being an inquiring activist concerned with normative values of the American system." It is much better for American citizens to conclude, after rational thinking, that America is a "good society," rather than succumb to propagandizing socialization such as, "My country, right or wrong," or "Better dead than red."
6. Inquiry as a teaching method should be instituted in the elementary school social studies program.
7. More emphasis should be placed upon right, justice, and good rather than law and order, patriotism, authority and pluralism, etc.
8. Law-related curricula in elementary schools should focus on the results of political socialization, i.e., efficacy, cynicism, submissiveness, political knowledge, participation, etc.

REFERENCES

Banks, J. A., & Clegg, A. A. *Teaching strategies for the social studies: Inquiry, valuing and decision-making.* Reading, Mass.: Addison-Wesley, 1977.

Changes in political knowledge and attitudes, 1969–76. Denver: National Assessment of Education Policy, National Center for Education Statistics, 1978.

Gillespie, J. A., & Mehlinger, H. D. Teach about politics in the "real" world—the school. *Social Education,* 1972, *36,* 598–603.

Greenberg, E. S. Children and the political community: A comparison across racial lines. *Canadian Journal of Political Science,* 1969, *2,* 471–492.

Greenberg, E. S. Children and government: A comparison across racial lines. *Midwest Journal of Political Science,* 1970, *14,* 249–275. (a)

Greenberg, E. S. Black children and the political system. *Public Opinion Quarterly,* 1970, *34,* 333–345. (b)

Greenberg, E. S. Orientations of black children and white children to political authority figures. *Social Science Quarterly,* 1970, *51,* 561–571. (c)

Hirsh, H. *Poverty and political socialization: Political socialization in an American sub-culture.* New York: Free Press, 1971.

Jaros, D. *Socialization to politics.* New York: Praeger, 1973.

Lyons, S. R. The political socialization of ghetto children: Efficacy and cynicism. *Journal of Politics,* 1970, *32,* 288–304.

Massialas, B. G. (Ed.) *Political youth, traditional schools: National and international perspectives.* Englewood Cliffs, N. J.: Prentice-Hall, 1972.

Orum, A. M., & Cohen, R. S. Development of political orientations among black and white children. *American Sociological Review,* 1973, *38,* 62–74.

Wolin, S. S. *Politics and vision: Continuity and innovation in Western political thought.* Boston: Little, Brown, 1960.

REFERENCE NOTES

1. Hicks, M. G.; Miller C. M.; Miller J.; & Stone, D. The acquisition of black political identity in Petersburg, Virginia. Paper presented at the annual meeting of the American Political Science Association, Chicago, 1974. (Mimeographed)
2. Ramsey, D. Factors affecting black political participation in Petersburg, Virginia. Paper presented at the annual meeting of the Association of Social and Behavioral Sciences, Atlanta, 1974. (Mimeographed)

Cultural Democracy, Pluralism, and Group Identity in Public School Education

Christian K. Skjervold

One of the basic characteristics of American society is that it is composed of people from a broad spectrum of cultural heritages. A blatantly obvious statement and, yet, one which it seems cannot be made often enough. Unfortunately and seemingly inexplicably, this multiculturalism continues to be less than satisfactorily accommodated throughout the institutional structures of our society. In this regard, schools and other educational institutions are no exceptions.

This issue is of such importance that we are breaking the regular pattern of this book to have three articles focusing on this subject, rather than two. This paper sets the context for the two subsequent articles, which more explicitly address the implications of multiculturalism for law-related education. Tracing historical reactions to ethnic diversity, Chris Skjervold follows the American experience from the melting pot to the more recent emphasis on ethnic identity. He makes a strong case for the crucial role the schools played in the national denial of diversity and the vital role they must play in the emerging acceptance of multiple ethnic identities. He rounds out his argument for pluralism by noting that multiple allegiances to ethnic and other groups, the nation, and a global society are not only possible to develop and sustain but mutually enriching.

In the last decade and a half it seems that the concept of cultural democracy has gained some measure of creditability in American education. However, there is room for doubt about how thoroughly this creditability has been translated into action. In public education we spend much time speaking about the legitimate aims and aspirations of a great many groups within society. As a result, we have experienced the development of a myriad of programs designed to enhance, enrich or just enable the education of various individuals or groups who for one reason or another have not been able to realize their full potential within the existing system. We have witnessed the implementation of Title I Reading Programs and Bi-lingual/Bi-cultural Programs and Ethnic Heritage Studies Programs under Title IX. All of these efforts have been designed to meet some clearly demonstrable need, and they have, of course, met with varying degrees of success.

Many of these programs have as stated or implicit goals the broadening of student participation or the recognition of difference and, through

Christian K. Skjervold is Coordinator for the Ethnic Cultural Center of the Minneapolis Public Schools. He is also President of the Minnesota Project on Ethnic America and past president of the Upper Midwest Ethnic Studies Association.

these, the democratization of the educational process. However, in our haste to confront some immediate need, we have often skirted the fundamental issue of what a culturally democratic school environment or program would be. We have failed to define cultural democracy and have settled instead on examining and correcting bits and pieces of the total problem. One of the problems we have tinkered with is how to deal with the individual and group identity of the schoolchild.

The schools of the United States often appear to be schizophrenic in their objectives and the means of dealing with the question of group and individual identity. On the one hand, we speak of the uniqueness of each child, and on the other, we voice our concern that the child have a proper sense of the totality of humanity. This dichotomous feeling is typified by a statement emanating from the 1970 White House Conference on Children, which attempted to answer the question of what the twenty-first century *man* should be. "We would have him be a man with a strong sense of himself and his own humanness, with awareness of his thoughts and feelings, with the capacity to feel and express love and joy and to recognize tragedy and feel grief. We would have him be a man who, with a strong and realistic sense of his own worth, is able to relate openly with others, to cooperate effectively with them toward common ends, and to view mankind as one while respecting diversity and difference."

This short statement reflects very clearly the dualistic nature of the assignment which has been given to the school system—and particularly the public schools—of our nation. Schools, it seems, are to recognize that persons are often individuals in relation to groups. How do teachers and others deal with group identity within the framework of the educational process?

America is a nation of diverse social, economic, and ethnic groups. It is a curious phenomenon that although we in the United States have a highly developed social science structure in education, we have devoted relatively little attention to the various groups—particularly ethnic groups—which flourish within our society. Only recently have the schools begun to accept the legitimacy of studies which more accurately portray the multiethnic character of America. Standard textual materials have tended to give the impression that America is a highly homogenous society that has been forged through the common experiences of the Anglo-American heritage.

America as Melting Pot

"From many, one"—peoples as well as states—has been the glory of the American republic, and its torment. In the beginning, the New World offered its bounty to the curious, the lucky, and the brave, whatever their social status or nationality—to all, that is, with certain exceptions, including native people and the black slave.

We were pushed into the melting pot and told to form a new race of men. There was an early assumption that assimilation, both mental and physical, was unilinear. In this view individuals progressed through various stages of "Americanization" until they could emerge as "new" people. As soon as the language or customs of the old country were lost or replaced, the individual had taken several steps down the road to being an American. There was no need to consider cultural democracy, only the need to stoke the fires under the melting pot. As the early-twentieth-century play *The Melting Pot* put it:

It is the fire of God round his Crucible. There she lies—the great Melting Pot listen! Can't you hear the roaring and the bubbling? There gapes her mouth—the harbour where a thousand mammoth feeders came from the ends of the world to pour in their human freight. Oh, what a stirring and seething! Celt and Latin, Slav and Teuton, Greek and Syrian, black and yellow (Jew and Catholic). Yes, East and West, North and South.... Now the Great Alchemist melts and fuses them with his purging flame! Here shall they unite to build the Republic of Man and the Kingdom of God. [Zangwill, 1909]

Of the many institutional fires which were ignited to bring the melting pot to the boil, the schools were to have a critical role. The schools were a part of the broader context of public institutions and as such were charged with the major responsibility for the education of the child. This education would develop a feeling of citizenship and assimilation of the individual into the "American Dream," which would ensure the child's integration into the larger society. While this became a function of the school, at an earlier time or in another place it would have been a duty of the parents or extended family. Perhaps this is only one more manifestation of *in loco parentis,* but by emphasizing citizenship, loyalty, and a desire for sameness, the education of the melting pot became a political concept which in the end would promote political consensus and define citizenship and, thus, *American.*

Teachers and schools were encouraged to disregard ethnic and cultural backgrounds. Indeed, the schools were urged to erase or ignore all signs of the child's background, and through a few short years to mold the child into a useful citizen without regard to preexisting conditions. To do this, the schools most often found it efficient to strip children of their ethnic birthright by asking them to choose between the language, customs, and sometimes even the religion of their forebears and the chance of making it in America. This choice was not placed before the child and the family as a clear-cut decision but was rather disguised as the process of becoming a good citizen.

Many of the actions which led to the "Americanization" of the child were end products of a conscious plan on the part of school and other government officials. However, a great many of these results were unforeseen developments. In other words, they happened simply as part of the interaction between the school and the larger society. In the category of conscious policy can be placed the many efforts to destroy the tribal affiliations of America's native peoples through removal from their historic territories. The separation of African peoples, in slavery, from those with whom they could communicate, thus forestalling effective resistance to that "peculiar institution," was also part of a deliberate policy. In both instances people were physically and emotionally separated from the familiar and thus were made easier to control.

Unlike the laws which governed our official attitude toward blacks and Indians, immigration laws did not prescribe areas of settlement for the voluntary immigrant to America. We relied upon the natural selection process of ethnic enclaves. While there were a number of laws governing all phases of immigration, our national policy toward the immigrant in society seems to have been characterized by the development of the unforeseen. Nowhere was it mandated that one had to change one's religion or name, but many found it easier to do so than to resist the pressures of American society. The schools used English, and while the native tongue was not forbidden outside the walls of the school, the structure of society encouraged the abandonment of the immigrant language. These changes, though seemingly small in themselves, piled one upon the other to ensure the utility of the immigrant to American society through the melting pot.

Ethnicity and Cultural Democracy

While the concept of the "melting pot" helped describe the American people's need for political cohesion, it could not prescribe individual activity. While the schools called for a blending and the casting away of ethnocultural baggage, family and peer loyalty reinforced ethnic ties. Indeed, ethnicity often powerfully buttressed the individual personality in a volatile, atomistic society that was dedicated, in principle, to the natural capabilities of the single citizen. Thus our public education ideology often grated against private notions of how affairs should be ordered. The traditions of family and group did not always reinforce the substance and style of our institutions. Even though individual citizenship and loyalty to America were results fostered by education, they were not enough to resolve the dilemmas of a nation of ethnics. We insisted on maintaining individuality for ourselves and uniqueness for our group.

People are awakening to the realization that everyone is a member of a group, whether by choice or by chance. They have begun to identify with differences in sex, age, occupation, interests, geography, and physical and mental conditions, to mention only a few. One of the most common groups with which people are identified is their ethnic group. And, as has been pointed out, the schools have not responded positively to this identification.

The history of American public education has overwhelmingly demonstrated a lack of sensitivity to cultural and ethnic differences—a deficiency which has been commonplace throughout our society. Scholarship often has focused more on aspects of assimilation and absorption than on the diversity which is demonstrated through group identity and cultural democracy.

Advocacy of cultural democracy in the classroom and in society should not be based upon a desire for a transient period of tolerance to ease the pathway to full assimilation. Instead, it should be based upon the assumption or expectation that distinct—and often separate—groups will continue to exist in the United States, that

they have worth, and that there are both programmatic and moral reasons why the educational system should help maintain them.

Even though the schools were the heirs of either conscious or unconscious assimilationism, the process was never as effective as its proponents would have desired. While much of the feeling of group identity or cohesiveness was subjugated through the daily confrontation with economic necessity—the need to learn English for the job, two world wars and nation-wide depression—the very human group consciousness could not be entirely extinguished. By admitting essential human feelings, the schools are faced with the problem of how to cope with diversity. The American Association of Colleges of Teacher Education (1972) has lately adopted a statement, "No One Model American," which takes a position on the attempt to deal with diversity. The statement says in part:

Multicultural education rejects the view that schools should seek to melt away cultural differences or the view that schools should merely tolerate cultural pluralism. Instead multicultural education affirms that schools should be oriented toward the cultural enrichment of all children and youth through programs rooted to the preservation and extension of cultural alternatives. Multicultural education recognizes cultural diversity as a fact of life in American society, and it affirms that this cultural diversity is a valuable resource that should be preserved and extended. It affirms that major education institutions should strive to preserve and enhance cultural pluralism.

However, there are serious obstacles to acceptance of the above as a policy for American education. Pluralism and differences are often seen as barriers to national or even global unity. Some people would categorize feelings of ethnicity as aberrations which prevent the development of an all-encompassing human identity and thus narrow the scope of humanity. Often people are given only the either/or choice of ethnic identity as a narrow allegiance only to one's own group or a broadly diffuse human identity. This choice should not have to be made. However, the forced-choice argument is still with us.

Recently it has become fashionable to lament the Balkanization of America. Implicit in these lamentations is the assumptions that at some time in the not too distant past there was a golden age of America and Americanism that has been all but destroyed by current trends toward a recognition of group identity within education. The fear that America is fragmenting is not limited to concerns about the educational system but extends even to the role and function of government and law within society.

An article in *Harper's* points out the irony that even while American technology has produced products such as Krazy Glue, the "bonds of

American society itself should be weakening or dissolving. All too many examples suggest themselves: the congealing of the melting pot and the reemergence of ethnicity;...the narrowing of loyalties; the fragmentation of government; the twilight of authority" (Phillips, 1978). What is indeed ironic is that even as this commentator on the American scene speaks of narrowing loyalties and reemerging ethnicity, he admits that "regionalism, separation, fragmentation, and rampant ethnicity are hardly new in the United States....On the contrary they are as old as Jamestown, New Amsterdam, and Plymouth."

Even though America had as one of its basic tenets the creation of a "New Man in the New World," the very human ties that have bound people together have persisted since "Jamestown, New Amsterdam, and Plymouth." Further, one cannot overlook the native American societies and the heritage of Spain in America. As a result of a myopic allegiance to the melting pot, we have been unable to define the American character in other than the most simplistic or superficial terms. We have attempted to define America as the crucible that boils off all impurities until the final product is just like everyone else. One is led to assume that in this picture the impurities mean language and customs that are different from those of the perceived majority. What is then left has little room for cultural diversity and democracy.

If there is to be cultural democracy within America, individuals as well as groups must have the opportunity to pursue their own course of fulfillment—within the framework of a general society—without ethnic background being a limiting factor. Further, a parallel right must exist in which each individual is allowed his/her own ethnic and cultural identity, without the pejorative connotation embodied in the words "parochial" or "narrow" being attached to those feelings. Ideally, the uniqueness of each individual or group would be allowed to enrich the experience of each other individual or group; provincialism would not bind anyone to his/her background. The schools are in a central position to implement this acceptance of intergroup understanding and cultural democracy. The converse of acceptance is continued intergroup friction, throughout society.

The Role of the Schools

One cannot assume that the schools will provide the solution to group conflict merely by attempts to teach youngsters to understand or appreciate each other. Just as teachers have not developed lesson plans with the express objectives of fostering mutual hatred or distrust based on ethnicity, it is not hard to conjecture that much prejudice and ethnocentrism has been allowed to take root because of a lack of positive efforts by the educational process to break down barriers to understanding. Certainly the schools are not the sum of children's educational experience. Simple multiplication shows that the average high school graduate will have spent less than 15,000 hours in all classroom experiences, while a recent study reports that this same average graduate will have given approximately 18,000 hours to television. Time spent with television, family, friends, and other groups certainly has an effect upon what we call the education process that produces the adult within our society. However, the schools are able to provide a time when youngsters may have their attention directed toward those human relations questions that they will need to consider in order to function in the larger context of American society. Undoubtedly, one of the human relations questions should deal with ethnicity and ethnic identity.

Many objections have been raised to the inclusion of ethnic studies within the curriculum. These objections have ranged from academic uncertainty over the educational soundness of ethnic history to the possibility of creating dissention and conflict within the classroom. The answers to these objections are not singular. We all have some knowledge of failed or failing experiences with ethnic studies, but we must bear in mind that there have been failures with other subjects as well. Not all industrial arts or classical literature classes are raving successes. Ethnic studies programs, like other curricula, depend upon teachers and appropriate content. In answer to the second question, concerning possible ill will, it must be pointed out that ethnicity is not of itself devisive; rather, it can be a powerful force for unity. Some people believe that the more you talk about differences the more you tend to separate yourself from the whole. This is not the case, however, as was pointed out in "Toward Educational Renewal in the Seventies: A Report on Racism in Education for the Minneapolis Public Schools." The report explored the effect of a monocultural curriculum on the development and perpetuation of institutional racism:

Historically, in an ethno-centric society institutions of learning have perpetuated one set of norms, values and philosophies through the curriculum. All ethnic groups which aspired to be American were required to move in the direction of a white, Anglo-Saxon Protestant base. The melting of atypical cultures and the severing of ethnic ties were prerequisite to becoming Americans.... If diversity among white ethnics is suppressed, then obviously racial distinctiveness is enhanced. One's race becomes paramount at the expense of one's ethnicity. Accordingly, when the curriculum is designed and supportive of the "centrism," outsiders (non-white racial groups) would be lost. [Task Force on Racism in Education, Note 1, p. 36]

As Robert Wood, director for the Joint Center for Urban Studies at MIT and Harvard University, has stated: "It is urgent, then, that we face directly, honestly, vigorously the challenge in ethnic relations today. That challenge to our open society has never been greater, but the need to meet it has never been more imperative for the country and the world" (Wood, 1969, p. ix).

Ethnic relations and group identity have been seen as the direct opposite of education for the individual, in which the expressed desire of our school system is to allow each child to realize his or her maximum potential. Looking at children as members of a group has somehow even connoted being un-American. It is only recently that we have come to accept as legitimate the aspirations expressed by such groups of people as the handicapped or aged, and we still have far to go in reconciling ourselves to positive measures in employment or job security. It is not my purpose here to explore the issue of affirmative action, but rather to urge acceptance of the position that one is not an American only as an individual.

This recognition helps to determine one of the functional dimensions of ethnicity and ethnic groups. American schools do not graduate thousands of homogeneous individuals into the mainstream. The schools and society must deal with a plurality of groups. Not only have ethnic groups not been assimilated, but ethnic identification has been seen as a useful organizing focus for pursuit or defense of legitimate interests. This becomes particularly true when government seems to rely upon ethnic and racial criteria in the allocation of resources. Ethnicity, as a means of self-interest/defense, then, works toward a more democratic and egalitarian society.

Ethnicity and ethnic groups mean many different things to different people. Otto Fienstein, through his experiences with ethnic communities and curriculum, has developed the following definition of ethnicity: "Ethnicity means peoplehood, a sense of commonality or community derived from networks of family relations which have over a number of generations been the carriers of common experience. Ethnicity, in short, means the culture of people and is thus critical for values, attitudes, perceptions, needs, mode of expression, behavior and identity" (in Herman, 1974, p. 17). To this description perhaps could be added Andrew Greeley's statement, which defines an ethnic group as people bound together by "real or imagined common origin" (1969, p. 18), as often ethnic origin cannot be precisely traced, nor can one exclude persons from an ethnic identity because they have several ethnic backgrounds from which to choose. In short, then, ethnic identity is a process, not an achieved and ossified quality. One's ethnicity is a commitment to a social grouping which exists within a larger society of diverse ancestral origins but which shares some values, behavioral patterns, or symbols distinct from those of the larger society.

It can, perhaps, be said that ethnic groups are people in whom the past endures, and in whom the present is inconceivable without moments gone by. Genuine understanding occurs only when the events of the present disclose the meaning of the past and offer an anticipation of the promise of the future. The question of the relevance of this kind of history has often been raised. But to state that ethnic history in schools is not relevant is to negate the relevancy of our own actions for tomorrow; today's existence will become history.

The schools have tended to remain conservative in their approach to learning, and to back off from discussion of basic human issues. Changes in our social systems have not kept pace with the rapid economic and scientific advances of our era. Intergroup conflict flourishes not only in the United States but in many places throughout the world, and schools have tended to ignore these conflicts except as political or military events. In our own country it has been hoped that other institutions would defuse the issue before it had to be discussed in the schools.

The schoolroom has been seen as sacred, exempt from the very real issues that confront American society. As long as the basic skills are taught—and they are viewed as reading, writing, and arithmetic, or to be more modern, comprehension, communication—that is all the school need concern itself with. The issues of law and humanities need never be touched in the classroom. Law can be taught by tracing the passage of a bill and then dismissed by the phrase "obey it," and the humanities can be covered by English class discussion of great novels. There need be no exploration of how we arrived at where we are, and only the most superficial attention need be devoted to where we are going. Children are urged to perform their civic responsibilities, attend class, hand in their homework, and, when they graduate and reach the age of 18, vote. Most time in the classroom is to be devoted to developing the youngster as a useful (i.e., producing-consuming) member of society. To many observers of American education this means that children should be classified early so that they can be taught a marketable skill.

Cultural democracy in the school environment does not preclude the teaching or learning of these "useful" objectives, but it recognizes that there are a number of different ways in which they may be taught and learned and that there may be differences in what is thought of as useful. Cultural democracy recognizes that youngsters may enter the school system from a bicultural background which also may be bilingual or monolingual non-English-speaking. As the authors of *Cultural Democracy,* Ramirez and Castaneda, pointed out: "Cultural democracy is a philosophical precept which recognizes that the way a person communicates, relates to others, seeks support and recognition from his environment (incentive motivation), and thinks and learns (cognition) is a product of the value system of his home and community" (1974, p. 23).

We in the schools must attempt to strengthen the positive bonds of mutual exchange between the home and formal education. And a greater concern for a culturally democratic school environment will enhance the chance for success for both. The chance must be given for the cultural reality of the child to be reflected in the educational program that the school offers.

The schools have acted—until very recently—as though the melting pot were a fact, or, if not, should have been. As described above, the cultural aspects of immigrant life were treated as so much unnecessary baggage that could be disposed of much as one discards a worn-out pair of shoes. The choice had to be made, to be American or to cling to the "old ways." The reality embodied in this forced-choice concept does not illustrate the reality for thousands of Americans who desire to function in a bi- or multi-cultural America. The schools must begin to appreciate the challenge and opportunity presented by this reality.

REFERENCES

American Association of Colleges of Teacher Education. *Bulletin,* 1972 (November).

Greeley, A. *Why can't they be like us?* New York: Institute on Human Relations Press; American Jewish Committee, 1969.

Herman, J. *The schools and group identity.* New York: Institute on Pluralism and Group Identity; American Jewish Committee, 1974.

Phillips, K. The Balkanization of America. *Harper's Magazine,* 1978 (May), pp. 37 ff.

Ramirez, M., & Castaneda, A. *Cultural democracy: Bicognitive development and education.* New York: Academic Press, 1974.

White House Conference on Children. *1970: Proceedings.* Washington, D.C.: Government Printing Office, 1970.

Wood, R. C. Foreword. In A. Greeley, *Why can't they be like us?* New York: Institute on Human Relations Press; American Jewish Committee, 1969.

Zangwill, I. *The melting pot: A drama.* New York: Macmillan, 1909.

REFERENCE NOTE

1. Task Force on Racism in Education. Toward educational renewal in the seventies: A report on racism in education for the Minneapolis Public Schools. Mimeographed, Minneapolis Public Schools, 1974.

Multicultural Law and Humanities Education: Preparing Young People for a Future of Constructive Pluralism

Carlos E. Cortés

The theme of multiculturalism is continued in this paper as the author discusses its implications for law-related education. After briefly addressing the relationship between law and ethnicity, Carlos Cortés presents what he terms "a selectively annotated multicultural adaptation of oft-stated goals of law-related education." This listing, while admittedly incomplete, should serve as a catalyst and guide for making certain that the goals of any law-related education program explicitly and positively address the needs of a multicultural constituency. The sampling of strategies for implementing multicultural law-related education with which the paper concludes should similarly serve as useful models for others. The author's central admonition is significant enough to bear repeating here: Ethnic and cultural factors must be continuously considered throughout the entire law-related curriculum and not left to be treated now and then in special units. As Cortés notes: "Ethnicity and culture, like law, are too important as societal realities to be marginalized or dealt with only 'in their place.'"

Ours is a nation of laws and a nation committed, at least in principle if not always in practice, to "justice for all," as symbolized in our Pledge of Allegiance. It is also a nation of individuals and of groups—political groups, social groups, economic groups, religious groups, professional groups, geographical groups, and, most important for this paper, ethnic and cultural groups.

What is the relationship of law and ethnicity in our nation? It is all around us and always has been. U.S. government treaties with Indian nations. Slavery. Treaty of Guadalupe Hidalgo. Abolition of slavery. Reconstruction. Chinese Exclusion Act. *Plessy* v. *Ferguson*. Segregation. Immigration laws. Japanese internment during

World War II. Civil rights struggle. *Brown* v. *Topeka Board of Education*. School desegregation. Sit-ins and bus boycotts. Affirmative action. *Lau* v. *Nichols*. The undocumented alien worker. *Bakke* v. *Board of Regents, University of California*.

This close, continuous, often ignored, often misunderstood relationship of law and ethnicity presents a challenge to schools—how to help prepare young people for life in a culturally pluralistic nation of laws and a rapidly shrinking, interdependent world. Too often such questions are incorrectly viewed as the special, exclusive province of the social studies. While well-conceived, well-coordinated, and well-implemented social studies programs can help meet this challenge, educators should not overlook the critical contribution that can be made by an imaginative multicultural law-related humanities program.

Educators have an obligation to try to develop citizens with "cultural literacy" (Banks, 1973)—a thorough understanding of culture and ethnicity in our society and in the world—and "legal literacy"—"a clear understanding of the concepts, skills, and processes associated with the American legal system . . . and personal and societal values in relation to that system" (Falkenstein, 1977, p. 77). These "literacies" are inexorably linked. One cannot be culturally literate without understanding the law-related aspects of ethnic and cultural

Carlos E. Cortés is Professor of History and Chairman of Chicano Studies at the University of California, Riverside. His many publications include *Three Perspectives on Ethnicity* and two major book series on Mexican Americans. He is currently writing books on Chicanos, multicultural education, and the history of ethnicity in U.S. motion pictures. The author would like to thank James Banks, Cheryl Biles, Eleanor Blumenberg, Don Brown, Peter d'Errico, Lynda Falkenstein, Elizabeth Farquhar, Ricardo García, Roy Harris, and Jimmie Martinez for their comments on a preliminary draft of this paper. Research support for this paper was provided by an Intramural Research Grant of the University of California, Riverside, Academic Senate.

experience. Nor can one be legally literate without understanding the ethnic and cultural implications and impact of our system of laws, legal institutions, and law-related processes, including its role in helping or hindering the struggle for social justice.

Survey research gives an indication of the problem. Yankelovich recently reported (1974) that young people (ages 17–23) expressed massive support for "more emphasis on law and order," acceptance of "the power and authority of the police," and the belief that "there is too much concern with equality and too little with law and order." Another national survey revealed that American adolescents knew little of the problems faced by members of minority groups in their struggle to achieve equality before the law (National Assessment of Education Progress, 1976).

The imperative for cooperation between multicultural and law-related education is clear. Multicultural educators need to make law-related concerns an intrinsic part of the multicultural approach. Conversely, law-related educators should include ethnic and cultural factors throughout the law-studies curriculum. All of us need to work to see that multicultural law-related education becomes a continuous, integral part of the entire school curriculum, including the humanities.

Societal Curriculum

In reality, multicultural law-related education has been going on for a long time . . . but not, for the most part, in the schools. It has been going on in the "societal curriculum"—that massive, ongoing informal curriculum of family, peer groups, neighborhoods, mass media, and other socializing forces that "educate" all of us continuously throughout our lives. Part of this informal societal curriculum is education (or miseducation) about the law (Hess & Torney, 1967; Niemi et al., 1974). Part of it is about ethnicity (Clark, 1969; Cortés, Metcalf, & Hawke, 1976). Part of it educates about the relationship of law and ethnicity. According to Comstock:

> Several writers have argued that television is a powerful reinforcer of the *status quo*. The ostensible mechanisms are the effects of its portrayals on public expectations and perceptions. Television portrayals and particularly violent drama are said to assign roles of authority, power, success, failure, dependence, and vulnerability in a manner that matches the real-life social hierarchy, thereby strengthening that hierarchy by increasing its acknowledgement among the public and by failing to provide positive images for members of social categories occupying a subservient position. Content analyses of television drama support the contention that portrayals reflect normative status. [1977, pp. 20–21].

Whenever I present in-service training courses on multicultural education, I ask teachers to keep a "societal curriculum journal" on culture and ethnicity—the education they observe taking place around them *outside* of schools. Even the most "aware" teachers express surprise about the amount of multicultural education in the societal curriculum. Much of this education deals with members of ethnic groups in law-related situations—committing, being accused of, or being victimized by crime, having confrontations with the law, or participating in other law-related activities.

What is the impact of the societal curriculum on young people? Studies have shown that many children develop well-informed attitudes about ethnic people, including prejudices and stereotypes, by the time they reach school (Goodman, 1964). A recent survey of fourth, eighth, and twelfth graders found that television had the greatest impact on their attitudes toward foreign nations and peoples. In a 1975–76 state social studies assessment project, more than 12,000 seventh-grade students in 65 California public schools were asked to select one of four answers to: "Which of the following is an example of an ethnic group in the United States?" Fourteen percent selected "The United Auto Workers," 24% each answered "All the people who live in the same town" and "The Chinese," and 34% answered "People on welfare"!

It takes little imagination to realize the potential impact of such films as *The Godfather, Shaft, West Side Story,* and *Geronimo* on people's "knowledge" of the relationship between ethnic groups and our law-related institutions, particularly when such films are consonant with prevailing societal attitudes. During its fall 1977 presentation of "The Godfather Saga," NBC repeatedly cautioned the viewing audience that: "*The Godfather* is a fictional account of the activities of a small group of ruthless criminals. The characters do not represent any ethnic group and it would be erroneous and unfair to suggest that they do." This gratuitous and totally ineffective posturing probably did little to soften the film's effect on perceptions about Italian Americans. However, it dramatized an awareness of the power of the multicultural societal curriculum.

Goals of Multicultural Law-related Education

Clearly, we face a formidable and critically important task in developing a multiculturally valid law-related education—a law-related education, which, among other things, helps students develop a sensitive understanding of the relationship between law and ethnicity in our society and in the world. A major step in achieving this aim is to reconsider the goals of law-related education in light of the realities and needs of our culturally pluralistic society and to redefine them with explicit consideration of relationship of culture and ethnicity to laws, legal institutions, and law-related processes. Following is a selectively annotated multicultural adaptation of oft-stated goals of law-related education. I feel that multicultural law-related education should:

1. *Help students function more effectively as responsible citizens in a multicultural society of laws, including developing the competence to use the tools of law to achieve personal and group goals.*

2. *Help students develop an understanding of basic concepts relating to law and legal processes, particularly as they function in a multicultural society.* A multicultural law-related program should seek to develop student understanding of such concepts as justice, equality, diversity, responsibility, perspective, discrimination, prejudice, tolerance, stereotyping, minority rights, and tyranny of the majority. The historical record is replete with the impact of prejudice on law-related situations, the role of laws and law-related institutions in maintaining, justifying, or eradicating discrimination, and the pervasiveness of stereotypes among persons involved in law-related processes. To omit such concepts from continuous consideration within law-related education would be to distort student conceptualization of the operation of law in our multicultural society.

3. *Help students develop an increased knowledge of the principles, ideals, and realities of the U.S. system of laws, legal processes, and government, including its differential impact on persons of different ethnic and cultural groups (as well as of different sexes, age groups, economic situations, and physical conditions) and its relationship to the quest for societal justice and human dignity.* To truly understand the reality of our law-related system, students need to explore the past and current relationships between our legal system and U.S. ethnic groups. In some respects, the legal system has functioned positively for U.S. ethnic groups, as in the *Brown v. Topeka Board of Education* Supreme Court decision of 1954 and the passage of the Civil Rights Act of 1964 and Voting Rights Act of 1965. In some respects it has had an inequitable and devastating impact on them. Among these deleterious historical phenomena have been slavery; loss of land by Native Americans and Mexican Americans; proscription of voting rights; legalized discrimination treatment of members of ethnic groups by government officials in law-related capacities. While many of these abuses are historical, with some having been rectified, the legacies in attitudes and behavior for citizens of all backgrounds have been profound.

4. *Help students develop an understanding of the relations of laws and legal institutions to other social forces, social change, and the constructive addressing of societal problems, including special problems faced by members of ethnic and cultural groups.* As Hennig has stated: "Another essential element in law education is the development of an appreciation of the scope of the law and of its effective limits. To what extent is law an effective means of regulating social behavior? Perhaps even more important, to what extent is law *not* an effective means of regulating social behavior? Other social mechanisms administered informally by individuals, families and communities are often more useful than law" (1973, p. 10). Ethnic social mechanisms have often functioned as truly alternative community-based legal systems. In some cases these ethnic alternative systems are recognized and supported by mainstream law—for example, tribal councils on Native American reservations whose special rights and status are guaranteed by tribal treaties with the U.S. government. In other cases, alternative systems have developed autonomously within ethnic communities in response to perceived group needs and dissatisfaction with inequities in mainstream legal institutions—for example, the Chinese Benevolent Associations and the northern New Mexico Penitentes. The study of the origins and function of ethnic intragroup legal processes would shed considerable light on the historical and contemporary relationships between ethnic groups and law-related institutions.

5. *Help students understand conflict as a normal characteristic of society, including conflict between individual liberties, group needs and hopes, and the functioning of society at large.* Falkenstein has argued that law-related concepts "should underscore that controversy is an adherent and healthy feature of a democratic society and an inextricable feature of the legal system itself" (1977, p. 81). Without controversy and conflict, most gains by minorities in our society would not have occurred. Yet, preadolescents (seventh and eighth graders) tend not to understand or appreciate this essential aspect of our national process (National Assessment of Educational Progress, 1973).

6. *Help students learn to examine conflicting ideas and various points of view on social phenomena, including ethnic, cultural, and various national interpretations and perspectives on laws, the legal system, the implementation of laws, and law-related events, values, and behavior.*

7. *Help students clarify their own personal values and attitudes in relation to the views, values, and ideals of society and of the various groups (including ethnic and cultural) which make up our society.*

8. *Help students develop their skills of inquiry, critical thinking, analysis, and synthesis, including an understanding of ethnic perspectives and the impact of cultural factors on attitudes and behavior.*

9. *Help students learn to identify alternate courses of action appropriate in various situations, including those involving ethnic and cultural groups, and to assess the potential consequences of these actions.* The history of ethnic groups in the United States has often involved selecting alternative courses of action to challenge the status quo in the quest for social justice. While most such actions have occurred within the system, at times they have fallen outside of traditional or even legally sanctioned (at the time) bounds. For example, the struggle to eradicate law-supported segregation in public conveyances was spurred by Rosa Parks's "criminal" refusal to sit in the back of a Montgomery, Alabama, bus. It may be that many future gains may depend on such alternative actions. A valid law-related curriculum should provide for the effective exploration of alternatives, including their potential positive and negative results.

10. *Help students make informed, considered decisions and take effective action appropriate within the framework of a multicultural, democratic society, including participation in the political system, effective use of the legal system, and the changing laws.* For ethnic groups, change is a *must* for the attainment of equality and social justice in our society. Law-related education should be a force for such change, not an impediment by reinforcing adherence to the status quo.

11. *Help students become aware of the societal curriculum on law, including the manner in which the societal curriculum "educates" about the relationship between ethnic groups and the law.* This seldom considered goal is a critical one, particularly when we consider that ex-students will continue their multicultural law-related education through the societal curriculum after they leave school. We cannot immunize students to the societal curriculum's potentially noxious effects, but we can help prepare them to deal with it throughout their lives.

12. *Help students understand the fundamental principles and values of U.S. law and their similarities to and differences from those of the legal systems of other nations.* Schools should prepare young people to be not only citizens of our nation, but also future actors of the culturally complex, ever shrinking, increasingly interdependent, constantly changing state of the world. Yet recent studies indicate that, compared with young people of other nations, young Americans lack global understanding, including understanding of law-related subjects. As our lives become increasingly international, it will be increasingly impor-

tant for us to understand the law-related aspects of international relations and the similarities and differences between the U.S. system and other legal systems.

Implementation of Multicultural Law-related Education

To attain these goals, law-related education should be continuously multicultural in conceptualization and implementation. Many current law-related educational programs devote *some* attention to culture and ethnicity, usually through special units on diversity, discrimination, and civil rights. But, while useful, this approach cannot substitute for the continuous consideration of ethnic and cultural factors throughout the *entire* law-related curriculum.

Moreover, the failure to deal with culture and ethnicity throughout the law-related curriculum creates "conceptual ghettoization." This has become too common in education—providing special ethnic days, units, or courses, while continuing with "business as usual" throughout the mainstream curriculum. Special units on such topics as diversity, discrimination, and civil rights—like special ethnic studies courses and units in other subject areas and disciplines—have values. But ethnicity and culture, like law, are too important as societal realities to be marginalized or dealt with only "in their place."

How can this fusion be achieved? Among the strategies which have been suggested for law-related education are case studies, mock trials, field experiences, use of visual media and literature, role playing, simulation games, and historical analysis. Many of these strategies are also being used in multicultural education. How simple and doubly effective if these two thrusts were used through the humanities to reinforce each other and to achieve the common goals I have outlined!

At any grade level where law-related case studies are used, cases should be selected which explicitly deal with ethnicity, and in all cases there should be a consideration of cultural and ethnic implications. Similarly, in the selection of mock trials, situations with ethnic and cultural implications should be used at each grade level in which the mock trial strategy is adopted. In providing field experiences for students, teachers should make certain that students have the opportunity to see law-related processes from the perspectives of the various ethnic and cultural groups which compose their communities and to see ethnic and cultural groups from the perspectives of members of law-related institutions. The study of values should include not only clarification of personal values and learning of societal values, but continuous investigation into values of the nation's ethnic and cultural groups (as well as values of various foreign nations).

Film can be used effectively to achieve multicultural law-related goals. At the University of California, Riverside, Dr. Leon Campbell and I offer a series of film-and-history courses in which film is the principal document for student analysis. In one of our courses, we explored the theme of "The Conflict between Law and Justice." To provide an international multicultural perspective on this law-related theme, we selected feature films from different nations expressing cultural variations of this universal conflict (Cortés, Campbell, & Curl, 1976).

A similar approach within the humanities would be to use literature—for example, novels or short stories dealing with ethnic people in various law-related situations. A combination of films, novels, and short stories can be used. Television, too, provides and excellent source for multicultural law-related education. Pioneering work in this area has been done by Prime Time School Television. One of its strategies has been to have students critically analyze current television shows for their presentation of law-related activities, particularly those involving law enforcement agencies (Prime Time School Television, 1977).

Moreover, the use of films and television links nicely with the study of the societal curriculum. Effective law-related education should help students learn to perceive and understand the process by which their law-related "knowledge" and attitudes have been influenced outside of school. This would include developing an awareness of the societal curriculum on the relationship between law and ethnicity. Students, like teachers, can keep societal curriculum journals on law. How is law—including its relationship to ethnicity—dramatized on television? In books? In movies? In magazines and newspapers? In advertisements? On bumper stickers? What is the "street wisdom" they may be learning from their friends and the "home wisdom" of their family about law, legal processes, government, and ethnic and cultural groups? By making the societal curriculum part of the multicultural law-related curriculum, we help prepare students for a more aware and effective future.

But wait a minute! Advanced literature and complex feature films at the elementary level? Of course not, but the base for later study of films and literature should be established at the elementary level. That is the place to begin creating an understanding of the relationship between individuality and the nature of groups (similarities and differences), developing student awareness of the societal curriculum, and establishing student "perspectivism"—the ability to view events, issues, ideas, and other phenomena from the perspectives of the different individuals and groups involved. The latter quality, "perspectivism," is vital for citizens in a multicultural society.

Piaget suggests that beginning elementary school students are highly concrete in their thought processes and egocentric in their perceptions. As they proceed through school, particularly from ages 8 to 12, they develop more abstract, less egocentric thinking. Yet this does not necessarily lead to perspectivism. In fact, some studies have shown that, particularly around age 12, students tend to become more knowledgeable about international issues, but also more firm in their stereotypes and less flexible in their perceptions of people of other nations (Hicks & Beyer, 1970; Lambert & Klineberg, 1967). If we are to develop perspectivism in students, we must make special efforts as students move from their early egocentric stage to this 12-year-old hardening of the perceptual and attitudinal arteries. For example, the San Diego Unified School District's "US: A Cultural Mosaic" program provides an imaginative, effective, and humanistic approach for helping young people come to grips with critical concepts and perspectives for understanding individual and group similarities and differences. The importance cannot be overemphasized. As Torney and Morris have pointed out: "The ability to take the perspective of another person may be prerequisite to the acceptance of different or unfamiliar characteristics of others (those common to persons from other countries, for example); similar role-taking ability is required to understand processes of conflict resolution either on the international level, as in war, or closer to home. Until a child has overcome cognitive egocentrism in his orientation he will gain minimum benefit from training requiring such ability" (1972, p. 9).

Role playing and simulation games provide myriad opportunities for students to gain insights into law, culture, ethnicity, and their interrelationship, while at the same time developing perspectivism. In my own work I have used role playing within the story lines of fairy tales to help early elementary school students understand perspectives and develop perspectivism. For example, I use a situation in which students take the roles of the three pigs and the wolf in a meeting 50 years after their well-known fictional confrontation. Students are asked, in their new roles, to discuss what went wrong "way back then" and to try to explain to other students how their points of view were misunderstood by the other three characters in the story.

For the advanced elementary level, a number of stimulating perspectivist simulation games exist. In *Rafá Rafá,* students split into two groups, form two distinct cultures, and then visit and try to function in the other culture for a predetermined amount of time (Shirts, 1976). This involves coming to grips with and trying to understand the values of the other culture, as well as the impact of those values on that culture's laws and customs...a marvelous blend of multicultural and law-related education. In Powderhorn, students form a frontier society, which is transformed from a fluid, mobile, free-wheeling society into a rigid, highly structured, class society with little upward mobility and in which the upper class establishes all of the laws (Shirts, 1971). Once again, a simulation game is used to develop student perspectivism and an awareness of the relationship between laws and the nature of groups.

In my own work with making the teaching of U.S. history multicultural, I have consistently blended law-related and multicultural education: for example, a 1-week unit on colonial governments in which students comparatively examine Spanish, French, and English colonial charters and the Iroquois Indian constitution...ending with a simulation exercise in which groups of students form their own colonies and establish their own legal processes; a 1-week unit on the California gold rush in which students read multiple cultural and ethnic perspectives on the gold rush, including law-related aspects of this event...ending with a simulation exercise of a gold field court, to which different individuals and groups, including members of ethnic groups, bring their cases, claims, and complaints.

We certainly would not expect second graders to deal with the complex, conflicting perspectives of the *Bakke* case (in fact, most adults seem unable to grasp them). But the work which we do with second graders in developing their perspectivism, legal literacy, and cultural literacy could be the basis for understanding *Bakke* at a later stage of their education. Or to be more negative about it, if we fail to develop these attributes in a child at the elementary level, we may, by default, contribute to reinforcing that child's ethnocentric blinders and create obstacles to later curricular efforts to help students understand multiple perspectives on issues.

School desegregation. Sit-ins and bus boycotts. Affirmative action. *Lau* v. *Nichols*. The undocumented alien worker. The *Bakke* decision. How much we have heard and read about these issues! How much of what we have heard and read has been nonsense, stemming from rigidity of perspective and ignorance of both the true functioning of our system of laws and the societal context of our ethnically and culturally diverse nation! How much it makes me wish that all adult Americans had received the benefits of a multicultural law-related education!

We cannot change the past or control the present. Neither can we determine the future through education, but we can certainly influence it. Multicultural law-related education—the preparation of all young people to go forth into a multicultural nation of laws and into a complex, interdependent world—provides a hope for the future.

REFERENCES

Banks, J. A. Teaching ethnic literacy: A comparative analysis. *Social Education,* 1973, *37,* 738–750.

Clark, C. C. Television and social controls: Some observations on the portrayals of ethnic minorities. *Television Quarterly,* 1969, *8*(2), 18–22.

Comstock, G. *The impact of television on American institutions and the American public.* Honolulu: East-West Communication Institute, East-West Center, 1977.

Cortés, C. E.; Campbell, L. G.; & Curl, A. *A filmic approach to the study of historical dilemmas.* Riverside: Latin American Studies Program, University of California, 1976.

Cortés, C. E.; Metcalf, F.; & Hawke, S. *Understanding you and them: Tips for teaching about ethnicity.* Boulder, Colo.: ERIC Clearinghouse for Social Studies/Social Science Education, and Social Science Education Consortium, 1976.

Falkenstein, L. C. Law-related study: Some curriculum guidelines. In D. Tavel (Ed.), *Law studies in the schools.* Toledo, Ohio: College of Education, University of Toledo, 1977.

Goodman, M.E. *Race awareness in young children* (Rev. ed.). New York: Collier, 1964.

Henning, J. F. Law-related education: What works and what doesn't. In S. Davison (Ed.), *Reflections on law-related education.* Chicago: American Bar Association, Special Committee on Youth Education for Citizenship, 1973.

Hess, R. D., & Torney, J. V. *The development of political attitudes in children.* Chicago: Aldine, 1967.

Hicks, E. P. & Beyer, B. K. Images of Africa. *Journal of Negro Education,* 1970, *39,* 158–166.

Lambert, W. E., & Klineberg, O. *Children's views of foreign peoples: A cross-national study.* New York: Appleton-Century-Crofts, 1967.

National Assessment of Educational Progress. *Political knowledge and attitudes.* Denver: Education Commission of the States, 1973.

National Assessment of Education Progress. *Education for citizenship.* Denver: Education Commission of the States, 1976.

Niemi, R., et al. *The politics of future citizens: New dimensions in the political socialization of children.* San Francisco: Jossey-Bass, 1974.

Prime Time School Television. *Television, police, and the law.* Niles, Ill.: Argus Communications, 1977.

Shirts, R. G. *Powderhorn.* Del Mar, Calif.: Simile II, 1971.

Shirts, R. G. *Rafá Rafá.* Del Mar, Calif.: Simile II, 1976.

Torney, J. F., & Morris, D. N. *Global dimensions in U.S. education: The elementary school.* New York: New York Friends Group, 1972.

Yankelovich, D. *The new morality: A profile of American youth in the 70's.* New York: McGraw-Hill, 1974.

Multicultural Law and Humanities Education: Preparing Young People for a Future of Constructive Pluralism

Stephen Conn

This paper takes a slightly different tack regarding multicultural law-related education than the one taken in the previous paper. Here Stephen Conn advocates the study of legal traditions of societies other than one's own in order to gain an understanding of the basic nature and functions of law as well as of the legal system of one's own society. He argues that by setting one's own experience side by side with another's one averts the bias of ethnocentricity and develops respect for other cultural perspectives.

Carlos Cortés, in his excellent paper, suggests that, as a practical matter, one cannot be legally literate without appreciating the historical impact of American legal behavior upon diverse ethnic groups in our society.

If we focus upon the relationship between American law and ethnic groups, we receive more than a recitation of injustice committed in the name of state authority to racial, religious, and cultural minorities:

1. We view our own law system and American legal culture through new eyes, eyes less likely to view the values and intent of the law as inherently correct because they are the law in a particular American time and place.
2. We come to see that one aspect of ethnic diversity is a diversity of legal traditions, traditions which suggest both problems and opportunities for the consumer or supplier of American justice.

What multicultural legal education offers students who are not ethnic minorities is a new and important way of looking at American law, not as rules and procedures fixed in time and place, but as an instrument of society, reflective of social values, capable of manipulation and change.

If there is confusion or even anger over demands that minorities make upon the legal system, one source of that confusion and anger is

our failure to understand that legal process is shaped by demands generated within an American legal culture.

What is a legal culture? It is that network of values and attitudes about the appropriate use of state power which determines: (*a*) demands a particular group make on the system; (*b*) which part of the system those demands are made upon; and (*c*) whether or not that part of the system responds through changed activity.

At the root of all conflicts over the definitions of crime, appropriate punishment, concepts of liability in tort or concepts of contracts in courts, legislatures, administrative bureaucracies, or station houses are conflicts in social values. Some of these social conflicts that become legal conflicts emerge from ethnic difference. The response of the legal system to these demands varies over time.

Consider that less than 25 years ago many state legal systems arrested and prosecuted blacks who drank from "white" water fountains or sat in the wrong place in restaurants or trains. Did the legal system change, or did its response to demands made upon it change?

Even the very meaning of law is subject to social definition. Japan and America have police. But what police do, their self-image, and society's image of them differs in each place.

The role of a legal system varies from society to society. Again, a comparative view of legal cultures enables us to view different ways that law might act or has already acted in our own society.

The role of law varies in time and place because different ethnic groups have different legal traditions. These traditions are reflected in:

1. The rights and duties of group members and

Stephen Conn is an attorney, Professor of Justice at the University of Alaska, Anchorage, and co-author of two sets of bicultural legal education texts: *The Law of the People* and *Alaska Natives and the Law.*

strangers regarding personal rights and property rights.
2. The appropriate way to avoid disputes and define disputes when they arise.
3. The appropriate sequence for dispute adjustment.
4. The social implications of employing formal law systems.

Legal traditions shape a person's attitude toward law even when that law is formed out of a second legal tradition.

So when an immigrant from Mexico sits down to discuss a family problem with a poverty lawyer from Ohio, client and attorney are influenced by two legal traditions. A clash in conceptualization of the problem and the role of the lawyer in its resolution is inevitable.

This clash between legal traditions can become an important vehicle for learning about law.

Cortés describes the way both media and classroom educators either underplay ethnic differences or treat it stereotypically. This same rigidity in defining the legal process denies the student of law an appreciation of his own legal culture and its influence upon law.

A multiethnic approach will then provide insight into an ethnic legal tradition. But, more important, by describing at least two traditions at work when minorities confront the American legal system, students will discover their *own* "missing" legal culture and its significance in the way law works for them.

How many persons who read *Bury My Heart at Wounded Knee* (Brown, 1971) considered that most of the conflicts described between white Americans and Native Americans could be characterized as conflicts between legal cultures?

I do not suggest that placing one's students in the position of outsiders to the American legal system will merely convey a sense of the law as oppressor.

My direct experience with squatters, Indians, and Eskimos suggests to me that these minorities are especially cognizant of the existence of multiple legal systems, and the influence of more than one legal tradition on problem solving. They seek the most favorable forum from their own perspective and not from the system's perspective. Sometimes they choose or are forced to opt out of the dominant society's legal system entirely.

Brazilian squatters with real property disputes are denied access to state courts because they lack title to land (Conn, Note 1). They do not seek out informal assistance of police or establish *favela* courts out of legal illiteracy or a desire to be separate. They react to official options of legal help, offered or denied, as options to be employed or rejected according to a single criteria—which forum will offer me the remedy I desire?

Rabbinical courts, Eskimo village councils, Chinese Benevolent Associations, and other extralegal forums represent something other than ethnic insularity. They are employed by persons who have realistically assessed and rejected options afforded by the official legal system. They have improved upon the options available by creating new options.

There is little to be gained by understanding the clash between legal traditions in education programs. The clash will not be resolved by printing the United States Constitution in Spanish or by training police to read the *Miranda* warnings in an Eskimo dialect.

But the non-ethnic-minority student who steps outside of his or her own legal culture and into another has everything to gain.

As Cortés suggests, the key to postconventional legal thinking is a pragmatic assessment of a legal process as a prelude to demands for change in that process.

To demand change in the value orientation of law is perhaps the most predictable request in the working relationship between any society and its laws. Ethnic minorities are not alone in seeking to bring about change.

Consider the shift in the American law of contracts from its affirmation of "buyer beware" as a legal standard to greater concern for unknown consumers who might be injured in the marketplace. Consider the change in tort law from its protection of fledgling industries against claims of injured workers to its shift of social cost through workman's compensation legislation in another country.

If you seek the logic of these legal changes or the dynamics of these changes within the legal system only, you will not find it.

And what of ethnic minorities? Should their legal education be indoctrination into American law as an ideal, exclusive system? Or should we continue the process of comparison between legal traditions as a vehicle for legal education.

Bicultural Legal Education

In developing legal education for Alaska Natives (Eskimos and Indians) (Barthel, Conn, & McDearmon, 1977) and for Navajos (Vicenti, Jimson, Conn, & Kellogg, 1972), I have found that teaching American law comparatively is superior. It involves:

1. A consistent focus on problems and problem solving as they occur within the student's and his or her family's community. Recourse to American law becomes then only a part of the picture.
2. A constant evaluation of the practical options for grievance processing afforded by both legal

traditions, whether or not these options are institutionalized.

3. Opportunities or problems which flow from the existence of more than one legal tradition in operation at the same time.

Does this mean that Navajo or Eskimo students are aware of their own legal culture in a way that middle American students are not? No, these students must learn to recognize the practical signficance of mechanisms and approaches to resolving social conflict that they may have assumed to be sublegal or "old fashioned."

Students should consider the significance of learned experience in one legal tradition for participation in another. For example, an Eskimo who is confronted with a charge against her in her village council knows that it is appropriate to confess immediately and set in motion a process of conciliation. But if that same Eskimo appears in an Alaska court, her admission of legal guilt will not be similarly rewarded.

Suppose, again, an Eskimo educated about his constitutional rights challenges the authority of the council and requests a trial in court? What impact will this have on the council's continuing significance as a kind of neighborhood justice center to resolve problems between persons with ongoing relationships? What impact will it have on his village relationships?

Students should be aware of the options available in both systems and weigh their acts accordingly—this is the message of what I term bicultural legal education.

A second legal tradition may offer options for problem solving. It will certainly offer values that may or may not comport with those of the American common law tradition as interpreted by the law givers, be they judges, lawyers, social workers, or police. The process of legal education as multicultural education becomes one of discovery and self-discovery for student and teacher.

And now the hard part. There is nothing easy about developing bicultural legal education. The process of teaching becomes, itself, a process of inquiry.

Recently, a teacher who had received *Alaska Natives and the Law* (Barthel et al., 1977) in his Eskimo village school told me how impressed he had been to read that in some villages councils resolved minor problems and headed off more formal confrontations. I surprised him when I said that it was in that very village that I had discovered councils. A council met not 50 feet from where we sat and had done so for over 50 years.

Teachers must explore not only the American legal environment in which they teach but the second legal system afloat in the environment.

But what of elementary school teachers?

If we follow the logic of symposium papers, then it appears that elementary school children may have preconventional attitudes about law, fixed more by age than by culture. Certainly, then, we cannot expect to make young Clarence Darrows of these children.

What I have described, a comparative legal education program, will be built on an assessment of values at the elementary school level. These values, so well described by Charles Lavaroni (in this volume), come to form and to be reaffirmed in a legal tradition, be it ethnic or American.

Our legal education materials for Alaska Native children, in kindergarten through sixth grade, focus on identification and clarification of values through lesson plans and activities: We focus upon:

- The child's role and relationship to family (rights and duties of parents and children).
- The child's role and relations within the school community.
- The child's role and relations with the larger community.

As jobs and activities are discussed, rights and duties emerge. As rights and duties emerge, a picture of those social values which underlie legal values come to the fore.

Problem solving and authority within small and large groups are considered in relationship to activities familiar to younger children—for example, the child's perception of consumption, where and how he gets things. Primary school children have social experiences to build upon—experiences which relate to the larger market and to consumption in the family and neighborhood.

Group activities, property use, land use, and many other topics can be dealt with.

The word "law" or the role of law is not very relevant as a starting point.

Curriculum development in this arena calls for a team approach. In Alaska and New Mexico we have employed: (*a*) a lay person trained to do social science interviews on traditional or alternative legal approaches, (*b*) an attorney with an ethnic clientele who can provide actual problem cases he has confronted with members of the target population, and (*c*) an educator experienced in instruction of the target group who can assist in developing instructional materials and in teacher training.

The material is then value- and problem-oriented. Material developed for an Eskimo population to deal comparatively with legal traditions can be used to draw non-Eskimos out of their own ethnocentric perspective. They can view their own system from another place.

Teachers often think that legal education can begin only when constitutional law or the criminal law system can be defined. But more sophisticated legal education is far more concerned with civil law than criminal law matters. Extraordinary blind spots to the legal overtones of civil problems exist in even otherwise worldly students.

And civil law, dealing with ongoing personal relationships, is at the heart of most legal traditions of small groups. So, again, small and large traditions lend themselves to comparison.

The challenge of legal education for elementary school students is that the teacher must curb any instinct he has to indoctrinate, and listen, listen, listen, and observe.

No textual materials on ethnic legal culture can compensate for this. Materials can point the way. But if they must accomplish more than this, then stereotyping rather than considered comparison will probably be the negative result.

So is cross-cultural legal education worth the risk and the effort?

I believe so. As Cortés argues, it more clearly reflects the world in which we live. It offers us an opportunity to view our own legal world without the bias of ethnocentricity—for the first time.

REFERENCES

Barthel, F.; Conn, S.; & McDearmon, P. *Alaska Natives and the law* (7 vols.). Anchorage: Alaska Legal Services Corporation, 1977.

Brown D., *Bury my heart at Wounded Knee.* New York: Bantam, 1971.

Vicenti, D.; Jimson, L. B.; Conn, S., & Kellogg, M. J. L. *The law of the people: A bicultural approach to legal education (4 vols.). Ramah, N.Mex.: Ramah Navajo High School Press, 1972.*

REFERENCE NOTE

1. Conn, S. The neighborhood law of Brazilian squatters. Unpublished manuscript, University of Alaska, 1978.

Real Problem Solving through Law and Humanities Education

Earle Lomon

One of the strengths of law-related education has been its strong emphasis on student participation and active learning. This paper discusses a program for science and math that emphasizes such student involvement and appears readily adaptable for law and humanities. In this program children are challenged to solve and guided in solving real social problems. In describing actual cases of children's problem-solving experiences, Earle Lomon demonstrates that issues related to law and humanities permeate the fabric of society and, therefore, quite naturally are confronted in such problem solving, which develops math and reading skills while instilling a sense of political efficacy and social responsibility. Those wishing a more complete description of the program and the attendant evaluation should contact the author.

Law is embedded in complex social patterns. The understanding and effective use of law by lawyers or citizens requires a grasp of a multifaceted, multidisciplinary activity. The needed process skills cannot be achieved through formal, structured learning by itself. Professional schools of law, medicine, and business emphasize the case method, and apprenticeship to the real thing is part of the preparation of executives, doctors, and lawyers.

The Unified Sciences and Mathematics for Elementary Schools (USMES) curriculum was developed to put the principle of learning through involvement in real problems to very wide use. The success of humankind in dominating its environment and improving its lot is dependent on the ability of people to respond flexibly and logically, rather than instinctively, to the challenges of life, including those of law and government. Recently, as the complexity of the problems facing us has rapidly increased, the effectiveness of isolated problem solving by a few leaders has diminished. The solution for one problem often exacerbates real or perceived grievances in another area. Thus in modern times it has become important for a substantial fraction of the populace to be able to participate effectively in the problem-solving activity and the consequent decision making. Only in this way can a

Earle L. Lomon is Professor of Physics at the Massachusetts Institute of Technology. He directed the Unified Sciences and Mathematics for Elementary Schools and Real Problem Solving in Secondary Education projects.

consensus be reached and acted upon, without being stymied by the reaction of politically effective interest groups. We are not likely to resolve conflicts such as energy versus environment unless a mode of problem solving in which the majority of citizens participate becomes effective.

Yet the educational systems of the democracies, which depend on such able and widespread participation, do almost nothing to promote in young people the development of those cognitive strategies needed for handling complex, real problems. Of course, many individuals become superb problem solvers and decision makers, but they must develop these skills through out-of-school involvement with life, or perhaps at a late stage of professional education. If the schools would turn some attention to the matter starting in elementary grades, might we not greatly increase the proportion of people with a high level of cognitive strategy, and thus transform society?

In 1967 a group of people experienced in mathematics, science, and education met in Cambridge, Massachusetts, to discuss the correlation of mathematics and science in the schools. They left with a broader vision of the effect of introducing elementary school students to investigation of and action on real problems of obvious concern to them and the adult population. They asserted that such exposure would not only develop the desired problem-solving process skills, but would at the same time give the student a sense of the power of learning and a better grasp of the use of basic quantitative and communications skills. In this way the basic skills themselves would be better learned, and attitudes of the young toward education, society, and their role in society would be improved. (See Cambridge Conference, 1969.)

Their conclusion implied that problem solving and decision making were best learned by practice in actual situations rather than in more formal ways, and that learning of basic skills would profit from the motivation of seeing their application to important uses and from the concrete, understandable context of such an application. On the acquisition of the problem-solving process skills, it was argued that formal statements concerning the steps of the scientific method or any other such problem-solving hierarchy were both too abstract and too simplistic to be effective. It is not the steps of problem solving which are most difficult to learn, but the interfaces between those steps and deciding when to use each step.

In any substantial, nonsimplified problem, cognitive strategies (such as defining the problem, deciding on the important variables, obtaining data, analyzing data, hypothesizing partial solutions, and testing hypotheses) must be returned to again and again as dictated by the developing situation. The strategies may be used in parallel by different individuals or groups who must frequently correlate results and revise strategies. As there are no simple rules for such complex activities, individuals must develop an innate sense of those strategies by repeated exposure to situations carried through from problem definition to solution implementation.

Short circuits or simplifications prevent learning of critical strategies, and lead to a misunderstanding of the essence of real problem solving. An individual trying to apply to real problems process skills gained from an artificial or incomplete experience becomes frustrated. This results in negative attitudes about the usefulness of school and education and about the role of the individual in society. Research by many schools and our own internal evaluation have confirmed this view, as we will discuss later.

With respect to the learning of basic skills and the organizing concepts of the disciplines, the evidence of the curriculum reforms of the fifties and sixties shows that the first, more formal, approaches were not adequate. Exposure to even the best written material did not succeed with the majority of youngsters, who lacked the motivation, maturity, and background of the specialists who constructed the course. The context of real and important situations could be a channel for improved learning of basic facts and skills not only in the sciences and mathematics, but in social studies and language arts as well.

The USMES program was a direct outcome of the 1967 Cambridge conferences, which recommended that learning through investigation and action on real problems should start early, and

that elementary schools, with their undepartmentalized setting, would be a relatively easy place to introduce such a curriculum. When USMES began in Janaury 1970, it had as its central hypothesis that involving elementary students in the improvement of practical situations would positively affect three major domains of learning:

1. The higher-level cognitive strategies of problem solving and decision making would be acquired. Not only is the USMES approach directly related to such process skills, but it may be the only successful way of acquiring them. (This is not to say that a person with sufficient maturity and grasp of these processes may not further improve his or her capacity by explicit and formal consideration of individual problem-solving strategies.)
2. The learning of basic observational, quantitative, and communication skills and an appreciation of the central concepts of the disciplines would be fostered by seeing the need for them arise in an important situation, which also provides the context against which to check their understanding.
3. Positive attitudes of students toward the power of learning, toward their own ability to cope, and toward their role in improving society would be fostered by early experience of real problem solving.

Many studies have been made of the effectiveness of learning in a real context. The USMES program also set out to obtain evidence from its own rather large-scale application of the method. This was accomplished in various studies by research groups at Boston University, at the University of Minnesota, and within USMES.

The results of many of these studies will be described later. First, in the next section I will try to make the particular approach of USMES clear through examples and to show how these cases have had direct bearing on the learning of both principles and specifics of law and government. We may see how real problem solving can be an effective way of fostering law-related education in elementary school, and also how problems centered on legal issues will present new, excellent "challenges" for use in real-problem-solving education.

Examples of USMES Real Problem Solving

The examples below are from actual cases, and not necessarily the most dramatic. I will first describe in some detail the variety of things that occur in the challenges categorized as Pedestrian Crossings. This variety of challenge occurs frequently in USMES and elicits a wide variety of problem-solving foci and strategies. Accidents or bottlenecks at crossings on the way to school are frequently news and recognized as problems of importance of both adults and children, have often led to spontaneous discussion by children. An inquiry by the teacher will often elicit chagrin about delays in crossing or concern about evident danger.

Not only does this immediacy provide internal motivation for the students' subsequent work, but it establishes a criterion for the correctness and effectiveness of their work. The students themselves can check if a pedestrian crossing has been made more efficient or safer. On the other hand, the "correct" solution to an academic or an artificial problem may depend on the framework of the poser of the question.

Once the students agree about the importance of the challenge to them, they discuss their experiences at several crossings and decide on the one or two that are most hazardous and most needed for getting to school. Then they specify their challenge: improved safety at the semirotary at one side of the school, and the convenience of a pedestrian crossing with a walk light on the other side of the school.

During the follow-up discussion the children list specific complaints and possible solutions on the board. At the rotary there isn't enough time to get across between cars. Many cars don't slow down for the children. A warning sign, a traffic light, or policeman at school opening and closing times are suggested. The walk light at the crossing is said to take too long to come on, and to go off too quickly. "But maybe the cars won't have enough time to get through, and it will lead to a traffic jam." The children decide that to check these assertions they will have to measure crossing times, the width of the street, gap times between cars, and light cycle times. They form task forces to get all these data.

At their first outdoor session they begin to make their measurements. The group measuring crossing times at the semirotary (cars go two ways on one side, one way on the other) notice that many cars fail to give turn signals and the crossing children get no warning of whether the cars will be coming in their direction. Those measuring the width of the road find that they cannot get their tape measure down safely in the traffic. The students timing the light cycle realize they will also need to know how many cars arrive at each cycle and how quickly they get through on the green light.

Back in class the students discuss their results and decide that (1) they should count the number of cars that signal and the number that don't; (2) they will construct trundle wheels that will

measure the road for them as they cross it (after they have consulted USMES "How to" cards on "How to Measure Long Distances" and "How to Make a Trundle Wheel"); (3) some of them should study the "How to Use a Stopwatch" cards because of the difficulty of measuring gap times; (4) they should count the number of cars that queue up at the light and their rate of departure; and (5) they should measure the speed of some cars, as they suspect that many are going over the speed limit.

They go out to observe and measure several more times, refining their questions and their techniques each time. They begin to analyze their data, subtracting to find the gap times between cars, and averaging their measurements. With the help of "How to" cards they decide how to organize their variable data into histograms. They find the ratio of the number of cars that signaled to the total number that turn at the rotary.

The last number tells them that only 59% of the cars that should signal do so. They decide that a sign should be put up reminding drivers to signal. They make such a sign in the Design Lab and try it out. They count signaling cars again and find that with the sign up 95% of the drivers signal.

From their frequency distributions of crossing and gap times, they note that nine out of 10 people cross in 10 seconds or less, but that there are only three gaps between cars of 10 seconds or more in a 5-minute period. They point out that impatient children may not wait for about 2 minutes for a safe interval and may dash across, endangering themselves. They feel that a patrol will be necessary for children coming to and going from school. The walk time at the light is 14 seconds, which gives almost all waiting children enough time to cross. But there are 35 seconds between walk lights. On cold days not all of the children wait for the walk light. The task force that had been measuring the queuing of cars remarks that only two or three cars in every 10 light cycles were not able to get across on one green light. They decide that the green light for cars should be reduced to 25 seconds, making it more convenient for the pedestrians.

Having decided on several improvements, they talk them over with their principal. He says that he will establish a patrol, with the town's permission, and that they should find out who is responsible for decisions about signs, light cycles, and patrols. They find out that there is a town traffic department and write a letter to it with their recommendations. An official of the department visits them and asks them questions about their data. He says that setting up a patrol at the semirotary is justified, and that the traffic department will also examine the timing of the walk light and determine if it will go along with their recommendation to shorten the green light for cars. But, he says, new types of signs cannot be put up without a new state law. He suggests that they conduct an educational campaign to convince motorists to signal and not to speed.

The children talk over what they have heard from the official. They decide that a film can be used both to educate drivers and to warn the younger children in their school about the dangers of crossing without a walk light or a big gap between cars. They decide that a scale model of the intersections will be needed, and use the "How to Make a Scale Drawing" cards. Also, a model of a driver in a car is made to determine visibility. They borrow a Super-8 camera and practice using it. Working with first graders, they make a film and show it at the school. They are then invited to show it at the town hall.

These children have not only learned much about observation and analysis, they have learned how people behave and how to communicate with each other and with adults. They have also learned about rules of the road and the need to balance the convenience of different groups; about safety laws; about authority and responsibility for roads and public safety; about costs of lights, signs, and traffic officers; about the town process of mandating expenditures and the restrictions on putting up signs in public areas. Moreover, they themselves have entered into the process of modifying group behavior for the public good.

Law-related issues in challenges. A list of the "challenge" categories is given in Table 1. From the topics the reader will be able to surmise many of the activities that young students would undertake and the topics of law that would be relevant. Some of the law-related activities that have occurred follow.

In Consumer Research–Product Testing youngsters have often checked advertising claims (of how many cups a wet paper towel will hold up, of the nutritiousness of cereals, or of the runproofness of pantyhose, for example). If the claims prove false, the children have done some counteradvertising in the schools and sometimes have protested to the advertising medium. In the cases of which I am aware (consumer research has probably been done by thousands of classes), the students have not pursued legal avenues to stop false advertising. Whether some have done so or not, providing teachers with background information on legal aspects would increase the range of such endeavors pursued by the classes.

Consumer Research, or some other unit such as Classroom Management or Manufacturing, has often led to the establishment of a school store by the students. Rules limiting selling within schools, the articles which may be sold, or the use of prof-

its have often arisen. The distinction between rules imposed by the principal, the school district, or a legislature has had practical consequences. For a school store students usually became involved in the borrowing of money and sometimes in the selling of shares. Accounting procedures must be set up. In at least one case the children incorporated themselves—then in April they realized that they had to make an income tax declaration!

A Design Lab (or general workshop) has been set up in many USMES schools to facilitate the testing, designing, and building of articles related to the challenge. In other cases tools are brought into the classroom for such activities. Safety rules and rules of supervision are an important consideration. The students look into these issues when they undertake the challenge of Design Lab design. Many of their products, such as tables or study carrels, are made out of Tri-Wall (a three-layer cardboard). Fire inspectors have rules in some locales that such material cannot be allowed to remain in the school. In some cases spraying the articles with a flame retardant has satisfied the law; in other cases it has been necessary to get rid of the articles.

The School Rules challenge brings up many facets of authority and governance around issues such as the chewing of gum, or truancy.

Eating in School has raised many issues of food ordinances, and of federal regulations governing the provision of subsidized food.

Bicycle Transportation brings up safety and riding regulations. Children have also raised funds for a bicycle path and entered into contractual relations with a contractor.

In School Zoo the issues of cruelty to animals and of regulations concerning animals on schools property have come up.

In many challenges the children need to leave the school building or school property to gather data, contact people, etc. They have to deal with the clearance and supervision requirements for such excursions.

Protecting Property is concerned with secure lockers, with educational campaigns to cut down theft and vandalism, or with the improvement of fire drills. In these activities children have had to be knowledgeable about legal aspects and have had to interact with relevant public officials.

This list could be lengthened considerably, but the reader will in any case be able to think of more examples. It is clear that such activities bear directly on the three issues which Morris (1973) has indicated to be of mutual interest to the ABA and to educators in supporting law-related education.

1. The children experience the functional and not-so-functional aspects of a community and

Table 1: The USMES Challenges

Challenge	Description
Advertising	Find the best way to advertise a product or event that you want to promote.
Bicycle Transportation	Find ways to make bicycle riding a safe and convenient way to travel.
Classroom Design	Change the classroom to make it a better place.
Classroom Management	Develop and maintain a well-run classroom.
Consumer Research	Determine which brand of a product is the best buy for a specific purpose.
Describing People	Determine the best information to put in a description so that a person can be quickly and easily identified.
Designing for Human Proportions	Design or make changes in things that you use or wear so that they will be a good fit.
Design Lab Design	Improve or set up the Design Lab in your school or class for the benefit of those who use it.
Eating in School	Promote changes that will make eating in school more enjoyable.
Getting There	Overcome the difficulties in getting from one place to another.
Growing Plants	Grow plants for ———. [Children determine the specific purpose, such as for gifts, for transplanting into a garden, for selling, etc.]
Manufacturing	Find the best way to produce in quantity an item that is needed.
Mass Communications	Find a good way for us to tell many people about ——— [topic, problem].
Nature Trails	Develop an outdoor area to help others appreciate nature.
Orientation	Help yourselves and/or others adapt to new situations.
Pedestrian Crossings	Recommend and try to have a change made that will improve the safety and convenience of a pedestrian crossing near the school.
Play Area Design and Use	Promote changes which will improve the design or use of our school's play area.
Protecting Property	Find a good way to protect your ——— [property in desks or lockers, bikes, tools, animals, Design Lab tools, etc.]
School Rules	Find ways of influencing rules and the decision-making process in the school.
School Supplies	Find effective ways to manage and/or conserve school supplies.
School Zoo	Collect and maintain a variety of animals in the classroom to help your class and others learn about them.
Soft Drink Design	Invent a new soft drink that will be popular and can be produced at a low cost.
Traffic Flow	Recommend and try to have a change accepted so that the flow of traffic will be improved at a nearby problem location.
Using Free Time	Find things to do during your ——— [recess time, lunch time] that would be ——— [educational, useful, fun].

are directly involved in trying to make it work better.

2. Real problem solving requires the development of clear thinking and an analytical approach. In particular, the nature of *evidence* is often challenged in the debates among students making a decision.

3. Familiarity with and experience in influencing law and society at the local level are surely good groundwork for a fuller understanding of how American society and the Constitution work.

Starr (1973) has said that "the attitude developed by law studies should be one of the honest inquiry," and points out that this differs in important ways from "being led through a complicated series of exercises to foregone conclusions." I submit that real-problem-solving education is the epitomy of such honest inquiry and provides exactly the right ambience for law-related education for the young. The resources of the law-related education program can build upon real-problem-solving opportunities in three ways:

1. By providing background materials of direct relevance to the investigations being undertaken by students.

2. By developing more formal materials which students are motivated to learn by recent problem-solving experiences, and which they can better understand by having had concrete experiences.

3. By formulating and trying in classrooms new real challenges which focus on issues of law and government.

How Well Does Real Problem Solving Work?

Above I have made many assumptions and claims about the role of real problem solving in education and about the effectiveness of USMES. What is the evidence for any of this? First, what about the overall assumption that experience is the best teacher for the attainment of proficiency in the complexities of problem solving and decision making?

Fortunately in this matter we have the research and conclusions of Robert Gagné, who paradoxically is best known for his work in the behaviorist approach of teaching through a highly structured, hierarchical method. He showed that breaking down a task into its smallest components was an effective way of teaching many things, such as flying airplanes (see Gagné, 1977).

However, in the sixties he began to examine the efficacy of teaching strategies in specific domains of learning—verbal information, intellectual skills, attitudes, and cognitive strategies. The last, cognitive strategies, he defines as "the internal controls which make [the student] an efficient learner, an efficient rememberer, an ingenious problem-solver" (Gagné, 1971).

He affirms on the basis of his research his earlier proposition that "intellectual skills...the basic skills of the elementary curriculum...require prior learning of prerequisite skills" (Gagné, 1972). On the other hand, for "cognitive strategies" his research shows "such strategies are not learned...as intellectual skills seem to be...a teacher...must provide many opportunities, throughout the course of his instruction for [the student] to encounter, formulate and solve problems of many varieties" (Gagné, 1971).

Another general assumption that was made in the founding of USMES was that basic skills are learned at least as well when partly in a context of real application, as they are in the more structured learning activities. There is much evidence (see Bruner, 1970), some of it collected by Rowe (1975), to indicate that using meaningful activity for part of the school day improves learning with respect to the useful application and retention of basic skills.

A large-scale and well known field trial of an approach very close to that of real problem solving was the progressive education movement of the 1920s and 1930s. This movement featured student involvement in complex, interesting projects (although they were usually not the practical, relevant problems emphasized by USMES). Its effectiveness was attested to by the 8-year longitudinal study of its graduates (Smith & Tyler, 1942). This study showed them to be more than averagely successful in later life. The failure of the progressive movement was not in its effect on students, but in the absence of any development of dissemination techniques beyond that of setting an example.

Now it is time to turn to research specifically directed to the efficacy of the USMES curriculum itself. The USMES approach is specialized, and its materials and training methods are specific. While real problem solving may be a good thing, is USMES an appropriate manifestation of it?

In spite of all the USMES implementation there has been to examine, it has not been easy to get definitive, objective evidence. There are few instruments in the literature that test real-problem-solving efficacy and none that probe the interdependence of the cognitive strategies or the more complex achievements of problem solvers.

Evaluative research on the real-problem-solving process in USMES was done by Bernard Shapiro

(Notes 1, 2) at Boston University; on real problem solving, basic skills, and attitudes, by a group under the leadership of Mary Shann at Boston University (Shann, Note 3; Shann, Reali, Bender, Aiello, & Hench, Note 4); on math skills learning, by S. Krairojananan (Note 5); and on real problem solving and basic economic skills, by A. K. Ellis and A. D. Glenn (Note 6). In addition, USMES has conducted research on all aspects of the program, the results now being published in three studies, one on student outcomes, one of the effectiveness of USMES programs in the school, and one on the dissemination teams (all available from USMES, Education Development Center, 55 Chapel St., Newton, Mass. 02160). I can only summarize the results here of six voluminous and three short reports.

Problem-solving process results. A unique approach to examining problem-solving process ability, that of the situational test, was developed by Shapiro (Notes 1, 2,) in collaboration with USMES. A small, but real, problem involving choice of variables, observation, and decision making is given to one or more subjects at a time. The subjects are given some time to deal with the problem in an open way while being observed. Then they are asked some structured questions. As a practical test, each administration can take no more than about a half hour; thus many aspects of problem solving, such as persistence and the refinement of procedures, are not examined. In the first situational test, the student was asked to recommend which of three differing notebooks was best for purchase in quantity by the school.

Shapiro administered this test in 1971–1972 to about 250 students in 53 USMES and non-USMES classes in a variety of grade levels and communities. His report concluded that "it would appear that in terms of the two dependent variables studied (measurable reasons given and tests performed), the USMES experience had, irrespective of units of teachers involved, a marked and positive effect on the students' problem-solving behavior" (Shapiro, Note 1).

The study by Ellis and Glenn (Note 6) of 78 fifth- and sixth-grade students compared USMES students with students who studied economics from a commercial economics workbook and a control group studying geography. They were tested on their progress in real-problem-solving ability. With respect to the latter: "The direction from low number of solutions to high number of solutions moved from control group, discussion workbook, contrived problem solving to real problem solving....A similar directional trend occurs when analyzing the difference across groups related to the specific number of quantifiable solutions suggested."

The USMES Student Study of 1976–1977 (Arbetter, Cooper, and Stalker, Note 7) developed a variant of the Notebook Test called the Pencil Problem, administered to several students at a time. On all three outcome variables ([1] total number of factors considered; [2] number of investigations carried out; [3] responses to "How would you convince the students that the pencil you chose was the best one?") students with substantial USMES had higher mean scores than students with no USMES. A regression analysis of all the data also indicated positive results for outcome variables 1 and 3, but a negative result for variable 2.

Two other other types of evidence bear on real-problem-solving process attainment. Classroom interaction scales were administered both in 1972–1973 (Shapiro, Note 2) and in 1973–1974 (Shann, Note 3) to large numbers of classes. These showed that, during USMES sessions, classroom organization and interactions were radically altered. There was much more small-group work, and groupings changed more often. There was much more cooperative interaction between students, and students suggested many more ideas and made many fewer change-of-subject or random comments.

An analysis of classroom activities according to specific problem-solving processes was made from 1,043 class session reports in the USMES School Study of 1976–1977 (Stalker, Note 8). In these reports each process occurs in 20%–43% of the sessions. Furthermore, at least one process occurs in 96.7% of the sessions.

Less objective than the situational tests, but perhaps better informed, were the teachers' views obtained from structured interviews (Shann, Note 3). The report states: "almost without exception teachers using the program felt that the program taught problem-solving skills and that children's behavior had been changed in that area,...the very favorable teacher responses were consistent across interviewers, across geographical areas, across grade levels, across units, across school community socio-economic levels."

Basic skills results. The difficulty in measuring these effects may be ascribed to the many non-USMES influences on the basic skills, whose pursuit takes up at least half the time of the elementary school program. Only a small fraction of the subjects spent as much as 20% of their time on USMES and most spent only about 10% of their time on it.

Boston University studies of basic skills improvement (Shann, Note 3; Shann et al., Note 4; Shapiro & Aiello, Note 9) were based on standardized tests. Reading comprehension, mathematics computation, science, social studies, and mathematics applications subtests were exam-

Table 2: Students' Responses to Questions about Attitudes toward USMES

Question	% of Students Responding "Agree a Lot" or "Agree a Little"
21: "I think USMES work is fun."	92.3
22: "I thing USMES work is boring."	12.5
23: "Doing USMES is hard work."	51.6
24: "I don't know why we do some things in USMES."	44.4
25: "Doing USMES makes me think."	89.5
26: "I think USMES work is confusing."	29.0
27: "I think USMES work is important."	89.3
28: "In USMES it's hard to decide what to do next."	58.5
29: "I would like to do more USMES."	86.9

SOURCE: USMES Student Study (Arbetter, Cooper, & Stalker, Note 7).

ined. In virtually every study where differences appeared between USMES and comparison groups, the trends favored the USMES group. Most of these differences were small, but they are encouraging and indicate the need for further investigation.

Krairojananan (Note 5) did a 9-week in-depth study of every mathematical topic arising in four classes doing four different USMES challenges. He found that almost every math skill that could be associated with elementary school came up in the real-problem-solving context and that many came up very frequently.

The investigation by Ellis and Glenn (Note 6) compared students' knowledge of basic economics according to the four treatment groups described above. A Test of Elementary Economics was given to all the students at the conclusion of the 4-week unit. The results were definitive: "Students in the real problem solving and contrived problem solving group had significantly (beyond .05 level) higher scores than the students in the discussion-workbook and control group. The largest difference occurred between the real problem solving group mean, 15.15, and the discussion-workbook mean, 12.10. The contrived problem solving group mean [was] 14.47."

The structured teacher interviews (Shann, Note 3; Shann et al., Note 4) also bear on the question of skills attainment: "teachers also cited student growth in data collection abilities, graphing, hypothesis testing, decision making and verbal communication amongst peers as decided strengths of the program."

The USMES School Study of 1976–1977 (Stalker, Note 8) sharpens up the information on the use of USMES in the basic skills. Basic mathematics, language arts, science, and social science skills were employed in, respectively, 67.1%, 65.9%, 48.0%, and 62.3% of the USMES sessions.

Student attitude results. It is important to know how students react to participating in USMES classes. Without students' interest and involvement, the philosophy of USMES is sure to fail. This was investigated three times. The results of the USMES Student Study shown in Table 2 were nearly identical with the results of a survey of 85 Edina, Minnesota, students in 1975 and of 900 Lansing, Michigan, students in 1973. The results are remarkable not only for the strong student enthusiasm for USMES, but also for the consistency among the three surveys, taken in six communities over 5 years. I always like to note that children enjoy USMES and desire to do more even though about half of them think "doing USMES is hard work." Are we really reversing the tendency to look for the easy way out?

The 1973–1974 and 1974–1975 Boston University studies (Shann, Note 3; Shann, et al. Note 4) compared the attitudes of USMES and non-USMES students toward such things as science and mathematics. It was found that the program may have significant positive effects on appreciation of science.

The 1976–1977 USMES School Study posed 20 questions to both USMES and non-USMES students. Eight of these questions were focused on attitudes toward working on real problems and producing effective solutions, seven on attitudes toward group interaction, and five on attitudes toward specific problem-solving activities. In all three categories students with over 20 hours of USMES (approximately 600) were substantially more positive in their attitudes than students with no USMES (approximately 400).

In many ways the effect on students' attitudes seems to be greater than we have been able to quantify. Their enthusiasm keeps them working after hours. At the end of a school year a class asked its teacher if they could meet with her at lunch time the next year to continue their work on improving the school cafeteria. The attendance of children who are often absent increases. Parents get involved in many schools. In one school all the children are involved in USMES challenges to improve attendance (there are many migrant children in this school), to clean and beautify the school, and to make sure that fire drills are effective. One student who was jailed for car theft returned to the school on all his furloughs to help with these challenges.

I cannot prove it now, but I believe that this type of education may be as effective as family or peers can be in modifying youngsters' behavior for the better. A single well done USMES unit should entail more than 20 hours of work, and one would like to see one or more units done each year from grade K through 6. The hypothesized power of USMES was based on about five times the exposure obtained by the average student in the evaluated "substantial USMES" group. In spite of this, the positive effect of USMES is quite evident.

The utilization of USMES. In this last section I address the ways in which USMES is best utilized and how successful the utilization strategies are. The evidence comes from an early study by Welch and Ward (Note 10) and the recent USMES Team Study (Arbetter, Cooper, & Stalker, Note 11) and USMES School Study (Stalker, Note 8). There are, in addition, some confirmatory data from a recent survey of USMES teachers and random non-USMES teachers on the nature of their classroom and on their response to various elements of curricula and classroom strategies.

The study by Welch was of USMES's first two attempts at implementation at a district level—one in Lansing, Michigan, in 1972–1973 and the other in Area A of Chicago (South Shore) in 1973–1974. Results were mixed. In Lansing the resulting implementation in the initial year was very high, 42 of the 50 teachers involved. However, only 16 teachers used USMES in the second year, perhaps because, with a major share of responsibility being taken by USMES and Michigan State University, the school district was not adequately responsible at an early stage. In Chicago the initial implementation rate was much lower, about 35 of 100 teachers. However, attrition of those who started USMES was proportionately much less than in Lansing. In the second year 64% of the original teachers taught USMES again. USMES is probably being used now by 50–100 teachers in Chicago. Strong support by the Chicago Board of Education and weaker support at the district and principal levels seem to be the cause of this mixed pattern.

USMES learned much from the successes and failures of the first two district implementation attempts. Out of this came the Resource Team program, which prepared school district and regional personnel to train teachers and support implementation in their own areas. This has the ad-

vantage both of cost effectiveness and of obtaining early district commitment and involvement. In 1976–1977 an intensive study was made of 15 teams representing various models throughout the nation (Arbetter, Cooper, & Stalker, Note 11). The results were gratifying:

> In general, the quality of workshop training afforded to participants by the 15 teams was good. Among teachers trained by the resource teams, 62.5 percent tried USMES with their classes. Of this group, the mean number of challenges conducted by 1 January 1977 was 3.6.... It was found that team-trained teachers were following the recommendations of developers on number-of-students involved, use of discussions, session length, and number of sessions per week.... A positive correlation was found to exist between the values selected by team-trained teachers and those selected by central staff members.

The USMES School Study (Stalker, Note 8) addresses itself to the school strategies and supports that best promote successful USMES. Five schools were studied in depth, while many others contributed information through the class session reports and a survey. The in-depth examination revealed sharply what was already suspected from the many school implementations—the intelligent and enthusiastic support of the principal is the chief single requirement for quality implementation by many teachers in a school. Another finding was that challenges of 16 or more sessions long were more successful that shorter series.

A recent survey of USMES (Note 12) and a randomly selected set of non-USMES teachers confirms the above findings as well as many of those relating to the teaching of skills through USMES. In addition, it affirms that USMES users find the needed preparation, the USMES materials, and the classroom strategies agreeable and acceptable.

The response of the non-USMES teachers tells us something else—that a program like USMES has the potential of very widespread acceptance in the schools. Over 90% of the respondents indicated their willingness to consider a curriculum that included interdisciplinary studies, teaching skills through (nontextbook) problem solving, class brainstorming sessions, small groups of students working on different aspects of a task, the teacher using open-ended questions to stimulate discussion, or hands-on activities. In other words, the majority of teachers would be willing to use a real-problem-solving curriculum if its quality were good enough. Could we conclude from that and the previous information that putting law-related education in the context of real problem solving would be an efficacious way of introducing large numbers of elementary school students to the essentials of law and government?

REFERENCES

Bruner, J. The skill of relevance or the relevance of skill. *Saturday Review*, April 18, 1970, pp. 66–68, 78–79.

Cambridge Conference on the Correlation of Science and Mathematics in the Schools. *Goals for the correlation of elementary science and mathematics.* Boston: Houghton Mifflin, 1969.

Gagné, R. M. Instruction based on research in learning *Engineering Education,* 1971, *61,* 519–523.

Gagné, R. M. Domains of learning. *Interchange,* 1972, *3*(1), 1–8.

Gagné, R. M. *The conditions of learning* (3rd ed.). New York: Holt, Rinehart & Winston, 1977.

Morris, E. F. Developing law-related studies: The roles of educators and lawyers. In S. E. Davison (Ed.), *Reflections on law-related education.* Chicago: American Bar Association, Special Committee on Youth Education for Citizenship, 1973.

Rowe, M. B. Help is denied to those in need. *Science and Children,* 1975, *12*(6), 23–25.

Smith, E. R., & Tyler, R. *Appraising and recording student progress.* New York: Harper, 1942.

Starr, I. Reflections on law studies in the schools today. In S. E. Davison (Ed.), *Reflections on law-related education.* Chicago: American Bar Association, Special Committee on Youth Education for Citizenship, 1973.

REFERENCE NOTES

1. Shapiro, B. J. The Notebook Problem: Report on observation of problem-solving activity in USMES and control classrooms. Boston University, May 1973. Available from Unified Sciences and Mathematics for Elementary Schools, Education Development Center, 55 Chapel St., Newton, Mass. 02160.

2. Shapiro, B. J. USMES evaluation report on classroom structure and interaction patterns. Boston University, June 1974.

3. Shann, M. H. An evaluation of USMES: Its effects on student performances in problem solving and basic skills. Boston University, School of Education, September 1974.

4. Shann, M. H.; Reali, N. C.; Bender, H.; Aiello, T.; & Hench, L. Student effects of an interdisciplinary curriculum for real problem solving: The 1974–75 USMES evaulation. Boston University, 1975.

5. Krairojananan, S. The mathematical behaviors derivable from the program of USMES. Unpublished doctoral dissertation, Michigan State University, 1973.

6. Ellis, A. K., & Glenn, A. D. Effects of real and contrived problem solving on economic learning. University of Minnesota, 1977.

7. Arbetter, C.; Cooper, D.; & Stalker, G. USMES Student Study. 1976–1977. Available from USMES (see Note 1 above).

8. Stalker, G. USMES School Study. 1976–1977. Available from USMES (see Note 1 above).

9. Shapiro, B., & Aiello, T. USMES report on basic skill development. 1974 (preliminary draft). Available from USMES (see Note 1 above).

10. Welch, W., & Ward, W., Jr. Evaluation of USMES implementation project. Minnesota Research and Evaluation Center, University of Minnesota, 1975.

11. Arbetter, C.; Cooper, D.; & Stalker, G. USMES Team Study. 1977. Available from USMES (see Note 1 above).

12. Report of USMES survey of teachers. 1977 (summary). Available from USMES (see Note 1 above).

Another view . . .

Real Problem Solving through Law and Humanities Education

Valerie Hess

In this paper Valerie Hess identifies several critical aspects of a curriculum for real problem solving that were not explicitly addressed in the previous paper, although actual application of the USMES model may accommodate some of her points. Anyone attempting to apply the curricular techniques advocated in the preceding paper would do well to consider the issues raised here. For example, the author points out that group problem solving does not always occur through consensus as the former paper suggests. She suggests that the strategies described could well be applied to relevant local controversies. She also cautions teachers not to turn problem solving into trial-and-error learning—teachers need to define their goals and procedures clearly *before* involving the children. The paper closes with an extended discussion of the politics of curricular change or intervention that would apply to the type of experience-based learning described here.

How can we apply what we know about children's learning to a law-related elementary curriculum? That the question is even asked indicates a change from the attitude which prevailed in 1972 when an influential book called *Children's Learning* made no mention of education because, the author noted, the two areas traditionally have been separate (Stevenson, 1972).

Earle Lomon has written a paper which addresses issues in both learning and education. One hopes the two are not separate in fact, no matter what their relationship in academia. Even the title of Lomon's paper, "Real Problem Solving and Law-related Education," is interesting. Does "real" refer to the kinds of problems being solved, to the solutions, or to the solving of problems, whatever they are? In any case, further questions immediately come to mind. What are real problems? What constitutes a real solution? What evidence do we have to indicate we are witnessing the real solving of problems?

In terms of the curriculum program which Lomon outlines, "real" can refer to all three cases: real problems, real solutions, and real strategies for solving problems.

Model

The USMES program follows a learning-by-doing model. Using the inductive method he recommends, Lomon supplies us with a marvelous example of a USMES "challenge" (problem) called Pedestrian Crossings. The real problem involved is how to make pedestrian crossings safer. As Lomon points out, the immediate relevance of this kind of problem to the students' lives eliminates the need for the teacher to construct an external motive for student involvement.

A real solution to this, and the other challenges in the USMES program, appears to consist of observable changes in conditions in the direction agreed upon by the students. The makers of USMES believe students not only learn cognitive strategies necessary to solve problems by working on these kinds of practical issues but also improve their basic academic skills, which are called upon in finding solutions. Finally, by developing workable solutions to actual everyday problems, the students are said to develop a belief in their ability to be useful members of a participatory democracy.

There can be no doubt that the discovery method proposed by USMES is workable. It certainly does overcome motivational barriers. Although Lomon does not specify grade levels of recipients, learning by doing is also in keeping with what we know about the cognitive level of elementary children. The Piagetian term for their level of functioning is concrete operational. At this level concrete problems and concrete solu-

Valerie Hess is a specialist in early childhood socialization. She has been especially concerned with the sex differences in socialization.

tions are most readily understood. The cognitive developmental approach has a parallel in Kohlberg's work on moral development and Tapp's explorations of children's understanding of the law. Incidentally, these two researchers have developed a theory of legal development based on their individual research (Tapp & Kohlberg, 1977).

As presented, the USMES model is a consensus model. Group decision making is emphasized. Social interaction is indeed an important learning situation. In regard to the kind of group decision making used in USMES, many specific management techniques have been developed to facilitate the process, for example, force field analysis, management by objective, etc. Teachers who use USMES-style programs to teach law-related curricula may benefit from learning about these techniques and then helping students try them. Learning by doing should not be a fancy way of saying trial and error. Even with a discovery method of learning, guidelines and methods for structuring group interactions can improve efficiency without sacrificing flexibility and spontaneity or creativity.

While our society does try to operate according to the sort of consensus notion intrinsic in USMES, this is not always easy. It seems to me that in a law-related curriculum an important lesson for students to learn is that it is often not possible to get consensus in terms of either statement of problems or methods of solution. Conflict is inevitable in any social organization. It has also been posited that conflict is a necessary part of cognitive growth.

Perhaps the USMES technique could be extended to include exploration of local, and therefore, relevant, controversies. For example, in Minnesota three such controversies that come quickly to mind are pollution control for large industries, permission for the building of high-power electrical lines, and regulation of utilization of the Boundary Waters Canoe Area. Alas, there are many others. None of these issues is easily resolved; yet some legal resolutions will ultimately be made. Students studying such cases and trying to come up with their own solutions will learn something of the power and limits of power the individual holds in our legal system.

Let me give one example to illustrate what can happen when students are confronted with such lessons. The Women's Studies Program of the Minneapolis Public School System has developed a unit on media which includes a project for which students monitor the sports page of the local newspaper. The children are often appalled by the sex bias in sports coverage. Classes often write to the newspaper to protest sexist practices. One fourth-grade girl reportedly wrote: "I think there should be more women in the sports section than there are now. We women can play sports too. I suggest you check out more women's sports and if you don't, I'm going to keep writing and complaining."

Learning

We have explored the real problems and real solutions of USMES. What can the USMES model tell us about learning? According to Lomon, in regard to the "higher-level cognitive strategies of problem solving and decision making...[n]ot only is the USMES approach directly related to such process skills, *but it may be the only successful way of acquiring them*" (italics added). This is certainly a strong claim.

Supposedly theory and practice are tied together in science. Observation leads to theory which can be empirically tested and then refined. If we have not been successful in formally teaching problem solving, this may be because our theoretical statements are incomplete. Thus in practical situations, such as those used by USMES, participants must work through the steps which are missing from our formal statements of problem-solving strategies in order to arrive at an actual solution. By analyzing what is actually done in such situations, we should be able to improve our theoretical statements. We may eventually know enough about problem solving to propose many ways to facilitate development of problem-solving abilities.

If practical experience is now the best teacher of problem-solving and decision-making skills, it may be simply because our understanding of the processes involved is now so minimal. We can, then, consider the practical approach not only as a way to learn problem-solving skills but also as a way to learn *about* problem-solving skills, and how such skills are acquired. For example, can we discover instances in which people have acquired the requisite skill but do not use it? What variables control the acquisition of skills? Which factors influence the evocation and use of these skills? Does a person monitor the application of a problem-solving skill and then use that feedback to reexamine the problem and come up with a new solution if needed? How does this happen? Are there developmental or age-related changes in the use and application of these skills? The questions go on and on.

Politics

In discussing a curriculum intervention program, I cannot resist saying something about politics. I would suggest that Lomon's comments on evaluation and utilization have to do with what I call the politics of curriculum intervention. There are at least four constituencies whose interests must be considered: teachers, students, administrators, and the community.

Teachers feel overworked. Anyone interested in selling curriculum changes had better remember the teacher's perspective. There seem to be two ways to approach curriculum change, namely, units versus revision. New units, covering content areas, concepts, activities, etc., can be developed and presented to teachers as a package for classroom use after field testing and in-service training with these materials. Often teachers resist these new units because they already feel overloaded and cannot squeeze additional curriculum items into an already tight schedule.

Another approach is to ask teachers to revise their current curriculum to cover a particular topic which previously has been omitted, slighted, or distorted. In this case project staff must work closely with teachers in clarifying just what needs to be covered and in suggesting what kinds of resources can be substituted for existing material.

With any method, evaluation of student response is critical. Lomon notes that much of learning theory and learning research supports the principles behind USMES. Clearly no curriculum is attempted without some theoretical and research backing. The proof, of course, is in the pudding. However, assessment is usually easier said than done. Thus every educational project becomes a "pilot project." Lack of appropriate measurement instruments and lack of adequate controls are but two real problems which evaluators must grapple with if not solve.

The best sorts of measures of success of an educational program would involve evidence of transfer effects. We can usually get indication of improvement in areas we specifically teach, but is there any generalization? Task-specific skills have limited utility, especially when we are interested in something as broad as principles of law and government.

Sometimes our evaluations reveal unanticipated effects of our educational program. A recent study of an antisexism educational project revealed that some children became more sexist after participating in the program because focusing on the issue only served to clarify and rigidify otherwise vague sexist beliefs.

Administrators are interested in measured effectiveness, since they decide whether or not to support implementation of a particular educational program on the basis of a cost/benefit analysis. Administrators are concerned with the issue of accountability because they must answer ultimately to community pressures.

Currently all school systems, from elementary through postsecondary, are under pressure because of declining enrollments and rising costs.

For our purposes two trends affecting education are important: interest in a "back to basics," or fundamental, education, and questions about teaching values in the classroom.

Criticism of public school education as neglecting the teaching of basic academic skills is what leads some teachers to feel hassled by requests to include new units on sexism, racism, problem solving, or law. If a program like USMES can be shown to relate directly to the learning of so-called basic skills, the concerns of many may be quieted. Revising rather than adding to a curriculum is also a way to answer such criticism. Furthermore, this technique makes the topic to be covered an integral part of the whole educational plan, rather than a "frill" which can be sacrificed to budget considerations.

The issue of teaching values is a difficult one. Educators often claim education is a means for expanding options. However everyone will not agree as to what options should be made available. If educators try to soft sell new programs with language that is vague, they risk the wrath of those who are pushing for a "back to basics" education.

Conclusion

I have tried to explore some of the implications of the curriculum model behind the USMES program Lomon presented in his paper. The model outlined, that of learning by doing, is appropriate for the cognitive level of the target population, that is, elementary school children. Focusing on concrete problem situations also provides intrinsic motivation for students to participate. The situations described in USMES involve a group problem-solving approach. The program might be refined to facilitate group decision making and expanded to explore the limits of consensus when dealing with social problems.

By teaching problem solving we can also learn about problem solving. Important developmental trends in the acquisition and performance of problem-solving strategies might be exposed and contribute to our understanding of cognitive development.

More complete theoretical statements may, in turn, improve our educational interventions in this area. While Lomon seems to feel that the practical approach is the only way to acquire problem-solving abilities initially, he does suggest that, once acquired, these processes can be improved "by explicit and formal consideration of individual problem-solving strategies." This would be an important consideration in working with people at later developmental levels.

I might add here that, although there is evidence that the USMES approach does facilitate problem solving, this does not mean it is the actual way such skills are acquired, or the only way. It may be a way to amplify, accelerate, or improve skills which children have already acquired, or are in the process of acquiring. We know, for example, that children can learn problem-solving strategies through observational learning. The question of how children learn to use observational learning as a problem strategy has been the subject of extensive and intensive research and theorizing.

Finally, I have tried to point out some political considerations in implementing curriculum intervention programs of any sort. Such considerations involve the needs of teachers, students, administrators, and community.

REFERENCES

Stevenson, H. W. *Children's learning.* New York: Appleton-Century-Crofts, 1972.

Tapp, J. L., & Kohlberg, L. Developing senses of law and legal justice. In J. L. Tapp & F. J. Levine (Eds.), *Law, justice, and the individual: Psychological and legal issues.* New York: Holt, Reinhart & Winston, for Society for the Psychological Study of Social Issues, 1977.

The Relationship of Law and Humanities Education to Values and Moral Education

Charles Lavaroni

As this author suggests, good law-related education programs are careful to demonstrate the close association between law and value issues addressing questions of morality and ethics. The explicit linkage of law and humanities makes the treatment of value and morality imperative. In this paper Charles Lavaroni gives a concise overview of two approaches in values education, values clarification and values analysis, and indicates how both approaches can be applied in law-related education. He also sketches the developmental theories of Piaget and Kohlberg, noting how these may be applied in structuring learning experiences. The paper opens with a few cogent observations on the natural affinity of law and humanities which are helpful guidelines for educators and developers.

For the past decade or more, teachers, administrators, curriculum developers, and educational theorists have been paying a great deal of attention to the whole nation of values education and/or moral education. Their efforts have produced many models, programs, and classroom strategies. Some of these have been in conflict with each other, some have been mutually supportive. Many have been biased upon some clearly defined philosophy or theory, while others seem merely to reflect the "gut-level feelings" of their proponents. Throughout the profession arguments and debates have focused on definitions, process, and the appropriateness of specific activities, as well as on the purpose and effectiveness of these programs.

Almost simultaneously, the law-related education movement has developed. Again, similar arguments have ensued. While there appears to be general agreement that a comprehensive law-related or citizenship education program must be concerned with inherent value/moral issues, as laws are society's institutionalized values, there has not been evidence of agreement as to how that concern might be met. At one extreme of that argument we have people who suggest that personal values are a direct result of knowledge, and that knowledge alone will ensure the establishment of appropriate values. These people would

use law-related citizenship education programs to "teach what is right and wrong." Others agree with the importance of values/moral education as part of a total program but seem to limit their pedagogical techniques to an affective exploration of how students "feel" about particular situations, issues, and ideas. These people would argue that values/morals cannot be taught, only experienced. They would say that there are not clear definitions of "right and wrong" but merely degrees of appropriateness.

Without stretching the imagination too far, one, until recently, might describe many values education programs as "process in search of content." Conversely, some law-related programs could be described as "content in search of a process."

Overriding these two issues, a third and directly related issue has more recently emerged: the role of the humanities in law-related education. That role can be simply—I hope not simplistically—stated as the recognition that traditionally the overall function of the humanities is to study, interpret, and improve upon the human condition. This same function has often been cited as the function of law-related education.

To be human is to be able to reason and to feel. The humanist recognizes the processing of law-related concepts and values as a human endeavor. The humanist also recognizes that experience, feelings, beliefs, and attitudes are appropriate data which children use to help them study, interpret, and improve their world. The humanities, in the formal academic definition, give us a wealth of

Charles Lavaroni is presently Dean of Admissions at Dominican College of San Rafael. For the past several years he has served as a consultant to several law-related projects throughout the West.

data and theories from others who have studied and interpreted their world. These can in turn be used by students to help then in that same process. The art, literature, music, and philosophies of the present and the past give many examples which can help students explore the concepts inherent in law-related education. What is the role of freedom in the dance? Does it change in different cultures? In different dance forms? What about responsibility as manifested in literature? How are diversity and privacy interpreted in drama? When students are exploring what is just or unjust, right or wrong, are they not engaging in philosophy?

One last point needs to be made about the humanities as integral to law-related education. The humanities constantly remind us that personal learning is not, I repeat *not*, a cognitive experience, an affective experience, or a psychomotor experience but instead the result of experiences which utilize the mind, the body, and the spirit. Thus the activities of a law-related education program can and must be structured so that children use their minds, bodies, and spirits not only to take in information but also to express their ideas: ideas about justice and the various political and legal systems which surround them.

It is the intent of this article to explore some concrete ways to bring a more definitive structure to a law-focused values/moral education program for elementary-age students and thereby attempt to make a reasonable connection between the content of law-related education and the processes of values/moral education. It also intends to do that with the attitudes of the humanities serving as its foundation. Much of what follows is not new, but instead a synthesis of theories and strategies which I have found helpful in making personal sense out of some of the arguments surrounding the close relationships among four programs: law-related, values, moral, and humanistic education.

Therefore, while this paper speaks to the ideas in its title, it is really a very personal history of one educator's move from an undergraduate music major to elementary classroom teaching, to an interest in inquiry, values clarification, and values analysis, to application of these processes in global education and law-related education, and finally through the notion of moral reasoning to a perception of law-related education as a values/moral education program grounded in the humanities.

Definitions

While there are many available definitions of law-focused education, this article will use the one developed by the Tri-County Law-related Education Project of Portland, Oregon, as a frame of reference: "Law-Focused Education is a kind of citizenship-education emphasizing the concepts, processes, skills and values of the American legal system. Essential to this approach are the thorough exploration, understanding and application of societal and personal values in relation to that system. Development of moral and ethical frames of reference appropriate for citizenship in a democratic society are prime goals of Law-Related Education."

This definition clearly includes the development of values as an integral ingredient of a law-focused program. However, to get any kind of consistent communication and meaning from this statement in relation to the topic of this paper, we need to define some of the concepts used or implied within it.

■ *Values* are the ideas of worth and importance people hold; they are the concepts upon which choices and judgments are made, upon which dreams are built.

■ *Societal values* are the ideas of worth as exemplified by the mores, processes, and accepted rules of the society. As mentioned earlier, laws are the formalization of society's values at any given time in history.

■ *Personal values* are the conscious and sometimes unconscious standards which influence an individual's behavior.

■ *Values education* is a program which focuses on helping students see their choices more clearly and make more consistent and rational connections between their dreams and their behaviors. The emphasis in values education is on what is "good and/or bad." It deals with the individual's experiences and concepts in relation to the society in which he finds himself and, in turn, the interpretation of what those values appear to be collectively in that society.

■ *Moral education* is closely related in that it too focuses on values, but it extends the notion of "good and/or bad" to include the discussion of "right and wrong." While building on the individual's own experiences, it further extends thinking to include society's experiences, expectations, and application of those values to its variety of social, political, and legal systems.

■ *Values/moral education* programs emphasize thinking as well as feeling and behaving. They recognize that feelings and thoughts are closely related. They recognize the obvious fact that the "affective and cognitive domains" exist in one human being, and for feelings to have meaning or for meaning to be personal, learning experiences must deal simultaneously with thinking and feeling. Values/moral education deals with both "good and bad" and "right and wrong."

It is important for me to distinguish between values education and moral education as they seem to be popularly viewed, not merely to be semantically precise but to bring some clarity to this discussion. An example from a dialogue with Calvin Miller of Virginia State College should be helpful. Cal tells of an innocent young black man who pleaded guilty to a charge of burglary in exchange for his immediate release. This man *valued* his freedom and made a decision. While that decision may have been "good" for him, it certainly points out the *immorality* of the system which spawned it—a system which seems to have lost concern for the *human condition*. A values/moral program would reflect all three of these concerns while constantly looking at the sociological, historical, and legal ideas which help define and explain such a situation. A program rooted in the humanities would also use such a dilemma to explore and illuminate such concepts as truth, love, and faith.

Rationale—Law-related Education

While there are many law-focused program projects and curricula, there seems to be more agreement than disagreement on their "content." Practically all programs emphasize the many concepts considered fundamental to our free society. Concepts such as justice, freedom, authority, diversity, property rights, and responsibility serve as the central themes for study. The programs all use data as well as human resources from the various institutions which influence and determine our political, legal, and enforcement systems. They emphasize the need for active student involvement, real understanding, and personal meaning.

There are two theoretical ideas which I find particularly useful when thinking about, making decisions about, or describing how to organize the concepts and resources of law-focused education to ensure that necessary involvement and meaning.

The first is a theoretical model which originally came out of some curriculum development work in the 1960s (Costa, Lavaroni, & Newton, 1967). This model, the Data/Theory Cycle, was developed to help describe what goes on when a human being inquires and brings his own knowledge and experiences to a problem and, in solving that problem, develops personal meaning for the concepts inherent in that problem. It is introduced here (see Fig. 1) as a means to remind developers and teachers what kinds of cognitive behaviors are involved in that process and how those behaviors are interrelated.

In this model *data* are considered the "stuff" of the world. External law-related data would include, among other things, rules, laws, pro-

cedure, codes, decisions, regulations, and, possibly most important, the Constitution. Personal data include the experiences, feelings, attitudes, and beliefs that students have as a result of their direct contact with the rules, laws, and people that make up the formal and informal "systems" in which they live. These systems include homes, schools, classrooms, playgrounds, and community organizations, as well as the courts, legislative bodies, boards, and police departments.

Theories are the "ideas" of the world. Law-focused theories include the assumptions, generalizations, relationships, explanations, and values which underlie our justice system.

The many learning behaviors which we, as human beings, use to bring meaning to a particular situation, issue, event, or decision, can be classified according to the four categories of the Data/Theory Cycle. *Data collecting* includes: remembering, observing, interviewing, polling, interrogating, measuring, reading, counting, recalling, etc. *Data organizing* includes: contrasting, graphing, classifying, categorizing, comparing, ordering, labeling, etc. *Theory building* comprises: explaining, synthesizing, generalizing, inferring, concluding, abstracting, theorizing, etc. Under *theory using* can be classified: predicting, hypothesizing, testing, controlling, voting, evaluating, modeling, etc.

In developing law-related curricula, the Data/Theory Cycle can be used to help determine: the law-related data and resources which must be made available to students and the means by which they can get it (data collecting); the kinds of learning experiences which must be structured to help students use those data to develop and refine their law-related concepts (data organizing); the various law-focused activities which need to be planned to ensure students' use of those concepts to explain, generalize, or create new ideas and values (theory building); and the situations to be set up or questions to be asked which give students the opportunity to test and evaluate their law-related ideas and values (theory using).

The second theory which has been important to me in my quest to understand and prescribe appropriate educational elements in law-related education is the cognitive developmental theory of Jean Piaget (see Inhelder & Piaget, 1958).

Piaget believes that thinking is the result of a developmental process. From the time of birth to age 2 (the sensory motor period), the child's range of cognitive operations develops from mere reflex actions to a more differentiated view of self and the environment. Cause-and-effect relationships are beginning to be formed, but they are limited to direct physical phenomena and the recognition of

Figure 1: The Data/Theory Cycle.

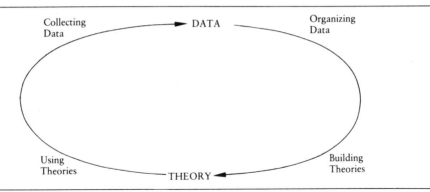

parental limits and controls. The ability to think out different "means" to achieve particular needs begins.

Between the ages of 2 and 7 (the preoperational period), the child approaches the ability to function symbolically. This is a period of rapid language and concept development. However, the language and concepts are egocentric, limited to the child's point of view. Conceptualizations are formed from single features of an object or event. While children at this stage can recognize oranges and bananas as food, they cannot successfully deal with multiple attributes, such as large, yellow, smooth-skinned bananas and small, green, rough-skinned bananas. And, as nursery school teachers know, children early in this period have difficulty dealing with teachers as shoppers or family friends. They also have difficulty thinking of police officers as men or women but view them as policemen regardless of sex. During this period, reality and fantasy frequently become confused. Thinking, during the preoperational period, becomes more internalized and increasingly less exclusively tied to specific actions.

Between ages 7 and 11 (the concrete operational period), children learn how to return to the original point in thought (reversibility), to organize objects and events into categories (classification), and to arrange items along a continuum of values (seriation). In other words, they become more efficient in organizing data (conceptualizing). During the concrete operational period, they acquire the ability to discriminate the relative variable. For example, in the problem, "The lawyer is older than the defendant and the defendant is older than the judge; who is the oldest?" Children can recognize that age is the important variable, not position or social status. It is during this period that problems are solved mentally and logical thought operations develop, but the child is still limited to the observable. Children at this general stage of development need the con-

crete (object/events) or representations (pictures, films, models) as props in their problem solving. Complex verbal problems cannot yet be solved.

According to Piaget, youths between the ages of 11 and 15 (formal operations period) take the final steps toward abstract thinking and conceptualization. Preadolescents and adolescents are able to develop and test hypotheses, to evaluate, and to reason. All types of complex verbal problems can be solved. Young people at this stage develop the abilities to use and link together all of the cognitive behaviors which make up the Data/Theory Cycle.

While this very condensed version of Piaget's theory appears to set specific ages for the various periods, they are not rigid. Children do not all move through the periods at exactly the ages listed. Furthermore, any individual child may function at more than one stage, depending upon the activity, past experience, and/or motivation. It should also be noted that, while the periods may not be universally experienced at exactly the same ages, no period can be "skipped." Each serves as the foundation for the next. Using language, talking about experiences, is important in moving from stage to stage. At least one other consideration must be pointed out when thinking about Piaget's theory, namely, that there seems to be evidence that not all adolescents or adults attain the formal operations level of reasoning.

Nine important considerations for an elementary law-focused education program can be synthesized from these two theories, the Data/Theory Cycle and Piaget's developmental theory. They are:

■ Learning activities should reflect changes in students' thinking abilities as well as changes in their knowledge base.

■ Learning activities should reflect movement from the concrete to the representational and finally to the abstract.

■ Learning activities in the primary grades should emphasize the collection and organization of data into concepts.

■ Learning activities which require more complex operations, such as generalizing and synthesizing several concepts, should be held off until the upper elementary grades.

■ Learning activities which encourage discussion, dialogue, and communication should be encouraged.

■ Learning activities in the primary grades should utilize and emphasize data from the students' real world.

■ Learning activities should be designed to help students legitimately recognize and use the personal data they bring to the classroom.

■ Learning activities should help students see the difference between data and theory and become increasingly competent in their world.

■ Learning activities at all grades should always have data readily available as the students need them to conceptualize and theorize.

Values Education Rationale

As in law-focused education, there are many theories, programs, and projects available for use in identifying a rationale for a values education program. However, there appear to be more confusion, controversy, and alternatives to review in establishing such a rationale.

I will limit my discussion primarily to the input from two existing values education models. Although I may seem to ignore the important contributions of people such as James Shaver (Shaver & Strong, 1976), Jack Fraenkel (1973), and Howard Kirschenbaum (Kirschenbaum, Harris, Howe, & Simon, 1977), I will, at least indirectly, employ these people's contributions, as it is my intent to affirm their apparent philosophy. They believe, as I do, that values, while individually processed, are learned; that they are learned through thinking; that specific skills are necessary for that thinking; and that thinking in general and the development of those specific thinking skills can be dramatically influenced by teachers and their programs.

Values Clarification

In *Values and Teaching* Raths, Harmin, and Simon (1966), describe a values processing model which has seven requirements. The authors offer this model as a means to help students clarify what is good or bad, important or unimportant, or of value to them in their lives.

According to this model, values are more than beliefs, attitudes, feelings, and/or interests. These are not values but value indicators. Frequently these indicators are in conflict with each other, causing confusion and a lack of direction. The authors present their model as a means to help clarify these indicators to a point where a clear, comprehensive, and consistent "value," which includes many of them, becomes operable. In fact, the authors say that unless these indicators are processed they will remain indicators and never provide the clarity, direction, and power of a value. They outline the valuing process as follows: (1) choosing freely, without coercion; (2) choosing from among alternatives; (3) choosing after thoughtful consideration of the consequences of each alternative; (4) prizing and cherishing; (5) affirming, making public those choices; (6) acting upon those choices; (7) repeating in some pattern. The three major valuing behaviors then are: choosing, prizing, and acting.

The proponents of this values clarification process recommend that teachers create situations where students have an opportunity to use their experiences along with their value indicators as data for clarifying their emerging values. They suggest a variety of strategies to do this, including rank ordering, voting, public interviewing, role playing, and using the values continuum. In each of these strategies the student is asked to take some kind of value position. The teacher then uses "clarifying responses"—in reality, questions—to help the student see if that position is chosen, prized, and/or acted upon. And, as this process is repeated, the underlying values become clearer and clearer to the student.

Teachers can use this model to plan questions which help students identify their value indicators in relation to such law-related concepts as justice, authority, and property.

Values Analysis

The 1971 National Council for the Social Studies Yearbook (Metcalf, 1971) provides a significantly different model for values education. While "values clarification" tends to limit the data students use to process their value indicators to their own experiences, "values analysis" emphasizes data collected from many other sources external to the student. Values analysis emphasizes the teaching and learning of specific thinking skills, while values clarification focuses on the questioning processes involved in determining choice, prizing, and action. Possibly even more significantly, the clarification model concentrates on what is "good or bad," while the values analysis model extends questioning to include the notion of "right or wrong," and therefore deals with morality as well as valuing.

Coombs and Meux (1071) identify six tasks

which they feel are critical to a values analysis, a values decision-making process. They are:

1. Identifying and clarifying the value question;
2. Assembling a wide range of purported facts;
3. Assessing the truth of purported facts;
4. Clarifying the relevance of facts;
5. Arriving at a tentative value decision;
6. Testing the value principle implied in the decision.

The first task centers around the need to ensure students' clarity about what is at issue. In the value question, "Is it bad to take drugs?" Students must first clarify what is meant by the value term "bad." Does it mean bad for health, morally bad, too expensive, or psychologically bad? Also, they must look at what is meant by the value object, "drugs." Are all drugs considered in the discussion, including heroin, coffee, beer, aspirin, cocaine, and tea? The purpose of this task is to help students learn how to move from the ambiguous to the clear, from the vague to the precise.

The second task, assembling facts, has several components. As part of this task, students first learn to distinguish between value claims and factual claims. They can recognize that statements such as, "Laws should be obeyed," "All guns should be prohibited," "The ERA is a good amendment," and "Welfare is bad," are value assertions (claims), not factual assertions (claims).

A second major component in this task is the collection of a wide range of facts. To help with this part of the task, the teacher asks the students to consider a variety of concerns or interests such as economic welfare, freedom, health, aesthetic enjoyment, recreation, or justice as they collect and organize their facts. They also learn to seek out information from a wide range of people who represent diverse backgrounds and points of view.

The students learn several specific skills to help them deal with the complexity inherent in collecting and organizing a multitude of facts. Some important ones are:

a. Identifying the concern or concerns each fact represents;
b. Rating those facts as supporting a positive or negative position;
c. Subsuming specific facts under more generalized facts;
d. Ranking facts in terms of their importance;
e. Recording the collected facts on a Fact Assembly Chart which provides space to include the results of analysis indicated in a., b., c., and d. above.

As part of the third task, assessing factual claims, students learn how to evaluate the three types of facts: particular facts, general facts, and conditional or "if-then" facts. Students learn that particular factual claims are verified by observing specific events, that general factual claims are verified by finding a series of specific facts which support them, and that conditional claims are verified by seeing whether there have been in the past similar relationships between the "ifs" and the "thens" to those now being proposed.

The student also learns that, in most cases, the verification process must rely on input from second-hand sources. Therefore, students learn how to assess the source of any claim as well as the claim itself.

The fourth major task, according to Coombs and Meux, is *clarifying the relevance of facts*. Simply stated, this is learning how to analyze the facts to see which ones reflect a particular personal conviction. To do this, students must first identify the value criterion a fact represents. They then must determine whether they believe that criterion and finally whether they have reasons for believing it. Coombs and Meux believe that unless the facts the student uses are relevant, there is little chance for the ensuing value decision to be rational.

Arriving at a tentative value decision is the fifth task recommended by the Coombs and Meux model. This is not a distinct task. It is instead the synthesis derived from the processing of the previous four tasks. If the student has worked through the other tasks, then making a tentative value decision is the next logical step.

The sixth task is *principle-acceptability testing*. The authors offer four tests which students might use in determining the acceptability of the value principles implied in their value judgments. The first step in each of these tests is identifying the value principle which underlies the value decision. Each of the four tests is briefly described:

1. New Cases Test: Can the student accept that same principle when applied to other relevant cases?
2. Subsumption Test: Can the student identify and assemble facts which indicate consistency between this specific value principle and a more general acceptable value principle?
3. Role Exchange Test: Can the student change roles with someone else affected by the principle? Imagine how that person might react to the principle and still accept it?
4. Universal Consequences Test: Can the student still accept that principle after considering the consequences which might occur if everyone faced with similar situations acted consistently with that principle?

Obviously, for the elementary teacher there is at least one other important difference between values clarification and values analysis. The difference is in the level of abstraction that each of these programs represents. No matter how the two programs are interpreted, it is evident that the tasks which make up values analysis are much more abstract than those which make up values clarification. Therefore, it seems clear, at least to me, that the kinds of experiences found in the values clarification program are most appropriate for the primary grades. As the students' thinking abilities grow, through the upper elementary grades, then the more abstract analytical skills can be introduced.

Given these two value education models and the learning models presented earlier, we can begin to see a general sequence for a values/moral education program for the elementary grades.

Kindergarten/primary—value awareness:
Identifying value indicators (feelings, beliefs, interests)
Exploring alternative indicators
Exploring possible effects of personal choices based on those indicators

Intermediate—value clarification:
Clarifying values choices
Clarifying the terms in those choices
Identifying possible consequences of those choices
Estimating probability of those consequences occurring
Determining appropriateness of various consequences

With these kinds of experiences as a background, the increasingly more abstract processes and skills can be effectively experienced and learned at the junior high and high school levels.

Junior high—values analysis:
Collecting factual claims
Assessing the validity of factual claims
Projecting consequences over a wide range of concerns
Rating consequences as desirable/undesirable
Verifying the possibility of consequences
Stating and assessing the value position inherent in the value judgment

High school—Values verifying:
Applying the Role Exchange Test
Applying the Universal Consequences Test
Applying the Subsumption Test
Applying the New Cases Test

This general values/moral education sequence can be used to help teachers determine the kinds of personal and external data as well as learning experiences necessary for programs which help students identify, develop, and internalize values inherent in the concepts which make up law-related education.

A primary-grade learning experience reflecting the above sequence might well be:

After a discussion of people who help other people make and carry out rules, students cut pictures of those who are in positions of authority from a variety of magazines and paste them on sheets of paper to form a collage. The teacher then asks questions which help identify and organize data about the various value indicators represented in the collage: "How can you tell they are in charge?" "How are some of these people the same?" "How are they different?" "Who are some of the people who make rules for you?" This activity could then be duplicated, using popular magazines from Mexico, Canada, Germany, or any other foreign country. Similar questions could then be asked to help students recognize similarities between various cultures.

An *intermediate-grade* example might be:

After reading the "John Peter Zenger Case" (Quigley, 1976), the students, through the teacher's questions, clarify the various issues involved in freedom of the press. Freedom of the press, a value object, should be clarified in terms of *truthfulness, propaganda, accuracy, slander,* and *fairness.* The case then should be used to help students think about the appropriateness of various consequences: "What if it led to revolution?" "What if Zenger gave up and was appointed to a government post?" "What if his readers didn't care one way or the other?" Some of the songs which have been used throughout history to rally people around a cause should be reviewed. Then students could form groups to write words to a well-known melody to encourage people to support Zenger or the idea of freedom of the press.

Moral Reasoning

At least one other theoretical notion must be considered for this paper. That is the work of Lawrence Kohlberg, who presents a developmental theory of moral reasoning. His theory, which incidentally reflects Piaget's theory of moral realism/moral relativism, presents a six-phase framework which indicates the kinds of criteria people consciously and unconsciously use as they make decisions about what they "should" or "should not" do. (See Doris, Note 1.)

Each stage reflects a particular mode or style or reasoning. As a whole, the stages reflect a movement from a narrow, egocentric notion of the individual and society as a whole. The first two stages are grouped and identified as the preconventional level of moral reasoning; stages 3 and 4 are called the conventional level; and stages 5 and 6, the postconventional level. Kohlberg sees

Table 1: Kohlberg's Levels and Stages of Moral Development

Level	Stage	Characteristics
I. Preconventional moral development: Moral value resides in external force, happenings, acts or needs, rather than in persons and standards.	1	Orientation toward obedience and punishment: Social order is conceived as an egocentric deference to superior power and to the avoidance of trouble or punishment.
	2	Instrumental, naively egoistic: Right action becomes that which satisfies one's own needs. Characteristic of this stage is naive egalitarianism and orientation to exchange and reciprocity, e.g., "You scratch my back and I'll scratch yours."
II. Conventional moral development: Moral value resides in performing good or right roles, the expectations of others, and maintaining the conventional order.	3	Good boy, good girl orientation: At this stage reasoning is oriented to pleasing and the approval of others. This stage is commonly called the "Charlie Brown" perspective.
	4	Respect for law and order: There is a shift toward fixed definitions of duty and responsibility. Doing one's duty, showing respect for authority, and maintaining the given social order are necessary to maintain order.
III. Postconventional moral development: Moral value resides in conformity by the self to shared or sharable standards, rights, or duties. Autonomous, principled moral judgment is the most developed form of moral reasoning.	5	Legalistic, contractual orientation: At this stage is a recognition of an arbitrary element or starting point in rules or expectations for the sake of agreement. Duty is defined in terms of social contract, majority will and welfare, and a general avoidance of violating the will or rights of others. (The United States Constitution is a stage 5 document.)
	6	Orientation to rational, universally prescriptive principles: The orientation here is not only to actually ordained social rules, but to principles of choice involving appeal to logical universality and prescriptivity, i.e., what one believes everyone else in similar circumstances ought to do and what one ought to do oneself.

SOURCE: Doris, Note 1.

the aim of moral education as that of stimulating moral reasoning from one stage of development to the next.

Characteristics of Kohlberg's levels and stages of moral development are outlined in Table 1. Several points need to be reviewed to interpret this model of developmental levels and stages according to Kohlberg:

1. Movement from stage to stage or level to level is not directly related to the age of the person involved.
2. People tend to remain at any level until they have an opportunity to be frequently exposed to the kind of thinking reflected at the *next* higher level.
3. People confronted with reasoning which reflects thinking typical of two or more stages higher than their own cannot understand or internalize that reasoning.
4. People who are functioning at a higher level can understand the reasoning of a person functioning at a lower level.
5. Two people functioning at the same stage may not come to this same conclusion, but their reasoning will reflect the same characteristics.
6. People tend to use the highest stage they have at their disposal when making moral decisions.

One very important classroom application of Kohlberg's theory is in the presentation of dilemmas. A dilemma is a hypothetical situation in which a person must make a difficult decision. The student is asked first to decide what that person should do or should not do and then to explain why that particular act should or should not be taken. As the explanations are made and discussed, the teacher asks each student probing questions in order to encourage thinking and, incidentally, listening. It is through this process of discussion, clarification, and analysis that the student may begin to recognize, understand, and use a higher-level, more abstract base for making moral law-related decisions.

Interestingly, from a law-related perspective, Kohlberg identifies the following issues as central to most moral dilemmas: authority, civil liberties, contract, life, personal conscience, property, punishment, sex, and truth.

In the primary grades a hypothetical situation may be set up in which a girl has to decide whether she should take some money from her mother because her best friend tells her she needs it and will never like her again if she doesn't. Should she take the money or not? Why or why not?

In the upper grades a boy might be faced with the dilemma of whether to report a petty theft by his best friend to the authorities. What if the theft were made by another boy who was not a friend? What if the boy were bigger? Smaller?

Summary and Conclusion

Many ideas and theories have been presented, however briefly, in this paper. Each reader will draw his or her own conclusion about the relationship between values and moral education and law-related education. However, my conclusion is: law-related education is, in fact, values/moral education. When we are dealing with laws, we are dealing with values. When we are dealing with personal or societal application of those laws, we are dealing with morality. To ignore that is irresponsible. To ignore the work of the many theorists who have given us some models to use in planning programs which are consistent with what is known about learning and the development of rational, responsible, and caring human beings is unforgivable. To make the kind of progress hoped for in those programs without constantly referring to their humanistic underpinnings is impossible.

REFERENCES

Coombs, J., & Meux, M. Teaching strategies for value analysis. In L. E. Metcalf (Ed.), *Values education: Rationale, strategies, and procedures* (41st Yearbook). Washington, D.C.: National Council for the Social Studies, 1971.

Costa, A.; Lavaroni, C.; & Newton, F. *Inquiry development extension service: Unit VI.* Chicago: Science Research Associates, 1967.

Fraenkel, J. R. *Helping students think and value: Strategies for teaching the social studies.* Englewood Cliffs, N. J.: Prentice-Hall, 1973.

Inhelder, E., & Piaget, J. *The growth of logical thinking from childhood to adolescence.* New York: Basic, 1958.

Kirschenbaum, H.; Harmin, M.; Howe, L.; & Simon, S. In defense of values clarification. *Phi Delta Kappan,* 1977, *58,* 743–745.

Metcalf, L. E. (Ed.). *Values education: Rationale, strategies, and procedures* (41st Yearbook). Washington, D. C.: National Council for the Social Studies, 1971.

Quigley, C. N. *Your rights and responsibilities as an American citizen: A civics case book.* Lexington, Mass.: Ginn, 1976.

Raths, L.; Harmin, M.; & Simon, S. *Values and teaching.* Columbus, Ohio: Merrill, 1966.

Shaver, J., & Strong, W. *Facing value decisions: Rationale building for teachers.* Belmont, Calif.: Wadsworth, 1976.

REFERENCE NOTE

Doris, D. Kohlberg's moral reasoning. Unpublished manuscript, Santa Rosa, Calif., 1977.

The Relationship of Law and Humanities Education to Values and Moral Education

Jack R. Fraenkel

This article is a useful companion to the Lavaroni paper in that the author discusses the possible limitations of the values education approaches delineated by Lavaroni. In addition to critically analyzing these approaches, Jack Fraenkel identifies other scholars whose work he feels should be consulted by anyone implementing values education. The author closes his remarks by outlining learning experiences to help students understand the relationship between values and law.

Charles Lavaroni's paper is primarily an accurate description of two of the most popular and widely known approaches to teaching about values that are now available. It is clearly written and correct in what it says about these approaches, but it is lacking in specific suggestions about how these approaches might be used in law education. Examples are needed to illustrate how these approaches and the other ideas he describes (the theories of Jean Piaget and Lawrence Kohlberg) might be used to develop a model law-focused education program for the elementary school. There is no assessment of the strengths and weaknesses of the ideas and approaches described.

The ideas of many scholars whose work is fairly well known and frequently cited is not mentioned (e.g., Fraenkel, 1973, 1977b; McPhail, Ungoed-Thomas, & Chapman, 1972; Scriven, 1966; Shaftel & Shaftel, 1967; Shaver & Strong, 1976; Wilson, 1972, 1973). Much of this work has considerable implication for the development of values in law-focused education programs, and deserves attention in a paper of this nature. Furthermore, the paper ignores what many values educators consider to be a crucial aspect of values education—the necessity for developing moral empathy, which is so crucial to acquiring an understanding of different points of view. This seems a significant oversight. Finally, the paper does not indicate to what degree and why the approaches described are particularly appropriate

Jack R. Fraenkel is Professor of Interdisciplinary Studies in Education at San Francisco State University. He is the author of several works on values education, his most recent being *How To Teach Values: An Analytic Approach* (Prentice-Hall, 1977).

for use in the elementary school. In my critique, therefore, I wish not only to make some comments about specific parts of the Lavaroni paper, but also to offer a few suggestions about how the ideas in the paper might be applied to law-focused elementary education programs.

Some Comments about the Paper

Lavaroni is helpful in pointing up the polarities in viewpoint between those who want to teach students the "truth" about what is right or wrong and those who see their role as primarily helping students explore their feelings in this regard. Neither viewpoint is adequate as a basis for dealing with values in law education because (*a*) laws are not matters of truth or falsity, but rather indications of actions people consider desirable at a particular time (although they may not consider them so at another time), and (*b*) laws are not merely feelings about how one should behave, but rather official guidelines designed to regulate behavior. Hence, laws reflect the values of a society.

This is an important idea for students to understand, for it enables them to realize that laws do not exist independently of human beings "out there" somewhere in the cosmos, handed down somehow from "on high" for all human beings to obey without question or understanding, but that they are made by men and women (mostly men) to serve as rules to live by in order to maximize harmony and minimize discord. Since they are made by humans, they can be changed, abolished, or replaced by humans when they no longer work (i.e., when they create more discord than they do harmony). Many laws are in fact ignored because they reflect values that most people in the society no longer endorse. A law-education program to help children understand what law is really about (i.e., the purposes of law) must take a position on values, which it expresses and implements in its materials, that falls somewhere between these two extremes.

The definition of law-focused education quoted by Lavaroni is not as clear as one might wish. It is difficult to disagree with, or even react to, primarily because it is so general that one is not sure just what it means. One wonders what *specific* values are to be emphasized and in what ways, or what moral and ethical frames of reference the formulator(s) considers to be appropriate "for citizenship in a democratic society." The definition, to be sure, is not Lavaroni's, and he does attempt to define some of the key terms in more detail; but more specifics are needed concerning how these definitions apply to the concept of law. Furthermore, he offers no suggestions or ideas about what kind(s) of moral/ethical frames of reference would be appropriate for (effective) citizenship in a democracy. This latter point is especially important for a law-focused program (not to mention crucial to any values education program), for it provides students with a means of evaluating various laws (values) in order to determine if the laws (values) are worth obeying (holding) in the first place.

Consider the applicability of these criticisms to law-focused education. Viewing values as "ideas of worth" which people hold points up again that the laws of a society reflect his values. A law is a statement about what people believe at a particular time should (or should not) be done. This is an important fact for students to grasp, for it provides them with insights, not only into why some laws appear outmoded (values have changed), but also into why some individuals in a society do not obey certain laws (they may not value that which the law endorses; they may hold conflicting values which possess greater valence for them; they may not understand the values of others which cause them to attribute importance to a particular law; etc.). As Lavaroni suggests, law educators need to take pains to help students understand the value base which underlies all laws. This can be done in part by continually discussing with students (in different forms and contexts) such questions as: "What values would you say this law reflects?" "Why do you think the people who wrote this law considered it important?" "Is it important?" "Why or why not?" etc.

I do not have enough space here to develop a complete notion of what an adequate moral/ethical frame of reference might be, but a few comments are in order. A frame of reference is a way of looking at the world, a conception of how things are and how they might be. An ethical frame of reference is a way of looking at questions of right and wrong so as to come to some conclusions about how things *should be*. Helping students develop such a framework should be an integral part of any law-focused program, since much of the law (and its interpretation and enforcement) implies questions of right and wrong. Judicial decisions, for example, are influenced by the values of the judges involved; the manner in which certain laws are enforced (or whether they *are* enforced) is frequently influenced by what certain police officers consider to be appropriate (i.e., "right" or "proper") behavior; etc.

The important concept to teach in this regard is the notion of *criteria* (i.e., that there are various sets of standards which exist—or which can be formulated—by which actions can be judged). The law is one set of such standards. There are others. Hence we can discuss the appropriateness of certain kinds of standards (e.g., legal, aesthetic, economic, ecological, moral, etc.) as means by which to judge, and thereby regulate, human behavior. Of course, this has to be done very simply and slowly with elementary-age students, but certainly the notion of *standards* can be introduced, even in the primary grades, and students encouraged throughout the grades to think about and discuss various ways that behaviors and rules can be judged. It is especially important for students to realize early in their schooling that legality and morality are not the same thing. Just because something is legal does not make it right. Unjust laws do exist. What makes a law unjust? Should unjust laws be obeyed? If so, under what circumstances? If not, why not? Is it ever *right* to disobey the law? Questions like these can help students begin to think about criteria for evaluation of laws. Developing criteria appropriate to various situations (individuals, objects, actions, etc.) is essential if students are to become ethically mature adults able to make intelligent decisions when matters of right and wrong intrude upon their lives.

Lavaroni's definitions of values education, moral education, and values/moral education programs are similarly unclear. As defined, values education seems indistinguishable from general education. Certainly a major purpose of education in general is to help students become "clearer in seeing their choices," and certainly education must deal with an individual's "experiences...in relation to the society in which he finds himself." It is true that concepts like *good, bad, right, wrong,* are central to values education, but Lavaroni does not indicate in what way(s) they are central. Questions immediately arise. What does it mean to say that "the emphasis in values education is on what is 'good and/or bad'"? Good and/or bad for whom? With regard to what? How do we determine if something is good or bad or right or wrong? Are there not degrees of goodness/badness, rightness/wrongness? Do such concepts apply when it comes to the law? If so, how? To say that values/moral education programs must deal with both thinking and feeling, with both "good and bad" and "right and wrong," is to voice an opinion that probably few people would disagree with; but it isn't very helpful in conceptualizing and justifying how to proceed in teaching about the law in elementary school classrooms.

A large part of Lavaroni's paper consists of a clear and accurate, although uncritical, description of the values clarification approach of Raths, Harmin, and Simon (1966), the value analysis model of Coombs and Meux (1971), and the developmental stage of theories of Jean Piaget (Inhelder & Piaget 1958) and Lawrence Kohlberg (1971, 1975). (Lavaroni cites Inhelder and Piaget [1958] as the reference for his comments on Piaget's theory, but he overlooks another of Piaget's works more appropriate to the topic of his paper, namely, *The Moral Judgment of the Child* [1932].) Again, I would have liked more examples of how these approaches and ideas might be used in teaching about the law, particularly in the elementary grades. A further concern is that no mention is made of the fact that all these ideas and approaches have been criticized, often severely, by various scholars questioning not only their appropriateness in certain contexts or if used in a cookbook- or recipe-like fashion, but also the validity of their claims to success in teaching about values (e.g., Bennett & Delattre, 1978; Fenton, 1977, Fraenkel, 1976, 1977a, 1977b; Napier, 1976, 1977; Shaver & Strong, 1976; Stewart, 1975).

All three approaches do have potential for use in elementary law-education programs, although their appropriateness varies with the grade level of the students. Many values clarification exercises (open-ended statements, checklists, rank ordering, value continuums, examining alternatives, etc.), can be used to help elementary-age children identify and express how they *feel* about various aspects of the law (e.g., particular laws, court decisions, methods of enforcement, tactics of lawyers, methods of punishment, types of laws needed), and compare their feelings with those of others, thereby beginning to determine what sorts of laws and law-related behaviors they consider important. Values analysis techniques (e.g., defining terms, determining facts, exploring the short- and long-range consequences of existing or proposed alternatives) can help students evaluate the desirability of different actions and behaviors (e.g., various alternatives open to police officers, judges, lawmakers, prison officials, probation workers).

The work of both Piaget and Kohlberg suggests that curriculum developers try to match the work set out for children to their intellectual level, but at the same time provide opportunities that create enough cognitive dissonance in students to challenge their views about the conceptual and moral adequacy of their ideas, so they will try to restructure and justify their viewpoints in ways that are increasingly more rational and humane. The Piagetian and Kohlbergian stages can serve as a series of goals that teachers might consider trying to attain in order to bring about such restructuring and justification. The discussion of value dilemmas (i.e., situations in which individuals are faced with a choice between two alternatives, both of which have value for them), used by Kohlberg and his students as their major research tool for determining stage level, should, I think, be a basic ingredient in any law-focused program. The notion that laws often conflict with inclinations, indeed that this is inevitable in most (all?) societies, is important for students to understand. Legal conflicts *are* value conflicts, and the discussion of value dilemmas is an effective way for teachers to help students realize this. Even in the early elementary grades (e.g., grades 3 and 4), students can be presented with a variety of simple value conflicts arising out of law-related situations (e.g., a classroom monitor who, to help a friend, would have to break a classroom rule; two children faced with a decision of whether to obey a class rule they feel unfair; deciding whether a student who is saying unpopular things should be allowed to continue doing so in class; deciding whether to punish a classroom offender or give him or her another chance).

Despite their obvious usefulness and appeal, however, these approaches and ideas must be used carefully and sensitively, particularly with shy or less verbally inclined children. Teachers need to be made aware of and cautioned against certain weaknesses, even dangers, which the uncritical use of any of the three approaches may promote. Some values clarification activities, for example, have been criticized as emphasizing the clarification of values to the exclusion of their justification, of ignoring the fact that values often conflict, of inducing conformity to the most popular or frequently expressed values, and of failing to teach students how to appraise values critically. Values analysis techniques have been criticized for being too difficult for many students to master, for being boring, and for ignoring other aspects of development, besides the intellectual, that are important for moral growth. Kohlberg's theory has been attacked as being too sweeping in its conclusions and too limiting in its techniques, as failing to stress the importance of facts in the resolution of ethical disputes, and of ignoring the development of moral sensitivity which full moral maturity requires. Law-focused education programs need to make teachers aware of these (and other) criticisms, and to ensure in both their teaching-training efforts and their classroom materials that guidelines and activities to guard against these dangers are provided for.

Implications of Values Education for Law Education

Given the above concerns and caveats, what else (besides what has already been suggested) might those concerned with law education do to help students understand the relationship between values and laws? Space prohibits an exhaustive treatment, but let me offer a few additional suggestions to consider.

1. Provide lots of opportunities for students to discuss increasingly more difficult and abstract ethical issues, topics, and questions as they move upward through the grades. Students in the very early elementary grades (grades 1–3), for example, can be helped to consider concepts like fairness, conscience, responsibility, etc., while older students (grades 4–6) can be encouraged to think about the conflict which often occurs between such notions as rights and responsibilities, duty and conscience, authority and responsibility, obligation and inclination, etc.

2. Provide lots of opportunities for students to observe (either directly or vicariously through stories, films, news accounts, etc.) individuals acting in law-related endeavors (a Supreme Court justice dissenting from the majority opinion of his fellow justices; a police officer deciding to break into a home without a search warrant; a superior reprimanding a young officer for failing to advise arrested suspects of their rights; a prison warden arguing for prison reform; jury members discussing why they voted as they did in a trial; two law students discussing the meaning of the term "fair trial"; etc.), and then discuss what values the students think motivated the individuals to act in the ways that they did. The important thing here is, whenever possible, to give both sides of the story, and to present as wide a range of human behaviors (ways of acting) as possible in order to avoid the development of stereotypes.

3. Provide lots of opportunities for students to *role play* (i.e., try out) various individuals (judges, lawyers, police officers, legislators, parole officers, etc.) faced with ethical dilemmas, and then to discuss their feelings during the role playing. It is important to give students opportunities to role play a variety of roles, and to switch roles frequently. This is crucial to the development of moral empathy as well as moral insight.

4. Provide lots of opportunities for students to *work* with rules—that is, to participate frequently in rule making, rule changing, rule following, in order to develop not only an understanding of what laws mean, their strengths and weaknesses, but also to begin to develop a notion of the kinds of laws students think are desirable.

5. Provide lots of opportunities for students to evaluate laws and law-related behaviors, using a variety of criteria. Particular attention should be paid to the consequences of various laws for the human rights of individuals.

6. Provide lots of opportunities for students to experience (again, if only vicariously) and reflect on alternatives open to individuals involved in law making, law enforcement, and law interpretation, together with the consequences which may result from choosing certain alternatives rather than others. This frequently can be accomplished, as suggested above, through role playing or other simulations (e.g., having students role play judges and juries considering hypothetical or real cases and analyzing them in terms of what alternatives might be pursued).

7. Provide lots of opportunities for students to explore the meaning of various terms which must be clear in order to determine if a legal question is involved (e.g., if there is a law which states, "No vehicles in the park are permitted on Sundays," it is important for law enforcement personnel to be clear about what constitutes a vehicle).

8. Provide activities which will help students move from the mere *expression* of their feelings about laws and law-related behaviors, to an *awareness* of their own attitudes, beliefs, and values concerning the law, to an *awareness* of the attitudes, beliefs, etc., of others, to an *appraisal* of the goodness or badness of various laws and law-related behaviors, to *acting* in some way that will allow them to experience the consequences of acting in certain ways rather than others.

Of vital importance in all of this, however, is that *teachers* involved in teaching about the law (and the values which laws reflect) consider the image of the law which they themselves give to students through their own behavior in the classroom (e.g., Do they always determine what the rules in the classroom are to be? Do students have any say in the governance of the class? etc.). Helping teachers think about the image of the law which they project and asking them to consider if it is one which will help students develop a respect for law and an understanding of what lawful behavior involves is a responsibility that all law-education programs should not ignore.

A Final Caveat

It is crucial in all of this that curriculum developers and others involved in law education not forget one vital fact: for any of the above suggestions to have much impact on students, the students *themselves* must perceive the issues they discuss as important and worthy of discussion; must feel they have a stake in what is going on in the class; and must be helped to draw their own conclusion about the law and those involved in the law rather than simply being given the conclusions of others to remember. Many a program has failed to have much of an impact because it ignored this fact.

REFERENCES

Bennett, W. J., & Delattre, E. J. Moral education in the schools. *Public Interest*, 1978, No. 50, pp. 81–98.

Coombs, J., & Meux, M. Teaching strategies for value analysis. In L. Metcalf (Ed.), *Values education: Rationale, strategies, and procedures* (41st Yearbook). Washington, D.C.: National Council for the Social Studies, 1971.

Fenton, E. The relationship of citizenship education to values education. In *Planning for moral/citizenship education* (Occasional Paper No. 2). Philadelphia: Research for Better Schools, 1977.

Fraenkel, J. R. *Helping students think and value: Strategies for teaching the social studies.* Englewood Cliffs, N. J.: Prentice-Hall, 1973.

Fraenkel, J. R. The Kohlberg bandwagon: Some reservations. *Social Education*, 1976, 40, 216–222.

Fraenkel, J. R. *How to teach about values: An analytic approach.* Englewood Cliffs, N.J.: Prentice-Hall, 1977. (a)

Fraenkel, J. R. Values clarification is not enough! *History and Social Science Teacher*, 1977, 12(1), 27–32. (b)

Inhelder, B., & Piaget, J. *The growth of logical thinking from childhood to adolescence.* New York: Basic, 1958.

Kohlberg, L. From is to ought: How to commit the naturalistic fallacy and get away with it in the study of moral development. In T. Mischel (Ed.), *Cognitive develpment and epistemology.* New York: Academic Press, 1971.

Kohlberg, L. The cognitive-developmental approach to moral education. *Phi Delta Kappan*, 1975, 56, 670-677.

McPhail, P.; Ungoed-Thomas, J. R.; & Chapman, H. *Moral education in the secondary school.* London: Longmans, 1972.

Napier, J. The ability of elementary school teachers to stage score moral thought statements. *Theory and Research in Social Education*, 1976, 4(2), 39–56.

Napier, J. Content influence while stage scoring moral thought statements. *Educational and Psychological Measurement*, 1977, 37, 519–525.

Piaget, J. *The moral judgment of the child.* London: Routledge & Kegan Paul, 1932.

Raths, L.; Harmin, M.; & Simon, S. *Values and teaching.* Columbus, Ohio: Merrill, 1966.

Scriven, M. *Student values as educational objectives.* Boulder, Colo.: Social Science Education Consortium, 1966.

Shaftel, F., & Shaftel, G. *Role-playing for social values.* Englewood Cliffs, N.J.: Prentice-Hall, 1967.

Shaver, J., & Strong, W. B. *Facing value decisions: Rationale building for teachers.* Belmont, Calif.: Wadsworth, 1976.

Stewart, J. S. Clarifying values clarification: A critique. *Phi Delta Kappan*, 1975, 56, 684–688.

Wilson, J. *Practical methods of moral education.* London: Heinemann, 1972.

Wilson, J. *A teacher's guide to moral education.* London: Chapman, 1973.

The Elementary School Years as an Optimal Period for Learning about International Human Rights

Judith Vollmar Torney

Education that is predominantly nation centered is by definition inadequate for children growing up in today's interdependent world. Starting from this premise, Judith Torney identifies the issue of human rights as a case in which educational approaches have been nation centered where a world-centered approach is indicated. She cites extensive research evidence indicating an almost universal consensus on basic human rights, and calls into question the typical practice of exposing students to the concept of rights only in the context of the U.S. Constitution and Bill of Rights. The author notes that cross-national studies show children in the United States have little understanding of the internationl political arena. The elementary schools bear a special responsibility for correcting this, as research further indicates that the elementary years are optimal for developing an international or global perspective and for teaching about international human rights. The paper closes with an explication of the vital role the humanities can play in human rights education.

The topic of international human rights and the concept of middle childhood as a critical or optimal period for education about this topic have an important thing in common. Both have been given too little attention in education program development.

A Consensus Definition of International Human Rights

The phrase "human rights" appears frequently in the headlines, but is not well understood by the majority of the American public who read the newspaper stories. According to GIST, a publication of the Public Affairs Department as a "quick reference" on foreign policy issues, the U.S. government is operating on the following definition:

The definition of human rights is based on our historical documents and experience, the UN Charter and other international instruments. One of these, the UN Universal Declaration of Human Rights, approved by the UN General Assembly in 1948, recognizes basic human rights at the international level. The specific rights we pursue include:

– Freedom from arbitrary arrest and imprisonment, torture, unfair trial, cruel and unusual punishment, and invasion of privacy
– Rights to food, shelter, health care, and education; and
– Freedom of thought, speech, assembly, religion, press, movement and participation in government....

All UN members have accepted the obligation under the UN Charter to observe and respect basic human rights. [GIST, 1978]

This paragraph sets forth the framework within which American foreign policy is conducted with regard to human rights. The first set of rights specified above is often referred to as "basic human rights," since they deal with the integrity of life and person.

Since the establishment of the United Nations, a substantial body of international law norms relating to human rights has been developed (see Sohn & Buergenthal, 1973). This development has led scholars of international law to conclude that there exists an international consensus regarding basic human rights, and that these rights are defined by the Universal Declaration (Buergenthal & Torney, 1976). Although the Universal Declaration was adopted by the UN in

Judith Torney is Professor of Psychology and Head of the Division of Developmental Psychology at the University of Illinois at Chicago Circle. She is co-author of *Civic Education in Ten Countries* and *International Human Rights and International Education*.

1948, when its membership was one-third of its present size and included very few African and Asian nations, it is not correct to assume that the declaration does not reflect the human rights conception of these nations, especially with regard to basic human rights such as freedom from arbitrary arrest, torture, and cruel and inhuman punishment. In the past three decades the Universal Declaration has been invoked with increasing frequency by African and Asian states, and the vast majority of UN members treat it as a legally authoritative instrument.

Even the fact that many governments give lip service to the Universal Declaration while at the same time violating its provisions supports the view that a consensus exists about human rights. There would be little reason for a government to defend policies which fly in the face of the Universal Declaration to its own people or to other countries unless it believed that there was strong support for these rights both internally and externally. It is generally agreed that *good* governments should not violate human rights. When violations occur, they demand elaborate justification.

There is substantial interest among scholars of international law in the process by which universal consensus (especially about basic human rights) has been reflected in legally binding documents. And human rights has become an especially important guiding principle in the conduct of American foreign policy since 1974–1975, when the Foreign Assistance Act was amended as follows: "Sec. 116   No assistance may be provided under this part to the government of any country which engages in a consistent pattern of gross violations of internationally recognized human rights, including torture or cruel, inhuman or degrading treatment or punishment, prolonged detention without charges, or other flagrant denial of the right to life, liberty, and the security of person, unless such assistance will directly benefit the needy people in such a country." In 1977, additional force was given to the importance of human rights when President Carter emphasized their role in the conduct of American foreign policy. There is little understanding among the American public about what internationally protected human rights are and what the implications are of making them central to the conduct of foreign policy.

Orientations toward Domestic and International Human Rights

For many reasons, historic and political as well as educational, Americans tend to be oriented much more toward the domestic than toward the international aspect of politics. An empirical confirmation of this was the recent analysis of data from 30,000 adolescents from nine countries provided by IEA Civic Education Project testing in 1971 (Torney, 1977; Torney, Oppenheim, & Farnen, 1975).

Students were asked how frequently they discussed domestic and international politics with parents, friends, and teachers. Respondents in the United States ranked quite high on total amount of discussion. There were considerable differences, however, in the particular *topics* which students discussed with parents and friends. On the average, 14-year-old students in the Federal Republic of Germany, Finland, Italy, the Netherlands, and New Zealand discussed "what is happening in other countries" more frequently than "what is going on in our country." National politics were of somewhat greater interest than international politics to Irish and Italian students. The United States was the only country (of those eight) where 14-year-olds reported substantially *less* interest in discussion of foreign politics than in discussion of national political matters.

Scores summarizing students' knowledge of domestic and of international politics were also available. The average American 14-year-old was more knowledgeable about domestic political institutions and processes than the average 14-year-old in any other country except Israel. In contrast, American 14-year-olds were *less* knowledgeable about international institutions and processes than the 14-year-olds in any other nation except Ireland. In other words, students in Israel, like those in the United States, know more about domestic politics than they know about international politics. In contrast, higher scores on items concerning international processes and institutions than on those concerning domestic institutions and processes characterized students of this age in the Netherlands and the Federal Republic of Germany.

In summary, American students beginning high school appear less knowledgeable and less interested in international issues than their age-peers in other nations. Although some of this deficit could presumably be overcome by programs in secondary schools, the IEA study showed few substantial increments in international interest and knowledge when 14-year-olds and 17–18-year-olds in the United States were compared. The later years of elementary education seem to be an important place to look for influences on these orientations.

There is substantial interest among American educators in programs of global and international education. Some of these programs, many of them implemented in the last 5 years, may result in a greater knowledge of and interest in international issues by adolescents in the future. However, the movement to create a global dimension for social studies programs has not extended to law-related education. These substantial programs have concentrated upon domestic legal processes and procedures at both elementary and secondary levels and have virtually ignored topics from international law.

American children, almost without exception, are exposed to the concept of rights only in the context of the U.S. Constitution and Bill of Rights. Laws in all of the 50 states mandate the teaching of the federal constitution (either in a separate course or as part of an American history course). To my knowledge none of the 50 states mentions the Universal Declaration of Human Rights. All textbooks devote substantial attention to the U.S. Constitution; very few mention the U.N. Declaration. In the teaching process, an attempt is often made to involve the student personally in an understanding of rights guaranteed in the U.S. Constitution by discussing examples of the child's own exercise of the right to go to the church of his/her choice or read the newspaper of his/her choice. Because the U.S. Constitution, and not the Universal Declaration, is the source of all the examples of rights, it should not be too surprising that American children have a tendency to view human rights as an American invention and monopoly. In fact, in a recent National Assessment Survey, a substantial number of children indicated that they believed the United States was the only country in the world where certain political and legal institutions (such as written constitution and political parties) exist.

It is not only that international human rights are infrequently mentioned in children's textbooks and curriculum materials. More serious is the fact that the material to which the average child is exposed has such a dominant focus on the domestic political and legal system that the child understandably draws the conclusion that the American political system is the only important framework for defining rights.

An important step in this area would be to introduce the concept of rights by a study of the Universal Declaration of Human Rights and then to study the U.S. Constitution in this framework. (An approach similar to this has been tried in a special social studies project in Pontiac, Mich.) Thus, before considering American institutions, the child would understand the definition of rights as people all over the world have defined them. This need not result in a lessened stress on domestic civil and political rights, only in a different order of presentation. This sequence of presentation might also be advantageous from the educational point of view, going from the more general to the more specific. It can also be a powerful component of a truly global and humankind perspective on educational programs.

Cultural Relativism and International Human Rights

American children face another difficulty in learning about international human rights. In most social studies curricula the child is exposed at a very early age to the idea that people in other countries have customs and values which are very different from his/her own. Television presentations about other nations also try to rouse children's interest by showing them strange and exotic aspects of other countries. At a recent symposium on the presentation of human rights issues in newspapers, a former Latin American correspondent for a major paper reported that the stories she wrote were much more likely to be printed if they had an unusual human interest angle.

As a result of these in- and out-of-school sources, a child develops the idea that his or her family is not like an Eskimo family, which is unlike a Japanese family, and so on. Every culture is presented as having its own particular values which determine such things as clothing and family structures, which frequently differ in very striking ways from those the child knows. It is little wonder then that children have a hard time realizing that there are certain values and matters of basic human rights which are widely (if not universally) shared within the human community. Although cultural differences are important, children need to understand that there are also qualities of being human which transcend cultural relativism. Educational experience can play a vital role in stimulating this understanding.

Universal Conceptions of Rights

The differentiation between values which one might reasonably expect to differ by culture and others which are seen to be universal has been addressed in several pieces of recent research. Gallatin (1976) interviewed young people from the United States, Britain, and the Federal Republic of Germany. Hers was primarily a study of conceptions of domestic social and political order and of the rights connected with it. Some of the findings are interesting nevertheless. Although there were some differences between the students of different nations, the differences between age groups were far more impressive. Gallatin concluded as follows about the political philosophy and concepts held by young people in these three countries: "Whatever their differences, these three nations share, at least, in recent history, a common political philosophy which stipulates that the rulers serve the ruled and the government is obligated to furnish certain basic services for its citizens and grant them a set of inalienable rights" (1976, p. 323).

A second study dealt with university students in Hong Kong, France, and the United States. Bloom (1977) found two separate dimensions of judgment in all of these cultures, "social principledness" (the ability to differentiate between a conventional and a personal standard of morality in making sociopolitical decisions) and "social humanness" (giving priority to the human implications of decisions). The latter is closely related to support for human rights.

Turiel, a developmental psychologist, distinguishes between social conventions and moral issues. He believes that previous work on moral development has frequently failed to see the important differences between them. Social conventions are "behavioral uniformities which coordinate the actions of individuals participating in a social system.... Uniformities in modes of dress, usages of forms of address... are arbitrary in that they do not have an intrinsic prescriptive basis" (Turiel, 1977, pp. 79–80). He reserves the term "moral" to apply to a more limited set of issues—the value of life, physical and psychological harm to others, and deprivation of something to which a person is entitled. These issues, which he defines as moral, are very similar to conceptions of universal human rights. They are related to not specifics of a cultural or social system but to underlying concepts of justice which "stem from factors intrinsic to actions: consequences such as harm inflicted upon others, violations of rights, effects on general welfare" (Turiel, 1977, p. 80).

Nucci and Turiel (1978), in one of their studies, observed the behavior of preschool children in 10 schools and interviewed the children about these events soon after they had taken place. They reported that it was possible to distinguish between children's responses to acts which violated social conventions (e.g., engaging in actions different from the group, such as sitting rather than standing while eating) and acts which were moral transgressions (one person intentionally hitting another). Eighty-three percent of the events were classified into the same category by adult observers and by children who were interviewed.

In another study (Turiel, 1979), elementary school and secondary students were asked whether a given act would be wrong even if no rule existed prohibiting it. In the case of a social convention, a country where everyone decides to play a game by different rules, more than 80% of children aged 6–17 said that *would not* be wrong. In the case of what Turiel called a moral issue, stealing in a country where no rule or law existed against it, more than 70% of the students at all ages said that *would* be wrong.

In summary, recent psychological research indicates that there is considerable consensus about issues relating to basic human rights—among adults who have grown up in quite different cultural settings (as well as in the U.S.) and among children in the United States. Although more extensive research is called for, this confirms the conclusion that it is inappropriate to consider the process of establishing human rights as requiring the export of American values or legal institutions. There are concepts of basic human rights and values which are widely shared. Furthermore, this international consensus can serve as a starting point for education. After grasping this general definition of human rights, young people can examine its exemplification in domestic legal and political institutions.

Elementary Years as Optimal for Social Studies Education

In a recent book on Piaget's theory of intelligence, Brainerd (1978) highlighted the importance of assessing the child's current level of cognitive and social functioning in designing effective educational programs and avoiding materials which are beyond the child's current level of development. Another idea from developmental psychology which gives positive guidance to program design is that of the critical or optimal period. This concept was originally used by psychologists and ethologists to describe an age-bounded period during which the social behavior and learning of young animals demonstrates a high degree of plasticity. Once such a period ends, there is a kind of turning point after which behavior organized in a given pattern is extraordinarily difficult to reorganize (Scott, 1962). It may be appropriate to consider the elementary school years as such a critical or optimal period for the development of attitudes toward other nations and global issues in general and toward human rights in particular. This is not an easy notion to test empirically; a fully adequate investigation would require a longitudinal study of different generational cohorts exposed to different kinds of educational experience at different ages or stages of development. However, some research evidence which shows particular peaks of attitudes or abilities during the elementary school period can provide useful information about the psychological characteristics of children.

Middle childhood appears to be a time of important developmental changes in attitudes and a period during which certain barriers to a global perspective have not yet been erected. Beginning at about the age of 6 or 7 a child enters a period of rapid cognitive development; although cognitive growth continues through adolescence, at about the age of 17 there appears to be a loss of attitudinal plasticity in many young people; opinions seem to become rigid as they are used more frequently as a way of confirming peer group solidarity and excluding those who are different. Middle childhood is thus a period when both cognitive and social development may be optimal for social education.

First, a number of studies which show rapid growth in cognition about social events will be reviewed. Gollin (1958) found a large difference between an 8/9-year-old group and a 10/11-year-old group in the ability to reflect conflicting themes in the perception of persons. Schultz, Butkowsky, Pearce, and Shanfield (1975) found 9-year-olds to be greatly superior to 5-year-olds in attributing psychological events in stories to multiple causes. In a study of person perception, Livesley and Bromley (1973) concluded that the year between age 7 and age 8 is a critical period in the development of descriptions of others based on regularities of behavior across time and situation rather than upon appearance or possessions of the person being described. In this study the differences between the 7- and 8-year-olds were often greater than those between the 8- and 15-year-olds. Flapan (1968), in a study of girls' reactions to a simple story in a movie, found the greatest shift in inferences about behavior to occur between age 6 and age 9.

Researchers in the Federal Republic of Germany, France, Great Britain, Czechoslovakia, and the United States showed children two films highly judged in an international competition (*Findings on the Television Perception, 1969*). The researchers contrasted the behavior of 8–9-year-olds with that of 10–12-year-olds. The younger children appeared to concentrate on the story line but not to remember details. The older children not only remembered details but used them as clues to the story's meaning.

Even more extensive reviews of research have led psychologists to similar conclusions: "... one is attempted [*sic*] to predict that middle childhood will turn out to be *the* developmental epoch so far as basic role taking and allied skills are concerned, with the preschool period contributing the prologue and adolescence the epilogue" (Flavell, 1966, p. 176). Selman arrived at the same conclusion: "Whereas late adolescence can be seen as a critical period for the development of principled moral thought, the age of 8 or 9 to 12 can be seen as an important period for the development of general social thought and interpersonal experience" (Selman, 1976, p. 307).

Second, studies of conformity will be reviewed. Young people are observed in a controlled situation when they are required to make a perceptual judgment which may either conflict with or conform to a judgment made by their peers. Allen and Newston (1972), using first, fourth, seventh, and tenth graders, found that conformity decreased with increasing age until about 7, then increased up to grade 10. Strassberg and Wiggen (1973) also found that conformity decreased with age between 8 and 11 but then increased up to age 13. Pasternack (1973) investigated yielding behavior among first through eighth graders. Conformity decreased through this period for girls; for boys, however, conformity decreased until the seventh grade, after which it increased. This evidence also suggests that middle childhood may be an optional period for social education.

Finally, evidence which deals specifically with children's attitudes toward persons in other nations and toward human/global perspectives will be reviewed. Montemayor and Eisen (1977) asked young people to answer the question, "Who am I?" The response "a person" or "a human" was given by fewer than 5% of the 10-year-olds but by a striking 80% of the 12-year-olds. That proportion was cut in half for 14- and 17-year-olds. This response was by far the most frequent for the 12-year-old group and suggests their readiness to adopt a global or humankind point of view.

Four European psychologists, Jaspars, van de Geer, Tajfel, and Johnson (1966), based their study upon Allport's three-stage theory of prejudice. During the first stage of pregeneralization, according to this theory, children seem aware of group differences but do not have strong negative feelings toward different groups. The next stage is total rejection and is thought to reach its peak in early puberty. At adolescence greater differentiation and less generalized prejudice is expected to characterize young people's approach to ethnic and national groups. Allport's theory predicts a maximum intensity of negative attitudes in early adolescence, with more positive attitudes in middle childhood and later adolescence.

The theory was tested on a group of Dutch students, who showed a clear preference for the Netherlands when asked to compare pairs of countries and show which they liked best. The intensity of this preference increased between grades 2 and 6, and the total amount of differentiation between preferences for these countries also increased. With regard to the cognitive judgment of similarity between one's own country and other countries, there was a change from the second grade (when one's own country was seen as different from all others but other countries were seen as relatively similar to each other) to grade 5 (when differences between all countries were perceived). Some of the measures used in this study showed the relation with age which Allport's theory predicted. For example, the correlation between preference for five other countries and the cognitive distance of these countries from the Netherlands reached a peak at grade 4 (and declined thereafter).

Lambert and Klineberg (1967) completed an interview study of 3,000 children at three age levels (6, 10, and 14) from 11 parts of the world. They concluded that American children of about 10 years of age were particularly receptive to approaches to and information about foreign people; these young people were interested in individuals who were dissimilar to themselves as well as in those who were similar. By the age of 14, American young people appeared to be less open to positive views of foreign nations. Stereotyping of foreign people also showed an increase between age 10 and age 14. Jahoda (1962) also found that attitudes about other countries shifted in Scottish children beginning at about 10 or 12 years of age. A study of 3,000 American seventh and twelfth graders using a map-related technique found that stereotypic concepts associated with Africa (natives, tribes, cannibals) and with Russia (enemy, dictatorship) increased from the seventh to the twelfth grade (Hicks & Beyer, 1970).

The conclusion one may draw from research, even with differences in method and in the year which change appears to be most rapid, is that the elementary school period is optimal for education about other nations, global issues, and international human rights.

Humanities in International Human Rights Education

There are many ways in which one might justify the stress upon the humanities in elementary law-related education including international human rights. One justification, which may be unfamiliar to many, is by reference to the 1974 UNESCO Recommendation on Education for International Understanding, Cooperation, and Peace and Education Relating to Human Rights and Fundamental Freedoms. This recommendation, which the United States as a member of UNESCO has a responsibility to implement and report upon, refers in several articles to the importance of interdisciplinary approaches to education at every level (beginning in the preschool years). Article 12 urges member states to "use methods which appeal to the creative imagination of children and adolescents." Article 17 says, in part: "Such study should, among other things, give due importance to the teaching of foreign languages, civilizations and cultural heritage as a means of promoting international and inter-cultural understanding." Article 38c highlights the importance of the visual arts and music.

This recommendation was written by government representatives of countries whose diversity mirrors that existing among the nations of the world. In it UNESCO member states agreed on a comprehensive set of principles and policies governing international programs, including education, regarding human rights as an important element. It serves, therefore, as a complete agenda for international education in which the topic discussed in this paper has a vital role. (See Buergenthal & Torney, 1976, for a discussion of this recommendation.)

Conclusions

This paper makes three major points. First, a substantial consensus exists in the world about the definition of basic human rights and about the importance of international education in furthering the observance of these rights. Second, because of substantial development in social-cognitive abilities, the elementary school years are an optimal period for education about international human rights. Third, the humanities have an especially important role to play in international human rights education. Literature and art are fruitful sources of illustrations of the universal human quest for values and rights. Children need to be helped to make explicit connections between universal themes expressed in literature and art and particular articles of the Universal Declaration of Human Rights. It is possible to link almost any piece of fiction both to the experience of the child and to the experience of those from other cultural settings (either in this country or in other countries). Both of these links—to the personal, social, and cognitive development of the individual and to the concept of humanity—are important.

The inclusion of international human rights in law-related programs in the humanities has tremendous potential for elementary education. And it is interesting to note that even the poet Auden has recognized, at least for girls, that the years of middle childhood are important. "A girl of 11," he wrote, "can be a most remarkable creature." He continued to describe the discipline, sense of identity, orderliness of mind, and imagination which characterize that age and to add that such a child represents "what, after many years and countless follies and errors, one would like in the end to become." A better melding of psychology and the humanities would be hard to find!

REFERENCES

Allen, V. L., & Newston, D. Development of conformity and independence. *Journal of Personality and Social Psychology,* 1972, *22,* 18–30.

Bloom, A. H. Two dimensions of moral reasoning: Social principledness and social humanism in cross-cultural perspective. *Journal of Social Psychology,* 1977, *101,* 29–44.

Brainerd, C. J. *Piaget's theory of intelligence.* Englewood Cliffs, N.J.: Prentice-Hall, 1978.

Buergenthal, T., & Torney, J. V. *International human rights and international education.* Washington, D.C.: National Commission for UNESCO, 1976. U.S. Government Printing Office No.044-000-01651-6.

Findings on the television perception and cognition of children and young people. Munich: Internationales Zentralen Institut des Jugend, 1969.

Flapan, D. *Children's understanding of social interaction.* New York: Teachers College Press, 1968.

Flavell, J. H. Role-taking and communication skills in children. *Young Children,* 1966, *21,* 164–177.

Gallatin, J. The conceptualization of rights: Psychological development and cross national perspectives. In R. P. Claude (Ed.), *Comparative human rights.* Baltimore: Johns Hopkins University Press, 1976.

GIST (Bureau of Public Affairs, U.S. Department of State), January 1978.

Gollin, E. S. Organizational characteristics of social judgment: A developmental investigation. *Journal of Personality,* 1958, *26,* 139–154.

Hicks, E., & Beyer, B. K. Images of Africa. *Journal of Negro Education,* 1970, *39,* 158–166.

Jahoda, G. Development of Scottish children's ideas and attitudes about other countries. *Journal of Social Psychology,* 1962, *58,* 91–108.

Jaspars, J. M. F.; van de Geer, J. P.; Tajfel, H.; & Johnson, N. B. On the development of national attitudes. *European Journal of Social Psychology,* 1966, *1,* 360–370.

Lambert, W. E., & Klineberg, O. *Children's views of foreign peoples: A cross-national study.* New York: Appleton-Century-Crofts, 1967.

Livesley, W. J., & Bromley, D. B. *Person perception in childhood and adolescence.* London: Wiley, 1973.

Montemayor, R., & Eisen, M. The development of self-conceptions from childhood to adolescence. *Developmental Psychology,* 1977, *13,* 314–319.

Nucci, L., & Turiel, E. Social interactions and the development of social concepts in preschool children. *Child Development,* 1978, *49,* 400–414.

Pasternack, T. L. Qualitative differences in development of yielding behavior by elementary school children. *Psychological Reports,* 1973, *32,* 883–896.

Schultz, T. R.; Butkowsky, I.; Pearce, J. W.; & Shanfield, H. Development of schemes for the attribution of multiple psychological causes. *Developmental Psychology,* 1975, *11,* 502–510.

Scott, J. P. Critical periods in behavior development. *Science,* 1962, 949–958.

Selman, R. L. Social-cognitive understanding: A guide to educational and clinical practice. In T. Lickona (Ed.), *Moral development and behavior.* New York: Holt, Rinehart & Winston, 1976.

Sohn, L. B., & Buergenthal, T. International protection of human rights. Indianapolis: Bobbs-Merrill, 1973.

Strassberg, D. S., & Wiggen, E. Conformity as a function of age in preadolescents. *Journal of Social Psychology,* 1973, *91,* 61–66.

Torney, J. V. The international attitudes and knowledge of adolescents in nine countries: The IEA civic education survey. *International Journal of Political Education,* 1977, *1,* 3–20.

Torney, J. V.; Oppenheim, A. N.; & Farnen, R. F. *Civic education in ten countries: an empirical study.* New York: Wiley, Halsted, 1978.

Turiel, E. Distinct conceptual and developmental domains: Social-convention and morality. In *Nebraska Symposium on Motivation* (Vol. 25). Lincoln: University of Nebraska Press, 1977.

Turiel, E. The development of concepts of social structure: Social convention. In J. Glick & A. Clark-Stewart (Eds.), *Studies in social and cognitive development.* New York: Gardner, 1979.

The Elementary School Years as an Optimal Period for Learning about International Human Rights

Thomas E. Fox

If elementary schools are to teach about human rights from a global and/or international perspective, what resources are available, what instructional strategies are appropriate? In this paper, Tom Fox discusses some of the instructional strategies which he feels this approach calls for. Among these is the necessity of giving what he terms "a thorough and realistic presentation of social conflict." The author goes on to identify a number of curriculum materials and agencies which are concerned with expanding children's understanding of the world and the global context for the extension of human rights.

Developing international understanding among children has long been a high-priority goal of social studies educations (Education for Understanding, 1948). The National Council for Social Studies devoted its 1954 Yearbook to the teaching of world affairs (Anderson, 1954). That same year Washburne (1954) published *The World's Good, Education for World Mindedness,* to be followed shortly thereafter by Kenworthy's (1956) widely read *Introducing Children to the World in Elementary and Junior High Schools.* The American Association of Colleges for Teacher Education published a committee report in 1956 that suggested programs and projects elementary teachers might use to facilitate international understanding (*Programs and Projects,* 1956). In the mid 1960s the National Council for the Social Studies gave us, *Improving the Teaching of World Affairs: The Glens Falls Story* (Long & King, 1964). Then in 1969 the National Society for the Study of Education Yearbook appeared with an article by Harold Shane that sharply criticized elementary and secondary schools for failing to provide students with better "value-paradigms" and significant experiences that bear on international education (Shane, 1969).

In the last decade a number of social studies programs have addressed the very shortcomings

Thomas E. Fox is Associate in Higher Education, New York State Department of Education. He is currently coordinator of academic affairs for College Proficiency Examinations/Regents External Degrees Programs, University of the State of New York.

Shane pointed out. Increasingly concepts such as "spaceship earth" and "global village" are used to stress the interdependence and commonality of humankind. Values education and moral reasoning models have been incorporated into social studies curricula at the elementary as well as the secondary levels. We seem to be moving away from cultural-relativistic approaches, stressing the quaint or exotic aspects of particular cultures, toward a more global perspective, underscoring cultural universals that transcend national boundaries. The November/December 1974 and January 1977 issues of *Social Education* were devoted to global education from this new perspective. However, in advocating a law-related curriculum for upper elementary school students that explicitly includes the subject of international human rights, Judith Torney goes considerably beyond most existing programs and practices.

Central to the teaching of international human rights, I feel, is the thorough and realistic presentation of social conflict. The school has a major responsibility in the political education of the young, which at the minimal level calls for avoiding blatant ignorance or complete rejection of the political mechanisms used to manage or resolve social conflict. Six years ago I examined 58 social studies textbooks widely used across the country for grades 3, 5, and 9 and found the relative absence of social issues, or the treatment of social issues rarely in terms of social conflict (Fox, Note 1). Torney cites more recent cross-national research that indicates American youth in general know less about international issues than their foreign counterparts, and that upon entering high school our students tend to be natio-centric and naive about international human rights. Part of the blame, she contends, must be ascribed to the emphasis the mass media and some social studies programs continue to put on the different and unusual aspects of other peoples. I certainly agree. I also support her contention that the practice of teaching human rights almost exclusively in terms of domestic issues has led our youth to feel that human rights were "invented in this country or can be defined only within the framework of the American political experience." Clearly more needs to be done at the elementary school level if we are to expand our children's understanding of the world.

Torney has made a case for the existence of a universal conception of human rights, and cites research indicating that even young children can distinguish between social conventions and moral issues. Her contention that the upper elementary school years are crucial in the formation of children's attitudes and beliefs finds considerable support in political socialization literature. The general argument is that children form basic political dispositions during their elementary school years (Easton & Hess, 1962), and that formal instruction about government in high school seems to have little effect on previously held values (Adelson, 1971; Adelson & O'Neil, 1966; Sigel, 1970). Like Torney, most political socialization researchers conclude that children should learn about the "real world" early in their school experience (American Political Science Association Committee on Pre-Collegiate Education, 1971; Easton & Dennis, 1969). Torney, however, specifically identifies middle childhood—the years between 8 or 9 and 12—as the optimal period for learning about international human rights. For during these 4 or 5 years, she argues, children acquire sufficient social and intellectual ability to understand global issues, while yet remaining flexible and receptive enough to accept information about foreign people.

If we assume Torney's hypothesis is correct, what then should we teach children about international human rights? While the U.N. Universal Declaration of Human Rights gives us a standard definition, even Torney admits that the phrase "human rights" is not understood by the majority of American adults. Law-related concepts, I would contend, are often best understood by studying violations of them. Might not the same hold true for international human rights? The U.N. declaration notwithstanding, the international community today is far from agreement on a definition of human rights. In fact, the 1974 UNESCO Recommendation on Education for International Understanding, Cooperation, and Peace, and Education Relating to Human Rights and Fundamental Freedoms, cited by Torney, was not adopted by the United States, Australia, France, Canada, and the Federal Republic of Germany because of a Peruvian amendment to it attacking "monopolistic" groups who practice exploitation and foment war (Buergenthal & Torney, 1976). Also, it is clear that the emphasis placed on individual freedom and rights in multiparty democracies like the United States is not found in Communist countries like the Soviet Union. Should young children be taught that developing nations are likely to be more concerned with supplying basic needs (food, clothing, and shelter) than they are with protecting "basic human rights" (arbitrary arrest, invasion of privacy, etc.)? Could these children understand the resentment developing nations feel when criticized by foreign politicians? For isn't the realization of one's own national perspective a prerequisite for gaining a global perspective?

Recently I asked David Hawk, executive director of Amnesty International, if his organization had any material related to international human rights that elementary social studies teachers might use. He replied that complex transnational legal questions are usually involved in the human rights violations his group uncovers, and considerable editorial effort is made to describe them so the adult layperson can understand them.

Even if the relatively complex ideas basic to understanding and accepting the concept of international human rights can be taught to children in the upper elementary grades—a contention that will probably bring Torney many arguments from learning theorists as well as classroom practitioners—social studies would have to undergo massive reform before such instruction could occur on any widespread basis. For it is still common to find children being taught that America is the "land of the free," where citizens can read, say, or do virtually anything, while artists, free thinkers, and so on are supressed in totalitarian countries like the Soviet Union and the People's Republic of China.

Fortunately some instructional materials have been developed that avoid such false comparisons. For example, the Center for Teaching International Relations and the Center for Global Perspectives have developed a curriculum to teach elementary children about social conflict from a global perspective. Their material is currently being field-tested in grades K–3 in Connecticut, and preliminary results are very promising. Supporters of Torney's thesis should also be encouraged by a Boston University study involving third graders in social studies classes using the *Family of Man.* Torney herself described this curriculum as one of the few "identifiable internationalized programs" available for elementary schools (Torney & Morris, 1972). The study found that children using the *Family of Man* materials developed a more positive view toward foreign people, and concluded that a carefully designed primary grade social studies program with a strong global focus "can have a significant effect on the understanding that children develop of other nations and other people" (Mitsakos, 1978, p. 12).

In these times of accelerating social change and global awareness, social studies educators must seek out and capitalize on every opportunity to help children and youth understand and feel responsible for the condition of our "shrinking" planet. The international and future orientation of global studies combined with the dignity and responsibility of all people stressed by humanities and law-related education provide many new opportunities to develop rich and significant learning experiences for students of all ages. It will be unfamiliar, and in the case of teaching about international human rights completely uncharted, territory for most elementary social studies teachers. It won't be easy even for some social studies specialists to move in this direction, but with exemplary books like *The American Way* (Branson & Coombs, 1978) and publications like the Center for Global Perspectives' *Intercom,* at least it appears it can be done.

REFERENCES

Adelson, J. The political imagination of the young adolescent. *Daedalus,* 1971, 4, 1013–1050.

Adelson, J., & O'Neil, R. P. The growth of political ideas in adolescence: The sense of community. *Journal of Personality and Social Psychology,* 1966, 4, 294–306.

American Political Science Association Committee on Pre-Collegiate Education. Political education in the public schools: The challenge for political science. *PS Newsletter of the American Political Science Association,* 1971, 4(3).

Anderson, H. R. (Ed.). *Approaches to an understanding of world affairs.* Washington: National Council for the Social Studies, 1954.

Branson, M. S., & Coombs, F. S. *The American way.* Boston: Houghton Mifflin, 1978.

Buergenthal, T., & Torney, J. V. *International human rights and international education.* Washington, D.C.: National Commission for UNESCO, 1976.

Easton, D., & Dennis, J. *Children in the political system: Origins of political legitimacy.* New York: McGraw-Hill, 1969.

Easton, D., & Hess, R. D. The child's political world. *Midwest Journal of Political Science,* 1962, 6, 229–246.

Education for understanding in American schools. Washington, D.C.: Association for Supervision and Curriculum Development and National Council for the Social Studies, National Education Association, 1948.

Kenworthy, L. S. *Introducing children to the world in elementary and junior high schools.* New York: Harper, 1956.

Long, H. M., & King, R. N. *Improving the teaching of world affairs: The Glens Falls story.* Washington, D.C.: National Council for the Social Studies, 1964.

Mitsakos, C. L. A global education program can make a difference. *Theory and Research in Social Education,* 1978, 6, 1–15.

Programs and Projects for International Understanding. New York: American Association of Colleges for Teacher Education, 1956.

Shane, H. G. International education in the elementary and secondary school. In *The United States and International Education* (NSSE Yearbook, Vol. 68, No. 1). Chicago: National Society for the Study of Education, 1969.

Sigel, R. S. *Learning about politics: a reader in political socialization.* New York: Random, 1970.

Torney, J. V., & Morris, D. N. *Global dimensions in U.S. education: The elementary years.* New York: Center for Global Perspectives, 1972.

Washburne, C. *The world's good, education for world-mindedness.* New York: Day, 1954.

REFERENCE NOTE

1. Fox, T. E. The treatment of social conflict in social studies textbooks for grades three, five, and nine. Unpublished doctoral dissertation, Stanford University, 1972.

Bringing It Together

There are many ways to approach the papers in this section and the ideas developed here. But perhaps the most useful for our purposes is to tease out the assumptions about the nature of childhood and the world of the child which should guide law and humanities program development.

The basic assumption is that law and humanities programs are most relevant to that aspect of childhood which can be characterized as the political/legal world of the child. There appear to be three general observations about the nature of the political/legal world of the child which are especially useful to developers and other educators. These are: (1) The political/legal world of the child is pregnant with a rich and varied array of problems, issues, and experiences related to law and humanities. (2) The political/legal world of the child is influenced by developmental factors. (3) The political/legal world of the child is influenced by sociocultural factors. Each of these observations is elaborated on here:

1. The political/legal world of the child is pregnant with a rich and varied array of problems, issues, and experiences related to law and humanities.

This political/legal world of the child is comprised of two grossly distinguishable dimensions. One dimension is the world of private or informal law and politics as encountered in such settings as families, playgrounds, and classrooms. The other dimension is the world of public or formal law shared with adults. It is the world of stop signs, police officers, warnings on medicine bottles, and restrictions on activities in parks and other public places.

The early experiences children have in both the informal and formal legal structures influence the ways they can and will respond to parallel situations as adults. Children continually ask questions about fairness and equity. They make and attempt to enforce or change rules. They exercise, challenge, or acquiesce in authority. They invade and respect privacy. In this society in particular, children grow up working through problems of property rights and responsibilities. The types of guidance—or lack of it—children have while confronting these problems are critical for society's future well-being. We cannot afford to wait until youngsters are through the elementary grades to introduce law and humanities programs into the curriculum. By that time, children have already formed opinions and perspectives relevant to such study. If they are left to their own devices, much of this prior learning may be negative. At the very least, leaving them to their own devices is simply a waste of a wonderful opportunity. A far more constructive approach would be to consciously structure learning experiences relevant to the children's everyday experiences with fairness, authority, privacy, property rights and responsibilities, equity, etc. And, as these authors and others repeatedly remind us, such learning experiences must develop skills as well as knowledge while handling responsibly any relevant values issues.

2. The political/legal world of the child is influenced by developmental factors.

The political/legal world of the child is "constructed" by children. That is,

104

children see and experience a political/legal world that is different from that which adults see and experience. Furthermore, the political/legal world of the child changes over time, reflecting changes both in children's social experiences and in their level of cognitive and moral development as they mature.

Many theoreticians and researchers have expended a great deal of time and energy attempting to describe accurately these processes of growth and development. These people and others have expended equal and even greater amounts of time and energy determining the implications and significance of the described processes and patterns of development.

Anyone faced with the practical task of curriculum development and implementation in law and humanities for young children will do well to become acquainted with at least the major works in this area. Armed with this information and range of insights, one can then make informed, reasoned judgments in selecting, adjusting, and applying aspects of appropriate theories to the task at hand. In some cases, in relation to a specific problem, perhaps the Kohlbergian-Piagetian perspective of stages of moral-cognitive development would be most useful. For another problem or task, insights from the work of the social learning theorists might be most useful, while for yet another task, aspects of both perspectives might be called for. What we are implying is that the social education of growing, developing young children in a complex, pluralistic, democratic society is a challenging task best met with a full arsenal of information, theories, perspectives, and insights.

3. The political/legal world of the child is influenced by sociocultural factors.

The political/legal world of the child is embedded in and reflects a larger culture. The child's cultural universe, like the cultural universe of adults, is multileveled. One level is the micro-culture of family, neighborhood, ethnic group, and class. This micro-culture shows marked variations along ethnic, racial, social, and class lines. The other level is the macro-culture of the larger society. It is the culture of large business firms, law offices, public bureaucracies, and the mass media. Increasingly, the macro-culture which children experience is global in scope and scale.

Any viable, responsible curricular/educational effort must take into account both these cultural levels and prepare children to function effectively and constructively across levels. Law and humanities programs are drawing from a resource base which has strong potential for achieving this goal.

Schools and
Schooling

An Introduction

The topics addressed in these papers are intended to be suggestive—certainly *not* definitive—of the aspects of schools and schooling that need to be considered when introducing law and humanities topics into the curriculum. The approaches to law and humanities which are outlined are also suggestive. We have tried to treat a few key aspects of the setting and the subject which knowledgeable observers would consider critical (but *not* exhaustive) and to treat them in ways that could be fruitfully modeled in further exploration. These authors focus on dimensions of the formal curriculum, the informal curriculum, instructional strategies, and factors outside the school setting that affect children's learning. Among the observations and recommendations that recur in several of these papers are the following:

1. The knowledge, attitudes, and competencies developed through sound instructional strategies focusing on law and humanities are essential to a pluralistic democratic society; therefore, schools should assume responsibility for making these an integral part of the curriculum.
2. Law and humanities permeate both the informal and formal curricula of elementary schools. Therefore, teachers must be aware of and understand these themes so they can, as Don Bragaw advocates, "recognize those themes in *any* lesson, in *any* subject, and in *any* classroom situation"—and, we would add, *grasp* these teaching/learning opportunities.
3. It is possible and preferable to infuse law and humanities into existing curricular areas rather than attempt to squeeze another subject area into an already overcrowded curriculum.
4. The humanitarian democratic ideology that undergirds this law and humanities thrust dictates that both the formal and informal curricula help all children develop esteem for themselves together with a sense of sociocivic responsibility.
5. The informal curriculum offers many opportunities to capitalize on the fact that young children learn by doing and by observing and modeling the behaviors of significant adults in their lives.
6. Many of the vital issues and principles associated with law and humanities are effectively explored and grasped by children as they participate in decision making, conflict management, and other governance activities.
7. Children pick up information and attitudes about law and humanities issues outside the school setting. This learning needs to be critically assessed and appropriately accommodated in planning and providing school learning experiences.

108

Law-related Education and Elementary Social Studies Programs

Donald H. Bragaw

Social studies seems to be a particularly appropriate entry point for law and humanities, but Don Bragaw identifies two major and, perhaps, related roadblocks: (1) an already overcrowded curricular agenda in which social studies gets short shrift, and (2) the current "back-to-basics" movement. In spite of this, he argues, law and humanities can become an integral part of the entire elementary curriculum—not just the social studies strand—if teachers have a firm grasp of the principles and issues. This argument is based on the premise that both the formal and the informal curricula already contain much law-related content. And where it doesn't already exist, there are natural entry points. Bragaw demonstrates that sensitive and knowledgeable teachers can, for example, teach law and humanities content simply by focusing on the content in basal readers while developing reading skills. They can teach such law-related skills as conflict management by appropriately handling classroom and playground disputes. Without heightened awareness and understanding of the basic concepts and reasoning skills associated with law and humanities, teachers will not grasp these opportunities and the potential will remain unfulfilled. But with such awareness teachers can provide rich learning experiences.

Being a juror was a terrible thing . . . I'm not smart and I'm not educated, and I don't know if it's right to put a person like me in that position of being the judge. It was awful. I had to think like I've never thought before. I had to try to understand words like justice and truth. . . . If it hadn't been for the foreman of the jury I don't know what we would have done. He didn't finish high school, you know. . . . why do they make people like us the judges?— quoted by Victor Villasenor in Jury: The People v. Juan Corona.

"Infusion" in social studies or any other curriculum area is best accomplished when it is the teacher who is "infused." Infusion units come and go. Teachers whose consciousness has been raised and skills and knowledge increased go on until retirement. Effective law-related in-service education programs must provide teachers with greater knowledge of such major concepts as justice, equality, and liberty, and they must develop teachers' reasoning skills. Teachers are rarely exposed to this type of education in their preservice

Donald H. Bragaw is Chief, Bureau of Social Studies Education, in the New York State Education Department. The department is in the process of producing an elementary law studies guide.

training. Much of what this paper proposes depends on such heightened teacher awareness and knowledge.

The first problem faced by any movement trying to infuse itself into elementary social studies at the lower levels (K–3) is to find social studies as a regular part of the social program—despite the illusion of its existence in local district or state prescribed curriculum guides and text materials.

At the intermediate levels, when content takes on its more formidable role, the afternoon social studies lesson (social studies is never the day's opener!) is often an arduous exercise in reading, and then responding to chapter-end questions (which may or may not be discussed). The role of social studies is as a soporific, or at best a palliative, for restless or exhausted physically exercised or "lunched-out" students. Indeed, elementary social studies is not considered basic to the majority of school district programs; it is not considered by most teachers, administrators, teacher education programs, or parents as part of the "basic skills"; and strong evidence exists that even the national organization espousing social studies education has surrendered to other subjects at the elementary level.

Education budgets at all governmental levels do not recognize citizenship training as a basic. Even patriotism, long the blind and powerful master of social studies, no longer has the power of bygone times—and rightfully so, considering the recent political and legal examples of its dominion.

It is not hard to understand why existing law-centered projects with major elementary segments create and publish their own K–6 curriculum guides, lessons, and materials which may exist apart from any other so-called social studies program. It is their commercial hope that such materials be adopted whether or not a regular social studies program exists. Elementary-oriented law education demonstrators of the last 5 years have gone to great lengths to create frequently fascinating action lessons (modules, units, etc.) which are largely outside the regular program presently defined as social studies in most schools.

The introduction and, occasionally, infusion of law-related education into a confused or even absent elementary social studies picture may reawaken awareness of the need for a better approach to citizenship education. Such an approach should constitute the entire framework of an elementary school's program. If we must go through the back door—using reading, for example—then let us unashamedly do so. But let us suggest further, and intrude ourselves into the front parlor.

This paper can only be suggestive, and I have chosen to deal with several selected topics in a superficial manner to point up areas needing concentration. Not adequately detailed here, and subject to critical evaluation, is my very broad perspective of citizenship as social conflict, and the correlative view of citizenship/law education as due process at all levels of the curriculum (Coser, 1956).

It is not too much to suggest that the law-related education movement's main contribution to elementary and secondary education is not law, per se, but the clear recognition that the emphasis in social studies must be on the first word of that term: *social*. Social studies should focus on people's relationships to society and how those relationships constitute conflicting claims. Law and legal processes can serve as a major way to highlight and attempt to resolve such conflicts. Social conflicts. Social conflict must, however, be accepted as a positive force in people's lives, unlike the view of it as negative and violent which even today pervades civic thinking.

In like manner law must be seen as positive, enabling, protective, and useful. From the earliest school experiences one of the main emphases must be on increasing students' civic skills: reasoning, and social interaction and conflict-resolving skills foremost among these. Where content is emphasized, the ultimate achievement would be greater attention paid to, and an increased understanding of, the concepts of justice, liberty, equality, property, and power and the conflicting claims to each of these which is the essence of social life. (Long conversations with Isidore Starr and reading in his works have convinced me that these five concepts govern not only law-related education, but citizenship as a whole.)

This paper will suggest several premises as bases for the "infusion" of law studies into elementary social studies:

- Social studies is both "content" and socialization in elementary programs; it should be the pervasive subject and guide to *all* activities, formal and informal, hidden and revealed, and its motivating nature should be found in human behavior, and in social conflict.
- Infusion of law studies can occur only when teachers are conscious of, and acquainted with, basic themes and concepts of law-related/civic education; the teachers must begin to recognize those themes in *any* lesson, in *any* subject, and in *any* classroom situation.
- Reading is not neutral. Students increase their reading skills only when the reading has meaning, and major meaning areas have to do with law-related/civic conflict factors.
- A major goal of all law studies is to increase reasoning skills—which eventually can be formalized in certain situations to "legal reasoning." The process is not unlike other social studies designs already presumably existent in school programs. The program should not be law *qua* law, but how people interact and resolve their points of conflict: law is one means to do that.
- In K–3 programs the concentration must be on infusing law and humanities into the classroom, not just into a specific subject. In levels 4–6 this same emphasis should be continued, but specific law-focused units and materials relating to social conflict could be introduced where levels of abstract thinking are higher.

More than Just Social Studies

Because the elementary curriculum tends to be 20-minute doses of a lot of things—with heavier doses of reading and mathematics—it may be best to attempt to get teachers (and curriculum writers, materials producers, publishers, et al.) to accept into their thinking and acting patterns major law/citizenship themes which, while presumably "social studies" in nature, are really pervasive civic ideas which encompass all "content" areas *including* social studies. This would assure that even if "formal" social studies is not taught every day, law/civic education ideas would still be incorporated into the day's work.

This suggests a greater infusion framework than just "law studies." It suggests that such themes govern not only content but classroom and school governance and, in general, greater civic competence in a total environment. I am not suggesting 12 themes for first grade and 12 others for each successive grade, nor do I have a definitive listing. But one might include, though not be limited to, the following:

1. Rules and laws influence our daily lives.
2. Rules and laws can encourage fairness and help settle disputes.
3. Conflict creates a need for rules and laws.
4. Rules and laws may vary from setting to setting/situation to situation.
5. Rules and laws protect people, property, and ideas.
6. Rules and laws are developed through interaction of persons as individuals or in groups.
7. Laws provide for the needs of people.
8. Rules and laws reflect a society's values.
9. We ourselves, and others, help make sure that we follow the laws we make.

I do not mean to suggest that these are simplistic, or necessarily easy to deal with in reality. I do suggest that teachers, given some understanding of these themes and their application to what they are teaching and having students learn, will tend to point these up with greater care as they encounter them in books, materials, and life situations. It should be further noted that such themes are not totally alien to most teachers; what tends to be alien is their understanding of the nature of conflict and law. What is needed is that these themes, as they relate to social conflict, be emphasized in in-service courses, materials, texts, etc. Because elementary teachers rely more heavily on teacher guides than do secondary teachers, every attempt should be made to have writers and publishers emphasize these themes in all of their aids to teachers.

Tying Legal Content to Reading

Reading is not a neutral decoding process; even McGuffey's readers were not content eunuchs. The books that children learn to read by are content oriented—most of them with greater "social studies" content than assigned social studies texts. Seldom do elementary teachers pursue the content, whatever it may be. They are trained not only to operate in 20-minute time segments, but also to be content separatists: "We will 'do' social studies this afternoon (if we get to it!) from 'the' social studies book."

It is not necessary to infuse law studies *into* reading, for it is already there, along with other social studies, like a rich untapped motherlode. The thematic approach suggested above would not only help alert teachers to the broader virtues of the basal readers, but would also help learners realize the real purpose of reading.

Few basal or supplementary readers, or library books, are without redeeming law content. The essence of all literature is to deal in some way with human behavior—even when a story is told through animal metaphor; and behavior generally involves in some way the previously cited Starr pentateuch: justice, equality, liberty, property, and power, and the conflictive nature of each. What is needed is a resource to accompany such books/texts to help teachers identify clearly the "law-relatedness" of the stories. A law studies concordance should be developed for each publisher's basal reader series, and a crash effort made to assist librarians in the same manner with easy cross-referenced guides to "law" in children's books. Such a concordance would include such topics as: What key social conflict is involved? What major concept? What law elements? It should also provide cues to follow-up activities of a law/civic nature.

Because the basic themes and concepts in the stories deal with human behavior, such stories offer a galaxy of opportunities for follow-up activities. Stop the story before the ending and have students develop and consider alternative endings through role playing, drawings, or paintings, puppet or real theater enactments, or additional stories.

Each of these reading situations could be explored by a "legal reasoning" process. Returning to the story's ending, after one or another of the above activities, would provide the teacher with an opportunity to say: "The author of the story chose to end the tale by.... Why do you suppose she/he did this? Let's compare it to other possible endings." Students would be encouraged to return to the story and other sources—their own created endings—to check evidence, issues, arguments, and logical thought. Whenever possible, class/real-life analogies would provide a transference of learning not offered by the story alone.

For example, in "The Magic Rings," Pat and Harriet send away for an advertised special: magic rings (Fay, Ross, & La Pray, 1974, pp. 39–61). When the rings arrive they are disappointed to find that both rings are damaged or broken. Each ring was to have a whistle attached. A friend temporarily "solves" their problem by putting Harriet's good whistle on Pat's good ring. The resulting "magic ring" turns out to be a dog whistle and neighborhood dogs come scrambling. Now that is the book's version. But let us return for a minute to the point in the story when the pair discover both rings deficient.

■ What is the situation?
■ What if you (your parents) order something and it arrives broken or damaged?
■ What can a person do? (What are your rights under the circumstances?)
■ What is the responsibility of the company?
■ Are there any laws involved?
■ What are some ways to deal with the situation?

The consumer conflict/law involved in this story is made to order for discussion, for role playing (transfer the scenario to a local store), for varied story endings, for "add to's": What about a large item like a piano? What if: The company refuses to replace the rings? The store manager accuses you of breaking the rings after leaving the store, or after they arrive at your house? What is "civically" correct? To accept the rings as they arrived and try to repair them, or return them to the sender?

The wealth of social studies (in the guise of law studies) in this one story could sustain a week's social studies' program: problem identification, hypothesizing, valuing, and resolution; giving opportunities to think more deeply about justice, property, power. This is dependent, of course, on the teacher's personal adequacy, and/or publisher's (or other) assistance. Introducing such elements as consumer complaint agencies, lawyers, and courts (reconcilers of conflict) is not beyond the reach of elementary school children. The teacher, however, must either have some basic consumer knowledge and know what action may be taken under the law, or have access to such expertise. This story would help develop the theme of protection of individual interests as well as the theme of laws being used positively to obtain or regain property or redress grievances. This incident also allows the basic legal reasoning elements to be pointed up: What are the facts? What are the issues? What are the arguments? What are the possible solutions/decisions?

If this is true of basal readers, the rich resources in the library are almost boundless. For example, Bernice Myers's delightful tale of *The Apple Wars* (1973) deals with property rights and extends the idea to dealings between kings/nations. Again, it is not reading or language arts but "life," and life consists of many occasions of social conflict. Reading is social studies; social studies is reading—but only when recognized and utilized as such.

In the law studies movement let us not be guilty of continuing the unnatural separation of reading skills from reading content. Some library stories like the above have already been tapped by filmstrip makers and filmmakers. The key,

though, is in helping librarians and resource center people become alert to various stories' potential and to the nature of social conflict. We must provide more than annotations in library lists if the law education effort is to go beyond other "movements."

Law studies cannot assume teacher/librarian knowledge, time, and desire; we must provide detailed keys to the use of stories, and encourage their translation into imaginative audiovisual and tactile materials and activities. (I want to express my deep indebtedness to the work of Nancy Wyner, Judy Wooster, and Harriet Bickelman, who have used children's literature for law-related lessons.) If we are to make progress, basal readers must be seen as the key to this infusion area; and law studies at the elementary level should begin to encourage the development of special readers. In such readers, both social conflict and law could be treated positively.

Overcoming the Textbook Blahs

A brief word about social studies textbooks. Present texts tend to be descriptive, expository, or broad antiseptic narratives. Seldom do they involve human behavior except by implication. Thus, grade 1 "family" books—so much better now in their multicultural case studies approach—tell about six or eight families, and students are encouraged to make contrasts and comparisons and, one hopes, come to realize that all families desire and seek much the same kind of well-being the world over. While expressing and encouraging many good "new social studies" concepts and skills, most texts remain nonconflictive and therefore do not develop the reasoning skills or have the conceptual impact that law studies could promote. Again, as with reading texts, some kind of teacher's guide or supplement, or special story collections to foster the ideas, must be provided (see Fox & Hess, Note 1).

One way to overcome a certain amount of the textbook blahs is through a device called a "Law Walk." Adapted from the "Mind Walk" activity, it is an attempt to help students recognize how much and in what ways law touches their lives.

One of the "natural" activities pursued by elementary teachers is the nature walk: the leaf-collecting walk, the small-creepy-crawlers walk, the seasons walk, etc. These frequently result in the building of science and language arts facts, observation/experience charts, art activities, etc. Translated into a law-related activity, such a walk could be a central activity for K–6 programs in social studies which would go beyond subject matter per se. It would also have the advantage of adapting a known activity to an "unknown" or alien context—a key to learning.

In the early grades, for example, a class could take a "safety walk," observing classroom windows and doors, hallways, exits, fire extinguishers, custodian's office, the front office telephone and its emergency numbers, etc., and outside the school, fire hydrants, firehouses, etc. Such walks might make the annual "trip to the firehouse" a more rewarding experience. Then, using the experience charts, the teacher would have a base to explore such ideas as:

■ There is a law which says doors in all public place must open out. Why?
■ There is a law which says we should practice escaping. Why?
■ Why do we have these laws?
■ Do these laws help us? How?

Law(s) can thus be related to the known, and be seen as positive: as resolving difficult issues of the rights of door owners and the rights and safety of people. With the increasing television sophistication of children, it is not too much to ask them to think about what action could be taken if doors in a school or another public place (stores, etc.) do not open *out* but *in*. The basis would thus be laid for helping students understand the legal means of bringing about change—a theme worthy of more than one lesson. Such a project would also encourage greater reasoning skills. Should such an example of safety violation be revealed, it could even motivate a civic action project to bring about correction. Such a project is well within the capability of the elementary grades (New York State Education Department, 1976). The imaginative teacher can be helped through this model to adapt it to other areas of the curriculum, contemporary and historical.

The "Basics" of Citizenship

What training does it take to be a juror? The same question might be asked of any citizen, or legal person. While the "back to basics" movement in citizenship centers on a "return to" the institutional-structural aspects of government and the court system, the juror in the *Corona* case cited at the beginning of this paper identified the more crucial elements that she needed in order to operate as a citizen sitting in judgment on other citizens: the thinking processes and an understanding of the nature of justice.

While all experiences have some law content, most law-related education in elementary and secondary schools might well focus on legal/civic socialization elements (Tapp & Levine, 1974). Indeed, those elements should be considered as fundamental to all school programs, and within those programs social studies should assume a major role. Programs should emphasize reasoning, social interaction, and conflict-/problem-resolving skills which encourage participation and mutual cooperation among students/citizens. Such skills should be looked upon as developmental and sequential. We cannot give jurors a full law course, but we can provide training and experiences in skills which will help them reason and interact with others so as to grapple more ably with justice.

Can young students (K–6, ages 6–11) begin to develop "legal reasoning" (Tapp & Levine, 1974)? I believe they can in terms of learning to think logically and apply reasoning to areas such as problem solving, conflict resolution, and valueing. Such "legal" reasoning includes:

■ Identifying the facts;
■ Determining the issues;
■ Developing the arguments;
■ Weighing the facts, issues, and arguments;
■ Reaching a decision.

This is a process fully compatible with and incorporating cognitive skills already associated with social studies and stressed by most current materials and text writers. (i.e., Chapin & Gross, 1973; Newman, 1977; Winston & Anderson, 1977):

■ Identifying the problem (conflict, value dispute, decision needing to be made);
■ Hypothesizing;
■ Gathering data;
■ Evaluating data/weighing evidence against hypotheses;
■ Reaching a solution/decision in light of considered consequences.

The problem-solving/conflict-resolving pattern in the elementary program could be incorporated into most topics in content areas at all levels (e.g., water and desert living; family meeting needs; New England settlers surviving severe weather; establishing government in early river valley civilizations). The use of legal reasoning can only be developed when materials dealing with such topics focus on behavioral case studies—increasing in sophistication at each level—which involve a person or persons in conflict with each other or with their society.

Such conflicts could include: early claims to an oasis by one individual who prohibits others from using the water; unequal division or theft of food from a common storehouse in a New England colony; father/mother loses a job and needs to feed the family; a Babylonian farmer diverts irrigation water away from his neighbors land to his own land. Students could deal not only with the basic "legal" reasoning steps involved, but with the concepts of justice, liberty, etc., localized in time and place as well as comparatively.

The areas in curriculum or text series that could present individuals coming into conflict with other individuals, groups, or the government are potentially numerous. Most of the current curriculums and texts, however, are still uninvolved with human behavior and detached from reality. A fourth-grade text which, while extolling the achievement of an Alexander Graham Bell, also dealt with the legal battle waged by Albert Meucci to challenge Bell's claim would make history exciting and real. It would also provide a magnificent opportunity to deal with the theme of protecting a claim to an idea or property (patent and copyright law). Some of the best 1960s project materials still in prominent use are those incorporating the jurisprudential approach, such as the Public Issues Series, Xerox Education Publications, Columbus, Ohio. James Shaver's *Public Issues Program* (1970), while more complex in execution, had a similar reasoning model as its base. The key to these publications was that people were involved and often in conflict with events; people had to work themselves out of real situations.

Progressing from such curriculum skill situations as those involving people or groups in dispute over law can provide stimulating lessons. But the greatest relevance to smaller children, and where we should be encouraging greater reasoning powers, is in concrete everyday classroom occurrences. Experiences such as establishing class rules and responses to class incidents promote the process of discussion and argumentation, which can not only bring about recognition of the need for rules, but initiate the kind of citizen reasoning and action which a rational society presumably desires.

The process requires occasional expenditures of time over an extended period to allow the rules/laws to emerge from experience, over time, as they do in adult society. Students entering a classroom for the first time with rules/laws already posted by the teacher encounter authoritarianism, not democracy, and come to experience a sense of citizen hopelessness about law. Recognition by the class, individual students, and the teacher that rules once made are also subject to change—and occasionally to be eliminated—should be a normal occurrence.

When developed, the rules, prominently posted, and always written in positive, clear language, should reflect both the individual's *and* the society's interests. Class meetings that are real decision-making sessions concerned with such matters as field trips, animals in the classroom, interest corners, chores, etc., in which the class develops a real stake in its achievement and possible failure, are time consumers but citizenship builders. Whenever disputes arise about any issue in the class, time must be taken to explore alternative solutions. These are social opportunities—if citizenship skill building is considered social studies.

From this base—and as each year's (K–6) experience becomes more developed and responsible, and more formalized—it may also be possible to develop procedures for handling more difficult classroom problems, such as discipline problems which do not endanger others:

- Merrie doesn't carry out her classroom job.
- John takes a pencil from Kathleen's desk.
- Peter disobeys a playground rule.
- Sarah deliberately breaks a jar of paint.
- Jennifer writes on the bathroom wall.

All are citizenship occasions, involving social conflict, and each could help develop reasoning skills, procedures for resolving problems, and a better understanding of justice and liberty, etc.

To the degree possible, modified due process procedures might be encouraged. Problems could be handled in a manner similar to the processes of the adult justice system. Classes might proceed from group rule-making experiences (simplified to age level and maturity) to treating actual class rule violations or "problems" in a procedural manner, offering, in part, "training" for jury duty and for active citizenship. "Legal thinking" and "legal acting" might help avoid confrontational situations, and give students training in seeking alternatives and negotiating (Gallagher, 1977; Newman et al., 1977; Winston & Anderson, 1977). Adaptations of the following may provide more worthwhile content than any infused unit on community helpers and self-governing compacts at Cape Cod Bay:

1. Class discussion ("Town Meeting") using legal reasoning/problem-solving guidelines.
2. Investigating teams, made up of representative students (not elite, or chosen for their obedience, or other goody-goody qualities), who are called upon to investigate the classroom crisis for facts, issues, and arguments and present both sides to the class in expository form—using pictorial or role-playing representations where appropriate.
3. Mock trial experiences, built around reader stories, other literary sources, or social studies materials. These might be followed by simulated court hearings on classroom incidents. Both sides present arguments and facts to support their views. Eyewitness accounts are given through testimony. The teacher's role here must be to guide, and help students avoid falling into kangaroo court fallacies. What happens when two honest, good, and sincere people see the same accident with different eyes?
4. Lawyer/client relationship or student om-

budsperson system: one of a classroom's "chores" is to act as representative or go-between in cases where conflict arises between students or between student and teacher (or school). Observation of student in a tense classroom reveals that students frequently seek the intervention of others when an explosive situation occurs. Teachers tend to react less violently to the intervenor. There may be a key here to "legal" management of classroom behavior.

Beginning with minor incidents will increase both teacher's and student's acceptance of such justice-dealing situations. The teacher must always keep in mind the need to broaden and deepen the concepts of justice, liberty, equality, property, and power. Teachers and administrators, however, must expand content experiences and minor incidents to real experiences involving crucial decisions.

If, as in New York, one legislative mandate is that all schools shall provide instruction in civics and citizenship, we should reconceptualize citizenship as due process, both procedural and substantive. Students will gain skills to prepare them not only for jury duty, but for other citizen action as well. Perhaps we need to infuse law and law behavior into civics and citizenship, and recognize, finally, that the goal of social studies is citizenship understanding and civic action. History, geography, socioeconomic culture studies, etc., are all aiming toward better citizenship, and are not ends in themselves. So, too, with law education. To avoid being just another fad, law studies must not be seen as an end. Rather, it must be given the more modest role of contributing to better "juror preparation," toward better citizen skills, and toward allowing justice to be an everyday guiding force in our lives—not the sole possession of 12 angry people, or a hanging judge.

REFERENCES

Chapin, J. R., & Gross, R. E. *Developing social skills.* Boston: Little, Brown, 1973.

Coser, L. A. *The functions of social conflict.* Glencoe, Ill.: Free Press, 1956.

Fay, L.; Ross, R. R.; & La Pray, M. *Magic rings and funny things* (Level 5). Chicago: Rand McNally, 1974.

Gallagher, A. Negotiation, I and II. *Law in American Society,* 1977, 6(3, 4), 36, 39.

Myers, B. *The apple wars.* New York: Parents Magazine Press, 1973.

Newman, F. M., et al. *Skills in action.* Madison, Wis.: Citizen Participation Curriculum Project, 1977.

New York State Education Department. *Law related education through a community study.* Albany: Author, 1976.

Shaver, J. *Public issues program.* Boston: Houghton Mifflin, 1970.

Tapp, J., & Levine, F. Legal socialization: Strategies for ethical legality. *Stanford Law Review,* 1974, 27 (November), 1–72.

Winston, B. J., & Anderson, C. C. *Skill development in elementary social studies: A new perspective.* Boulder, Colo.: Social Science Education Consortium, 1977.

REFERENCE NOTE

1. Fox, T. E., & Hess, R. D. An analysis of social conflict in social studies textbooks (Final Rep., Project OEC 9-72-0007). Washington, D.C.: Office of Education, 1972.

Infusing Law and Humanities Content and Skills into the Elementary Language Arts Curriculum

Judith S. Stecher

Can law and humanities become an integral part of the elementary school curriculum? Can teachers find ways to slip it in easily and "naturally" without causing imbalance or dislocation in the existing curriculum? Judith Stecher answers "yes" to both these questions in her reflective analysis of the congruity between the goals, processes, and content of language arts and those of what she terms "law studies." The author solidifies her position further by outlining a scope and sequence design for a "law/language arts" curriculum at the conclusion of this paper.

The most cogent reason for infusing law-related content and skills into the language arts curriculum is the probability that the structures and functions of students' thinking will be improved. Law, no less an art of language than literature, merits consideration as a humanities component of a language arts program.

The law/humanities/language arts relationship is both relevant and timely. Elementary law study emphasizes the skills and symbols inherent in language. In fact, the recent movement for its inclusion is perhaps an attempt to restore the ethical and linguistic content lost to language arts curricula when the purposeful content of readers such as McGuffy's was replaced by the trivial content of many contemporary reading texts. Language arts curricula need retooling.

Whether elementary educators, the principle retoolers, will "infuse" law-related study depends on their perception of law study as a way to improve student reading. Although language arts consists of listening, speaking, and writing, as well as reading, it is to reading skills that public and professional attention is paid.

The relevance of law study becomes more apparent when language arts are perceived within the broader framework of communication com-petence rather than as ends in themselves. The distinction made by sociolinguists between speech (or talk) and language relates language to thinking and reenforces its communicative function. Even when language encompasses mental processes such as remembering, imagining, reflecting, and judging, a communicative intent is implied. Language always requires an audience even if that audience is oneself, as in thinking (Olson, 1977). Although law programs for elementary children frequently utilize the "talk" dimension, their objectives concern language development as a mental activity. Similarly, listening, writing, and reading are language based with a communicative function. The current effort to integrate law and language arts was recognized in 1916 by Dewey, who suggested the "wedding of free social inquiry to the art of full and moving communication."

Similar Goals and Skills of Law Study and Language Arts

Law study and language arts share the same goals: (1) interpretation of symbols (alphabet, headlines, traffic lights, etc.); (2) interpretation of documents (novels, Constitution, newspapers); (3) understanding of social reality (playground fights, drama); (4) provision for personal expression (diaries, law suits); (5) sharing of values (holidays); and (6) participation in group decision making and group action.

A position paper of the New York State Board of Regents (Note 1, 1971) stated: "the ultimate goal of reading education is people who can and do use reading for full participation in social and

Judith S. Stecher coordinates a right-to-read teacher training program. She developed a course in "Law and Elementary Learning" for the Education Department of Queens College, University of the City of New York, and directs a program in elementary law study designed for the Dalton School and modified for other independent schools.

civic life. There is no more important priority for education in New York State than adoption of such a program in every school."

The similarity of law and language arts goals is paralleled in the skill area. Reading comprehension requires (1) understanding explicit facts of a text; (2) understanding inferences implicit in the text; (3) understanding implications beyond the text. Starr has frequently mentioned almost identical elements as required elements in case study: (1) legal facts, (2) legal issues, and (3) legal opinion.

Reading comprehension and comprehension of a legal case do not seem to require dissimilar mental processes. "But," one educator sputtered, "isn't the print on legal documents too small for young children's eyes?" That educator's unspoken question may have been, "Is this appropriate for young children who are certainly not able to read cases?" A reasonable question that requires response. The language arts/law program does not propose that children's reading will be improved if they gain skill in reading law content, but rather that the content they do read in primary and elementary grades can be related to law concepts with significant consequences for their social and mental development.

Law Study and Reading

Although Moffett (1968) and other language arts curriculum developers have stressed that reading is an intellectual process, most classroom teachers emphasize the sounds of words and memorization skills without providing adequate opportunity for the K–6 child to think about content.

...the national pattern of high scores at the lower grades and lower ones at the upper elementary grades, suggest that reading comprehension activities cannot be postponed.

"We're finding it all over the place," said Roger Farr, a reading specialist at Indiana University, "but it's especially pronounced in the inner cities. We reviewed the scores in Cleveland two years ago, for example, and found that once you get above fourth grade the number of kids reading at grade level begins to decline. By the time you get to high school, you have a large number below the national average."

Educators also note that a major shift occurs at about the fourth grade level in the content of reading instruction. In the early years, reading instruction consists primarily of teaching students to read words they already know by sound. "You're essentially substituting written language for oral," said Thomas H. Sticht of the National Institute of Education.

Beginning in the upper elementary grades, the tasks become considerably more difficult, and students begin to encounter words, and ideas they do not already know. "It's the difference between learning to read and reading to learn," Mr. Sticht said. [*New York Times*, 1978]

The need to emphasize reading comprehension was confirmed by the Resnicks (Resnick & Resnick, 1977), who studied the efficacy of the current back-to-basics movement.

Although the claim is frequently made that a return to basics would improve our educational system, the consequences of such a program are not clear. Presumably, proponents of basic education want schools to stress skills of literacy and mathematics more than certain recent additions to the curriculum. This much is reasonable. But unless we intend to relinquish the criterion of comprehension as the goal of reading instruction, there is little to go *back* to in terms of pedagogical method, curriculum, or school organization. The old tried and true approaches, which nostalgia prompts us to believe might solve current problems, were designed neither to achieve the literacy standard sought today nor to assume successful literacy for everyone.... There is no simple past to which we can return. [P. 385]

Acceptable levels of literacy considered in terms of either goals or instructional strategies have reflected a society's religious and political objectives. Today's situation does not differ. Perhaps the unique contemporary element is the quickened pace and greater complexity of a democratic, striving society in which familiarity with symbols, chants, and TV slogans no longer constitutes communication competence. Specifically, reading requires more than the decoding of familiar content. Reading content and method must activate consciousness. Law study may provide an ideal paradigm for this critical instructional problem.

Law Study as Language Arts Content

One successful model that improved communication competence was designed by Paulo Friere. He improved the reading levels of adults in Brazil, Chile, and impoverished areas of New York City. He provoked communication by arousing the social consciousness of his students. He got them to talk about justice, police brutality, and police power. He taped their discussions and used the transcriptions for reading texts. The students who had started the program with reading levels of zero to second grade achieved fifth, sixth, and seventh grade levels quickly.

Friere (1973) attributed student achievement to the high motivation that resulted when the written texts referred to situations significant in students' own lives. "Just as important as learning to read was the growth of social consciousness and action. Learning to read was more than a step in education. It was a means of helping citizens of oppression to change their situation in an unjust society."

Student preoccupation with problems of justice is not unique to Friere's adult students. Piaget characterized childhood mental activity as a quest for justification. Cahn (1949) recommended it as a way to teach law:

Why do we speak of the "sense of injustice" rather than the "sense of justice"? Because "justice" has been so beclouded by natural-law writings that it almost inevitably brings to mind some ideal relation or static condition or set of perceptual standards, while we are concerned, on the contrary, with what is active, vital and experimental in the reactions of human beings.

Where justice is thought of in the customary manner as an ideal mode or condition, the human response will be merely contemplative and contemplation bakes no loaves. But the response to a real or imagined instance of injustice is something quite different; it is alive with movement and warmth in the human organism . . . not a state but a process, not a condition, but an action. [P. 13]

Justice is not the only topic of student concern. Any nursery school which permits verbal spontaneity reverberates with students' concern for each of the concepts of law categorized by Isidore Starr as justice, property, equality, liberty, and power. The children can be heard saying: "It's not fair." "It is so mine." "I had it first." "You're bigger." "Who sez so?" "You're not my boss." "I will so."

Children's conversations are filled with examples of real and imagined injustices that provide topics for a language-law program. In fact, the methods Friere used are reminiscent of early childhood experience charts based on children's own observations, written down by adults and then used as beginning reading texts by children themselves. The approach is called, of course, the language approach to reading. The progression in this system, as in Friere's, goes from personal metaphor to more general verbal symbols. The progression may serve to explain not only oral language acquisition, but also the developmental stages of writing competence, or reading comprehension, and of the acquisition of social concepts (Torney, Note 2). Therefore the scope and sequence of a law/language curriculum should probably develop the need to talk about social justice.

Infusing Law Concepts

One illustration of how a law-study/language program can accommodate itself to children's linguistic development might use an authority-justice concept. After children had become aware of the reason for rules, to take one example, and had expressed their feelings about rules, they would be ready to articulate some criteria for a rule. Second and third graders might collect school rules and write a rule book, taking into consideration the perspectives of all the people (and property) protected by the rule.

But could a rule book intended for use by an indigenous population also serve the needs of a more remote population, such as visitors, new students from other classes, other schools, other countries? Thus children would have to do a certain amount of perspective-taking distancing, or decontextualizing when *writing* the rules.

And finally, how does this rule book compare with other written (and unwritten) rule books from home, other schools, other governments? What are the dilemmas, problems, decisions, that "I," "we," "others" have to solve? How has law solved these problems in other times? (see Law and Youth Citizenship Project, in press). Such an activity views a child as an active information processor who can understand, transform, and select from a range of options in varying circumstances when making judgments. This view of the child remains valid both for law learning and for language learning. The Fischers' sledding episode (Fischer, Fischer, & Fischer, in this volume) is an excellent application of this perspective to law/humanities/language arts in elementary schools. Another excellent example was supplied by Moffett (1968) when children "talked out" and "wrote up" a stealing situation in school.

Development of Communication Competence

Law-related activities can intersect with, expand, clarify, and make significant established language arts programs. They can be initiated by children themselves or by teachers in connection with early childhood socialization, through peer discussion groups, during beginning reading lessons, as a dimension of children's literature, through specific word analysis, and by the staging of mock trials. These activities should however, correspond as closely as possible to children's own patterns of developing communication competence.

Children's competence in language arts seems to progress from spontaneous expressions requiring unique and idiosyncratic experiences to a more formal consideration of text.

One illustration of how children move from "talk to text" (Olson, 1977) may serve to clarify the process.

Initially, language (including mental acts such as imagining, reflecting, judging) is context dependent; that is, the meaning is obscured unless the audience is familiar with the elements of the speech act such as time, place, speakers, situation, and purpose. When a toddler says, "Mine," or "Down," for instance, the speech context must be known by the listener. Eventually, "text" as written language can be understood independent of context. An example would be the child's understanding of "red." At first, redness is not perceived

Table 1: Entry Points for Law/Humanities Study Using Basal Readers

Series	Type of Material	Reading Level	Concept of Law	Title
Heath	Basal reader	A	Equality	*How to Tell a Mother from a Father*
		A	Property	*How to Tell a Bird from a Boy; A Pet Is not a Pit*
		A	Power	*The Anger Book*
		B	Liberty	*I Don't Want to Go to School*
		C	Justice	*A Lesson for Mrs. Gomez*
Harper & Row	Basal reader	First	Contracts	*Stick to Your Bargains*
Phoenix Reading Series, Prentice-Hall, middle grades, remedial	Photographs and text	A	Environmental law; liberty	*Call of the Wild*
		A	Property, federal housing, participation	*House Wanted*
		B	Indians and the law	*Smoke Signals*
		B	Environmental law	*Down in the Dumps*
		C	Freedom of the press	*What's News*
Houghton Mifflin	First reader	. . .	Legitimate authority	*Signposts*

as distinct from the objects that are red, but eventually, after perceiving many red objects in connection with the spoken word "red," the word "red" evokes the color and can be understood independent of a specific context.

Although the "red" example is most appropriate to preschool language learning, the process of organizing thought by confronting ambiguous situations holds true for other ages as well. Primary and elementary school children need many opportunities for oral discourse and informal writing related to their own perceptions before they encounter communication in language that is formal or frozen as in a written form.

The bias of written language toward providing definitions, making all assumptions and premises explicit and observing the formal rules of logic produces an instrument of considerable power for building an abstract and coherent theory of reality.... Yet, the general theories of science and philosophy that are tied to the formal use of texts provide a poor fit to daily, ordinary, practical, and personally significant experience. Oral language with its depth of resources and its multitude of paths to the same goal, while an instrument of limited power for exploring abstract ideas, is a universal means of sharing our understanding of concrete situations and practical actions. [Olson, 1977, p. 278]

Law/Language Arts Curriculum

The scope and sequence of an experience-based law-humanities language arts curriculum might be developed as follows:

Level 1: prekindergarten–kindergarten. The most appropriate activities to begin with are prob-

ably the improvisations, "acting out," described by Moffett (1968):

Younger children ... seem to have to be themselves by being something else ... they wish to test out adult roles symbolizing powers they wish to have. They work out realities through fantasies and thus prefer the symbolic and ritualistic to the actual and original.... They are less interested in what they are—weak, fearful dependent—than in what they want to be—powerful, fearless, and self-providing. Sometimes they act out both roles at once by assigning to a toy or a puppet the weaker role and assuming the more powerful role themselves. Realistic role-playing, imitating various kinds of adults, may be both an assumption of power roles and also an effort to understand adults. [P. 36]

Any activity selected for this age group should enable children to express themselves in unique rather than standardized symbols. Archer's (Note 3) fantasy animal stories provide children with opportunities to encounter regulatory procedures. Moreover, she has provided children with individual modes of response to rules perceived as unfair.

An introduction to citizenship can come through informal decision making so that children can communicate their choices about allocations of time, space, materials, and work/play groupings. On a more formal basis they can be introduced to the conventional flag and allegiance rituals through first designing individual flags celebrating something about themselves—their birthdays, a family banner, a feeling flag, etc. This personal relationship to an expressive symbol can be expanded on a group basis by making curriculum collages or banners. One class in District 3 in Manhattan made a "math banner." The flag salutation need not be static. Patriotic expressions in the form of original dances, songs, and poems are both educationally appropriate and legally acceptable substitutes for what is usually a monotonous series of malapropisms and the worst language experience possible.

Level 2: grades 1–2. Law study can enliven and add depth to both reading lessons using basal texts to children's literature. Through teacher training and by use of supplemental guides, any basal reading series can be explored for law-humanities application. The illustrations cited in Table 1 have already been used by teachers using Dalton Law Study. The basal readers served as entry points.

Teachers can be provided with reading guides, complete with instructions for organizing small-group discussions, allowing for individual expression, organizing games, and introducing skits related to the content of the basal reader. The Dalton Law Program included teacher workshops and in-class consultation. At times remedial reading teachers have utilized individually designed work sheets for those children who have participated in law study and have been highly motivated to talk, write, and read about it. Don Bragaw's suggestion for basal reader use would extend this list provided that the author's purpose is not subverted to that of the social studies teacher.

Almost every elementary law program has included trade book use. Recommendations have ranged from the presentation of picture books to the use of fiction for dilemma discussions. Some examples of the books and the programs initiating their use are listed in Table 2.

Classroom experiences in role taking—that is, the ability to realize and respond to the perspective of another—are integral both to curricula concerned with communication competence (Flavell, 1968) and to law-humanities study. One of the most coherent strategies for teaching role-taking skills to primary grade youngsters was suggested by Flavell (1968), who modeled his communication competence curriculum along a continuum suggested by Piaget. The five skills identified are described below, along with children's books that would provide the role-taking experiences (Mansell, 1974):

1. *Existence of perspective of others:* Pooh and Piglet perceive what is to them a pile of twigs but to Eeyore, his house (A. A. Milne, *The House at Pooh Corner* [London: Methuen, 1956]).
2. *Need to recognize another's perspective:*

Sylvester needs to realize that lions, mean and hungry, like to eat donkeys (W. Steig, *Sylvester and the Magic Pebble* [New York: Simon & Schuster, 1969]).

3. *Predicting what information a listener needs in order to understand a situation:* the missing piece of a jigsaw puzzle (B. Shecter, *If I Had a Ship* [Garden City, N.Y.: Doubleday, 1970]).
4. *Maintaining one's own point of view intact but neutralized, while being aware of another's perspective:* impulse control, concentration (E. Arrizzone, *Wrong Side of the Bed* [Garden City, N.Y.: Doubleday, 1970]).
5. *Application framing and expressing the message that will persuade and/or inform the listener:* Berta describes a tree to a blind grandfather (A. Lindgren, *Christmas in Noisy Village* [New York: Viking, 1964]).

Level 3: grades 3–6. Two new elements can be added to the law/language program which supplement but do not supplant the individual experiences and group talk introduced in the earlier grades. The new elements consist of an introduction to the trial as an art of language and an intensive study of the language of law. The first element would simultaneously introduce concepts of justice and communication skill practice. The second would endeavor to increase vocabulary.

While the most familiar trials may be from *Alice in Wonderland* and the "Trial of Peter Zenger," the amusing *The Cats Stand Accused* (Townsend, 1961; see Stecher, 1978) and the historically interesting trials collected by Raskin and Raskin (1975) are also worth investigating for possible scripts. It is at this point that many elements of the trial can be introduced as reading comprehension exercises: identification of main conflict, sequencing episodes of a trial, examination of roles, identification of rationale for decison making, empathy for various perspectives.

Postman (1976) suggests that a trial presents us with a specific semantic environment in which "the witness is required to confine himself to *descriptive* statements ('Please keep your conclusions to yourself . . . and tell the court what you saw'); while the judge's sentences are most likely to be *prescriptive* ('I won't have any noise in this courtroom.'); the jury's evaluative ('We find the defendant, Mr. K., not guilty.'); and our greatest lawyers, such as Clarence Darrow, have always specialized in impressive *explanatory* sentences ('Mr. K. committed this crime, but we are all guilty for having been indifferent to the suffering that society has inflicted upon him.')."

While Postman admits to oversimplification, his apt use of courtroom talk describes *why* peo-

Table 2: Entry Points for Law/Humanities Study Using Children's Literature

Author	Title and Level	Law Topic	Classroom Use Suggested by
Adams, F.	*Mushy Eggs* (pre-K–2)	Equality/nonsexist	*Children's Literature: An Issues Approach* (Heath)
Aesop	*Fables*	Justice, etc.	Lincoln Filene Center for Citizenship and Public Affairs, Tufts University, Medford, Mass.
Andersen, H. C.	*The Ugly Duckling* (K–2)	Diversity: benefits and costs of being different	Law in a Free Society, Santa Monica, Calif.
Alcock, G.	*Turn the Next Corner* (primary)	Urban boy copes with father's imprisonment	*Children's Literature: An Issues Approach*
Brown, D.	*Someone Always Needs a Policeman* (primary)	Authority	New York State Education Bureau of Social Studies, *Living under Law*
Burch, R.	*Queenie Peavy* (5–6)	Personal growth within framework of criminal justice system	Child Study (New York) Annual Book Award
Carrol, L., adaptation	*The Trial of the Knave of Hearts* (4–6)	Justice	Lincoln Filene Center for Citizenship and Public Affairs
Clifford, E.	*The Year of the Three Legged Deer* (4–6)	Indians and justice	*Children's Literature: An Issues Approach*
De Paola, T.	*Strega-Nona* (primary)	Authority/justice	*Living under Law*
Distad, A.	*Dakota Sons* (5–6)	Friendship between a white boy and a Dakota Sioux	*Children's Literature: An Issues Approach*
Dr. Seuss	*The Cat in the Hat* (pre-K–2)	Lack of authority	*Living under Law*
Fox, P.	*Good Eathan* (primary)	Authority	*Living under Law*
Galdone, P.	*The Little Red Hen* (pre-K–2)	Justice	*Living under Law*
Goldreich, G. and E.	*What Can She Be* (pre-K)	Role: lawyer	Women's Action Alliance, New York
Hoban, R.	*Best Friends for Frances* (K–2)	Diversity: how different?	Law in a Free Society
Klagsbrun, F. (ed.)	*Free to Be You and Me*	Liberty	Women's Action Alliance
Lionni, L.	*Tico and the Golden Wings* (3–4)	Equality/conformity	Law in a Free Society
Raskin, J. and E.	*Guilty or Not Guilty* (4–6)	Historical trials; justice	Susan Davison Archer, YEFC
Townsend, D.	*The Cats Stand Accused* (4–6)	Cats stand trial for murder of a guinea pig	Dalton Law Program, New York
White, E. B.	*Charlotte's Web* (3–4)	Participation	Law in a Free Society
Winn, M. S.	*Shiver, Gobble and Snore: A Story about Why People Need Rules; The Thief Catcher: A Story about Why People Pay Taxes* (K–2)		Special Committee, YEFC
Yashima, T.	*Crow Boy* (primary)	Equality/diversity (rural Japan)	Women's Action Alliance
Zolotow, C.	*William's Doll* (pre-K)	Equality-sexism	Women's Action Alliance
Bishop, C.	*Five Chinese Brothers*	Trial	Dalton Law Program

ple talk: to inform, predict, explain, control, find out, judge, persuade, etc.

When the mock trial is over, experiences can be compared with those of contemporary adult models and with literary, historical, and television models. When these can be related to magazine and newspaper reports, elementary students are provided with learning experiences which reach beyond classroom walls.

A valuable evaluation tool is available utilizing videotape (or audio cassettes). When it is possible to tape a rehearsal, students are able to reflect on their own communication skills and at the same time teachers are provided with a language assessment. The tapes provide information about extensiveness of vocabulary; patterns of use of simple, compound, or embedded sentences; convergent or divergent questioning; correct use of referents; relevant subordination of ideas; ability to describe, recall, elaborate; ability to use language for a variety of functions: interpersonal, informative, persuasive, heuristic, etc. Bloom's *Taxonomy* provides one possible model (Bloom, 1956).

An important task of the elementary school teacher is to help students augment the 2,000-word vocabulary acquired (one hopes) from the first reading books to the 10,000 words required for high school work. This task cannot be accomplished by spelling tests and beginning dictionary skills only. Word study needs to go beyond features such as spelling and pronunciation. Words need to be related to each other in terms of their structure, which in turn is determined by their history and geography. Roots of words are no less fascinating than roots of families.

The language approach to literacy does not preclude disciplined word analysis. A semantic or meaning approach to vocabulary development seems more sensible than meaningless memorization. A law program can contribute to vocabulary development in at least two ways.

The first is an emphasis on semantic analysis and historical etymology. Semantic analysis is the study of word structure for the purpose of identifying similarities and differences between words. For example, the word "judge" can be used to demonstrate that the same word can have a nominative and predicative use, and that suffix, prefix, compound, and inflectional modification of the root yields *judgmental, judgment, judicial, adjudicate, judicious,* etc. One excited fifth-grade student derived the meaning of *prejudice* from just such word analysis. Semantic and etymological analysis not only develops key words identified with law but helps youngsters understand the logic of language through a discipline in which language is particularly logical.

Teachers are often amazed to hear children speak words considered "beyond them." We explain this by saying the word has meaning for the child. Perhaps what we ought to say is that the child has meaning for the word. The process of developing vocabulary through meaning was demonstrated recently when an elementary school child was furious that a notice of a canceled class had not been posted prior to the time that the class was to have met. She exclaimed, "That's ex post facto!" It is certainly not important for an elementary school child to add "ex post facto" to her basic vocabulary, but it is very important for her to know that language is a tool to express and evaluate social obligations.

Summary and Suggestions

Law-related activities, as we have seen, can intersect with, expand, clarify, and make significant established language arts programs. They can be initiated by children themselves or by teachers in connection with early childhood socialization,

through peer discussion groups, during beginning reading lessons, as a dimension of children's literature, through specific word analysis, and by the staging of mock trials. Teachers can feel reasonably well assured that the fusion of law-language programs will strengthen children's communication competence, particularly when the programs are consonant with children's language acquisition patterns, which develop along a continuum from "talk to text."

When innovative ideas proliferate for the pre-K–6 curriculum, educators who do adopt them rarely take the time to analyze and transform them. Too often, "infusion" becomes diffusion. The tendency of educators to paste one idea onto another in a meaningless collage can be destructive to the school, to the learners, and to themselves. It defies natural law, which suggests that new systems are created to accommodate new functions. Educators tend to "divide and conquer," amoeba-like.

In art, in dance, and in literature, new ideas are represented by new forms. Too often, in education a fully developed curriculum means only another workbook, another group of multiple choices with only one choice accepted as correct. A law program which would simultaneously develop the art of language and an exploration of law would rely on the language children bring to school. It is this form of language that the child must "transform" in order to progress from the stage of producing "utterances" to the reading of texts. A law-language program should reinforce this progression.

The program ideas, as well as the K–6 curriculum described in this paper, were derived from a linguistic learning model which places high value on the communication function of language. A law-related program intended to develop communication competence cannot be a footnote to the language arts curriculum. How, when, and why infusion occurs is a matter of rethinking, not merely of rescheduling, the elementary curriculum with respect to language learning.

REFERENCES

Bloom, B. S. (Ed.). *Taxonomy of educational objectives.* New York: McKay, 1956.

Cahn, E. N. *The sense of injustice.* New York: New York University Press, 1949.

Dewey, J. *Democracy and education.* New York: Macmillan, 1916.

Flavell, J. H., et al. The development of role-taking and communication skills in children. New York: Wiley, 1968.

Friere, P. *Education for critical consciousness.* New York: Seabury, 1973.

Law and Youth Citizenship Project. *Guidelines for an elementary law curriculum.* Albany: New York State Department of Education, in press.

Mansell, M. *Seeing the other point of view, elementary English*. Urbana, Ill.: National Council of Teachers of English, 1974.

Moffett, J. *A student centered language arts curriculum, grades K–6*. New York: Houghton Mifflin, 1968.

New York Times, January 11, 1978, B6.

Olson, D. R. From utterance to text: The bias of language in speech and writing. *Harvard Educational Review*, 1977, 47(4), 257–281.

Postman, N. *Crazy talk, stupid talk*. New York: Delacorte, 1976.

Raskin, J., & Raskin, C. R. *Guilty or not guilty*. New York: Lothrop, 1975.

Resnick, D. P., & Resnick, L. B. The nature of literacy: An historical explanation. *Harvard Educational Review*, 1977, 47(3), 370–385.

Stecher, J. S. *A time for law, a place for law*. New York: Dalton School, 1978.

Townsend, D. *The cats stand accused*. Boston: Houghton-Mifflin, 1961.

REFERENCE NOTES

1. New York State Board of Regents. Position Paper No. 12. Albany, 1971.

2. Torney, J. V. Child development, socialization and elementary political education (National Science Foundation Political Education Project, Working Paper). Unpublished manuscript, University of Illinois at Chicago Circle, 1973.

3. Archer, S. Workshop given at Dalton School, New York, October 1977.

Another view . . .

Infusing Law and Humanities Content and Skills into the Elementary Language Arts Curriculum

Margaret Stimmann Branson

This paper complements the previous by looking beyond the language arts curriculum and the elementary school. Margaret Branson gives an insightful overview of the current public debate about education in this country. Focal questions of this debate are noted, as well as possible reasons behind it. The author argues that infusing law and humanities into the elementary school curriculum has the potential not only for strengthening and revitalizing the curriculum but for meeting critical social needs.

Certainly suggestions, such as those made by Judith Stecher and others whose work appears in these pages, that law and humanities be infused in all of the subjects traditionally taught from kindergarten through eighth grade are to be applauded. In fact, the efforts currently being sparked by the American Bar Association to revitalize the elementary school curriculum could hardly have come at a more propitious time. Americans are involved in what may prove to be the most significant debate about the nature and purposes of education at all levels in which any people has ever been engaged. They are asking

themselves and each other some very simple but profound questions. Among them are these:

■ What knowledge, skills, and attitudes are essential for students who will come to maturity in the last quarter of the twentieth century and whose productive years will extend into the twenty-first century?

■ How can we introduce students to our common historical and cultural background without causing them to esteem less their own individual and group heritages?

■ How can we as a people continue to celebrate our diversity without losing sight of the shared goals and common values inherent in our democratic society?

■ How can curricula be devised which enable students to learn how to identify issues, clarify terms, differentiate facts from values, invoke the processes of reasoning, appreciate the consequences of alternative positions, and make wise decisions?

Margaret Stimmann Branson is Director of Secondary Education at Mills College and an Associate Professor of Education at Holy Name College in Oakland, California. She also serves as a curriculum consultant. She is the author of more than a dozen elementary and secondary social studies textbooks.

■ How can the experience of schooling help students learn to live their lives more humanely in an increasingly crowded, complex, and interdependent world?

When, Where, Why the Current Debate Began

Just when and where the current debate about the nature and purposes of general education was touched off is uncertain. Most people, however, tend to credit Harvard University with being first to embark on a full-scale reassessment of its core curricular requirements. Whether or not Harvard was first is unimportant. What is important is the fact that the nation's oldest and perhaps its most prestigious collegiate institution publicly acknowledged the need to reexamine itself. By doing so, it encourages others to follow suit. For that reason, a brief history of Harvard's continuing efforts at curricular reform may be instructive.

In Harvard's case, the dean of the faculty, Henry Roskovsky, acted as the gadfly. Dismayed by what appeared to him to be the chaotic condition of undergraduate education, Roskovsky shared his disquiet with others on the faculty. At a faculty meeting in late 1974, Roskovsky lamented: "At the moment to be an educated man or woman doesn't mean anything. . . . It may mean that you've designed your own curriculum; it may mean that you know all about urban this or rural that. But there is no common denominator. . . . The world has become a Tower of Babel in which we have lost the possibility of common discourse and shared values" (*New York Times*, 1976).

Roskovsky called for a reformation of undergraduate education. The faculty responded by naming some of its members to a Task Force on Core Curriculum, which Professor James Wright was asked to chair. It did not take him long to come to the conclusion that Roskovsky did indeed have good cause for alarm. Wright avowed publicly that "an educational nutritionist would say that we no longer are requiring a balanced diet."

Although Harvard's efforts have attracted worldwide attention, it certainly is not the only institution which has become concerned with the "educational diet" being offered students. Many state legislatures have. So, too, have increasing numbers of state and local boards of education, parent-teacher and citizen groups, and professional associations.

Unfortunately, discussions about what is or ought to be the nature and purposes of general education, particularly at the elementary and secondary levels, are not always as enlightened or as enlightening as they should be, given the seriousness of the present situation. Neither is participation in that discussion/debate as widespread as it ought to be, given the far-reaching consequences which are likely to result. Therefore, efforts such as those initiated by the American Bar Association are terribly important. It is to be commended for providing the forums and some of the leadership essential for healthy, informed discussion/debate among a variety of audiences concerned with the nature and purposes of general education.

Why the Time Is Ripe for Reassessing/Redirecting

All of the reasons why the time is ripe for reassessing, refocusing, and redirecting general education cannot be examined here in detail. Some of the most compelling reasons, however, are summarized below in staccato fashion.

■ There is widespread dissatisfaction among people generally with the learning achievements of students in the core areas of the curriculum.

■ That dissatisfaction has prompted many people to propose very simplistic solutions. On every hand, one hears cries about "getting back to the basics." Why politicians have made "back to basics" a rallying cry is perhaps understandable. Why educators—who ought to know better—often join in the chorus is less comprehensible.

■ Despite the veneration currently tendered the "basics," there is very little understanding of what they really are. Popular opinion holds them to be just reading, writing, and computing. And in deference to that opinion, increasing amounts of time are being devoted to them. One recent study showed that in northern California counties, for example, 70% of all in-class time now is being devoted to just reading and computing (Nalty, Note 1).

■ Research shows that attempts to teach skills alone or any skill in isolation are doomed to failure. Skills are interrelated. To be taught successfully, they must be related to the processes of problem solving, conflict resolution, and valuing.

■ Reading, writing, and computing are not "subjects" or "disciplines" which have content or concepts of their own. In order to teach those skills, teachers must "borrow" or depend upon the ideas and concepts generated by other areas of the curriculum. One must read about something; one must have something about which to write; one must compute for a purpose. From whence does substance —content or concepts—come? It comes, of course, from those studies which we label history, the social sciences, literature, law, music, art, philosophy, mathematics, and the sciences. Sadly, those are precisely the subjects which now are being neglected in the elementary schools.

■ Both experience and research remind us that skills are taught most successfully when they are natural outgrowths of attempts to answer the really consequential questions which concern each of us as human beings. Each of us must ponder for ourselves questions such as these: Who am I? How should human beings behave toward one another? Under what conditions should I as a member of a family, a citizen of a school, city, nation, or the global community, be loyal to and proud of my group and when should I be critical? What is the good life, and how can I live such a life?

Those questions and others similar to them are precisely the kinds of questions with which the law and the humanities are concerned. It stands to reason, therefore, that law and humanities ought to be at the very heart of the elementary school curriculum.

Why Inclusion of Law/Humanities Curriculum Is Critically Important at the Elementary School Level

What children learn and how they learn during their early years is probably more critical than what or how they learn subsequently. Indeed, one might say that the most unique feature of the elementary school is that it serves children at what is probably their "prime time." There is an abundance of research which corroborates the statements just made. Here—again in staccato fashion—are just a few of the more important conclusions reached by researchers:

In early childhood children begin to learn what styles of interpersonal interactions are rewarded by adults and by peers. Thus, siblings are urged to share with each other, and mothers and nursery school teachers set up norms for behavior by saying, "Wait your turn," and, "That's not fair." Experiences of this kind may lay a foundation not only for the development of personal morality (Piaget, 1965; Kohlberg, 1964) but for normative expectations of a political system. [Schwartz, 1975, pp. 230–231]

There is evidence that beginning about the age of seven, the child enters into a period of rapid perspective and role-taking. Middle childhood (before the onset of puberty) might even be called a critical period in attitudinal development since after this there is a decline in the malleability of attitudes. [Buergenthal & Torney, 1976, p. 106]

On the whole, children, particularly those between approximately 8 and 12 years of age, seem relatively open to new approaches to and information about foreign people; by the age of 14 they are less open. [Lambert & Klineberg, 1967]

Each individual builds up a repertoire of ways of obtaining satisfaction of his needs in the social context. Those that are perceived to have been successful are retained, and those that have not produced success are not. *By the time an individual approaches his early adult years, these modes of relating to the world are largely fixed.* [Renshon, 1974, p. 72]

Research findings such as those just cited are indeed sobering. They remind us that the elementary school years are too important to be squandered on mean pursuits or the minutiae of learning. They are indeed the very years during which the most critical questions of human existence must be addressed and during which norms for behavior are examined.

Next Steps

Given the desirability of infusing law-related, humanities-centered content in the elementary school curriculum, what means of persuasion or courses of action are open to concerned citizens? There are, of course, a number of possibilities. Instead of relying on just one or two, there ought to be simultaneous movement on a number of fronts. Each of those possible fronts needs more careful and complete exploration than can be afforded here. But for purposes of stimulating thought, the following suggestions are offered.

The first and most critical effort that needs to be made is that of taking the case for law-related, humanities-centered curricula directly to the many publics concerned with education. Several years ago, a little book appeared with the intriguing title: *How to Talk Back to Your Television Set.* That title might well suggest the advisability of beginning at once to:

■ "Talk back" to the propounders of simplistic slogans and programs.
■ Set the record straight, making it clear that there is no one sure, easy, quick way to educate all of the children of all of the people.
■ Disseminate broadly findings from research relevant to the teaching of skills and sources of content, being careful to see that the language used is jargon-free and comprehensible;
■ Insist on a balanced curriculum.
■ Remind people of the many statements of goals for education in a democratic society that have been made over the years. Those statements almost without exception constitute ringing endorsements of humane purposes.

A second effort might be made to increase opportunities for staff development and in-service training. While it is true that a number of law-related projects have been offering in-service training for several years, most teachers in this nation have not as yet been reached. Furthermore, it is probably safe to say that, thus far, only the most competent and open teachers have been reached. Such teachers generally are the ones who seek out opportunities for increasing their competence. Those who most need assistance generally do not.

Little has been done as yet in the area of staff development in the humanities for elementary teachers. More needs to be done to help teachers learn to use music, poetry, drama, and art to teach listening, speaking, reading, and writing and to explore law-related concepts.

A third effort which is essential is to increase the variety and availability of high-quality, immediately usable materials. Teachers in the elementary school receive many exhortations to incorporate law-related studies and the humanities into their day-to-day work with students, but they are poorly supplied with specific unit/lesson plans, imaginative textbooks, filmstrips, films, audiotapes, and trade books. Already overburdened, elementary teachers cannot and should not be expected to produce their own materials.

To increase the availability of suitable materials, educators ought to apprise publishers, particularly those who supply the major basal reading series, of their needs. They should encourage publishers to expand the law-related, humanities-centered content of basal readers. Further, educators should indicate the need for questions in the texts at the upper ends of the cognitive taxonomies and for suggestions for pupil activities which will further affective objectives.

Finally, they should insist upon materials which have global humanity-wide orientations.

REFERENCES

Buergenthal, T., & Torney, J. *International human rights and international education.* Washington, D.C.: National Commission for UNESCO, Department of State, 1976.

Lambert, W. E., & Klineberg, O. *Children's views of foreign people.* New York: Appleton, Century, Crofts, 1967.

New York Times, November 10, 1976, p. B4 L.

Renshon, S. A. *Psychological needs and political behavior: A theory of personality and political efficiency.* New York: Free Press, 1974.

Schwartz, S. K. Preschoolers and politics. In D. C. Schwartz (Ed.), *New directions in political socialization.* New York: Free Press, 1975.

REFERENCE NOTE

1. Nalty, D. Report on an unpublished study conducted by the Sacramento Area Council for Social Studies, 1977–1978. San Jose, Calif.: San Jose State University.

Nonverbal Tactics for Teaching about Law and the Humanities

Francisco Reynders

People—especially very young people—learn and express themselves through a broad range of modalities. But most schools in our society neither accommodate nor capitalize on this fact. Francisco Reynders, who has perfected the art of expressing himself and teaching others to express themselves through mime, has some provocative observations to make about the effects on children of various types of restrictiveness in schools. He sees the seeds of teenage trauma—indeed, of criminal behavior—cultivated, if not planted, in the formal educational structures of elementary schools. Drawing on his craft, the author sketches what might appropriately be called a "preventive" curriculum. It calls first and foremost for the development of a healthy *self*-discipline in which, as Reynders puts it, the mind and body work as one.

I am an artist by profession. As an artist, I try to educate myself and others in the common truths of life, so perhaps I am a kind of educator as well. And I spent 9 years of my life teaching mime and stage design at a small college in Oregon.

But the young people I worked with there happened to have already behind them 18 or 20 years of experience apiece. They had ideas of their own about education, and habits built up from years in the system.

Happily my present work often brings me in contact with the young children of America. Mime shows them a possibility in life their parents and teachers never, or rarely, thought of —creative expression achieved without uttering a single word, with the strictest discipline, with the whole body.

Let me tell you a little of what I have seen in our fifth graders.

I've seen them walking in straight lines in the halls of their schools. They are well dressed, clean and groomed. Bells ring at regular intervals, and as if by magic, columns of fifth graders move from class to gymnasium to cafeteria back to class, until yellow buses come and bring them back home.

In class they sit in neat rows facing the teacher. They are anchored in their steel chairs, and silence is the whip of discipline.

They behave well.

In the play yard they play the same games over and over again. They yell and scream with the same high pitch, and theirs is a sameness of vocabulary. Their bodies move in short uncoordinated movements. They're fine.

Their beautiful little faces chew rubber masses from cheek to cheek in the rhythm of their mothers' heartbeats.

They are all the same. They are good little soldiers responding to the discipline of the school.

Their interest in knives and pistols at play is artificial, no more. With the plastic weapons they act out their favored scenes and heroes from TV or motion pictures, with sound effects and all.

The girls rock their make-believe babies, prepare food, change diapers, play nurse, etc. They are playing "little mothers." Most of the girls know that they will grow breasts, and they hear rumors about menstruation.

They are healthy young children, it seems.

And that's my observation from the schools I have visited in the last 15 years, from Texas to Alaska, from New York to California, and all states in between.

Things change drastically when the fifth graders graduate into the teenage world.

They seem truly unprepared to face the physical and psychological surprises they encounter. Their bodies are changing. Their desires are changing. If they fail to gain perspective, survival seems impossible.

Education has become, for them, more compulsory than ever. They alienate themselves from learning, their parents, and themselves. Aided and abetted by ignorance, they create a no-man's-land for teenagers.

Francisco Reynders is Artistic Director of the Oregon Mime Theater. He and his company tour throughout the United States, performing before over 90,000 people per year.

The domain of too many teenagers is without intellectual stimulation or positive creativity. It is a primitive world, with its own borders, law, and heroes.

Teachers and school administrators have a small place on the periphery of this teenage society. Their guidance counts for little.

Dissidence and dissatisfaction stimulate the teenage world. Music, clothing, and drugs give it substance.

To American business, this world I have described is a most important part of our society. To maintain that world has become important, because there is profit in it.

As an observer, I cannot help but be fascinated with the teenage phenomenon. In a way, it is beautiful. From a theatrical point of view, the teenage world has spawned a pure form of tragedy—it is a keenly, passionately self-destructive world.

But this tragedy is too young and too painful. It is at the beginning of life, not at its maturity. My artistic involvement with theatrical possibilities is too selfish, and should not be a part of this paper.

Still, it is this that I think about when I start to devise my own curriculum for the happy fifth graders who may become unhappy, alienated teenagers.

As I see them, here are some of the problems:

1. Formal education produces a physical and spiritual imbalance in the young. The fifth graders need to be prepared to face the physical and psychological surprises they encounter later on in their development.
2. Most students do not understand why they are at school. A deep distance exists between student, teacher, and administration.
3. The growth of the educational process is interrupted by disciplinary rulings. A teacher uses half or more of the time in school to maintain physical order.

The problems of our educational system have pushed it into chronic chaos. Many teenagers have become defiant of teaching. Ignorance is a virtue. As the students get older, teachers find it more difficult to maintain control.

The common truths of our society also are made confusing by the way in which they are taught. I have examples.

The killing of human life, and of some animal species, is not permitted. So we understand from our constitutional law and most religions. But within the law of our society elimination of life is permitted and even encouraged. Those who perform the act well may become heroes and examples for others. I'm speaking, of course, of war. This is a double standard. If not well and fully ex-

plained, it creates confusion among our youth.

Stealing is not permitted. The law of the land says so. But business depends on it. Instead of labeling the act "stealing," we accept it as something good which creates "profit." But to my mind, this is again an unexplained double standard.

The United States is known to be a free country. By law all citizens have equal rights. But no one is free. The fact is that we all are conditioned to behave in a particular pattern designed by the need to maintain order in our society. We are free, in a prison.

At the same time, we are told to exercise our unique individual talents, in order to continue the necessary growth of our society. The environment best suited for people to exercise their unique talent is often not in harmony with the law, with the rules set forth by our rigidly designed social structure.

Let me present to you a curriculum of my making: It has six courses.

A. Motivation. "Why should I be a student?" a young person asks. "Why should I go to school?" Within any educational building, from the first moment the child steps inside and becomes formally a student, these questions must be answered.

B. Self-investigation. This course would involve a psychological, biological, ethical, and artistic study of the self. It is my passionate belief that children at a very young age can sometimes understand, grasp, things more keenly and intuitively than older people can. The shades between love and hate, the chemistry of the body and the brain, who they are and where they came from, should not wait until children are too old for natural understanding to be taught.

This course would launch students upon a thorough investigation of what they, individually, are about. Each one must recognize the similarities and differences between himself and others. Thus he may acquire a knowledge of the things that could otherwise make him afraid, and rob him of his sense of security.

C. Logic, in creative thinking. Logic is used as a discipline to limit confusion. It is a thinking technique, a style of thinking. Mathematical logic recognizes that one plus one is two. Another kind of logic recognizes the process of creation.

All people, whoever and wherever they may be, experience the need to investigate those things they do not understand. On investigation, they travel parallel to chaos, and may become blinded by a complexity of findings.

The two logics I have named, taught together, can help the left and right halves of the brain develop in harmony with each other.

D. Social structures. This course would encompass the teachings of social systems —capitalism, socialism, communism, etc. Students could learn the differences between them, and how to appreciate—or perhaps not —the system in which they live.

Someday these students will leave school. They may get married, work and make money, buy a house. They must make all their learning pay off for them. As far as their formal education can see to it, they must not be misplaced in society. It is a part of them, and they are a part of it, and they must realize this truth.

E. Communication. All information gathered by an individual needs to be expressed to others and thus shared, to make the process of learning complete, or, like still water, it will rot.

Communication is not a special privilege, but a necessity for survival. It is important to discover that one's self is not alone. Loneliness and ignorance can be detrimental to survival.

F. Common courses. Here I place courses that are important, but not all-important. The familiar courses of school: arithmetic, English, history. Some part of each course I described above must find its way into each of these "common" courses.

Once a young person has learned who he or she is, that person has a fair chance to develop a sense of respect for our democratic system and its laws. He or she will become willing, not afraid, to become a part of it because it will be no mystery.

A true pride of country grows from understanding. When a man flies from America to the moon, our pride would be greater if we understood the meaning of the event.

When I first began to perform at colleges in this country, I went to a small college in upstate New York. The students there were demonstrating. "We are for the Negroes," they said, "and we want freedom."

The president of the college said, "Good. But show me that you really understand the black's plight. Tell me what you know of black history."

They knew very little, but they wanted to demonstrate.

"Go back and learn the history of the blacks in this country," said the president. "Show me you understand what you're protesting. Then come back and proceed with your demonstration."

Mime and Nonverbal Education

I have presented to you some directions in which, I believe, education should go. Now let me show you how I use my specialty to improve communication between human beings. Let me give you a glimpse of how a system of nonverbal education could develop.

But first, I have a startling confession to make. I hate rules. I love to sabotage things.

For the common laws of humanity I have nothing but respect. When I saw them being violated in my native country many years ago, I joined the Dutch Resistance.

But simple rules often stand in the way of a person who is out to create something new. Over mindless regulation, I prefer self-enforced discipline, which comes when a person understands what his or her objectives are and what must be done to reach them.

Without discipline, I would have no technique. Without technique, I could not speak the language of mime. Without mime, I would not have been invited to come to this symposium.

Discipline is a lonely thing. It comes from within. Our bone-bound island of flesh and blood was born alone and will die alone. Loneliness in this sense is an essential state of being, our only motivation to communicate with ourselves and with others.

Our life, between birth and death, is lived through a chain of communicative efforts. These efforts are part of the creative process.

The degree of excellence in communication determines the degree of happiness, fulfillment, and satisfaction we reach in our life. It is the responsibility of formal education to teach the understanding, technique, and materials of the process of excellent communication.

The disciplined body for the use of communication is fundamental to a complete, healthy awareness of self and others. Sports and physical fitness are fine in themselves, but they are not communication and they do not fit my requirements.

In my business, the foot is on equal terms with the brain. The chest is as eloquent as the hands. The eyebrow speaks as loudly as the mouth— because the mouth does not say a word. All are part of the whole body, a thing which conventional education has ignored.

When I teach mime, I first ask the students to explore themselves alone. Establish a territory around you, I tell each of them, and work inward.

Like newborn babies, they learn of and use muscles they never dreamed they had, and they are fascinated. Their heads move about in curious new directions. They find that their chests have their own muscles too, and can move without the rest of the body helping out.

None of these students is afraid to appear foolish in front of the others, because everyone is taking part in the foolishness.

Using her arms and body in a new way, a student may be transformed into a bird on the wing. Using her imagination and her experience in the world, she may convincingly ride a bicycle that seems not to exist. She picks and sniffs a flower out of thin air, and by her motions she makes others watching see and smell the flower with her.

And these little mime exercises make her happy with her body, even proud of its new accomplishments.

You see, I like to introduce parts of the body to the mind, and watch friendship arise between the two ancient enemies of our modern civilization. In this way, the young people become ready to work honestly with each other.

I like to see a healthy interest on the part of one body for another. I ask the students to take the air before them, and build with the movement of their hands another human being. Build a woman, I might tell the boys. Build a man, I might tell the girls. Be as precise as you would be with your words.

One student will lie down on the floor, and another will place hands above the prone body, without touching it. The hands may become hot. This little mystery brings with it implicit understanding of the power of the body.

A few together, or a large group, or the entire class, can join to build mimes of a moment's devising. I have seen some very bad ones, but I also have seen masterpieces of instantaneous creation, expressing more in a few minutes than could the longest written essay or term paper.

And I have seen students hone and refine their individual mime creations into beautiful and lucid statements of the human condition.

I have seen even in college-age young people an innocent and uninhibited physical relationship grow up. They don't forget sex (would that be healthy?), but they see that there is more to bodily communication than sex. They learn the art of silent eloquence.

But my students have been late, very late, in coming to this. They were in college by the time they used their bodies in school for more than push-ups or tackles in football. The process should have begun with the beginning of education.

Neglect of the discipline of communication through the body results, I believe, in disorderly behavior of the individual that has a lot to do with insecurity and ignorance of his or her own body.

Vandalism, rape, thievery, assault, murder, and involvement with drugs are all physical acts. To me, they are derailed acts of creativity, gone terribly astray. The mind has alienated itself from the body, and the body has become a rumor—an accident—a disturbance—a hindrance—a crucifix.

Our ambivalence toward the body in Western civilization has done tremendous harm. Bodies are filthy things. We don't talk about them in school.

Without the knowledge and discipline that has been left out of teaching, the body is a stranger to the mind. The things that they do together, then, can be strange, aberrant, and lawless acts.

When you look at a class of students, even as early as in the fifth grade, do you see the patterns already beginning to form?

Do you see those who are less sure of themselves, less happy, more lonely? Whose few friendships seem unhealthy ones? Do you see some of your academically bright students who are painfully shy and withdrawing into isolation?

My chief message to you, who think to change education for the better, is this: Give the children an opportunity to know themselves and each other through their bodies when they are young. Help them know why they are in school, what society they live in, and how education will help them to survive.

Put as much emphasis on creative logic as is now placed on mathematical logic.

Above all, don't take away the ability to communicate with the whole body that all children have at birth. Let that ability grow and refine itself.

These are the rough ideas of a man who has watched American education and thought much about its deficiencies. I am not an educational theorist. I am not used to putting my ideas down on paper, or speaking them aloud to a group of professionals. I am more comfortable doing the things I know best—designing, painting, performing.

But I believe in the truth of my observations and the value of my ideas. I am grateful for this chance to communicate them.

Nonverbal Tactics for Teaching about Law and the Humanities

Dorothy J. Skeel

This paper offers the theoretical and pedagogical underpinnings for the type of curricular approach advocated by Reynders. Dorothy Skeel sketches the cognitive-developmental stages of elementary school children and indicates appropriate learning experiences. She notes the limitations as well as opportunities existing in childhood and juxtaposes these with a realistic view of the elementary school setting.

As I read Francisco Reynders's paper, it reminded me of the *bill of rights* for children by Gladys Andrews, (1954, p. 19), which states:

> Let me grow as I be
> And try to understand why
>   I want to grow like me;
> Not like my Mom wants
>   me to be,
> Nor like Dad hopes I'll be
> Or my teacher thinks I
>   should be.
> Please try to understand
>   and help me grow
> Just like me!

Everyone agrees that each child is unique, an individual with different capabilities, talents, and desires. Most teachers would not argue that children should be permitted to develop their uniqueness and be themselves. But how does the school as a *system* foster this development.

Children entering kindergarten or first grade are egocentric, concerned about self. Many have come from safe, secure home environments where their individual needs and desires are central concerns of the family. Others have come from environments where there is little regard for them as individuals. They come with tarnished self-concepts. Both groups of children enter this new environment with little understanding of what their role is to be. How do you become a student in school? What are the rights and responsibilities of a student? Suddenly there are other people to

Dorothy J. Skeel is Professor of Social Studies Education at George Peabody College for Teachers, Vanderbilt University. She is directing federally funded projects in law-related education and global education and is author of *The Challenge of Teaching Social Studies in the Elementary School*.

consider—the teacher, children in the classroom, a person called the principal who seems to have much authority, nurses, cafeteria people, and those who clean the school. But the child wonders, How do I fit in? There are toys to share, the teacher says to be quiet, to listen, to take a nap, to have cookies and juice, to go to the bathroom and get drinks at certain times. Children quickly recognize the expression of disapproval on a teacher's face when inappropriate behavior is exhibited. Or how many well-meaning teachers use this technique of control to suggest the proper behavior to the child: "I like the way Kevin is sitting quietly on the rug," or "Look at Nancy, she knows where the toys belong when she's finished playing with them"?

The initial concerns of the school are often to organize the environment and to teach conforming behavior. Schools readily defend these concerns as legitimate, since little can be accomplished in chaos and the safety of all children is crucial. But what of the individual and the desire to develop his/her unique talents? Unfortunately, at the age when children are attempting to understand their roles in school, to cooperate with others, to respect their rights and show concern for them, they are, according to Piaget, cognitively egocentric and not able to take the *perspective* of another person. Therefore, the children model behavior pointed out to them as good to avoid punishment. Kohlberg suggests that they have reached the stage in moral development at which they obey to avoid punishment, or they are at stage 2, at which they conform to obtain rewards, such as a smile from the teacher or an opportunity to be first in line to go out for playtime. Piaget indicates that most children do not overcome this egocentric perspective until they are seven or eight years old. In most cases the modeling behavior by this time has become complete; they continue to conform and receive the rewards of that conformity. In many classrooms, those who do not conform are looked upon as discipline problems rather than as exerting their individuality. Children do not question whether they are being themselves or conforming, and if they are not given the opportunity to be themselves, much of their individuality and creative talents may be lost.

If the problems Reynders suggests are real—students do not understand themselves, do not understand why they are in school, are not motivated to learn, and are discipline problems—what can be done to avoid them? Two crucial points in children's elementary schooling occur: when they enter school, and when they reach the stages in cognitive development at which they move away from their egocentrism, can begin to solve problems, and can apply role-taking skills in resolving conflicts. At these points the school as a system is important, since it establishes expectations for children and teachers. Teachers often have no control over rules for conformity such as lining up for walking through the halls. However, when one views the roles of the teacher, it is obvious that the teacher is the key. More will be said later about the curriculum of the school.

Seaberg (1974) identifies the roles of the teacher as relator, mediator, diagnostician, and choreographer. In the context of this paper we are most concerned with the roles of relator and choreographer. In the relator role, the teacher establishes the environment of the classroom, which should be a place where the children are comfortable, where they are viewed with respect and worth. "Respect and love of the teacher is not purchased by behavior conforming to the teacher's wishes.... The pupil is not dependent on the teacher for a sense of self through praise for conforming. Rather, the teacher helps the child to discover and trust his uniqueness, and to express himself in the ongoing activities of the classroom.... The teacher relates to each on the child's own wavelength, so that children begin to recognize and value their own special qualities and their own individuality" (Seaberg, 1974, p. 24).

Much of this communication is nonverbal—a smile that is real, the look in the eyes that says, "You're important, you're a person," the touch of the hand that communicates, "I understand" or "Don't be angry." "A non-verbal espirit de corps develops, which enables the children to become active in discovering their own goals" (Seaberg, 1974, p. 24). Children who feel adequate and comfortable with themselves reach out and discover one another. Much can be communicated in the classroom about justice, equality, freedom, and fair play through nonverbal means.

In this atmosphere, the teacher functions in the role of choreographer. "In dance as well as in teaching, choreography is a flexible, creative art that involves far more than merely assembling movements or manipulating the environment.... An educational experience comes to life when the learner taps his creative and rational powers.... When the pupil choreographs his own learning, through the facilitating function of the teacher, he too is a creator, and his educational experience evokes beauty and joy both for himself and for his teacher" (Seaberg, 1974, p. 51).

I agree with Reynders that a part of the curriculum should deal with exploration of self. Within the previously described classroom atmosphere, the young children are not inhibited but feel free to move their bodies to express themselves. As facilitator, the teacher provides opportunities for expression of feelings of love, hate, anger, frustration, happiness, and sadness. For example, the teacher may describe a situation such as a child losing a pet, receiving a new bike, or attempting to reach a water fountain. Children are asked to use their bodies and without words show how each would behave in that situation. Older children can act out more complicated problem situations, in which a child has broken a school rule or is confronted with a decision about fairness. Children soon discover the feelings they have are not so different from those of others, but the feelings are their own and they have expressed them as individuals. Also, abstract concepts of authority, justice, and equality become more meaningful, since children have observed or participated in the behaviors related to them.

Only after children have explored who they are does communication with others become more meaningful. Nonverbal communication is a vital part of the elementary classroom as it contributes to the humanistic atmosphere. How do children learn about nonverbal communication? An early experience should be through the use of mirrors to investigate how one appears to others when smiling, frowning, etc. Then through the body movement experiences as described by Reynders, children realize how much can be communicated through the use of the body. Upon this foundation can be built a curriculum that takes children beyond themselves to explore the world around them.

One can readily see the value that comes from learning about one's body and the use of it to express feelings and to communicate, but realistically, is it likely to become a part of an already crowded curriculum? With the concern for "back to the basics," career, global, and values education, what chance does nonverbal communication for teaching about law have in the curriculum? Certainly understanding one's self and communicating are basic to learning, and the other curriculum concerns of career, values, and global education should begin with these aspects as well. Schools will more readily use cognitive means to teach about law, such as learning the Declaration of Independence and the Constitution, than an aesthetic approach. Obviously, it should not be an either/or decision. The aesthetic quality of the humanities, such as nonverbal communication, removes some of the harshness and stark reality from law. It adds the feeling or affective dimension which we hope will produce citizens who are humane and concerned about justice and equality.

REFERENCES

Andrews, G. *Creative rhythmic movement for children.* Englewood Cliffs, N.J.: Prentice-Hall, 1954.

Seaberg, D. *The four faces of teaching: The role of the teacher in humanizing education.* Pacific Palisades, Calif.: Goodyear, 1974.

Governance in Elementary Schools: An Exploration in Law-related Education

Barbara Bree Fischer, Louis Fischer, and Valerie Bäng-Jensen

The formal and informal curricula are being increasingly recognized as having a tandem impact on school learning. When law and humanities is the curricular topic, certain dimensions of the informal curriculum become especially vital. Among those dimensions are the amount and kind of civic participation experiences children are afforded and through which they learn basic law-related attitudes, skills, and knowledge.

In this article the authors discuss the potential for and possible limits to student participation in school governance. They note that young children learn more quickly and thoroughly through direct experience. And while they eschew the traditional student government model as an inappropriate learning tool for the total population in elementary schools, they are able to identify a wealth of opportunities for involving children in worthwhile governance experiences. This discussion includes a convincing delineation of basic law-related objectives which can be achieved through a sound governance program.

Our approach to "governance in elementary schools" differs from commonly held conceptions. Rather than focusing on formal structures, offices, and procedures related to them, we emphasize the educative impact of the informal systems that operate school-wide as well as in the classrooms. It is our opinion that these systems, and the authority implicit in them, teach concepts, attitudes, and values that are the necessary foundations of democratic governance.

Our assumptions. The following eight propositions are accepted as the working assumptions of this paper. These propositions themselves could be the subject of scholarly investigations, some empirical, some analytical, and some both. However, since everything cannot be investigated at the same time, they are accepted as true for present purposes.

Barbara B. Fischer is Director of the Smith College Campus School and Lecturer in the Department of Education and Child Study. She has published and consulted in the areas of elementary curriculum, instruction, and organization.

Louis Fischer is Professor of Education, University of Massachusetts, Amherst. He has written widely on civil rights and education and is currently President of the John Dewey Society.

Valerie Bäng-Jensen is an elementary school teacher at the Riverdale Country Day School, Bronx, New York. Her special areas of interest include language arts and children's literature.

1. Schools can be significant, growth-enhancing influences in the lives of children.
2. While many agencies, institutions, and environmental forces educate our children, schools are the only institutions created specifically to educate. Thus they have special responsibilities. Among these, schools are typically charged by their governing boards to teach concepts, skills, and attitudes that are useful in governance-related social studies.
3. Although there are scholarly disagreements about theories and models of stages and phases of human development, a developmental approach to schooling makes good sense at the elementary level.
4. Educators must take stands and make decisions even in the absence of reliable knowledge. In circumstances where scientific knowledge is incomplete, carefully considered professional experience is a sound basis for decision making.
5. The grounds of educational decisions as well as their probable consequences must generally be available to public scrutiny and discussion.
6. The informal (or hidden) curriculum is probably just as powerful in school learning as the explicit or formal curriculum.
7. Attitudes and dispositions such as fairness, cooperation, and respect for people, rules, property, and authority can and should be taught in the elementary schools.
8. Ordinary people can learn to participate in

self-governance. Elementary schools along with families are important institutions in which to begin learning such participation.

The meaning of governance. The ordinary and generally accepted meaning of governance is the direction and control of the actions and conduct of a group, based on either established laws and rules or an arbitrary power. In schools, governance refers to the way that the behavior of various people in schools is controlled and directed, the way that power is allocated, and the way that various decisions are made. Experience shows that school governance, like governance outside schools, is at times based on established laws and rules, at times on arbitrary power, and often on a combination of the two.

Our proposed meaning for governance in the schools is broader than the traditionally accepted conception indicated above. We include not only the formal machinery of governance with its specified roles and statuses accompanying those roles, but also the informal means that function in schools as in other institutions. This view is not new or unique to us, and the powerful influences of the school's social system and its subcultural patterns have been carefully analyzed and documented by various scholars (e.g., Dreeben, 1968; Gordon, 1957; Henry, 1963).

However, insufficient scholarly work has been done so far on the topic of governance in the elementary schools, when governance is broadly conceived to include both the formal and informal means of maintaining the orderly, efficient, and effective functioning of such schools. And while there is extensive literature on political socialization in the secondary schools, extrapolations from such work to life in the elementary schools is, at best, problematic.

Within such a broad conception of school governance, one that encompasses both formal and informal processes and influences, two major purposes can be identified. One purpose of governance here, as elsewhere, is to maintain order, efficiency, and an effective machinery for conflict resolution. The second purpose, not found in other institutions, is *to teach* a variety of concepts, skills, and attitudes. We assume that the latter is the prime purpose of governance at all levels of compulsory schooling. Thus, through the way governance functions, we can reinforce the stated goals of the formal curriculum and model what we teach.

Developmental considerations. While a systematic analysis of human growth and development is the subject of other papers, in discussing elementary school governance we cannot ignore developmental issues. It seems to us that enough is known about commonalities and variations in

patterns of child development to alert us to its complexities and place us on guard against over-simplification. While even more definitive knowledge is in the making, we know that inter- and intraindividual differences are impressive and useful in the educative process. As we look at principles and processes of governance in classrooms and school-wide, developmental notions will repeatedly enter. For the time being, it is important to note that the typical elementary school enrolls children within a very large developmental span. For example, it is now known that there is a greater difference in cognitive abilities between the 5-year-old and the 12-year-old than between the 15-year-old and the 30-year-old. We also know that the cognitive abilities of a child are necessarily part of his/her social abilities. Therefore, there is a tremendous difference in what one can expect from the very young and from the oldest children in elementary schools. We speak of the 5–12-year-olds as the typical span of ages within elementary schools, though we realize that some include children as young as 3 and/or as old as 14. The latter is particularly the case in schools organized on the eight-four plan as contrasted to the six-three-three type of school organization.

For example, the 5- or 6-year-old views the school as almost exclusively the classroom and tends to view the teacher as an extension of the parent. Contact with the rest of the school is seen through very egocentric eyes: "The nurse helps me when I get hurt." At the other end of the age range, the child can perceive how adults in the school function as support systems for the classroom. These older children can also view the school as a small community and can learn to apply this understanding to the institutions of a town or city, looking at functions such as protection, regulation, and provision of needed goods and services.

The general "climate" of the classroom and the school plays a vital part in helping the child accept the school's authority. In discussing the elementary child, Dreeben contends that "the emotions aroused in schooling derive from events in which the pupils' sense of self-respect is either supported or threatened....this influences the pupils in deciding whether or not they will find their early experiences at school enjoyable enough to act according to the standards governing school activities" (1968, p. 39).

Formal governance in elementary schools. On the basis of our understanding of human development, cognitive, affective, social, and moral, we conclude that as a general rule a school-wide governance structure is not appropriate for elementary schools. Some schools use school councils of various forms, whose membership is selected in different ways. Participation in such organizations has been significant in the experience of some children, but, in our estimate, the educative impact on students in general cannot be considered impressive. All too often, the organization is merely window dressing, creating a make-believe democracy, or a thinly veiled machinery for adult control. (Similar co-opting of student government in high schools and colleges might well have been a contributing cause to the rebellions of the 1960s, as students objected to "playing in the sand box.")

Developmentally, for the elementary school child, unlike the high school student, a year, or even a semester, is a *very* long time for serving on a "governing council." Furthermore, it is not effective as a teaching device, for very few children have the opportunity to serve. Later in this paper, we will describe an alternative conception of total-school governance we consider more appropriate for elementary schools.

There are those who consider traffic squads to be a form of governance. Undoubtedly, they perform useful services for schools and, if wisely conceived and guided by the faculty, they can be educative for all the students and particularly for the members of the squads. There are also classrooms that use a set of "officers" selected by various means and for different terms of office, to perform some needed functions. We shall comment on these later.

Informal governance in elementary schools. For some time now, it has been recognized by insightful observers that all of life educates, not only school life (see, e.g., Dewey, 1916, chap. 1). In his recent book Cremin (1976, p. 4) reiterates this thesis and gives credit to Dewey for recognizing and explicating it over half a century ago. Cremin, in presenting Dewey's ideas, asserts: "In the ordinary course of living, education is *incidental*; in schooling, education is *intentional*" (1976, p. 4, italics in original). In our opinion, this is an overstatement. Much of education within classrooms is intentional, but in each classroom there are unintended or concomitant learnings, incidental and often accidental, at times referred to as the "hidden curriculum." Furthermore, classrooms and schools have subcultures and social systems of their own through which the hidden, or implicit curriculum makes an educational impact.

Authority systems always operate within classrooms as well as school-wide. The explicit rules of such systems, the positions and roles in a school, the way adults work with each other and with students, the "educational atmosphere" they create, influence children's learning of governance-related ideas, values, and skills. It is our conviction that these are the areas of elementary school life where governance-related learning will make the most lasting impact. And, although they are inextricably related, it is possible to look separately at the classroom dimensions of governance and those of the school-wide system.

Before we do, however, some basic ideas should be stated. These might be very obvious, but without constant reference to them, some adult behaviors in school appear arbitrary. The two basic ideas against which various behaviors in school must be judged are: (1) each child in school has a right to learn, and (2) each child in school has a right to be safe. Safety is a necessary condition for learning, and learning is the basic reason for schooling. Governance-related activities are at times the means for insuring safety, while at other times they are the means for providing other proper conditions for learning. Simultaneously, governance-related learning also constitutes an end or goal of instruction. Thus, in both the explicit and the implicit curriculum of the school, governance-related learning and activities constitute some of the ends as well as some of the means of education. We trust that the following pages will explain these ideas more fully.

When we talk about governance as an education *goal* or an *end* of instruction, we consider the concept to include such ingredients as: respect for all individuals; respect for property; understanding of "fairness," cooperation; understanding of "responsibility"; understanding of the need for rules; and understanding and acceptance of proper authority. Governance as *means* includes: understanding and obeying rules, developing skills in conflict resolution, and developing problem-solving skills.

Governance and the Classroom

As a guiding principle, we accept the proposition that elementary-school-age children learn most quickly and thoroughly through direct experience. This general principle applies to governance-related concepts as to other abstract ideas. Subsequently, this learning may be transferred to vicarious experiences such as courses in history, civics, and government, when students have developed the ability to do abstract thinking and have built a personal foundation of ideas based on their own experiences. This does not mean that at any stage of schooling concrete experiences with governance should be completely replaced by formal study. We recommend that instructional techniques and classroom organization should continue to provide direct experience with governance, for the concepts thus learned through participation and those taught in the curriculum will mutually reinforce each other.

When organizing and implementing classroom

procedures and activities that will provide children with opportunities for governance-related learning, two considerations must be explored thoroughly in order to design an appropriate and effective program. They are: (1) the developmental characteristics of each age group, and (2) the students' background in relation to self-governance, responsibility, and functioning in organized groups.

Since governance-related learning is an aspect of social (as well as cognitive) development, the classroom teacher must remember that in terms of responsibility a young child begins with learning to be responsible for self and develops toward responsibility for self within a group as well as of self to the group. A young child is egocentric and can be expected to accept responsibility for himself/herself. This can range from getting one's own snack and cleaning up after eating it, to putting away blocks after using them, to learning to take turns at the slide on the playground during recess. As children grow older and more competent in self-responsibility, sharing, cooperating, and taking turns, they are ready to try their social skills in group situations. (These opportunities reinforce responsibility for the self, as well.) When they enter middle childhood and become increasingly peer-oriented, interest in the group can provide opportunities in leadership, both positive and negative.

A second developmental consideration relates more directly to the curriculum and has to do with *who* sets up goals, expectations, and evaluations of what is learned (in terms of management of instruction, rather than objectives or curricular units). While the young child is still adjusting to school and functioning within a new structure, the expectations are primarily set by the teacher. At a later stage of development, the student contributes to the activity—the story she dictated needs another sentence, it doesn't sound quite right, or he wants to spend the morning finishing a project in math, having been exposed to and participated in other areas last week.

In middle childhood, the students, with their newly developed cognitive skills and with increasing competence in abstract thinking such as drawing inferences and making comparisons, can contribute to the evaluation of individual or group behavior and work. In social learning and the evaluation of social behavior, they are increasingly able to project what is required for identified tasks, establish criteria for themselves and others, and become committed to their decisions.

Thus, social learning can be placed on a continuum wherein students' responsibility develops from a focus on self toward becoming a functioning member of a group. Paralleling this development is a shift from articulation of expectations by teachers toward students taking over this role, with the help of teachers.

A second important consideration, previously mentioned, relates to the student's prior experiences. The teacher must attempt to diagnose what experience his or her students have had with responsibility, organization, and group work. Expecting students who have always worked alone to produce a project in groups of six or eight will probably create difficulties and frustrations. Responsibility and the ability to work in group situations require both developmental readiness and skills acquired through experience.

Procedures and activities. There are two major ways in which children can learn about governance-related ideas in the classroom. One is the formal program, including the explicit rules and procedures that govern daily classroom activities. For example, during reading instruction some stated rules guide the behavior of children working in an instructional group with the teacher, as well as those engaged in other activities around the room. These rules and procedures relate quite directly to certain learning outcomes (reading skills).

There are also rules which govern activities such as sharpening pencils or preparing for recess, rules which relate to the reasonable, fair, and safe use of materials and equipment within the classroom.

The second way in which children learn about these concepts in the classroom is more often overlooked and is more difficult to plan and to implement. This has to do with the classroom interactions that relate to conflict, and the conflict resolution techniques employed by the teacher.

Many aspects of the elementary school classroom may be set up to facilitate the development of concepts such as cooperation, responsibility, and respect for others, for rules, and for authority. For example, students learn some of these by being responsible for cleaning their room, both after work periods and at the end of the day. If the expectations are clear, students can easily understand and internalize them. Rotating jobs insures fairness, and a student supervisor in groups of older children gives opportunities to develop leadership skills and to understand better the concept of authority. Being exposed to all aspects of the jobs gives students the information they need when they become the supervisor or authority. Children in the upper elementary grades should be encouraged and expected to determine what jobs should be done and what the criteria should be for selection for those jobs. The consequences for failing to do the job adequately should be decided by the students, with teacher help, or by the teacher if the children are too young, and should relate to the job. (If supplies run out and none were reordered, drawings will have to be done in pencil; if Mary forgets to take attendance, it is she who must write and deliver a note of explanation to the office.)

Students should have opportunities to discuss and suggest classroom rules or guidelines. Those created by the school or by the teacher should be thoroughly discussed so that the reasons for them are explicit and to some degree understood, even if not agreed with. (All this, of course, must take into account the children's level of development.) After rules have been established, changes may occur which necessitate the formulation of new procedures (the acquisition of a guinea pig, the construction of a teepee, etc.). Teachers who can anticipate the change can use the opportunity to help students identify the possible effects of the change and draw up new guidelines as needed. In doing so, students become familiar with rule-making procedures and also gain in understanding that (1) rules should fit each situation, and (2) when a change occurs, new rules are sometimes necessary.

It is a common practice to specify a period of "free time" or "choice time" during each week (called "open" time, "home base" time, "home room" time, etc.). Students can learn important skills by having responsibility for careful management of this time. Its purpose should be discussed with the group, suggestions shared and considered, and, through such a process, criteria developed for its use. Groups of students can take responsibility for planning each week, with their plans checked by the teacher, and later by the students, against the criteria developed earlier. The activity should proceed, with time saved for evaluation. Again, teachers are responsible, just as in other areas of the program, for diagnosing the capabilities of the students and for helping set criteria appropriate for the group at different times of the year. Student growth should be anticipated through this activity in the areas of responsibility and decision-making abilities.

Although rules may have been created in collaboration with students and may be clearly understood, developmental characteristics leading to experimentation, bids for power, or home influences may cause children to ignore rules, test limits, and wind up in conflict with each other or with the teacher. These occasions are useful in developing a variety of governance-related social values, including the concepts of fairness, responsibility, and authority. By listening to each child's point of view, by determining (or having the child choose) a consequence that is related to the undesirable behavior, one can teach respect for individuals as well as the foundational attitudes for due process. (In part, this is what Dewey meant when he said that "children learn by doing and undergoing the consequences of their actions." Popularization of this idea led to the slogan "Learning by doing," and to much mindless activity, or activity for the sake of activity.) Furthermore, by following through on consequences and being held to them, and by going back to the premise on which the rules were based, children can learn that there are reasons for rules and that each member of the group has responsibilities to self, teacher, and group. (Children thus learn that "fair" does not necessarily mean equal, but that fairness does have rules and precedents. They are also reminded of the two basic referents for decisions in classrooms and schools: the right to learn and the right to safety.)

The foregoing indicates the pervasive tenor of a classroom that is likely to develop knowledge, attitudes, and skills that lay the foundations for governance in a democratic social order. It is our conviction that a steady, consistent, and knowledgeable management of the classroom, in light of the principles explained above, is more productive of the learning we desire than emphasis on formal and often ritualistic classroom governance structures and procedures.

What transpires in classrooms, however, is only part of the subculture and social system of the school. School-wide activities and procedures also make an educative impact on children, and the fact that they are ignored in too many schools does not make them any less powerful. What is learned as a consequence of school-wide governance should be consistent with what is learned in classrooms; the two subsystems should mutually reinforce each other for optimal learning to occur. "Pupils learn to accept principles of conduct, or social norms, and to act according to them" (Dreeben, 1968).

Some Aspects of School-wide Governance

For purposes of emphasis we note that all the principles related to human development, cognitive and social learning, and learning based on experience apply with equal force to school-wide governance as to classroom learning. Furthermore, the twin rights, the right to learn and the right to be safe, are again the pervasive criteria against which all behavior should be assessed.

While we noted earlier that, in our estimate, a total-school governmental structure is not appropriate for elementary schools on a continuing basis, some more desirable alternatives are available. We rule out the standing, school-wide structure, primarily on developmental grounds as noted earlier. We are also convinced that, at this age level, learning decreases as children serve on governing councils that meet routinely throughout a semester or a year, but learning becomes vivid and is enhanced if participation is organized when common problems arise. The following examples (based on an experience in 1976 at Smith College Campus School, Northampton, Mass., under the supervision of Kent Lewis) will, we believe, illuminate our meaning.

In an elementary school in New England, the first snow of the winter brought great excitement to the children, and the school's newly acquired plastic flat slides were enthusiastically put to use on the sledding slope. Since this area was the only outdoor recess area usable during the snowy season, almost the entire school population used it at some time during the day. Problems were rampant, and when some minor injuries had to be treated by the nurse, children complained and the teachers feared that more serious injuries were likely to occur if the situation continued. An outline of a school-wide approach to their problem follows:

Step 1. After a discussion with the teachers, the principal requested each class to send two representatives to a "sledding crisis" meeting. The representatives were to be selected on the basis of: (*a*) a generally constructive attitude toward problems, (*b*) an interest in solving the sledding problem, (*c*) a real liking for sledding shown by active participation in it, and (*d*) an ability to listen to ideas and to explain what was done at the meeting.

Step 2. Each class representative was to bring to the meeting a statement of the problems the class members could identify. (Collisions and taking turns were the main concerns.)

Step 3. In the meeting, through discussion, the representatives clarified and summarized the problems (too many children on the slopes at once, etc.).

Step 4. The representatives then took the summary statement to their classes for discussion and for possible solutions (new recess schedule, space out sledders, etc.).

Step 5. Class representatives returned to the school-wide group for discussion of solutions, selection of a solution, and its clarification in the form of a set of rules that each representative could explain fully (new schedule, plus two rules: [1] wait for 5 seconds, and [2] come up slope outside of sledding path).

Step 6. Class representatives returned to class and explained the solution selected. Classes raised questions and recorded them (Will there be enough time for our class to sled? etc.).

Step 7. The whole school tried out the new rules.

Step 8. Each class discussed the trial in relation to its questions or raised new questions (worked very well; request for bales of hay at the bottom of the hill, etc.).

Step 9. The school-wide group ironed out any serious "bugs" remaining (bales of hay ordered, schedule is OK, rules are OK).

Step 10. Representatives reported back to classes.

The crucial ingredients of this process are:

1. All children participate in articulating problems, proposing and finding solutions, and establishing rules, thus giving substance to the reasons for the rules.
2. Children elect someone they consider qualified to represent them in relation to a meaningful problem. (This is recognition of authority at a simple but meaningful level.)
3. Trying out the new rules promotes recognition that rules and laws are established to solve problems and that they can be changed when the need arises.

Other school-wide problems, from food throwing in the cafeteria to gang fights, can be addressed in this fashion. In these situations, school-wide governance is clearly at work, organized when meaningful problems arise. To have real reasons for decision making, to participate fully in the process, and to experience the school-wide process at least once or twice a year are necessary parts of a child's experience related to civic education. (Perhaps it is even arguable that a school wherein no school-wide problems arise is too tightly structured and controlled by administrators and/or teachers for optimal social learning to occur.)

What can be learned? Ideas such as authority, fairness, justice, respect for individuals and property, and the need for rules can be understood and accepted at a very practical level in the upper elementary school years, if the school provides direct experiences in a suitable program. Havighurst, for example, states that "middle childhood is the period when the basic social attitudes are learned.... These attitudes may be changed by later experience, but they do not change easily." He further states that "attitudes, or emotionalized dispositions to act, are learned in three ways: (1) by imitation of people with prestige in the eyes of the learner; (2) by collection and combination of pleasant or unpleasant experiences associated with a given object or situation; (3) by a single deeply emotional experience—pleasant or unpleasant—associated with a given object or situation" (1972, p. 34).

School-wide governance-related ideas can be referred to the twin basic rights of children in school: (1) the right to learn, without undue disturbance and with the use of the resources provided by the community (thus destroying school property denies the use of such property to others); and (2) the right to be safe, free from physical and psychological harm, ridicule, or degradation, or the threat of such harm. To help achieve the goals of schooling, it is important for the child or the group to know when behavior is appropriate or inappropriate and why. The adult must intervene when the child's behavior is damaging to another, physically or psychologically, or to opportunities for learning.

Where does the learning take place? Possibilities for learning occur in various situations outside the classroom in relationships with other parts of the school, in informal settings and in organized group situations.

The way the school is organized to provide a fair share of materials and facilities to each classroom is important. Children should be aware, for example, that they have time in the gym as do other groups. "Fair" in this case means appropriate and reasonable (though not necessarily equal). Children will come to understand these ideas after "living them" in many situations where these terms have meaning for them.

The way the school handles problems, including "sending children to the office" because of misbehavior, also teaches governance-related concepts. A cooperative teamwork approach makes good sense here, one that is based on mutual respect and clear communication among teachers, administration, and office personnel. A nurturing atmosphere or climate must prevail, and such incidents should be used as opportunities for teaching. Certainly the child's (or children's) version(s) of an incident should be sought and considered.

A variety of informal settings, such as hallways, bathrooms, playgrounds, and cafeterias, are places where problems may arise, which may relate to safety, fighting or other conflicts, overcrowding, racism, etc. Careful enforcement of rules is crucial in these situations, for if clear violations are ignored, children are deprived of the experience of moving, playing, eating, and relating in a fairly predictable and safe environment. This broad base of experience is necessary for the child eventually to recognize the need for rules, to understand conflict resolution, and to value efforts to respect each person in these settings. When problems arise, discussion or explanation should focus on the immediate situation, so the consequences of the behavior in question become evident to all. Everyone's explanation should be considered, in order to show respect for the rights of every individual involved.

Organized group situations outside the classroom present further opportunities for learning. Children are in large group situations in assemblies, in the cafeteria, on the bus, and in physical education classes. Order is important in each of these activities, and there are excellent transfer possibilities for the learning that occurs because, unlike the classroom, which is unique to schools, these school-wide experiences are more like the life outside of the school which all children experience. However, the kinds of learning to be gained on the bus, in the cafeteria, etc., are very different from each other.

On the bus, learning relates to safety rules and fairness in the order of entering, taking seats, and disembarking. In the cafeteria, where the school is attending to one of the primary needs of the child, comfort and health considerations are important. The child should become aware of the need for order to ensure fairness in access to food and to encourage an atmosphere free from tension, noise, and unpleasant sights to facilitate proper digestion and pleasant social exchange. Assemblies and other large group gatherings should allow each child to see, hear, and, when relevant, participate. The rules and the atmosphere should allow each child to make mistakes and to have his/her presentation accepted with serious attention.

For all large group situations, preparation (planning and discussion) must be made in the classroom as well as attention paid to problems as they arise in the various settings. Raising to a conscious level the underlying considerations in each setting gives meaning to rules and a framework within which to examine problems.

Attitudes, understandings, and skills the adults must have. The *attitudes* and values that adults must have to facilitate governance-related learning in school-wide settings are at least the following:

1. A willingness to assume responsibility for the behavior and learning of all the children in the school (not just one's own classroom, busload, etc.).

2. An awareness that for children to accept and value authority they must understand *what* they are learning and why rules and procedures are necessary. (Even a glimmer of understanding is worth the effort for the very young because it shows respect for them—at least a respect for their potential to understand.)

3. A valuing of the principles of fairness, cooperation, authority, and respect for individuals and a willingness to spend time exploring the meaning of these principles and developing strategies for teaching them.

4. A cooperative attitude among the various segments of the school's adult population. Such cooperation shows mutual respect and, if visible to children, provides excellent models for them.

Adults must *understand* at least the following:

1. The cognitive development of 5–12-year-olds and what this means for social/moral development. All school personnel (teachers, administrators, office staff, nurses, cafeteria workers, custodians, bus drivers, etc.) will interact with children of all ages. They should know what responses are appropriate when problems arise and what statements are likely to be effective when trying to emphasize children's learning of positive social behavior.

2. The basic concepts children should learn in each large group setting. Terms which can

have meaning now and usefulness after the elementary school years, in citizenship education, should be used consistently.

3. The conditions under which these concepts are best understood; how attitudes and values are internalized (the affective taxonomy) and what this means for law-related education in the elementary schools.
4. Educative ways of dealing with conflicts between individuals or between groups. Ways to deal with individual or group violation of rules.
5. Distinctions among different types of problems (individual, group, and total school): (*a*) single occurrence of a minor problem, (*b*) single occurrence of a serious problem, (*c*) repeated occurrence of a minor problem, (*d*) repeated occurrence of a serious problem. Children gain perspective by learning to distinguish the differences between minor and serious violations as well as the significance of repeated violation.

Necessary *skills* include the following:

1. Modeling desirable behavior. This is a powerful teaching device; adults in schools must demonstrate consistently, in daily behavior, the values they espouse.
2. Leading discussions.
3. Guiding decision-making processes.
4. Working with children and adults so that opinions and feelings are expressed and respected.

In sum, the underlying principles for encouraging governance-related learning are the same for the classroom and for school-wide experiences. The differences lie in the learning situations peculiar to each, the characteristics of both adult and student populations, and tasks and complexities. The overall goals are the same, the principles of human development equally apply, and a mutually reinforcing set of attitudes and approaches creates the most desirable learning environment.

Conclusions

Governance in the elementary schools is a little-studied topic. (An interesting recent treatment, though more clearly related to curriculum than to governance, is that of Berlak, 1977.) Perhaps it is little studied because of a widespread realization (though seldom expressed) that formal systems of all-school governance are inappropriate to children of this age. Formal governance within classrooms has not been used for much more than taking care of daily routines.

Our paper looks at the more complex and subtle forms of governance that constantly function in classrooms and school-wide. We propose that explicit recognition be given to the fact that such systems always operate in every school and that they should be consciously used to teach governance-related concepts. Learning related to cooperation, respect for individuals, property and authority, fairness, the need for rules, and responsibility can and should be taught in schools, and ultimately forms the foundations upon which democratic governance rests. Such concepts are best taught when based on the direct experiences of children and when the schools themselves provide models who constantly function in terms of these values.

This social learning, like all other parts of the curriculum, must be based on sound knowledge of human growth and development and should constantly be evaluated in light of two rights basic in all schooling: the right to be safe and the right to learn.

REFERENCES

Berlak, H. Human consciousness, social criticism and civic education. In J. P. Shaver (Ed.), *Building rationales for citizenship education* (National Council for the Social Studies, Bulletin 52). Washington, D.C.: National Council for the Social Studies, 1977.

Cremin, L. A. *Public education.* New York: Basic, 1976.

Dewey, J. *Democracy and education.* New York: Macmillan, 1916.

Dreeben, H. *On what is learned in school.* Reading, Mass.: Addison-Wesley, 1968.

Gordon, C. W. *The social system of the high school.* Glencoe, Ill: Free Press, 1957.

Havighurst, R. J. *Developmental tasks and education* (3rd ed.). New York: McKay, 1972.

Henry, J. *Culture against man.* New York: Random, 1963.

Governance in Elementary Schools:
An Exploration in Law-related Education

Ron Wetterholt

How much responsibility for self-governance in schools can young children assume? Ron Wetterholt suggests that the answer becomes apparent when we look at children operating in their own private worlds unconstrained by adults. He notes that by carefully observing children at play and on their own, teachers can determine children's capacities for self-governance and adjust the responsibility they give children to the capacities and needs of individuals. The author expands the concept of self-governance to include having children help make decisions about what they learn as well as how their school social environment is managed.

Having been a student, then later a teacher, in public school for many years has been an experience somewhat similar to swinging on a pendulum. I have had many moments when I was unsure of myself. Was I, in fact, grasping the tail of a tiger? Was I, perhaps, part of a strange construction, the creation of a latter-day Edgar Allan Poe?

Indeed, from all my recollections—elementary school: depression of the thirties; high school: World War II; university: McCarthy; teaching: "A Mighty Fortress Is Our IBM," followed by "Off the Pig," "Burn, Baby, Burn," "Hell No, I Won't Go," "Do Your Own Thing," and finally, "Back to the Basics"—I get the feeling that students and parents, no less than teachers and administrators, are reeling.

We would all like a panacea, I know, but that isn't likely. What we do need in place of pedagogical Valium is a continuing, developmental stability within the larger educational community: a stability at little cost (our dollars are disappearing along with the fanny patches on the Levis), a stability that would be unaffected by rapid and erratic political swinging and swaying.

Certainly, the stretching, contracting, expanding, and approaching financial bankruptcy of school systems go far in confusing adults about the roles we must play out in education. If we are confused, God help the kids.

I have the good feeling, however, that the ideas on governance in schools, as defined and so well

described by the Family Fischer, will help solve some of the problems.

With all that, let's move to the Fischer paper. May I say at the outset that I believe in the ideas—in my heart, and from 10 years' continuous experience where I presently teach—and I have seen them work. For ease of understanding, I'll attempt to review and react, in the paragraphs that follow, in the general order of presentation of the Fischer paper itself.

In the opening pages the Fischers call attention to informal systems that operate in a school, and they state that these systems are probably just as powerful as the formal systems in school learning, that they teach concepts and influence the development of attitudes and values. It is my feeling that this statement should have more teeth added. These informal systems are the *real* systems in schools. Established bureaucratic systems are cumbersome, and easily paid off with lip service once the classroom door is closed.

But the informal systems! They are born of strong belief and immediate necessity. For good or bad, they work, and it is those systems that have the real impact on students: Are conflicts resolved by discussion, face-saving, and compromise? Or does everybody get chewed out for swamping the teacher's canoe? How much consideration is given to children's expressed needs in curriculum planning (within the larger taxonomy)? How far away from the first 10 amendments to the Constitution does the teacher operate?

My own experience tells me that it is the powerful hidden curriculum that must be altered and improved if real governance involving children is ever to take place on more than a spotty basis across the nation. Teacher training institutions

Ron Wetterholt is a classroom teacher of a multi-age group and team coordinator at Martin Luther King, Jr., Experimental Laboratory Schools (K–5, 6–8), Evanston, Illinois. He has served as editor of and contributor to *Motivations,* a publication of the faculty.

are changing—and improving. My student teachers have a better understanding that human rights and responsibilities apply to the 9-year-old, just as they apply to them—college students—in their late teens. The late-sixties campus revolution on the grass of the quadrangles appears to have had good effect at the lecturn in the adjacent School of Education.

So, it appears to me, governance that involves the governed—the children—should have good possibilities for the future, as more and more recently graduated young people join the professional ranks. And new professionals help change old institutions. But there is a danger: The continuing—and worsening—financial situation in education is creating ever greater demands for simplicity and efficiency in education. And governance that involves the children can never be either simple or efficient. As the economy worsens and inflation continues, more and more parents—frightened by the balances in their charge accounts and by ever-tightening conditions for student entrance into college—demand simpler curricula with more and more statistical measures to prove the present—and future—success of their children.

Educational authoritarianism of the worst sort would satisfy many of the parents, and even some of the students. And it might even help balance the budget. But I think that such authoritarianism would produce lousy human beings, lacking those human qualities that would emerge if schools and curricula would take time to involve students in decision making in the classroom and in the school.

Self-Governance at the Elementary Level

Developing governance learning in the early elementary grades *is* a delicate procedure. And the Fischers are both perceptive and astute in their discussion. Their point that the students' background in relation to self-governance is of great importance is well taken. It has been my experience that even partners in the most open marriages tend to be authoritarian with regard to the children. Children are accustomed to this authoritarianism, and, as they view the homeroom teacher as an extension of the parent, so they expect—even demand—authoritarian structure in the school, at least at the beginning of their careers. And the school, too, for reasons of physical and mental safety, must have many reasonable, but also many arbitrary, rules. How these rules are explained, how they are applied, makes the difference. Explaining the "why" of rules to 5-year-olds is an initial step in helping youngsters take their own first steps in accepting

responsibility for their own actions. And the education lasts a lifetime.

I continue to be interested in the Fischers' points that (1) the developmental characteristics of each age group, and (2) the students' background in relation to self-governance, responsibility, and functioning in organized groups must be considered in organizing classroom procedures. I should like to make some observations about a special problem, that of developing ideas about self-governance with students in the inner city. (And here I am, calling the awful slum by its most recent euphemism: inner city. But then, I'm not middle-aged, I'm in my prime. Later I'll be a senior citizen, not an old man. And I'll eventuate a transition to tranquillity.)

Students in the inner city, more than many other students in the "better" parts of town or in the suburbs, have strong backgrounds in self-governance. It means their survival. Many, in the inner city, have highly developed backgrounds in functioning in organized groups. The problem is that this experience is seldom recognized because the philosophies of the groups are not compatible with or acceptable to the established school systems. But the experience exists. The expertise of these students—some as young as 7 and 8—probably could be tapped and used for governance in the classroom.

One last point about developing ideas about self-governance with the young of the inner city: Their expectations about creating and following rules in the school may be different from those of students in middle-class and affluent systems. Most teachers, I think, would teach children that if you do something "good," "good" things happen to you. If you do something "bad," the consequences are similar. But many students know that whether they do good or bad—or, indeed, do nothing (which could be good or bad, depending upon context)—*bad* things are the only things that happen to them.

I have never lived in the inner city, nor have I ever taught there. My acquaintance with the problem is through reading and through contact with people who have had personal experience there. Others—perhaps some in this gathering—could be precise informants.

When, as a teacher, one does examine a child's previous experience in self-governance, one should look, I think, at the child's play experience. This play experience, more than a lot of other factors, provides valid indicators. Does the student opt for low-organized games when at play? Or does he or she opt for more complicated games, such as soccer, football, or one of many forms of baseball? Does the child play alone on a swing, or wander, inactive, during a recess?

Games play involves rules and adjustment of rules, sometimes with yelling and fighting when rules are too confining.

Conflict resolution among children on their own is another good indicator of experience and maturity. Are conflicts "settled" with fights and abusive language? With real argument? In difficult situations does the child resort to an adult as lawyer/arbitrator/King Solomon?

Loner students—those who studiously avoid any entangling alliance—provide special challenges for teachers. These students generally make rules only for themselves and have little experience with compromise. Some loners are highly creative, but, unless helped to learn to function in groups at least part of the time, helped to make and understand political decisions, will never be adequately prepared to function (even solo) in the larger adult society.

Now, what really works at the elementary level in developing self-governance? The Fischers have given some excellent examples, and I'd like to add some that work in my school setting.

Handling conflict resolution. We try, as much as our energies and emotional capabilities will allow, to examine conflicts as honest attempts at settlement that went wrong. (I'm always reminded of one student, years ago, who explained to me about a fight, "It all started when he hit me back.") Regardless of the conflict—whether it involves a fight, or an insult that grows from anger or vice versa, or one of a hundred things that go wrong in the course of a single school day—the approach is (or attempts to be): "Tell me what you think happened. What do you think went wrong? How do you suppose you could handle it better the next time?" And I'm the first to admit that on burned-out Fridays I am liable to say, "Quit it." Nobody's perfect.

In my school we like to have big units of study that present several (not reams of) big ideas, and at the same time have students (mine are 8-, 9-, and 10-year-olds) elect particular areas of concentrated study within the larger core. Students sign up for individual or small-group research projects. They tell us what they wish to accomplish. They tell us how they plan to meet their own goals. (And if that is difficult for some, we help them on the spot.) This means that we, as teachers, can examine, along with individual students, what responsibilities are involved. We can check with the students to make certain they really understand what they are undertaking, whether the goals and activities are realistic with regard to the individual student. Teachers, then, are not instructors, but resource people and facilitators. They help students produce work of quality; they don't abstractly demand quality. Students, we feel, can then learn to govern themselves, push

themselves, rearrange goals and aims in the light of experience on the job.

The eventual evaluation to be read by parents (the "report card") is often written by the students themselves.

An example: About the time of the Nixon visit to China, we studied China. The team of students received a large body of information from books, films, TV tapes, and resource people: big ideas about geography, history (old and recent), commerce, and industry, including agriculture. Individual projects elected by students included (but were not restricted to) studying Chinese ideographs (and learning to mix ink from an ink block and using a brush to write), studying the abacus (and making one) and the Chinese counting system, Buddha, traditional costume, what children study in school, what Chinese people eat, what games Chinese children play, what songs they sing, folk tales, Yang and Yin, dragons, Mao, and *The Sayings of Chairman Mao*.

And, by the way, parents were involved. They attended a series of weekly evening talks and discussion on Red China given by a Northwestern University professor. He was Chinese, had been there on the heels of Kissinger, and lectured to packed houses.

I include this extended description to give you an example of the wide-ranging planning that is necessary when self-governance is a major consideration in curriculum design.

With regard to school-wide governance, I am in full agreement with the Fischers. Student government organizations are flashy, and work for just about the time it takes to elect officers. Kids, too, know that they don't work. Elections for such "front" organizations are generally used by students as popularity contests, and are best forgotten. (We have used some, however, to simulate registration and ballot-marking procedures.) At the junior high and high school levels, some schools have PTSAs (parent-teacher-student associations). I've never had any direct contact with them. Perhaps they work. Or perhaps they are merely an opportunity for parents to co-opt their own children. I don't know.

Our best successes at school-wide governance involved ad-hoc committees of children (similar to those described in the Fischer paper). Some helped design and install new landscape plantings for the schools grounds; another helps police the school campus. Probably our greatest success has been with major, school-wide curriculum projects. They are big enough and handle subject matter over a long enough period of time to allow us to involve children in the construction of aims and evaluation. The China unit is one such example. We have had other all-school themes that lent themselves to governance-related concepts: communications, Africa, prejudice.

Teachers need *time* to do these things. Fast in-and-out units of study demand too much efficiency.

Concluding Thoughts

Some general thoughts occur to me:

Governance-related concepts at *any* level of public education—kindergarten through grade 12—are most likely to be learned when teachers themselves practice professional self-governance in their own careers in the school system. So it comes down to this: the ideological center of any such law-related philosophy depends upon the intellectual set of the principal. At my school we are blessed with an administrator who helps make things happen, who, as an intellectual leader, fosters independent thought and responsible freedom of action in her faculty.

If, however, the principal is an authoritarian and dogmatist—paying lip service to ideas concerning self-governance in the faculty and student body—such law-related projects as those described today have little chance of getting off the ground—unless, of course, the teacher has the emotional strength of Saint Catherine, the patience of Job, and the skin of a walrus.

Real and lasting change in curriculum—formal and informal—has best chances for success when its origins are at the classroom level and blossom upward. But...Up the Republic! What we are about here is good for children and their families, good for schools, and good for government.

Bless the work.

Television Violence and Youth Attitudes toward Law Enforcement: A Proposal for Critical Viewing Skills

Helen A. Britton

When planning instruction and designing curricula, responsible educators must be cognizant of and allow for the multitude of factors outside school environs which affect learning within the school. One such factor which has received considerable attention in these last few years is the influence of television on children's learning. Both the medium and its messages are being scrutinized. When reading test scores decline, television viewing becomes suspect. Sex and violence spice up weak plots, but what are our children learning? Many television shows derive from legal contexts or address law-related issues. What, for example, are "Starsky and Hutch" and "Cass" teaching our children about law in our society? Helen Britton explores issues such as these and concludes that "television does not represent reality on issues of law enforcement" and does encourage violence and/or the condoning of violence. To counteract such negative influences, the author advocates a curriculum to teach critical viewing skills which will enable children to evaluate and control the messages sent by the television medium.

The suspicion that television has profound effects on our society has been present ever since the medium was introduced to American life almost 30 years ago. But only within the past decades have social scientists, psychologists, and educators begun to study seriously the effects of television on socializing the young.

"The American public has been preoccupied with governing our children's schooling," says Alberta Seigal, a psychiatrist at Stanford University. "We have been astonishingly unconcerned about the medium that reaches into our homes. Yet we may expect television to alter our social arrangements just as profoundly as printing has done over the past five centuries" (Seigal, 1974).

Still, with the fear of television persisting in some quarters, the American people have become the world's leading consumers of television sets and television programming. In 1976, it was estimated that there were 125 million television sets in the United States, with more than 90% of the households possessing at least one operating set (*A. C. Nielsen Report*, 1977).

According to Nielsen (1977), children under the age of 5 watch an average of 23.5 hours of television per week. While less than the average weekly television diet of adults (44 hours per week), its effects are incalculable. Over a lifetime, that rate of viewing means that by high school graduation, a student has spent at least 15,000 hours in front of the television screen—more time spent than on any other activity except sleep. And at present levels of advertising and violence, that teenager will have been exposed to 350,000 commercials and 18,000 murders.

It seems clear that a very large number of Americans like television, whatever effects its programs may have. And if these millions of people believe that television may be harmful to anybody, they do not believe it is harmful to them. In fact, most of the furor over violent television has been centered on its effects on children and youth. There is fear that children may imitate the violent acts of a television program and/or may become insensitive to the violent treatment of other people as a result of their television viewing.

This paper examines the evidence to support claims of negative effects of television in our society. In addition to looking at television research evidence, the paper considers the dynamics of mass communication effects as related to attitudes and beliefs about our law enforcement and criminal justice system in America. Finally, it presents ways in which educators might influence our societies' television viewing habits, the primary way being a curriculum for teaching critical viewing skills.

Helen Britton is currently a free-lance consultant in New York City and is doing research and writing for television. She was formerly Coordinator, Television Programming, San Diego County, California, Department of Education.

Media Content and Social Learning

It is a given that all human social behavior is learned. Much of this process occurs through trial and error, which involves differentiated feedback. Television, an unresponsive communication system, does not enter into trial-and-error learning.

A great deal of human social behavior is also learned through imitation and observation. As children mature, they acquire the ability to model their behavior after that of others, independent of punishments and rewards.

Although the mass media offer rich and powerful personalities, lovers and friends, artists and criminals, saints and neurotics, as objects for identification, we may assume with certainty that identification with the content of mass media does not play as decisive a role in the socialization process as identification with parents and other more intimately related persons (Seigal, 1974).

In a summary of research on identification theory and children's mass communication experience, Feilitzen and Linné (1975) conclude that children whose relations to parents and playmates are less harmonious tend to seek models in the world of mass media to a greater extent than others. They may also be assumed to seek other kinds of models. It has been shown, for example, that children who watch television and attend movies most frequently, as well as those who prefer more violent programs and films, often lack positive relations with the people around them. Also, these same children are the most influenced by what they have seen. Feilitzen and Linné list two types of media identification—similarity identification and wishful identification. They also report that identification tendencies seem to change around the age of 8. Until then, children's programming for similarity identification is preferred; later, adult or family programming speaks more to wishful identification.

To explain children's observational behavior, we should consider the observational learning opportunities which are available. We know that children watch television. Do they imitate what they see there? The authenticity of television and movies in American society makes it seem credible that they may.

Research Studies on Media Violence and Behavior

In a series of studies at Stanford University, Bandura and his associates (Bandura & Huston, 1961; Bandura, Ross, & Ross, 1961, 1963a, 1963b) have concluded that children learn aggressive behavior from television and that they enact this behavior in their play under suitable circumstances. In earlier studies, Bandura showed that children will imitate acts of aggressive behavior they observe in an adult. He then conducted a study which concluded that children will imitate aggressive acts of adults, whether they were seen on film or observed at first hand. Bandura has conducted many such studies, using different subjects and different films. Each confirms the first conclusion drawn.

Each of these studies also showed that children who observed film-mediated violence later manifested more nonimitative aggressive behavior than children who observed either no film or a nonviolent film.

In another vein, studies (Hartmann, 1969; Walters & Llewellyn-Thomas, 1963) exposed adolescents to either violent or nonviolent films, after which they were placed in a situation in which they thought they were actually administering shocks to another person. In both cases, subjects who had viewed the more aggressive films gave much longer "shocks" than did their controls. From these studies, researchers have concluded that film-mediated violence may not only teach specific aggressive behaviors, but may generalize to a class of aggressive behavior.

Moreover, relative to other kinds of film-mediated behavior, aggressive behavior appears to have a high probability of being learned. For example, media violence occurs in contexts of emotion, action, and conflict, contexts that increase children's attention. Media violence is often committed by characters with whom children identify. When the hero triumphs through aggressive behavior, that behavior is often portrayed as inherently effective and rewarded.

Today, even the most adamant network executives concede that some children, under certain conditions, will imitate antisocial acts that they witness on television. Given these conclusions, social scientists have begun to focus on less obvious evidence of psychic dysfunction. Evidence is now beginning to emerge that watching violence on television increases children's tolerance of violent behavior in others. In an experiment by Drabman and Thomas (1975), several hundred fifth graders were asked to act as baby-sitters for a group of younger children shown on a TV screen, who were supposedly playing in the next room. The baby-sitters were instructed to go to a nearby adult for assistance if their charges began fighting. Those who had been shown a violent TV film just before taking up the duties were far slower to call for help than those who had watched a pro baseball telecast. While the exact psychological mechanism governing this behavior remains to be discovered, the overall conclusion is cause for concern. It is even more chilling when one combines these data with the older modeling research. Television violence may be having the dual effect of exacerbating some children's violent behavior while at the same time teaching the rest to tolerate their aggression. A future society subject to such dynamics could well be an unfortunate place to live.

Gerbner and his associates corroborate these findings and contend that television provides a sense of false reality (Gerbner, Brouwer, Clark, & Drippendorff, 1969). In their research, 3 years of tests on television violence established that heavy TV watchers tend to exaggerate the danger of violence in their own lives, creating paranoia in the young. Gerbner contends that the prevailing message of television is to generate fear.

While research studies offer evidence that children are affected by viewing acts of violence on film or television, consideration should be given to how this may alter their attitudes and behavior in our everyday world. In a study, commissioned by the American Broadcasting Company, of 100 juvenile offenders, 22 confessed to having copied criminal techniques from television. In 1977, a Los Angeles judge sentenced two teenage boys to long jail terms after they held up a bank and kept 25 persons hostage for 7 hours. In pronouncing the sentence, the judge noted that the entire scheme had been patterned after an "Adam-12" episode the boys had seen 2 weeks earlier ("What TV Does to Kids," 1977).

The Ronald Zamora trial in Miami, Florida, based a defense for murder on television violence. A 15-year-old who was convicted of murdering his elderly neighbor in a robbery attempt contended in his defense that watching so many murders on television had distorted his judgment of right and wrong (Grant, 1978). Another case, scheduled to come to trial in San Francisco, contends that the networks are liable for damages that result from imitation of violent acts on television. The case revolves around a controversial movie shown on television, *Born Innocent*. It contains explicit scenes of an adolescent homosexual rape like one later carried out on two young girls. The girls' lawyer contends that the network advertised the movie along with another adolescent movie, *Born Free,* and therefore encouraged a youthful audience for this explicit violence. They further contend that the network (NBC) should have known that this act could be imitated, and therefore the network has culpability. The outcome of this trial may set a precedent for future trials involving imitation of violence from television.

Adult behavior, as well as children's, may be imitative. On December 13, 1966, the National Broadcasting Company presented a filmed drama entitled *The Doomsday Flight*. The plot of the film centered on the placement of a bomb on a transcontinental airliner. The plane emerged safely because it landed at an altitude above that at which the bomb was triggered to go off. The supposed suspense lay in tracing the deranged man, who kept teasing officials with information on his deadly act (Gould, 1966a, 1966b).

While the film was still on the air, a bomb threat was telephoned to one U.S. airline. Within 24 hours of the show, four more had been phoned in. Within the week following the show, eight such hoax calls in all were received by various airlines. These eight bomb threats in 1 week equaled the number of such calls received in the entire previous month, according to the Federal Aviation Agency.

Numerous efforts were made by the Air Line Pilots Association to keep the program off the air in the interest of air safety. These efforts proved unsuccessful. The film was shown, and a rash of bomb hoaxes did ensue. Fortunately, there is no record that a bomb was in fact placed on any plane.

Prosocial Learning from Television

Evidence has been presented establishing a causal link between viewing televised violence and later aggressive behavior. But on the opposite side of the coin, couldn't televised positive social examples have just as much effect on imitative behavior? Considering the importance of this possibility for the socialization of the young, it is striking that so little is known about the potentially positive influence of television.

A study (Sprafkin, Liebert, & Poulos, 1975) was designed to determine whether the presence of a specific act of helping would induce similar behavior in young viewers who were later placed in comparable situations. Children were exposed to episodes of prosocial "Lassie" television programs and a neutral episode of "Lassie," and a control group viewed a situation comedy program, "The Brady Bunch." The researchers concluded, that at least under some circumstances, televised social examples can increase a child's willingness to engage in helping behavior.

More research is called for in this area, but indications are that television has potential to influence children's prosocial as well as antisocial behavior.

Cross-cultural Analysis and Media Violence

While the evidence points to television violence being imitated in American society, little cross-cultural analysis has been done. One recent analysis of the effects of television in Japan (Barnard, 1978) brings a rather disconcerting note into American research and conclusions about the effects of television violence. Although the Japanese have been thoroughly exposed to the purportedly degenerative effects of television since 1953, their national crime statistics improve each year. Murder, rape, assault, and other violent crimes have been on the decline for 30 years. Juvenile delinquency is simply not a problem, nor is street crime. The ever-present police officer is a respected figure who salutes smartly when a citizen speaks.

Granted that Japan differs from the United States in many ways, but Japanese television is very much like our own, violence and all. The Japanese have just as many television channels, some programming up to 20 hours a day, and, like Americans, rate television ahead of newspapers as their prime source of news and as a necessity of life. In the prime-time evening hours, over 62% of all Japanese television sets are turned on. American and Japanese researchers agree that Japanese television is at least as bloody, brutish, and frightening as is American. Japanese authorities consider television violence to be an old issue. "Television simply does not have that kind of effect on Japanese youth," says Fumio Mugishima of the Psychological Research Section of the Police Science Laboratory (Barnard, 1978).

Speculation among Japanese psychologists is that violence in Japan does not have the same effects as in America because the family is still too strong, too influential in the lives and conduct of young people. Educators in Japan suggest that most children's viewing is limited to between 4:00 and 6:00 P.M. because after that they are too burdened with schoolwork to spare the time. A Japanese advertising executive promotes a widespread opinion that while the Japanese like violence in their entertainment, it is all fantasy, not real. In real life, it is difficult to get away with a crime. If the man on the street sees a crime being committed, he will do something about it. He is not afraid to become involved. If a woman screams rape in a Japanese house, everyone in the neighborhood will surely hear her. Also, Japan has strict gun laws—3 years in jail for possession of a gun, 10 years for using a gun in a crime. So, even if young Japanese see robberies and killings with guns on television, they simply do not picture themselves doing such things . . . it is beyond possibility.

Television and Attitudes toward Law Enforcement

An important question to consider for the purposes of this paper is that of attitudes on law enforcement and its relationship to viewing of television crime shows. One study by Bouma (1969), a sociologist, surveyed 10,000 students in several Michigan cities. He found that attitudes toward police were related to race, social class, sex, and actual contact with police. Low-income black males with personal contact with police displayed the most negative attitudes.

In a content analysis (Dominick, 1973) of crime and law enforcement as portrayed in prime-time television, several stereotyped portrayals were found:

1. TV crime is unsuccessful (90% of all TV crimes were solved at the end of the program.
2. Compared to its relative frequency in real life, murder is overrepresented on television.
3. When a TV crime is witnessed by the general public, the witnesses generally remain passive.
4. TV police are seldom portrayed as villains (only 2% were judged to be villains).
5. Law enforcers in a major role usually commit a violent act (92% according to the content analysis).
6. Violent crime among family members is underrepresented on television (only 7% of the violent crimes were in this category).

In another study (Dominick, 1974), designed to gauge (1) the amount of exposure to police and crime shows and (2) the relative importance attached to this content as an information source, it was found that the amount of time a child spent watching crime and police shows was unrelated to the judged importance of television as an information source. The viewing of crime shows was positively correlated with (1) identification with a television character associated with law enforcement; (2) belief that criminals usually get caught; and (3) knowledge of civil rights when arrested. However, it was also found that the more important television was to the child, the less likely he or she would be to inform police about a witnessed crime. For both boys and girls, the strongest predictors of general evaluation of police were the perceived attitudes of friends and family. For boys only, more personal contact with police was associated with negative evaluation. Finally, legal terms and processes shown frequently on television were better known than those items not commonly portrayed.

Another study (Rarick, Townsend, & Boyd, 1973) shows that young people's image of television police is not correlated with their image of actual police, and television images held by delinquents and middle-class youths are not much different. Six distinct patterns of perception, three of actual and three of television police, were found. Perceptions of actual police are diverse, ranging from highly favorable to openly hostile, with some mixed feelings. Perceptions of television police are relatively homogeneous and positive. Among three groups of adolescents sampled there is widespread belief that television police are idealized dramatizations different from reality. Adolescent adjudicated delinquents perceive television police in much the same way as do nondelinquents. However, the adolescents agreed that most people dislike and distrust the police and that police recognize this hostility.

This research points to the need for making actual police relationships with the community more positive. Television does not appear to be generating negative attitudes toward law enforcement officers.

Television does give information to young people. In the Dominick (1973) study, almost all subjects knew about rights upon being arrested, while few knew legal terms uncommon on television. This reflects the fact that on television the legal process generally ends with arrest. Television shows seldom focus on what happens to a case as it goes through the court system. As a result, youngsters know one part of the judicial process but know little about the workings of the system in other equally important areas.

What Can the Schools Do?

That television does not represent reality on issues of law enforcement, offers examples of violent behavior for possible imitation, and presents psychological forces that seems to engender tolerance of violence for others can be concluded from the foregoing analysis. Television does offer information on certain areas of our legal system, but none in other areas. But the solutions to these problems are far more complex than they might appear at first, and simple statements of blame will not suffice. Some members of the general public, academia, and Congress sometimes assume that the federal government does, or should, decide what programs are suitable for public consumption. In fact, people often believe that the Federal Communications Commission should take off the air programs it does not like or does not find acceptable. The FCC does not censor for two basic and wise reasons. First, the First Amendment guarantees free speech for all forms of communication which applies to the nation as a whole; second, Section 326 of the Communications Act states: "Nothing in this ACT shall be understood or construed to give the Commission the power of censorship..." (Hartenberger, 1977).

If the FCC should not exercise controls on television programming, who should? There is considerable merit to the broadcasters' claim that parents are at fault if they do not regulate their children's viewing habits. By the time the Family Viewing Hour was struck down by the courts, it had already proven unsatisfactory because so many parents were not cooperating. Nielsen (*A. C. Nielsen Report,* 1977) found that 10.5 million youngsters under the age of 12 were still watching television after 9:00 P.M., when the Family Hour ended. And a recent Roper study reported that only two-fifths of the parents polled enforced rules about what programs their children could watch.

Dr. Robert L. Stubblefield, child psychiatrist and medical director, Silver Hill Foundation, New Canaan, Connecticut, recommends ("What TV Does to Kids," 1977) that parents should be prepared to turn the television set off and pick up a book if a child wants to watch an "adult" show after 9:00 P.M. Children still model most of their behavior after their parents—so the best way is for the parent to set the example.

If parents are unwilling to provide positive models for their children, can the schools contribute to a solution to the television controversy? After many years of schools being mandated to provide a variety of food, bus, and health services to students, many educators are reluctant to take responsibility in a new area. Also, many people believe that the schools should stick to the basics—reading, writing, spelling, and arithmetic. The opposite position points out that the average person is using television as a replacement for reading in the one-way communication process. Those who hold this point of view will say that times have changed since 1945, and one of these major changes is a shift away from depending upon print for information and entertainment. Just as the schools recognized that students need to learn about science and new health discoveries, so should the schools accept the responsibility for teaching children skills needed to deal with television messages.

Parents must regard with an understanding eye their own extensive use of television and their own turning away from reading. If the average adult does not read for leisure activity, children cannot be expected to embrace reading in the face of the pleasure of television watching.

Some educators have begun to harness commercial television's power in positive ways. A few years ago the Philadelphia school system started tying reading assignments to television offerings. For example, scripts for such documentary dramas as *The Missiles of October* and *Eleanor and Franklin* were distributed to more than 100,000 students before the television programs aired.

Prime Time School TV (PTST), a nonprofit Chicago organization, has designed an innovative approach. PTST uses some of television's most violent programs to examine positive social values. In one 7-week course, students were given questionnaires and told to fill them out while watching "Kojak" and "Barretta." The questions were later discussed in class and dealt with everything from illegal search and seizure to forced confessions.

These are sadly isolated positive approaches to using television. The power of television, for good or harm, must be harnessed by our society. Students must be taught to be intelligent consumers of television fare, not mindless recipients of a myriad of television messages. The teaching must be organized and systematic so that all students have the benefit of being informed viewers.

To accomplish this goal, a curriculum for teaching critical viewing skills, acceptable for national adoption, must be designed and implemented in our schools with all deliberate speed. That one generation of children has grown up under the influence of television violence is enough for many parents and advocates of youth to cry for change. However, that the change process in the form of educational programs may take a long time to accomplish is no reason for some television critics to attempt regulatory short-cuts with implications for censorship.

A Proposal for the Study of Television

Amidst the charges and countercharges, new generations of Americans continue to be inducted into our television society with little if any more understanding of the medium-institution-industry than their parents or grandparents had as a result of their formal education. What is proposed is an inquiry-oriented introductory study of television which may be undertaken at the intermediate, junior, or senior high school levels. The curriculum should be designed to provide students with opportunities to gather their own data, draw their own inferences, compare their analyses with other studies, and examine objectively major conflicting positions on the impact of television on our society.

The curriculum for teaching viewing skills is indicated in the following outline:

I. The Nature of Human Communication
   A. Mass media as social systems
   B. The structure and function of communication in society
   C. Mass media as a communications institution
II. Mass Communication Audiences
   A. The television audience in the United States

   B. Selective exposure to information—perception and television
   C. Messages for audience persuasion
   D. Audience responses to slanted messages (propaganda)
III. Historical, Social, and Technical Factors Affecting the Emergence of the Modern Television Industry
   A. Television and radio operations—scientific/technical background
   B. Historical background and the beginnings of television
   C. The economic structure of television
      1. The beginnings of national networks
      2. Television networks today
      3. The economics of advertising
   D. Alternative systems of mass communications; global perspectives
      1. The British Broadcasting Corporation and ITV
      2. European television
      3. Television in the Third World
IV. Critical Issues in United States Television
   A. The public interest and television regulation
   B. Stereotyping of minority groups and women in television
   C. Political socialization and television
   D. Social learning and television violence
   E. Television and prosocial behavior
   F. Television and the dynamics of changing society
   G. The future of television—emerging technology and information systems.

Ultimately, teachers and curriculum writers can integrate instruction about television into the present curriculum areas of the social sciences, such as history, sociology, economics, and consumer education, as well as into language arts and communications.

A different approach to teaching critical viewing skills could be developed using the model of Ploghoft and Anderson (1977) at Ohio University. They suggest that a program should include these components for children in upper elementary and high school classes:

1. *Television and You,* a student textbook which examines the institution of television.
2. A personal diary study in which each child studies his/her own uses of television.
3. Entertainment programs and values. Students are guided in sorting out value statements in entertainment programs and consider the consequences of these values.
4. Commercials. Students analyze professionally prepared commercials for the persuading

statements and finally produce their own commercials to get a first-hand feel of the persuasive process.

Students can be taught, on a simple level, some of the sociological and psychological effects of heavy television consumption so that they may exercise informed judgment on what they see on television and regulate their own and their children's television viewing in an intelligent manner.

Implementing a Critical Viewing Skills Curriculum

That television news is the most widely used source of information has been known for some years. Moreover, a Lambert and Klineberg study (1967) emphasized that pedagogues are rarely mentioned by their students as important sources of information about foreign peoples, while the mass media are claimed as the almost exclusive sources of such information.

Teachers still find it difficult to make students' many hours of television viewing relevant to their classroom experience. Nor do teachers receive much guidance from methods texts, which seem to view television in the classroom as an afterthought. Teachers often site such difficulties as student access to a television set at home, concern for advertising on assigned programs, and inability to preview television programs for planning, as reasons for not using commercial television in the classroom.

These problems may be minimized if teachers will: (1) recognize that television can be profitably used in the classroom, (2) extend extra efforts to plan for TV programs, and (3) relinquish the idea that all students must have a common experience before a classroom discussion can take place.

To implement properly a curriculum for critical viewing skills, student learning materials must be purposely developed with a strategy for diffusion into the school curriculum. Student materials, such as text materials with accompanying visuals, can help, but what better way to teach about the medium than to use the medium itself? For example, a television series could examine the issues and provide information on the topics listed in the curriculum outline. To encourage teachers to use the newly developed learning materials, a strategy for diffusion is essential for adoption. Finally, to implement further the concepts of critical viewing skills, teacher institutes or courses in teacher education programs could be created.

From the evidence reported in this paper, it can be concluded that behavioral and social learning does occur from imitating what is seen on television. However, both positive and negative (ag-gressive) behavior can be learned, depending on the models presented. While more evidence and analysis are in order, a tentative conclusion is that existing social values are operating in conjunction with TV viewing to cause violence in American society. A cross-cultural analysis shows that in Japan television programming is just as violent as in America, but there is little violence in Japanese society generally.

Rather than impose guidelines for censorship on the television producers and writers, a curriculum for critical viewing skills, to be taught in the public schools, is suggested. Informed viewers, capable of evaluating and making independent decisions about what they will watch, are the goal of such a curriculum.

REFERENCES

A. C. Nielsen Report. New York, 1977.

Bandura, A., & Huston, A. C. Identification as a process of incidental learning. *Journal of Abnormal and Social Psychology,* 1961, *63,* 311–318.

Bandura, A.; Ross, D.; & Ross, S. Transmission of aggression through imitation of aggressive models. *Journal of Abnormal and Social Psychology,* 1961, *63,* 575–582.

Bandura, A.; Ross, D.; & Ross, S. Imitation of film-mediated aggressive models. *Journal of Abnormal and Social Psychology,* 1963, *66,* 3–11. (a)

Bandura, A.; Ross, D.; & Ross, S. Vicarious reinforcement and imitative learning. *Journal of Abnormal and Social Psychology,* 1963, *67,* 601–615. (b)

Barnard, C. N. An oriental mystery. *TV Guide,* January 28, 1978, pp. 2–8.

Bouma, D. *Kids and cops.* Grand Rapids, Mich.: Erdman, 1969.

Dominick, J. R. Crime and law enforcement on prime time television. *Public Opinion Quarterly,* 1973, *37,* 241–250.

Dominick, J. R. Children's viewing of crime shows and attitudes on law enforcement. *Journalism Quarterly,* 1974, *51,* 5–12.

Drabman, R. S., & Thomas, M. H. Does TV violence breed indifference? *Journal of Communications,* 1975, *25* (Autumn), 86–89.

Feilitzen, C., & Linné, O. Identifying with television characters. *Journal of Communications,* 1975, *25* (Autumn), 51–55.

Gerbner, G.; Brouwer, M.; Clark, C. C.; &)rippen-dorff, K. Dimensions of violence in television drama. In R. S. Baker & S. K. Ball (Eds.), *Violence in media.* Philadelphia: University of Pennsylvania, 1969.

Gould, J. *The Doomsday Flight. New York Times,* December 15, 1966. (a)

Gould, J. A bomb backfires. *New York Times,* December 16, 1966. (b)

Grant, M. N. Can youngsters really catch the violence bug from TV? University of California at San Diego, *Medical News,* March 6, 1978, p. 9

Hartenberger, K. S. Sex, violence and the FCC. *Public Television Review,* 1977 (November/December), pp. 37–40.

Hartmann, D. P. Influence of symbolically modelled instrumental aggression and pain cues on aggressive behavior. *Journal of Personality and Social Psychology,* 1969, *11,* 280–288.

Lambert, W. E., & Klineberg, O. *Children's views of foreign people.* New York: Appleton, Century, Crofts, 1967.

Ploghoft, M. E., & Anderson, J. A. *Children and television.* Columbus: Ohio State University, October 1977.

Rarick, D. L.; Townsend, J. E.; & Boyd, D. A. Adolescent perceptions of police: Actual and as depicted in TV drama. *Journalism Quarterly,* 1973, *50,* 438–446.

Seigal, A. E. The effects of media violence on social learning. In W. Schramm & D. F. Robert (Eds.), *The process and effects of mass communication.* Champaign/Urbana: University of Illinois Press, 1974.

Sprafkin, J. N.; Liebert, R. M.; & Poulos, R. W. Effects of a prosocial televised example on children's helping. *Journal of Experimental Child Psychology,* 1975, *20,* 119–126.

Walters, R. H., & Llewellyn-Thomas, E. Enhancement of punitiveness by visual and audio-visual displays. *Canadian Journal of Psychology,* 1963, *17,* 244–255.

What TV does to kids. *Newsweek,* February 21, 1977, pp. 63–70.

Another view . . .

Television Violence and Youth Attitudes toward Law Enforcement: A Proposal for Critical Viewing Skills

Barbara R. Martinsons

According to Barbara Martinsons's analysis, television conveys a fairly primitive notion of justice. From the examples explored, she concludes that "the members of TV society are not sufficiently free or rational to forge their own social contracts, to be responsible for the maintenance of justice." If these observations are generalizable to the bulk of television fare, the models TV presents to our children are surely both inadequate and inappropriate for a democratic society. Any sense of dis-ease this observation gives the reader won't be relieved by this author, who concludes her remarks by reminding us of the limitations of schooling for affecting children's orientations.

The evidence is coming in, and it appears, as Helen Britton indicates, that kids do indeed learn aggressive behavior from television and that they subsequently enact this behavior. In addition, there is emerging proof that watching TV violence leads to increased apathy when one is exposed to actual violence in others. I agree with Helen Britton that there is cause for concern, and an urgent need to explore televised situations that might result in prosocial learning in young viewers.

The issues of law enforcement and viewer attitude toward the police which are ably explored here are, I believe, a single (although important) aspect of a larger moral and philosophical issue. As Helen Britton points out, on TV the legal process tends to end with the arrest. The assumption

seems to be that once a lawbreaker has been identified, tracked down, and caught, justice has been done. It appears, from this well-taken conclusion, that not much is learned of the nature of justice; questions of justice, equality, and equity are largely ignored by TV.

The issue of aggression/violence is a vital one—but I think that it is possible to look "behind" it at some germinal concepts, background, underpinning. One might choose from a list including (but not necessarily limited to) liberty, power, fairness, authority, etc. I will consider justice.

I would like to examine the concept of justice as portrayed on television and its relationship to the elementary-school-age audience. First, however, two preliminary points might be useful. The first of these is a brief statement of our Western, twentieth-century view of justice in society.

Justice, as Rawls (1971) points out, is the first virtue of social institutions and of human activities. We tend to start with an intuitive conviction

Barbara R. Martinsons is currently a doctoral student in American history at Columbia University. Previously she was Vice President, Acquisition and Development, Prentice-Hall Media, Tarrytown, New York.

of the primacy of justice, on which we attempt to structure our political and social lives. While this intuitive notion of justice has historical roots in our Judeo-Christian background and in the utilitarian tradition, it is drawn largely from the contractarian tradition of Locke, Rousseau, and Kant. This social contract notion of justice stresses three points important for this discussion. They are: (*a*) that people are rational, that society is composed largely of "individuals as moral persons, that is, as rational beings...capable...of a sense of justice" (Rawls, 1971, p. 12); (*b*) that people are equally able to enter into contract, and are equally able to make the necessary moral decisions, that there is "equality between human beings as moral persons...and each man is presumed to have the requisite ability to understand and to act upon whatever principles are adopted" (Rawls, 1971, p. 19); and (*c*) that people have the capacity for "disinterestedness," that the individual can waive his/her own good for the good of society.

Justice, then, is interpreted as a cooperative venture for the mutual advantage of all members of society in which "the well-being of each [member] depends on a scheme of social cooperation" (Rawls, 1971, p. 103). What I want to stress here is that justice must be consented to by people who are equally able to arrive at such rational consent.

There is a second preliminary point to consider before going on to consider the impact of TV on kids' concept of justice. It seems reasonable to establish some kind of development "state of the art." What does a 6-year-old mean by "it isn't fair"? What does a 12-year-old understand of "liberty and justice for all"? What kinds of concepts of justice are kids able to handle?

A variety of developmental models are available that focus on the social and moral growth of children; Kohlberg's is one of the better-known schemes for guiding kids from one stage to the next. Kohlberg's work, however, like everyone else's in this area, is based on the concepts and experimental findings of Piaget (1965), who still provides the most coherent and most useful model.

On the concept of justice, Piaget points out that there is an "evolution hierarchy" through which kids progress (more or less). Children of 6 and 7 combine two ideas about justice, both of which are aspects of retributive justice. The first he calls immanent justice. This is the notion of justice in *things;* at this age, he suggests, the child believes that the world will get even for misdeeds—a tree will fall on you, or it will rain on your picnic, or you will get stung by a bee, or as one 7-year-old put it, "nothing will go right all day." Paralleling immanent justice, kids of this age also accept an

ethic of constraint, or authority. Little cooperation is possible, and punishment which is seen as expiatory and often vindictive, is valued by the kids according to its severity—the more severe the "better."

By 7 or 8 years the ethic of cooperation begins to be grasped as a concept. Appropriate punishment is now seen as reciprocal, with clear relationship between the punishment and the crime. According to Piaget's model, distributive justice, based on the ideas of cooperation and equality, replaces retributive justice, which is based on authority and vengeance.

There is one more step in the Piagetian model, which begins, in the children Piaget studied, between 10 and 11 years, although I have encountered it in American 8-year-olds. This is the ethic of equity. After the idea of equality, during the period when the ethic of cooperation and distributive justice is grasped, is accepted, the child begins to realize that equality is frequently absent, that some kids are older or bigger or stronger than others. The ethic of equity acknowledges inequality and compensates for it: "Give him a head start; he's only 7."

Piaget stresses that this development sequence is largely independent of adult influence and "requires nothing more for its development than the mutual respect and solidarity...among children themselves" (Piaget, 1965, p. 198). The ethic of equity, which kids approach by adolescence, sounds very much like the basis for contractarian notions on which we base our idea of justice; Piaget concludes: "Authority as such cannot be the source of justice, because the development of justice presupposes autonomy...resting as it does on equality and reciprocity, justice can only come into being by free consent" (Piaget, 1965, p. 319).

TV and Children's Concept of Justice

Keeping in mind the contractarian view of justice, the Piagetian developmental model, and the notion of covert as well as overt "curriculum" in all learning, we come to television.

To prepare myself for this discussion I've been watching TV; I watch it a good deal anyhow—I like it. But during the past weeks I've been looking at the stuff that 6–12-year-old kids watch a lot of (Striker & Bonney, 1974), primarily cartoons, sitcom, and drama like "Wonder Woman" and "The Waltons." Consider a couple of examples:

On a "Wonder Woman" episode, the villains, called Skrill, are from another galaxy and don't have faces. They are described as a species that is mean for the sake of meanness, and they live up to their description. They are vanquished by Wonder Woman and a friend and banished to an out-of-the-way planet. There is no hope for them, in terms of human justice, and they don't deserve any. Thus Piaget's early-stage formulation of retributive, authoritarian, vindictive justice, in which the participants are hardly capable of moral decisions, since they are neither moral nor human, is acceptable.

On an episode of "The Waltons" another early-stage formulation is given legitimacy. Jim Bob, who loves machines and once built his own car, hears of an after-school job in an airplane plant close by. It seems heaven-sent. The pay is good and the family could certainly use the money. Most important, Jim Bob, who is considered something of an incompetent at home (somewhat clumsy and graceless; although the family loves him nonetheless, they tend to boss him around and tease him), knows that he's good with machines and can't wait to get his hands on airplane components. It seems a dream come true on several levels. He is under age, however, and must get consent from both parents to get the job. Unfortunately for Jim Bob, his mother is going through menopause and refuses, in a moody moment, to sign the application. Then, to scotch it completely, she runs away from home. The job is to be filled soon, and in desperation, knowing it's wrong, Jim Bob decides to forge his mother's signature. He parks behind some bushes and spreads the application on the car seat—when the local reverend, whose car has just broken down a few feet away, comes along and discovers the culprit. The mother recovers, and Jim Bob, who isn't big on schoolwork and whose handwriting is terrible, is forced by not so subtle blackmail on the reverend's part to take the job of copying out the reverend's sermons instead of working on airplanes. During the course of the episode the frame of a house that the father of the family has spent a lot of time and effort on blows down in a storm. Perhaps the father wasn't sufficiently understanding of the mother's problems. In any event, the episode ends with Jim Bob beaten by unjust circumstances and the other children teasing him (lovingly) about his new "job."

Here the audience is given a perfect example of immanent justice (or injustice, depending on one's point of view). If you break a rule as by lying or forgery, the world will get you somehow. Even an emergency does not temper the letter of this law—and Jim Bob's attempt at a reasonable interpretation of the spirit of the law does him in.

Finally, consider the world of Saturday morning cartoons: I've watched only a few of these, but I expect that they will serve as examples of the rest.

On "Scooby Doo Laff A Lympics" three teams compete in a variety of athletic events. The first team, called the Rottens, is composed of Charles Addams-like monsters who are named things like Creeply, Dread Baron, and Mumbly. This team cheats all the time. The second team, called the Yogis, is composed of animals with names like Grape Ape and Yankee Doodle Duck. The third team, the Scoobys, is made up of teenagers, superheroes, and dogs. The Rottens' motto is, "It's not how you play the game, it's the winning that counts," but they are constantly being penalized for booing the judges, having double contestants, and cheating. They *never* win. According to one steady 8-year-old viewer, the same team has won every contest but two over the past couple of years.

The judges are never seen, but are apparently omnipotent and are manifested by the scoreboard. When all of the Rottens' points were wiped out due to cheating, one of the Scoobys said: "See, there is justice after all." But is there, on Laff A Lympics? (If you're willing to pass on the question and settle for fun, instead, follow the advice of the accompanying commercial, which over a high-stepping red-white-and-blue parade, sings: "Where do you go for the good times?/You don't have to go far/Just put your hand in Nabisco/America's cookie jar.")

A second kind of cartoon, which includes "Superfriends," "Batman"/"Tarzan," and "Space Ghost," has more plot and more clearly evil "bad guys." On a recent Saturday morning of random channel changing I encountered:

■ Huge red army ants who are marched "over that cliff to the bottomless darkness" by the human good guys;
■ One "giant scaley ape" who crushed the good guys' (teenagers this time) spaceship on one hand;
■ Gigantic red bats with malevolent demeanor and intent;
■ An alien named the Creature King, who has a giant green head, fangs, yellow serpent-like eyes, and a spindly black body.

The only human bad guy was a preserved Neanderthal man, who, waving his club, chased the teenaged good guys around, and who turned out, in the last few minutes, to be a greed-crazed college professor disguised in a Neanderthal-man suit.

Once again, the villains are evil by design and intent. They are seldom human and have little communication, apart from malevolent snarls, grunts, and occasional plans to take over the universe, with human heroes and heroines. Although the human characters tend to be more or less integrated in terms of sex and race, justice is still a question of "them," generally unredeemedly evil and usually alien, against "us," the teenagers and superheroes and our pets. There are exceptions: I saw a "Fat Albert" in which cigarette smoking was the villain, but most of the programs planned for kids by educator types with good intentions ("Carrascolendas," "Big Blue Marble," "Zoom," "The Electric Company") are considered babyish by the 7–12 set and are not watched much.

So: the members of TV society, as portrayed in these few examples, are not sufficiently free or rational to forge their own social contracts, to be responsible for the maintenance of justice. The TV characters also display a lot of what Piaget would call retributive justice, immanent and vindictive, as if that's the way the world is. If, as the evidence suggests, kids learn a great deal about violence and aggression from TV, it is likely that they also learn a lot about other things, including what justice is all about. We must remember, though, that most lessons must be presented, reinforced, and re-presented over and over before attitudes are learned. Indeed, this is just what happens; TV is not the only American institution that characterizes or treats people as if they are not equally able to forge and maintain justice. Neither society in the real world nor society as portrayed on TV allows much room for the kind of questioning of basic premises needed if justice is to be *consented to.*

Schools do not encourage much questioning of basic premises either, nor do they tend to consider their clientele sufficiently free or rational to establish and maintain justice within the school community. In the early grades, of course, kids are not able to assume this task, if we accept the Piagetian model.

But, still following Piaget, in the normal course of things they *will* get there—become able to. For this kids need to develop a sense of autonomy, of daring to take risks and be wrong, of self-esteem, of efficacy, as well as the ability to think carefully, to reason clearly. Legitimate participation in school governance might be one way of getting there; law-related case studies and mock trials might be another; formal exploration of concepts such as justice, authority, or liberty might be still another. Perhaps critical viewing skills are part of the picture as well. Before we advocate school-oriented solutions, however, it might be wise to consider some of the recent thinking on the role of schooling and its purpose.

This recent thinking is concerned with the amount and kind of impact that schools have on the knowledge and lives of students. Once limited to schooling, today, thanks to the work of Lawrence Cremin and his students, the definition of education has broadened to include all the institutions that educate, including families, churches, zoos—and television. This expanded definition of education, combined with the idea of a "hidden curriculum" which exists in the classroom as well as in the TV program, leads to a series of questions about how important schools are, as well as about what is *really* being taught—and learned—inside and outside of school. Are schools, as Christopher Jenks suggests, "marginal institutions" that don't have much impact on the lives or attitudes of students? To what degree does the learning that kids do in school connect with what the teachers and curriculum writers think they're teaching?

Although this kind of question is, perhaps, beyond the scope of this symposium, I am uncomfortable supporting any curriculum, particularly those of the more formal, academic sort, until we have a clearer sense of the goals, impact, and outcome of schooling.

REFERENCES

Piaget, J. *The moral judgement of the child.* New York: Free Press, 1965.

Rawls, J. *A theory of justice.* Cambridge, Mass.: Harvard University Press, Belknap, 1971.

Striker, L., & Banney, N. Children talk about television. *Journal of Communication,* 1974, *24* (Summer), 54–61.

Bringing It Together

The introduction to this set of papers explicitly noted that the topics addressed were intended to be suggestive. The papers made no attempt to give an exhaustive overview of the nature of schools and schooling and how law and humanities programs might become a part of the elementary school curriculum. While we continue to make no claim for comprehensive coverage in this brief discussion, we would like to share with the reader some of the insights on the subject that have evolved both from the ideas presented in the papers and from the subsequent development work of these past several months.

The role that teachers play apparently cannot be emphasized enough. In his paper, Don Bragaw makes a strong plea for "infusing" the teacher with understanding of and commitment to the principles underlying a law and humanities focus. He makes the case that such "infused" teachers can then grasp the opportunities for teaching law and humanities which permeate the curriculum. The recent study of the status of science, mathematics, and social studies commissioned by the National Science Foundation's Education Directorate suggests that it is *absolutely imperative* that classroom teachers understand and concur with stated educational goals. This study shows that the extensive social studies development efforts of the sixties have had very little impact on actual classroom practices. A National Council for the Social Studies interpretive paper observes, "The reports remind us emphatically that the teacher is the key to what social studies will be for any student" (Shaver, Davis, & Helburn, 1979). This analysis demonstrates that teachers' perceptions of the purposes of education, in general, and social studies, in particular, are not the perceptions underlying the "new social studies," which are generally shared by social studies specialists. This interpretive report, which, by the way, is much more sympathetic to teachers than it is critical of them, describes both the teaching practices and teacher attitudes which predominate in classrooms across the nation. A careful study of this report should be on the "must read" list of any would-be educational change agent. Creative innovators should be able to use this information to design strategies for overcoming possible obstacles and capitalizing on apparent opportunities.

At least three observations about schooling which are made in the papers warrant being restated here. One observation is that television is only one of a multitude of out-of-school factors influencing what children are learning about issues related to law and humanities. Among other influences are: other public media, families, peers, the formal and informal governing structures of neighborhoods and communities, and visible authority figures at all levels of government. This list is also only suggestive, but it should serve as a reminder of the many influences impinging upon children which must be recognized and accommodated in any instructional program. A second observation is that the "hidden" or informal curriculum is an especially critical dimension of schooling related to issues associated with law and humanities. When the focus is on issues of justice, equity, authority, and other constructs which are manifest only in

157

social contexts, the impact of the informal curriculum has to be reckoned with. Strategies for doing so must be developed. The third observation is really a blueprint for action. It is—"infuse, don't add on." There is no room for another distinct subject area in an already overcrowded curriculum.

What else have we learned about getting law and humanities into the curriculum of the elementary schools? Perhaps the most useful—certainly the most optimistic—way of communicating this is through the following list of opportunities for law and humanities programs in elementary schools:

- Both educators and the general public are concerned about the apparent lack of respect for public institutions and public and private property, and the lack of discipline among children and young people. Good law and humanities programs involve children in meaningful citizenship experiences which promote both healthy social attitudes and civic responsibility.
- While the "back-to-basics" movement would seem to be working against us, it is possible to demonstrate that basic skills can be promoted through law and humanities programs.
- The flexible scheduling of elementary schools lends itself fairly easily to implementing such law-related strategies as using community resources.
- The core of ready-made community support which characterizes law-related education should make a law and humanities emphasis attractive to elementary school administrators.
- Most elementary schools have some form of school safety program which offers "entry" points for law and humanities.
- Elementary school teachers are not subject-matter specialists but specialists in children. Law and humanities programs are similarly concerned with developing well-rounded, socially responsible, and competent human beings.
- According to the NSF report, teachers believe one of their major responsibilities is to teach citizenship. Law and humanities programs offer these teachers support in achieving an objective to which they are already committed.
- Elementary teachers are concerned with school and classroom "management," which can be demonstrated to be a spin-off of a good law and humanities program that teaches conflict management, the nature and function of rules, and other group management processes and values.
- Textbooks—which the NSF study found to be teachers' major tool—already contain a significant amount of material related to law and humanities. This material could be pointed out to teachers and extended by curriculum developers. Where the material is missing or limited, it can (and should) be infused.
- Successful law-related programs in high schools can and should be pointed to as examples of the potential for such programs in elementary schools.
- In the same vein, it can be legitimately argued that if a solid foundation is *not* built throughout the elementary years, law-related education programs in high schools will necessarily be more remedial than developmental.
- Since few teachers have had previous exposure to law or to law and humanities curricular efforts, the subject offers them something new to learn themselves. This can be very attractive to a teaching force that is made up largely of war-weary veterans who have probably heard everything they ever wanted to know about reading and math—and then some.

■ Elementary classroom teachers have greater influence over their own pupils' total school experience than do high school teachers. Good law and humanities programs can help them shape both the formal and informal curriculum to reinforce educational goals and make them more successful teachers.

These are only some of the opportunities for law and humanities within elementary schools. Creative, innovative, dedicated, determined, informed persons will find or be able to develop many others. Individuals possessing these characteristics would probably even be able to ferret out "opportunities" within what appear to be "obstacles." The real challenge will be to find a way through or around such obstacles. The NSF studies referred to earlier identified several characteristics of classroom practices and teachers' perspectives which appear to work against successful implementation of law and humanities programs in elementary schools. The Executive Summary of the interpretive report, for example, concluded:

The dominant instructional tool continues to be the conventional textbook, and longtime bigsellers continue to dominate the market.

There is little interdisciplinary teaching, and little attention to societal issues.... The dominate [*sic*] modes of instruction continue to be large group, teacher-controlled recitation and lecture, based primarily on the textbook.

The "knowing" expected of students is largely information-oriented. [Shaver et al., 1979, p. 151]

The earlier list of "opportunities" suggested a way of turning the potential obstacle of textbook reliance into an opportunity. Can we find ways of achieving the same miracle with other perceived obstacles?

REFERENCE

Shaver, J.; Davis, O. L., Jr.; & Helburn, S. W. The status of social studies education: Impressions from three NSF studies. *Social Education*, 1979, *43*, 150–153.

Introducing,
Nurturing, and
Maintaining

An Introduction

Many steps can be counted between germination of an idea and its practical implementation. This chapter focuses on a range of vital, often intersecting issues which can be found somewhere on that continuum. The issues appear so diverse that it initially seemed impossible to find a single title to accommodate the range of ideas and concerns presented. Close reading of the total collection of papers revealed, however, that not only can a common element be found among them, but it is of considerable significance to virtually every aspect of law and humanities education. That thread is the recognition that any attempt to promote a curriculum innovation—in this case law and humanities in the elementary school—*must take into account the context or total system into which that innovation will go.*

The common thread reminds us that education does not occur in a vacuum. A variety of competing, conflicting, and often uncooperative factors impinge on the innovation and the anticipated consumer. To ignore this fact is tantamount to encouraging failure of the innovation.

Many of the points raised in this chapter are applicable to innovation generally and should be seriously considered whenever and wherever such an effort is undertaken. Some of the issues, however, are especially germane to law and humanities. Readers will find that the key points raised in this chapter include:

1. The context or overall environment into which educational innovations are introduced today is not a friendly one. It is one both actively inhibiting change and highly resistant even to accommodating innovations.
2. Perhaps as a result of this hostile environment, teachers find themselves in a precarious economic and psychological position. At times they are lonely; nearly always they are overburdened.
3. Specialists in law-related education may become so enamored of its goals and zealous about its potential that they forget that not everyone feels the way they do. In fact, many teachers remain unconvinced about law-related education's virtues and potential.
4. The system within which educational innovations must be made is a political one. That political nature is greatly magnified for a law and humanities effort.
5. Educational priorities virtually mandate that innovations be infused rather than added on. Teachers cannot and will not tack on another subject.
6. Careful, thoughtful planning with respect to all aspects of implementation and innovation is an absolute must. This mandate emerges throughout all the papers included in this section.
7. Existing resources and networks should be used to their maximum potential, rather than reinventing linkages and products already existing.

Educational Priorities: How They Link to Law and Humanities Education in the Elementary Grades

Allen L. Dobbins and Peter H. Taylor

Elegant curriculum projects and innovative new programs come and go and, much to the chagrin of the developers, make little or no difference in the education of children. While this may be a gross oversimplification of the situation, it also has a large share of truth. One of the major reasons why these efforts have attained and continue to attain less than maximum success is that they are eclipsed by the realities of education—that is, practical educational priorities.

This paper identifies and describes the various educational priorities which exist today and provide the context for any educational innovation. Virtually all of the issues outlined by authors Dobbins and Taylor can be seen as difficult ones to deal with. Some may view them as impossible. It is essential, however, that they be understood and seriously considered as part of the total system into which a curriculum and/or program developer's product will go.

Each of the issues developed by the authors is significant, but one point stands out above all and is worthy of the reader's most careful attention. That is the authors' discussion of the nature of teaching. Described by Allen Dobbins and Pete Taylor as the lonely and defensive profession, teaching obviously involves a world more than a simply formal written curriculum.

Pity the poor teacher! How difficult it is to decide what to teach!

As our society hurries on its way toward a new century, as the problems we must confront along the way become ever more complex and pressing, and as the evidence of our inability as individuals to resolve many of them becomes more and more apparent, it seems inevitable that the schools will be asked to play an ever-increasing role in addressing major social and educational issues.

We would like to start off by discussing briefly some implications of the increasing politicization of important segments of our society. Whether because of what our children learn in school or in spite of it, increasing numbers of subgroups within our society are organizing to confront critical problems that exist within the social body.

Allen L. Dobbins is Curriculum Administrator with the Portland, Oregon, Public Schools. He has worked as a high school teacher, guidance counselor, and vice-principal and has taught curriculum and methods courses at Harvard and Pacific University.

Peter H. Taylor is Assistant Superintendent of Tigard School District, Tigard, Oregon. He has published articles in the *Journal on Child Development* and *Synergy* magazine.

Emerging interest groups clamor for attention to their favorite subject, hoping to reduce or resolve their particular concern. And they come charging to the public schools for help, applying pressures to cause the emergence of some new school priority. Thus, school boards, administration, and teachers are set upon by various groups, understandably exercised and calling for an emphasis on themes or topics that range from career education, consumer education, environmental education, and safety education to cardiopulmunary resuscitation training, bicycle and boating safety, and Frances E. Willard Day. We must—and should—focus on improving the education of the handicapped "in the least restrictive environment." Pressure is mounting to attend to sex education and VD education in the schools, while others say the classroom is no place for any attention to sex education. (Archie Bunker said, "Get sex education out of the schools and back into the streets, where I learned it!") What ever happened to the instruction of modern foreign languages? And Latin? The Creationists argue for equal time in the classroom along with those in support of the theory of evolution! Affective education is a priority! Many, if not most, of our school districts are struggling with issues of multicultural and multiethnic education. Some districts are doing so because of moral suasion, others because of pressure to comply with various civil rights legislative provisions. Major urban districts are doing so, not only for these reasons alone, but also for sheer survival! And, in no way least important, school people *must* be responsive to the understandable pressure for emphasis on the basics. What, indeed, should a teacher teach? What, indeed, are the priorities to which teachers, as mere mortals, and school districts, as imperfect and impersonal institutions, should be responsive?

The quest for a legitimate place for law and humanities education in the elementary school curriculum, it would seem, will not be an easy one. Not only is the competition tough, as indicated, but contemporary curriculum trends seem to be in other directions. Whether because of such economic reasons as inflation, declining student enrollments, and scarce tax dollars, or because of a new philosophical shift toward a pragmatic job awareness and vocation orientation, or because of whatever else underlies the accountability- and competency-based education movement, the humanities are getting lost. We have fewer art and music teachers per capita than two decades ago. Less history is taught; one can't find philosophy and religion in the curriculum. And, of course, law-related education as a recognized part of the elementary curriculum, except in the rarest of circumstances, simply doesn't exist. The challenge is before us.

In order to understand better some of the challenges which we face and to maximize the chances to bring a new focus on law and humanities education in a time of priority overload, this paper will attempt an analysis of the "priorities game": Where do priorities come from? What are the forces that influence and modify them? And why, in the face of new social needs and pressures, do schools and their inhabitants seem to be unresponsive to new priorities? What has to happen for teachers to give new priorities attention? We will explore several characteristics of schools as institutions, operating formally according to predictable rules and procedures, and also informally, perhaps for reasons that are more bureaucratic, self-serving, and self-preserving than for the purpose of helping children grow and learn. We will also comment on the special significance of published material as an influence in the curriculum. Then we will turn to a review of the ever-increasing role of government in influencing educational priorities. We will conclude with a distillation of considerations, which we think can help influence educational priorities and classroom implementation of such new curriculum themes as law and humanities education.

Priorities and the Local Setting

1. *Formal action of the school board.* Most school districts have an articulated statement of philosophy from which can be derived statements of district priorities. These statements are usually written at a high level of generality, and deal with such issues as "helping each child maximize his or her human potential," or "obtaining knowledge in the areas of the basic skills." (You know how Lewis Carroll defined the basic skills. "I only took the regular course," said the mock Turtle. "What was that?" inquired Alice. "Reeling and writhing, of course, to begin with, and then the different branches of arithmetic—ambition, distraction, uglification, and derision.") The statements often include mention of job training and, not infrequently, some reference to citizenship, or stewardship, or helping students fulfill their civic responsibilities. The statements of philosophy are usually broad and general enough to introduce as little controversy as possible. In fact, statements of philosophy at the level of the school board are often so general as to be of little use to, and have little impact on, the classroom teacher attempting to decide what to incorporate into the curriculum and what to ignore or downplay.

Another product of school board action may be more helpful. School boards may take a position, by resolution, which states that such-and-such concept is "a high priority of this school board." District administrators and teachers, under these circumstances, are to fall into line and begin attending to that issue. However, it is the view of many observers that such statements are more enabling or facilitating than assuring that teachers will focus on that topic. Thus, the teacher who is sympathetic to the need to attend to a given theme, concept, or priority will be more comfortable in addressing it in the classroom if there is a board resolution endorsing it as part of the curriculum. However, the endorsement itself will have little impact, in many instances, on the teacher not personally inclined to deal with the theme.

2. *The workings of the central or school administration.* The district superintendent or his or her staff may wish that a particular theme or content area in the curriculum receive more emphasis. The administration could issue directives and in other ways publicize to teachers their desire in this regard. And to the extent that time devoted to teaching this theme in the classroom is monitored, the administrative directive approach can be reasonably effective. However, we are mindful of the analogy articulated by Kenneth Hoyt of the U.S. Office of Education (Note 1). He suggests that schools work according to what he terms "the marshmallow principle." As long as external pres-

sure, such as a finger, is applied to the marsh-mallow, it will assume and maintain a new shape. Similarly with schools and the curriculum: as long as a new emphasis is stressed by board and/or administration, instruction will take new shape and direction. Remove the pressure, or the emphasis, either consciously or by neglect, and the marsh-mallow, as well as the curriculum, will return to the *status quo ante digitus*. Thus, sad to say, it appears that new priorities receive and maintain operational status only to the extent that districts have the time, energy, and interest to monitor what they want teachers to deal with; in other words, we receive not what we *ex*pect, but what we *in*spect.

This analysis exposes something of a dilemma in implementing change in school districts and classroom instructional priorities. The logic of Hoyt's views suggests that school districts should operate according to principles and practices of directive management frequently found in industry. This kind of thinking assumes that the employees of an institution lack purposeful direction and self-determined commitment to the aims of that institution, and need explicit direction and guidance regarding how they should spend their time and energies. Thus, leadership has the clear responsibility for providing precise directions about what employees (labor) should do. Little initiative should be left to the workers—in this instance the teachers—to identify and be responsible to what is best for that institution or its clients.

However, one of the problems with directive management as applied to schools is that some of the people who make up the management or administration in school districts are uncomfortable in employing a directive management style. They perhaps have philosophical reasons relating to their sense of the potential of humankind, and, further, they are not confident that, at least in schooling, directive management works. Moreover, teachers also resent and resist such a style. As a generalization, administrators and teachers alike prefer a sharing, participatory mode of decision making, one that explicitly and formally operates in such a way that people who are affected by a decision are, as far as possible, involved in shaping that decision. To summarize this issue, while the implications of the "marsh-mallow principle" support the use of directive management to bring emphasis to new priorities, such a process or decision-making style does not fit comfortably into "the culture of the schools."

3. *District budget.* Another interesting institutional feature affecting priorities is the budget. The history of school innovation is clear in that no program, project, or content area can be emphasized if it does not find support in the budget. Indeed, it is interesting to analyze a school district's statement of philosophy and priorities as compared with the budget. Logically, one would presume that priorities of a district would be reflected in the budget, and to some extent they are. Yet it is not unusual to hear loud statements about basic skills only to find that, for example, the athletic budget is proportionally quite oversized. And rarely does one find "winning the state tournament," in our state a matter of enormous importance, in the district priorities. An analysis of the budget often reveals a different set of priorities from the formally stated set. And the teachers know the difference.

It is important to note—and say—that the amount of revenue available to a typical school district for innovative projects and for emphasizing new themes or content areas is quite limited. This is especially true, and critical, in most small school districts. The major reason for this is that such a large percentage of every district's budget is tied up in teacher salaries. (My friends in industry are invariably surprised, actually disbelieving this reality of school districts, because they put such a large proportion of their budget into development and research activities.) Putting substantial numbers of dollars into teacher salaries is an effort which is understandable, given the mission of a school district, one which we support and which we do not see diminishing. The implication of this reality is clear, however: for focus to shift to a new theme such as law and humanities education, it must be able to do so with limited resources.

4. *Locally developed curriculum documents: district curriculum guides and scope and sequence statements.* School systems, especially large ones, often have teacher-developed curriculum documents which are supposed to guide teachers as they decide what they are going to teach. The guides are also supposed to present ideas to teachers about activities and strategies other teachers have used successfully in the past to teach a certain content or set of concepts. Curriculum guides can be very helpful to teachers if they present practical, down-to-earth ways to teach a new theme or content area and work it into the regular curriculum. But, as with so many educational "secondary documents," district curriculum guides are often identifiable only by the dust they collect.

School districts also often have a statement of what students are to be taught (as opposed to what they should learn, sad to say) and roughly in what order. The statement usually contains considerably greater detail than the typical statement of district philosophy or priority. Frequently organized along traditional subject matter lines, however, the statement of scope and sequence usually presents content that is broadly representative of the standard curriculum. New and emerging content areas are *not* typically found in the scope and sequence, so in effect such a document can function as a bastion against change.

However, there appear to be times in the life of school districts when they are more open to change, more responsive to new priorities, and more able to institutionalize new themes. An example of such periodic, and admittedly infrequent, openness to confronting new areas of need was apparent in Portland, Oregon, recently, when that school district—the twenty-sixth largest in the country—elected to develop a new version of its scope and sequence. This effort was, to some extent, a reaction to the "relevancy" movement, with its resultant curriculum diffusion, which characterized so much of the sixties and early seventies. It was also in part a response to our declining basic skills test scores, and the national "forward to basics" effort. But it nevertheless provided district educational leaders with the opportunity to stress the need to attend to several pressing new educational priorities, including law-related education.

The way we proceeded was to bring together several teacher committees, one for each of the eight major subject matter areas in the curriculum. The teachers represented different grade levels and different sections of the city, but all were competent, well-respected teachers in the district. Each teacher committee was given the task of describing a combination of "what is" and "what should be" in its domain: teachers were to draw upon the existing curriculum combined with their judgment to describe the content desired for each subject matter area. Importantly, law-related education—one of four special-emphasis themes—was described for "infusion" into the program of instruction wherever possible. A major review process was developed, so that every teacher in the district, whether he or she wanted to or not, had ample opportunity to react and provide input to the teacher review committees. This input was considered with great care and was used in the final version of our new scope and sequence documents.

The extent to which our scope and sequence acutally influences instruction is, of course, problematic. Many teachers refer to it frequently. Others couldn't care less, and use it only when pressured by the administration. Clearly, the marshmallow principle is germane here. However, at the bottom line, we think the thrust to redefine the Portland curriculum through the scope and sequence development project, incorporating attention to special-emphasis themes, has been well worth the effort and represents one promising means to implement new priorities in the school program.

And yet we would be overly sanguine were we to suggest that merely writing a special-emphasis theme into a new scope and sequence or describing, in a curriculum guide, creative ways to teach that theme would get it introduced and established in the curriculum. Bruce Joyce of Stanford University points out that "secondary documents"—that is, supplementary pamphlets, resource books, handbooks, manuals, teacher guides, district curriculum guides, and scope and sequence documents—are used much less frequently and are much less influential in determining what is taught, and how it is taught, than are what he terms "primary sources": the published textbooks.

5. Published and adopted text material. A moment's reflection will confirm that once the teacher closes the classroom door, all the statements and efforts of the district, the board, the administrators, the parents, even the federal government, will not influence what the teacher teaches unless the teacher is open to be influenced. If the teacher wants it thus, scope and sequence be damned.

Truly, for the vast majority of classroom teachers, what is contained in the published and adopted textbook is what enters the mainstream curriculum of the schools. Teachers are under far too many pressures—from the overloaded curriculum, from children, from the administration, from work overload, from the bureaucracy, and from various and competing outside pressures—to be able to select carefully and rationally what they should teach and what should be omitted. Clearly, such a generalization is inaccurate and terribly unfair to many highly skilled teachers. Many teachers make excellent decisions based on professional judgments as well as legitimate district recommendations and pressure. However, for all too many, the textbook is the reality. Indeed, most observers of the change process in curriculum and instruction look to the textbook as the primary vehicle for influencing what is taught and what is learned.

At first glimmer, then, and we hear it suggested frequently, it would seem that people with a special proposed priority should influence publishers to incorporate their point of view or theme into text materials. And indeed, efforts to influence publishers should so proceed. But to do so is neither easy nor likely to bear results, especially in the short run, for several reasons.

In the first place, the process which publishers must go through in order to publish a new text and also to get it adopted is complex, lengthy, and expensive. It generally takes as long as 7 years, and costs several hundred thousand dollars, to generate new text materials, to get them through the process of editing, field testing, revision, and pilot testing, and then to prepare them for publication. And even at that time, another series of hurdles must be overcome. New text materials usually have to go through a review and approval process, usually by agencies in the various state departments of education. Material for a specific discipline usually is considered once every 5–7 years, so the opportunity for publishers to introduce, for example, a new social studies test in a particular state only occurs once in a great while. The publishers don't want to muff the chance for adoption because of inappropriate or novel text material.

Second, it is clearly in the publishers' interest to publish what the large states which operate according to a statewide adoption process—26 states, including New York, Texas, and Indiana, have such a process—will want several years in the future, and for many years thence forward. Gaining adoption status in a big state is well worth ignoring the conflicting wishes of several small states.

Third, since major textbook series are designed for entry into classrooms 5 or so years after development begins, and for continued use—with replacement purchases as incentive for remaining in print—for the better part of another decade, any concept that might become faddish is suspect. Is it any wonder that the textbooks emphasize conventional content?

But even after publication, and before publishers make a dime on a new series, they must become involved at the local school district level. There, most school districts go through another set of procedures, usually—and appropriately—involving classroom teachers and parents, whereby materials offered for consideration by publishers are assessed against district criteria for appropriateness for use in that specific local district. Again, there is little incentive for publishers to support a new concept or theme and encourage its incorporation into text material only to determine that, by the time of publication, it is no longer of central concern to educators and school board members, and therefore is not salable.

6. *Communication with the public.* One of the most neglected areas in innovation in curriculum programs is effective communication with the public. Too often innovators fail to adequately describe and discuss the merits of their particular program with parents and patrons of the school district where the program is to be implemented. This lack of communication often results not only in a lack of public acceptance and understanding of the innovation, but in active opposition to the program itself. The implications for law-related education are that not only should the public be informed of the programs, but they should be given opportunities to participate and to review the materials. Parent meetings, back-to-school nights, and presentations to community groups and other parties are only some of the ways in which schools districts can communicate with the public. Press releases, television reviews, and booklets describing the new program are also helpful in establishing acceptance of and participation in the innovation. The days of teacher-proof curriculum and the authority-centered curriculum which is handed down from above went out with the new math and the new science of the 1960s—any program which is to survive within the climate of today's public schools must have not only public understanding but public support as well.

7. *Proposition 13 and other tax cuts.* The national trend toward tax reform has had a devastating effect upon curriculum programs of the public schools. The tax reform movement, coupled with the back-to-basics drive, has created a climate in the public schools in which only the basic skill are seen as relevant and necessary for students. Therefore, it becomes increasingly important that law-related education be emphasized as a basic skill which is important for all citizens. Legal literacy must be defined as a basic skill along with reading and writing. It will be critical to the success of law-related education projects that they demonstrate that this type of education contributes substantially to a student's ability to reason, write, and read. Programs which appear to the public to be just another educational frill and which emphasize only those activities which are fun, such as field trips and mock trials, will not gain wide public acceptance.

8. *Testing and other forms of assessment.* The emphasis upon testing for student achievement in the last decade has created a climate in which those areas of the curriculum which are difficult to test are often neglected. Yet, as educators, we know that current testing instruments are often suitable for testing only those skills which can be easily measured. It might be argued that our ability to test student achievement effectively is directly proportional to the triviality of the content to be tested. While it is fairly simple to test a student's ability to add and subtract numbers, it is far more difficult to assess a student's understanding of values and social concepts. For these reasons, law-related education faces a formidable challenge in attempting to evaluate the impact of its progams.

Characteristics of Teaching

We would like now to turn to some brief observations about some unique, and we think important, characteristics of teaching and the hidden curriculum and of teaching as a lonely profession, as one often characterized by defensiveness, and as one enmeshed in the labor movement.

1. *Teaching and the hidden curriculum.* In recent years, some attention has been directed

toward the study of the sociological climate of schools. Expanding numbers of researchers agree that the school climate, or, as it is often called, the hidden curriculum, has as great or perhaps more of an influence upon the lives of some students as the formal and explicit curriculum of the school. This notion is a particularly fertile one, for it suggests that those who would establish law-related education as a high educational priority must also carefully study the operation of schools to determine whether the implicit message of the institution through its very operation is teaching lessons which are in conflict with the explicit curriculum of the school. For example, the elements of due process can be learned in a textbook fashion at one level of understanding. But the key question in the minds of many students might well revolve around the issue of due process in the day-to-day operation of the school. What will students learn, for example, about due process taught as subject matter but not practiced as a characteristic of the school environment?

Many such contradictions exist within current curricula. Since what children really learn is, more often than we might suspect, the subtle and informal messages from the institution itself, school people need to examine many of our current classroom practices and schoolwide norms at both the elementary and secondary levels and assess the consistency between what we might want the institution to stand for and what we actually do. Perhaps we might analyze our institutional super ego against its id.

2. *Teaching: the lonely profession.* Unlike so many of the other professions, the teaching profession can well be characterized as the lonely one, one in which the practitioner, all too often, works in isolation from other professionals in the same field. Indeed, the teacher works separately not only from other colleagues but often from other adults as well. The lonely profession indeed.

Although this point may bring dispute, we want to argue that this very isolation helps explain why teachers resist change and quietly oppose the introduction and incorporation of new special-emphasis themes into the curriculum. It seems clear to us that those advocating a new theme would be wise to build a support system of some kind, a means or mechanism to overcome the loneliness and isolation of the job and to provide sustenance for teachers embarking on new efforts to teach new content, perhaps through new instructional procedures. Team teaching, team planning, the "cadre" concept, the leadership team or consultant group—all of these organizational suggestions contain some potential for helping strengthen and support teachers undertaking new endeavors. Some form of support for teachers seems essential in efforts to change the curriculum and instructional programs. This is especially true when the proposed new priority or program is something not widely recognized as filling a legitimate place in the curriculum.

An interesting, if somewhat discouraging, corollary of the "teaching as a lonely profession" observation is that perhaps teachers *want* to be isolated; perhaps they want to avoid outside observation, assistance, and support. We frequently hear teachers complain, after attending a workshop or seminar taught by someone from outside the school or district, "He/she certainly doesn't understand *my* kids/circumstance/problem/classroom!" or "Why didn't someone tell him/her that we tried that some time ago and it didn't work!" Sad to say, the outside expert is neither welcome nor trusted by a great many teachers.

3. *Teaching: the defensive profession.* An informal characteristic of the culture of the schools, one that gives it remarkable staying power and intractability and should not be underestimated, is the implied criticism and threat inherent in change. If people "out there" propose that attention suddenly be given to a new topic, theme, or content area such as law and humanities education, the specter of negative criticism arises immediately. "They think we aren't doing the job," many teachers feel. And thus teachers are forced to look at what they are doing, what they will have to give up in order to "add on" the new topic, and it all becomes unpleasant and threatening, something to be resisted and opposed. Strategies for influencing instructional priorities should avoid being perceived as a burden and a threat to teachers if at all possible, because if the teachers dig in their heels against the program, it simply won't attain legitimacy as a useful part of the curriculum.

4. *Teaching and the emerging role of the teacher organizations.* Another important fact in the establishment and implementation of new priorities is the new role and importance being assumed by teacher organizations. The most obvious implication of this trend has to do with teacher support: no longer is it as easy as in the past for school administrators to work in collegial, supportive mode with teachers, despite the need, as suggested above. The trend toward unionization fosters a schism between labor and management which requires that teachers look elsewhere—and we hope with the help of administration—for the support structure necessary, in our view, for curriculum and instruction change.

An additional consequence of the emerging role of the teacher organizations is that in many states and districts teacher organizations are bargaining to have their involvement in the process of selecting curriculum materials formalized in the negotiated contract. As this is a fairly recent development in school district collective bargaining, it is difficult to foretell what implications this development may have for implementing new priorities within the curriculum. However, given that teacher involvement in the selection process is essential in any event, the trend is probably not a complicating one.

Influencing Priorities at the National Level

A brief review of federal involvement in education over the past 200 years reveals a major and escalating tendency toward federal requirements upon state and local education agencies.

The impact of federal legislation. Perhaps the first effort by the federal government to influence policy through education occurred under the Articles of Confederation when Congress passed the Survey Ordinance of 1785, an early attempt to provide support for public education. Another major event in federal involvement began when Congress passed the Morrill Act of 1862, which established the land grant colleges. It was the first instance of a federal act for specific educational purposes, and it demonstrated a role which the federal government was to take increasingly in later years, that of taking action when it appeared that states were not responding to a persistent national need.

The next milestone was reached in 1917, when Congress passed the Smith-Hughes Act, which was designed to increase the number of skilled craftspersons in the country. Smith-Hughes provided matching funds for vocational education in agriculture, the trades, and industry. This act represented a major shift of government policy in education in that it provided resources for the first categorical grant program to mandate specific outcomes. It was the first program to be administered primarily by the state educational agencies, and the first which required states to match federal dollars. These characteristics can be seen in many of the later federal acts.

In 1957, the debate on educational priorities suddenly focused on a major issue of the cold war: how could American education help us catch up with Russian technology? As a result of the lead demonstrated by the Soviet Union in the exploration of outer space, Congress urgently passed the National Defense Education Act of 1958. This program promoted improvement of educational programs in specific areas of science, mathematics, and foreign languages and was later extended to other subject areas in the public schools. However, a barometer of congressional reluctance to become continually involved in shaping public elementary and secondary "traditional" curricular

areas was the fact that involvement was rationalized as being a function of national defense, not education for its own sake; hence, NDEA.

In the 1960s, schooling increasingly became one of the major weapons in the domestic war on poverty. The Vocational Education Act of 1963, in order to improve existing educational programs and to develop new programs to train youth for gainful employment, increased federal support for vocational education fourfold.

By 1965, however, Congress dropped the rhetoric and rationale relating to defense and, as we all know, through the Elementary and Secondary Education Act, created the potential for massive use of federal funds primarily to meet the needs of the educationally disadvantaged and the urban poor.

The recent enactment of Public Law 94-142 is yet another extension of the concept of providing educational equality—really providing for the civil rights of the handicapped—under the sanction of federal law. (Right now we have the mandate and the sanction, but *not* the resources.)

In reviewing federal legislation as a source of educational priorities, it becomes evident that during the past 200 years federal legislation has had an increasing impact upon policy making in public education. In general, the focus of federal involvement in education has shifted from short-term programs of general support to long-term and highly specific programs. This trend suggests increasing influence of federal legislation upon policy making in American education in the coming years. It seems likely that the influence of the federal government upon public schools will create an increasing role for state education agencies as monitors of federally mandated programs at the local district level. It also seems predictable that pressure groups will increasingly use federal school legislation as a means of achieving their goals, and therefore federally mandated programs will become more specific in the terms of their impact.

Before leaving our discussion of the potential for federal legislation to influence local priorities, it is probably important to note the small proportion of dollars that actually comes from the federal level. An analysis of typical school districts' budgets shows that as little as 6%, an average in suburban and rural districts, and somewhat more but usually not exceeding 15% in urban systems, of the dollars for operating school comes from the federal government. And most of these funds are categorical; that is, they can only be used for special, predetermined purposes, such as school lunches and breakfasts, vocational education, compensatory education with emphasis on the basic skills, etc. Only through the Elementary and Secondary Education Act amendments do we find support for such new programs as Innovative Programs (Title IV), Bilingual Education, Women's Studies, Metric Education, Teacher Centers, Gifted and Talented, the Arts, etc. And competition for the all too scarce funds for these programs is fierce. Thus, for new programs (with exceptions), even though the clamor at the federal level is great, the impact is not without limitation.

The impact of court decisions. While Congress has had a major effect upon the establishment of school priorities through legislative action, a second and perhaps even more significant impact of the federal government has been through court decisions. In 1954, the classic decisions of the U.S. Supreme Court in the *Brown* v. *Board of Education* desegregation case clearly established a new priority for the public schools. *Brown* created the legal cornerstone for the enforcement of civil rights in public education. It is significant to note that the task of desegregating public schools remains unfinished today. However, the federal mandate is clear.

Recent court decisions are, in our view, an indication of the increasing impact which court decisions will have upon decision making within the public schools in the coming years. It seems likely that the courts will continue, at an increasing rate, to influence what schools can and cannot do, especially in the domain of personnel and civil rights. Even though it seems unlikely that the courts will enter the area of what we may or may not *teach*, the attention given by the courts to legal rights and obligations, both of schools and individuals, may very well provide added impetus to local districts to emphasize law-related education as a needed part of the curriculum.

Influencing Priorities at State and Local Government Levels

Another source of educational priorities could be identified by those coming from state and local government organizations. Due largely to the increased availability of federal dollars, state departments of education have grown rapidly in recent years. Federal funding has not only caused rapid increase of staff in state education departments; it has mandated that the state monitor programs legislated at the federal level. This has created imbalances at the state level: some departments, such as career education, have experienced enormous increase in staff, while others, such as those dealing with such inconsequential areas as the basic skills, have hardly increased at all. The piecemeal style of legislation described earlier has created serious imbalances in the way state departments respond to new educational needs.

Another source of priorities within state departments of education is programs or procedures initiated by local legislatures. One such effort is the recent reform movement toward competency-based education, which currently has so many districts in turmoil over its implications. Since state legislative action regarding new programs often brings with it the presumption that the state department must provide leadership in implementing as well as monitoring these programs, a new custom or ethic seems to be emerging: for a new need or priority to become legitimized, it is increasingly important to involve and gain the support of state departments of education. If new curriculum programs are to be implemented, it is critical for developers and advocates of those programs to have some insight into various means of influencing state departments of education to support and expand those programs. A recent study by the Rand Corporation reviewing the impact of Title IV (old Title III) on ESEA and other projects makes this point by arguing the need for continuing local support at the state and district level if the adoption of new priorities is to continue.

Considerations

1. People who wish to influence a school district's priorities—for example, to encourage the teaching of law-related education and the humanities—must approach the task with the recognition that teachers, in the parlance of race driving, are at the "red line" point already. We had better appreciate the fact that the initial mind set of all too many of our colleagues in the classroom, when they hear of a proposed new program or a recommended new priority, is, "My God, if we are asked to do one more thing, it will blow us apart!"

2. When a new priority is about to be surfaced by its advocates, they must make a special effort to obtain understanding and support for it from representatives of as many levels of the educational system as possible; especially important is support, early on, at the level of the school board. In addition, opportunities for involvement by central administrative and curriculum personnel, certainly principals and teachers at several grade levels, and, to the extent possible, parents and other representatives from the community, must be encouraged. It is probably also prudent to involve state department personnel as well.

3. In order for new priorities to stay in place and to remain operational, at least two conditions pertaining to teachers are essential. First, teachers must be part of a support structure, an organizational pattern perhaps of col-

leagues who can talk together and support each other as they work through the new and perhaps intimidating aspects of a new program. We mentioned several such support structures, of which the teacher consultant team may be the most promising. We further think that some form of organizational support structure can be a major asset, both in dispelling the loneliness that occurs when the teacher closes the classroom door and in overcoming the defensiveness teachers often manifest when asked to become involved in and committed to a new and perhaps anxiety-provoking project. A second necessary condition is the opportunity for teacher training, in order that teachers may understand better and in more detail the complexities and implications of a new concept. We are categorically of the view, however, that the kind of preservice training that teachers often receive before they enter the classroom—that is, a program usually provided at some distance from the classroom, probably in a sheltered university location—will not work to meet this need. The training we have in mind here must take place closer to the setting where the action is. And, critically, the program must be designed taking into account the wealth of experience and wisdom that teachers have gained on the job. A clinical field setting can be helpful in this regard.

4. Like it or not (notwithstanding those of us who think all teachers are intrinsically motivated to work for the betterment of kids), if a change in priority and practice is to be maintained, a school district must provide not only the support structure described above, but also a monitoring service to audit what teachers are doing to implement the change, and thereby make sure the teachers are doing what is expected. (Our skeptical view is that, lacking extensive motivation, the half-life of unmonitored innovative projects is perhaps 1 year.)

5. Secondary documents can be extremely helpful to teachers. Perhaps one of the reasons why they often fall into disuse is that they are too rigid, and unadaptable to the unique needs of a given teacher. Therefore, it seems to us that if the documents which support an innovation allow for a variety of uses and can readily be molded to fit different circumstances, as long as there are other motivating forces for staying in the project (especially support and monitoring), the documents will in fact be well used by the teachers.

6. Efforts should be made to assure that the new priority is reflected in the district budget. State and federal or other grant monies may be needed as well, but the local district commitment, sooner or later, is essential. Furthermore, if the cost for establishing and maintaining a major priority change is excessive, it is unlikely to be sustained over the years.

7. Even though the process is complicated and time-consuming, the ultimate goal of those in support of a new concept must be its incorporation into standard, published texts which will eventually make their way through the development-selection-adoption maze and into the classroom.

8. Regarding the informal curriculum, those who support emphasizing law and humanities education at the elementary grade levels should encourage school people to look at the consistency, or its absence, between what the explicit curriculum says—for example, fairness and justice for all—and what the informal curriculum expresses. Inconsistency between the formal and informal curricula, we believe, communicates a garbled message about the law-related society of the school, to the detriment of the students growing up in that society and ultimately moving into the society of the real adult world. We all will be the beneficiaries if the young make that transition with a well-developed sense of the power and potential for living in a society governed by laws, seeking the best for all.

REFERENCE NOTE

1. Hoyt, K. Paper presented at a meeting of the Oregon Council of Career and Vocational Administrators, April 27–28, 1978.

Educational Priorities: How They Link to Law and Humanities Education in the Elementary Grades

Michael Radz

This paper extends discussion of educational priorities by focusing (as did authors Dobbins and Taylor) on the practical realities of curriculum innovation within the educational system. Drawing from his personal perspective and experience as a school district assistant superintendent, Michael Radz provides additional and important insights into the issues often working against progress and advancement of educational goals.

Readers will find two areas of particular interest in this paper. The author explores implications of the media for curriculum innovation and, along with authors Dobbins and Taylor, underscores the need to proceed with an infusion approach, thus "neutralizing" the effect of "add-on-finitum."

Who controls determination of priorities in the curriculum? This question has been addressed on numerous occasions, and the response is invariably the same: "No one." If the question is, "Who influences curriculum decision making?" the answer is, "It all depends." Allen Dobbins and Pete Taylor have tackled a difficult assignment and have done a commendable job. While they offer little that is new, my colleagues from Oregon have managed to capture the dynamics of the shifting waters of curriculum priority setting.

Given a topic of this breadth, the authors had to decide whether they should attempt to cover the waterfront or focus on a few critical forces. Obviously, they selected the former. This, of course, opens the door to a reactor to say, "Yes, but." Therefore, with all due respect and admiration for Dobbins and Taylor, I propose to (1) pursue several influencing forces which are of particular concern to me, (2) remind symposium participants of several well-known reasons why curriculum seeds fail to take root, and (3) suggest several guidelines as we approach the task of infusing law and humanities concepts into a curriculum which is at once on the verge of bursting with "mandate inflation" and being stripped to its basic bones.

I am distressed and disappointed with the media. I feel they have done education a great disservice by deliberately deciding to accentuate the negative and ignore the positive. There is no doubt in my mind that the mass media are a powerful catalyst in the back-to-the-basics, competency-testing movement. Admittedly, test scores on a number of well-known instruments have declined over the past decade. Both educators and laypersons have a legitimate cause for concern. However, it seems to me that the press has been all too quick to point an accusing finger at the school, saying, "You and you alone are to blame!" Furthermore, the public has been shown the dark cloud, but seldom a glimpse of the silver lining.

Stanley Elam (1978) provides a case in point. He cites a recent syndicated column by Martha Engle and Robert Walters entitled, "Teenagers Have Lost Ground in Understanding Citizenship." In the best traditions of the irate critic, Engle and Walters looked at data comparing the political knowledge of 13- and 17-year-olds on the 1970–1972 and 1975–1976 National Assessment of Educational Progress Citizenship tests. They expressed their indignation at the fact that only 65% of the 17-year-olds knew that the Supreme Court was a part of the judicial branch of government and that less than half could name their U.S. representative or one of their senators. Elam, however, discovered, buried in the midst of the column, a bit of news that a less careful reader would have overlooked (to say nothing of a "headline skimmer"). "Older teenagers in particular showed an increased respect and tolerance of people of another race and a growing understanding of the problems of the poor. Moreover, youngsters of both ages improved their ability to

Michael Radz is Assistant Superintendent for Instruction for the Olympia Community Unit School District in Stanford, Illinois. He has served as a Teacher Associate with the Social Science Education Consortium and on several committees of the National Council for the Social Studies.

'suggest methods of avoiding future wars.' " As a former social studies teacher, a parent, and a citizen of the global community, this is one of the greatest pieces of news I have heard in a long time! Should not the headline have read, "American Teenagers Show Increased Tolerance"? Sadly, this is not an isolated case. Examples of this type of journalism abound. Make no mistake, the media are a force to be reckoned with in the process of determining curriculum priorities.

Coming from Oregon, one of the first states to mandate competency testing, Dobbins and Taylor are fully cognizant of the role of the politician in setting educational priorities. In fact, it can be argued that curriculum decision making is a highly political process. It is not my intent to argue the pros and cons of competency testing. However, it offers a classic example of how state legislators can shape the educational destinies of parents, teachers, administrators, and students. The cover of the October 1977 issue of *Educational Leadership* presents two political outline maps of the United States. One, dated January 1977, shows 17 states with some type of competency-testing legislation. The second, dated September 1977, adds nine to the fold. The number continues to grow. Again, this is but a single example. Mandates almost too numerous to mention are repeatedly laid on local districts without the financial means to provide for implementation. Illinois is typical. By law and/or resolution of the Illinois Office of Education, the curriculum of all schools must include career education, consumer education, conservation education, citizenship education, health education, metric education, physical education, a program of media services, the constitutions of Illinois and the United States, driver education, safety education, special education, guidance services, and, of course, the basic academic subjects. This is a partial listing. While Governor Thompson has called for a moratorium on mandated programs, the legislature is more inclined to listen to the folks back home, the media, and what is going on in other states.

Switching to the politics of local curriculum decision making, another point mentioned by Dobbins and Taylor that merits fuller development is the financial crunch. Declining enrollments, spiraling inflation, disgruntled taxpayers, and unrealistic state aid formulas have placed school districts, large and small, urban and rural, in a financial vise. As every administrator and board member knows, 75%–80% of a district's budget is devoted to teacher salaries and benefits. When it comes time to reduce costs, the only way it can be done is to cut personnel, and when personnel are cut, programs are cut. Add the back-to-the-basics movement to the financial crunch, and you get such tragedies as the elimination of

art, music, physical education, and meaningful extracurricular programs. For those of us in the trenches at the local level, as Dobbins and Taylor can attest, the battle is often a matter of how to keep what we already have rather than how to add new programs. The militant taxpayer, by the way, is only one vested interest in a group at the local level. Numerous others stand waiting in the wings.

I would also like to make note of external forces which can and have made their presence known in local communities. This is a particularly frightening topic, for our knowledge of such groups and their tactics is limited. Most of us viewed the Kenawka County, West Virginia, situation with horror. Most of us also assumed an "it can't happen here" posture. I fear we are mistaken. There is evidence to suggest that these small groups are linked in a semiformal network which can be activated at a moment's notice. Any community torn over such curriculum issues as values clarification, sex education, evolution, patriotism, or the basics could become the target for these organized opposition groups. Most of us simply are not prepared to cope with an intensive, targeted attack by a committed, articulate pressure group based outside our own district.

While I have now partially relieved some of my personal frustrations as a curriculum worker, I feel that I have done little to clarify the muddy and turbulent waters of setting curriculum priorities. The truth of the matter is that we have an ebb and flow of forces. At a given time in a given district one or more of the influencing agents mentioned by Dobbins and Taylor may emerge as the dominant force. When caught up in shifting currents, what is the curriculum developer to do? Go with the flow? Row against the current? Holler for help? Panic? Pray? Apply one's knowledge and experience to making the best of the situation? Not go near the water?

To a large extent, however, there has always been pressure exerted upon the school to give priority to a particular vested interest. One could argue that the highly religious nature of the curriculum of our first schools was the result of the power, prestige, and position of the church fathers. One would hope that, given 200 years of experience to draw upon, we have developed the knowledge and skill not merely to survive but to lead.

I think most of us know why curriculum reform, be it the "new social studies" or a law and humanities approach, fails to achieve its intended mission. At the risk of restating the obvious, allow me to suggest four reasons why innovation often fails to reach the intended audience—the children behind the classroom door. I do so at the risk of generalizing, thereby alienating curriculum developers who have been successful. To you I say, you have been successful because you have managed to negate the factors I am about to list. We have much to learn from you.

1. We are guilty of failing to take into account what is known about the ways in which children learn. For example, assuming we accept Kohlberg's stages of moral development, how many of us as teachers and curriculum developers have given kids stage 4 concepts when they are at a stage 2 level of development? Those of us who were weaned on Ralph Tyler's curriculum model read with interest that distinguished educator's thoughts in the October 1976 issue of *Educational Leadership*. Tyler asserts that he "would now give much greater emphasis to the active role of the student in the learning process and...to the need for a comprehensive examination of the non-school areas of student learning as they relate to curriculum development" (p. 62). We would do well to heed Tyler's advice.

2. Far too often curriculum developers and curriculum administrators have neglected the teacher or, what is worse, assumed that they were developing "teacher-proof curricula." Those who did conscientiously provide for adequate in-service training often overlooked the absolute necessity of developing a support system. No teacher likes to feel like the Lone Ranger. Districts are guilty of adopting programs without the benefit of even a minimal in-service effort. In spite of the graying of America's faculties, many school districts have not committed themselves to ongoing staff development programs. Preservice training leaves much to be desired in terms of preparing prospective teachers to develop or implement curricula.

3. In spite of the rhetoric on community involvement, schools have generally done a poor job of involving the community in *meaningful* ways. I am using "community" in its broadest sense to include students, teachers, parents, and community groups.

4. Many an innovation has been subverted by the hidden curriculum. The learning that takes place as the inhabitants of the school interact with each other, with the physical environment, and with the prevailing customs, attitudes, and regulations is not to be underestimated. The hidden curriculum can reinforce the formal curriculum and help make it relevant. On the other hand, it can activate the student crap detectors and make learning an exercise in hypocrisy. While the building principal is the key determiner of school climate, all adults in the building need to recognize their role as models. Students are not at all impressed with a "do as I say, not as I do" approach to living and learning.

Dobbins and Taylor conclude with a list of eight conclusions about the process of influencing educational priorities in general and law and humanities education in particular. Their points are well taken. In fact, I wish they had more fully developed these points rather than concentrating so heavily on the factors involved in setting curriculum priorities.

A particularly appropriate suggestion relates to use of an infusion approach in order to neutralize the "add-on-finitum" syndrome. While a good deal has been written on infusing, it is my observation that most of us have only a vague idea as to how one proceeds to do such a thing (in the best traditions of "interdisciplinary" programs). There is a need not only to develop a workable model but to train the infuser. If infusion is nothing more than a new format for a curriculum guide, I see no reason to believe it will advance the cause of law and humanities education. As I see it, legal and humanities concepts, as legitimate as they may be, are going to find expression to the extent that they are infused into the existing "basic skills" curriculum.

In closing, I would like to quote four educators. As we attempt to cope with curriculum change, we would do well to be guided by their words:

The single school is the largest and the proper unit for educational change. The single teacher is too small a unit to be a focus for significant change. Cultivation of teachers' necessary knowledge, skills, and attitudes is no assurance that the culture of the school will support their use. The school system is too large a unit and it is structural, not organic. What is good for its maintenance frequently is a destructive pollutant for the school. Ideally, the system exists to nourish each individual school, in the way the school should exist to nourish its inhabitants: to legitimate the authority it needs to fulfill its responsibilities, to channel needed resources, to provide it with a protective umbrella, to nourish its individuality, and to encourage the risk-taking involved in productive change. [Goodlad, 1975, pp. 110–111]

The school can also continue its long-accepted role of providing within its environment a democratic society closer to the ideal than the adult community has yet been able to achieve. It can provide a setting in which young people can experience concretely the meaning of our democratic ideals. In the school, every student is to be respected as a person, regardless of his background. In the school, the students can experience a society where justice and fair play dominate, a society where people care about each other and where all have an opportunity to share in planning activities, executing them, and gaining the rewards of what they have accomplished. It is not always easy for teachers and administrators to provide this kind of environment, but it is crucially important for children to see firsthand a society that encourages and supports democratic values. [Tyler, 1977, p. 23]

It is becoming clearer that the old ways of updating our schools through add-ons, appendages, and remediation will no longer be appropriate. Our present school system has not only spread itself thin but has surely developed unnecessary duplication. As society has become more complex, it has delegated increased responsibility to the schools; but the schools are designed for schooling, not education. We therefore need to convert a school system into an educational system. To accomplish this goal, the school cannot go it alone. A much broader conception of resource utilization will have to be considered. The new educational system will systematically link a complex of institutions and agencies. The school will be linked to the strengthened family; to the multicultural neighborhoods; and to the cultural scientific, and recreational agencies in the communities. [Fantini, 1977, p. 170]

All schools need regularly scheduled faculty meetings to develop an educational philosophy for the school. Once a working philosophy is agreed upon, it should be implemented by using new approaches and new techniques where old ones have not done the job. The schools differ, not only from most businesses, but from all other agencies that work to improve human behavior in that little or no working time is devoted to staff meetings. Unless the teachers can meet together and as committees work with the principal and with the grade-level chairmen to develop programs to solve educational problems, nothing new will happen. I hesitate to write the previous sentence because so many readers have had bad experience with committees that waste time and accomplish little. Unless school committees are given a mandate to implement their recommendations, they too will be meaningless. [Glasser, 1969, pp. 117–118]

REFERENCES

Elam, S. Diamonds found in a garbage pile. *Phi Delta Kappan,* 1978, *59,* 514.

Fantini, M. D. Toward a redefinition of American education. *Educational Leadership,* 1977, *35,* 167–172.

Glasser, W. *Schools without failure.* New York: Harper & Row, 1969.

Goodlad, J. I. Schools can make a difference. *Educational Leadership,* 1975, *33,* 108–117.

Tyler R. Two new emphases in curriculum development. *Educational Leadership,* 1976, *34,* 61–71.

Tyler R. The total educational environment. In National Task Force on Citizenship Education, *Education for responsible citizenship.* New York: McGraw-Hill, 1977.

Identifying and Evaluating Law and Humanities Education Content in the Social Studies

H. Michael Hartoonian

This paper addresses one of the key issues faced by educators introducing law and humanities into the elementary school. Early in his article, Michael Hartoonian emphasizes that such educators must avoid tacking on additional content areas. Instead, they should facilitate smooth integration of content and processes associated with law and humanities into existing curricular areas. This point is made very clear by the author's suggestions that "one more set of things for elementary teachers to do might prove to be dysfunctional." Integration, then, is paramount.

Hartoonian goes on to provide several important categories which educators can use in their effort to understand the nature of law and humanities curricula. He identifies the following areas for our consideration: (1) ethical responsibility, (2) legal/political knowledge, (3) inquiry, (4) school environment, (5) larger community, and (6) history.

Readers will be particularly interested to follow the author's theoretical discussion of the categories through to his suggested operational stage, which is described through a valuable checklist for identifying law and humanities content in the elementary school.

A Common Rationale

The discipline of law has been an implicit component of social studies education from the turn of the twentieth century. But it has only been within the last decade that law has surfaced to take its place with the humanities, history, and the social sciences as a legitimate area of formal social study—legitimate in the sense that the discipline of law involves knowledge constructs, skills, and attitudes that have pedagogical usefulness.

This emphasis upon law in the social studies curriculum should not be surprising, since a primary purpose of education in general and social studies education specifically is the development of enlightened citizens. If we compare the goals of law-related education with those of social studies education we find a great deal of congruency. The goals of law-related education address: (1) critical thinking abilities, (2) perception of law and the legal system, (3) knowledge of society and its system of laws, and (4) relationships between societal values and the legal system. The goals of

H. Michael Hartoonian is Program Coordinator and Supervisor of Social Studies Education for the Wisconsin Department of Public Instruction. He has served as a classroom teacher, university professor, and administrator; his current research interests are in reasoning and language skill development.

social studies education address: (1) the development of a just society; (2) the ongoing social needs of citizens; (3) the record of the past and keeping that record alive; (4) the legal, political, and economic systems of our nation; and (5) the intellectual development of students.

From their stated goals it would seem that the purposes of law-related and social studies education are directly associated. Further, if we look at the major concepts of history, the social sciences, and law, we find more useful similarities (see Table 1).

A study of the goals and major concepts of law-related and social studies education suggests a fundamental relationship. Law seems to add a dynamic dimension to the study of society, and it provides the student with the necessary understanding for the creation of a more just society.

In addition to the goal and concept similarities between law and social studies, there is an even more important relationship between these components of the curriculum and the content needed to bring instruction to life. That content, particularly in the elementary school, can best be described as inclusive. In other words, all disciplines are useful in meeting the goals of citizenship education. For example, there are "laws" in the discipline of music—for instance, three beats to a measure. There are also songs about the helpful police officer. As we look to art,

Table 1. Basic Concepts from History, the Social Sciences, and Law

Field	Concepts
Anthropology	Human being; needs; culture; culture change (dynamic of society); cultural ecology; symbols
Economics	Scarcity and choice; economic systems; specialization; interdependence; market; money; factors of production (land, labor, capital, management); economic growth, stability, and security; business cycles
Geography	Spatial relationship; map; region; linkage (spatial interaction); geographic change (new geographies)
History	Story; record; change; continuity; time; cause and effect relationships; nature of evidence; philosophy and beliefs
Political science	Political system; legitimacy; decision making; law; institutions; interdependence; citizenship
Psychology	Personality; behavior; perception; conformity; deviance; experimentation
Social psychology	Personality; social situation; social interaction
Sociology	Social system; role; society; social problem; institution; family
Law	Law; freedom; legal system; property; justice; voluntary compliance; due process; authority; participation; contract; ethics; order; responsibility; legitimacy

literature, and history, we find example upon example of useful materials, narratives, and processes that can tie the study of law to the content of the humanities as well as the content of the social sciences.

The human community. The human community is what students study in elementary school social studies programs. As can be seen in Figure 1, emphasis is placed upon people, self, and others, and the interrelationships among knowledge, skills, and values across time and space. These relationships form the systems into which human beings are born and within which they function throughout their lives. These systems present opportunities, challenges, and problems with which all of us must cope in our daily lives. When the child enters school, he or she moves into a new culture, a new system that must be understood if the individual is to grow and function as a total human being. This is also true as students and adults move into different settings and, indeed, as institutions change around them. Thus, it becomes imperative that we understand the systems within which we operate in as much depth as possible. This means attention to all of the subtle attributes of culture that make up any human community, including the human knowledge we call "the humanities."

In the elementary school's social studies program an understanding of a "system" or "community" means that the student not only knows that there are school or community helpers, for example, but understands the relationships that exist among students, teachers, administrators, janitors, cooks, counselors, etc., as they all func-

tion within a total system. The notions of community and system are appropriate at all sequence levels, from the study of the home and school to the study of the world.

Different disciplines play different roles in helping students understand "system" or "community," and law can perform an extremely important function here, particularly when we investigate those attributes of the system which help hold the pieces together. The process of law and citizens' understanding of it make it possible for all other community or system functions to take place. Law becomes the oil in our social machinery.

In addition to the importance of law as the element of social cohesion, it also plays two other important roles. First of all, it offers protection of those basic rights which give meaning and dignity to life. There is an interesting scene in the play *A Man for All Seasons,* in which Thomas More is talking to his son-in-law Roper about the protection of the law. Roper insists that to catch the devil he would cut down the thicket so that the devil would have nowhere to hide. The thicket is used in the discussion as an analogue for the law. But, More asks, what would happen if there were no thicket and the devil turned on you? Where would you hide then? The thicket of the law may be difficult to live with at times, but it does offer protection to those who know and understand their legal rights and responsibilities.

Second, understanding the law makes manifest the concept of "government of law." In a free society we should understand that the law—for example, our Constitution—is and must be a liv-

Figure 1

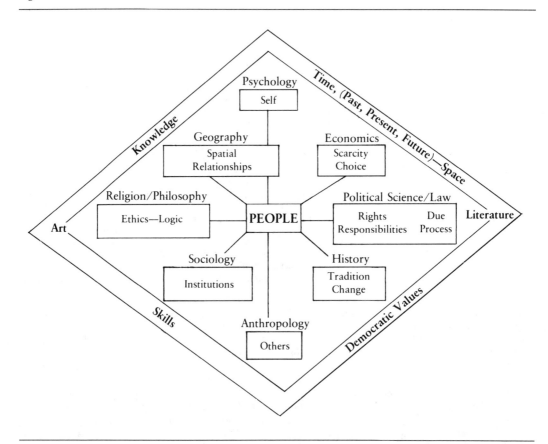

ing institution, alive within all citizens. This means more than a visit to Washington, D.C., to view the Constitution as opposed to a visit to Moscow to visit the tomb of Lenin. It means that no one person is above the law, and yet the law is the servant of all citizens. This is at once the most simple and the most profound principle of democratic citizenship.

Components of an Elementary School Law-related/Social Studies Program

To discuss components of a law-related education program suggests a new conceptual framework of some kind. However, one more set of things for elementary teachers to do might prove to be dysfunctional. We need, instead, to consider ways in which programs can be made more manageable, more integrated, and more efficient. What is there about law education that can help simplify and improve the elementary social studies program? Can the study of law help the humanities assume their rightful place in the elementary curriculum?

Can we develop a set of principles or themes that will address the larger issue of guiding citizenship education?

Themes of Civic/Legal Education

The following themes do not establish a new orientation in schools but reflect the continuing educational obligation made explicit by Thomas Jefferson in the statement he made to William Jarvis in 1820: "I know no safe depository of the ultimate powers of the society but the people themselves; and if we think them not enlightened enough to exercise their control with a wholesome discretion, the remedy is not to take it from them, but to inform their discretion by education."

A. Ethical responsibility. The student (teacher-child) should be aware and understand that legal and political action or behavior is an ethical act, since it affects other individuals as well as the community, and that all institutions have ethical responsibilities which need to be continually checked with institutional practices.

Civic/legal education involves at least two ethical responsibilities. First, students need to develop an awareness of how government and politics actually function. This understanding, though, should not be just passive. Students need to develop standards in order to judge whether what is occurring is just and equitable. Second, civic/legal education involves student responsibility in determining policies important to their daily lives. While the degree of complexity in civic/legal learning will vary from younger to older children, it is an educator's obligation to consider how students at all ages can increase their understanding and participation.

These two themes reflect a classical meaning of democracy. The purpose of a democratic political process is, in part, to enable people to gain tangible benefits. To do so, people need to have accurate knowledge about how political decisions are made, who makes those decisions, and how that process can be influenced. Democracy has another just as important dimension, and that is the belief that individual self-development is dependent upon being able to participate in public affairs. Self-esteem and human dignity are viewed as related to the opportunities individuals have to express themselves in public affairs. Educators need to consider both dimensions of democracy in planning instruction.

B. *Legal/political knowledge.* The student (teacher-child) should be aware of the basic concepts and processes of law, and other disciplines related to civic/legal education.

The honesty of what students are asked to know must be guaranteed. Knowledge about the political and legal process should be accurate. It should focus upon the ways in which the legal system works and not only upon formal or ideal models. For example, the passing of laws should be understood as only a part of governmental and political processes. Further, students should have opportunities to consider the continual political and legal tension within our society—that is, the ongoing struggle between the demands of society and the rights of individuals. Educators should not teach patriotism as blind obedience to authority. Watergate and the CIA revelations, for example, demand that governmental agencies continually be open to public scrutiny and debate. On the other hand, individuals need to consider themselves as part of a community to which they have obligations and responsibilities.

C. *Inquiry.* The student (teacher-child) should be able to use the skills of inquiry in the investigation of political and legal issues.

The need to scrutinize and criticize political/legal institutions demands that students do inquiry. The notion of inquiry has verb qualities; that is, it is a form of work which involves investigating questions about political and legal events. It demands seeking data which can help answer the question(s). Inquiry also demands time to put all the data together in some coherent fashion. It is the *doing* of inquiry that can enable students to consider where there is conflict between ideals and practices.

D. *School/environment.* The student (teacher-child) should understand the school setting as an environment in which to practice the skills of political/legal behavior.

The school environment has to encourage democratic behavior. All classrooms need to be places where ideas can be argued and debated. The ongoing experiences of school must provide a range of activities which call upon students to practice responsibility and initiative. Those school practices which are paternalistic or demand uncritical acquiescence need to be considered as antithetical to the purpose of democratic citizenship education.

E. *Larger community.* The student (teacher-child) should possess the skills necessary for inquiry and action in the community.

The activities of civic/legal education must also extend beyond the classroom. Students should have experiences testing their ideas in the general community in which they live. These experiences may be those of inquiring how local government works, who actually makes decisions or how legal issues are resolved. Although participation in the community will vary according to children's ages, involvement in situations beyond the school is necessary in order to understand the values, attitudes, and practices which comprise the political and legal world.

F. *History.* The student (teacher-child) should understand the traditions and historical perspective of the American democratic experience.

Civic/legal educating requires historical understanding. Students need to be able to place what now exists in a context of what people have thought and done in the past. The legitimacy of institutions involves giving attention to why political and legal structures have emerged and the intent of those who have come before us. This involves an accountability to Plato, Jefferson, Lincoln, Martin Luther King, Jr., and so on. It is within a historical perspective that we can gain greater insight into our current legal practices.

Major Content Areas

The six themes just discussed are (or can be) developed within the major K–6 social studies content areas. Listed below is a national synthesis of social studies content areas.

Table 2: Major Law Concepts

Concept	Grade						
	K	1	2	3	4	5	6
Rules (law)	•	•	•	•	•	•	•
Fairness (justice)	•	•	•	•	•	•	•
Authority	•	•	•	•	•	•	•
Order	•	•	•	•	•	•	•
Responsibility	•	•	•	•	•	•	•
Participation	•	•	•	•	•	•	•
Property	•	•	•	•	•	•	•
Contract	•	•	•	•	•	•	•
Freedom			•	•	•	•	•
Voluntary compliance			•	•	•	•	•
Legitimacy				•	•	•	•
Due process				•	•	•	•
Legal system					•	•	•
Ethics						•	•

Kindergarten. Emphasis is placed upon the self and family. The student develops an understanding of those items that people need. Study is made of the concept of change as the student makes the transition from home to school.

Level 1. Emphasis is placed upon the school environment. Students study what goes on in school and why. Students have opportunities to investigate the fact that learning goes on at home and in the community as well as in school.

Level 2. Emphasis is upon the interrelationships in communities. A community operates as a system of interrelated acts, and students study industrial, commercial, and residential "regions" or sections of the community and their linkages to one another. Students study how people find their way around a community or city and how different sections of the community exchange ideas, goods, and people.

Level 3. Emphasis is placed upon a set of selected communities around the world and a comparison of cultural attributes taken from these communities. A community: is a geographical or physical setting; is held together by means of transportation, communication, and the sharing of common values; helps meet individual and group needs and provides opportunities for exchanging ideas; contains families, places of worship, economic institutions, and educational settings; reflects degrees of continuity and change; and can be very small in terms of geography and population or as large as the planet Earth. A community encompasses all forms of relationships that are characterized by a high degree of personal and emotional involvement, moral commitment, and continuity. The cultural attributes studied include: family, work, play, travel, tools, language, art, and beliefs.

Level 4. Emphasis is placed upon the interrelationships between and among regions of the United States and between the United States and selected regions of the world.

Level 5. Emphasis is placed upon the geography and social history of the United States. Study is made of important people and their social, economic, and political activities.

Level 6. Emphasis is placed upon the study of culture in areas such as Europe, Africa, the Middle East, the Far East, and South America. Each area is studied in terms of location, demography, terrain, and other factors of spatial relationships and resource potential. Each area is also studied to allow for a historical perspective. Finally, institutions of socialization, economics, politics, and recreation are studied, with special attention to the following concepts: language, law, tools, art, beliefs, and customs.

Major Law Concepts and Social Studies/Law Skills

Within the social studies content areas listed above, major law concepts and social studies/law skills can be identified (see Tables 2 and 3). Knowledge of these items will help educators see the relationships between social studies and law content. For example, such concepts as rules, fairness, and responsibility can play a significant part in the kindergarten social studies sequence that wishes to address the content of self, home, and family.

On the skill dimension, one can observe the appropriateness of general skills to the discipline of law. Skills such as formulating operational definitions, locating and gathering information, and giving and accepting constructive criticism find their rightful place in law as well as in social studies educational programs.

By noting the K–6 social studies content areas, major law concepts, and general skills, one can

Table 3: Social Studies/Law Skills

Skill Area	Students Should Be Able to:
Social science processes (critical thinking)	Formulate operational definitions; form hypotheses; test hypotheses; interpret data; communicate; classify; observe; measure; predict; infer; formulate models
Locating and gathering information	Use reference books, audiovisual materials, current periodicals, people
Maps and globes	Orient directions; learn to make maps and globes; devise symbols for maps and globes; interpret flat maps; learn names of cardinal directions; become familiar with and interpret map symbols; interpret political maps; interpret product maps; locate places on maps and globes; trace routes; interpret topographic features; interpret scale of miles; interpret weather maps; use parallels and meridians; interpret town-state road maps; interpret outer space maps; interpret degree of latitude into miles; interpret degree of longitude into time; interpret polar projection maps
Time and spatial relationships	Relate dates to personal experiences; make use of the calendar; relate cause-and-effect relationships among events and dates; develop and use vocabulary of time expressions; place related events in chronological order; develop numerical chronology
Interpersonal relations and group participation	Help organize and plan tasks; develop ability to listen carefully; give and accept constructive criticism; accept others as persons; contribute to the accomplishment of the task; accept views of others; practice courteous behavior; anticipate consequences of group discussion or action; follow rules and laws; follow parliamentary procedure; accept responsibility for own actions
Social mathematics	Make or use approximations, measurements, continuity, discreteness (clearly define domains and range of variables), frequency data, sample techniques, randomness

see the complementary nature of these items. In essence, law and social studies educational programs are or should be one and the same.

Criteria for Identifying and Evaluating Law-related Content in Social Studies Materials

The following are procedures curriculum committees and others can use in selecting worthwhile law-related content.

The first step in identifying and evaluating law-related content in a social studies program is to establish that the basal program has internal integrity or congruency—that is, that the program rationale, objectives, content coverage, teaching strategies, and evaluation design are congruent with each other. For example, if objectives call for student involvement and participation and all the learning strategies are teacher-centered, then we have a lack of congruency and a breakdown in the logic of curriculum design. Internal integrity is one of the standard basic criteria for identifying a sound curricular program.

Once it is established that the material for review is sound, criteria for identifying and evaluating the law-related content of the material/program can be applied. Sound law-related education content should address in part or in whole the following themes, discussed above: (A) ethical responsibility, (B) knowledge, (C) inquiry, (D) school environment, (E) larger community, and (F) history. These six themes provide a scope for the criteria and establish necessary and sufficient conditions for content selection. The identification and evaluation instrument shown in Table 4 applies these criteria. To use the instrument read and review the social studies program under consideration and rate its law-related content on a five-point scale.

Note that there are two sets of scores to be obtained. The first rates the overall quality of the total law-related content. The second rates the content on its balance or distribution relative to the six themes. Scores for overall quality are as follows: 1–100 = poor, 101–150 = fair, 151–200 = good, 201–250 = very good, 251–300 = excellent. Scores for distribution among themes should be rated as follows: theme A: should score at least 25; theme B: should score at least 50; theme C: should score at least 25; theme D: should score at least 13; theme E: should score at least 25; theme F: should score at least 13.

Table 4: Identification-Evaluation Instrument

A. Ethical responsibility

The material helps students understand:

A1. That *ethical* judgment is a component of all political and legal behavior because it affects the lives of other people.

A2. The value of pluralism and the difficulties and opportunities that it presents to the *legal system*.

A3. That although citizens delegate *authority* to elected officials who make up government, they (citizens) still have obligations to be informed, influence, and judge the actions of officials.

A4. That citizens have an *ethical responsibility* to practice democratic behavior.

A5. That voting is only one part of active democratic citizenship (*participation*), which also includes influencing, judging, and informing oneself and others.

A6. That home and school share *responsibilities* to encourage behavior and attitudes which are favorable toward the establishment of a *just (fair)* community.

A7. That there is a direct relationship between an individual's *rights* and *responsibilities* in a democracy.

A8. That as the world becomes increasingly interdependent, citizen roles (*participation*) in the global society are more important.

A9. That *laws* (rules) are created to influence the behavior of people.

A10. That in a democracy, *order* can only be maintained through the *voluntary compliance* of citizens with the law.

B. Knowledge

The material helps students understand:

B1. How penalties and sanctions are provided for violations of *law*.

B2. How people make *rules* in their homes, schools, and communities for their safety and health.

B3. How *governments* are established.

B4. How the pressure of *interest groups* sometimes results in the establishment of laws.

B5. How governments gain *legitimacy*.

B6. How government and laws change as people respond to different needs and situations.

B7. How local, state, national, and planetary agencies can provide different yet important services to the communities of the world.

B8. How the *Constitution* of the United States provides for a system of checks and balances among the three branches of government—executive, legislative, and judicial.

B9. How the purpose and operation of each branch of government are determined by the state and federal *constitutions* as well as their interpretation by the *courts*.

B10. How as people feel increasingly *powerless,* the level of social *responsibility* drops.

B11. How various means are used to hold the *judicial system* accountable—i.e., election of judges, passage of new laws, etc.

B12. How *law enforcement* agencies and the courts are constrained by the federal and state constitutions.

B13. How *penalities* and *sanctions* for law violations are determined by legal restrictions, designation of judges, etc.

B14. How *administration* of the law affects the intent of the law.

B15. How the *judicial system* interprets, changes, expands, or nullifies law as passed by the *legislative system*.

B16. How individual rights granted by the *Constitution* are not automatically protected by the *courts*.

B17. How the judicial system is structured and operates in the *criminal justice* area, including law enforcement, court procedure, the *jury system,* the protection provided for individuals, and the weaknesses of the system.

B18. How the *juvenile justice system* differs from the adult system in jurisdiction, procedures, and philosophy.

B19. How courts provide a means of *redress of grievances* and how they operate.

B20. How many administrative *governmental agencies* serve a quasi-judicial function in the enforcement of administrative rules and in the resolving of conflict of interest—i.e., WERC, ICC, etc.

C. Inquiry

The material helps students discover:

C1. How to use the inquiry skills of observing, communicating, classifying, inferring, predicting, formulating models, measuring, interpreting data, formulating operational definitions, formulating questions and hypotheses, and testing hypotheses.

C2. How *rules* are made.

C3. How to identify *legal* questions.

C4. How *political involvement* is a learning process in a democratic setting.

C5. How individuals and groups can behave *legally* as well as *illegally*.

C6. How appropriate questions can be asked about any *institution*.

C7. How *legal issues* have many sides which an informed citizen must examine.

C8. How *information* without evaluation and judgment is of little use.

C9. How *legal decisions* are reached.

C10. How the study of issues can produce *new* inquiry *questions*.

Table 4: Identification-Evaluation Instrument

D. School environment
   The material helps students understand:
   D1. That political *decisions* in a democratic setting must be *shared.*
   D2. That the environment of school is a *legal,* political, and *ethical* setting.
   D3. That personal *responsibility* must be taken before learning can occur.
   D4. That there must be *mutual respect* among all individuals in the classroom.
   D5. That open discussion and *debate* are necessary for reaching *democratic decisions.*

E. Larger community
   The material helps students be aware:
   E1. Of and able to take a *local issue* and follow it through the complete *decision-making process.*
   E2. Of and able to identify the source of *power* and special *pressure groups* affecting decision making in the local community.
   E3. Of how to use the skills needed in organizations for *collective action.*
   E4. Of how to use tactics and strategy to *influence* the decison-making process.
   E5. That they must assume more *responsibility* for future and continual involvement in government.
   E6. That an election is only part of political involvement and that skills are needed to participate in politics both during and between *elections.*
   E7. Of and develop skills needed by active citizen observers, having knowledge which is the key for keeping a governing body *accountable.*
   E8. Of his/her task of *decision making* in an increasingly wider variety of social setting.
   E9. Of and able to see and argue two sides of a given *issue.*
   E10. Of and able to *communicate* his/her concerns to those in power.

F. History
   The material helps students understand:
   F1. That ideas and *values* based on *tradition* are strong, lasting influences upon the structure and actions of government.
   F2. That the *Constitution* (state and national) is a "living" document that must be studied, understood, and celebrated with each new generation.
   F3. That government and laws *change* as people respond to different needs and situations.
   F4. That historically citizenship has involved varying degrees of *obligations and privileges* depending upon the form of government.
   F5. That the *democratic system* is a very fragile one and only constant watchfulness has preserved it and will continue to do so.

NOTE: The scale assumes that the material being examined is a complete K–6 basal social studies program.

Another view . . .

Identifying and Evaluating Law and Humanities Education Content in the Social Studies

James E. Davis

This article supports the basic arguments of Michael Hartoonian's paper. James Davis lends his own perspective to the issues involved in identifying and evaluating law-related content in the social studies by emphasizing the importance of making rational decisions in this area. Davis says, in fact, that he would "support any process that would enable those charged with adoption of curriculum materials to make more rational decisions."

The author goes on to raise several other questions suggested by the Hartoonian paper. The issues of separation versus integration of law and humanities content and competition of major curriculum themes for visibility and space within existing curricula are among those raised by this article.

I am pleased to react to Mike Hartoonian's paper, in which he has done his usual, thoughtful job in laying out some of the major concerns of law-related education in the elementary curriculum. He obviously has an in-depth understanding of elementary social studies that is worth listening to. While I might quibble about his "national synthesis" of elementary social studies content areas, I think in general that he is pretty much on target.

Hartoonian's six major themes reflect, I think, a good compromise between what some might think of as "pure" law-related education and a general social studies program. I agree with him that the first task in incorporating law-related content into an elementary social studies curriculum is to identify those substantive content areas that might be appropriate entry points. With the exception of one or two of the more creative elementary social studies text series, Hartoonian's six themes would seem to fit quite well with elementary series now on the market or in use in elementary classrooms.

Another general comment is in order here. I would support any process that would enable those charged with the adoption of curriculum materials to make more rational decisions. One of the greatest tragedies in elementary education is that we are often confronted with a host of new

James E. Davis is Associate Director of the Social Science Education Consortium and the ERIC Clearinghouse for Social Studies/Social Science Education. His main areas of interest are in curriculum analysis and planning, and in educational dissemination.

curriculum materials and given a very short time in which to decide on an adoption. Those involved in the decision-making process have little time to analyze the material thoroughly in order to make the best decision. The categories Hartoonian offers and the checklist would be good starting places for developing an analytical tool for local use in examining law-related curriculum materials. However, given the practical considerations of the adoption process, I would recommend that a list of questions be confined to about 20, and that the task of analysis be divided among various people. Further, the analytical work on any given set of materials should be done by a minimum of three different individuals. In this way, some interjudge reliability on the quality, usefulness, etc., of a given set of materials might be attained.

As I read Hartoonian's paper, a number of issues come to mind concerning law and humanities curricula at the elementary level. I raise them because they must be addressed squarely, and should provide food for thought for those who are concerned with this project.

1. Should law and humanities education become a separate part of the social studies curriculum, or should it be an integral part of a "basal" or "standard" elementary social studies curriculum? Part of this issue is whether social studies is actually taught to any substantial degree in U.S. elementary schools.

2. A closely related issue is the competitiveness among and between the various areas of study to be "infused" into the social studies cur-

riculum. Some subject areas that come to mind are: free enterprise (economics?), career education, health education, sex education, teaching about religion, and ethnic studies.

3. To what degree is it possible to foster rational decision making concerning curriculum selection?

4. There are other important issues related to the whole business of analysis and selection of curriculum materials. These include reading-level assessment; analysis of materials regarding race, ethnic and sex bias; and procedural concerns, such as negotiated contracts which often preclude extensive curriculum analysis work, involvement of community people in the selection process, and certain state mandates that may require districts to teach the "basics."

5. Of what relative importance are the various substantive areas of law and humanities in the elementary curriculum?

6. There has been some discussion of late about the climate of the schools for providing a humane education. To what degree should curriculum people address what has been called the "hidden curriculum" and begin to organize programs that would expose the hidden curriculum and turn the organization of the school into a humane climate for students, teachers, and parents?

Teacher Education: The Key to Effective Law and Humanities Programs in the Elementary School

David T. Naylor

In this paper, David Naylor describes features which are important to effective teacher-training programs in general and those focusing on teaching about law and humanities in the elementary school in particular. Several points are subject specific and warrant close attention by the law and humanities teacher/educator. The author points out, for example, that despite what leaders in the law-related education movement may perceive about the growth of the field, large numbers of teachers remain unconvinced about its virtues. These same teachers are not well informed about the nature and goals of law-related education. An especially interesting point made by the author is that extremely careful efforts must be made to integrate presentations of substantive law into teacher education and methodology workshops.

Perhaps one of the most important points made by Naylor focuses on teacher education in general. He reminds us that, as with attempts to teach younger students about law and humanities, no single or monolithic model for teacher education can or should be identified.

Teacher education is the sine qua non for widespread acceptance and successful implementation of law and humanities curricula in the schools of this nation. Unless that point is grasped, efforts to promote law and humanities programs are doomed to failure, victims of a malady that has so often afflicted other promising education reforms. Successful law and humanities programs cannot be established on a wide scale without the existence of large numbers of teachers who understand the nature of such programs, who are convinced that these programs are important—indeed, essential—areas of the curriculum, and who possess the necessary content background and methodological skills to teach law and humanities curricula effectively.

But such a cadre of teachers does not exist at the present time, especially at the elementary school level. Despite what its proponents may wish, law-related education has not yet won universal acceptance by American teachers. Although the 1970s have been a time in which law-related education has been given increasing attention and visibility, a time when we have witnessed the appearance of a mushrooming number of law-related projects, teacher education courses and workshops, articles in professional books and journals, presentations at national, multistate, and state-wide conferences, and curriculum materials designed for use in the schools, the fact remains that far too many of America's teachers have been untouched by these efforts. Too many teachers remain unaware of the nature of law-related education and unconvinced of its importance. And far too few of America's elementary and secondary students have been exposed to effective law-related education programs in the schools they attend. If law and humanities education is to become an integral part of the curriculum in the elementary and secondary schools of this country, a major effort in teacher education must be launched, at both the in-service and preservice levels.

The task will not be easy. Financial considerations aside, teachers are still troubled by many aspects of law-related education, not the least of which is the most basic question: Why do it? Successfully addressing this issue is the most important task, the most significant challenge confronting advocates of law-related education. The problem is especially acute at the elementary school level. Likely to be least affected by recent developments in law-related education, elementary teachers are often unaware of the nature or scope of law-related education, troubled by the mystique of law that plagues many of our citizens,

David Naylor is Associate Professor of Education and Director of the Center for Law-related Education at the University of Cincinnati. His latest publication is a textbook for secondary students, *Law, Order, and Justice* (Hayden Book Co.).

educators and noneducators alike, and skeptical of the relationship of law-related education to the elementary school curriculum.

While many teachers may be willing to concede the value of at least an acquaintance with law for students in the secondary school, such a concession is much more difficult to obtain at the elementary school level. The paucity of law-related materials available for use in the elementary school compounds the problem. There is a critical need for instructional materials which incorporate the basic goals and components of law-related education and are suitable for use with elementary school children.

Yet, despite such obstacles, it is at the elementary school level that the greatest potential exists for the development and implementation of widespread, high-quality law and humanities education programs. It is on elementary school teachers that the major emphasis of teacher education must be placed.

During the elementary school years, children are engaged in the process of socialization as they move from the limited frame of reference of the home environment to the more complex environment of the school and the larger society. Political socialization studies attest to the critical importance of these years in the development of citizenship concepts, attitudes, and behaviors. These are formative years for elementary school children, a time when they acquire a basic understanding of rules and law, of the nature of authority and one's relationship to it, of concepts of justice, responsibility, diversity, and freedom. Yet, these studies remind us that traditional elementary school programs have not done very well in meeting that challenge.

The theories of Jean Piaget and Lawrence Kohlberg point to the key developmental stages children experience during the elementary school years. For Piaget, this is a time when children move from the stage of preoperational thought to the stage of concrete operations, a time when they acquire the capacity for logical thought. For Kohlberg, the elementary years represent an important time in the development of the child's capacity for moral reasoning, moving from preconventional reasoning characterized by a preoccupation with self to conventional reasoning and a concern for others and the larger society. Advocates of both theories recognize the critical importance of the developmental processes children experience during the elementary school years and call for curricula which provide appropriate, sequentially ordered learning experiences that recognize and facilitate the child's developmental growth.

Carefully planned law and humanities curricula can contribute significantly to these important developments in the life of elementary school children. More than just another addition to an already crowded curriculum, well-conceived, well-developed law and humanities programs are essential elements of the elementary school curriculum. Their basic goals, content focus, and methodological approaches, approaches which emphasize understanding as opposed to blind conformity, can do much to enrich and strengthen the elementary school curriculum and the lives of elementary school children.

The qualities of those who teach in the elementary school and the nature of the elementary school itself hold much promise for the growth of law and humanities curricula. By training and expertise, elementary teachers tend to be generalists, as compared to secondary teachers, who tend to be specialists. As such, elementary teachers are more likely to be receptive to curricula that emphasize interdisciplinary learning experiences, curricula that successfully fuse the social studies, the traditional province of law-related education, with language arts, music, and art, the traditional province of humanities education, and with other subjects such as science. And elementary school teachers are more likely to identify ways in which they can provide such experiences for their students.

The organizational patterns found in American elementary schools are highly compatible with law and humanities program goals and objectives. Given its nature and scope, the traditional self-contained classroom provides many opportunities for teachers to implement interdisciplinary learning experiences. The team teaching approach frequently utilized in nongraded and departmentalized organizational modes affords many opportunities for teachers to engage in cooperative planning, to take advantage of respective strengths and interests, and to supplement and reinforce the instructional efforts of each member of the teaching team.

Compared to secondary teachers, elementary teachers are likely to have a greater awareness of the instructional goals and efforts of other teachers at similar grade, subject, and/or developmental levels, greater opportunities for planning and implementing instructional programs, and greater flexibility in scheduling classroom instruction, in arranging for field experiences, and in grouping students with similar interests, needs, and abilities. By contrast, secondary teachers often face inflexible schedules, larger numbers of students with fewer opportunities for flexible grouping, and subject matter fragmentation due to departmental organization, greater student choice in course selection, and a lack of articulation within large teaching staffs.

How, then, does one address these problems

successfully, capitalize upon these strengths, and move to infuse law and humanities programs into the elementary school curriculum? The key is the use of widespread, effective teacher education programs. As the American Bar Association's Special Committee on Youth Education for Citizenship (YEFC) report *Law-related Education: Guidelines for the Future* (1975) concluded: "Effective teacher training is the most important component of law-related education. While lawyers, judges, and law enforcement officials can help by making occasional classroom visits, only teachers can be expected to bear the instructional burden and implement the goals of law-related education" (p. 31).

Describing what needs to be done in law-related teacher education programs, Assistant YEFC Staff Director White (1976) wrote:

[I]f teachers are to carry the instructional burden in this important area, we have to provide them with the tools they'll need. We have to give them an accurate knowledge of important points of law and legal process. We have to advise them of the many pedagogical techniques that are particularly suitable for law-related education.... We must help them gain confidence to use these techniques in their own classrooms. We have to suggest ways in which law may be infused into the existing curriculum. We have to increase their familiarity with law-related materials. We have to help them learn to use the wide variety of community resources available to law-related programs. [P. 1].

This task is compounded for law and humanities teacher education programs, for the merger of law-related education and humanities education requires additional efforts with substance, methodology, and integrative strategies and models. Law and humanities teacher education programs must recognize and address these needs successfully.

YEFC has initiated many programs to stimulate interest in law-related education. One of that committee's most important contributions is *Teaching Teachers about Law: A Guide to Law-related Teacher Education Programs* (1976), which contains articles by many of those actively involved in law-related teacher education. It is a "how to" book, a book which includes descriptions of 11 different models for law-related teacher education programs—their purpose, their nature, and their potential. It is an invaluable source for anyone interested in designing and implementing a law and humanities teacher education program.

An analysis of the 11 models described in *Teaching Teachers about Law* reveals a strong emphasis upon secondary teacher education. All 11 models include programs for secondary educators. However, only seven provide programs for elementary educators, and, of these, only five in-

clude programs for teachers in grades K–6. While consistent with the thrust of law-related teacher education efforts in this decade, the models included in this book make clear the great need for widespread teacher education programs involving large numbers of elementary teachers, programs which speak to the special needs of elementary teachers and which capitalize on their potential.

The 11 models reveal clearly that law-related education is not a monolithic movement. Describing the great variety of approaches within law-related programs, YEFC Staff Director Gross (1977) wrote: "Programs in law-related education vary as much as law itself. They span the spectrum from those concentrating on practical aspects of the law...to those with a jurisprudential or conceptual focus.... Even within these particular categorizations, one finds a rich substantive diversity.... Most programs combine, to varying degrees, these different approaches and emphases" (p. 3).

Just as program emphases vary, so too do the means by which law-related programs are initiated, implemented, and sustained. Hence, there is no one model for law and humanities teacher education that will fit all situations. Nevertheless, law-related teacher education efforts share a number of common characteristics, the prevalence of which attests to their value. Described below, they deserve serious consideration by those interested in providing law and humanities teacher education programs for elementary school educators.

Characteristics of Law-related Teacher Education Programs

Virtually all of the 11 models stress the importance of an interdisciplinary approach to law-related teacher education, an approach which, as Gross (1977) has observed, involves "the combined efforts of lawyers and educators, with civil and criminal justice officials and other community leaders contributing to many programs. This involvement includes serving on advisory committees, marshaling community support, educating educators, arranging field experiences, assisting in the development of curricula, and participating in classroom presentations" (p. 4). For programs which seek to fuse law-related education and the humanities, the interdisciplinary approach is even more essential. Law and humanities teacher education programs require an expanded effort to utilize persons with expertise in both of these areas and to draw upon a wide variety of subject matter. Such programs are likely to involve persons and resources not previously considered part of traditional law-related or humanities education efforts.

Another common feature of law-related teacher education programs is the emphasis upon instruction in substantive law and in appropriate methodology for teaching children and young people about law, and the utilization of field experience as integral parts of the program. These three elements constitute the heart of law-related teacher education. No law and humanities teacher education program can afford to ignore any one of them.

That teachers need to become more familiar with law and legal processes should be obvious, as should the vital role that field experiences play in law-related teacher education programs. Not as obvious to some, however, is the critical need for teachers who participate in such programs to rethink pedagogical approaches and techniques. Law and humanities teacher education programs must equip participating educators with an appropriate rationale, with methodology suitable for use in classroom situations, and with an awareness of the types of materials available for use in elementary and secondary classrooms.

The high quality of the instructional staff is another characteristic of successful law-related teacher education programs. Those who assume responsibility for administering and for providing instruction in law and humanities teacher education programs must be selected with great care. Their role is critical to the program's success. Resource persons (e.g., lawyers, judges, police officers, university professors, etc.) must be thoroughly informed of the nature of the program and what is expected of their presentations (i.e., purpose, content, and methodology). Field experiences must be carefully planned and meaningfully chosen. Those who assume responsibility for instruction in educational methodology must have a thorough understanding of the nature of law and humanities education, must exhibit appropriate teaching behaviors in the instruction they provide, and must provide a variety of methods and techniques appropriate for use at the grade levels represented by those teachers participating in the program.

The preparation of a law-related curriculum unit for use in a specific course, a specific grade, or a specific program is commonly used as a culminating experience in law-related teacher education programs. Asked to select one of the basic topics or concepts presented in the teacher education program, teachers develop a unit appropriate for use with their students, utilizing a number of the instructional approaches presented in the program. In this way teachers explore possible entry points for integrating law-related education into their own school curriculum and identify at least one specific area of that curriculum to which a law-related unit is particularly well suited. Thus the transition from teacher education program to a specific school situation is facilitated, and teachers have at least one law-related unit suitable for use with their own students in their own school.

These features of law-related teacher education programs are applicable to both in-service and preservice law and humanities teacher education programs. The former comprise the great bulk of attention devoted to law-related education; the latter represent the future of the law-related education movement. If law and humanities education programs are to realize their potential, large-scale preservice programs of the kind described above must be developed and implemented in America's colleges and universities (i.e., interdisciplinary approach; blending of instruction in law and educational methodology; use of field experiences; high quality of instructional staff well grounded in law and humanities education; and curriculum development). I have advised: "Not only is it more logical for long-term success to make instruction in law-related education part of the training received by all of those who are about to embark upon a teaching career. But, by shifting the emphasis to pre-service education, the financial burden can be alleviated through institutionalization and the training responsibility will be primarily assumed by those who are presently involved in the training of teachers, the nation's colleges and universities" (Naylor, 1977, p. 73).

In light of the dominance of in-service law-related teacher education efforts and the relative ease in establishing in-service programs, it is likely that initial efforts to foster law and humanities teacher education programs will concentrate on in-service education. Given that, those who wish to establish such programs need to consider the following factors. One of the most important is the need to foster teacher awareness of such programs and to attract teachers to participate in them. This is a task of special concern to in-service teacher education efforts, for preservice programs have certain inherent advantages, not the least of which are the program course requirement and advising systems prevalent at the college and university level.

Presentations at workshops and clinics as part of regularly scheduled sessions at meetings of such organizations as the National Council for the Social Studies and its regional and state affiliates have been used as one approach for fostering teacher awareness. But such an approach is of limited value, especially if one's target is the elementary teacher, since elementary teachers are not as likely as secondary teachers to be involved in these organizations or to attend meetings sponsored by them. Hence more localized efforts are needed, including presentations as part of regular in-service programs and/or as part of special awareness workshops conducted in specific, limited geographic areas.

Grass-roots involvement in the planning of such programs and workshops and in the mechanisms used to recruit teachers to participate in them is another necessary factor, one that is stressed by many who are involved in in-service law-related teacher education programs. They emphasize the need to involve representatives of local school districts (i.e., administrators, curriculum supervisors, and teachers), bar associations, and colleges and universities to jointly plan and participate in law-related teacher education programs. For widespread in-service law and humanities education programs to become a reality, especially if such programs are expected to reach large numbers of elementary teachers, localized programs and workshops of this nature are a prerequisite.

Once mechanisms have been developed for providing in-service law and humanities teacher education programs, special incentives will likely be needed to attract teacher participants, if, as Sullivan and Baker (1976) suggest, "for no other reason than to get their attention" (p. 28). Incentives used in law-related teacher education programs have included the awarding of free or low-cost graduate university credit, the granting of stipends, the distribution of free books and materials, the inclusion of teacher education programs as part of a school district's in-service offerings, and the use of released time for participation in teacher education programs. As I have advised: "The value of these benefits should not be underestimated. . . . The awarding of one or more of these benefits is as important in attracting qualified elementary school participants as it is in attracting qualified secondary school participants, for, while descriptive information may serve to spark interest, the failure to provide adequate benefits may financially exclude a number of otherwise highly qualified elementary school educators" (Naylor, 1976, p. 55).

The importance of a strong university base for in-service teacher education should be evident. The ability to marshal university resources— faculty, graduate credit, reputation, and facilities—is a critical variable for legitimizing a law and humanities teacher education program and for providing various incentives. Hence it is not surprising to find that of the 11 projects described in *Teaching Teachers about Law*, seven have a strong university affiliation.

Another important issue relates to the nature of the target population. A number of projects provide law-related teacher education programs for both elementary and secondary teachers. Some of these have separate course offerings for the two groups. Some involve both groups in a common program. Advantages are claimed for both approaches. For example, those with separate course offerings emphasize the differences between elementary and secondary school students and the need for programs to recognize and deal specifically with those differences in terms of both substantive law instruction (i.e., content; concepts) and methodological instruction (i.e., goals; curricular approaches; strategies and techniques). Those whose programs involve both elementary and secondary teachers point to the commonality of law instruction and basic methodological approaches (though some divide teachers for the latter) and the value of increasing articulation between elementary and secondary teachers and thus providing a greater awareness of and increased possibilities for sequentially developed law-related curricula. Both approaches merit careful scrutiny by those advocating law and humanities teacher education programs.

Another issue to be considered is when and where in-service programs are to be offered. Many projects find a once-a-week, multisession program of teacher education advantageous for attracting large numbers of teachers. Frequently held in local schools distributed strategically throughout the state or geographic region, these programs provide greater accessibility (an important factor for attracting elementary teachers), permit a series of courses to be offered which focus on special concerns or special needs common to particular communities or groups of teachers (an important factor for curriculum implementation), and increase the likelihood of involving teams of educators from the same school or school district, including administrators (another important factor for attracting elementary teachers and enhancing curriculum implementation).

The location of teacher education centers constitutes still another critical variable. Those projects which seek to draw participants from many states or many hundreds of miles away have limited potential for involving large numbers of teachers or securing large-scale curriculum implementation. Those projects with more modest objectives must also contend with geographic considerations. With too few centers, sheer distance may exclude many teachers from participating. Yet, with the addition of each teacher education center, more staff, greater administrative coordination, and additional financial resources are needed. Hence, the number and availability of teacher education centers are likely to influence heavily the design of a project's teacher education program, whether it is to be a 1-, 2-, 3-, or 4-week summer program, or whether it is to be a once-a-week afternoon or evening program, or whether it is to include both types of programs or some variant of them.

The particular model one chooses for a law and humanities teacher education program will depend upon a variety of factors. Most likely, those factors will include: (*a*) the goals and scope of the teacher education effort; (*b*) the characteristics of the target population; (*c*) the nature of the instructional offerings; (*d*) the degree of acceptance and support the program enjoys; (*e*) the amount of financial resources available; and (*f*) the quality, number, and capabilities of those responsible for implementing the program.

Having outlined the special features common to successful law-related teacher education programs and emphasized some special considerations in the design and development of law and humanities in-service teacher education programs, we still need to identify some other issues which are of special concern to many elementary teachers. Discussed by me in a previous article (Naylor, 1976), they include whether, for elementary school children, law-related education is: (*a*) too irrelevant; (*b*) too complex; and (*c*) too value-laden. Such issues must be confronted and dealt with effectively in a law and humanities program for elementary teachers, whether at the in-service or preservice level.

In summary, law and humanities teacher education must emphasize and help teachers recognize the value of this important educational reform and develop an appropriate rationale for its inclusion as an integral part of the elementary school curriculum. These programs must help elementary teachers become more knowledgeable about law and the humanities and their relationship to each other and feel intellectually comfortable with them. And these programs must help teachers become aware of methodology appropriate for teaching elementary school children about law and the humanities, skilled in the use of these teaching approaches and strategies, and willing to use them in the elementary school classroom.

The close coordination of substantive law presentations with education workshop sessions which stress classroom application will enhance the possibility of helping teachers identify and develop "appropriate subject matter and teaching strategies responsive to the [elementary school] child's dynamic range of developmental needs and capabilities" (Wyner, 1976, p. 41). In this way, the gap between the espousal of educational reform and the reality of achieving it can be successfully bridged.

In addition, law and humanities teacher education programs for elementary teachers must do more than merely conduct classes. Follow-up efforts are needed if the impetus is to be sustained. These efforts might entail additional educational opportunities through other course offerings, leadership training and opportunities, and special follow-up workshops. Or they might consist of a law resource service to facilitate the use of speakers in school classrooms and field experiences for schoolchildren. Or they might include the publication of a newsletter, magazine, or handbook. Whatever the method or methods employed, follow-up efforts are needed to sustain interest, refine skills, and maintain an important line of communication.

Those who are to be involved in law and humanities teacher education programs for elementary teachers are embarking upon an exciting journey. Though it is fraught with many obstacles, those who will make it can take comfort in the knowledge that they will not travel in totally unchartered waters. By capitalizing upon the lessons gleaned from the experiences of those presently involved in law-related teacher education, the journey may be made easier and its end reached more efficiently and more effectively. I hope this article will be of benefit to those who plan to be part of this expedition.

REFERENCES

American Bar Association Special Committee on Youth Education for Citizenship. *Law-related education in America: Guidelines for the future.* St. Paul: West, 1975.

Gross, N. Law-related education: Current trends, future directions. *Peabody Journal of Education,* 1977, *55*, 2–5.

Naylor, D. T. Effective training programs for elementary school educators: Selected issues and recommendations. In C. J. White III (Ed.), *Teaching teachers about law.* Chicago: American Bar Association, 1976.

Naylor, D. T. Preparing teachers to teach about the law. *Educational Comment,* 1977, *19*, 66–75.

Sullivan, B. R., & Baker, L. Planning and organizing a teacher education program. In C. J. White III (Ed.), *Teaching teachers about law.* Chicago: American Bar Association, 1976.

White, C. J., III (Ed.). *Teaching teachers about law: A guide to law-related teacher education programs.* Chicago: American Bar Association, 1976.

Wyner, N. Observations on the teaching of law in elementary schools. In C. J. White III (Ed.), *Teaching teachers about law.* Chicago: American Bar Association, 1976.

Teacher Education: The Key to Effective Law and Humanities Programs in the Elementary School

William Hazard

In responding to David Naylor's paper on teacher education, William Hazard has raised several intriguing and important points. Some may perceive the issues he raises as "devil's advocate" questions, but their importance should not be overlooked, for they challenge us to scrutinize our procedures and goals in teacher education as they relate to law and the humanities in the elementary school.

Readers will find the following points especially provocative: (1) Since each unit of education in the hierarchy tends to influence the curriculum of those units below it, perhaps it would be useful to "cultivate the idea that successful high school work in the social sciences and humanities" extends from such work at the elementary level. (2) Injecting the basic content of law and humanities education into the elementary school will precede any broad-scale development of such content in preservice teacher education. (3) The content of law and humanities is subject to "professionalization" and therefore may result in the trivialization of the knowledge, values, and understanding it seeks to impart. (4) Placing principal responsibility for teacher education on preservice may be a very poor idea. (5) Placing primary responsibility on elementary teachers for disseminating and institutionalizing law and humanities education may be inappropriate or, as Hazard suggests, "wrong-headed."

David Naylor's paper has outlined the principal arguments and issues related to the need for increased numbers of elementary school teachers who are prepared to deal with law-related education in their classrooms. If the basic tenets of such education are to take firm root in the elementary schools across the country, it seems rational to suppose that the seeds must be cast on fertile ground, nurtured with sound husbandry, and evaluated rigorously to develop the hardiest strains. As a novice in the gardens of elementary school teaching, I accept Naylor's major and minor propositions about the need for informed, confirmed believers in the content, methods, and purposes of law-related instruction among our colleagues in the elementary schools. I am prepared to believe that widespread diffusion of law-related education probably will happen only if the notion somehow is adopted and developed in the elementary schools across the country. I am

much less certain, however, about the most likely strategies to reach these goals.

There seem to be several discernible strategies for introducing intellectual content and appropriate teaching methods into our school machinery. The political mandate is one of the more obvious ways to inject specific substance into the curriculum veins. Through this strategy, the content is compacted into persuasive symbols (e.g. special education, driver education, consumer education), adorned with politically attractive rhetoric, and lobbied into the school code and thus into the rules and regulations via the state education agency. Article 14 of the Illinois School Code is a handy illustration of this approach for handicapped children. Article 27 of the Illinois Code (Illinois Revised Statutes, chap. 122) is another example of legislatively mandated symbolic education on a broader scale. That article mandates *inter alia,* the teaching of English patriotism, physical education, consumer education, and U.S. history, and permits instruction in a fascinating array of specific topics, such as safety, Arbor and Bird Day, and Leif Erickson Day. A number of these mandated or permitted content areas also carry a mandate to the teacher training institutions in the state of Illinois. Safety education, for example, is a permitted (*not* mandated)

William R. Hazard, a lawyer, is Professor of Educational Administration at Northwestern University. He is currently conducting research on the importance of Public Law No. 94-142 to educational practices for children in special education in selected public school districts and is author of *Law and Education*, a widely used textbook, now in its second edition.

subject of local district instruction; all state universities must include "an elective course of instruction in safety education for teachers, comprising at least 48 fifty-minute periods or the equivalent thereof." Politically mandated curriculum may stem from federal legislation. Ethnic studies and bilingual and bicultural education are well-known examples of content injected into our elementary schools by federal legislation and buttressed by court opinions.

What might be called a sociocultural imperative is a second strategy for implanting content in the school curriculum, and ultimately, in teacher education programs. Most elementary schools include some kind of instruction in art, music, sex education, and drug and alcohol education, and more or less sophisticated clinical experiences in political decision making. These areas, though not necessarily mandated by the state machinery, reflect widely held public notions of what is important for children and, hence, are included in the elementary schooling of most children. Perhaps these areas of instruction rest on the cultural and social values of adult society and derive their support from shared notions of a common-sense sort.

Beyond the politically mandated and the sociocultural imperatives, there may be a third strategy at work. Each unit of education in the hierarchy influences the curriculum of those units below it. Graduate schools tend to influence college curricula; colleges, the secondary schools; and they, the elementary schools. Despite our brave rhetoric and outrageous disclaimers, college-bound students seem to get the message that "solids" are safer than "frills." Perhaps we need to cultivate the idea that successful high school work in the social sciences and humanities properly builds on fundamental concepts of law-related education undertaken at the elementary school level.

There may be yet other strategies to plant, nourish, and harvest content and teaching methods in the elementary school program, but the point may be clear already: once law-related education is firmly planted in the elementary school curriculum, the need for teacher education will follow. In my judgment injecting the basic content of law-related education into the elementary school curriculum probably will precede any broad-scale development of such content in preservice teacher education. I think this for several reasons. First, the preparation of teachers is a public concern, with licensing or certification procedures under state-level control. The requirements for teacher certification currently are under extensive national debate, and the addition of law-related material to the credential requirements probably would involve a difficult political fight with the already entrenched interests. It is no

secret that the national and state teacher unions are taking an increased role in teacher certification decisions at the state level. There is considerable evidence that any effort to reshape elementary teacher certification requirements to include law-related components could raise substantial opposition and could very well constitute an irrelevant, though politically real, hassle.

There is yet another concern, which I find somewhat difficult to articulate. As I understand the fundamental elements of quality law-related education, they include a substantial component of law content, its relation to the social sciences and the humanities, and appropriate teaching methods, broadly supported by scholars and practitioners in the fields of law, political science, and the administration of justice. If we attempt to "professionalize" this content, so as to fit it into programs for teacher preparation, I am fearful of trivializing the important knowledge, values, and understanding central to first-rate law-related education. This may be an unduly harsh charge. I think, however, a review of the history of professional education would show some grounds for this concern. I will be even more blunt. I feel very strongly that the programs in law-related education delivered to elementary school children should continue to represent the joint effort of teachers, lawyers, and the best available talent in the related academic disciplines. If we attempt to develop and install law-related education as an integral component in preservice teacher preparation, I doubt that such interdisciplinary efforts will continue. At the present time, my sense is that scholars in the social sciences and humanities and the professionals in our judicial system contribute their invaluable perspectives to the law-related education movement because they feel that they can make unique contributions to the education of young people and thereby the betterment of society. If we should place the principal responsibility on preservice teacher education institutions, I frankly doubt that this interdisciplinary thrust would survive.

Finally, I feel strongly that placing the primary responsibility for the diffusion and institutionalization of law-related education on elementary teachers is a wrong-headed approach. Certainly, as Naylor points out, most elementary teachers must be generalists, and I perceive the content, implications, and objectives of law-related education to be substantially more specialized than we realize. The translation of legal concepts, values, and understanding from relatively abstract levels to more concrete teaching materials offers frightening opportunities for misunderstanding and mistranslation.

As I noted at the outset, Naylor has made a persuasive case for the need to reach a broader segment of classroom teachers in order to develop law-related education and make it available to all students. Few would quarrel with this logical objective. Given the recent national interest in our judicial system and particularly its role in shaping national social policies, there is good reason to expect continued support for an interest in the basic concepts, values, and social utility of this kind of instruction. It seems to me that the continued partnership of teachers, lawyers, judges, and other key participants in our judicial system is necessary if the quality of the programs and the momentum of the national movement are to be sustained. Consequently, I would urge that we examine very carefully any notion of moving toward a preservice thrust.

I think the likelihood of fruitful development will be greater through the in-service route than the preservice route. Without citing the discouraging statistics, I think it is safe to predict that the teachers we see in the schools are probably those we will have for the next several decades. Teacher turnover among the more than 2 million profes-

sionals will be quite low, and the responsibility for developing and nourishing law-related education will rest primarily on those teachers already in the classrooms. To sustain the active interdisciplinary base and the professional partnership already forged, it seems to me that in-service teacher education may represent the greatest short-range potential for law-related education. If this curriculum can become installed in the schools, particularly the elementary schools, the likelihood of generating the necessary political support for preservice education is enhanced. I hope that the research and scholarship concerning curriculum materials, teaching methods, and other pedagogical concerns will continue during this period of program development and implementation in the fabric of the elementary schools. I guess I am saying, perhaps simplistically, that it makes more sense to me to build on the known strengths in the pioneering disciplines than to move toward the professionalization of the concept in preservice teacher education.

Key Factors Affecting the Introduction and Retention of Educational Innovations: With Implications for Law and Humanities in the Elementary School Curriculum

Carole L. Hahn

It is increasingly recognized that even the most superb curriculum innovation is of little value if it is destined to sit on the classroom shelf 90% of the time or be hidden away in a dusty closet amidst other never used, old-new books. In other words, to be of any use, the innovation must reach the consumer. In this instance, of course, the consumer is first the teacher and ultimately the student.

Innovation issues range far beyond just getting the new curriculum into a given setting, to maintenance and support after the initial introduction. Carole Hahn's paper provides important insights into factors identified by major research studies as affecting the successful long-term use of a new product. Hahn's paper, like so many others included in this book, has significance well beyond the context of law and humanities in the elementary school. Readers from virtually any part of the educational system can extrapolate to their own situations. For those concerned especially about introducing law and humanities, the author lays out the steps with clues to the importance of each feature of the innovation in relation to the long-range success of the product.

In attempting to introduce law and humanities into the elementary school curriculum, one can simply jump in with enthusiasm and effort and hope for the best—or make careful, deliberate plans, utilizing the experiences of others and existing research on how to introduce innovations most effectively. The latter approach is suggested because much time, effort, and emotional strain can be saved by repeating actions which have proved successful in other similar situations. Time and energy are too valuable to risk failure or needless effort. For that reason, this paper will present key factors in educational innovations, factors identified by researchers (Hahn, 1977b) and curriculum developers (Becker & Hahn, 1977) and having implications for people who would like to infuse instruction in law and the humanities into elementary schools. Examples are suggested for curriculum developers/diffusers, for curriculum coordinators within school systems, and for individual teachers.

Several definitions will serve as a basis for our discussion. First, an innovation is any idea, practice, or product which is perceived as new by the receiver (Rogers & Shoemaker, 1971). The *idea* that young children ought to study concepts like justice and equality, the *practices* of using case studies, mock trials, and value analysis in the elementary class, and *products* like the casebook for *Your Rights and Responsibilities as an American Citizen* by Charles Quigley (1976) are all "innovations" if they are new to the decision makers or teachers in a school.

Research on the dissemination and adoption of innovations suggests factors which are important in spreading information about and promoting the use of new ideas, practices, and products. Recent research has demonstrated that the process is not complete once the decision has been made to adopt or use the innovation. New programs are often discontinued or changed so that they no longer resemble the initial intent (Fullan & Pomfret, 1977). The events that occur after adoption are referred to as the "implementation" phase.

What, then, is known about the dissemination, adoption, and implementation of innovations which may be of use to those of us interested in promoting law and humanities as part of the elementary school curriculum? Figure 1 summarizes the process of educational change.

Carole L. Hahn is Associate Professor, Division of Educational Studies, Emory University. She is the author of "Research on Diffusion" in *Review of Social Studies Research 1970–75* (National Council for the Social Studies).

Figure 1. How does educational change occur?

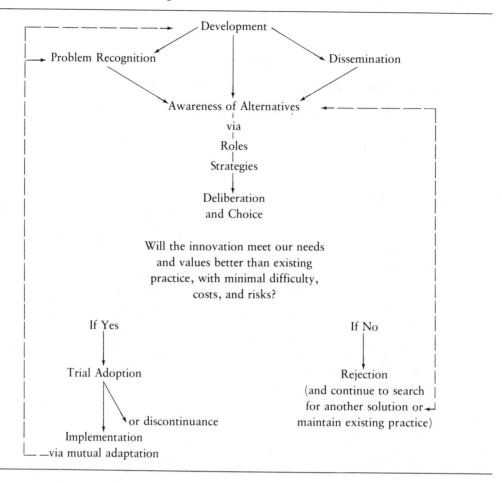

Development

First a word about curriculum development, because at this point few materials exist for teaching law and the humanities at the elementary school level. There is a need for research-based development. But that development should attend to research on curriculum adoption and implementation as well as on learning processes, political socialization, effective teaching strategies, and the fields of law and the humanities. For example, in developing materials one should consider that decision makers feel a greater need to adopt textbook series in social studies and reading than to purchase films or multimedia kits for a subject that is not now taught. Similarly, teachers will find it easier to adapt predesigned lessons to their own needs than to create their own instructional materials from scratch. Although millions of dollars, years of human energy, and much expertise went into curriculum development in the 1960s, there has been low utilization of the new

curriculum projects, to a great extent because the curriculum developers did not attend to the realities of curriculum adoption and implementation.

Let us turn now to the process by which people in a local school system become aware that innovations, which are the products of development, exist.

Awareness

Awareness may begin when an individual or group either feels a need to solve a problem or is exposed to dissemination efforts. People may become involved in law and humanities education because they are dissatisfied with the current curriculum, because they are troubled by national assessment data revealing students' lack of knowledge about constitutional principles, because their state mandated a course in citizenship education and they are developing course guides, or because in some other way they feel a need for change.

Alternatively, one may become interested in law education through exposure to dissemination efforts. Individuals may have atttended a session on law-related education at a convention, a publishers' representative may have told them about a new activity book, they may have read a copy of *Update*, or their local district may have sponsored an in-service workshop on legal education through a humanities approach.

If one has decided to promote law and humanities education in the elementary school, he or she can stimulate the change process by creating a felt need to solve a problem or by disseminating information about law education. The curriculum developer might share with key people in a school district the results of the recent National Assessment program which show that about half of the 13-year-olds tested think the press should not have the right to criticize elected officials, 40% feel that atheists should not be able to express their views publicly, and almost half feel people should not always have the freedom to assemble (National Assessment of Educational Progress, 1978). Curriculum developers could also stimulate felt needs by publishing for educators and the community needs assessment instruments related to law and humanities, or by publishing instruments to measure students' knowledge about laws. Such instruments could be used by people within the district who want to promote law and humanities education.

Individuals within the school system can conduct a needs assessment by surveying parents, teachers, and/or students to determine their satisfaction with the current level of instruction on law and the humanities. Similarly, they might assess student knowledge of laws and attitudes toward legal issues.

Times at which curriculum guides are revised, new schools are planned, or new textbooks are selected also offer opportunities for people to begin to feel a need for new content, or for new approaches which relate to law and humanities education. Once need is felt, people will be receptive to information about law and humanities education.

The second way to stimulate the change process is by conducting activities to disseminate information about legal education. An effective way of creating awareness of innovations is through the use of mass media. Curriculum developers can build interest in their particular product and in law and humanities education in general by mailing brochures, sending free newsletters, writing articles like those published in *Synergy* (Wyoming social studies journal), and advertising in *Social Education, The Reading Teacher, The Instructor,*

Learning, The Elementary School Principal's Journal, and journals which elementary school librarians read. Curriculum developers can also create awareness by making presentations at reading and social studies conferences at the local, state, and national levels. People within the school system can help their colleagues get to meetings where such presentations will be made. They can also circulate newsletters through teachers' mailboxes or call individual teachers' attention to articles like "Kids, Teachers and the Law" (1975) to stimulate interest in teaching about law and humanities through case studies, community resources, and the arts. Showing a slide tape or filmstrip presentation on "Why and How to Infuse Law and Humanities Education into the Elementary School" at meetings of educators and community members would be another mass media way one could create awareness of the topic.

In a more personal communication one could tell someone about the topic or about a particular approach or product. A publisher's representative, a college professor, a curriculum coordinator, or a teacher who is familiar with the innovation could talk with interested people about it. While all of the methods above are appropriate to informing people about law-related education, such information does not necessarily lead people to want to try the new approach. People have neither the time nor resources to use all the ideas and programs that are developed, and most innovations do not meet their particular needs.

If it is felt that infusing law and humanities instruction into elementary schools will meet the needs of a particular school, it will be necessary for decision makers to move from a state of awareness about the approach to consideration of its use in classes. In the second stage of the change process, when people consider whether or not to try an innovation, three factors are important: innovation characteristics, communication strategies, and influential roles.

Deliberation and Choice

What characteristics of innovations are important? We will consider first the characteristics of the innovation which influence whether people will decide to use it. Several studies have found that educators are more likely to want to use a new approach or product if they believe that it is compatible with their needs and values, and if it is not difficult to understand and use (Hahn, 1977a; Brennan, Note 1; Cameren, Note 2; Hahn, Note 3; Spencer, Note 4).

Because compatibility with values is important, people who value active learning and concrete experiences might be favorably disposed to the use of role play in elementary classes. People who believe children ought to examine values and practice decision making may see law and humanities education as a way to meet their goals. People who believe schools ought to teach children to be loyal, patriotic, law-abiding citizens will want to know if the new program will do a better job of achieving those goals than what they are now using. If people place a high priority on scores on standardized achievement tests, then one must be able to demonstrate that students will score at least as well on those tests when the new program is used as they have been scoring in the past.

Compatibility with needs is also important. If the content, approach, or packaging of a new program meets the needs of people, they are likely to develop an interest in it. Law and humanities education which is infused throughout an elementary social studies textbook series will meet the needs of people who need to adopt a K–8 hardback textbook series. A teacher's guide with sample lessons to supplement the reading or language arts program might be needed by a school which does not teach social studies or the arts earlier than the fourth grade. Adding a new subject like law and humanities is not going to meet the needs of teachers who feel there is not now sufficient time to cover all the subjects for which they are responsible.

People who believe that the law education program will meet their needs and is consistent with their values might become interested in the program if they also believe that it will not be difficult to understand and use and will not take more time and energy than what is currently used. If curriculum guides need to be revised or new lessons need to be developed to infuse law studies into elementary instruction, then release time, substitutes, and technical assistance must be provided to overcome the problem of additional time and energy needed.

It is important to remember that it is the *receivers' perception* of the innovations' characteristics, not the characteristics as seen by experts, which is important. Charles Quigley may believe that the case-study approach is easy to use, and the curriculum coordinator may say that the casebooks are written at a fifth-grade reading level, but if the people on the textbook selection committee think the UCLA materials would be difficult for students and teachers, then they are not likely to adopt those materials. Reports of teachers who found the materials easy to use would be helpful in creating a positive attitude toward them.

If one wants teachers to use mock trials, poetry readings, or creative dramatics to learn about law

in society, then teachers must be convinced that those approaches take no more time or energy than what they are now using, that they require no special skills or further training, and that they are not difficult to use. Step-by-step teacher guides, sample lessons, in-service training, demonstrations, and the opportunity to receive support from other teachers can reduce perceived complexity of use. To encourage teachers to use speakers and field trips in a law and humanities program, it would be a good idea to suggest community groups or parent volunteers who could help the teachers identify and select sites and speakers, make the detailed arrangements, and chaperone. A written step-by-step guide for making such arrangements would also reduce the complexity of using community resources.

In summary, new techniques and materials are more likely to be used if they are consistent with existing values, if they meet "felt needs," and if they are not more difficult to use than those currently in use. Cost, risk, observability of results, and whether a small-scale trial is possible also influence the adoption of innovations, but to a lesser extent (Hahn, 1977a, 1977b, Note 3).

Obtaining films or recordings on law and the humanities through the state department of education, through a service to which the school system subscribes, or by rental may cost no more than what the school currently spends. If buses are not available for field trips, that may be a new cost. Volunteer speakers and role playing are free. Will it cost more to replace the paperback casebooks over 5 years than to continue using the current textbooks? If there will be a new cost to purchase audiovisual materials, the librarian, principal, or parent-teacher organization could be persuaded to use their special funds to support law education.

If the new program can be tried on a small scale, perhaps as a single unit in one class, before everyone tries it, there may be greater interest in it. And if one can observe positive results when the program is first tried, it is more likely to be adopted. If students show more interest in class discussions, or if they do better on tests when the program is in use, then others are more likely to try it.

If one wants to infuse law and humanities education into the elementary school curriculum, one must begin by asking: Can others be convinced that the program is consistent with their values, that it meets their needs, that it can be tried on a small scale at first, that positive results can be observed, that there will not be a greater cost in time, money, or energy, and that it will not be more difficult for teachers or students than what is currently used? If those questions cannot be answered in the affirmative, then people are not likely to decide to use the law-related innovation. While perceived characteristics are important to the adoption of law education, however, there are other factors to which one must also attend when planning an educational change.

What change strategies should be used? While mass media can be effective in creating awareness in the early stages of the change process, people are not likely to be persuaded to try something just from mass media exposure. One-to-one personal communication is important for developing interest in and willingness to try some aspect of law and humanities education. One might talk to someone and share knowledge and impressions, or one might arrange for teachers to talk with someone else who has had personal experience with the innovation. In-service meetings might offer important one-to-one contact which would enable people to ask specific questions related to their particular concerns.

Seeing demonstrations and visiting schools where the innovation is in use can be very convincing (Brickell, 1961; House, Kerins, & Steele, 1970). If teachers can visit a school, even in another system, in which elementary children are investigating issues related to concepts like liberty and property, or if they can observe a class in their own school learning about due process and freedom of speech, they are more likely to try that approach themselves. Pilot classes, demonstration centers, and the provision of substitutes are thus important in developing support for an innovation.

To convince people to infuse law and humanities education into the elementary school, one should plan for personal contact with people who are familiar with the approach, for demonstrations of its use, and for visits to sites where it is in operation. Such plans should combine with attention to innovation characteristics discussed earlier and to particular roles.

Who should be contacted? Research on the diffusion of innovations has identified a pattern by which new ideas or practices are adopted or used (Carlson, 1965; House, 1974; Rogers & Shoemaker, 1971). At first just a few "innovators" who are high risk takers will try the new approach. Second, a few more "early adopters" will be persuaded to try it. The majority observe their trial and, if it appears successful, are likely to follow. The majority are followed by a few laggards who are the very last to try the new idea. This bell-shaped pattern suggests that everyone will not jump on the bandwagon for law-related education at the same time. Right now there are only a few innovative school systems across the country, and in a given school system there may

be just a few innovators who are teaching about law and humanities in elementary school classes.

Clearly, no innovation automatically spreads from a few to many. Rather, there are key roles which can influence whether it spreads further. Opinion leaders, inside advocates, and gatekeepers are particularly important.

"Opinion leaders" have much influence in convincing others to try or not to try a new program. "Opinion leaders" are individuals who, often informally, influence other people's attitudes. They are accepted as "one of us" by members of their social system (the school faculty, the local lawyers' group, the elementary principals in the school district, etc.), and they follow the norms of that group. Opinion leaders are not likely to deviate much from tradition, and they do not usually take great risks in trying new things. If they believe that a proposal for law education is a good one, others will notice and follow their lead. However, if they are against it because they think it is just another one of those fads that come out every year or so, or because they think it will be too hard or time consuming, or because they think students should be learning basic skills, not discussing controversial issues, or for any other reason, they will spread the bad word; then all one's efforts will be thwarted. Because opinion leaders can be so important, it is crucial that they be identified, and that one be able to demonstrate to them that the new approach is compatible with their needs and values and that it is easy to understand and use. To identify the opinion leaders, ask people whom they turn to for advice. At faculty meetings, in the teachers' lounge or lunch room, or at the principals' meetings, notice whose opinions seem to be respected and considered carefully by the others.

If one is an outsider to the "target group" which he or she wants to involve in law and humanities education, the assistance of an "inside advocate" will be needed. Curriculum developers will need to identify potential advocates within particular school systems. A curriculum supervisor would need to identify a teacher on a school faculty who might see it in his/her best interest to promote law education. For instance, the third-grade teacher who likes to teach social studies and thinks the whole day should not be spent in reading groups and math drill might work to persuade others to try the new law and humanities program. Or someone who has been teaching students to examine values might be a potential inside advocate.

The third role that is important is the gatekeeper or legitimizer. That is the person whose official approval is needed—whether to purchase materials, to hold an in-service meeting, or to arrange for a field trip. It is important to plan ahead in obtaining the support of gatekeepers/legitimizers. They will be interested in whether the proposed law program is compatible with their particular needs and values and whether it is low in complexity.

The perceived characteristics of the law-related innovation, the strategies used to expose people to it, and the attitudes of key people toward it, all contribute to the decision to try or not to try the new approach. But even if these factors come together in the formation of positive attitudes toward the innovation, adoption does not necessarily follow. One study found that people who wanted very much to try a new approach after visiting a demonstration center were not able to do so because of constraints in the local school system (House et al., 1970). No matter how much teachers like paperback booklets or multimedia kits, teachers may not be able to use them because instructional materials may be purchased only from the state-approved textbook list (Hahn, 1977a). One researcher found that, while people were quite satisfied with a pilot program, when the federal funding ended the program was discontinued because local funds were allocated first to areas which had relatively higher priority in the local system (Schumacher, Note 5). If the decision is made not to try an innovation, the process is not necessarily ended. Changes in personnel, in local priorities, or in change strategies, or simply time to observe others, may result in the reconsideration of law and humanities education at a later time.

Implementation

On the other hand, neither does the process end once the decision has been made to try a new approach and its use has begun. Recent studies have shown that much occurs during the process of implementation and that that stage should be carefully monitored (Berman & McLaughlin, 1975; Fullan & Pomfret, 1977; Goodlad & Klein, 1970; Gross, Giaquinta, & Bernstein, 1971; Smith & Keith, 1971; Wolcott, 1977; Schumacher, Note 5; Loucks, Note 6).

The very "newness" of an innovation means that it is inevitable that difficulties will arise. To minimize those difficulties, it is important to provide training before and during trial and to begin with a small-scale pilot. It is important to have other people nearby who can provide moral support, and who can brainstorm solutions to problems as they arise. Teams of two or more teachers have often been used successfuly when new programs are tried. Resource support in the form of adequate materials, space, equipment, time to plan, and time to work out the problems that develop are also important. Administrative support is crucial in providing both the needed resources and moral support.

While many of the problems that arise during trial can be solved by two or more teachers putting their heads together, sometimes they cannot be, or the solutions proposed may not be consistent with the original goals. For these reasons, it will be important to monitor the new law and humanities education programs carefully after they have begun. Teachers might find it easier and faster to tell students what the Supreme Court decided than to have students analyze and debate the underlying issues, but the goal of teaching decision makers through practice would not be met. Or principals might feel uncomfortable when the first parent calls objecting to the discussion of controversial issues, and the program might be thrown out before possible solutions are tried.

It is important to monitor the use of the new program by making classroom observations. After a curriculum guide has been revised to include new topics like "Our Community Laws" and "Rules and Norms in Colonial America," it might be assumed that law and humanities education has been infused into the curriculum; but classroom observation might show no change in actual teaching and learning about "our community" or "the colonial period" in most classes.

Most often a process occurs which has been labeled "mutual adaptation" (Berman & McLaughlin, 1975). That occurs when both the innovation and the users change each other. For example, materials designed to be role-play episodes may be used in debates with a class which prefers the latter approach. But in using the adapted materials, students are now reflecting upon legal issues which they did not previously reflect upon.

Further, a new program sometimes fails, not because of dissatisfaction with the program itself, but because of hostilities that develop over the way in which it was installed (Fullan & Pomfret, 1977; Wolcott, 1977). Again, careful monitoring of the implementation stage should alert one to such problems in time to eliminate them.

And, finally, we should keep in mind that implementation is successful as long as the approach used is the best available to meet local needs. As new problems are identified and/or new innovations are developed, the process of educational improvement begins anew.

It is clear that developing a systematic plan for infusing law and humanities into the elementary school curriculum is a time-consuming task, but it will be well worth the effort if students, teachers, parents, and community members are satisfied that elementary students have a deeper appreciation for values reflected in law and the arts: respect for individual liberty, equality, community welfare, the democratic process of decision making, and government by people through laws.

REFERENCES

Becker, J. M., & Hahn, C. L. *The wingspread workbook for educational change.* Boulder, Colo.: Social Science Education Consortium, 1977.

Berman, P., & McLaughlin, M. W. *Federal programs supporting educational change.* Vol. 4: *The findings in review.* Santa Monica, Calif.: Rand, 1975. (ERIC Document Reproduction Service No. ED 108 330)

Brickell, H. M. *Organizing New York State for educational change.* Albany: New York State Education Department, 1961. (ERIC Document Reproduction Service No. ED 002 714)

Carlson, R. O. *Adoption of educational innovation.* Eugene: University of Oregon, 1965.

Fullan, M., & Pomfret, A. Research on curriculum and instruction implementation. *Review of Educational Research,* 1977, 47, 335–397.

Goodlad, J., & Klein, M. F. *Behind the classroom door.* Worthington, Ohio: Jones, 1970.

Gross, N.; Giaquinta, J. B.; & Bernstein, M. *Implementing organization innovations: A sociological analysis of planned educational change.* New York: Basic, 1971.

Hahn, C. L. Attributes and adoption of new social studies materials. *Theory and Research in Social Education,* 1977, 5(1), 19–40. (a)

Hahn, C. L. Research on the diffusion of social studies innovations. In F. P. Hunkins et al., *Review of research in social studies education, 1970–1975.* Washington, D.C.: National Council for the Social Studies, 1977. (b)

House, E. R. *The politics of innovation.* Berkeley, Calif.: McCutcheon, 1974.

House, E.; Kerins, T.; & Steele, J. M. *The demonstration center: An appraisal of the Illinois experience.* Urbana: University of Illinois, 1970. (ERIC Document Reproduction Service No. ED 047 396)

Kids, teachers, and the law. *Social Education,* 1975, 39(3), 155–169.

National Assessment of Educational Progress. *Citizenship goals.* Denver: Education Commission of the States, 1978.

Quigley, C. N. *Your rights and responsibilities as an American citizen.* Lexington, Mass.: Ginn, 1976.

Rogers, E. M., with Shoemaker, F. F. *Communication of innovations: A cross cultural approach.* New York: Free Press, 1971.

Smith, L. M., & Keith, P. M. *Anatomy of educational innovation: An organizational analysis of an elementary school.* New York: Wiley, 1971.

Wolcott, H. *Teachers vs. technocrats.* Eugene: University of Oregon, 1977.

REFERENCE NOTES

1. Brennan, L. Teacher acceptance and rejection of innovation in classroom practice. Unpublished doctoral dissertation, Teachers College, Columbia University, 1971.

2. Cameren, R. J. Innovation as a factor influencing the diffusion and adoption process. Unpublished doctoral dissertation, University of California at Berkeley, 1966.

3. Hahn, C. L. Social studies textbook adoption in Georgia: A case study in innovation adoption. Paper presented at the meeting of the Georgia Association of Educational Research, Atlanta, 1978.

4. Spencer, E. N. Variables affecting the adoption rates of educational innovations in selected school districts of Oakland County, Michigan. Unpublished doctoral dissertation, Wayne State University, 1967.

5. Schumacher, S. Limitations of a research, development, and diffusion (RD and D) strategy in diffusion: A case study of nine local implementations of a state adopted curriculum. Paper presented at the meeting of the National Council for the Social Studies, Boston, 1972.

6. Loucks, S. F. An exploration of levels of use of an innovation and the relationship to student achievement. Paper presented at the meeting of the American Educational Research Association, San Francisco, 1976.

Key Factors Affecting the Introduction and Retention of Educational Innovations: With Implications for Law and Humanities in the Elementary School Curriculum

Jack E. Allen

This paper emphasizes that development is but one phase in the effective curriculum innovation process. Agreeing with Carole Hahn's basic argument for a second rationale for planning and dissemination, Jack Allen focuses on dissemination issues. He goes on to identify and explore several important issues which are raised in Hahn's paper.

One of the most important points raised in this paper has to do with the *use of existing networks*. Educators are encouraged not to "reinvent wheels"—to maximize that which already exists to disseminate innovations. The author's point is well made, as he provides several examples of existing networks which curriculum developers can look to for disseminating innovative programs and materials.

Any organization which organizes and funds a curriculum development effort must certainly be aware of sound curriculum and learning theory, and must attend carefully to building the new curriculum around this theory. However, if the developer wishes the new curriculum to impact upon schools other than those involved in the development, other very important issues need to be thoroughly studied, thought through, and planned for. One such issue is dissemination. Because of the significance of the dissemination problem, it is very appropriate that the American Bar Association has requested a paper on introduction and retention for presentation at this symposium.

The paper developed by Carole Hahn presents a sound rationale for planning the dissemination strategy or strategies concurrently with the development strategy. Although not in so many words, the paper makes clear that there are a number of different actors involved in the development who will also have important roles in the dissemination activities. They should be preparing, during the development stage, for those future roles. From the paper, the following set of actors who have significant dissemination roles can be identified: the American Bar Association program staff, administrators of developer

school districts, and teacher developers in local school districts. As indicated in the paper, these people should be actively engaged in planning dissemination strategies.

The paper points out that, over the past several years, many millions of dollars have been spent upon massive curriculum development projects; yet these projects have brought about little change (new mathematics, NSF science programs, etc.). When it finally became apparent that development did not automatically bring about change, many studies were organized and conducted. These studies basically revealed that the developers had not planned for and carried out effective dissemination activities. There now exists, as a result, a whole new body of knowledge about educational dissemination. It contains information, as Hahn notes, on how to identify the appropriate audience, how to attract the attention of the audience, how to secure involvement, and how to support adoption by the audience. If developers study this body of knowledge and apply what they learn, then the first step to changing current school practices successfully by developing and introducing new curricula will have been taken.

A careful study of Hahn's paper will produce a set of questions for the development agency (ABA). By addressing these questions, the agency can establish specifications for its dissemination functions. Some of the questions to be considered are:

Jack Allen is Director of the Curriculum and Administrative Services Program of the Northwest Regional Educational Laboratory, Portland, Oregon.

■ How do we verify that the new product is educationally sound?

■ How do we determine if the product is cost effective?

■ How do we package the product so that it will be attractive and easy to use?

■ How do we let the educational community know that the new product exists?

■ How do we market the product—through education channels or commercial channels?

■ Does the product require teacher in-service training? If so, how do we provide it?

While this list does not exhaust those questions which Hahn implies, it does begin to point out the range of issues which must be considered.

From a somewhat different point of view, but also of vital importance to the ultimate dissemination of the newly developed product or products, are those questions which Hahn implies must be answered by the administrators of the local school districts which accept developmental responsibilities. Those questions are:

■ Is the district willing to make the commitment necessary to follow a rigorous set of procedures so that, when development has been completed, there will be solid data about expected educational results, start-up costs, and operational costs?

■ Is the district willing to define its role in development to board members and the public in a manner that clarifies the reasons for teachers or administrators working for periods of time outside the local districts?

■ Is the district willing to make and implement plans for involvement of local staff, other than the developers, so that district-wide implementation of the new curriculum can take place?

Also, the teachers involved in the development have some important questions to deal with. Some of them are:

■ Do I have the necessary research background to conduct a sound development program which not only produces a new curriculum but also produces information necessary for effective dissemination?

■ Am I willing to make the necessary time and energy commitments both to conduct curriculum development and to continue teaching?

■ If the newly developed curriculum meets expected standards, will I be willing to do the travel, conduct the workshops, and do the monitoring which will promote adaption/ adoption by other school districts?

Looking at still another point of view, that of the potential users of the new curriculum, both the development agency and developers in the schools must keep in mind another set of ques-

tions. Hahn describes the problems of adopt/ adapt districts as:

■ Do we want to modify our current curriculum to include the new curriculum? Why?

■ If we buy into the new curriculum, should we start with a pilot, then adapt and expand, or should we attempt a district-wide adoption?

■ What are the start-up and operation costs to the district?

■ Is there support—human, fiscal, or both—available to the adopting district?

■ How many problems will the district face in terms of resistance from teachers, principals, community?

■ How long can we expect it to take from the time the new curriculum is adopted until we can see demonstrable results?

These questions, which arise in local school districts thinking about adopting new curricula, must be considered early and logical answers prepared prior to active dissemination.

The problems, questions, and concerns identified above are not an exhaustive list of those identified or implied in Hahn's paper. They are complete enough, however, to demonstrate the complexity of the responsibility educational developers have in relation to dissemination of their product.

At this point it seems appropriate to digress from the paper to deal with a part of the topic not included there. A number of agencies and organizations are currently involved heavily in the emerging field of educational dissemination. Anyone embarking upon the effort of curriculum development should be aware of who these agencies are, what they are doing, and what the possibilities are of joining them or at least indirectly using their networks to reduce costs which might result from duplication.

As Hahn points out, the early 1960s were disastrous in terms of dissemination and implementation of nationally developed curricula. Needless to say, the U.S. Office of Education and the National Institute of Education have both been made painfully aware of this fact by the Congress. As a result of this new awareness, several activities related to dissemination are now in progress. In this new activity the two leading agencies, which have money and power, are the U.S. Office of Education (USOE) and the National Institute of Education (NIE).

Let's first examine some of the efforts of USOE. In the final years of the Title III Elementary and Secondary Education Act (ESEA), the commissioner devised an effort, through the use of the discretionary funds available to him, which was called the State Facilitator Project. The plan was to provide funding to nationally validated Title III projects which would enable them to package their materials, prepare themselves to conduct in-service programs, and pay for expenses they might face in a national dissemination effort. It also involved the establishment of state facilitator offices in local school districts. These offices were charged with promoting the national projects, funding local district personnel for on-site visits to projects they might wish to adopt, and helping support costs of adoption.

Certainly the projects and the facilitator offices made numerous errors and frequently wasted funds, but the results looked promising. The project was continued and the processes were refined until that first effort, now supported under Title IV, has become the National Diffusion Network (NDN). Almost any developmental project willing to undertake the rigorous evaluation process required by the Joint Dissemination Review Panel (JDRP) for national validation can apply for validation and for funding related to the NDN.

USOE is making other dissemination efforts, such as that related to career and vocational education and other individual programs. However, the other one which may have implications for the ABA effort is also a part of the Title IV ESEA. Each state which receives funding through Title IV, Part C, is being encouraged to build into its state plan a dissemination component. At this time in most states, locally developed projects, especially those developed with money from Title IV, Part C, can apply for dissemination grants for the purpose of helping other schools within the state adopt/adapt their programs. Also, in many states, schools wishing to adopt/adapt an approved program may apply for limited funds to help offset the expenses related to the adopt/adapt procedure.

NIE has taken a somewhat different approach to dissemination. Since the result of much NIE funding is research reports, and additions to the knowledge base other than curriculum and instruction packages and programs, NIE has concentrated on information dissemination. Much effort has gone into broadening and updating the ERIC data base. Many improvements can presently be seen or soon will be seen in this important program. NIE has also made a great effort to define and support the dissemination role of state departments of education (SEAs). If you are not familiar with the Interstate Project on Dissemination (IPOD), it might be helpful in this early stage of developmental effort to review the project report (1976).

The IPOD report, among other things, defines dissemination, and then defines the role of the SEA as that linking resources to needs. This role can be more clearly understood by examining the visual model displayed as figure 1 of the report (Interstate Project on Dissemination, 1976, p. 33).

In addition to funding the long-range study done by IPOD, NIE has established a funding mechanism for SEAs called Capacity Building Grants. These grants support SEAs in their effort to develop and institutionalize policies and procedures related to implementing a program along the lines recommended in the IPOD report.

Another major activity presently being developed by NIE is that of the research and development exchange (RD$_x$). Regional exchanges operate in defined regions of the country. The five regional exchanges and their cooperating states are:

1. Appalachia Educational Laboratory, Charleston, West Virginia (Alabama, Florida, Kentucky, Mississippi, North Carolina, South Carolina, Tennessee, Virginia, West Virginia).
2. CEMREL, Inc. St. Louis, Missouri, with Mid-Continent Regional Educational Laboratory (Illinois, Indiana, Iowa, Kansas, Michigan, Minnesota, Missouri, Nebraska, Ohio, Wisconsin).
3. Northwest Regional Educational Laboratory, Portland, Oregon (Alaska, Colorado, Hawaii, Idaho, Montana, Oregon, Utah, Washington).
4. Research for Better Schools, Inc., Philadelphia, Pennsylvania (Delaware, Maryland, Pennsylvania).
5. Southwest Educational Development Laboratory, Austin, Texas (Arkansas, Louisiana, New Mexico, Oklahoma, Texas).

Activities of the RD$_x$ are carried out primarily through intermediate linkages affiliated with state departments of education. That is, each cooperating state department has one or more contact persons. Schools, then, call on these linkers when in need of human or material resources. The linker, in turn, refers questions or requests as necessary to the regional exchange.

CEMREL, Inc., produces a magazine entitled the *R&D Report*. If you wish to keep up to date on this effort, you may subscribe by sending your name and address to:

R&D Report
Suite 206
1518 K Street, N.W.
Washington, D.C. 20005

It is a free publication!

In addition to the major funded dissemination agencies, there are other agencies which are involved in dissemination to some degree. Some of these are regional service agencies in individual states, such as BOCES in New York or ESDs in Oregon. Also, one should not forget the National Parent Teachers Association, NEA, NCSS, and, finally, private publishers.

This lengthy description of the major actors in the dissemination field and their roles or activities has been included as a reminder to the decision makers for this major curriculum development program that there are a number of established networks which are currently recognized by the educational community as legitimate. With some careful investigations and planning, the ABA's "Law and the Humanities: A Design for Elementary Education" might be able to join one or more

of the current networks rather than developing its own. By joining a current network, it might enjoy a limited amount of additional funding. If it can receive some limited funding and/or join an existing network, then the results of this developmental effort should move rapidly and smoothly into the schools, thus shortening the time lag between development and implementation.

REFERENCE

Interstate Project on Dissemination. *Report and recommendations of the Interstate Project on Dissemination.* Produced pursuant to a grant by the National Institute of Education, January 1976. (ERIC Document No. ED-125.552)

A Design for Community Education: Its Implications for Law and Humanities Education at the Elementary School Level

Frances R. Link

While the term "community education" is used with increasing frequency, the dimensions of its definition seem limited to those describing public relations and brief information sessions. This paper greatly expands upon that perception of community education and challenges readers to conceptualize—indeed, invent—a whole new approach to educating for citizenship.

Frances Link's paper describes the role of a "parallel curriculum" for the community. This is a curriculum offering more than token information but an opportunity for two-way communication and negotiation about school curricula. Link's paper further considers the nature of the curriculum critic and the general influence of the ultraconservative point of view on education.

While this paper focuses on the implications for teaching about law and humanities in the elementary grades, its significance does not rest there. Link's observations and suggestions have relevance throughout the educational institution and for all readers.

It is the purpose of this paper to stimulate both discussion and debate on issues related to curriculum design and community education. The report on the nature of community education for the next decade has not been written. Perhaps it is because a concept of community curriculum has never been conceived. Perhaps it requires an "invention" if one is to proceed seriously to think about community education beyond the trivial level. Perhaps we have too little experience with inventing modes of access to the dynamic nature of the culture. Perhaps the nature of community as an instrument for education is very unclear in our highly technological universe. Perhaps the perfecting of education begins earlier than we thought, and goes on for a lifetime. Certainly, citizenship education must become a lifelong process.

Do we have fine enough tools to transmit what we have discovered? Surely we will not progress or realize our full potential as a culture or as a na-tion unless we invent better ways for educating the young and the community simultaneously. I think we are at the crossroads again in education and in curriculum development. There is a sharp increase in interest in the problems of economy and management of learning, in reemphasis of the "basics" (math and reading), in reexamining the role of the school, the media, and the community, even in questioning the worth of organized "new" knowledge and skill to amplify the powers of thinking and questioning. In fact, we are in a state of crisis. Any movement which advocates going back to the basics is lagging behind fearful, or unwilling to respond to changing social needs.

In the forties the textbooks of Harold Rugg, in the fifties and sixties films and sometimes library books and literature like *To Kill a Mockingbird*, and in the seventies Man: A Course of Study, funded by NSF, and the Nuffield Humanities Curriculum, supported by the School Council in England, all have been challenged or banned. All of these curricula or books or films dealt with moral, social, cultural, and controversial issues which require analysis, thought, and questioning of established behavior and practices. Of the curriculum projects named above, Man: A Course of Study has survived the challenges in places where community education and parent involvement created an informed public with the ability and

Frances R. Link is Vice-President of Curriculum Development Associates, Washington, D.C., and formerly teacher-counselor-director of curriculum, Sheltonham Public Schools, Pennsylvania. She has contributed to educational journals, including *Education Forum,* ASCD's *Education Leadership,* and the ASCD yearbook on evaluation.

power to relate the curriculum challenges to other issues of public policy in their communities and in the nation.

The Concept of the Unfinished Curriculum

A curriculum—if it is in fact a curriculum—must have a *design* which can be described, analyzed, and tested. Although clarity of design is essential, if a curriculum is to contribute to staff development, it must also be sufficiently open-ended so that teachers may adapt the materials to their styles of teaching and to their students' styles of learning. The process of examining and testing a clear and identifiable curriculum design with teachers enables them to understand it well enough to have a sense of control over the objectives, materials, and pedagogy. It *empowers* them to adapt, modify, and go beyond the original structure. This is the paradox of the "unfinished curriculum": because it has a finite clarity, it creates conditions for infinite modification.

A design for curriculum, when viewed as an "unfinished curriculum," serves as a framework:

Enabling teacher educators
■ To create new forms of preservice and inservice programs which relate to innovative curricula in the social sciences.
■ To apply existing in-service and preservice objectives and techniques to a concrete set of goals or set of materials.
■ To experiment with curriculum adaptation as it relates to teacher development.

Enabling scholars
■ To bring new knowledge and their own orientation to the organizing questions and design of the curriculum.
■ To invent new problems and contents for curriculum development.

Enabling learners
■ To expand their thinking by asking universal questions which lead to new knowledge and a changing perspective in the mind of the questioner.
■ To relate organizing questions to their own concerns.
■ To pursue independent investigation stimulated by their own curiosity.
■ To extend and test with parents and peers theories derived from course materials and experiences.

Enabling teachers
■ To experiment with teaching styles and learning sequences.
■ To create curriculum spin-offs.
■ To relate curriculum ideas to relevant and current social issues.
■ To capitalize on unique student interests and school settings.

Ideally, for law and humanities education, the materials and teaching strategies in the curriculum empower "teachers" to shape alternative learning environments. Operationally, this means adding new materials of their own and altering sequences to fit the particular situation created by students' needs and their own school community settings. Further, it means providing options for learners and encouraging youngsters to go beyond the limits which course design or materials often imply.

Teachers need a sense of "inventing," as well as time to create, test, and adapt, to enable any curriculum to transcend the image of a prescriptive, finished curriculum. A significant task of inservice and preservice leadership personnel is to make operational for teachers the nature of an "unfinished curriculum" and its infinite possibilities for curriculum adaptation. The challenge is to create an *expectation* similar to the one which the original teachers, scholars, and curriculum designers and developers had.

Thus, there is a difference between a curriculum and a "collection" of instructional materials. Most books (texts) or other isolated instructional aids—the newspaper, a film, a filmstrip, or any document which cannot be justified as relating to an overall design—may inform but lose power to develop skills and understanding. A body of related experiences and knowledge exists to help learners see the connectedness of knowledge. This is the essence of a humanities approach to the curriculum.

The *content* of a law-related curriculum is well documented. It is involved with basic concepts of liberty, justice, equality, power, and prosperity. When we add the connectedness of the humanities to the curriculum, we must be willing to face the changing nature of culture and technology in our times. Both connectedness and content are value laden and marvelously fraught with controversial issues. New courses of study or revising a curriculum for elementary school children will not suffice for our times. What is required is a more fundamental restructuring of our idea of a school curriculum to include a parallel curriculum for community education. The cry "back to the basics" comes from a highly organized minority effectively using the political process to influence the educational system to return to a way of educating that maintains a monolithic curriculum and a class system—a group at the bottom! Whatever the design of a law and humanities curriculum, it must relate to all children and the citizens of their communities. It must encompass a problem-solving approach which will face the appalling effects of racism, a culture of ghettos and poverty, and the uses of power. It must encompass "honest" inquiry. Isidore Starr wrote in 1973:

Honest inquiry, as I view it, is a never-ending search for viable alternatives in real-life situations. Controversial issues, when law-related, force each of us to face issues realistically and honestly. Inquiry is an attitude that recognizes that all of life is the story of never-ending value differences, forcing us to live with questions that defy instant solutions. The great equations of life and of the law seem to me to be the following: My right and your need, liberty and license, right and responsibility, freedom and security, liberty and equality, free press and fair trial, the right of property and the quality of life. Some of these rights and values are on a collision course. We know that in many neighborhoods peaceful resolution of disputes is on a collision course with civil disobedience and even violence. All of these equations are, for me, the calculus which forces us to think in terms of priorities and hierarchies of values. That is part of the great story of the law. We have to make decisions. We cannot wait for the long run. We make decisions the best way we can, provided we have some conception of what it means to be living in a country of liberty, justice, equality, property and power.

It seems to me that Starr's statement is as relevant now as it was in 1973—and that it must become a framework for the design of a curriculum for children with a parallel community education program. I am not referring only to using community resources. I think we need to become more sophisticated in that respect as well. I am suggesting that the designers of the elementary school curriculum conceive of "learners as a community," and design experiences and materials which include children, teachers, parents, and citizens at large as the learners. Curriculum designers should also conceive of "teachers" in a new way; for example, the educational role of senior citizens in a number of communities is emerging.

What is the teacher's role in handling controversial issues and value-oriented literature and questions? The role will be "new" for most elementary teachers and citizens and is still controversial among secondary teachers. Examine an episode in Montgomery County, Maryland. A high school teacher was temporarily dismissed for telling students where to have marijuana tested for dangerous pesticides which may have been sprayed on the plants. Prior to a hearing with the superintendent, she was interviewed by press and media. In response to the question, "Did you tell your students that smoking marijuana was illegal?" she said, "They knew that already, I was concerned about their dying." The teacher was reprimanded but reinstated and told she had not broken school policy. Teachers appearing with their lawyers on TV, students testifying for or against their teacher, these are becoming common items on the news in many communities. The clash of values and ideas and the role of the teacher and the curriculum in relation to school personnel and community members are reaching more and more courtrooms than ever before.

The community program we need is long overdue. We have failed to educate about education and the role of citizens, and what I am proposing would develop an instructional role for parents and other adults to involve them directly with materials and experiences which would be an integral part of the design of the school curriculum.

Perhaps I am proposing more than some educators think is their job or want to become involved in; I hope not. For if the initiative is not taken by the schools, sooner or later segments of the community are likely to take another kind of initiative that is now sweeping the country in communities where the extreme right is being elected to local school boards and state legislatures. In at least three states, laws have been passed which have determined the nature of the economics curriculum—without the knowledge of the chief state school officers, or school people in those states.

Censorship is on the rise in our country. Much of it is being initiated by small, highly organized groups whose familiar cry is that today's books, programs, films, homework, etc. are anti-Christian, antiparent, antigovernment, immoral, and obscene.

There is evidence to suggest that American public education may be entering another round of attack from the far right. Aided by increased taxes, unionism, liberals in power, and godlessness in the public schools, a number of ultraconservative, far-right groups are showing a remarkable success in developing a grass-roots political structure designed to restrict social legislation, reduce spending, elect like-minded persons to public office, and turn education back to a monolithic curriculum. During a time of distrust of government, public apathy at the polls, and conflicting results of educational programs, the conditions are ripe for any well-organized group of true believers to exert influence far beyond their numbers.

American education can never be entirely removed from the political process. Educational support is a function of public opinion, and we are caught in the web of changing, diverse, and conflicting debate about the future and the nature of schooling. Education is a function of the law; therefore, it is a necessary ongoing task for educators to consider carefully the political climate that appears to be emerging at any time in the nation, and particularly in their own communities. Many of our citizens seem to be seeking a retreat from a changing world in a society, as Toffler observed in *Future Shock* (1970), that appears to be in the midst of a veritable value vertigo. As a society changes, it is to be expected that some will seek the easy comfort of absolutism.

Any "new" curriculum project which has federal funding must be aware of the efforts and goals of the organized groups, and of their publications. It is the responsibility of educators to know the variety of points of view which reflect special interest groups. For example: *Education Update* appears to be designed to establish communication among conservative and fundamentalist private school organizations regarding funding, curriculum content, and educational issues at the state, local, and national levels. A booklet published by Heritage Foundation argues that the cause for the precipitous deterioration of learning achievement in our schools is humanistic education: "Children are . . . being taught at school that moral and social beliefs and behavior are not necessarily based upon Judeo-Christian principles being taught by most families at home, but should be fashioned instead to suit the wishes and convenience of the majority of society as a whole" (McGraw, 1976, p. 5).

The American Legislative Exchange Council (ALEC), whose board of directors includes the last three presidents of the Heritage Foundation, publishes a booklet intended for "conservative" state legislators throughout the nation. The booklet includes, word for word, legislative bills that can be introduced on a number of topics, including education. Among the bills affecting education, the 1977 edition of *Suggested State Legislation* included items on free enterprise, parental rights, teacher proficiency, school discipline, and a bill prohibiting forced busing.

With growing sophistication, large numbers of grass-roots citizens have demonstrated effectiveness in writing letters and visiting congressmen at the state and national levels, protesting passage of the Equal Rights Amendment. At the center of the anti-ERA movement is the Eagle Forum, which is estimated to have some 50,000 core members. The stated goals of the Eagle Forum include a provocative educational dimension in the anti-ERA movement. Included in the statement of purposes is a reference to education which claims belief in the right of parents to insist that schools permit voluntary prayer, teach the precepts of holy scriptures, use textbooks that do not offend the religious and moral views of parents, permit children to attend schools of the neighborhood, and use textbooks that honor the family and woman's role as wife and mother.

The John Birch Society continues to hold its own through local chapters, local libraries, and several publishing companies. Booklets concerning public education are a frequent item in the Birch bookstores, generally labeled American Opinion Libraries and Bookstores.

The Institute for Creation Research, Inc. (ICR) is devoted to "a revival of belief in special creation as the true explanation of the origin of the world." ICR will send free materials to any person who will present them formally to their school board. Among the publications that have generated controversy is a textbook, *Biology: A Search for Order in Complexity* (Moore & Slusher, n.d.). In Indiana, Texas, Arkansas, Tennessee, and California the text has raised debate. In Indiana, the text was adopted by the state textbook committee, but later ordered removed by Judge Michael T. Duggan, who asserted: "The book's claim that it presents a balanced view is a sham that breaches the separation between church and state voiced by Thomas Jefferson" ("Biology Text Banned," 1977, pp. 17–18).

Third Century Publishers present materials designed to mobilize a conservative Christian political base. Chapter 6, "Are Public Schools Ruining Our Children?" of *One Nation under God* suggests that the root evil is compulsory education, curriculum, and financing (taxation) (Walton, 1975a). In the study guide, students are asked to "consider the parents in Kanawha County, W. Va., and other school districts. Are there similar problems in your area?" (Walton, 1975b, p. 27). In *In the Spirit of 76: The Citizens Guide to Politics* (1975), Third Century Publishers provide details on how to organize a political campaign.

Conclusion

The future of public education is more than a function of public opinion—it is a matter of law and of policy at the state and local levels. Thus we are well advised to consider the increasing importance of local school board elections and state legislation. If, as seems predictable, we are on the verge of another round of distrust of the schools, what might educators expect for the future when local boards are elected by very few citizens?

It is not too early to predict the specific issues that may surface in education. It appears that taxes, social issues, curricula in the areas of multicultural studies and human relations, sex education, and federal funding for educational projects will become prime targets. So, too, we may expect to see increased concern about program developments involving the treatment of women in textbooks—specifically, a review of text materials relating to the traditional role of women. We may also expect concern about godlessness, in the form of secular humanism, in the schools.

At issue here is not the right of persons within society to express their views regarding public education. Indeed, too few viewpoints are being expressed. At issue is the capability of educators to respond effectively to organized pressure from any groups. To be effective in the political arena requires tools and strategies that are effective in influencing curricular decision making and implementation and the goals of education. Teachers and administrators do not relate easily to the political realities which face them as professionals, on the one hand, and as citizens, on the other. One has only to look at the difficulty of such organizations as UNICEF, SIECUS, ERA, and others to observe the harm that can occur when organizations become embroiled in political debate without an *informed* public and often with an uninformed professional group.

Knowledge and a sense of the history of controversy in education are important. During the sixties and seventies, American public education experienced a number of pressures from the far right and far left through such issues as students' rights, integration, and sex education, from such organizations as Students for a Democratic Society, the John Birch Society, Black Panthers, Christian Crusade, and others. A review of the controversies reveals many common characteristics. Political literature, accusing the schools of conspiracy, was the basic tool. The antischool campaign was often controlled by a highly organized group within the community which was tied to a national organization. Sometimes the groups had interlocking memberships. Educators and the community were often caught by surprise, and when the schools are in a climate of distrust and not prepared to speak with conviction, firmness, and courage, prepared critics are successful in using controversy for political gain. In the forties and fifties, similar pressure groups attacked textbooks which were considered un-American, and many publishers responded by eliminating controversial issues from their instructional materials.

What is particularly noteworthy is that the literature, tactics, and style of community conflict caused by any extremist groups are predictable. Educators need awareness of the problems that can and will occur, desire and courage to stimulate and become involved in public debate, mechanisms to handle challenge, and support systems that will assist in bringing issues and facts to the attention of the public. This is one part of a curriculum for community education. Such a curriculum for community education does not exist. At the present time major educational organizations do not have the facilities, nor have they plans, to deliver consultant services to schools experiencing difficulty from challenging groups, and study of these problems is all too often lacking in teacher and administrator preparation programs. Further, controversial value issues must be professionally understood and used as an instrument for local community education.

It is important to create the conditions that would make education a dynamic process, with new breakthroughs in curricula and educational structure. What we need is models of more effective citizenship education programs.

I think a breakthrough in curriculum development is possible in a law and humanities curriculum project which focuses on how the concepts of liberty, justice, power, and education can become the subject matter of a controversial-issues curriculum for community education. The goal must be to foster debate rather than the current monologue. The unfinished-curriculum model can keep the relevant values and issues for elementary school children in a context which involves community, home, and school together developing an understanding and appreciation of the law in human situations.

REFERENCES

American Legislative Exchange Council. *1977 Suggested State Legislation.* Washington, D.C.: Author, 1977.

Biology text banned. *Church and State,* 1977 (June), pp. 17–18.

In the spirit of 76: The citizen's guide to politics. Washington, D.C.: Third Century, 1975.

Moore, J. N., & Slusher, H. S. *Biology: A search for order in complexity.* Grand Rapids, Mich: Zondervan, n.d.

Starr, I. Reflections on law studies in the schools today. In S. E. Davison (Ed.), *Reflections on law-related education.* Chicago: American Bar Association, Special Committee on Youth Education for Citizenship, 1973.

Toffler, A. *Future shock.* New York: Random, 1970.

Walton, R. *One nation under God.* Washington, D.C.: Third Century, 1975. (a)

Walton, R. *Study plan and leader's guide: One nation under God.* Washington, D.C.: Third Century, 1975. (b)

A Design for Community Education: Its Implications for Law and Humanities Education at the Elementary School Level

Roger K. Wangen

Roger Wangen's paper is a strong support to Frances R. Link's arguments in the preceding paper. In addition to underscoring her premises and the need for a new concept of community education, Wangen goes on to suggest some practical activities whereby the community might become involved in various levels of decision making about the educational establishment. He suggests, in particular, that school and community people should make a joint effort to clarify such things as educational assumptions and educational goals.

The Special Committee on Youth Education for Citizenship of the American Bar Association has undertaken, with support from the National Endowment for the Humanities, a major effort to encourage development of law-related education activities at the elementary school level. It is not the intent of this project to establish consensus regarding the best or a singular approach to the law-related education of young children. Rather, it will promote models which can be implemented by local projects according to their own needs and circumstances.

Frances R. Link makes three extremely important points. Her first point sounds an alarm, describing pressure group organizations and their impact on educational decision making at the local level. The case studies of how these pressure groups catch educators by surprise are impressive and should alert all community educators to become knowledgeable about the pressure groups and how to deal with them effectively. Her second major point is the need for an informed community that acts as a support group to educational decision makers. To involve parents in student curricular materials is one way to have informed, supportive parents. The third major point of her paper is the need for a curricular design that is open ended and flexible. Her design will be helpful to a variety of teachers, teacher educators, scholars, and learners.

Roger Wangen has been the Social Studies Specialist with the Minnesota Department of Education for the past 11 years. He is co-author of the student text *The Student Lawyer: A Handbook on Minnesota Law* (West Publishing Co.).

I will attempt to contribute to the law and humanities project by further discussing the processes of creating informed community support groups, the need to clarify educational assumptions that guide decision making, and a design for a law and humanities elementary curriculum.

Creating an Informed Community Support Group

In recent years, educators' concerns about the community have generally related to quantitative aspects of providing for growth of staff and facilities to handle the growing numbers of students. Communities seemed content and committed to support this growth. However, with student numbers declining, decisions to close buildings, lay off staff, and eliminate programs have resulted in conflicting views. These conflicting views are intensified by interest or pressure groups motivated by declining test scores, humanistic curricula, increased costs, and the desire to return to basics; they make diverse, conflicting demands on the educational decision makers. Many educational decision makers do not have the skills and means to cope with these diverse demands. Common problems are ambiguity about what education is trying to do for students and lack of evidence to show how poorly or well education is doing. Many curricular programs just happened. They were not carefully designed. Some call this curriculum anarchy—each teacher doing what he or she feels best meets the needs of students and/or society.

To remedy this, many legislative bodies are requiring educational institutions to seek advice

211

from the community about what the goals should be and what the instructional program to meet the goals should be. Some major problems emerge. One is how to involve busy citizens and what activities work so the involvement is meaningful, productive, and not too time consuming.

Many local school districts have a long history of involving community speakers in the classroom and sending the student into the real world of the community. A few communities have devised a family-based learning technique of sending home learning activities that encourage or require the total family's participation. An example of this might be an analysis of home energy consumption which identifies what kinds of energy are consumed, by whom, and when as well as possible ways of reducing consumption. Additional ways of involving the community need to be identified.

One successful way of involving the community is known as the Phi Delta Kappa Goal Setting Activity, in which individuals rank 18 general educational goals and then in small groups seek agreement on the ranking. Procedures for total community perceptions of performance are also identified. The processes of this 3–5-hour activity are as important as its product. See Wangen (1978) for a revised set of educational goals that can involve the community in clarifying community values that can be helpful for decision makers.

Another activity that can involve the community is a questionnaire concerning a rationale for social studies education (Wangen, 1976). Again the process used can be as important as the product. The end product can be used to clarify community values, as participants agree or disagree with educational assumptions. The activity allows a community to *know* what some citizens assume about the nature of people, about the good society and good citizens in a democratic society, about trends and issues in society, about knowledge, about the nature of learning, about the school as a social institution, and about what the role of a school *should* be in a democratic society. This process document can be modified to reflect the community's values.

The Goal Setting and Assumption activities are long-range activities that can help guide decision makers. Each activity does require creative ideas for involving sufficient numbers of citizens to reflect community norms. Many smaller advisory groups, each given small tasks which require a minimum time commitment, work best. Some districts have formed small teacher-parent-student teams to discuss the implication of selected goals or assumptions. Many communities are selecting community groups like the chamber of commerce, the Lions, and the League of Women Voters to nominate representatives to discuss educational matters. Other districts create short instruments for mailing to a representative cross section of the community.

The creative ideas will emerge if educational institutions are committed to involving citizens and at the same time provide lifelong learning opportunities for the adults.

Law and Humanities Curricular Design

A curriculum is a written descriptive plan that contains a conceptual frame, content to be "covered," skills to be learned and used, attitudes to develop, alternative strategies for learning, and materials to be used. A good curriculum also contains a rationale which outlines the developers' beliefs, reasons for those beliefs, and implications for students in a democratic society.

One important component of any curriculum is content, and one needs to be explicit about the "content" of a law-related curriculum. A most important step is to identify and state in student-learning terms the conceptual framework, listing *some* essential knowledge, skills, and attitudes that students should demonstrate at certain identified checkpoints. This list should be shared with community members along with an invitation to place a 1 in front of each statement they think is essential for students to know and a 3 by each statement they think should be omitted. They should also be invited to add statements to the list.

One such framework was developed by the Pennsylvania Department of Education. It has three broad categories of knowledge, skills, and attitudes. The major headings are: "Groups Establish Certain Acceptable Behavior," "Groups Differentiate between Acceptable and Unacceptable Behavior," and "Groups React in Varied Ways to Acceptable Behavior" (see Schell, 1971). Under each heading one finds substatements that further clarify specific concepts which together form a very comprehensive law-related curricular framework. Examples of substatements include the need for law within and between groups, who makes the rules, how laws are made, what rights are protected, ways of settling disagreements, and why one must accept responsibilities in observing rules and laws.

A second important component of developing any curriculum is for curricular decision makers to choose what context or problem area they want to use as a vehicle to teach law-related concepts—for example, community conflict, court systems, lawmaking in Minnesota, or a historical problem. The real test for any conceptual framework, however, is whether it will work as a system for analyzing contemporary community differences that are surfacing around educational issues such as the back-to-basics movement, the role of parents in curricular decisions, community value differences, and identifying what students need for successful living in a dynamic democratic society.

Another component of a curricular design is identification of the skills the students are to know and use. An evaluation instrument I developed for process objectives (Wangen, 1977) gives *some* of the basic inquiry skills that help in conflict analysis and resolution. Again, community members should be invited to agree or disagree on whether each skill is essential for students to acquire, and to modify and add to the list.

A fourth component of any curricular design is the identification of attitudes to be focused on. (See Wangen, 1978, for *some* attitudes identified by educators and lay citizens.) Built into this activity is another opportunity for community members to agree or disagree with each statement as well as modifying or adding to the list.

Developing the teaching strategies and specific materials to impart the knowledge, skills, and attitudes of the curricular design needs more time and expertise than I can give here and is best done by small groups of expert classroom educators. These strategies and materials must be diverse in interest and difficulty, to meet the diverse needs of students, teachers and communities.

Because this curricular design carries the word "humanities" in the title, I feel compelled to describe some of the characteristics of humanities as a concept. "Humanistic," "humanities," and "humanism" are currently controversial words. Humanism is the quality of being human or concerned with the interests and ideals of people. A humanist is a student of human nature and human affairs and is interested in these questions: What makes human beings human? How did they get

that way? How can they be made more human? Humanities is the study that leads one to deeper comprehension of time and place in the world and to more intelligent realization of one's obligation to world citizenship, to sound moral and spiritual values, and to an expanded opportunity for creative participation in holistic learning concerned with human thought and human relations.

In conclusion, I have attempted to make a case for creating an informed community by involving them in a number of activities which help educational decision makers by clarifying such things as educational assumptions and educational goals. The processes used and the products developed both contribute to a law-related humanities program for students as well as to parents' learning about education. The challenge is to create varied formats and incentives to encourage community involvement.

I have also attempted to organize activities for identifying, clarifying, and seeking agreement with some concepts or knowledge, skills, and attitudes students ought to have prior to completion of the program. Participating in these activities will expand one's knowledge about law and humanities education.

REFERENCES

Schell, R. L. *Legal education rationale.* Harrisburg: Pennsylvania Department of Education, 1971.

Wangen, R. K. *Social studies education rationale.* St. Paul: Minnesota Department of Education, 1976.

Wangen, R. K. Process objectives. In R. K. Wangen (Ed.), *Some essential learner outcomes in social studies* (Bulletin 43). St. Paul: Minnesota Department of Education, 1977.

Wangen, R. K. *Learner goals.* St. Paul: Minnesota Department of Education, 1978.

Community Involvement in Law and Humanities Education at the Elementary School Level

Ira Eyster

This paper underscores that effective use of the community requires attention to specific concerns and situations. As with any other area of the curriculum, community involvement must be the result of a carefully thought-out plan and design.

Ira Eyster provides readers with practical suggestions for extending the elementary school student's experience to the community in a way that expands upon and provides a context of reality for the written curriculum within the school.

This paper acknowledges that community involvement is really a two-way street and provides useful tips to those individuals involved. A helpful checklist addresses apprehensions of resource people and teachers.

One of the most salient points made by this paper is at the same time one so obvious it might be overlooked. The author reminds us that community involvement is an imperative aid to the classroom teacher, whose job cannot be accomplished solo.

Four questions immediately present themselves as one considers community involvement in a law and humanities program: (1) What is inferred by law and humanities, particularly in the elementary grades? (2) Why is community involvement essential to a law and humanities program? (3) How may community involvement and learning be integrated? And (4) what constitutes effective community involvement?

Law and Humanities: What Is It?

Although law education resists simple definition or categorization, it has perhaps best been described by the American Bar and others as "those organized learning experiences that provide students and educators with opportunities to develop the knowledge and understanding, skills, attitudes and appreciations necessary to respond effectively to the law and legal issues in our complex and changing society" (U.S. Office of Education Study Group on Law-related Education, 1979, p. 50).

Paul Freund of the Harvard Law School designates three widely accepted objectives of law education: (1) the learning of moral reasoning and

ethical analysis by continued practice in reaching moral decisions and justifying them; (2) developing an appreciation of the legal process and an understanding of the functions of law; and (3) acquiring information about the law (Freund, 1972).

To many, law education is a process through which viable, highly motivating quests for knowledge can be directed, with a resultant development of basic skills and increased appreciation and understanding of law, the processes of law, and the persons involved in law. Given these definitions of law education, what then is implied by the addition of the word "humanities"?

The humanities are often defined in terms of specific academic disciplines because human experience has been primarily preserved through books, art works, and other cultural objects. From another viewpoint the humanities, according to the National Endowment for the Humanities, is that family of knowledge that deals with what has been—and is to be—human, to make value judgments and to select the wiser course of action. Again, according to this source, this making of value judgments—selection of the best course of action—is achieved by examining human experience and its implication for the present and future.

Upon examining the definitions of law education and those of the humanities, one finds certain

Ira M. Eyster is Associate Director of the Southwest Center for Human Relations Studies, University of Oklahoma. He has been Director of a state-wide law education program in Oklahoma for the past 6 years.

214

common threads. Both stress ethical analysis—the making of value judgments and the justification of those judgments. Both indicate a response—a change in attitude or appreciation and/or a selected course of action. Essential to the response are discovery, quest, examination, process. Last, but not least, both infer or state a reaching out and encompassing of human experiences and understanding, both past and present.

Although threads of commonality can be found in law education and the humanities, it should not be inferred that they are similar in all respects. Where law, through the courts, sets the parameters of human interaction, the humanities define the nature of such interactions if they are to enhance rather than debase social realities. Ultimately, law speaks the language of authority, through enforcement. The humanities add the vocabulary of humaneness and consideration, which appeals to the people to fulfill their responsibility through obedience to the law.

However, for purposes of this paper it is important to realize that both law education and the humanities seek changes in attitude, appreciation, and/or action. To accomplish this common purpose, both the humanities and law education reach out to encompass human experiences both past and present. It is in this respect that community involvement appears to be most essential to a law and humanities program.

Community Involvement: Why?

Community involvement is the catalyst of an effective law-humanities endeavor. It adds to the law-humanities process the ingredients of characterization, experience, humaneness, identification, and universality. It is based on the assumption that the classroom teacher alone cannot maximize the impact of all such ingredients. The human experience is given blood, flesh, and characterization as students share with other community persons their frustrations and successes in coping with issues of liberty, justice, equality, property, and power. The elements of humaneness and identification surface when children realize that certain legal roles are performed by real live people whom they have talked with and touched. Likewise, the resource person becomes more sensitive to the probability that the decision he/she makes may ultimately affect these or other children. Universality is sensed when children become aware that few experiences are unique, that most experiences have been or are being shared by a broad spectrum of humanity.

Practical objectives. From the elementary students' viewpoint, community involvement and participation provide for learning to respect other people and their property, taking responsibility for one's actions and accepting the consequences, and forming a stronger attachment to society by making young children feel like active participants. Finally, such programs should reduce delinquency and develop an appreciation of the need for fair rules, in terms of their purpose and function and how they can be achieved through the legal process.

Law education has never had as its objective the surrogate attorney, judge, or police officer in the classroom. Rather, it is grounded on the premise that the teacher organizes the learning experiences and sets the stage in such a way that appreciation and understanding of the legal system may develop. The degree to which attitudes change and appreciation and understanding develop will be largely dependent on the skills of the teacher in setting the stage and using legal resource persons at the right time and under the right conditions.

Integrating Community and Learning: How?

The well-known "No Vehicles in the Park" activity provides a classic example of the integrating of community and learning. "No Vehicles in the Park" refers to a law passed by a fictitious city council. Having passed it in all innocence, as a meritorious law, the city council did not anticipate the flood of protests resulting from their action to outlaw vehicles in the city park.

How does the teacher involve both community and students in the activity "No Vehicles in the Park"? As a first step in setting the stage for meaningful interaction between the community and students in this activity, the teacher may arrange a class visit to the park. Prior to the visit students may beneficially develop an observation checklist. The checklist will guide them in a systematic observation of such law-associated items in the park as litter, no-trespassing signs, assigned play areas, locks, park lights, and abuses of the park. During the visit students may talk to the park director, maintenance personnel, and/or a member of the city council with a special interest in parks. At the conclusion of the visit the students may visit the police department or arrange to meet with a police officer to discuss questions of security and protection which may have arisen from their observations in the park.

From this exploratory experience, students write of their observations, identify and work on activity-related vocabulary, and make inferences about law, people, and responsibility. Perhaps just as important, students identify with legal persons, talk to them, and make associations between these persons and their own personal concerns.

Worthwhile as the previously described experience may be, the enterprising teacher has not exhausted the many learning possibilities to be found in the simple activity "No Vehicles in the Park." Exciting adventures in decision making, value judgments, basic skills, the balancing of rights and responsibilities, community roles, lawmaking, and a more in-depth interaction with community persons awaits students fortunate enough to have such a creative teacher.

How may all these promised things happen? What are the magic ingredients? How are they blended and timed? Drawing from the experience of visiting the park, some students may design and draw what they consider to be an ideal park. Another group of students may function as advisors to the park designers, securing information through interviews and surveys of civic leaders, family, and friends. Still another group may continue their investigation of park maintenance, safety, and security, while a fourth group of students continue their exploration of park governance. Students gain in communication and organizational skills as they design surveys, write interview questions, formulate letters, conduct person-to-person or telephone interviews, and organize information.

The stage is now set for culminating activities which provide students with opportunities to develop decision-making, critical thinking, and other law-related skills. Encouraged by the teacher, the governance group announces the passage of a law which reads very simply "No Vehicles in the Park." Exhibiting the drawing of a park previously done by students, the governance committee explain to the class that, conferring with the safety committee, they felt the best interest of everyone would be served by passing such a law. They also announce that anyone may voice such objections at the next meeting of the governance committee. In preparation for the next governance (council) meeting, the teacher encourages several students to prepare petitions of personal or organizational exceptions to the law "No Vehicles in the Park." One student, for example, may ask permission to ride a bicycle, another to push a baby carriage through the park. A student acting as a representative from the sanitation department asks permission to enter the park with a garbage truck, while a student acting as a member of the police department petitions the council for the right to drive a patrol car through the park when in pursuit of bank robbers. The list may go on and on as time and imaginations permit.

Other community resource persons can add tremendously to the learning possibilities in the interchange between the petitioners and the council. After the student council members have had an opportunity to struggle with the practical and value-oriented issues posed by the petitioners, and

have made decisions regarding them, some pertinent questions will naturally arise from the students or can be instigated by the teacher.

To the police officer who has been present during the simulation, the students or teacher may well ask how the police would feel about enforcing a law such as the one passed. This may lead to other associated questions, such as, "Do police officers have to follow the law when on duty?" or, "Are there laws, now on the statutes, which police officers do not attempt to enforce?"

To a member of the city council, students or the teacher may ask if it is difficult to make laws or regulations pleasing to everyone. Other associated questions may refer to lawmaking procedures or the politics of lawmaking.

An attorney provides excellent resource assistance as students try their hand at improving the law "No Vehicles in the Park" or answers student questions about the lawmaking process.

Effective Involvement: What Are the Ingredients?

In a recent survey conducted among teachers and potential community resource persons, they expressed various anxieties regarding community involvement in the classroom.

Teachers listed the following apprehensions regarding the use of resource persons, in descending order of concern. They feared that the resource person:

1. Might not be able to contribute at the students' level of understanding.
2. Might not be able to relate to students of this age group.
3. Might not be able to participate when needed or at the time arranged.
4. Might not involve students.
5. Might not do what the teacher wanted him/her to do.
6. Might be inadequately prepared.
7. Might be treated rudely by students.

In turn, the potential resource persons listed the following anxieties, in descending order of concern:

1. They might not have sufficient information about prior student involvement and orientation regarding the topic assigned.
2. They might not be fully informed regarding what they were expected to present.
3. They might not have sufficient information about the ages, achievements, and interest level of the students.
4. They might not be fully informed regarding the time, place, amount of time, conditions, and resources available.

Table 1: Checklist—Preparation for Resource Person

In preparation for the visitation of a resource person to my class, I, [name of teacher], have done the following:	Yes	No
1. Checked my school's policies and procedures regarding the use of resource persons (hereafter referred to as RP).		
2. Carefully thought through the contributions desired from the RP.		
3. Checked with the local bar association president or other key person for recommendations regarding RP to make the contribution(s) desired.		
4. Involved students in decision regarding use of RP.		
5. Provided the prospective RP with the following information:		
a) Exact time and place of presentation, name of school, street, room number, location of building, my name.		
b) Subject I teach.		
c) Where RP may park car.		
d) Amount of time for presentation.		
e) Presentation format—formal or informal, etc.		
f) Age of students.		
g) Number of students.		
h) Classroom arrangements.		
i) Unusual student situations.		
j) Exactly what I want the RP to talk about.		
k) Background students now have on topic to be covered.		
l) Probable student questions on the topic.		
m) Specific interest students have in the topic.		
n) Audiovisual materials available.		
o) Suggested approaches RP may effectively use.		
p) Materials RP may need to make presentation effectively.		
q) Ways I or students may assist with presentation.		
r) Sources where RP may get information.		
6. Followed up the initial communication with RP with further communication.		
7. Checked with RP 1 or 2 days before visit to class.		
8. Prepared my students for the coming of the RP by:		
a) Telling them something about RP.		
b) Involving students in identifying RP.		
c) Eliciting questions students may wish to ask.		
d) Informing students of sacrifice RP is making to visit class.		
e) Discussing format that will be used.		
f) Involving students in courtesy arrangements.		
9. Followed up the RP visit by:		
a) Evaluating the experience.		
b) Relating information brought by RP to unit of study.		
c) Reviewing major points with students.		
d) Sending RP note of thanks.		

5. Teachers might not adequately prepare students for the resource person's involvement.
6. Students might not be responsive or ask questions.
7. Students might have difficulty understanding the presentation.

Resource persons could take a giant stride in dealing with their own apprehensions if they would remember a few fundamentals such as: (1) speak in human terms, (2) demonstrate, (3) encourage student participation, (4) use lifelike examples and illustrations, and (4) be yourself.

Performing as stated above is easier said than done. The teacher, of course, does bear the major responsibility for providing the conditions under which such effective involvement may occur. Either the checklist shown in Table 1 or a more suitable one developed by the teacher will at least serve as a reminder of the items that should receive attention when preparing for community involvement.

Obviously not all community involvement occurs within the confines of the classroom. Both students and parents can be immediately involved in the objectives of a law and humanities program by soliciting their suggestions of agencies and persons who might make contributions. How rewarding it is to discover and use the unique experiences of a juror, probation officer, judge, FBI agent, welfare worker, parent, etc., who may live within the extended boundaries of the classroom.

Some innovative elementary teachers collaborate with other classroom teachers where the particular subject emphasis and student maturity level provide the potential for conducting community surveys. Through the community survey the teacher develops a list of agency sources, their possible contributions, and the conditions under which such contributions are available in a law and humanities program. In the absence of a collaborative teacher arrangement, parent volunteers are often available and willing to assist in such educational searches.

The resource agencies, along with the classroom contributions of resource persons, should be constantly evaluated. An evaluation may include such questions as: (1) Did this agency/resource person contribute toward my overall objectives in a law and humanities program? (2) Does the involvement with the agency/resource person improve school-community understanding? (3) Can the services of this agency/resource person be utilized with a minimum of inconvenience to the agency, the resource person, the student, and the school? (4) Was a field trip to the agency worthwhile? (5) Did the field trip provide opportunities for students to interact and identify with persons who perform roles in the justice system? (6) Are students positive toward the experiences provided through involvement with this agency or resource person? (7) Were the experiences conducive to the development of such basic learning skills as reading, writing, listening, communications, reasoning, and decision making? (8) Have the people who perform roles in the justice system now taken on characterization, humaneness, and reality to students as a result of this experience? (9) Have the concepts of liberty, justice, equality, property, and power been enlivened in the minds of students through these encounters?

In the elementary school one finds most of the necessary ingredients for a law and humanities emphasis as well as a successful school-community mix. Discovery, quest, and inquisitiveness, so essential to law and humanities education, are found in abundance at this level. Also significant for the law and humanities emphasis and for community involvement is the spontaneity of children in the elementary grades. Such spontaneity enhances the building of relationships between resource persons and students and provides for a more informal sharing of experiences and for identification with such persons and their experiences.

Other factors which make the elementary school a natural place for law and humanities education supported by community involvement are flexibility and availability. Flexibility, deriving from the nature of self-contained classrooms, provides for more adaptable blocks of time, which in turn lay the foundation for the effective use of resource persons.

Given the climate for law and humanities education, the flexibility of self-contained classrooms, the professed desire of resource persons to contribute, and the commitment of the elementary teacher to the involvement steps outlined earlier in this paper, one can only expect a successful and worthwhile venture in the elementary school.

REFERENCES

Freund, Paul A. Law in the schools: goals and methods. *Law in American Society* (journal of the National Center for Law-focused Education), 1972, *1,* 1, 9.

U.S. Office of Education Study Group on Law-related Education. Final report, September 1, 1978. Washington, D.C.: Government Printing Office, 1979. (OE No. 79-43000)

Community Involvement in Law and Humanities Education at the Elementary School Level

Richard Weintraub

This paper provides readers with both practical suggestions for effective community involvement and important reminders about the rationale for such involvement. Referring to the "gap between theory and practice," and the fact that "children learn what they live," Richard Weintraub strengthens the argument for such programs.

This paper is particularly helpful for its attention to existing curricula. It explores the relationship between education in the "basic skills" and community involvement. Most important, it describes such involvement as needing to be a series of progressive learning experiences. Again, an author underscores the need for thoughtful, well-articulated planning.

Richard Weintraub has provided a series of checklists which readers will find helpful in assessing and proceeding with their own community involvement programs.

Students in a traditional school setting are very isolated. The four walls in a classroom cut them off from the realities in the community. A gap will always exist between what students learn about law in the classroom and what lawyers and law enforcement officers and other professionals experience in the field. This, however, should not prevent us from developing programs for teachers and for children at the elementary level which provide experiences in the community that will help bridge the gap between theory and practice.

Practical Goals

As Ira Eyster points out, community involvement and participation for elementary-level children should include: "learning to respect other people and their property, taking responsbility for one's actions and accepting the consequences, and forming a stronger attachment to society by making young children feel like active participants." Such programs should also help reduce delinquency and "develop an appreciation of the need for fair rules, in terms of their purpose and function and how they can be achieved through the legal process.

A humanities project implies a multidisciplinary approach which will focus on the human interaction between members of society and representatives of the legal system. Community involvement means the opportunity for children to become involved in community law-related programs, and, concurrently, it means involving the "legal" community in school-based law studies programs. Our textbooks should be professionals and resource experts from the community, and the school and the city should be settings for students to learn to take responsibility, to gain feelings of personal worth, and to focus on present as well as futuristic issues and problems.

Specific Kinds of Community Involvement

Before children can begin to comprehend the concept of a legal community, I recommend that 10 steps be considered:

1. Children must first begin to recognize, name, and identify the players in the system—for example, police officers, attorneys, judges, criminologists, social service workers.
2. The students need to be able to define the purpose and function of these vocational specialists and understand the connection between purpose and service performed. Ask the children to imagine what their community would look like without the police, courts, etc.
3. Students must begin to view their own classroom as a microcosm of the community at large. What rules or guidelines should the community establish and live by? Students are entitled to know their rights and responsibilities as members of that community.

Richard Weintraub, Associate Education Director, Constitutional Rights Foundation, is also President of the California Council of Children and Youth. He is co-author of numerous simulation games including *Liberation*, *Jury Game*, and *Kids in Crisis*.

4. All classroom discussions must highlight issues that are directly related to things young children can understand—for example, street and bicycle safety, keeping the community clean, the correct care and training of pets, respect for other people and their property.

5. Involve students in planning which resource experts to invite to visit the class. Having played such a role, the students will be better prepared to meet and talk with professionals involved in the legal system.

6. A "Justice Ride" through their community provides students with a sense of where the legal agencies are located. Take a bus ride, with a legal expert as the tour guide, through the community—stopping at appropriate sites, so students can get a view of all the agencies involved in the administration of justice.

7. The traditional walk through the neighborhood can now be converted into a creative search for things we normally forget to associate with the study of law and humanities—for example, locks, stop signs, fire alarm boxes, broken windows, playgrounds, liquor stores, law offices, banks. What do these places or objects tell us about the need for law in our community?

8. Ask students to conduct surveys or interviews with their families and friends about what they like and dislike in their communities and their perceptions of the need for law and justice.

9. Take a field trip to a community agency (court, law office, police station, social service center, etc.) Let students interact with agency representatives on their turf.

10. If all students cannot go on field trips, have those students who can go develop peer teaching lessons; this will serve as a way for students to share their newly acquired information and experience.

Guidelines for resource people inside and outside the classroom. I have found it helpful to provide teachers with guidelines for the use of resource experts both inside and out of the classroom.

Resource experts have a natural tendency to talk at students. In order to minimize this approach, resource people should be given the following helpful hints for classroom presentations: (a) Make all presentations short and at a level the children can understand. Don't oversimplify. Speak in human terms. (b) Studies indicate that information is more likely to be remembered if you "show 'em while you tell 'em." (c) Encourage student participation. Do not lecture! (d) Information relevant to the children's

lives should be used. Your audience will not respond to facts that don't touch them. (e) Be yourself! (f) Make the cases, situations, or problems as lifelike as possible.

Specific strategies for involving resource experts outside of the classroom include: (a) Make arrangements for a legal resource expert to meet the students at the court to observe with the students and discuss with them what they have seen. (b) Observe an attorney in action in court. (c) Have students visit an attorney in his or her office.

Checklist for teachers. The following checklist is offered as a guide for determining needs and avoiding potential problems when planning field experiences with justice agencies.

1. How much time will be required to organize and administer a community activity?
2. Should the school be responsible for the program?
3. How can students be more effectively utilized to help identify and coordinate resources in their own community?
4. What organizations and agencies must take part if the program is to achieve its objectives?
5. Which individuals can be asked to lend their support to the organization and implementation of the program?
6. Has the agency been properly notified?
7. Are students familiar with the background of the agency?
8. Have students returned the parental consent slips?
9. Have transportation arrangements been finalized?
10. Do the students have information about the agency?
11. Are students prepared to wear certain types of clothing for certain field experiences?

Guidelines for evaluating community activities. Every community activity worth doing should be evaluated. Questions to be considered should include the following:

1. Were there any problems in making arrangements to visit the agency?
2. Was the agency receptive to your group?
3. Was the time spent realistic for obtaining an overview of the agency? Too long? Too short?
4. What kinds of services did the agency provide?
5. How were the clients referred to the agency?
6. What did you do?
7. What did you learn about the individuals who worked there?
8. What types of questions did you ask?

9. Were they willing to answer all of your questions?
10. Would you recommend the agency to other teachers, parents, students?
11. Were there any transportation problems?
12. What could have been done to make this a better field experience?
13. How does the agency fit into the overall justice system?
14. Would you someday like to work in this agency? Why? Why not?
15. What changes would you make within this agency?

Law-related Education and Basic Skills

Law-related education at the elementary level is the perfect vehicle for promoting basic skill development. Children at this level must be prepared with the basic skills so that they will be able to cope with everyday situations which require cooperation, compromise, inventive thinking, and respect for authority. Community involvement provides students with the perfect opportunity to practice communication and reasoning skills. The communication skills we are seeking include reading, writing, research, and speaking. The reasoning skills include judgment, decision making, thinking, and persuading. Law-related education should begin to engage students in problem solving. At the same time children will be developing analytical and thinking skills to test mental reasoning.

To provide practice in basic skill development, have the children write about and reflect upon the experiences which they have in the community or the classroom. One technique for achieving this is to have students keep personal journals about speakers and field experiences. Data recorded in the personal journals can include: (1) a summary of what the children saw on the visit and (2) what they felt about the people and environment they saw.

Future Potential

The elementary level is the most fertile ground for establishing positive attitudes toward, and behavior consistent with, a law-based society. It is at that level that children are at their most eager and enthusiastic in terms of learning.

Children must begin early to understand the role of law and justice in their lives and in the lives of those around them. They need to understand that resolving interpersonal and intergroup conflicts through a rational, "rules of fair play" approach is what keeps families, schools, communities, the entire society "running," not always smoothly, but certainly without constant breakdowns.

All of the successful programs have at least one factor in common. They are predicated on the belief that children learn what they live. How do children growing up today learn to be responsible and self-actualizing human beings? The ways in which they come to feel a sense of personal responsibility for, and understanding of, our law-based society may be the key ingredient in achieving that goal. An effective law studies curriculum requires that we provide additional humanities lessons and cocurricular programs to pick up where law studies leaves off.

Law and Values in American Society

Murry Nelson

"Values are already in the classroom, and no complaining or investigating will ever get them out." Murry Nelson suggests that what is needed is a clearer idea of what values are and how they interact with ideas of law in American culture. The changing idea of values is presented in this paper, as well as a discussion of how values are of concern to the humanities, particularly in the area of law.

Three relationships between law and values are discussed, followed by a discussion of law as a gatekeeper of American culture. Finally, the implications of these relationships and the ways in which law functions in this society are explored as they might affect the elementary school curriculum, elementary school teachers, and parents of elementary school children.

Values have no place in the classroom. Now, I do not believe that for one minute, but some readers may, and they may wish to be warned that I take the above statement as both a null hypothesis and someone's wishful thinking. The latter idea will probably be most fruitful to pursue.

Values are already in the classroom, and no complaining or investigating will ever get them out. "You're late—school starts at 9:00, not 9:05." "Eyes on your paper only." "Please rise for the pledge to the flag." "No talking." "Let's treat our guest as we wish to be treated."

Does this sound like a typical classroom? I think it does, and each statement implies or describes a value. Still not convinced? How about this statement: By denying the discussion or recognition of values in the classroom, the teacher is imposing his or her values directly upon the students.

Of course, the above is a simplistic argument for the inclusion of values education in classrooms, and it will be difficult to agree or disagree with it unless there is some definition of and rationale for values understanding in elementary classrooms.

Rokeach defines values as a "type of belief, centrally located within one's total belief system, about how one ought or ought not to behave, or about some end-state of existence worth or not worth attaining" (Rokeach, 1969, p. 124).

Values are always present in our choices of action, and those choices may indicate which values are *more* important to someone at a particular time than some other values. Take, for example, the dilemma facing many school systems—the

Murry Nelson is Assistant Professor of Education at The Pennsylvania State University. He is the author of *Law in the Curriculum*, a Phi Delta Kappa Fastback.

diminishing tax base in the face of rising costs. If voters fail to pass bond issues to aid the schools, does it mean that schools are not of value? Not necessarily (though that *may* be the case). What it may more accurately indicate is that citizens feel they cannot afford to have increased taxes, to spend more on schools, without cutting what they value as more important things in their lives. What these are may vary, but I strongly doubt that, if queried, many people would say that they do not highly value public education. All cultures possess particular human values, but some may become obscured when viewed from a position of ethnocentrism (cultural bias) or a misunderstanding of value priorities. For example, numerous writers (who shall go nameless) have said, in so many words, "Life is cheap in Asia," implying that wars and high infant mortality rates have caused people to view life as less important than Western culture groups do. Emergent nations have far less money to build hospitals, provide services, and educate their inhabitants. But these facts in no way can be construed as a disregard for human life. During the Vietnamese war, innumerable photographs of grieving families brought this point home.

To *other* nations the carnage that occurs on our highways each holiday weekend may indicate that Americans hold life in low regard, but again cultural bias may be warping the picture.

What should be clear, then, is that values are in a constant state of flux, being reordered in one's own mind. Actions and ideas based on those values also may change from time to time as people (and cultures) "grow."

As values vie for internal precedence in our lives or in a culture, external choices and actions change. Certain values are then given priority over

222

others, and one's actions will usually change in a commensurate manner. Those actions, though, are again subject to constant scrutiny and change as one's values are reassessed.

This symposium focuses on law and the humanities, and within that context one may rightfully ask, Where do values fit into all this? Humanities refers to knowledge that is humanistic, that is, concerned with human values and expressions of the spirit of the human being. Within this definition fall language, creative and practical arts, literature, history, jurisprudence, et al. The underpinnings of all these fields, however, are the values held by the humanists who work in them. An artist's sense of human dignity and values is reflected in his or her work, whether it be sculpture, painting, musical composition, dance, interpretive language, or law. The choice of how or why one pursues an area of the humanities is clearly based on one's values rather than on purely objective descriptions of the world.

Law, however, is a bit harder for many people to see related to values than an impressionistic artist's painting. A more precise relationship of law and values should be described. Laws may be seen as formal statements of the values of a society. They do not always reflect the whole society, however, and disenchantment with parts of the law by some individuals may cause values of the majority to be reexamined and laws changed. This is again a simplistic explanation, but this point is vital and I shall expand upon it later. It does seem appropriate, then, to deal with values in a conference such as this. In fact, *fundamental* is probably a more fitting word than appropriate.

American Cultural Values

I said earlier that there are many human values that transcend individual cultures. Are there, then, also particular cultural values that seem to be pervasive in America (though not exclusively so)? Some scholars believe that there are, and I would agree with their contention. Robin Williams (1965, pp. 415–468) has identified the following as major American value orientations: (1) achievement and success, (2) activity and work, (3) moral orientation, (4) humanitarianism, (5) efficiency and practicality, (6) progress, (7) material comfort, (8) equality, (9) freedom, (10) external conformity, (11) science and secular rationality, (12) nationalism-patriotism, (13) democracy, and (14) individual personality. (Williams notes that, since values are constantly shifting, the list here is not in any rank order. Williams "compiled" this list from his participation in the Cornell Values Study Group in the 1960s. This group consisted of noted experts from many disciplines who met regularly and "hammered out" these value orientations.)

Williams sees these as "criteria for deciding what we want," and, as I mentioned above, these values priorities are constantly changing. For example, material comfort may have seemed less important to a college student of the 1960s than freedom and equality. As that student started a family and assumed responsibility for more than himself, he may have altered his priorities somewhat. He does not value freedom and equality for all any less. He "merely" sees material comfort as being of greater value to him. (Politically this may sound like a classic case of liberalism, but this is not a political essay.)

Overriding all of these values may be the constant desire for achievement and success. This was seen in terms of the student's fight for freedom and equality at age 20. It may be viewed as providing material comfort at age 30. These examples are merely possible illustrations of American cultural values, not advocacies of them.

At this point I would like to use the frame that I have constructed to illustrate three very important relationships between values and law.

These relationships are reinforced by the way in which law is viewed in our society. The law is usually seen as a vigilant watchdog, and this function may often influence the role that the law ultimately plays in the shaping of values.

A very general illustration of the cultural gatekeeping that the law provides is the Bill of Rights. These amendments aid in maintaining the culture, protecting (ideally) both the culture and the individuals within it.

The very notion of the three branches of government (or four, if one views regulatory agencies as distinct) reflects the belief that the law should and does operate as a gatekeeper, sheltering the culture and its citizens from ideological or personal abuse.

There are many instances, however, when the views of a society and its citizens may be in disharmony concerning the extent of legal paternity. At other times the values and laws of a society and its citizens are quite harmonious. I would like to explore briefly these relationships.

Law and Values as They Reinforce One Another

Ideally the relationship between laws and values should be complementary. The values that the majority of people hold should be felt by legislators (or supreme judiciaries) and reflected by the laws that they pass (or uphold). New law, because it usually reflects values, is almost always a "victim" of cultural lag (a term coined by William Ogburn and the Chicago school of sociology). No matter how swiftly legislation is passed, it usually lags behind societal values by a period of months or years.

Let me illustrate this with a rather innocuous law—the Twentieth Amendment to the Constitution, the so-called lame duck amendment. This amendment reflects "national" values of efficiency, practicality, and progress in moving up the date for presidential inauguration and providing more thoroughly for succession in the executive office.

For many years technology had made it possible to know the next president within 24 hours after the polls had closed in November. Yet the values of tradition and resistance to social change had prevented a change in the law setting a March 4 inauguration date. The romantic picture of a messenger slogging through Tennessee in December 1828 to tell Andrew Jackson of his presidential election was no longer valid when a president could fly to a nominating convention (as Roosevelt did in 1932). The values of efficiency, practicality, and progress, then, overrode other values to the point that the law was changed to be consonant with those values, moving the inauguration up to January 20. For the most part laws passed in this country fit in the category of reinforcing values that citizens agree with. Thus many of the laws may seem innocuous or even superfluous, since they merely codify what has been the practice. Because most laws readily illustrate the above point, I see no reason to dwell on this area further.

Values and Law in Conflict in American Culture

Even when values and laws do reinforce each other for the majority of people, there are still dissenters. These individuals, or groups, may see the law as antithetical to their personal values, despite overwhelming societal support for certain laws. For instance, during most of our country's history it has had to tax its inhabitants in some way to raise revenue to govern. Despite complaints from citizens, taxes have usually been paid and the government supported. Occasionally however, individuals have seen the law as conflicting with their personal values and have refused to pay taxes. Thoreau went to jail rather than pay a tax to the government because it defended slavery for black people. Over 100 years later Thoreau's principles and tactics were adopted by individuals who also felt their personal values in conflict with the law.

The law, then, often becomes a source of conflict to citizens because it opposes their personal values. By creating conflict situations in our society, these citizens hope to enact resolutions that can accommodate both the law and their values. Conflict should not be seen as violence, since this is only one form of conflict and has been held in low esteem almost universally in our culture. Conflict may mean verbal confrontation; it may mean civil disobedience; it may mean labor slowdowns or sabotage.

These conflicts are common not only to American culture. What is unique, however, is our constant reliance on the courts to reconcile these differences. In many other cultures resorting to legal courtrooms for conflict resolution would not only be held in low esteem but would also be inefficient. In rural Mexico, taking problems away from the village often means neither party will achieve satisfactory redress. The Kpelle people of Liberia use a so-called moot that allows parties to air their differences and find compromising solutions swiftly. This unwillingness to enter formal courtrooms for conflict resolution is not limited to "less developed" cultures. In Norway compromise is the essence of conflict resolution. Only in a relatively few instances, when all other avenues have been exhausted, will disagreeing parties resort to the legal courtroom process.

One may argue that these cases in other cultures are relatively petty, two-party offenses compared to the larger policy issues that have been used as illustrations in this paper. That is true, but I did not mean to imply that the idea of values and law intg only applies to these so-called big issues. Most of them started as smaller issues.

An example of a "small" issue that illustrates the conflict of law and personal values is the famous *Tinker* v. *Des Moines Community School District* case (1969). The Tinker children wore black armbands to school to protest the war in Vietnam. School officials suspended them when they refused to remove the armbands. The school officials saw their action as disruptive to classrooms and the school at large. The case finally reached the Supreme Court, where the Tinkers' right to protest in this manner was seen as an exercise of their right to free speech guaranteed under the First Amendment. A small issue involving the conflict of law and personal values.

Sometimes the conflict is over a larger issue, but a smaller law becomes the focus of attention. The 1968 Chicago riots, for example, were largely precipitated by enforcement of the law concerning the closing of public parks at 11:00 P.M. This conflict was actually over the war in Vietnam, however, and was only one of many conflicts over that war.

The draft law also became a focus of antiwar feeling. During previous drafts there had also been disagreement over the law. It was only during the Vietnam war, however, that a great number of people finally came to protest the selective services law. Conflict in the Vietnam era was inspired by personal feelings against the legality of the Asian conflict. Many people resisted army service through conscientious objection; others avoided it by emigrating or hiding. The ultimate result was a dissolution of the draft and a new law mandating a volunteer army.

Values and Laws as Change Agents of American Culture

More controversial, usually, are laws that change values or, conversely, laws that are directly changed because of changing values.

As I stated above, citizens have never been particularly fond of paying taxes, but they have done so. The income tax amendment (Sixteenth Amendment), while not universally popular, was accepted by a populace that recognized the cost of humanitarianism and material comfort for all. This was an example of valuing of social reforms being codified by a law that generated more revenue to provide for them.

The 1957 launching of Sputnik brought a great deal of fear to this country—fear that our scientific prowess had become second to Soviet technology. The idea that our technology, our achievements, our *progress* were not first rate resulted in a greater value being put on improvement in these areas, particularly in schools. At that point, cost was of less relative value than achievement and success. Americans seemed willing to accept less material comfort if we could increase our scientific achievement. Thus the law creating the National Science Foundation was clearly a reflection of current American values. It is easy to find other significant instances where values lead to a change in the law. For example, the recognition of the value of youth was instrumental in the passage of child labor laws.

Besides values shaping laws, we can find noteworthy instances of laws that have shaped values. Many jurisprudential scholars feel that this ought not to happen, and, of course, many disagree. I am not a jurisprudential scholar and am not prepared to defend a stand on either position. I am, however, prepared to illustrate how laws have *contributed* to a change in values. It should be noted that I say contributed to a change in values, not led to such change. It would be fatuous to believe that the law could generate such change without the aid of other social factors, such as population distribution, poverty, war, environmental concerns, increase in crime, etc.

Two interlocking legal decisions, *Plessy* v. *Ferguson* (1896) and *Brown* v. *Board of Education of Topeka* (1954), are examples of law leading to change in national values. Of course, one can immediately argue that the *Plessy* case was merely the culmination of the erosion of the 1875 Civil Rights Act and other civil rights legislation that began with the famous slaughterhouse

cases (1873). I would contend, however, that the value of the doctrine of separate but equal was not firmly fixed in America's values, except in the South, until the decision in *Plessy* v. *Ferguson*. From that point, there was a given principle—separate but equal access and facilities were not unconstitutional. The law, then, aided many citizens' acceptance of this notion as a "proper" value.

Fifty-eight years later the Supreme Court found that separate but equal facilities (in public education) had no place because such "educational facilities were inherently unequal." Many critics saw the court as engaging in social engineering, and indeed, it did, as Chief Justice Warren's opinion makes clear. The law, again, had become an important factor in the changing of values— changes that are still going on in this area. The *Brown* decision was instrumental in the development of the civil rights movement, which culminated in the passage of the Civil Rights Act of 1964. The passage of this act illustrates again how values lead to a change in the law. It seems apparent that this entire process is dynamic, and to freeze illustrations in time can be deceptive. I am doing so to show that dynamism more clearly, rather than to obscure it in a shower of examples.

Breaking down all of these events into a scheme of action, we can see the following pattern. First, a conflict arises over some issue that pits the law against one's own personal values. That conflict causes those values to become better known and to have a pervasive effect on society. Society begins to modify (or adapt) its views, and this culminates in a law that more reasonably reflects the new feelings of society. (Of course, if the conflicting values are too outrageous for society ever to agree with, the law may and often does stop such change.)

This design attempts to cover *all* instances of the interaction of values and law, not just conflict resolution, because certainly all laws do not arise out of conflict, though many do. In addition, my illustrations are not meant to be fixed examples of my points, since the law and values are dynamic. Thus I have attempted to show how values and law are integrally related as both change agents and "gatekeepers" of our culture. What effect this interrelationship has, or should have, on elementary programs is important. In the final section I explore the possible implications of dealing with values and law in elementary schools.

Implications

Values and law share one very important characteristic in their introduction into elementary programs: any attempt to teach either or both of these areas separately is bound to be unsuccessful in the elementary school. Ultimate success, I believe, will only come by integrating the concepts of law and the process of valuing throughout the existing curriculum. There are at least two good reasons for these contentions. The first is that in a time of curricular cutbacks it would be suicidal to propose an additional curricular program for the elementary school. The second reason is that introducing the law as a separate discipline would not be true to the spirit or the intent of law-focused education. One of the most salient objectives of law-focused education is to allow students to "live the law." It seems absurd to ask them to do this only during 6 weeks in school.

How, then, can we develop a program of law and values in the elementary school?

A first step is to involve parents and community in the development of such a program *and* in the teacher training for such a program. "Even before the child enters school, a system of values has been developed in a variety of ways resulting from influence of home and neighborhood contacts" (Ploghoft & Shuster, 1971, p. 46). The child's value system is shaped by so many factors *outside* the school, that not to include some of them in a law-related program seems ineffective and wasteful.

One of the Carter administration's biggest thrusts in education is intended to be parents' involvement with schools and the education of their children. The administration is strongly urging schools to attempt to get parents involved and to train teachers and administrators in how to *keep* parents involved in schools during the school day (Abramowitz, Note 1).

A developing thrust like law-focused education is perfect for the reinforcement of such ideals. The teacher can work with parents to secure insights and understanding about their view of law, police, and justice. To ignore or undermine familiar attitudes is to put the young child in a position of undue stress. Teachers should work to reinforce a parental value system, but that means such a value system must be clear. Parents should be given the opportunity to learn about law-related education through a short evening course at the school.

Teachers should reassure parents that their values are sound or, if parents *wish* guidance in this area, suggest how values may be attained. This fostering of a positive relationship among school, home, and community is crucial in areas as potentially misunderstood as law and values.

It may be argued that the school (or its teachers) should not reinforce what it may perceive as "negative" values of the parents. This type of selective moralizing almost certainly will be counterproductive in nurturing the school-community relationship. Teachers should not, however, condone values that lead to illegal actions by parents. Thus, teachers may see themselves in a classic double-bind situation. To condemn parental values in the role of moralizer means that the teacher will almost certainly lose further voluntary parental contact. To condone parental values that the teacher is averse to is personally unhealthy.

What I am proposing here is neither of those polar opposites. Instead, I am suggesting that parents and teachers should have the opportunity to recognize each others' values and to appreciate the rationale behind them. This is basically a simple human relations idea that seeks to provide parents and, ultimately, students with the tools to be aware of others' values and to appreciate diverse points of views.

Values awareness. Students in elementary school must recognize their own values and how values are formed before putting them in a more complex legal framework. Values of other people should be recognized, and the understanding of such values should be attempted.

When values are brought into the framework of law, the teacher should try to get students to see laws as implying or assuming certain values. Understanding or recognizing these values will aid in the understanding of the meanings of certain laws. For example, in the first-grade curriculum students often study the family, and the study of law and values should tie directly into such study. Students might look at a law that says all persons must have their births certified when they are born. What values would underlie such a certificate? One, of course, is the value of efficiency and practicality: the orderliness that we assume is necessary for the longevity of our society. Another value assumed is equality of treatment for all. Another might be the technological value that we recognize in our society. Disease might be more easily fought by recording certain data at birth.

More values can, of course, be discussed, but the point seems clear—even first graders can examine laws for their implied values.

Teachers should set up genuine value-producing situations. These might be in the form of show-and-tell activities or sharing experiences in lower grades or more developed activities or case studies in middle and upper elementary grades. The National Education Association publishes a booklet that contains a number of good activities in this area (Naylor, 1976).

Other activities to enhance law and values. A number of other types of activities are available to aid teachers and parents in this area. For children of any age, sociodramatic episodes would be extremely helpful. Sociodrama refers to role playing for social values, rather than merely reenacting specific assigned scenes. The steps to sociodrama were developed by Fanny Shaftel, and her book (Shaftel & Shaftel, 1967) is still the best volume available on this subject. The last step in the Shaftel scheme involves sharing experiences and generalizing, and it is this step that may be the most useful for our concerns.

Legal conflicts may be dramatized with the focus on understanding various points of view. The underlying values of both the law and citizens can be a very fruitful source of discussion and ultimately social action by students, teachers, and parents.

Teachers should develop activities that allow students to make decisions—to make "laws." By doing so they can and should examine the rules that they follow in school, home, and community and those rules that they make in school. This examination should allow them to see the relationship among the values they hold, the values others hold, and the laws that are made. The relationship of values and laws as developed earlier in this paper can be scrutinized by students, parents, and teachers. In planning for decision making, it may be useful first to have students work in small groups that promote equal-status interaction (Nelson & Singleton, 1977). Later large-group decision making can lead to effective lawmaking.

Many avenues for research may very well be generated by the three categories of law and values that I have differentiated. One area that seems quite important is researching whether certain age groups of children seem to see the law in one of these categories. The results of such research might affect the entire introduction of law-related education into the curriculum.

This whole framework of values and law would seem to fit comfortably within the "typical" elementary curriculum. The primary grades seek to give students foundational knowledge in content areas as well as social and personal "basics" necessary for all persons to function in our society. Students can look at rules that they follow and the values implied (as described above). The need

for and value of leadership can also be studied within this framework.

The middle grades usually spend time on state, national, and cultural study. Values and laws inherent within this study can be examined in order to help students understand the reasons events take place rather than memorizing the facts about them. For example, in the study of Pennsylvania history, students could more thoroughly examine the values underlying treaties made between William Penn and the Pennsylvania tribes. Treaties are as important today as then, and students could examine what values are brought into play by each side, as well as the legal status and potential effect of those treaties.

The elementary curriculum is ideally shaped for the introduction of law and values. By recognizing the way law and values interact, we can begin to integrate these concepts into elementary schools to make healthier, more responsive schools.

REFERENCES

Naylor, D. T. *Values, law-related education and the elementary teacher.* Washington, D.C.: National Education Association, 1976.

Nelson, M., & Singleton, H. W. Small group decision making for social action. In D. Kurfman (Ed.), *Developing decision making skills* (47th Yearbook). Arlington Va.: National Council for the Social Studies, 1977.

Ploghoft, M. E., & Shuster, A. H. *Social science education in the elementary school.* Columbus, Ohio: Merrill, 1971.

Rokeach, M. *Beliefs, attitudes, and values: A theory of organization and change.* San Francisco: Jossey-Bass, 1968.

Shaftel, F., & Shaftel, G. *Role playing for social values.* Englewood Cliffs, N.J.: Prentice-Hall, 1967.

Williams, R. M. *American society: A sociological interpretation.* New York: Knopf, 1963.

REFERENCE NOTE

1. Abramowitz, E., Assistant Director for Education of the Domestic Council of the President. Remarks, Washington, D.C., December 7, 1977.

Law and Values in American Society

Margaret A. Carter

This article is an interesting complement to the one prepared by Murry Nelson. Margaret Carter's remarks have particular implications for the elementary school classroom. She suggests, for example, that it would be profitable to focus classroom discussion on the relationship between law and values as they are evident in public conflict. She also suggests that it is useful to consider a system of laws as opposed to a collection of individual laws. Of particular interest is Carter's description of law as codified morality. Readers will find that this article has significance in a range of areas associated with curriculum innovation and implementation.

Murry Nelson's article helps the reader focus on some of the major issues that must be considered in any decision to include values and the law in an elementary curriculum. Nelson immediately takes on one of those issues when he gives a definition of values and uses Williams's value orientation to analyze and explain behavior. But is Williams's framework adequate for classroom use? Can that list aid us in clarifying the causes of participation in the march to Selma or a march in Skokie? What is it about that list that explains the actions of the citizens who took part?

The citizens' view of reality, in each case a view formed through their experiences as individuals and as members of groups, needs to be considered in order to understand the interplay and conflict among the many values available to them.

The example of the young student of the 1960s who supposedly loved freedom and equality more than material comfort does not take into account that someone else was taking care of his needs. The student did not make a choice between food and marching. His choice was also a personal one which affected few others.

The focus for discussion of the relationship between law and values should be on public conflict, as in the later example of the schools.

Perhaps the interpretations of American values by Gunnar Myrdal (1944) or Stuart Chase (1962) might be more useful in approaching American society and its laws. The excellent discussion of core values in Oliver and Shaver's *Teaching Public*

Issues in the High School (1966) offers insight into the major values of a democratic society.

It is also helpful to think of a system of laws rather than of a collection of individual laws. That system operates between the society's assumed values (ideals) and the actual experience of citizens. A law can be viewed as an established regulation which is backed by society in its struggle for order.

A law can be passed by a legislature or ruled by a judge, but if the law does not fit, if it is not consistent with other laws, it will not be obeyed or enforced. The lawmaker does not operate outside of society, but rather within it, subject to the same morality or interlocking system of core values. (I owe what is good about this argument to James K. Feibleman of Tulane University. Its inadequacies are caused by my interpretation.) Members of a society live together by means of that set of moral values. "When that society becomes a state, its morality is established by codification: laws are codified morality. The established laws and law practices endeavor not only to particularize the accepted morality but also to enforce and defend it" (Feibleman, 1975, pp. 108–109).

Since laws are established, there is a lag between the movement of public morality and the shift of the law to reflect it. Something happened in American Society between *Plessy* v. *Ferguson* in 1856 and *Brown* v. *Board of Education* in 1954. It is doubtful that people gave up *valuing* the doctrine of separate but equal. It is unlikely that anyone ever valued it, except as an out, an excuse for what he or she was really protecting. Blatant racism was no longer acceptable to many people. What was accepted was the value of education and the right of all Americans to have access to

Margaret A. Carter is the Coordinator for the Social Studies in the Ann Arbor, Michigan, schools. She is currently directing a Title IV-C Staff Development Project and is one of the authors of *Discrimination: A Global Perspective* for Holt-Saunders (Australia).

education and all that it can supposedly do for an individual.

It seems there was a whole package of values making demands on the system, directing the law away from inequality in the public sector to equity. Public schools, public transportation, and participation in public policy formulation came under scrutiny. Law was altered to meet the requirement of morality.

Of interest at this point is the question, How do we know when the morality has changed and that we are ready to alter the laws? The Warren Court did not run a Gallup Poll. But if it had, what would have been the point at which a shift could have been made? 51%? 66⅔%? Or is the number who believe less important than who believes? Where does the final authority come from? Is it in the streets? Is it more mystical, what Mill called "the sentiment of justice" or the feeling of what is right? (Bring on the humanities!)

The draft laws during the Vietnam war and the conflict raging around those laws illustrate another area for exploration in understanding (or in confusing) the shift in public morality. There were great numbers of people involved in the draft riots in Northern cities during the Civil War. But they were generally from the new immigrants and the lower classes. The wealthy were able to buy substitutes and to avoid the mayhem and death of the battlefield. In the 1960s and 1970s the draft was more evenly administered, and middle-class and upper-class young men were more apt to be called. Equity raised the level of argumentation, and the sons of blue-collar workers and corporation executives joined forces to avoid and to change the laws.

While there is currently a volunteer army, has the draft issue really been resolved, or is it merely in abeyance? Has the morality of the society changed sufficiently to require a new codification, or will the old one be recalled? What dissolved may have been the myths about classic battles and lights at the end of tunnels in Vietnam swamps.

Implications

Mr. Nelson correctly points out that values are in the schools. They come in the door with the teacher and students, and they exist in the procedures and the demands of the classroom.

For instance, who gets rewarded? What is valued? Do the people who fought on the playground or the ones who did 10 problems correctly get to feed the guppies? Which child never gets chosen to greet a guest, and why not?

Children ought to have an opportunity to make rules, study them, amend them, and live by them. They ought to analyze why a move from the classroom to a ball diamond changes the "rules" and the expectations about noise and movement. They are able very early to understand the "system of rules" and can be helped to view that system in terms of the need for order and, therefore, justice.

The upper elementary classroom is the place to begin serious discussion of basic documents that embody the core values of society. The Bill of Rights and the Universal Declaration of Human Rights ought to receive special attention so that young people can recognize rights, the reasons why they are important, and the consequences of their denial.

Rosa Parks, Fannie Lou Hamer, and Cesar Chavez are but three people whose "stories" ought to be part of the elementary curriculum. Their lives are intertwined with the core values of our society, and they are touchstones for the fit of the legal system.

The necessity for curriculum development in the field of law and American values and the enormous task of bringing everyday actions closer to the ideals we assume can be seen in the following anecdote from real life today. The people involved were all public school administrators. No one held less than a master's degree or had been with the schools fewer than 10 years. The program had received rave reviews from administrators in school districts in several states and at the AASA national meeting. It concerned procedures for dismissing teachers, implying "You can do it in spite of the tenure law if you pay attention." The 4 hours were well organized and well paced. The excellent case studies were ticked off, one by one, as the "legal technicality" that lost each case was examined. There must have been a dozen statements about the courts and lawyers and "technicalities."

In the final moments of the program, during the comments and questions, a voice protested, "Gentlemen, sometimes those 'technicalities' you have been discussing all evening are referred to as the Fifth and Fourteenth Amendments."

REFERENCES

Chase, S. *American credos.* New York: Harper & Row, 1962.

Feibleman, J. K. Philosophical perspectives. In T. Taylor, C. B. Motley, & J. K. Feibleman, *Perspectives on justice.* Evanston, Ill.: Northwestern University Press, 1975.

Myrdal, G. *An American dilemma.* New York: Harper & Bros., 1944.

Oliver, D. W., & Shaver, J. P. *Teaching public issues in the high school.* Boston: Houghton Mifflin, 1966.

Building on Secondary Programs and Materials

Mary Jane Turner

This paper suggests that it is necessary to examine and classify secondary-level legal education materials and to consider typical elementary school curriculum patterns in order to determine: (1) what elements of secondary-level programs might be adapted for use in elementary schools; and (2) how to prepare elementary-level students better to cope with secondary legal education curricula. A categorization scheme for legal education materials is offered, and two elementary curriculum models are discussed. The author argues that materials dealing with the role of law in society or with concepts related to law may hold the most promise for elementary-level students and suggests that the focus should be on developing analytical skills and positive attitudes.

Secondary-level legal education has evolved in response to certain needs, many of which have not been seen as germane to the goals commonly prescribed for elementary education. Some of the secondary programs which first emerged in the 1960s were in large measure a part of the "new social studies movement"—cognitively based and dependent upon inquiry modes of instruction. Others had as their primary focus the development of compensatory skills in the law. These programs sought to teach students something of the content of law as well as the skills for living in an environment which is largely structured by legal prescriptions. A third kind of program was directly related to rising crime rates among the young. It was suggested that teaching about law and the consequences of antisocial behavior would have a deterrent effect upon "crime-prone" adolescents.

A critical examination of the presumptions underlying these early efforts has led many practitioners to question both the locus of instruction and some of the content thrusts. Discovery learning and the social sciences, for example, have trickled down into elementary social studies programs. Political socialization experts have noted that support for the system and compliance with its rules may be a phenomenon engendered in early childhood rather than in secondary schools. At the same time, secondary developers have been moving beyond simplistic notions such as "using the content of law to improve student attitudes

toward the police" and "teaching what the law says to deter criminal behavior."

The broadening and deepening of objectives for law-focused education have still not redressed the imbalance between elementary and secondary offerings, however. With few notable exceptions, legal education materials are still designed primarily for secondary-level students. In addition, the majority of the elementary programs that are available are best suited for upper elementary grades.

If curriculum developers and writers have failed in preparing instructional materials and strategies for elementary schools, so have teacher trainers and university methods professors. The task of translating secondary-level legal concepts and content into something useful for elementary students has been left for the teachers, who are largely unprepared to assume the burden for several reasons. First, their backgrounds in the substance of law and appropriate methodologies for teaching it are usually inadequate. Second, time constraints for these teachers are generally severe; and finally, many have not been made aware that law studies constitute a legitimate and important area which should be included in the elementary curriculum.

I believe that elementary curriculum developers should consider two major aspects of secondary-level law-related programs and materials. The first has to do with translation. What is there in the secondary-level materials and strategies that might be useful for elementary levels, given existing elementary curriculum patterns? The second has to do with preparation. What is inherent in secondary-level programs that requires a unique understanding not usually provided in

Mary Jane Turner is Co-Director of the Colorado Legal Education Program and Staff Associate at the Social Science Education Consortium. She is currently involved in citizenship education.

typical elementary programs? Answering these questions requires that we examine secondary-level programs and materials with some precision, and that we identify those areas and/or levels of the elementary curriculum where infusion of new content would seem to be most appropriate.

Generalizing about materials is always risky. There are literally hundreds of published programs, from student materials, teacher resources, and audiovisual components to games and simulations. Examination of these in terms of their general goals and objectives would lead one to believe that they are more similar than dissimilar. For example, we find that most programs are intended to:

1. Develop an understanding of such concepts as justice, freedom, equality, fairness, law, legal institutions, legal sanctions, due process, and so on.
2. Demonstrate the necessity for law and a government of laws.
3. Reduce alienation.
4. Increase feelings of efficacy.
5. Demonstrate that law is not static and further show that it can be changed.
6. Develop appreciation of and respect for the merits of our legal system and its representatives.
7. Encourage willingness to participate in the legal system and to expend energies affirmatively to improve it.
8. Encourage reasoned and constructive criticism of our legal system.
9. Develop an appreciation for the complexities of social problems on which law works.
10. Develop tolerance of and reduce frustration about the imperfections of our legal system.
11. Develop an understanding of the consequences of breaking the law and the values, personal and social, of obeying it.
12. Teach youth to make reasoned judgments.
13. Develop analytical skills.

It is obvious that few of the programs succeed in achieving all of these objectives. It is also true that some materials are of much higher educational quality than others. Comparing materials is beyond the scope of this paper, however, and we can, without resorting to comparisons, differentiate between programs by analyzing them in terms of their specific objectives and major content foci. When we view the materials in this way, a useful classification scheme begins to emerge. Although there is considerable overlap among categories, I believe the following typology can be utilized in assessing materials and in making testable hypotheses. Law-focused education materials tend to focus on: (1) the role of law in society, (2) concepts related to law, (3) constitutional law and civil rights, (4) criminal law and the criminal justice system, (5) the interrelationships of social problems and law, and (6) substantive law.

Materials in the first category, the role of law in society, generally deal with such topics as the need for laws, the techniques of law, basic legal functions, process values, the limits of law, law and social change, and constitutional protection of basic social values. The second category, concepts related to law, focuses on such concepts as justice, equality, liberty, responsibility, participation, diversity, property, authority, power, and decision making. Materials in both these categories tend to be more abstract and philosophical than those in other categories. Many in the first category, for example, use a jurisprudential model, while those in the second category may emphasize conflicting definitions and/or perceptions regarding the various terms.

Content related to constitutional law and civil rights can be found in nearly all law-related curriculum materials. Justice, a concept treated in the second category, is often discussed in the context of the constitutional provisions that ensure and secure it. However, much of the material dealing with the Bill of Rights of the United States Constitution has been developed according to the structure of that document. Such materials, which typically are focused on freedom of expression, freedom of religion, freedom from search and seizure, due process, and equal protection under the law, can, I believe, appropriately be included in this category.

Due process and equal protection under the law, along with administration of the justice system and various rationales for punishment, are content foci of the fourth category, criminal law and the criminal justice system. Interestingly, it is materials from this category that secondary-level students (initially, at least) find most exciting because most of the emphasis is on juvenile rights and protections afforded to wrongdoers. Enforcement, the role of police, and trial procedures constitute the substance of this category.

Social problems and issues—poverty, welfare, pollution, energy, discrimination, and prejudice—are among the themes which are examined in category 5 materials. The pervasiveness of the law in structuring remedies and solutions means, however, that much of the content is devoted to providing an understanding of the role of law in dealing with conflict situations. To a large extent, solutions to complex problems in modern societies are basically legal remedies.

Documents and materials in the last category, substantive law, deal with what the law actually says. Torts, contracts, and statutes governing taxation, poverty, insurance, welfare, the family, and business are among the topics examined.

Although some materials from each category can be found for all grade levels, most elementary curricula fall into the first two groups. (Among the exceptions are bicycle and pedestrian safety materials that describe and explain traffic laws.) In some regards, this confounds the conventional wisdom that abstract concepts and ideas cannot be taught to students in lower grade levels. I do not mean to suggest that developers are preparing elementary materials using the same levels of abstraction that are reflected in secondary-level materials. Rather, they are designing activities which convey abstract ideas in concrete and familiar forms.

Most secondary-level materials fall into categories 3, 4, and 5. Substantive law, the sixth category, is the least represented. Teachers tend to find it difficult, and when they do present material from this category, it is usually with the cooperation of a lawyer.

The course patterns predominant in legal education are as diverse as the materials designed to implement them. For example, some program planners and curriculum developers believe that the study of law should be incorporated into ongoing programs of American history and American government. Others believe that legal education is an integral component of civics instruction and therefore should be taught at the elementary level as well as in the traditional ninth- and twelfth-grade programs. Still a third group believes that the law offers a unique body of content and thus should be treated as a separate discipline in the social sciences or the humanities.

The legal education programs being offered in American schools today reflect all of these conceptualizations. Some elementary-level teachers are incorporating new content and strategies into traditional approaches to history, civics, and government. Many schools are offering 9-week or 1-semester elective courses that focus on consumer law, juvenile law, and judicial and civil processes.

None of the remarks in the preceding two paragraphs should be taken as inferring that legal education can be found in the majority of American school systems, particularly at the elementary level. Furthermore, what legal education there is is generally provided as a part of the social studies offering. Thus, the language arts and reading specialists have scarcely been involved at all, nor are there presently many materials which would be appropriate for use in these settings.

Now that we have examined, albeit briefly, the "what is" of legal education, we must consider the environment—the elementary school—into which we propose to inject this content, as well as suggest strategies for better preparing students for the demands of the secondary curriculum. If generalizing about legal education is risky, generalizing about existing elementary course patterns is formidable.

One statement can be made fairly simple, however. Most elementary teachers are more concerned about teaching the skills of reading, writing, arithmetic, and spelling than they are about teaching concepts and/or skills derived from the humanities or social sciences. A reading teacher might be willing to utilize law-reflected content in teaching reading. Nonetheless, the major objective would still be to provide facility in reading, not to provide legal understanding. Furthermore, there is nothing available among the secondary offerings which these teachers could use, regardless of their objectives. Thus, because of the commitments of elementary teachers and because of the nature of available secondary-level materials, it is necessary to look at only two portions of the elementary curricula—the social studies and humanities offerings.

Typical of basal social studies programs is the so-called expanding-horizons construct, which teaches about school or helpers in kindergarten; families in grade 1; the neighborhood in grade 2; communities in 3; state history and geography in 4; American history in 5; and selected world cultures or the Western hemisphere in grade 6. A second model is similar but features world geography at grade 4. It is interesting to note that although many district-generated scope and sequence charts specify concepts, generalizations, or themes where are to be taught at each grade level, the content which is generally used to teach them is much as described above.

A totally different way for organizing elementary curricula first emerged in the 1960s. Although used to a much smaller extent than expanding horizons, described above, it is worth mentioning because some major elementary textbook series use the format. Concepts are drawn from the various social sciences and used in a cumulative sequence (as opposed to the random and eclectically selected concepts often utilized by school districts) to provide coherence in the curriculum. A variety of content foci can conceivably be used to teach discipline concepts.

Humanistic curriculum patterns are typically more fragmented and diffuse. Even the extent to which the humanities are emphasized varies from district to district. In almost all cases, however, humanities in the elementary schools are taught in social studies, in art, in music, or in language arts. Thus, what has been said about social studies patterns applies to humanities offerings also. Some areas of the social studies, however, tend to have a stronger humanities focus than others.

Some areas, for example, almost always are concerned with qualitative rather than quantitative questions and methodologies. History, cultural anthropology and geography, sociology, psychology, and political philosophy are among the more obvious of the genre. In addition, a considerable portion of the elementary curriculum is devoted to valuing activities.

Matching these content areas to the expanding-horizons model shows that in every grade level except grade 4 the chances are good that humanities will be emphasized. In those instances at grade 4 where the focus is on cultural as opposed to physical geography, a humanities orientation may also be central.

The humanities potential of curricula organized according to concepts derived from the social science disciplines is harder to specify. It can be argued that there is an evaluative aspect to all concepts. Thus, the approach to teaching the concept is the critical issue. It is probably reasonable to assume that most elementary teachers would spend considerable time emphasizing underlying values.

In addition to prevalent curriculum patterns, it is necessary for us to consider what it is that should be going on at elementary levels that would best prepare students to cope with the secondary curriculum. This question can probably best be addressed by considering, first of all, what is not important to do. There would be small pay-off in trying to teach substantive law. There is presently not a significant amount of "black-letter" law being taught at secondary levels, nor is there likely to be; whatever students did learn they would probably quickly forget because the content would be neither relevant to nor readily applicable by them. Moreover, the rate of change in the area of substantive law is so dramatic that laws learned today will be changed tomorrow.

Many of these caveats also hold true for some of the other categories we have discussed. The issue of relevance, for example, becomes critical in the area of social problems and the law. It might be useful to have elementary students consider such problems as littering, overconsumption of water and other resources, or poverty, if the issues were kept simple enough and related to their own experience base. But to expect them to devise social rules for solving complex problems is futile.

It might also not be fruitful for teachers of primary-level students to emphasize the historical antecedents of the Constitution, the structures of the rule-making branches of government, the nature of the court system, and so on. Students at this age do not relate adequately to the realities of the adult world. In addition, the existing curriculum patterns do not fit well with these contents. This is not true for the upper elementary grades, however. At some point during this time students become fascinated with the world

around them. They can, therefore, deal with constitutional issues, not in the historical, chronological mode that marks the traditional emphasis of the fifth-grade American history course, but by considering the implications of majority rule and minority rights, rule making, justice (fairness), and so on. Students in grade 6 might compare law and legal systems in various countries and cultures as part of the course of study.

In many ways, the approaches which are used to organize the first two categories of secondary-level materials may hold the most promise for structuring elementary curricula. Young students can and should discuss such issues as the need for laws (rules), the role or purpose of law in society, the pertinence of the law for managing conflicts, the methods and techniques of law, and so on. They can also examine and, more important, apply the criteria of fairness and equality to their own behavior. They can think of authority relationships in terms of the quality and the benefits that result. The long-term outcome of providing these kinds of educational opportunities for elementary students is that they learn to perceive law as a necessary component of social living and to understand that law is less likely to be a punitive than a positive force. Furthermore, this learning can be accommodated within the typical elementary curriculum patterns.

The question of how students can best be prepared to handle secondary-level law programs probably has less to do with the substantive content they have mastered than with the intellectual skills and attitudes they have developed. No one would argue that educational experiences should not be sequential and cumulative. This does not mean, however, that the elementary teacher should teach a little bit about torts, contracts, juvenile law, incarceration, and rehabilitation. Rather, the elementary teacher should introduce those concepts which have power in explaining the underlying principles relating to torts, contracts, juvenile law, and so on. Furthermore, the students should be provided with opportunities to analyze and to generate hypotheses about the content with which they are dealing. Teaching the skills related to inquiry has much more to recommend it than does teaching a compendium of unrelated and largely unprocessed facts.

In a similar way, attitudes and values ranging from valuing the process of inquiry to valuing justice, freedom, responsibility, and participation are necessary for an optimum secondary-level educational experience. In other words, I believe that, rather than focusing on the facts of law, elementary programs should emphasize the skills of processing information as well as the attitudes necessary for doing so. This is not to say that students in grades K through 6 should not be taught about the law and legal system. They should, but as they do so they should learn about the social values inherent in law and the relationship of law to democratic values.

I believe there are three educational implications of developing quality elementary-level law programs. The first has to do with content selection. If, as I have suggested, it is appropriate to build curricula around legal concepts and generalizations, content still must be selected to illustrate the concepts. It can be chosen from what is traditionally taught, or it can be drawn from other areas. There is no valid reason why all students must be presented with the same substance. Secondary materials are diverse. Elementary materials can be equally so.

Second, it is important that attention be given to the quality of the educational environment. Law-related instruction has to do with the values of democracy, just as law is a necessary cornerstone for preserving democracy. It is hard to believe that students can internalize these values unless they themselves are treated fairly and equitably in the classroom. I do not propose that students will be allowed to make curriculum decisions. I do think, however, that they should be

treated in such a way that they view as legitimate the authority figures with whom they interact in the schools.

The third point is directly related to the second. There should be extensive teacher training to assist teachers in implementing their own programs. Other than parents, teachers may be the most important authority figures students encounter in their early years. Supportive adult authority role models can encourage students to think about and feel positive about the values which laws are designed to preserve. In addition, teachers need help in refocusing old content or in selecting new. They also should be trained in the use of new strategies—inquiry, role play, debate, mock trials, and directed discussion. If the content and the generalizations are not new, the emphasis certainly will be. If the strategies are "old hat," their use with new content needs to be explained.

Legal education has great promise for revitalizing and enhancing civic education. It is too important to be left to the secondary years, and whether it will be taught to elementary students should not be left to chance.

Another view . . .

Building on Secondary Programs and Materials

Donald P. Vetter

This article is in basic agreement with Mary Jane Turner's argument that elementary-grade materials in law and humanities should focus on developing analytic skills and positive attitudes through a conceptual approach or through the examination of the role of law in society. Don Vetter's article expands on Turner's views and develops several additional ideas. The author also attempts to bridge what he describes as the gap from theoretical to practical by proposing a curriculum model for a law education strand in a K–12 citizenship education curriculum.

In her paper Mary Jane Turner focuses on two general questions. First, she analyzes, "What is there in the secondary-level materials and strategies that might be useful for elementary levels?" Then she considers, "What is inherent in secondary-level programs that requires a unique understanding not usually provided in typical ele-

mentary programs?" The purpose of this review is to expand on her responses and to develop several ideas which were not emphasized by her. In addition, I shall attempt to bridge the gap from the theoretical to the practical through a curriculum model for a law education strand in a K–12 citizenship education curriculum.

Turner is very thoughtful and thorough in her categorization of secondary law-related curriculum materials and her analysis of their possible use in elementary programs. The classification of existing materials into six categories is of great

Donald P. Vetter is Supervisor of Social Studies for the Carroll County Public Schools in Westminster, Maryland. He was the first Director of the Law-related Education Program for the Schools of Maryland.

value in making decisions regarding their possible use in grades K–6. I agree with her that categories 1 (the role of law in society) and 2 (concepts related to law) are the levels into which most elementary materials fall, while categories 3 (constitutional law and civil rights), 4 (criminal law and the criminal justice system), 5 (contemporary issues, or the interrelationships of social problems and law), and 6 (substantive law) are most representative of secondary materials. The reasons for this are made evident by James Davis (in this volume) in his list of the most common learning objectives of materials within each of the six categories. An examination of the objectives emphasized within the categories reinforces Turner's position because the majority of the objectives which are appropriate for elementary programs are found in the first two categories.

On the basis of her extensive analysis of law-related curriculum materials, Turner notes that relatively few law education materials have been developed for grades K–6. Also, she observes that teacher trainers and curriculum developers have largely left it up to the elementary teacher to adapt secondary materials for primary and intermediate levels. While this is generally true, one exemplary project is clearly an exception. I am referring to Law in a Free Society (LIFS), a K–12 curriculum with strong components in teacher training and program evaluation. Based on the concepts of authority, privacy, freedom, justice, participation, diversity, property and responsibility, the instructional materials include sound filmstrips, student workbooks, and teacher manuals. A particular strength of this project is the cooperative involvement of attorneys, police, and other justice system practitioners with teachers and school administrators. I am highlighting this project because I believe the materials published by LIFS should be carefully examined by the staff members of local projects before they set out to develop their own law-related activities for elementary school levels.

As Turner observes, existing law-focused curricula on elementary levels tend to be organized either conceptually or topically. While the first approach deals with abstract concepts such as the eight identified by LIFS, the topical approach is concerned with abstractions such as the need for laws, basic legal functions, the limits of law, and constitutional protection of basic social values. Because of the abstract nature of these concepts and topics, it is of critical importance that these ideas be presented to elementary students through concrete activities related to the classroom and the school. This strategy provides a vehicle for the schools to convey the ideals of our democratic society to children during the crucial formative ages of 5–9. Through planned school experiences

for the elementary student, an understanding of democratic processes could be promoted and a sense of social commitment could be fostered. Rather than emphasizing compliance with rules and authorities, a law-related curriculum should utilize student-oriented teaching strategies that promote an understanding of the rights and responsibilities of citizens in a representative democracy.

I am in complete agreement that the educational environment should be compatible with democratic values and foster self-discipline and mutual respect. Through the hidden curriculum of the schools, students very often are learning such values as obedience to authority, conformity to school rules, loyalty to the school, and respect for adults. Also, they recognize at an early age that such behavior traits as passivity, standing in line patiently, not speaking until recognized by the teacher, marching quietly to the cafeteria, and responding appropriately to bells are valued. My purpose is not to suggest that all of these things are inherently bad. It is obvious that controls are necessary if goals are to be attained and social chaos averted. However, are these the values and behaviors the schools should communicate to pupils 180 days or 1,260 hours a year? Given the realization that schools are dealing with values education in extensive and pervasive ways, it is of vital importance that elementary law-related curricula establish a strategy to deal with values in a planned and overt manner, and not just through the hidden curriculum. The opportunity for pupil participation, especially at an early age, in classroom or school governance provides both an understanding of democratic ideas and a strategy for presenting abstract concepts in a context that is meaningful to young children.

In considering "what it is that should be going on at elementary levels that would best prepare students to cope with the secondary curriculum," Turner highlights what is *not* important to do and suggests several implications for developing elementary law programs. She notes that development of intellectual skills and attitudes is more important than mastery of substantive content. While primary-level law curricula should be built around legal concepts, she points out, "there is no valid reason why all students must be presented with the same substance." I agree that diversity of elementary materials is desirable. However, I wish to add that the content areas must reflect carefully chosen goals and must be based on guiding principles of child development. Given a conceptual framework, the curriculum should integrate content of a relevant nature with the development of problem-solving and decision-making skills through personal analysis and intergroup participation. Fundamental ideas such as governance, responsibility, interdependence, and diversity can effectively serve as organizing concepts for the curricular structure. Because they are comprehensive, they are suitable for the creation of learning experiences geared to the general developmental level of the pupils.

Although the majority of the activities will undoubtedly take place in the classroom, an attempt should be made to engage primary-level pupils in activities that involve the school as a societal model. In the intermediate grades, programs should involve representatives of the justice system in classroom activities and take youngsters into the community for first-hand experiences. Ultimately, the classroom and community-based experiences will help the children develop the citizenship participation skills that will enable them to make thoughtful decisions about relevant personal problems and prepare them to deal with complex issues that will confront them in the future.

In an attempt to bridge the gap between theory and practice, I would like to present a model for incorporating law education as a major component of a citizenship education curriculum. Due to constraints on time and space, this overview, presented in Table 1, is very sketchy. It is intended to show that law education can be integrated into the K–12 curriculum through different approaches such as the three mentioned by Turner: (1) incorporated into ongoing programs of history and government, (2) treated as an integral component of civics instruction at elementary and secondary levels, and (3) taught as a separate discipline. Also, the model is designed to present a possible K–12 scope and sequence for law education and to highlight an approach that should prepare elementary students to cope with the secondary curriculum.

Finally, I wish to express agreement with the idea that extensive teacher training is needed to assist teachers in implementing elementary programs. A limited survey by Gross (1977) showed that less time is now being devoted to elementary-level social studies, as an apparent result of the current "back to basics" mania. Gross states that teachers in Colorado are averaging only 1 hour per week and that in Florida "less than one-third of the K–5 teachers reported positive attitudes toward the social studies and less than half regularly taught social studies."

If this survey is accurately depicting a national decline in social studies instruction in our elementary schools, it highlights a need for preservice and in-service training of teachers in the field of social studies. It also suggests an approach to the implementation of the new law education curriculum that focuses on the training of administrators and teachers and that clearly depicts the vitally important role of citizenship education during the early years of a child's formal education. Wyner (1976) concluded that this training should emphasize five areas: (1) increasing teachers' knowledge of the law to help them feel more confident in teaching about it, (2) increasing teachers' knowledge of developmental theory to help them understand the importance of gearing activities to the developmental age of the child, (3) demonstrating ways to incorporate law-related education into the daily activities of the school in order to point out the danger of the "hidden curriculum" and to present a positive model for the democratization of the classroom, (4) demonstrating ways to employ resource persons effectively in the classroom to foster constructive attitudes toward the legal system, and (5) demonstrating ways to use a variety of teaching strategies which provide for inquiry-oriented instruction and promote a pupil-centered learning environment. This type of training will enable elementary teachers to develop in their students the intellectual skills and attitudes needed to prepare them to cope with the secondary legal education curricula.

It is obvious that there is a dearth of law-related materials for the elementary level. Attempts to adapt secondary materials to the elementary classroom have failed to have much of an impact on our schools. It is of utmost importance that a variety of materials be created, especially on the primary level, that promote the development of concepts, skills, and attitudes in the broad field of elementary law and the humanities. As Turner has documented, the need for this type of program is tremendous. Once developed, it is likely to be implemented, especially if teachers and administrators can be trained through well-planned in-service presentations.

REFERENCES

Gross, R. E. The status of the social studies in the public schools of the United States: Facts and impressions of a national survey. *Social Education,* 1977, 41, 194–200.

Wyner, N. Observations on the teaching of law in elementary schools. In C. J. White III (Ed.), *Teaching teachers about law.* Chicago: American Bar Association, 1976.

Table 1: A Model for Incorporating Law Education into the K–12 Citizenship Curriculum

I. Levels K–4: conceptual approach
   A. Experiences based on inquiry processes and designed to build toward complexity
   B. Cumulative conceptual sequence: *possible concepts*
      1. Governance/fairness—formal and informal ways decisions are made in a democratic society to pro-mote fairness in the enforcement and interpretation of laws by persons in authority
      2. Responsibility—effect of one's participation in a group and the obligation one has to establish and support individual and group rights or to modify them in constructive ways
      3. Interdependence—the interaction of individuals and groups for the purpose of satisfying basic needs and the role of rules and laws in promoting equality and providing for safety and liberty among dependent peoples
      4. Diversity—ways individual/group differences and unique characteristics may lead to conflict but also promote cultural richness
   C. Development of concrete activities based on principles of child development
   D. Participation and decision-making skills fostered through democratic classroom environment
   E. Utilization of community resources

II. Levels 5–6: topical approach
   A. Emphasis placed on Constitution, branches of government, and nature of courts
   B. Activities integrated into ongoing programs
      1. Grade 5—lawmaking examined in context of unit on history and government of Maryland
      2. Grade 6—nature of courts examined in context of unit on urban communities
   C. Active involvement in community-based experiences
   D. Development of problem-solving skills
   E. Extension of democratic classroom environment

III. Levels 7–8: integrated approach in U.S. history and world cultures
   A. U.S. history: colonization to Reconstruction
      1. Foundations of legal system
      2. Role of constitutional law
   B. World cultures
      1. Laws of various cultures
      2. Role of law in resolution of international conflicts
   C. Implications of law-related topics examined in context of established curriculum
   D. Emphasis on intellectual skills

IV. Level 9: U.S. political/legal system
   A. Focus on legal education as integral part of civics instruction
   B. Reinforce and extend knowledge of functions of legal institution
   C. Designed to further thinking, valuing, decision-making, and problem-solving skills
   D. Curriculum is student oriented and develops participation skills through active involvement in hypothetical situations, actual case studies, and historic episodes
   E. Unit overview
      1. Citizenship
         a) Students' rights and responsibilities
         b) Vandalism
      2. Personal decision-making and communications skills
      3. Economic decision making as consumer and producer
      4. Political decision making
         a) Need for government: dissent and protest
         b) Judicial decision making
         c) Executive decision making
         d) Legislative decision making
         e) Political involvement
      5. Juvenile justice
         a) Nature and causes of juvenile crime
         b) Role of police
         c) Juvenile court procedures
         d) Dispositions and corrections

Table 1: A Model for Incorporating Law Education into the K–12 Citizenship Curriculum

---

   V. Level 10: integrated approach in U.S. history—1865 to today
      A. Historical, chronological examination of constitutional issues
      B. Impact of legal decisions on subsequent historic events

  VI. Levels 11–12: elective experiences
      A. Separate discipline approach
         1. Criminal justice
         2. Civil justice
      B. Issues approach
         1. Sexism
         2. Racism
         3. Peacekeeping
         4. Environmental concerns
            a) Energy
            b) Pollution
            c) Land use
            d) Population

The Politics of Curriculum Innovation

Todd Clark

Although educators have been resistant to accept the fact, theirs is a highly political professional world. Curriculum decisions are part of that arena of politics. Todd Clark describes the political context in which schools operate today and in which critical decisions about curriculum are made. In urging that educators accept the reality of politics, he suggests that teachers and administrators must themselves become political. Clarification of educational goals is one important step, he suggests, on the road to lessening public confusion regarding what schools are up to. Clark encourages use of plain language as a replacement for educational jargon understandable only to the professional establishment.

This paper raises a series of important questions regarding the responsibility of schools to the community, particularly where conflicting values may exist. Of particular value is a checklist of suggestions for undertaking a political action plan that will result in constructive relationships between the educational establishment and the lay community.

As educators, we are part of a political system. All others who have a stake in schooling are also constituents with levels of power that influence, for good or ill, the decisions that determine what American education is to be. Although we have long realized the power of our communities regarding school financing, we have not so often been made aware of the politics of education regarding curriculum policy and classroom practice. Over the years, as we have turned education into a profession, it has caused us to cut ourselves off to a larger extent than we should have from our own communities. A recent statement by William Haubner, of the NEA's Teachers' Rights Division, illustrates the ultimate polarity between the educator and the community. Haubner said: "Selection and presentation of materials falls within the purview of the profession. You don't tell a carpenter which saw or grade of wood to use. If you let inexperienced, unsophisticated, unknowing people make the decisions, teaching quality will be impaired" (Note 1). Such a position is the antithesis of what is needed. Too much polarization will diminish still further the opportunity which I believe does exist for educators and the public to agree on educational policy issues. After all, the use of compromise to reach consensus is not an unknown process in a democratic society and is, in fact, essential to its health.

Traditionally, education is a local matter. Taxes are raised and policies set by the community and its elected representatives. As educators, we were, perhaps for too long, able to function in a relatively autonomous fashion, giving little attention to the community because the community gave little to us. Such is no longer the case. Not only has concern for educational performance contributed to the back-to-the-basics movement, but various federal and state mandates now require direct involvement of the community in decision making. We must become more committed to and involved in that process. Our professional skills and knowledge must be used not only to educate children but to educate parents as well. To engage in the required level of community education is a part of what I mean by the politics of curriculum innovation. Community attitudes on education issues are now formed almost entirely without the benefit of our ideas. Television, newspapers and magazines, neighbors, tax rates, report cards, and candidates for office contribute more to the development of attitudes about education than do we. We must accept responsibility for the present state of education in America and actively involve ourselves in the politics of schooling. We must acknowledge our success at improving working conditions and benefits, and focus now on matters that concern curriculum content and instructional practices.

Todd Clark is currently National Education Director for the Constitutional Rights Foundation, Los Angeles, and President of the National Council for the Social Studies.

Origins of the Present Public Mood

What is the current state of the political system about which this paper is concerned? What factors have contributed to the present mood of adults concerned with educational policy? How does the present education climate determine the manner in which professionals and concerned adults should relate to one another?

During the 1950s, Sputnik caused great concern regarding the quality of American science education. New math, new chemistry, new physics stimulated the conceptualization of new social studies, an effort to use the structure of the disciplines in a social scientific way as the basis for curriculum and instruction. With some significant exceptions, the new social studies was a failure, as were the reform efforts in science education. The expectations of success were based on bad assumptions. Jerome Bruner, whose little book *The Process of Education* (1960) started the movement, has conceded that what he stimulated was based on the notion that *all* children wanted to learn and possessed what it later became clear were middle-class analytical skills. Many of us worked hard to foster what, in retrospect, was a middle-class reform movement.

Even so, many of the contributions that the "new social studies" made could have succeeded if we had done a better job of explaining this importance to our communities. The failure of "new social studies" is, in part, our failure as educational specialists to prepare the public for what we were doing. The drive to create new educational curricula resulted in the emergence of widely diverse products, among them materials bafflingly different from those previously used in schools. Whole new vocabularies were constructed out of the alliances educators of different disciplines formed to build new programs.

For a time, the public accepted our explanation that such changes were necessary to prepare well-educated young people. Suddenly, student scores on achievement and aptitude tests dropped. Annual reports indicated that SAT scores, of vital importance to the middle class, were also falling. Explanations were required, accountability was demanded, the schools suffered the consequences. We argued that the tests were out of synch with what was taught, that many variables affected academic performance— variables that educators could not control. While these explanations were, in part, correct, our communities were no longer willing to accept our explanations. Our credit had been used up.

Law-related Education—Bridge to the Basics

We had claimed the competency to achieve goals the public never really understood. What they do understand are basic skills. Sex education, global studies, death education, multicultural education, conceptually based education, all may be important to us. But the tests show and business persons (and college professors) have long been saying that many kids can't read, write, or compute when we graduate them. It is then an easy jump in logic for our public to demand that more attention be given to these tasks. Furthermore, who among us can argue that such skills are unimportant? (I have recently seen an article in a respected education journal which argued that literacy was no longer a needed skill.) Add to these community concerns a strong conviction by some traditionalists that social studies programs are irrelevant unless they teach patriotism, historical facts, and political structure. Also, concede that some among us thought basic skills were irrelevant.

The growing public disquiet over pupil achievement levels has stimulated a demand for change in the focus of the school curriculum. The results of public pressures are now to be found in the convergence of career education, basic skills, survival skills, and conservative notions regarding social studies into the competency-based education movement. Public dissatisfaction has led to more active parent groups and a wider demand for community involvement in educational decision making. It is appropriate for us now to look at ways to broaden our commitment to and concern for educational change. Certainly law-related education, focusing on improving the degree to which young people understand and learn to apply to their lives values related to the Bill of Rights and the legal system, represents what may now be called one of the fastest growing areas in the social studies and one which is perhaps most clearly in tune with the present public mood. In my judgment, this movement can provide the bridge between our concerns as educators and the expectations of our communities.

Given this background, how should we begin to become politically active? James Shaver, in his NCSS presidential address of 1976 (Note 2), criticized social studies educators, including himself, for the mindlessness with which we developed our programs. Quoting Charles Silberman, Shaver pointed out that nowhere is the lack of a carefully developed rationale more evident than in the almost universal claim that we make for our programs of citizenship education. Given the lack of evidence that our courses affect the quality or quantity of citizen participation, we are all in trouble in this era of accountability.

In law-related education, a basic strand of citizenship education, our first task, therefore, must be to identify clearly our goals, how we propose to achieve them, and how they relate to the preparation of citizens. A jargon-free descriptive rationale must be developed responding to the traditional concerns of our communities that we teach the history as well as the structure and processes of our government. The need to teach problem-solving and critical-thinking skills in a law-related context must be clearly explained so that it can be understood as a part of basic skills and survival education. Especially important is the need to convince our communities that educated students are those who are capable of making reasoned value judgments consistent with our national principles. Explicit attention must also be given to our responsibility to teach, in a social studies context, reading and writing.

I believe we are now moving rapidly in the direction of providing the clarity of purpose through a number of professional documents now available from the National Council for the Social Studies. The recent bulletin *Building Rationales for Citizenship Education* (Shaver, 1977) and the NCSS curriculum guidelines (1979) should both be carefully examined by every social studies teacher, for, in my view, they come as close to satisfying the need of which I speak as do any other current documents. The report on citizenship education by the United States Office of Education (Farquhar & Dawson, 1979) may also prove helpful.

The Cost of Public Confusion

Once we have put our own house in order, by developing goals which are clearly stated and closely linked to citizenship education and the development of basic skills which are analytical and value based as well as mechanical, we must learn to understand how our work relates our educational philosophy to that of our communities.

Today, more than ever, community standards prevail with regard to curriculum choices. That few overt community controversies over curriculum and teaching arise is due in large measure to the fact that, as educators, we intuitively mirror the values of our communities. The major conflicts in recent years have taken place when we failed to realize that the choices we were making were at significant variance with community standards. As a consequence, we were surprised and shocked at the strength of the negative reactions. The controversy which raged for several years over the NSF-supported Man: A Course of Study is one example. The beautifully prepared MACOS curriculum materials designed for use in the elementary grades were so exciting to all connected with the effort that no one asked how much the materials might arouse and anger parents. Cultural comparisons contained in the materials were intended to improve students' understanding of similarities between people. But many parents came to believe that the purpose of these materials was to undermine traditional family values. The fight that ensued was surprising to professional educators and was viewed by many as a well-orchestrated attack against educational innovation by the "right wing," which, in part, was true. However, no such attack could have been successful without a deep concern by many sincere individuals about the appropriateness of such an innovative curriculum. Community adults' confusion about the program provided fertile soil for extremist views. Professional exorcists and book burners of the right grew fat on confusion, which it was our responsibility to allay.

The violent public antieducation outburst in Kanawha County, West Virginia, grew out of the same soil. As a member of the National Education Association Task Force sent to investigate the origins of that conflict, I can attest to the deep feelings and sincerity of the people in that community. The precipitating factors behind that controversy were found to be suspicions which grew out of the failure of professional educators to work with and involve their community. Similar public concerns today relate to such movements in education as values clarification, which is attacked for teaching moral relativism; death education, which some see as too traumatic an issue for teenagers to deal with; and almost any effort to illustrate common bonds between people, which opponents often view as secular humanism, which they believe to be a form of religion. Over and over, the pattern repeats itself; inadequate community understanding, which leads to sincere concern, which provides the opportunity for extremists to stimulate conflict in the schools. We must break that cycle.

Adults want educational programs similar to those they knew as children or, at the very least, addressing agreed-upon needs in a manner they can understand. In my judgment, education has become a fertile field for right-wing attack because we have confused and upset good people who want good programs for the young. To improve the quality of education, we must learn to speak in plain language about programs which meet needs that can be agreed upon by educators and the public. To achieve this end, we are thrust, to a greater degree than has ever been previously true, directly into the political process. For, in addition to putting our own house in order with regard to our goals, and doing so in a manner which clearly expresses our purposes to our communities, we must also look at educational decision making as a political process and give attention to questions of public education and political strategy.

What Is Our Responsibility to the Community?

The era of the "new" is over in terms of educational change. Our communities insist that their schools reflect their values. Attention to the "basics" of reading, writing, and computation, rather than experimentation with new approaches to learning, is what communities expect today. Within such a context, how do we proceed? Is it our responsibility as professional educators simply to reflect the values of our community? Is it possible that significant and desirable change can still take place within the context of the present conservative view of the role that education plays in our society? Certainly the sixties and seventies, with the attention given to innovation, created today's educational climate. Adults now want schools to go back to more traditional educational activities.

Even if we chose to do so, it would not be possible to ignore the present public mood. And, although there are significant reasons for all of us to support more attention to the basics, there are still more reasons for us to work toward a broad-based definition of what is basic. As professionals, concerned with the educational process, we must not simply knuckle under to the wishes of our taxpaying public. We must accept our responsibility to educate our community parents, as well as their children. We must work to broaden public understanding of the significant purposes of schooling in our society. We must act as leaders directly connected to our constituencies, rather than professionals cut off from community concerns. As part of accepting this broader responsibility, we must give greater attention to what is unique about the political role in which we are cast. We must also become more sensitive to the legitimate concerns of parents, and make every effort to examine carefully the content of the curriculum in light of values of our communities.

Is Law Education Basic?

Politics of curricular innovation at the elementary school level is especially important. There has always been a greater degree of parental involvement during those early years than at any other. The formative nature of childhood, with regard to socialization and development, is profound. Demands that teachers of young children focus increasing amounts of attention on basic or fundamental skills have already altered the nature of the school curriculum. In many areas, attention to reading, writing, and computation drills have all but eliminated "frills." Recent studies all support the conclusion that there is little time devoted to elementary social studies. Greater demands by communities for teacher accountability require that attention be given to basic skills.

Elementary teachers working in self-contained classrooms also face a wider range of responsibilities for the children under their charge than do educators at any other level. Attention must be given to playground, hall, and classroom management, to build good citizens who perform to the standards of the school. It is in the process of achieving those goals that law-related education can best be emphasized. For it is in the development of student understanding with regard to laws and rules, and their fair enforcement, that the most significant early work must be done. After all, one of the basic purposes of education in a democracy is to ensure the survival of the system by providing the young with understanding, skills, and values necessary for intelligent and humane interaction with others. Although reading, writing, and computation are basic to effective living, a curriculum based on those skills alone is likely to produce generations of citizens without the values and understanding needed to maintain a democratic society. We must make this point forcefully in our communities, state, and nation. Already, the once stabilizing and socializing influences of family and church have diminished. The impact of the school has, at its best, been weak. The principle sources of values education today are the peer group and the media. Further weakening of the socializing impact of the school curriculum in the social studies, especially as it relates to standards of fairness, will leave Kojak, Starsky and Hutch, and the boy or girl next door in the role of teacher. I don't believe that is what our communities want.

We must, therefore, aggressively lobby in every way possible for a broad definition of the basic skills, so that reading, writing, and computation can serve as the foundation for the study of history, government, values, and social concerns necessary for our students to live lives based on individual freedom and a concern for human well-being. Basic skills should be viewed broadly to include knowledge of the social sciences, history, the humanities, and the arts, as well as the capacity to use that knowledge to organize, analyze, generalize, and act. Finally, basic skills must include an understanding of humanistic and democratic values before we can expect the quality of American life to reflect more accurately the hopes that the Founding Fathers had for this democracy.

In my judgment, law-related education has great potential to become the central focus for elementary social studies. Ours is a conservative society. We have common and humane values given expression in the Constitution and the Bill of Rights. While there is much disagreement over the implementation of those values in our daily lives, school programs which focus on the need for laws, how laws are made and enforced, and the values which underlie our system are not as difficult to justify as programs which may deal with the life styles of exotic cultures. While we recognize that there should be a place for both in the curriculum, we now find most elementary schools deal with neither. Programs which deal with practical problems of living in America are related to skills needed for the survival of the individual and the society. Therefore, it is my view that law-related programs should be presented as a part of the basic-skills curriculum of elementary educators. If we can successfully integrate law-related programs in the elementary schools, we can then broaden their scope and, once again, help students learn something of human interaction in our complex society and world.

Political Pitfalls of Law Programs

But even law-related education is political. Should law-related programs simply be recitations of laws and what happens to those who break them? Should these programs focus on Policeman Bill and Officer Friendly? Should they teach absolute obedience to authority or the right to practice civil disobedience as a part of our tradition? The answers to these questions are political, as well as educational. Educators are not free to make decisions on such issues without considering the values of their community. Therein lies the rub. Most communities would probably make the most conservative choice for law-related programs. "Law-abiding citizens," the average parent might say, "are those who obey the law, the rule, the authority figure without question."

The educator might design an elementary program whose broad goals and specific objectives are intended to develop skeptical, not quiescent, citizens. Gather facts, organize and analyze them. Draw conclusions based on skeptical analysis. Balance the rights and responsibilities of the citizens with those of the government. Question the rules. Make choices independently. Challenge those in authority. Such an approach, we might conclude, is consistent with American values. But, politically, how will most adults in our communities respond? In an elementary setting, such a program might involve students in classroom and playground rule making and enforcement. At what age should children be guided in such an effort? Or, as part of the program, police, lawyers, the school principal, and parents might be asked to discuss fair rule enforcement with children. How might these people respond to such requests?

How to Take Responsible Action

In my view, no program unrelated to elements of the child's life experience can successfully teach the basic tenets of our legal system. A program in law-related education which does not relate rule making and enforcement to children's lives will not succeed. But there are political risks, and, before becoming involved in a controversy over efforts to examine the basic concepts of our system rather than simply teaching absolute obedience, we must design programs we believe in, then become involved in the politics of our communities. I believe that there are 10 steps in the process:

1. In rough and incomplete fashion, design an "ideal" program. Roughly sketch out objectives, as well as ideas regarding program organization and classroom activities.
2. Study the nature of the community. What is its economic base? Political characteristics? General public attitude toward the schools? What is its political power structure? Have there been previous conflicts over educational policy? What is the level of sophistication of the power structure and the general population? Is there a significant difference between the point of view of the power structure and the general population?
3. Try to characterize the value structure of the community with regard to religious, political, economic, and social issues.
4. Who are the community opinion makers and leaders? Identify the groups and individuals as well as the media. Characterize the positions of each on public issues.
5. Analyze program goals and plans in light of the community profile. Make a list of those aspects of the program which the community would like and another list of those elements which the community would dislike.
6. Are the concerns of the community based on religious, racial, economic, political, or simply traditional grounds? As a professional educator, what responses to these concerns are consistent with your principles?
7. Design a strategy which appears likely to be effective in either resolving, managing, or avoiding the potential problem.
8. Develop a written rationale for the school program, intended to stimulate as broad a base of community support as possible.
9. Prepare a list of key groups and individuals whom you believe would be most interested in supporting the program. Contact them and try to educate them with regard to implementation of your plans.
10. Identify the most strongly supportive groups and organizations, and, whenever possible, ask their help in selling the program to the community and the school board—such groups as the local bar association, the police, church leaders, political leaders, etc. Advocate with allies from the community.

I believe we must all become involved as advocates for programs we believe in. To be effective advocates, we must develop our goals carefully. We must express our purposes more clearly than we have in the past, so that our communities can understand what we are about. We must relate our educational concerns to the values of our neighbors and be prepared to show how our programs contribute to a better life for the young and a better society for us all. We must develop effective and informed alliances with individuals and groups who can speak effectively for themselves, favoring what we propose. Such is the process of political advocacy that we must engage in. It is the only choice for us as professionals. We not only owe such action to our profession, we also have a responsibility to provide our students with a role model for political action which they can learn from. Creative and responsible action, based on sound principles grounded in American political values, is the very least our students can expect from us.

REFERENCES

Bruner, J. *The process of education.* Cambridge, Mass.: Harvard University Press, 1960.

Farquhar, E. C., & Dawson, K. S. *Citizen education today: Developing civic competencies* (Report of the Citizen Education Staff, U.S. Office of Education). Washington, D.C.: Government Printing Office, 1979. (OE Publication No. 79-07007)

National Council for the Social Studies. *Revision of the NCSS social studies curriculum guidelines.* Washington, D.C.: Author, 1979.

Shaver, J. P. (Ed.). *Building rationales for citizenship education* (Bulletin 52). Washington, D.C.: National Council for the Social Studies, 1977.

REFERENCE NOTES

1. Haubner, W. Report of the inquiry panel on the Kanawha County, West Virginia, textbook controversy. Teachers' Rights Division, National Education Association.
2. Shaver, J. Presidential address. Paper presented at the meeting of the National Council for the Social Studies, 1976.

Another view . . .

The Politics of Curriculum Innovation

Jerri Sutton

Jerri Sutton offers basic agreement with the propositions set forth in Todd Clark's paper on curriculum innovation. That agreement is underscored by her statement that she has put Clark's ideas into practice in her own experience as social studies specialist for the state of Virginia for 12 years. Such a test of reality is among the strongest statements one can make about the integrity of any argument!

Sutton suggests that readers faced with innovation issues would do well to follow a sequencing of questions. She urges educators to consider "what ought to be," "what is," and "what can be," in that order as the process of decision making is carried out.

Todd Clark has sought to distinguish the realm of "what ought to be" from the realm of "what is." He has rejected the first for the second. He develops a series of provocative ideas in his paper and suggests to the reader the realm of "what can be." Within this philosophical crucible, he encourages the reader to consider alternatives carefully. The measure of an educator is the ability to extend the sphere of the possible—what can be. If the paper were given a new title, it could well be

the "The A, B, C's of Political Realism for Making Law-related Education a Successful Part of the Elementary School Curriculum." In developing ideas on "how to get it together," he establishes a base for a call to creative and responsible action. He makes four important statements:

- Educators *are* part of a political system.
- Curriculum policy and classroom practice *can be* influenced by the concerns of the community.
- Educators and the public *can participate* jointly on educational policy issues.
- The public has many concerns about the elementary school, and law-related education *can be a bridge between* our concerns as

---

Jerri Sutton is past President of the Council of State Social Studies Specialists and served as a consultant for the President's Commission on Foreign Language and International Studies.

educators and the expectations of our communities.

The second part of the paper reviews "what it is the public understands and wants" and develops the idea of how law-related education might be and/or should be initiated. What the public understands and wants is basic skills. The way in which "basic" is defined is the key for unlocking an important door. The author then asks, Is law-related education basic? He proceeds to answer this pivotal question in one of the strongest statements of the paper:

One of the basic purposes of education in a democracy is to ensure the survival of the system by providing the young with understanding, skills, and values necessary for intelligent and humane interaction with others. Although reading, writing, and computation are basic to effective living, a curriculum based on those skills alone is likely to produce generations of citizens without the values and understanding needed to maintain a democratic society. . . . We must, therefore, aggressively lobby in every way possible for a broad definition of the basic skills, so that reading, writing, and computation can serve as the foundation for the study of history, government, values, and social concerns necessary for our students to live lives based on individual freedom and a concern for human well-being.

The author lets the reader know exactly where the issue must be confronted. "What ought to be" and "what is" cannot be neglected but *must buttress* "what can be." The S.O.S. is clear—educators must articulate a rationale and get into the arena for making decisions about curriculum matters. Law education—here we come!

The author then proceeds to list 10 steps for responsible action in developing and implementing law-related education programs for the elementary school: (1) design "ideal" programs; (2) study your community; (3) review value structures of the community; (4) know the community leaders; (5) compare program goals to community goals; (6) identify community concerns; (7) design strategies to resolve, manage, or avoid problems; (8) prepare rationale; (9) identify supporters for the program; and (10) identify supportive groups and ask their help in implementation. Step 1 concerns what ought to be; steps 2–5, what is; and steps 6–10, what can be.

In the course of the paper the author raises two very challenging questions but does not answer them directly. While the scope of the present paper does not allow a comprehensive review of these inquiries, they must be dealt with in the politics of making curriculum innovation successful. These two questions are: (1) "Is it our responsibility as professional educators simply to reflect the values of our community?" (2) "Is it possible that significant and desirable change can

still take place within the context of the present conservative view of the role that education plays in our society?" Clark implies, in my opinion, that the answer to the first question would be no—with an explanation that would encourage the educator to know the values of the community, discuss them with its members, and proceed with moderation. He makes a statement that will be a red flag to some: *"Educators are not free to make decisions on such issues without considering the values of their community"* (my emphasis). His answer to the second question is yes, because he has faith in educators, especially teachers, who are willing and able to get involved in the politics of curriculum innovation.

I agree with the author on all major points of his paper. I know that what he believes will work—for I have made it work. I have been confronted for 12 years with the responsibility for trying to make things happen in a state, the Commonwealth of Virginia, where sometimes change has been about as welcome as the plague. What has always been welcomed is a *sincere concern for making education better* for boys and girls. Now the rub is, How do I determine what is better? How does Todd Clark determine what is better? How do others in the community determine what is better?

- What ought to be: What do I think and what do others think?
- What is: What do I think and what do others think?
- What can be: What do I think and what do others think?

The most important thing to remember is the *sequence* of these three realms of discourse.

- Ask each question.
- Do not get them out of sequence.
- Spend equal time on each inquiry.
- Remember that no question is more important than another.
- Know the rationale for your answers and listen openly to others who may feel differently.

A few years ago the author and I attended a conference on controversy, censorship, and confrontation between educators and the public on certain issues. At the conference I shared five questions known as Sutton's Sieve. They have served me well. (1) Who is the quarterback in the baseball game? (2) Are the ducks in a row? (3) Why should people who live in glass houses not throw rocks? (4) How do yellow and red make orange? (5) How can holding hands with strangers help make new friends? These questions have provided me with an invaluable seismograph for the politics of curriculum innovation. These five questions may not seem too important on first glance, but the answers we give as we attempt to define "basic," develop and implement programs in law-related education for the elementary school, and prepare curriculum materials for law and the humanities may well determine the differences among premise, polemics, politics, phantoms of permanence, and pragmatism.

We can no longer afford to indulge mindlessness—new programs in citizenship education must have carefully developed statements of rationale (what ought to be). But even when we do develop a rationale, the program may not be suc-cessful if we do not understand the politics (what is) of our local communities.

And thank you, Todd Clark, for stimulating our thoughts on how we should go about getting our ideas and our programs implemented in the curriculum. Our programs are not useful if they remain on the shelf or if they run into the dead-end street of extreme community reaction and controversy.

Law and the humanities can provide exciting and challenging programs for elementary schools. Our task is to know what ought to be and what is and to prepare for what can be.

Bringing It Together

On the basis of the sum total of the foregoing papers, it would not be difficult to conclude that the state of educational affairs is so grim as to be hopelessly inimical to change, much less introduction of law and humanities on a systematic basis. Recognizing our own vulnerability as individuals firmly committed to a point of view (perhaps suffering from some of the same tunnel vision warned against in these papers), we do nonetheless offer an alternate interpretation. For the most part, the "lessons" of these papers are not overnight revelations with startling new conclusions. That they have long been unheeded, however, cannot be denied. Few will maintain that such "head-in-the-sandism" can persist without continued destructive results.

Perhaps the most loudly voiced lesson is that the day of the curriculum developer, teacher, administrator, or other educator operating effectively in isolation—from an ivory tower or intellectual cloister—is (or should be) well over. Educators must come to terms with the reality that schooling is but one part of a total system. Any significant impact on student learning must in one way or another affect this system, as well.

If we look at the lessons of these papers in a positive light, we can see considerable reason for optimism. They suggest stretching our creativity (perhaps even our psyches), taking some risks, inventing new ways for doing things, reconceptualizing ideas long since taken for granted. Most of all, *we must catch up with ourselves* by getting into the system, which keeps moving ahead and around regardless of our stance.

Some of the lessons of these papers are powerful—indeed at times poignant, especially in the continuous references to the "teacher's world." We are reminded over and over again that the teacher is not an isolate. The teacher *is a human being first,* responding to the environment in much the same ways as students do—with fear, with positive anticipation, with anxiety, with concern for self-preservation. The specialist in law-related education must keep in mind that the classroom teacher has other things to think about than the virtues of law and humanities in the elementary school! Another way of putting it is to remind ourselves of the oft-used phrase "to start where the students are." Perhaps we must also be equally concerned about "where teachers are."

Being sensitive to the culture of the classroom, then, requires that we also be sensitive to the culture of teaching. Today's culture is not replete with motivation devices—just the opposite. At one time, university credit provided important incentives for the teacher. Today, however, aging faculties "maxed out" on the salary schedules no longer need university credit for increment or contract renewals. The huge question emerges, What incentives are or can be provided to encourage positive change and learning—incentives for taking the time and trouble to make necessary commitments so vital for law and humanities education?

The educational system hasn't all of a sudden become political. As with several of the other issues discussed here, it is simply impossible to ignore this reality any longer. Such recognition requires that we take on a new view, a new intellectual posture—a new perception about education and politics. Rather than avoiding educational politics, we should develop appropriate skills and maximize the political process.

This new stance will require us to adopt a different perception as well as implement new strategies. Community education is but one area in need of such redefinition. Efforts must be made to take it beyond simplistic "parent-information nights" and public-relations mailings to students' homes. Indeed, a massive effort to educate and constructively involve citizens in the educational system must be made immediately. Such an effort should be characterized by citizens having access to the ongoing curriculum in the same way students do. It should provide adults with an opportunity to learn substantive information about the local curriculum and its educational goals, and with legitimate opportunities for ongoing dialogue regarding the curriculum and educational process. This altered perception of community education may be understood better if the term "teacher" is stretched a bit, to include parents and other members of the community who influence the intellectual and emotional growth of our youth. After all, aren't parents among the most influential teachers of all? What about TV and other media? If we allow the definition of "teacher" to grow as it should, there will be strong indications for new and modified training programs which universities will be called upon to invent. "Invent" is a word used several times throughout these summary remarks. The word in itself suggests another theme of the papers. We will need not just different ways of dealing with long-standing problems, but strategies reflecting different visions and understandings of a new reality.

Another thread found not only throughout the articles in this section but indeed throughout this entire collection is the need for deliberate, careful, and long-term planning. It rules out the desirability or usefulness of "one-shotism." Thoughtful planning allows developers to identify ways "connectedness" already exists among the various activities which need to be undertaken and among the various individuals who should be involved in implementing a curriculum effort.

This chapter is a collection of challenges. Perhaps the greatest one, however, relates directly to the title of this book and philosophical theme of this elementary education project—that is, the links between law and humanities. Nearly every paper (sometimes by omission) emphasizes that the total environment does not reward, much less offer sensitivity to, the humanities. Our authors acknowledge dissonance between the goals of the humanities and the visions of much of the population. If our efforts to integrate law and humanities into the curriculum of elementary schools are to be successful, considerable adjustments in fundamental attitudes and perspectives must be made by those on the outside—namely, the taxpayers and all who might be termed "teachers"!

Evaluation

An Introduction

Is evaluation the inherent nemesis of education? Can it ever be viewed as other than the bane of our existence? Few areas remain as little understood, as much neglected and generally resisted, as the field of evaluation. While considerable progress has been made in substantive and philosophical areas associated with teaching about law and humanities, evaluation has retained its tradition of being relegated to the background and generally regarded as an invention of gremlins and other mischievous beings.

To some extent its dubious position has been warranted. It does not take an expert in evaluation to know that many efforts have been perfunctory, political, and tenuously associated with key student learning. Neither does it take an expert, however, to recognize that such a situation *need not* be the case! Indeed, strong evidence exists suggesting that evaluation *can play* a valuable role in the overall educational processes within our schools.

In our attempt to clarify and finally distill the essence of that potential role, we became dramatically aware of the need to adjust—indeed, expand—our own thinking about evaluation in general. These adjusted visions have taken into account the varying and sometimes divergent perspectives provided by "authorities" in the field of evaluation. The incredible diversity of viewpoints emerges as a clear theme and important lesson for us to remember.

Out of this diversity, however, some other key themes have surfaced. The papers in this section appear to be in accord in emphasizing the following points:

1. Evaluation must be an integral part of the entire educational program. As with law and humanities content, evaluation should not be undertaken as an "add-on" or piecemeal activity.
2. Evaluation should begin at the earliest stages of program or curriculum development. It should flow logically from the clearly stated goals of the law and humanities program.
3. The evaluation design should be consistent with the rationale and philosophical basis of the program of curriculum.
4. No preexisting ideal model for evaluation can be found which is applicable for all programs and all situations.

Program Evaluation: A Collage of Views

Edward Hirsch, Edward Nelsen and John Wick

As with classroom evaluation, program evaluation in law-related education has received little serious attention. And as in the classroom, the ideas of what *should* be done in program evaluation are broad and diverse. It seemed obvious that a single paper on the subject could not adequately touch upon all the salient issues or, more important, reflect key philosophical perspectives. Thus, we invited three persons, each highly regarded in the field of evaluation, to share their views about evaluation in relation to teaching about law and humanities.

Two dominant themes emerge from these papers. First, no preexisting ideal evaluation model—suitable for all occasions—can be found. Second, whatever the final model looks like, it should reflect a logical flow from specifically stated goals of the project or curriculum.

Each of these papers' authors has served as the evaluator of a law-related education project and thus brings lessons of experience and practical application to the issues at hand.

Comments by Edward Hirsch

The guidelines for the design of this paper stipulate that it should provide teachers with information they can use to assess the effectiveness of law and humanities programs at the elementary school level. Since I believe that teachers have enough responsibilities already, I will address my remarks instead to those I think should bear the burden of this responsibility—program developers and program selectors. If teachers happen to be among their numbers, more power to them.

In the drama of instructional development, those who evaluate the effectiveness of programs often play the "heavy." Why? Are they inherently evil people, or does the role they play require them to act in ways which evoke hisses and boos? Since some of my best friends are evaluators, I must accept the latter explanation. To understand

Ed Hirsch develops instructional programs in consultation with a variety of organizations. He is currently exploring the instructional and commercial potential of programming for new and emerging electronic media.

Edward A. Nelsen is Associate Professor of Educational Psychology at Arizona State University and Associate Director for Experimental Programs in the I. D. Payne Laboratory. He is currently directing a study of computer-based simulations of behavior related to rules and laws.

John W. Wick is Professor of Education at Northwestern University. He recently served as Director of Research and Evaluation of the Chicago Board of Education and is author of a comprehensive assessment program for Scott Foresman and Company.

why evaluators feel compelled to act as they do, let's examine the role and see if we can transform it so that those who are asked to assess the effectiveness of law and humanities programs at the elementary school level can be the heroes they always wanted to be.

If you believe, as I do, that the major thrust of program evaluation is determining the extent to which instructional programs promote the achievement of prespecified objectives, then you must realize why evaluators are hardly ever satisfied with the way those objectives are stated. Evaluators require objectives which are as operational as possible. Therefore they constantly badger program developers to write objectives with the kind of precision and specificity that strain the patience and endurance of mere mortals. The process of refining and explicating objectives until they are operational enough for the evaluator to generate measurement instruments often seems a drain on the all too limited time and energy needed to develop the actual instructional program.

Just when you think you have evaluators where you want them, in their offices cranking out test items, observation schedules, and whatever other exotic devices they are capable of conjuring up, they begin to pester you again. Inclined as they are to use the jargon of their trade, now all they talk about is "formative evaluation." In case you haven't heard, formative evaluation is the collection and analysis of data which can be used to improve a program as it is being developed.

Formative evaluation involves the field testing of prototype instructional materials and procedures—lesson plans, treatments, scripts, story-boards, and illustrations—to determine the likeli-hood that more polished versions will facilitate the attainment of program objectives. It requires a commitment to successive approximations of the finished product. Moreover, it requires program developers to foresake the safety of their offices and theories in favor of the cold, hard reality of classroom experience. This process of trying out materials and procedures with individuals, small groups, and eventually entire classes is often regarded as an additional strain on the resources available for program development even though the most informal and least rigorous research designs may be employed. Is it any wonder, then, that evaluators are sometimes perceived to be wearing villainous costumes when they themselves believe they are actually models of heroic sartorial splendor?

Assuming that the development and field test-ing of prototype materials and procedures even-tually yields an instructional program which may reasonably be expected to promote the achieve-ment of its objectives, some individual, school, or agency will surely demand that the program be subjected to the rigors of what evaluators call "summative evaluation." The major thrust of this process is determining the quality of a completed program in order to decide whether to adopt it, reject it, or retain it. Whether they are working for the program developer or the program selec-tor, it is at this juncture that evaluators generally transcend villainy and become absolute monsters.

In order to demonstrate that student achieve-ment results from a program's implementation and not from other experiences, or maturation, or particularly effective teachers, or from the added charge that a new program may generate, evalu-ators historically have required that some form of control-group experiment be undertaken. To in-sure that the results of the investigation will apply to the population for which a program has been designed (the target population), they try to draw a representative sample of students to serve as an experimental group and a corresponding sample to serve as the control group.

Ideally evaluators would like to assign students randomly to both groups. But it is virtually im-possible to do that in a school setting where classes and instructional groups must remain in-tact. Therefore, they frequently resort to the use of the classroom as the experimental unit and ran-domly assign each classroom to either the experi-mental or control group. Since the ability of teachers is an important variable to control, it becomes necessary to assign enough classrooms to each group to minimize the influence teaching ability might have on the outcome. Inevitably, hundreds of students become involved in the

study. While it may be possible to analyze only a portion of the data generated and still draw valid conclusions, the planning and organizing required present formidable challenges.

Depending on the nature of a program's objec-tives, a variety of assessment devices might have to be prepared, field tested, and eventually ad-ministered to prospective students. Such devices include: written tests requiring selected or con-structed responses, oral interviews, and observa-tion schedules to document behavior patterns, both in and out of the classroom, which might be indicative of anticipated attitude changes. Each type of assessment device has a legitimate function in determining the efficacy of an instructional pro-gram. However, there are costs associated with each which merit consideration.

Multiple-choice tests are relatively easy to ad-minister and score but quite difficult to develop. This is particularly true of tests designed to measure the attainment of high-level cognitive skills and of survey instruments designed to monitor changes in attitude. On the other hand, instruments which are designed to elicit construct-ed responses, whether written or oral, are not on-ly difficult to develop but may also be hard to ad-minister and score. They are difficult to develop because of the necessity to explicate fully whatever criteria will be used to determine the adequacy of responses.

Even when criteria have been fully explicated, the evaluation of constructed responses is no sim-ple matter. It is usually so time-consuming that a scorer is required to demonstrate that criteria have been applied consistently from the first set of responses to the last set. When several scorers are employed, either to save time or to minimize scor-ing bias, they must practice the application of criteria until they can demonstrate that their in-dependent ratings of a common set of responses are highly consistent. Naturally raters should have a way of knowing whether they are rating the response of a member of the experimental group or the response of a control-group member. The collection and interpretation of interview data im-pose additional restrictions. Interviewers may not deviate from the established procedure. Nor should they be able to determine the experimental status of those being interviewed.

Since observations are supposed to reveal pat-terns of behavior, it is necessary to observe students as frequently and systematically as possi-ble. Practical problems abound. If forewarned, students and teachers are likely to behave in ways which are expected of them. However, unan-nounced classroom visits by outsiders are bound to be disruptive and anxiety-provoking. At any rate, observers must be careful not to invade the privacy of those involved in the study. Finally, in experiments involving many classrooms, there are seldom sufficient staff members to ensure frequent observations in every classroom.

Then there is the evaluator's report, replete with technical language, tables, charts, columns of figures, and all too often the revelation that there were no statistically significant differences found between the experimental and control groups. It is hardly surprising that evaluators are sometimes perceived to be the bane of their employers' existence. They are so very demanding and exacting. They see mountains where others see molehills. They consume vast amounts of resources in the performance of their duties. And, they add insult to injury by failing so often to provide their employers with evidence to support one decision or another. The situation is especially touchy when an evaluator is employed by the program developer, who naturally has a vested interest in the outcome of whatever study is undertaken.

What can be done to help us avoid perpetuating the somewhat facetious view of evaluators described above? How can we best take advantage of evaluators' genuine and much needed talents to ensure the development and implementation of effective law and humanities programs at the elementary school level? To answer these questions, let's first look at ways in which evaluation expertise might be employed in program development. Then let's examine how such expertise might be employed by program selectors.

It must be admitted that the descriptor "law and humanities" is quite vague. Under such a rubric any number of conceivable programs might be developed. How does one decide what to teach? It seems to me that the discipline of evaluation has a lot to offer those who must answer that question. Indeed, the phrase "needs assessment" is mentioned quite frequently in professional journals and touted at professional meetings. Although I am not familiar with many of the attempts to determine curricular needs in a systematic way, the idea appeals to me. Conducting a needs assessment is bound to involve collecting, organizing, analyzing, and finally evaluating information. Since that is what evaluators are paid to do, it seems reasonable to expect the evaluator's role to include helping plan and carry out a need's assessment.

Once the goals of a prospective law and humanities program have been agreed upon, the next order of business is to develop a set of objectives which can be used to generate assessment devices and a coherent and systematic instructional strategy. It is important to realize that some of the most worthy objectives may not be readily achieved. Students might require repeated exposures to appropriate instructional stimuli over a long period of time before achieving them. The attainment of other objectives, particularly those in the affective domain, may be extremely difficult if not impossible to evaluate. There may be legal and moral problems in obtaining relevant data. It is for these reasons that I suggest that objectives be divided into four nonexclusive categories: long range, short term, practical to evaluate, and difficult to evaluate. In this way program developers will not be promising more than they can reasonably be expected to deliver.

Before developing instructional materials and procedures, it will be helpful to develop a set of evaluation instruments for those short-term objectives which are practical to evaluate. These instruments should then be administered to a sample of students from the target population. This process serves two purposes. First, it provides program developers with baseline data they can use to determine the suitability of those objectives for that population. Second, by providing developers with graphic examples of uninstructed students' abilities as well as a more complete and refined picture of what students will be expected to accomplish after instruction, this process should render invaluable assistance in the selection and construction of suitable learning opportunities.

The next order of business is to establish the sort of relationship with nearby schools that will permit designated staff members to visit those schools frequently to try out materials and procedures while they are still malleable. It may strike some as hearsay if not blasphemy, but I believe that more valuable information may be gleaned from frequent, informal, yet well-documented contacts between developers, teachers, and students while a program is being developed than may be obtained from the most rigorous control-group experiment conducted upon completion of the program.

It is easier to conduct formative evaluation in elementary schools than it is to do so at the secondary level. Scheduling tends to be more flexible, and there seems to be less of a sense of urgency to fulfill established course requirements. But there is one major difficulty. Students are generally unable to express themselves adequately in written form. Therefore a much greater reliance must be placed on well-documented observations and on tape-recorded interviews and conversations with students. In spite of this problem, the techniques and devices which evaluators use to collect, organize, analyze, and evaluate pertinent data may be put to good use in the formative evaluation of law and humanities programs for elementary school students.

Does this mean that the rigorous experimental designs commonly associated with summative evaluation have no place in assessing the efficacy of these programs? My inclination is to say they do not. It seems to me that large-scale experiments designed to assess the effectiveness of instructional programs are only appropriate when a decision has to be made by program selectors regarding the adoption or retention of one of several programs designed to promote the achievement of a common set of objectives. For example, if a district must decide which of three competing geometry programs to adopt, it makes sense to conduct an experiment designed to determine which program must effectively promote the achievement of commonly accepted geometry objectives.

It is highly unlikely that there will be even two law and humanities programs at the elementary level with identical or even similar objectives. In most cases, deciding which program to adopt will depend upon three things: (1) an inspection of each program's objectives to determine if they are compatible with the district's goals; (2) documented proof that the program was field tested as it was being developed with students similar to those who reside in the district; and (3) a demonstration in selected schools that the program can be implemented with ease and effectiveness.

I feel confident that the application of the principles set forth herein will contribute to the development and implementation of effective law and humanities programs at the elementary school level. It should also result in a more suitable image for those of us who try so valiantly to assess the efficacy of such programs.

Comments by Edward Nelsen

Evaluation is often viewed as a terminal process. Typically, evaluators are employed as a project nears completion to assess its successes and failures. The evaluator's role resembles that of the accountant who is employed by an executor to assay the estate of a deceased person. For example, he or she determines the net value of the estate after assessing assets and liabilities of the deceased. However, evaluation need not be limited simply to retrospective accounting. Indeed, the evaluator's role should begin at a project's inception, and evaluation should serve both practical and productive purposes at any stage of the project.

The variety of functions an evaluation may serve is unlimited and may touch upon many aspects of a project. For example, evaluation studies may be designed to achieve any of the following purposes:

1. To assess needs and establish priorities for an instructional program—for example, as a basis for program planning.
2. To assist in the development and clarification of project goals.
3. To provide periodic appraisals of the curriculum, instructional materials, staff performance, etc.—for example, as a basis for improving the quality of program.
4. To identify problems and issues hindering the operations of the project and to recommend solutions or strategies to improve the effectiveness of program operations.
5. To assess student achievement—for example, as a basis for providing feedback, grades, or certification.
6. To document the accomplishments and benefits of a program—for example, to seek support for its expansion.
7. To fulfill an obligation to sponsoring agencies or administrators—for example, to provide interim or final accounting, documentation, or appraisal of a program.

The common elements among these evaluation activities are: (*a*) systematic analysis, (*b*) documentation, (*c*) evaluative judgment, and (*d*) prescription. In other words, the basic functions of the evaluator are first, to portray the essential components of the project systematically as a basis for formulating an evaluation design; second, to gather relevant qualitative and quantitative data that pertain to the essential operations and outcomes of the program; third, to analyze and interpret the data as a basis for judging plans, activities, and outcomes; and finally, to offer helpful and appropriate recommendations on the basis of the judgments.

Differing purposes for evaluation studies. The purposes for various evaluation studies may differ according to the nature of the projects. Depending upon the nature of a project, evaluation studies may be conducted at various levels of program operation or with varying scopes. For example, they might focus upon any one or more of the following purposes: (*a*) operational components, such as curriculum models or instructional activities; (*b*) impact upon students, such as attitude change or academic achievements; (*c*) broader impacts and benefits of individual projects; or (*d*) comparison of the effects of alternative models or project units.

It is important that project administrators and policy makers clarify the major purpose(s) and scope of the evaluation as a basis for developing the evaluation plan. Ideally, the purposes should be clearly specified and prioritized as a matter of policy. This can be accomplished by formulating major evaluation questions and determining what potential consequences and decisions might follow from the answers. Of course, the priorities and plans should be mutually agreed upon by project sponsors, administrators, staff, and other concerned parties, as well as the project evaluators.

Development of a program design and evaluation plan. Having established the purposes and scope of the evaluation, the next step in evaluation planning involves developing an overview of the program design. This design specifies major *program objectives* in relation to all relevant *program inputs* (resources) and *processes* (e.g., instruction, administration, materials development). With the major program components specified in a design, an evaluation plan can be prepared. This plan should propose the *evaluation objectives, evaluation questions, instrumentation* (e.g., variety, types, and formats), *evaluation schedules* (e.g., formative and summative stages, pilot studies, data collection timetable), *data collection responsibilities, statistical design,* and *report specifications.* The plan should be well conceptualized and feasible and should specify responsibilities, costs, or other required resources for all major phases. However, it should not be viewed as fixed or final—it should be regarded as a proposal that summarizes current thinking but is subject to revision and elaboration as the project progresses.

In preparing an evaluation plan, it may be helpful to keep in mind that the most common weaknesses in evaluation plans are: (*a*) lack of clarity about basic purposes of the evaluation; (*b*) failure to specify clearly the most relevant and important questions; (*c*) selection of instruments that are not relevant to the evaluation questions or the project objectives; (*d*) preoccupation with statistical methods and technicalities rather than program substance; and (*e*) overambition, that is, promising to measure and analyze too many variables.

Role and responsibilities of the evaluator. An evaluator should be designated early in the planning phase of a project. In making the selection the following considerations are important: general evaluation experience (communication skills, etc.); knowledge and experience related to the project mission (i.e., law-related education, humanities, elementary school curriculum); professional integrity and reputation; and institutional affiliation and obligations (e.g., sufficient independence versus supervisory or personal relationships with project administrators and staff).

The evaluator's responsibilities should be negotiated and structured so that they are clearly understood and separate from conflicting or incompatible project activities. For example, the evaluator should generally not assume a supervisory relationship to project administrators or staff, nor should the evaluator be responsible for directing project activities that he or she is also to evaluate. That is not to say that the evaluator must be entirely detached from the project. The evaluator might appropriately serve in planning, instructional, and/or mediating capacities, insofar as these involvements do not impede or bias the evaluation process.

The functions and duties of the evaluator will evolve or unfold as the project progresses through successive stages. During the planning phase he or she can assist with the development and improvement of the project proposal and plans. For example, an evaluator can contribute to planning by clarifying objectives, by delineating relationships between project activities and intended outcomes, and by assisting with documentation of the project design. Once a project progresses from initial planning to an operational basis, the evaluator's functions may include gathering data to identify and solve problems, documenting progress and successive accomplishments, compiling reviews of project curriculum and material, and/or development and pilot testing of various assessment instruments and procedures. In the latter stages of the project, the evaluator's role will presumably shift toward its more traditional form, involving assessment of project outcomes in relation to project objectives and formulation of summative judgments and conclusions concerning the project's accomplishments and limitations.

The role of an advisory committee. Development and implementation of an evaluation plan can often be aided by an advisory committee, comprised of key project staff and representatives of various constituencies involved in the project, such as administrators, teachers, students, parents. An evaluation committee can serve several functions, such as: (*a*) formulate, clarify, and prioritize major evaluation questions or issues; (*b*) review and clarify evaluation instruments; (*c*) explain evaluation issues and procedures to constituents and solicit their cooperation; (*d*) assist with various evaluation tasks, such as collecting or processing data, writing reports, etc.; and (*e*) formulate and critique conclusions and endorse recommendations emanating from evaluation reports, etc.

Problems and issues in evaluation of law and humanities education projects. The general discussion of evaluation purposes, functions, and strategies applies to most evaluation endeavors. Consideration of projects concerning law and humanities education raises substantive questions such as: (*a*) What are the relative effects of alternative models—for example, in terms of impact upon student attitudes and knowledge? (*b*) What are the most appropriate objectives, scope, and structure of various curricula, considering the existing school curriculum in the humanities and social sciences? (*c*) To what extent are teachers and administrators disposed to support a project concerning law and humanities education? (*d*) How are the various attitudes and interests of students supportive of or antagonistic toward the program? (*e*) What are the existing community standards, concerns, and viewpoints related to education?

Thus, an evaluation design relating to law and humanities faces a number of unique problems that evaluations of programs with more traditional subject matter might not face. The first problem concerns the clarity and scope of the broad goals of instructional programs. Because basic concepts of law, morality, and the humanities are abstract and potentially ambiguous, it may be difficult to specify and agree upon the goals of a program, except in the most general terms. For example, a program's goals might concern attainment of knowledge and attitudes relating to "responsible citizenship," "support for social justice," or "principled moral reasoning." Unless these concepts are carefully defined, the goal statements may be susceptible to diverse interpretations as a function of the interpreter's political biases, cultural background, academic specialization, or personal beliefs and values. Varying interpretations of the program goals may, in turn, produce differences in specific program objectives, operations, and contents. Moreover, with respect to evaluation procedures, the diverse conceptions of program goals are likely to result in conflicts or misunderstandings concerning the translation of project goals into specific objectives and measures for assessing project outcomes. Thus, if goals are misinterpreted, the evaluation could become controversial and be challenged on the basis of "invalid" or inappropriate measures.

The second problem that should be considered in planning and evaluating a law and humanities education program concerns the complexity of cognitive and affective characteristics related to law, society, and humanities education. For a law and humanities program to be effective, teachers must be aware of their own attitudes and also sensitive and responsive to the cultural and individual differences in attitudes of students. Moreover, for an evaluation plan to be germane and useful, comprehensive conceptualization and measurement of relevant teacher attitudes and of student attitude changes must be considered as part of the evaluation, as well as part of the program. In-

dividual and cultural differences in cognitive-developmental stages, moral reasoning, cultural values, personal attitudes toward law and authority, and literary, musical, and artistic tastes may affect the teacher's as well as the students' interest, involvement, and achievement in both humanities and law-related education programs. This is true, presumably, because both law and humanities relate to so many personal and cultural experiences in the lives of the students. Experiences related to police and crime, on the one hand, and literature, music, and art, on the other, may often arouse strong and diverse affective reactions among different groups of individuals.

Special consideration for evaluating elementary-level programs. Elementary-level programs are seeemingly more difficult than secondary or adult programs to evaluate, since most traditional self-report, paper-and-pencil measures of attitudes and characteristics are inappropriate for children below the junior high school level. For example, there are few, if any, self-report measures of authoritarianism, moral development, social responsibility, or social consciousness that are suitable for primary-age children. Moreover, young children are less able than adolescents to provide objective or written self-portrayals of their knowledge and attitudes. Thus, written materials and responses, especially at earlier grade levels and with lower-SES children, will have limited utility.

Nevertheless, limitations of existing self-report instruments and restrictions upon written materials do not preclude the development of valid, relevant, and useful measures for assessing program impact. A variety of data collection procedures and instrument formats may be employed, including direct observation, interviews, tape recording of orally presented questionnaires, sentence or story completion, drawings, teacher or parent reports, videotaping or transcription of responses in games or simulations, ethnographic or case studies, etc.

Ideally, evaluation procedures will be a natural outgrowth of the classroom activities, learning exercises, or instructional games. For example, children's drawings, stories, or poems may be used as an expressive learning activity, and they may also be scored for themes or schemas to assess changing concepts or attitudes. That is, pupils might be asked to write stories with illustrations concerning a crime, including a policeman, a law violator, a victim, and a bystander. The instrument could be administered on a pre-post basis and scored to assess changes in children's concepts of authority, power, crime, and responsibility. Likewise, plays or dramatic activities could be adapted to nurture and observe pupils' capacities to assume alternative roles or perspectives.

As an additional example, students could be surveyed concerning their attitudes toward capital punishment. Following a discussion or simulation (e.g., a mock trial), another survey could be taken to assess the degree of change in attitudes and concepts related to capital punishment.

Evaluation procedures, as well as instructional activities, may also be related to the school environment and natural events and situations. For example, children's understanding of and attitudes toward school rules may be a topic of discussion and may be assessed through interviews or questionnaires. Instruments are also available to assess characteristics of the classroom climate, such as "democracy," "rule clarity," or "authoritarianism."

Contributions of evaluation to curricular integration and improvement. A comprehensive evaluation plan could contribute to integration of law and humanities concepts into the broader school curriculum in a number of ways. First, development of a program integrating law with existing humanities and social sciences curricula might begin with a systematic review and evaluation of the objectives, instructional materials, and learning activities of an existing school curriculum. This review should consider the curriculum in all subject matter areas, including the natural and social sciences as well as the arts and humanities, to determine potential relationships and opportunities for integration. The curricular sequence from kindergarten through the elementary grades should also be reviewed and analyzed. From this framework, potential relationships of legal concepts to the existing curriculum should be noted in a creative and flexible manner. Thus, development of an integrated law-humanities program could begin with a review, analysis, and evaluation of the existing curriculum, and proceed with a creative analysis and formulation of an expanded curriculum.

There are many directions such an analysis and formulation might take. First, broad frameworks are suggested by Piaget's (1932) and Kohlberg's (1976) analyses of stages of moral development. Another relevant framework is suggested by Isidore Starr's conception (in this volume) of an integrated curriculum in terms of children's developing interests in and capacities to comprehend concepts related to power, justice, liberty, property, and equality. These concepts are sometimes explicitly discussed in children's literature, art, music, and drama, as well as in history and social studies. More commonly, phenomena related to these concepts are implicitly expressed, not only in these curricular areas, but in noncurricular aspects of the school environment, for example, in school rules and disciplinary policies, in student governance, in the teachers' relationships to the children and in children's relationships to one another. Second, a review of research and theory related to the project may facilitate the conceptualization of curricular objectives; student abilities, interests, and other characteristics; and forces affecting students' interests. Third, systematic data-gathering instruments for assessment of children's concepts related to the curriculum (e.g., assessing children's concepts of "justice") may provide teachers with concrete examples of existing viewpoints and attitudes as points of departure for instruction in law and humanities. Fourth, documentation of changes in children's attitudes toward rules or their concepts (e.g., pre- and post-levels of comprehension or interpretations of law-related situations) may provide evidence concerning the nature of attitude change and academic achievement that may be realistically expected with a particular age level or type of children.

Conclusion. The complex nature of evaluation plans and procedures for an innovative law and humanities education project implies that development and implementation of the plans and procedures must be guided and overseen by an experienced evaluator who has a broad repertoir of evaluation skills and substantive knowledge related to elementary school curricula, the humanities, and law-related education. For example, an evaluation team may be constituted of professionals with complementary skills and knowledge related to the program. These evaluators must work closely with the evaluation advisory committee to develop plans and procedures.

One must face many complex issues when planning the evaluation procedures. The following list of questions raises some of the issues that should be resolved as one begins the planning process:

1. Why evaluate? What are the evaluation questions? What decisions will be influenced by the results of the evaluation? How will the results be used?

2. Is there a relevant theoretical base for planning the project and the evaluation?

3. Who should be involved in the evaluation planning (e.g., central staff, local administrators, participating staff, etc.)? This relates to the questions of who will be most affected by the outcomes and results of the evaluation study and how the results will be used.

4. Should the evaluation design(s) and in-

struments for various projects be coordinated to facilitate comparability of results?

5. Who should conduct the evaluation (e.g., internal or external; central or local)?

6. How will the evaluation be financed and how will financial sponsorship affect the evaluation? What portion of a project's resources should be allocated to evaluation of the project?

7. What personnel are available to develop evaluation designs, plans, and instruments; collect and analyze data; and write interpretive reports that contribute substantially to the purposes of the project?

8. How much data should be collected and how often?

9. From what sources will the data be collected?

10. Who should be involved in interpretation of the results?

11. What form will the final report take and to whom will it be directed?

These questions raise critical issues that should be carefully considered as bases for evaluation planning. If they are satisfactorily resolved, a sound evaluation plan can be developed. More specific practical and technical issues will certainly arise as specific evaluation plans are developed and implemented. However, if the basic issues raised herein have been considered, the evaluation process is likely to contribute substantially to the effective implementation of an innovative, worthwhile project.

REFERENCES

Kohlberg, L. Moral stages and moralization: The cognitive-developmental approach. In T. Lickona (Ed.), *Moral development and behavior.* New York: Holt, Rinehart & Winston, 1976.
Piaget, J. *The moral judgment of the child.* London: Kegan Paul, 1932.

Comments by John Wick

The questions I have been asked to address in this paper are of necessity overlapping, and so I'm going to respond in some detail to a few of them, and very briefly to the others.

1. *Statement of rationale and assumptions respecting the role of evaluation generally, with application specifically to programs focusing on law and the humanities.* People usually develop a new educational program for one of two reasons. The first is a situation where the program developer believes that a void exists, that is, that no program currently is available to fill an existing need. The second reason for a new approach is a situation where the program developer believes that he or she can put together a substantially more effective educational program than the existing one in some particular area.

The very term "evaluation" implies assessing, measuring, and valuing. Assessing and valuing give one a good place to start in addressing the rationale and assumptions with respect to the role of evaluation. Evaluating the objectives of a project implies assessing the degree to which the objectives were met—not only assessing changes between the moment the project began until it ended, but assessing changes in a formative manner as the project develops. Assessing the degree to which objectives have been met presumes that the objectives have been stated in such a way that they can be measured and that the evaluator is clever enough to devise techniques for gathering objective information. Actually, developing the instruments or techniques to gather the objective information is the easier part of the evaluation process. Interviews, observations, tests, physical measures, all these information-collecting devices are available. The hardest part is stating the goals of the project in some sort of objective manner, so that these can be translated into measurable outcomes.

The second part of the definition of "evaluation," the valuing part, is the more difficult side to address in an evaluation format. Whereas the first part, the assessment, addresses the question, Did the project achieve the goals which it set out to achieve? the second part addresses the question, Were the goals this project set out to achieve worth achieving at all? Or, putting it another way, is pursuit of the goals of this project more important than what the students would be doing if this project did not exist. These kinds of questions, the valuing questions, go well beyond the scope of the evaluator, for these are the kinds of questions the general public and the people who make long-range decisions about what the educational process should be must answer.

The above statement is particularly appropriate to programs which focus on law and the humanities. Usually, at the elementary school levels, these programs are part of a social studies curriculum. Some groups feel that the social studies curriculum should focus on economics. Other groups say it should focus on citizenship. Others say children will be better off, in terms of liberal arts, if the social studies curriculum focuses on history. The demand for social studies time from people of various persuasions is great, whereas in some areas, such as reading comprehension and mathematical skills, one finds little disagreement among reasonable adults about what should be taught. Thus, both elements of the evaluation term, the valuing and the assessing, should be specifically addressed in any evaluation program dealing with law and the humanities.

2. *What are the programmatic features of evaluation designs generally regarded as "successful"? That is, how do you know a successful evaluation design when you see it? Perhaps make some reference here to the most common weaknesses found in evaluation designs.* This question is particularly hard to answer, since the nature of evaluation designs is that they respond to very specific and very different projects. Thus it is hard to come up with one simple statement about what a good evaluation design is. If such a statement were possible, there would be far more agreement among various evaluation programs, far less difficulty in interpreting evaluation results. However, these kinds of things are worth looking for, and in discussing this question I'm going to mix up the things to look for and the things to avoid.

a) Most evaluation results are difficult to interpret in an absolute sense. They only make sense in terms of trend analyses. Wherever possible, the measured data should be gathered at stated intervals over a substantial period of time. The well-documented decline in college board scores only became of some concern after 3 or 4 years of annual assessments. The changes each year were very small. It was the trend of the downward scores that finally caused people to sit up and notice. This is probably true of programs related to the law. The impact of the programs on certain important variables, such as respect for the law as manifested in a variety of ways, or avoidance of getting into trouble with the law as manifested in a variety of ways, will probably be small and only perceptible across a substantial period of time.

To be avoided are evaluation designs which deal only with initial and final measures, with no information gathered prior to the initial measure, between the two, or after the end of the program. When changes occur in a simple pre- and post-test design, it is difficult to figure out whether the changes are due to the program or to some other situation which occurred during the program, and whether the changes are going to last after the program ends.

b) I look for a clear, simple set of goal statements. If the person designing the evaluation program must go into elaborate detail involving the use of language and terms not comprehensible to the average generalist in the field, then one gets the idea that the evaluation is not going to provide any other information understandable to the average generalist. If the goals cannot be stated in clear, simple language, albeit in measurable terms, then one must question whether the project itself is an attempt at obfuscation.

c) Another thing to look for is an evaluation design specifically put together for the project at hand. As I stated before, projects are started either to fill a void or to improve upon the way current education is delivered. Projects, then, span all kinds of different areas and address all kinds of different concerns, and very few, even within the same area, are as much the same as they are different. Whenever a person or an organization attempts to superimpose essentially the same series of objectives or measures or techniques on one problem or project after another, I feel they haven't seriously considered the goals of a specific project, but instead are treating it superficially.

d) Another point is that the evaluation, in almost all cases, should not be based solely on standardized tests. If the objectives of the project can be stated in measurable terms and broken down into suitable hierarchical performance goals, then the best way to do the evaluation is to monitor the rate at which individuals master the objectives. Then the evaluation is based on average performance of the group and individual variations in performance within the group. Techniques for gathering information are widespread, and a design which is based only on standardized tests makes me wonder if the person who wrote it has had very much experience in evaluating projects.

3. *Description of the unique needs (if any) which a program seeking to integrate law and the humanities into an existing curriculum might have and which should be reflected in the evaluation design.* That is, does an evaluation design focusing on *law* as opposed to mathematics need to take any particular issues into consideration? What about the *humanities* component? How does the evaluation design address the unique needs (if any) of that area?

I touched on this question in my response to question 1, in saying that the second part of the evaluation definition, the valuing part, is particularly important as we decide or attempt to decide the extent to which one approach to law and humanities is preferable to a variety of others.

There is another answer to this item. When one measures objectives in mathematics, the sequencing of the topics introduced is relatively obvious. That is, one would not try to teach children to add three-digit numbers with three renamings involved until one had taught them to add one-digit numbers with a single renaming involved, or three-digit numbers with a single renaming. That is, the sequence of hierarchical skills is relatively clear. When one moves from mathematics and the sciences to somewhat less concrete areas, like reading, the topic becomes a little more difficult. Even here, however, we know what the outcome is to be, that the child, as time goes by, should approach reading comprehension at an adult level. The measurement of reading comprehension is not a particularly difficult task, although there is some controversy over this. Over the past 10 years, a variety of people have put together fairly acceptable series of hierarchical objectives which move a child in some 200–400 steps from the point of a prereader to being a fully functioning adult reader.

In the area of law education and in the humanities, placing things in a series of hierarchical objectives becomes more difficult. This is not because these areas are not important, but rather because the overall goals are not as clearly explicated as in fields like mathematics and reading comprehension.

It is here that the need for topics raised in the questions above becomes even more important. That is, because it is possible to be quite vague and because there may be widely divergent beliefs about the overall expected outcomes of programs, it is even more necessary to make clear, simple goal statements which can be fully understood by people in the field. Of course, when you state your goals in clear and simple words, it is easier for people who disagree to understand what you are saying and, therefore, disagree, which is, in my opinion, one reason why many people make goal statements in nonspecific, obfuscating language. It is also important to state the expected outcomes in terms which can be measured objectively so that everyone can understand what the project is trying to do and whether or not the goals are actually achieved.

4. *Description of the unique needs of elementary school programs in relation to the development of an evaluation instrument. Are there specific issues which must be considered when evaluating programs at the K–6 level rather than secondary grades?* Obviously, for the first 3 years of the K–6 program the evaluation techniques are difficult because the children cannot read. The usual standardized testing programs begin in the second grade, although all of them are in agreement that the tests must be read to the child, except in certain areas. Even at grade 3 a substantial number of children are not yet comfortable readers, in terms of reading comprehension; and it takes a very sensitive test writer to write questions which discriminate on the basis of the students' real knowledge of information in the area being tested, and not on the basis of the students' reading comprehension level. Thus, for at least the K–3 levels, evaluation design should include things like classroom observations, student interviews, tests read to the student by the teacher, tests presented via tape recorders or video equipment, and all sorts of things which do not accidentally measure reading comprehension rather than program performance. This advice is particularly true if the program is being introduced in

an urban area with substantial proportions of educationally disadvantaged students.

A second point specifically concerns programs involving law-related education for K–6 students. Of the many purposes for introducing law-related issues to elementary school children, one frequently stated is a belief that a better understanding of our laws and legal system in this country will result in more respect for law, better citizenship, and perhaps eventually less trouble with the law by students so taught. Students don't usually get in trouble with the law in the first 6 years of schooling, although obviously some students already exhibit citizenship behavior that is not what the normative group would like to see. If an important goal of a law-related program is indeed to develop adult citizens who are more respectful of and responsive to the law and therefore have less trouble with it and behave in a manner that we call that of a good citizen, then the outcome is not going to be measurable for a long time. Since most projects will not have life spans of 10 or 15 years, following elementary students into adulthood and obtaining measures then, one needs to find in the performance of young children surrogates for later performance. It is at this point that such projects run into trouble, for we have no convincing information that good citizens at the elementary school level will be good citizens as adults. On the contrary, the students who are most questioning and get into the most trouble in elementary school may well be the best citizens and have the greatest overall respect for the law when they reach adulthood. This is a serious problem with law-related educational programs, and one in which the second definition of evaluation, that of valuing, comes into major focus.

5. *What have we learned about the evaluation process as applied to existing law-related education programs? What are the implications for programs in law and the humanities for elementary students?* In all my time in evaluating the Law in American Society Foundation programs, one outcome stood out in my mind: using brief interviews with four or five randomly selected students in experimental and control classrooms, we found that we could get just as good a picture of what happened in those classrooms as could have been obtained via a very expensive classroom observation program. We found that teachers who have been given a 4- or 6-week summer in-service program, full time, about law-related education varied when they returned to their home school across an extremely wide range of implementation. We found some teachers who never used any of the books or equipment and especially never used any of the unique pedagogical techniques which we knew had been presented in the summer in-service program. On the other hand, we found teachers

who introduced nearly every book, film, document, teaching technique, play, field trip, and outside speaker that had been suggested and, in fact, broadly expanded the amount of time devoted to social studies and law-related education.

The outcome for the students was very clear. The extent to which the teacher used the unique parts of the program—the plays or the mock trials or the outside speakers or the trips to court or the various specific, unique pedagogical approaches suggested—the degree to which these were implemented, was directly related to the amount of outcome seen by the student. This doesn't seem like a very overwhelming conclusion and would be, I suspect, the conventional wisdom. What was always a little surprising to me is that we could get such a clear picture of what was happening in a classroom simply by having a 15-minute interview with four or five randomly chosen students, asking them very simple questions about what they did every day during their social studies period and prying just a little bit about field trips and outside speakers, and that that clear picture was tied so unambiguously to student performance on a variety of achievement and attitude measures that we used on a classwide basis.

6. *Brief suggestion of an ideal model or evaluation design appropriate for use in an elementary school law and humanities program.* I don't believe this has an answer. I don't believe that there is such a thing as an ideal model or evaluation design.

Another view . . .

Program Evaluation: A Collage of Views

Adrianne Bank

The last decade has been one of enormous growth for the field of evaluation. The present period may be looked upon as one of ferment about, and, to some degree, reexamination of the professional roles of the evaluator and the goals of evaluation.

With considerable diversity existing within the field of evaluation, Adrianne Bank was asked to explore the three preceding papers which individually examined evaluation in relation to law and the humanities in the elementary school. Her own paper pulls out key strands and themes evident in those papers. She goes on to describe three distinct views of evaluation: the evaluator seen as an analyst, the evaluator as a documentor, and the evaluator as an assessor. Finally, and perhaps most important, she enumerates key questions raised by each of these frames of reference.

Perhaps it is because I have recently spent several anxious hours searching for my own stage of development within the pages of Gail Sheehy's *Passages* that I see the concept of "stages of development" as a useful organizer for understanding growth within the field of evaluation. Presently, as evaluators, we are in our adolescence. Two of the papers being reviewed here, I believe, reflect evaluation ideas from an earlier stage of our professional development. The third incorporates many current notions and points to directions for future growth in evaluation of educational programs. After discussing the papers, I will try to outline the dimensions of a mature relationship between evaluation efforts and a curriculum development program such as this in law and the humanities.

Evaluation as a large-scale enterprise within the educational establishment is almost 15 years old, stimulated into existence by post-Sputnik concern with education and by expectations that technological thinking would quickly solve our social problems. The early hopes that evaluation data could simultaneously provide policymakers with information about allocating resources to the "best" program, provide teachers with information about improving instruction, and provide parents with information about what the school was doing for their children, have now been shattered.

Evaluators, sobered by experience, are putting

Adrianne Bank is Associate Director of UCLA's Center for the Study of Evaluation. She currently directs formative evaluation studies related to school improvement processes, to desegregation, and to lifelong learning.

away childish things, among them simple-minded views of the world, fantasies of perfection and control, reliance on ready-made solutions to non-standard problems. But the enterprise of evaluation is still growing. More and more people are calling themselves evaluators. Expenditures for education by federal, state, and private groups concerned with educational practice are also increasing.

Evaluation has grown in self-scrutiny as well as in size. Currently, evaluation is characterized by intense discussion of epistemological issues, of standards for "good" evaluations, of professional ethics, and of attempts at role distinctions. Are evaluators to provide—in essence—"consultant services" to curriculum developers and thereby become program advocates? Or are they to provide information to curriculum consumers and, by becoming consumer advocates, become also program adversaries? Or is the chief function of evaluators to provide a detached overview of a particular educational area so that policymakers, whether in government, in schools, or in other institutions, can make corrections and adjustments in their funding decisions? To summarize: there is a healthy ferment among evaluators who are reexamining their professional roles, functions, skills, rights, responsibilities, etc.

Reviews

Ed Hirsch's paper is part of this reexamination. He paints a dismal picture of an ineffectual evaluator carrying out a narrowly defined task in curriculum evaluation. With tongue in cheek, he describes the evaluator's role vis-à-vis the program developer. It is one of unremitting abrasiveness. The evaluator insists on endless restatements of objectives until they are operational; he makes developers go through expensive tryout and revision cycles and locate difficult-to-find comparison groups; he administers time-consuming tests or conducts intrusive observations. As a last indignity, the evaluator foists onto the program developer a complicated report whose findings are either negative or inconclusive. I must assume that Hirsch is painting a caricature, since the remainder of his paper discusses some positive uses for evaluation activities. Among these he notes that evaluators can assist in needs assessment leading to goal definition. He suggests that evaluators can make distinctions among program objectives and classify these according to time to effect (short to long range) and according to ease of measurement (easy to difficult). He suggests that evaluators recognize all the possible combinations of objectives but focus on assessing short-term or easy-to-measure objectives. Hirsch

describes the evaluator's responsibilities as doing an objectives-based evaluation almost in spite of what the developer wishes.

John Wick's paper likewise asserts that the evaluation of a program means "assessing the degree to which the objectives have been met." He recognizes that, to some people, evaluation also means assessing the worth of those objectives; but he implies that this determination rests with the public and policymakers and not with evaluators, particularly in law and humanities courses. He then describes what a good evaluation should contain: its own clearly stated set of goals, a design specific and appropriate to the program, and measurement instruments in addition to or instead of standardized tests. He strongly suggests that in-depth interviews with a few students per class are less costly and as revealing as extensive testing or observation. Wick's paper implies that the evaluation itself be planned, and that the evaluator and the program developer make some choices about what is to be evaluated.

The third paper, Edward Nelsen's, broadens the discussion of evaluation in a manner more characteristic of contemporary thinking. Instead of assuming that an evaluator's primary purpose is to assess the extent to which students achieve program objectives, Nelsen lists seven possibilities as examples of the range of issues evaluations might address. He then goes on to note that evaluations might examine any one or several of these issues at varying levels of program operation or scope. His main point is that the questions to be answered by the evaluation must be clearly specified and prioritized before making an evaluation plan. He then addresses the specific problems of evaluating programs in law and the humanities. He points to several sets of difficulties related to evaluating such programs. The objectives of such programs may be abstract and ambiguous; and simultaneously the responses of children to instruction may be idiosyncratic—dependent on their individual stage of cognitive development and moral reasoning and on their culturally related values, attitudes, and experiences. Furthermore, for elementary students traditional paper-and-pencil methods may be unsatisfactory as outcome measures.

As the foregoing brief summary indicates, there are differences in emphasis among the papers. Hirsch and Wick assume that assessing objectives attained is an all-important purpose, while Nelsen sees many other possibilities for evaluator assistance to program developers. Hirsch implies an independent role for the evaluator in relation to the developer, while Nelsen implies a collaborative relationship between decision maker and evaluator. But all three authors agree on some major points:

■ They urge the involvement of evaluators in the conceptualization of the program—specifically for the setting of goals and stating of objectives.

■ They urge that evaluation planning occur simultaneously with program planning and that the evaluation itself be flexible enough to conform to program requirements.

■ They are impressed with the difficulties of comparing programs with one another or with a no-program situation and therefore tend to favor formative rather than summative roles for evaluators.

■ They recognize special difficulties in the assessment of law and humanities programs, especially on the elementary level.

■ They propose exploring nontest ways for evaluating program outcomes.

What interests me now is how to supplement and incorporate their suggestions into an agenda for systematically dealing with the evaluation issues raised by curricular efforts in areas such as law and humanities.

Evaluating Law and Humanities Programs

We may begin such a task by defining our areas of knowledge and our areas of ignorance. We may then proceed, with a somewhat reduced anxiety level, to determine how to enlighten ourselves, perhaps by seeking assistance from other fields or by borrowing techniques developed by other disciplines.

Let us suppose that, as a presumed expert, we are called upon to evaluate an elementary school program dealing with law and humanities. An organizing question might be: How does this program differ from other programs that we do know—more or less—how to evaluate? But first, as a guide to developing our answers, let us array three general types of program/evaluation interactions, temporarily sequenced.

1. *Program as conceived/evaluator as analyst.* During the conceptualization and development stage, the evaluator's services can be useful in raising issues such as:

1.1 What do you expect children to learn from this program? That is, what are the major outcomes—knowledge, skills, attitudes—that you would want children to take away with them?

1.2 How do you justify these outcomes? That is, why is it important that children learn these things? The justification can be rooted in personal, social, political, humanistic values.

1.3 Why do you expect that children will learn from the components of this program? That

is, what is the reasoning that leads you to believe that the activities, materials, amount of time spent, etc., will actually produce learning? This reasoning should have a basis in learning, development, motivational, etc., theories.

2. *Program as taught/evaluator as documenter.* When the program is taught in the classroom, the evaluator's services can be useful in describing the delivery of the program.

2.1 What is the teacher doing? That is, what does the teacher appear to be doing both intentionally and unintentionally (e.g., conveying information, organizing activities, reinforcing student behaviors, modeling appropriate behaviors)?

2.2 What are students doing? That is, what activities are students engaged in that are program prescribed, not program prescribed? What materials are they using? How much time are they spending on task? etc.

2.3 What is the classroom setting? That is, what are the operative norms, rules, expectations within the classroom that support or conflict with the program as conceived?

3. *Program as learned/evaluator as assessor.* When the program is being taught in the classroom, the evaluator's services can be useful in assessing the extent to which students are learning from the program.

3.1 What do students report that they are learning? How satisfied are they with what they are doing?

3.2 What objective evidence is there that students are learning? That is, can they recall/apply/analyze/synthesize/evaluate what they have learned? Do others report, or can it be observed, that their behaviors have changed in any way?

If the foregoing are some of the general ways in which evaluators can be useful for program developers, from the conception to the implementation of the program, what are the evaluation problems specifically raised by programs in law and humanities? Do these programs raise evaluation problems different from those of other programs, and if so, how? Their differences from other programs and from each other may occur along a number of dimensions, as shown in Table 1. The first column briefly enumerates some of those dimensions. The second column describes evaluation activities for which techniques may not yet be available.

Table 1: Evaluation Problems Raised by Law and Humanities Programs

Dimensions of Law and Humanities Programs	Evaluation Needs Feasible Techniques for:
1 Program as conceived:	
1.1 Hoped-for knowledge, skill, and attitudinal program outcomes may be manifested: now, in the near future, intermediate, in adulthood; at school, at home, in the community, within the peer group, etc.; in accordance with individual preferences and values in complex and interacting ways.	1.1e Inferring and stating in measurable form: intermediate/long-term outcomes; outcomes as mediated by individual background, choice, experiences, preferences; complex and synergistic outcomes.
1.2 Justification of outcomes may be a combination of implicit and explicit values, preferences, opinions, utility factors, etc.	1.2e Clarifying, classifying, arraying value positions.
1.3 Program components may be a combination of experiential/vicarious, concrete/abstract, exploratory/directed, within-school/out-of-school experiences and tasks.	1.3e Operationalizing learning theories and examining the consistencies and contradictions among them.
2 Program as taught:	
2.1 Teacher activities may range from directive to facilitative, from didactic to providing experiences. Messages may be transmitted to students directly/indirectly, etc.	2.1e Recording complex teacher behaviors/body language/interactions with students.
2.2 Student activities may occur within school, within home, within community; may be cumulative, hierarchical, eclectic; may be teacher directed or personally selected.	2.2e Describing complex tasks, experiential learning settings, etc.
2.3 The "hidden curriculum" may be supportive of/in conflict with overt curriculum. Program may be integrated with/isolated from other subject area teaching.	2.3e Describing norms, expectations, roles, rules, "deep structure" of classroom.
3 Program as learned:	
3.1 Student interest/involvement/learning may be mediated by prior cultural, developmental variables not susceptible to change by instruction.	3.1e Measuring complex attitudes, synthesizing and interpreting data developed from measurement techniques which have differing logics (i.e., ethnographies, surveys, attitude measures).

For example, a law and humanities program that is primarily experiential and conducted outside of school, with expectations for affecting students' future adult behaviors related to political action, requires that an evaluator use very different analytic documentation and assessment techniques from those she/he would use in evaluating a math program which stressed immediate knowledge outcomes taught through workbook instructional activities. Evaluators have much work ahead of them in order to make their craft adequate to the demands that law and humanities curriculum projects place on it.

The existence of an effort which is simultaneously funding several curriculum development projects offers a good opportunity for evaluators and developers to work together to improve, after some time, each of their fields and the resulting products. Suggestions for organizing evaluation activities within and between individual curriculum development projects on law and humanities, so that mutual benefits can occur, are given below.

Within projects. Evaluators should, I believe, act so as to assist in making each curriculum project as good as possible. Specific tasks should be, of course, negotiated between evaluator and decision maker. However, evaluators should work

■ To develop an overall evaluation plan specifying evaluation audiences and evaluation questions, with justification in terms of anticipated use, design, instruments, reporting procedures, time line, budget, personnel.

■ To formulate evaluation questions whose answers will be useful, and ensure that sufficient project resources—time, money, personnel—are available to collect the data and, most important, to act on them once they have been reported. (This last is crucial. Often, project time lines do not allow sufficient time to make changes when it appears essential to do so.)

■ To examine project goals to see if they are realistic, that is, within the abilities of targeted students, capable of being done by teachers, and amenable to instruction in the time allotted to their achievement.

■ To examine the consistency between planned activities and intended outcomes. This conceptual analysis—requiring the application of theory or of logic—would indicate why there was reason to expect that the instruction would be effective. It would also assist in determining the appropriate amount of instructional time to be devoted to each objective alone and in combination.

■ To examine instructional techniques to determine if, on their face, they provide students with motivation, appropriate practice, reinforcement, etc.

■ To collect data in an economical and imaginative fashion to get at both objective (i.e., observable) changes and subjective (i.e., self-reported) reactions by pupils, teachers, community members, parents, and others during program implementation.

Between projects. Although it is likely that each project's evaluation will be idiosyncratic,

there may be enough communality among projects to make discussions among the evaluators attached to them profitable. Periodic meetings among these evaluators might include:

■ Identification of elements common to all law and humanities courses that need special attention from evaluators.

■ Sharing of instruments or analysis procedures useful to more than one project.

■ Development of procedures to document and conduct research on evaluation related to such programs.

Research on evaluation in those areas stimulated by the needs of law and humanities curriculum efforts might take the form of post hoc analysis and synthesis. If there were interest, research on evaluation might also take the form of a planned parallel evaluation study of a specific project so that two teams of evaluators using different evaluation techniques might try to answer the same evaluation question, or, alternatively, using common data, might use different analysis procedures to answer additional evaluation questions.

These thoughts sketch an outline for a productive relationship between evaluation efforts and curriculum development projects in law and the humanities.

They seem likely to turn evaluators prematurely gray.

Classroom Assessment in a Law and Humanities Elementary School Program

Ronald Gerlach

Classroom assessment remains the nemesis of most teachers. On one hand, it is carefully avoided, and on the other hand, it is increasingly recognized as potentially valuable—as well as politically necessary!

In addition to the discussion of objectives, Ron Gerlach's paper identifies and gives a full range of test-item examples for evaluating growth in the areas of knowledge, attitudes, and skills associated with a law and humanities program. His discussion not only clarifies the goals and processes of classroom evaluation, per se, but sheds additional light on the nature of law and humanities in the elementary school.

Evaluation takes place many times each day in elementary school classrooms as the instructor observes students and makes judgments about their behavior and work products. In turn, the children themselves often have a good idea about and reflect upon how well they are doing in Ms. or Mr. Johnson's class (Jarolimek, 1977).

Yet, as Jarolimek points out, classroom assessment may be the weakest link in the instructional process. Even with significant advances in teaching methodology and instructional materials for classroom use, evaluation seems to be getting more difficult and subjective as well as perhaps less rational and effective (Jarolimek & Walsh, 1969, pp. 466–467, 482–485).

At a time when teachers are asked to integrate or give greater emphasis to not only basic skills but also such things as critical thinking, valuing, and law within their instructional programs, they remain handicapped by the lack of adequate assessment instruments which reflect these recent trends and developments. In addition, as more and more parents and patrons of the schools clamor for more tangible evidence of and greater accountability for each child's educational progress, many teachers have neither the time nor the skills and knowledge to respond with an improved classroom assessment program (Keller, 1974, pp. 226–249).

Jarolimek adds that matters are made worse by the attitude which many instructors take toward

classroom evaluation. That is, they have come to regard it as an unfortunate appendage of teaching. As a result, some teachers rely heavily or almost entirely upon intuitive appraisals of student performance . . . feeling that as the days pass by in school, students will surely progress (Jarolimek & Walsh, 1969).

An Unfulfilled Potential

Heavy reliance upon hastily conceived and/or intuitively based assessments produces results that are quite limited in scope and of questionable accuracy. Moreover, the information that they provide can have an adverse effect upon the kinds of judgments which both teachers and students make about the instructional process and about themselves.

Teachers, for example, may be led to accept a distorted picture of the teaching/learning process. They may reach unwarranted conclusions about their teaching effectiveness and make decisions that are not in the best interest of their students. Take, for example, the case of an instructor who wishes to teach critical thinking; assigns a chapter in a text on the subject; quickly constructs a 50-item true-false quiz on the chapter; and concludes that, since the class did well on the exam, he or she successfully taught "critical thinking." All of which, in fact, is pure folly! Although the preceding example is extreme, improper assessment can and does help produce a significant gap between what a teacher says instruction *will* accomplish and what *actually* is achieved.

Classroom assessment based solely on teacher intuition or a poorly constructed test does not

Ronald Gerlach is Director of the New York State Law, Youth and Citizenship Program, sponsored jointly by the New York Bar Association and the New York State Education Department. He is co-author of the text *Teaching about the Law* (Cincinnati: Anderson, 1975).

contribute to a good learning environment. If anything, it helps nurture suspicion, distrust, and confusion among students in the classroom. It encourages students to view their teachers as poorly prepared and uncaring. Moreover, it prompts students to look upon assessment as a purely whimsical, capricious, and punitive process that has no real merit or meaning for them. From this perspective, instruction can become an extremely negative experience.

Preparing Young People for Citizenship

Education law in most states provides for instruction in the first eight grades that includes the teaching of history and "civics." As a result, the themes of patriotism and citizenship have had a long history in elementary school programs (Bureau of Social Studies Education, 1974). But what is it that should be stressed in instruction and, subsequently, evaluated?

Hess and Torney (1967) point out that the political and social development of children involves three things: the acquisition of specific *information* about the system; the acquisition of *attitudes and values* about the role the citizens are to play; and the learning of both general and specific *skills* related to citizenship. Although intimately related and generally overlapping, educational achievements in each of these areas seem to provide the central focus for citizenship education in the schools.

The Board of Regents (1974), for example, which heads the New York State education system, has issued a statement concerning elementary, secondary, and continuing education which clearly reflects these three areas of achievement. Included among its 10 comprehensive goals for educating New York State residents are the following: (1) mastering of the *skills* of communication, reasoning, and decision making; (2) *understanding* the processes of effective citizenship; and (3) achieving competence in the processes of developing sound *values*.

The Pennsylvania Department of Education (1975) seems to have taken a similar position regarding citizenship education. In addition to preparing a comprehensive list of law-related competencies for primary, intermediate, and secondary school students, the department stresses the need for substantial background *information*, general *respect*, and participatory *skills* in citizenship.

The implications of the above for classroom assessment become quickly apparent. If citizenship training and law-related instruction, K–12, are to be adequately assessed, classroom evaluation will have to reflect each of these overall goals and include measures of the following:

- Gains in student knowledge and understanding of the law and our system of government;
- Changes in student attitudes, values, and beliefs regarding related institutions and processes; and
- The achievement of essential participatory and decision-making skills.

Moreover, successful evaluation will require that each of the above measures be further delineated and clearly defined in terms of the daily aims of instruction (Mager, 1970). That is, objectives will need to be prepared which:

- Are stated in terms of *student* behavior;
- Focus on a final outcome of instruction;
- Are *realistic* in terms of what students are capable of achieving and what instruction is capable of promoting; and
- Contain clear, unambiguous *action verbs* which can be observed and assessed in one manner or another.

Finally, most elementary school authorities and experts in educational measurements would agree that classroom evaluation must proceed in a systematic, comprehensive, and continuous manner. That is, classroom assessment must truly reflect the purposes of instruction, involve the use of a variety of assessment practices on a regular basis, and yield information regarding *all* aspects of student behavior rather than only subject-matter achievement. In addition, it must be presented as a positive component of the teaching/learning process and not as a punitive measure.

Development of a sound evaluation program based on the above characteristics requires hard work and a strong commitment on the part of the instructor. Unfortunately, what is recommended is no easy task. It demands self-reflection by the teacher and careful scrutiny of instruction. In the process, intuitive thinking must give way to hard analysis. Only then is there a real chance that evaluation in the classroom will proceed according to the recommendations cited above.

But where does an elementary school teacher involved in a law and humanities program begin? Two options appear open to instructors. On one hand, they may try to identify and construct their own set of overall goals and daily aims for instruction for a law and humanities program. Or, on the other hand, they may elect to survey other published material and established listings of educational objectives, adopting and adapting those goals which best suit their instructional needs.

Identifying Law-related Content Objectives

In a K–6 curriculum package entitled *Living Together under Our Laws,* a committee of New York State elementary school teachers and university educators identified a series of themes or "understandings" which they felt could be developed through law-related studies (New York State Education Department, in press). On the basis of their exposure to selected law-related content and their involvement in a series of classroom activities, students would be expected to have reached the following conclusions about the law by the close of instruction:

- Rules and laws play an important role in our daily lives.
- "Worthwhile and fair" laws generally have certain characteristics in common.
- Rules and laws are made and enforced by different people in different settings.
- Laws help make it possible for people to live together by: (*a*) protecting differences of opinion and individual rights; (*b*) helping right wrongs and settle disputes; (*c*) protecting a person's property, privacy, and own well being; and (*d*) providing citizens with certain benefits as a group.
- Laws can be changed and/or cause change in a society.

Despite the fact that these themes are not all encompassing, they suggest one significant way of delineating *what* basic information students should possess, should "know," about law and our legal system and of identifying important instructional outcomes for assessment. (Starr [1973 and in this volume] suggests another way in which these goals can be accomplished. He recommends that law-related instruction focus on five key ideas or concepts involving the law and our legal system: liberty, justice, equality, power, and property. This approach has been used in the Law in a Free Society curriculum, which is based on the study of eight rather than five key concepts [Law in a Free Society, 606 Wilshire Blvd., Santa Monica, Calif. 90401].)

Encouraging the Development of Values

Hess and Torney (1967) point out that the development of political attitudes in young people seems to proceed at a very rapid rate, especially through fifth grade. Moreover, the findings of these researchers appear to indicate that the public school is the most important and effective instrument in the United States for inducting youth into political and legal systems. (Although Hess and Torney are highly critical of what values the schools stress and how they proceed with the political education of young people, these topics are beyond the scope of this paper.)

Law-related studies by their very nature cannot be taught as a "value free" subject. Most law-related content involves personal values, choices,

and emotions. It focuses on subjects about which most people, including youth, have opinions and, perhaps, even related experiences. More often than not, it involves or raises questions concerning societal problems and/or personal choices and decision making. To try to ignore this dimension of law-related studies or completely eliminate it from instruction would not only be nearly impossible, but would dilute much of its educational value and appeal to students.

Recent efforts to define "good" or "effective" citizenship as an overall goal of law-related instruction have tended to center on the development of student values such as the following (Board of Regents, 1974).

- Respect for the welfare and dignity of others;
- Appreciation of the need for governance by law;
- Support for the rights and freedoms of all people;
- Recognition of the need for active democratic participation;
- Prizing rationality in thought, communication, and action;
- Commitment to the maintenance and improvement of our democratic society;
- Acceptance of responsibility for one's own actions;
- Recognition of the need and right to oppose injustice; and
- Belief in the interrelatedness and general welfare of the entire world.

Unfortunately for evaluation, most of the work in law-related studies and citizenship education concerning attitudes and values has ended with preparation of lists such as the above.

Promoting Significant Life Skills

With public demand for a "return to the basics" increasing, educators have been prone to pay greater and greater attention to the development of basic life skills. As a result, elementary and secondary school students are being exposed to new instructional materials and curricular innovations which reflect this renewed commitment (Gilliom et al., 1977).

Law-related studies in elementary schools, for example, might help facilitate the development of each of the following skills (Carpenter, 1963; Bureau of Social Studies Education, Notes 1, 2):

- Observing.
- Reading.
- Writing.
- Working cooperatively in groups.
- Analyzing cases.
- Problem solving.
- Listening.
- Speaking.

- Expressing oneself creatively.
- Interpreting graphs/charts/maps/tables.
- Organizing ideas.
- Valuing.

Although this listing is not intended to be all inclusive, it does suggest a number of key skills that might contribute to the development of an informed, analytic, and actively involved citizenry. Once identified, however, each of these skills would need to be further defined in terms of specific student behaviors for assessment purposes.

The Humanities Role

Up to this point, discussion has tended to center on the development of a sound evaluation program and the overall objectives of a law-related school curriculum. Little, if anything, has been said about the contribution which the "humanities" themselves might make to instruction and assessment in an elementary school citizenship education program.

The humanities have been defined as the branches of learning concerned with human thought and experience. The study of literature, painting, sculpture, architecture, music, drama, and poetry generally is placed under this heading. On occasion, history, philosophy, and law are added to the list of subjects (Powell, 1969). Each of the subjects within the humanities presents, in one way or another, a view of life. Each relates the experiences of "people." By focusing on the often unique, human side of life within a social context, the subjects within the humanities offer another important dimension to the study of law and society.

Elementary school teachers, in particular, are likely to find the humanities of special value in teaching about the law in their citizenship education programs. More specifically, the humanities might help the teacher:

- Present law from a more "humane" perspective for elementary school youth;
- Stimulate student interest in citizenship by creating drama, evoking emotion, and stimulating thought about the subject;
- Facilitate students' awareness of societal values and the value choices they are likely to have to make during their lifetimes;
- Promote a general appreciation of the role which law has played in the development of civilization and the advancement of the human race; and
- Foster individual expression and creativity in children at a time when their imaginations are perhaps most active.

In addition, material from the humanities can be used to improve overall classroom evaluation and to enhance its attractiveness to students. Selections from or assignments involving art, literature, and music, for example, might be used to assess student knowledge, skills, and attitudes. Use of these materials, in turn, may help make classroom assessment less threatening and punitive, more interesting and challenging, and, perhaps, even fun for students.

Testing Student Understanding

Five types of test items are commonly used to assess student knowledge and understanding. These include the following four objective-type items and the essay question: (1) true-false, (2) fill-in-the-blank or completion, (3) multiple choice, and (4) matching. Most of these items can be adapted for use at grades K–12. At the primary grade level, for example, verbal questions and pictorial responses are likely to be used in place of items which require substantial reading and writing skills.

In preparing these kinds of items for assessing student knowledge and understanding, it is useful for teachers to check the following: Does the item assess something of significance regarding student achievement? Is the item clearly written and not wordy? Does the item avoid confusing or tricky wording that may mislead students as to what is being assessed? Can the item be scored numerically or in some other manner? Will there be adequate time to score the item? Will the item be scored consistently from one student to the next?

In addition, it is important for the instructor to recognize the strengths and weaknesses of each type of item. (A more detailed description and analysis of these types of items can be found in most standard measurement texts.) True-false and completion items, for example, are useful in testing student knowledge of a wide range of material. In the case of true-false questions, however, students have a 50-50 chance of selecting the correct answer on each item without knowing anything. Scoring of completion items, in turn, often is complicated by the variety of different answers that may show up on a given blank. In addition, both types of items tend to be difficult to adapt for assessing higher levels of thinking.

Multiple-choice items and matching exercises, in contrast, can reduce the chance guessing found in true-false questions. Unlike completion items, they can be scored rather quickly and by almost anyone. Moreover, the multiple-choice item is perhaps the easiest, outside of the essay test question, to adapt for use in assessing more complex modes of thinking. On the other hand, however, both the popular multiple-choice question and matching exercise have certain weaknesses that generally result from flaws in construction. Finding plausible alternatives and maintaining grammatical consistency, for example, can make these items somewhat difficult to prepare.

As already stated, the essay question perhaps lends itself best to evaluating the more complex thinking processes of analysis, synthesis, and evaluation, as well as related skills. It is, nevertheless, plagued with its own problems. Ambiguity in the question itself and/or a poor scoring key can make scoring difficult and time-consuming and produce questionable results.

Despite each test item's own specific limitations, all five of the above evaluation techniques can contribute to the assessment of student understanding in an elementary school law and humanities program. (For the purposes of this paper, student understanding is defined broadly in terms of the following behaviors: recall/recognition of previously learned information [knowledge]; interpretation of a given reading, visual, chart, etc. [comprehension]; use of previously learned information/material in new situations [application]; ability to break down a communication/material into its parts [analysis]; creation of something new based on previously learned information [synthesis]; and judgment of the merits of something, with reasons for choice [evaluation].) Careful construction and selective use of each type of item are essential to its success. In the sample items which follow, completion questions are used to appraise the students' ability to analyze a visual; multiple choice, to determine student comprehension of a reading selection; and an essay assignment, to ascertain student understanding of a designated topic.

In the sample completion items, students are asked to identify the major features of a police officer's badge (illustration by: Rochester City School District).

Look at the drawing. Then fill in the blanks in the statements below.

At the top of the object is a(n)_____.
The number on the object is _____.
The object is a(n) _____.
The person who would have this object is called a(n) _____.

Generally, it is best to pose completion-type items in the form of declarative or descriptive statements. Also, the blank space in each item should be placed near the end of the sentence rather than at its beginning.

Some follow-up classroom activities to the completion-type exercise presented above might include: discussing why certain things were found on the badge; having students make badges like the one in the test for their own police department.

The sample multiple-choice items which follow are designed to test student comprehension of a reading describing courtroom activities.

Read the description below carefully. Then select the best answer to each of the questions which follow. Circle the letter before your choice.

A large number of people are in the room. At the front of the room, sitting behing a large desk up on a platform, is a man dressed in a black robe who seems to be in charge of things. As we watch, two men face each other in front of the man in the black robe. One man seems to be holding a Bible. He says to the other man, "Raise your right hand. Do you swear to tell the truth, the whole truth, and nothing but the truth so help you God?" [Jarolimek, 1977, p. 240]

1) Who is sitting at the front of the room behind a large desk?
   A) A man dressed in a black robe.
   B) A man holding a large book.
   C) A large number of men and women.
   D) Two men facing each other.
2) What does the one man say after he asks another person to raise his right hand?
   A) "Do you wish to leave the room?"
   B) "Do you swear to tell the truth?"
   C) "Do you want some help?"
   D) "Do you wish to tell me something?"

A well-constructed multiple-choice item generally consists of a stem or introductory statement in the form of a question or incomplete sentence. This statement must include the main idea of the passage. A series of choices (one right answer plus several distractors) then are used to complete the statement or answer the question. All choices should be approximately the same length and have equal plausibility.

For the primary grades, the essay question may be used to elicit pictorial responses rather than written answers. A sample question follows:

Select 10 pictures from our classroom files/picture table or from a magazine at home which describe what the police do.

Or another version of the same type of question:

Draw a picture showing three ways that the law is involved in your life.

Older students, in contrast, might be asked to write on any number of different topics. In the sample item which follows, students are asked to solve a problem posed in case-study form.

Directions: Read the story below. (A) Describe Johnny and Jean's problem. (B) List three ways Johnny and Jean could choose to deal with the problem they face.

Johnny and Jean are classmates and good friends. One day in school last week, they saw a third friend, Tim, take a fourth student's milk money from her lunch pail. What should Johnny and Jean do? [Gerlach & Lamprecht, 1975]

The careful construction of essay-type questions is important. The questions must be clearly written and be answerable in the allotted time. A precise scoring key and/or list of acceptable answers must be developed to help maintain consistency in scoring the responses. Moreover, a special effort should be made *not* to restrict the use of this type of item to assessing the simple recall or restatement of information.

Measuring Attitudes, Values, and Interests

In addition to the preceding evaluation strategies that are designed to assess student understanding of law-related content, elementary school teachers have available to them a number of other useful techniques for measuring student attitudes, values, and interests. (For other suggestions and an in-depth analysis of the subject, see: Gerlach & Lamprecht; 1975; Raths, Harmin, & Simon, 1966; Krathwohl, Bloom, & Masia, 1964.)

These evaluation techniques involve the use of: (1) questionnaires and polls, (2) inventories, (3) checklists, (4) projective measures, (5) logs and diaries, (6) individual conferences, and (7) personal observation.

More specifically, these evaluation measures can help classroom teachers make warranted inferences about the following:

■ What *interests* do students possess? That is, what things are they likely to pay close attention to and/or be willing to participate in?
■ What *attitudes* and feelings do students have? That is, what things are they likely to feel positive toward or negative about; when confronted by what things are they likely to become happy, sad, angry, hostile, elated, etc.?
■ What *values* do students hold? That is, what things do they prize or hold so dear that they are willing to take a public stand regarding them and use them as guides to their behavior?

Several sample strategies for assessing student attitudes, interests, and values in a law and humanities elementary school program are described below. Included is the use of an attitude questionnaire/opinion poll, interest inventory, projective exercise, and student diary assignment.

Before proceeding, however, a word of caution regarding the use of these evaluation techniques.

These assessment devices are designed to be used in classrooms which encourage openness, honesty, and acceptance among students and teachers, as well as respect for one another and for individual privacy. Moreover, these measures are *not* intended to produce a specific grade for individual students. Any violation of these conditions is likely to discourage free and honest expression and, in turn, distort the results.

The use of attitude questionnaires and opinion polls in the classroom is increasing in popularity. Asked to respond with a show of hands or in writing, students are encouraged to "take a stand"—to express their own feelings about or reaction to a selected subject.

On a Likert-type questionnaire or poll, for example, students may be presented with a series of descriptive statements (what is/what has been) or prescriptive items (what should be/what ought to be) about a subject. They are asked to indicate *the extent* to which they agree or disagree with each item on the poll.

A sample Likert-type item is provided below:

The police should be more helpful to young people. (Circle your choice)

Strongly agree	Mildly agree	Undecided	Mildly disagree	Strongly disagree

Primary school children, in turn, might be asked to respond to the statement orally or through the show of hands. Or the standard Likert-type item might be portrayed visually as follows for use with primary school youth.

The police are good people. (Check your choice)

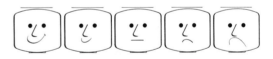

Student inventories have a long-established history. Generally, inventories are used to assess student interests and preferences (Jarolimek, 1977). A sample inventory follows:

What Would You Like to Do?

Place an *L* in front of each item if you would *like* to do it.
Place a *D* in front of each item if you would *dislike* doing it.
Place an *X* in front of the item if you are *unsure*.

_____ Visit a police station
_____ Ride in a police car
_____ Read stories about the police
_____ See a movie about the police
_____ Make a model police station
_____ Have a police officer visit class

The information obtained from inventories such as the one above can be used by an instructor to help plan instruction as well as to promote class discussion regarding the subject under consideration.

In contrast to student inventories, the use of projective measures in the classroom is a relatively new phenomenon. Its development as an instructional technique and assessment tool appears closely linked to values clarification theory and the experimental study of human personality. Projective techniques require students to react to partially structured stimuli, that is, to interpret or to complete an unfinished sentence, story, role play, picture without caption, etc. (Gerlach & Lamprecht, 1975; Raths et al., 1966).

Compared to the preceding evaluation measures in this section, the projective technique is *not* designed to yield any kind of numerical score. It is very difficult and often counterproductive to code the individual responses numerically and count them up for a total score.

Projective measures, instead, yield descriptive (qualitative) information about student feeling and attitudes. They encourage free expression by students rather than using forced-choice responses. One example of this technique is provided below:

Write *five* endings for the following statement. Make sure each ending expresses *your* feelings regarding the subject.

"I feel angry when the law ..."

The contents of student logs and diaries provide another valuable measure of attitudes, values, and interests. In addition, they are likely to promote self-reflection on the part of students as well as individual responsibility (Michaelis, 1968, pp. 519–552).

Each student might be asked to keep a log or diary in class that would be available for teacher inspection at specified intervals. Each day, for example, students might write a comment or draw a picture about how they felt, note some thing that concerned them, or respond to a specific request from their teacher. A sample item follows:

In your diary today, I would like you to draw a face or picture showing how you felt about our visit to the courts yesterday.

Can you also describe how your five senses were involved? Note one thing which you heard, ... saw, ... smelled, ... tasted, ... touched.

Assessing Skill Development

In addition to student "knowledge and understanding" and "attitudes and values," it is essential that classroom evaluation include appraisals of significant "life" skills. All too frequently, however, skill development is given only cursory attention in classroom evaluation.

Teachers' reluctance to do any substantive evaluation in this area perhaps can be attributed to the difficulties encountered in translating general skills such as "problem solving" into specific, observable student behaviors that can be easily assessed. It is important to note that once this initial hurdle is overcome, a variety of evaluation strategies are available that can be used to assess student achievement in this area.

These assessment strategies may involve the use of objective test items, role-play episodes, short-answer questions, class discussion exercises, student self-evaluation forms, and/or teacher rating sheets, among other techniques. Moreover, they may be used to assess the development of those skills associated with an elementary school law and humanities program—that is, a student's ability to read, observe, solve problems, write, discuss, and work together cooperatively in groups.

Several sample assessment procedures and exercises are described below for use in a law and humanities elementary school program. Taken together, these evaluation practices provide a brief survey of the wide variety of approaches open to teachers in assessing life skills in the classroom.

In the illustration which follows, a "case study" is used to assess students' reading comprehension as well as the thinking skills of application and analysis.

About a month ago, Mary received a wonderful birthday present. It was a book called a "diary." In her diary, Mary wrote about the things she had made and how she felt about what she did each day.

Yesterday, Mary caught her older brother reading her diary. She was very, very unhappy. She was so unhappy that she grabbed the book from her brother and ran crying to her room. [Gerlach & Lamprecht, 1975]

What did Mary receive about a month ago?

A) A dog   C) A doll
B) A diary   D) A doll house

[In this item, students are asked to simply extract information from the reading on the very *literal* level.]

Which of the following objects do we use in class that is similar to Mary's present?

A) A journal   C) A paper pad
B) A reading book   D) A desk

[In this question, students are asked to use the information contained in the reading and *apply* it to another experience.]

What is the main idea presented in this reading?

A) Mary wrote in a book each day about the things she made.

B) Mary received a wonderful birthday present.
C) Mary was unhappy because her brother did something she didn't like.
D) Mary's brother was older than she was.

[In this item, students are asked to sift through/*analyze* the information contained in the reading and identify the main thought.]

Whereas objective testing is likely to yield neat, numerical scores, a role-play/game format can provide useful descriptive information on the behavior of students. The sample activity below asks students to role play a "lost child" incident (adapted from an activity in Rochester City School District, n.d.). Teachers might use this classroom activity to evaluate the following observation skills: (1) how accurately and objectively students describe an object—that is, one another's physical makeup—from observation; and (2) how adept students are at giving special attention to key elements in a description and identifying a subject based on these descriptors.

"Lost Child"
Introductory Questions:
■ Have you ever been lost?
■ What did it (might it) feel like?
■ Was anyone concerned?
■ Let's suppose that a mother and father notice that their son or daughter is missing. What should they do?

Role Play:
■ Let's pretend that a police officer comes to the parents' home. He or she will need a description of the "lost child." (Select three members of the class to play the roles of [1] the police officer and [2] the mother and father of the lost child.)
■ Ask the "officer" to leave the room, and select a fourth student as the "lost child."
■ Instruct the "officer" that upon returning to the room, he or she will have an opportunity to question the mother/father, get a description of the "lost child," and identify the member of the class who is the "lost child."
■ The parents, in turn, should be told that they should try to describe the lost child (the third student) for

the officer as completely as possible. Have the "lost child" stand up in class in order for the "parents" to get a good look at him or her. Then have the lost child return to his/her seat in class.
■ Ask the class not to focus their attention on the student chosen as the "lost child," since that would "give it away." Finally, tell the parents that they may not use the real name of the "lost child," since this too would make it too easy for the officer.
■ Have the "officer" return and role play the situation in front of the class. Permit the "officer" to walk around the class while he/she is trying to "find the lost child."
■ Discuss the enactment with the class.

The successful use of role-playing episodes as an assessment technique is dependent largely on the observation skills of the classroom teacher. How well he or she has identified the behaviors to be assessed, and has proceeded systematically in recording the results, is likely to have a significant impact on the accuracy of the information collected. In many cases, it is best to construct a rating sheet. By listing clearly what is to be assessed, a rating sheet such as the one shown in Figure 1 can serve as an important guide for observation.

In essence, student behavior associated with listening, speaking, discussing, and working cooperatively together may be evaluated through systematic observation by the teacher. Moreover, students might be invited to participate. That is, they might be encouraged to use the same or similar rating sheets on occasion to help appraise their own skills as well as assess the performance of their classmates. In addition to promoting students' powers of analysis and objectivity, these assessment practices could provide the teacher with yet another measure of student growth in a designated skill area.

Looking Ahead

On the basis of the preceding discussion, it is perhaps safe to conclude that the task of classroom evaluation is formidable and complex and, at the same time, intellectually stimulating and challenging. Sound evaluation demands that

Figure 1: Sample Rating Sheet

Discussion Skills of: _____ (Name)		Date _____		
	Always	Usually	Seldom	Never
1. Listened to what was said.	X	X	X	X
2. Contributed own ideas.	X	X	X	X
3. Was willing to take turns.	X	X	X	X
4. Was willing to build on what others said.	X	X	X	X
5. Gave in when the group decided something didn't like.	X	X	X	X

assessment procedures and strategies reflect the goals and content of instruction.

Despite the promise which a law and humanities curriculum may have for both instruction and assessment on the elementary school level, classroom evaluation will not be easy. Teachers will need all the assistance they can obtain.

Participating elementary school instructors are likely to be confronted by problems associated with integrating new materials and/or a different instructional emphasis into their school programs. In addition, they are not likely to possess the requisite skill or have the time to prepare all of the essential assessment goals and measures for a balanced classroom evaluation program.

The above concerns seem to warrant substantial action by funded projects as well as personnel outside the immediate realm of instruction. If a sound classroom assessment program is to be achieved, it appears essential that:

1. The overall goals for the law and humanities program be clearly articulated;
2. Specific instructional goals for all new material and strategies be prepared;
3. Teachers be trained in both the content area and related techniques for achieving and assessing instructional goals; and
4. A compendium of assessment measures for each of the program's major goals be prepared and made available to the participants.

It is almost certain that the activities cited above will require a substantial commitment of time, energy, and resources. Nevertheless, their potential contribution to the development of a viable and effective elementary school program on law and humanities seems clearly to outweigh their costs.

Sound evaluation practices should facilitate the integration of instruction with a law and humanities orientation into existing school programs. Moreover, they should promote more effective teaching as well as encourage more productive learning. In essence, all of the principals involved in this educational enterprise are likely to benefit—this ABA/NEH project, its cooperating teachers, and, most important, elementary school students.

REFERENCES

Board of Regents, State University of New York. *Goals for elementary, secondary and continuing education in New York State.* Albany: State University of New York, 1974.

Bureau of Social Studies Education, New York State Education Department. Social studies in the elementary school: Implications for social studies programs K–12. *Newsletter,* 1974, 2 (March), 1–3.

Carpenter, H. M. (Ed.) *Skill development in the social studies.* Washington, D.C.: National Council for the Social Studies, 1963.

Gerlach, R. A., & Lamprecht, L. W. *Teaching about the law: A guide to secondary and elementary instruction.* Cincinnati: Anderson, 1975.

Gilliom, M. E., et al. *Practical methods for the social studies.* Belmont, Calif.: Wadsworth, 1977.

Hess, R. D. & Torney, J. V. *The development of political attitudes in children.* Garden City, N.Y.: Doubleday, 1967.

Jarolimek, J. *Social studies competencies and skills.* New York: Macmillan, 1977.

Jarolimek, J., & Walsh, H. M. *Readings for social studies.* New York: Macmillan, 1969.

Keller, C. *Involving students in the new social studies.* Boston: Little, Brown, 1974.

Krathwohl, D. R.; Bloom, B. S.; & Masia, B. B. *Taxonomy of educational ojectives: The affective domain.* New York: McKay, 1964.

Mager, R. F. *Preparing instructional objectives.* New York: Harper & Row, 1970.

Michaelis, J. U. *Social studies for children in a democracy* (4th ed.). Englewood Cliffs, N.J.: Prentice-Hall, 1968.

New York State Education Department. *Living together under our laws: K–6.* Albany, N.Y.: Author, in press.

Pennsylvania Department of Education. *Law-related education competencies.* Harrisburg, Pa.: Author, 1975.

Powell, T. F. (Ed.). *Humanities and the social studies.* Washington, D.C.: National Council for the Social Studies, 1969.

Raths, L. E.; Harmin, M.; & Simon, S. *Values and teaching.* Columbus, Ohio: Merrill, 1966.

Rochester City School District. *Officer Friendly says you are a V.I.P.* Rochester, N.Y.: Sears-Roebuck Foundation, n.d.

Starr, I. Reflections on law studies in the schools today. In S. E. Davison (Ed.), *Reflections on law-related education.* Chicago: American Bar Association, 1973.

REFERENCE NOTES

1. Bureau of Social Studies Education, New York State Education Department. Social studies competencies list. Albany, N.Y.
2. Bureau of Social Studies Education, New York State Education Department. Seven goals—effective citizen. Albany, N.Y.

Another view . . .

Classroom Assessment in a Law and Humanities Elementary School Program

Robert W. Richburg

Professional evaluators are generally critical of the assessment practices of classroom teachers. That criticism stems from their observation that teachers tend to use intuitive and subjective judgments rather than rigorous or systematic practices.

This paper offers several reasons why teachers resist the use of recommended assessment procedures, beyond those that will yield grades. It focuses on one use of assessment data—to make curriculum decisions. In addition, the paper provides important insights into how curriculum inferences can be made from group data in the affective or attitudinal realm, an area central to any law and humanities curriculum.

Dear Fellow Evaluators,

I just finished reading Ronald Gerlach's paper "Classroom Assessment in a Law and Humanities Elementary School Program." I am writing in part to recommend it to you, though his primary audience is the elementary school teacher. If I may be evaluative for a moment, it is an excellent paper. It includes a very comprehensive discussion of the process of determining objectives and also a practical explanation of procedures by which a teacher can develop assessment instruments for measuring student progress in the cognitive, affective, and psychomotor domains. His examples are appropriately drawn from law-related curricula, and the procedures he recommends are well suited to assessing a full range of academic growth in the elementary-age child.

After reading Ron Gerlach's paper, I have one concern that I feel we as a profession need to consider among ourselves. So much of what we write for teachers comes across as being critical and without understanding of their situation. We often self-righteously browbeat teachers for the way they use evaluation. Gerlach cites Jarolimek's judgment that evaluation "may be the weakest link in the instructional process." Teachers rely on subjective, intuitive practices rather than using the "systematic, comprehensive, and continuous"

assessment practices that we evaluators promote. There is little doubt in our minds that rationally conceived assessment procedures will yield valuable feedback as to how teachers and students alike could improve their performance. The question that baffles us is why conscientious teachers do not use these valuable tools.

We usually answer this question in one of two ways. Either teachers lack the knowledge of assessment procedures and don't know how to use them, or they are simply stubborn and lazy—they know what to do and simply won't do it. I think there may be some other explanations of why competent teachers resist implementing the good assessment procedures suggested by Gerlach and others in our profession.

Teachers, like most other human beings, make choices about how they will spend their time out of a perception of what will give them the greatest payoff. Let's assume that because we are talking about good teachers, that "greatest payoff" is seen as the "highest good" for their students. Creating a bulletin board about the duties of a police officer, developing a Likert scale to assess student attitudes toward the law, making up a study guide about the judicial process to go with a film, contacting the sheriff about a "ride with an officer for a day" project—these are but a few of the kinds of uses of her/his time. Even the most conscientious and hard-working teacher will not be able to do all, and will thus make choices. It is at this point that assessment that is not absolutely required for grading purposes loses out, not because these other assessment practices are not worthwhile, but rather because there appear to be more worth-

Robert W. Richburg is Associate Professor of Social Studies and Adult Education at Colorado State University. His interests include developing innovative teaching material for the social studies classroom and curriculum evaluation with an emphasis on the affective domain.

275

while activities that should take precedence.

Let me illustrate this point by asking you to react to the short simulation exercise below.

Put yourself in the role of an elementary school teacher committed to teaching about law and the American legal system. By district rule you must record two grades per week in your grade book, so you have to make up and grade some tests and quizzes and papers. You have no choice in that. But you do have a lot of choices about how you spend the rest of your time. Below are listed nine activities that would be "good" to do with and for your students. Even taking work home in the evenings, you can probably only get five of these things done. Which would you do? Rank your priorities from 1 to 5, with 1 being the first you would do:

_____ Plan a field trip to the county courthouse to see a trial. This involves your time organizing transportation, checking with teachers and administrators so as not to allow conflicts in the school calendar, getting parental permission and supervisory support, working with the judge to maximize learning, etc.

_____ Develop and use a simulation of a crime and the apprehension and trial of an accused person. A robbery of the school store could be staged. Students could play the roles of investigators and witnesses as well as the criminals. If there was enough evidence, charges could be brought and a trial held.

_____ Write specific behavioral objectives for the unit, being careful to include verbs that are observable, the conditions under which the accomplishment of the objective will be measured, and the criterion for successful completion of the objective.

_____ Take pre- and posttest data from the last unit that the class studied and relate each item on the test to some aspect of the curriculum materials and class activities which were used to help the students learn what you intended them to learn. Then make inferences from the test data about which activities were and were not successful in promoting learning.

_____ Make an appointment and visit the home of a student who seems withdrawn and lonely at school.

_____ Do some background reading in the development of law through history. This is an area you were never exposed to except superficially in your undergraduate teacher preparation.

_____ Construct a semantic differential on the attitudes of your class toward police to determine if your unit changed the way students feel about officers of the law.

_____ Spend time in the public library with one student trying to find information about what lawyers do. This student is bright and has shown a keen interest in being a lawyer but was unable to find anything on lawyers in the school library.

_____ Work out a program with the police department in town to bring a police officer into the classroom on a regular basis to talk informally, answer questions, and just be around the students.

Now, be honest, how did the evaluation activities fare in comparison with other worthwhile things a teacher might do?

If teachers are to move evaluation activities such as those mentioned in this exercise to a higher point in their scale of priorities, they must see evaluation as having more worth than some other activities that take their time. In communicating with teachers, we evaluators have overemphasized the explanation of how to collect evaluative data and neglected to show how those data can really help them.

Teachers participating in a law and humanities program will have some very important uses for evaluation information beyond what they will use in grading students. Of special concern will be the need to make some determination of the worth of a new set of curriculum materials, compared to what they have been using previously. They will also want to identify weak areas of the curriculum and, through an analysis of data on student performance, suggest how that curriculum can be improved. Both of these are valid and widely promoted uses of evaluation. The problem is that teachers are rarely shown how to organize evaluation data to be able to address such worthwhile questions. They are also not exposed to the pitfalls that one may encounter in making such assessments. It may be in this arena, however, that a teacher spends some of his/her most profitable time for students.

Gerlach correctly admonishes teachers to be comprehensive in their classroom evaluation. To get a complete picture of student performance the teacher must measure growth in knowledge, skills, and attitudes. As evaluators we know how often the knowledge domain is overemphasized in the evaluation efforts of teachers at the expense of other aspects of student learning. This is again evidence that most teachers have not been shown how to use evaluation data except to grade students. Teachers can give grades on knowledge and skills but not on the attitudes students hold. To illustrate how evaluation data can be useful to the teacher in other ways than in giving grades, let's focus on the affective or attitudinal domain.

Using Assessment Data from the Affective Domain

It is important for those planning an assessment program for a law and humanities program to give priority to the affective domain. It is becoming increasingly clear from the perspectives of research and reason that how a person feels is more important than what he or she knows. Feelings and attitudes act as a greater control on behavior than knowledge does (Ringness, 1975, p. 4).

As an example of how information about attitude change could be useful in making curriculum decisions, let's look at some questions which would reflect student attitudes.

1. Do you think police officers are pretty nice people?
2. Do you think the city would be better off with more police officers?
3. If you needed help would you go to a police officer?
4. Do you think the police treat black people and white people alike?

The response choices could be scaled in several possible ways to record the spread of student opinion. By turning the questions into statements, the students could be asked how intensely they agree or disagree with the statements. For example, question 1 above could become:

1. Police officers are pretty nice people.
   Strongly Agree Agree Uncertain Disagree Strongly Disagree

This is a Likert scale of the kind suggested by Gerlach, and with its five response options it has the advantage of spreading student opinion broadly. For younger students, however, a simpler three-response option to a question format may be better. For example:

1. Do you think police officers are pretty nice people?
   Yes   Not Sure   No

Teachers unfamiliar with the use of affective or attitudinal measures will naturally tend to use them to assess the attitudes of *individual* students. We are accustomed to assessing an individual's knowledge, again for the purposes of grading.

Why not assess the individual's attitudes in that same way? The answer is that in working with individuals, attitudinal measures tend not to produce much that is useful. First of all, the results cannot be used for grading. It would be immoral to grade a person on what he or she feels or values, and, if you tried, he or she could readily determine what you wanted and "fake" a response in order to better his or her grade. Beyond use of the data for grading, a teacher might try to develop individualized instructional programs on the basis of an assessment of each individual's attitudes toward the law. This would be so time-consuming to do for each member of the class that it is hard to imagine a teacher doing so.

A much more practical and useful approach would be to interpret the data from items or scales for a class as a whole. The attitudinal scales have much greater reliability when treated in this way. One item taken by 30 students gives you the same degree of realiability as 30 items taken by one student.

To interpret a Likert or other attitudinal scale you must assign each response a point value and then come up with a numerical average for the class on each item. For example, in the three-response example, "yes" responses would be given a value of 1; "not sure" responses, a value of 2; and "no" responses, a 3. For the Likert scale, which is a five-response scale, "strongly agree" would receive a 5; "agree," a 4; and so on down to "strongly disagree," which would receive a 1. The class average for each statement or question can be determined by multiplying the number of student responses by the point value assigned to each response. If there were 20 students in the class

---

Figure 1

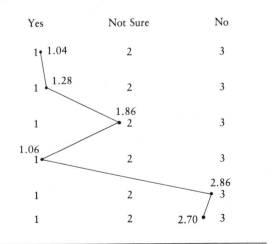

	Yes	Not Sure	No
1. Do you think police officers are pretty nice people?	1 1.04	2	3
2. Do you think the city would be better off with more police officers?	1 1.28	2	3
3. Do you think the police treat black people and white people alike?	1	1.86 2	3
4. If you needed help would you call a police officer?	1.06 1	2	3
5. Would it be better to live in our town if we didn't have any laws?	1	2	2.86 3
6. Should people obey even unfair laws?	1	2	2.70 3

Figure 2

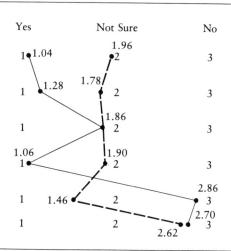

	Yes	Not Sure	No
1. Do you think police officers are pretty nice people?	1●1.04	1.96 ●2	3
2. Do you think the city would be better off with more police officers?	1 ●1.28	1.78 ● 2	3
3. Do you think the police treat black people and white people alike?	1	1.86 ● 2	3
4. If you needed help, would you call a police officer?	1.06 1●	1.90 ● 2	3
5. Would it be better to live in our town if we didn't have any laws?	1 1.46 ●	2	2.86 3
6. Should people obey even unfair laws?	1	2 2.62	2.70 3

NOTE: Pretest profile indicated by dashed line; posttest profile, by solid line.

their responses might be distributed in this manner: 13 "yes" responses, four "not sure," and three "no." To get a class average determine the sum of the responses times the value of each response:

13 "yes" × 1	=	13
4 "not sure" × 2	=	8
3 "no" × 3	=	9
		30

Now divide by the number of students in the class: 20 ÷ 30 = 1.5.

If this were done for each statement, you could construct a class profile which would reflect students' attitudes about the police or the law or whatever the scale concerned. Figure 1 shows such a profile. It is an actual profile for a class of students in Colorado that had just completed 6 weeks of instruction in legal education.

If this same instrument had been administered before as well as after the instructional unit, we would have a preinstruction and postinstruction profile like that shown in Figure 2. This would, of course, indicate changes in the attitudes of the class as a result of the lessons that had been prepared.

For the sake of discussion let's assume the teacher whose class these profiles represent had used the following kinds of activities and experiences to teach this unit.

1. A role-playing exercise in which students pretended to live in a mythical place where there were no laws. The incidents to be acted out would be intended to show the kinds of problems that could occur in this situation.
2. A movie which showed the kinds of things a police officer does in a community that citizens are often unaware of.
3. A field trip during which students visited a police station and in groups of three accompanied an officer as he cruised the city streets in his patrol car.
4. A reading and discussion about how police must relate to people of different racial and ethnic backgrounds.
5. A class discussion about what constitutes fair and unfair laws.

How would the information that could be derived from these attitudinal measures—administered before and after a unit of this kind—be useful in making curriculum decisions? Some attitudes held by the class were clearly changed and some were not. We could apply statistical procedures to be precise about this. Even without such precision we can be confident that after the unit the students were more positive than before about police being nice and approachable. They remained uncertain, however, that police treat whites and blacks the same way. Nor was there any change in attitude about obeying laws that they perceived as unfair.

If these results can be associated with specific activities or aspects of the curriculum, then there will be some good information about what to do and what not to do the next time this unit is taught. Having the students ride with a patrol officer, for example, appears to have been a good way to influence their thinking about police being friendly and helpful. The results of items 1 and 4 help us reach that conclusion for this class. In the same way, item 3 seems to indicate that the reading and discussion about police interaction with various racial groups were ineffective. The next time this unit is taught the teacher might want to plan some other kind of experience to attempt to have a greater impact on these attitudes.

The insights gained from associating pretest and posttest changes in class attitudes would be useful in helping a teacher replan a unit for teaching it another time. A teacher could see where the strengths and weaknesses in the curriculum were and what kinds of things could be done to improve it. The time and skill it would take to construct scales such as this, summarize the data for several classes, and generate reasonable interpretations should not be minimized, however, when we recommend such procedures to teachers. As valuable as such insights might be, we still need to acknowledge that in the day-to-day press of working with students evaluation may never have high priority.

REFERENCE

Ringness, T. A. *The affective domain in education.* Boston: Little, Brown, 1975.

Improving Law-related Elementary School Courses through Qualitative Evaluation

Gail McCutcheon

A major complaint about evaluation is that conventional procedures often do not reveal some of the most important things students learn. Similarly, such procedures do not allow for the most crucial goals of law-related education to be satisfactorily measured. Qualitative evaluation is not a panacea but does promise to be an important complement to the more traditional approaches.

This article introduces the nature and function of qualitative evaluation, as well as the potential role(s) of the evaluator. Most important, the author links the implications of qualitative evaluation procedures to instruction in law and humanities in the elementary school.

An integral part of planning for the development and implementation of a new program or course of studies is planning for evaluation of that program. Evaluations of courses are aimed at improving their development and implementation and facilitating decision making, and evaluators can have several roles. The evaluation of law-related elementary school programs raises several interesting and important concerns addressed in this paper. What functions does evaluation serve? What roles could evaluators have? What could we evaluate about a program? What new developments in evaluation might be particularly appropriate to law-related elementary school programs? How are these types of evaluation done?

This paper discusses an approach with potential for evaluating law-related elementary school programs. It is not intended to prepare people to do the evaluation. Rather, it provides information to help educators be better planners for evaluation, better hirers of evaluators, and better consumers of evaluation reports. Understanding the approach permits readers to know what sorts of questions a qualitative evaluation might answer, what information could be gathered, and what roles evaluation could play. For further information about the approach, readers are urged to consult the References and to seek out workshops and

Gail McCutcheon, Assistant Professor of Curriculum at The Ohio State University, recently completed research into elementary school teachers' planning, as reported in a forthcoming article in the *Elementary School Journal.* She is currently studying the uses of text materials in elementary school classrooms.

courses about qualitative evaluation, educational criticism, or educational ethnography.

Evaluation

Functions and types of information collected. The evaluation of school programs and curricula is undertaken to gather information and to make judgments about them. This information and these judgments can be used in course development, course improvement, and decision making about dropping or retaining courses. For example, an evaluation indicating that certain materials are poorly worded for children might lead to revisions. Or an evaluation might provide evidence of wide community support for a course—that it is enjoyed by children and teachers, provides worthwhile, exciting activities for the children, and meets the aims designated by the developers. Facts such as these might help an administrator decide whether to continue funding the course.

Information generated by an evaluation permits informed judgments to be made about the development, improvement, and continuation of a program. The information base should be complete enough to permit people to make warranted decisions about courses, preserving the excellent ones and revising or discontinuing those that are unsound. The information base should answer common-sense questions. These questions can be raised in advance, but they may also arise during the course of the evaluation or as the program is used.

Information for an evaluation can be collected about several types of phenomena. One type is evidence of student outcomes, such as test scores, examples of written work, tape recordings of class discussions, descriptions of group presentations, and photographs of artwork or other constructions. Another type is evidence about the materials to be used by children and teachers in the program. This evidence might include descriptions, samples, photographs, or films of the materials. A third type of information in many curriculum evaluations is evidence about the ongoing process of schooling provided by the program. Descriptions, videotapes, or photographs could provide this kind of evidence.

It is important to note that the three types of information—student outcomes, materials, and the ongoing process of schooling—can be helpful in each of the functions curriculum evaluation serves—to facilitate course development, to assist with course improvement, and to provide a basis for decisions about continuing or discontinuing a course. Information of several types can be used in one curriculum evaluation; a wealth of information is needed if we are to generate and maintain programs of quality.

Information is collected about the program and also about its fit with the rest of the school's curriculum. Both the overt curriculum—the stated one—and the latent, or "hidden," curriculum—the unintended outcomes and activities—can be considered.

Roles for the evaluation. In what ways could an evaluator assist with the development, implementation, and dissemination of law-related humanities programs for elementary schools? (Acknowledgment is extended to Gary Wehlage, with whom I discussed roles for evaluators when we attended a conference in Chicago in 1978.)

During the early stages when developers begin to conceive a program, an evaluator can help by raising issues and by analyzing goals and priorities. Retaining a scholarly stance is important here; as people get more involved in developing the program, they may tend to believe in it more, almost blindly. This belief is important for sustaining the efforts of the project, but it can do harm unless an outsider continues to ask pertinent questions and raise issues. Do some of the assumptions or goals of the project conflict with one another? Does research provide any clues about whether it might work?

In addition to the roles of issue raiser and goal analyst, an evaluator can also explore the context in which the project is being developed. What are the preferences of the community? Might structural limitations in the schedule, budget, staff, or buildings interfere with the program? How do the context and the program relate to each other?

Throughout the project, an evaluator can also function as a historian by documenting the development. Records can be kept of key decisions and arguments for them. Later, if a decision is called into question, the evaluator's notes might prove helpful in reconstructing the reasons for it. What are the visible or potential influences of such decisions? Also, if a lack of consistency grows in the program, developers can trace its path. Historical notes of this sort might be useful to the development team, but histories of curriculum development projects are important to maintain for their potential contribution to research and to theories about curriculum development. Many have noted the lack of fit between theories of curriculum development and practice. Collecting many case studies seems to be a likely early step in developing more useful theories.

During the development of a project, an evaluator can also have the role of monitoring what is being developed and piloted in successive trials. Evaluators can also point out data that developers may not have noticed. Evaluators can interpret this information, historically, psychologically, and socially, in terms of learning theories or some other context. The evaluator can keep track of the sorts of revisions that are going to be needed.

The evaluator can also be responsible for reviewing the materials and manuals after the program's development phase is completed. Do the parts fit together? Does the program have coherence and direction? Is it attractive, intelligible, and potentially interesting for students and teachers to use? What sort of school might find it a good program? What might be the hidden curriculum—the ancillary outcomes—of the program? Just as a play producer reads a script for a play before deciding whether to support a particular production, so can an evaluator review a "script" for a program.

Further, the evaluator can act as portrayer (see Parlett & Hamilton, 1976) of the program and its materials. What is their nature? What do children and the teacher do? What do they produce and appear to learn? Is it worthwhile? For what reasons?

During implementation the evaluator can continue to monitor the use of the project.

Evaluators provide evidence on which to base decisions about a program's development and improvement and about whether it should be used, modified, or dropped from a school's curriculum. Not all of these roles may be necessary or appropriate for the evaluation of every program.

Trends and issues. Historically, the information provided by evaluators has been based on test score data. In some evaluations, these data are compared to a course's objectives to discover the discrepancy between student outcomes (as measured by the test) and stated goals. This approach to evaluation has probably been popular for a number of reasons. Tests produce few problems when we administer them, are relatively inexpensive, provide easily compared numbers, are norm-referenced on a national basis, and provide at least a facade of consensus (even if tacit) about the goals of education.

If practice is any indication, prior to 1930 evaluation was viewed as nearly synonymous with the administration of standardized tests. As Taylor and Cowley (1972, p. 1) note about this era: "Comparisons, when these were appropriate, were made between two groups or between a target group and a set of norms. This kind of evaluation stemmed from the preoccupation with content objectives that characterized education in the early part of this century." After this period a few larger-scale curriculum evaluations (such as Tyler and Smith's Eight Year Study) were undertaken to collect more comprehensive and varied evidence. In the United States, at least, we are still concerned in early curriculum evaluation primarily with measuring student outcomes through the use of tests. We tend to focus on test-related student outcomes and to measure the achievement of objectives, rather than collecting information about a wide range of student outcomes, the materials used, what students actually do, or the educational setting.

A few evaluators in several European countries and the United States, however, have become increasingly concerned about collecting varied information. Hamilton (1976, p. 49) characterized these evaluations as follows: "A movement away from achievement measurement, they indicate an increased concern for contextual [studies]. ... Above all, they reflect a gradual move from the evaluation of curricula and materials to the appraisal of the entire social milieu relevant to teaching and learning." Objections to the achievement test score approach to evaluation include the following:

1. Two chief functions of evaluation are to assist with development and renovation of programs. If we administer achievement tests at the end of the experimental program and find our students did not perform well, what does this indicate about how to improve the program? Was the teaching poor, implying we need in-service courses or new teachers? Was the program poorly constructed? Were the activities dull or beyond the reach of the children? Or was the test not matched to the program? On the other hand, if the achievement test scores were marvelous, what do they indicate about how we can recapture our success? A major difficulty, then, with the achievement testing approach to evaluation is

that practical implications for improving the program or maintaining its excellence are missing. Without these implications, the decision maker is also left in a quandary about whether to continue the program. For example, children recently declined in their ability to define "democracy" in a nationwide poll. What does this mean? Poor teaching? That it is not included in curriculum? Is it symptomatic of a lack of clarity in the general society? Or was the test item itself unclear?

2. Examining only student products as evidenced by test scores disregards the quality of the experience undergone to achieve those results. What if the experience was dull, humiliating, or restricting, yet produced high achievement scores? (In medicine, surgeons might say the operation was a failure although the patient lived! And, conversely, what if the experience was mind-expanding, exhilarating, or creative, but produced low scores? Is it right for student outcomes to be the only criterion for success of a program?

3. Only certain kinds of items can be formulated for achievement tests, items that may not measure the true intent of the course. Can we provide test items, for example, about kinds of understanding essential to living in a democracy, or how people in a democracy must "balance the needs for individual rights with imperative for individual responsibility" (Morris, 1973, p. 3)? Listing the articles of the Constitution and checking off items guaranteed by the Bill of Rights are items easily put on a test, but they do not measure fundamental aims of law-related elementary programs.

4. Large-scale evaluations using test items are insensitive to the local context, to forces influencing the program and preventing or guaranteeing its success. Such items are lost to discussion but may be especially pertinent.

This paper should not be perceived as an argument for totally abandoning standardized achievement tests. Rather, it is an argument that they are not sufficient (by themselves) for evaluating a curriculum, for they do not provide us with enough information. (For further discussions of these points and other criticisms of achievement testing as course evaluation, see Easley, 1973; Eisner, 1979; Parlett & Hamilton, 1976, pp. 86–88; Stake, 1967.)

In general, then, evaluation is an activity aimed at providing information to practitioners for use in developing or renovating a program and making decisions about its continuation. Conceiving an evaluation in this way dictates that we collect a wealth of information, focusing on several aspects of the educational scene. Tests scores may be one piece of this information but cannot be viewed as sufficient alone.

Qualitative Evaluation

A definition. Several alternatives to the use of achievement tests have been developed by educators in Great Britain and the United States. Among these are evaluation as portrayal (Vallance, Note 1), illuminative evaluation (Parlett & Hamilton, 1976), educational ethnography, educational criticism (Eisner, 1979; McCutcheon, 1978, 1979), documentary evaluation (e.g., Bailey, 1976), and responsive evaluation (Stake, 1975). These forms of evaluation are qualitative, for their main attention is to the qualities of a program rather than to the collection of quantitative data. This dichotomy is rather deceptive, for numerical data may be collected as evidence for a qualitative evaluation. The important distinction here is that the *focus* is not on quantities, but on qualities.

The aim of qualitative evaluation is to collect information about the nature, the character, the essences of a program and to appraise the likely consequences of those qualities. Generally, an evaluator engaged in qualitative inquiry documents the nature of student outcomes, materials, or the program in operation. For example, with regard to student outcomes Davis and Greenstein (1969) documented one child's—Jennifer's—difficulties with subtraction, seen as an outcome of the mathematics program in her school. With regard to materials, Vallance (1977) portrayed a unit about the Great Plains by examining, describing, and commenting upon the television programs and accompanying materials used in a course developed by the University of Mid-America. And with regard to the program in operation, McCutcheon (1978) disclosed and commented upon the day-to-day activities of a fourth-grade classroom.

Principles and processes. Several processes are common to many qualitative evaluations. Generally, a qualitative evaluator gathers a broad range of information by observing the program in use or examining the program's materials or student work. On the basis of this evidence, the evaluator describes, interprets, and appraises the program.

When describing the program, an evaluator considers its nature. What do children and teachers do? What materials do they use? How frequently? What is the character of the materials? In looking at student outcomes, an evaluator describes the nature of those outcomes and the nature of things children say, write, and make. After examining these products, what can we say

students were given the opportunity to practice? As a result, what were they likely to have learned or not to have learned? What might they have learned along the way that was not intended? Description is one process of qualitative evaluation, and for many evaluators description is the main purpose of their effort.

A second process common to most qualitative evaluations is interpretation. After the information has been gathered and described, we must interpret it in one of several ways to derive meaning from it. One way of interpreting events or materials concerns the social meaning of happenings. Social events, even if reduced to discrete behavioral acts, must be interpreted before we can make sense of them. We use this type of interpretation in everyday life when we decide such things as whether a crowd standing by the street constitutes a menacing gang, a group of strikers, or commuters waiting for the 5:30 bus. Anthropologists interpret the meanings of acts in cultures they study. We can use this kind of interpretation, as well, to derive the social meanings of classroom events. What does it mean when three children raise their hands in a discussion about a news article, oohing and aahing to be called upon? And what if children quietly announce to their peers, "I'm done," as they turn in their work sheets about human rights? This description of physical behavior is less important than the social meaning of these events. Were the discussants eager to share? Were they competitive? Were they trying to exhibit all their knowledge of the answer? Did the children announce their work sheet completion to brag? Was a subtle form of competition operating? Is it symptomatic of pervasive achievement motivation operating in the class? Or were they relieved to be finished? (See Geertz, 1973, for elaboration of this type of interpretation.)

In a second type of interpretation the qualitative researcher analyzes the program or classroom by discussing its parts and resynthesizes them to form patterns that explain the relationships of the parts by their functions. How do the parts relate to each other and to the whole? The evaluator does not portray the actions of students and teachers and other elements as if they were random, isolated acts; instead, by constructing patterns, he/she gives them meaning by disclosing their affiliations to one another and to the whole.

For example, with respect to law and humanities elementary school programs, we may find many bits of evidence indicating the teachers genuinely do not understand some basic concepts they are trying to teach. In written work, class discussions, and lectures, teachers and children may demonstrate a lack of clarity and fundamental knowledge of these meanings. After further examination, we may be able to relate this to poorly worded teacher's guides or to the neglect of this topic in an in-service program. Constructing such patterns assists us in understanding internal relationships among events.

In addition to social meanings and patterns, a third type of interpretation in many qualitative evaluations relates local information to the external and broader context. That is, the evaluator compares phenomena peculiar to this case to historical events, to events in other schools or in society at large, to theories from the social sciences, or to philosophical positions. For instance, difficulties cropping up in a kindergarten program dealing with reasons for crosswalks and traffic lights might be better understood when seen in light of Piaget's theories about preoperational and concrete-operational thinking. The activities may be too abstract for the youngsters. This type of interpretation is reciprocal, for not only can a classroom or a program be more fully understood in light of the interpretation, but the event vividly exemplifies the theory, the event of history, the philosophical position, or the larger social context. It may also provide evidence of a new theory, a flaw in a theory, or a change in the times. As a result, we can understand the kindergarten better, but the interpretation also helps us understand Piaget's theories.

These three types of interpretation—interpreting the social meanings of events, patterns of events, and their relations to other theories and information—can be seen to varying degrees in different qualitative evaluations. One evaluation may focus on the first type of interpretation, while another may focus on one of the others.

Some evaluators, having described the context in some detail, leave interpretation up to their audience.

Two processes apparent in many qualitative evaluations, then, are description and interpretation. A third process is appraisal. Questions one asks when appraising a classroom or program appear to be easy to answer: Is the program worth teaching? Was it done well? But appearances do not tell the whole tale. The first question—Is it worth teaching?—provides an opportunity for the evaluator to consider the educational significance of the program. For example, in considering a program's educational significance, we might wonder about the sort of intellectual environment the program provides. What was the nature of the interpersonal climate created by the use of the program? What were pupils likely to believe and feel about the subject matter and the activities they engaged in? Are these beliefs and feelings worthwhile for children to possess and to carry with them into adulthood? Given all the things we could impart in schools and the relatively little

time spent there, is this program worth the time invested? The first question of appraisal weighs the aims of a program by examining its instructional materials or student products or the program in action. From these, goals can be inferred. Evaluators may also ask the program's authors about their goals, but these goals may not always have been put into operation. In addition, knowing the goals may focus our attention unduly on them while extremely important considerations escape our attention as a result. For these reasons, some evaluators, particularly at the beginning of their inquiry, choose not to ask developers about their goals. Other evaluators collect goal statements as one item of information for consideration. (See Scriven, 1973, for elaboration of this point.)

The other question of appraisal—was it done well?—addresses the instructional quality of the program. For instance, let us assume that the program being evaluated includes taking a field trip to the state general assembly to see how laws are made. Did the teacher tie the field trip into what went on in class? Did the trip help children understand the rather abstract written or discussion material, and did the material facilitate children's understanding of what happened in the assembly? Or was the field trip just an activity—fun, but not an integral part of the in-class learning?

These three processes—description, interpretation, and appraisal—characterize many qualitative evaluations. Evaluations differ regarding the extent to which each process predominates and the type of information gathered. It is important to note, too, that the three processes are highly interrelated. That is, we interpret almost as we describe, and appraise while we interpret. For purposes of discussion, though, it is useful to separate the three.

As a final consideration about principles and processes of qualitative inquiry, let us turn now to how the approach is made rigorous. Any form of scientific inquiry is governed by a set of rules for assuring or assessing its discipline and rigor. These "rules of the game" assure that an investigation was done in a scholarly fashion. The investigator should provide evidence of having followed these rules to permit readers to assess the study's believability.

In qualitative inquiry, several such rules or principles exist. For one thing, it is important to provide the evidence supporting an interpretation or appraisal. The evidence can be descriptive, photographic, or of any other kind but its value lies in providing support for the analysis. Just as a well-written detective novel includes clues leading to a crime's solution, so should qualitative evaluators provide evidence supporting their case. Second, it is important to reveal the line of reasoning behind an interpretation or appraisal. All the clues are present in a detective novel; at the end, the detective weaves them together coherently, enabling us to understand the line of reasoning behind the detective's deduction. To be sure, our line of reasoning must frequently be more involved than a detective's, and therefore all the more important to reveal. Unless the supporting evidence is included and the line of thinking is revealed, qualitative evaluations are little more than allegations, for their subjectivity, believability, and validity cannot be assessed by the public. (For elaboration of these processes and of techniques for assuring or assessing believability, see McCutcheon, 1978.)

Its application to law-related elementary school programs. Given all of the above, how might qualitative evaluation be applied to law-related elementary school programs? Indeed, why *should* it be?

For one thing, it could be helpful to educators engaged in the enterprises of developing programs, revising them, and deciding whether to continue them. By providing varied evidence about student outcomes, materials, and programs in use, qualitative evaluation could enable educators to make warranted decisions. Second, certain goals may be difficult to assess on quantitative achievement tests. If we resorted to that method alone, we might be forced to water down the goals to conform to the standardized testing model. It seems more reasonable and educationally sound to devise evaluation approaches appropriate to the goals rather than to twist the goals to render them appropriate to the evaluation approach. Third, if many different programs are devised, it may not be fair to measure all according to the same criteria. What were the strengths of the Los Angeles program? The one used in Winnetka? What about the one in Stony Point? Qualitative evaluation also responds to several criticisms of the testing approach to evaluation mentioned earlier. Let us now turn to a few illustrations specific to elementary school law programs and examine ways in which qualitative evaluation could be applied.

In considering human rights, over a period of several weeks, a sixth-grade class could attempt to define human rights guaranteed in the United States by examining our Bill of Rights, the United Nations statement on human rights, and other documents. Then they could read newspapers and news magazines and watch television news to collect examples of cases in which a right guaranteed in the United States was being denied to a citizen. The class could also discuss which right was being ignored, possible reasons for its denial, and whether they seemed just. Each student could choose a news article and write about these topics. Flowing from this could be an investigation of the responsibilities of citizens in a democracy. If these are our rights, what responsibilities result from them? What other responsibilities are necessary if the country is to function as a democracy?

In this case, an evaluation of student products might be called for, requiring collection of the articles they read, papers about the articles, and tapes of the discussion. These could be analyzed with respect to what children were likely to have learned about rights and responsibilities in the United States. If the products did not reflect deep understanding of rights and responsibilities, several possible reasons could be offered and explored. Perhaps the materials were too difficult for sixth graders to read. Perhaps the discussions were not skillfully handled. Perhaps the topic was not presented in an interesting or relevant way.

In another elementary school classroom studying democratic principles, evaluators might be observing the ongoing use of the program. They might observe that for 50 minutes twice a week children read about, hear about, and investigate democracy in action. But for the rest of the week, the classroom is run in a very authoritarian, undemocratic way. Might this lack of fit between the subject matter of study—democratic principles—and the way in which the classroom operates convey messages to children? What are they likely to understand deeply about democracy in the setting? Are there better ways to learn how to live in a democratic society?

In an upper elementary school classroom, children might be wondering about the roles of police officers. What do they actually do in the community? This could be compared to the children's initial beliefs about what police officers do and to mass-media images. To begin with, children might list what they believe police officers do. Later they might examine comic strips (such as "Dick Tracy"), television shows (such as "Kojak," "Police Woman," "Starsky and Hutch," "S.W.A.T."), and children's stories to discover how they portray the police. On another occasion, children could visit the police station and interview police officers to find out what they really do. Perhaps some could watch police at work. In a play, children could dramatize differences between the fictional police world and the real one. Or they could rewrite an episode of "Dick Tracy" or "Kojak" to correspond more to reality. Perhaps a discussion could follow about possible reasons for differences between the fictional and real worlds of the police and possible problems the fictional accounts could create.

In this case, an evaluator might tape the play or examine children's revised cartoons or TV shows to discern whether children appear to understand the roles of police in a democracy, or if they are still attuned to the roles presented by mass media. Examining the discussions might reveal the clarity and depth of understanding. An evaluator might also want to look at the entire law-related program to see where this goal fits. Does it accord with other goals? Is there order to the program, or are there many fun, involving activities, such as this one, but little commonality holding the program together, giving it direction and continuity? How can we maximize the opportunity for children to make connections among their experiences?

These examples are intended to serve as illustrations of the sorts of information that could be collected and the issues that might be addressed in a qualitative evaluation of a law-related elementary school program. Case studies are needed to provide a more comprehensive view of a curriculum evaluation in action.

Presentation. Information from quantitative evaluations is generally presented in tables. Sometimes a narrative follows to assist with interpreting the figures on those tables. How can information from qualitative evaluation be presented? Baily's evaluation (1976) of the European Architectural Heritage Year was presented through photographs of students' projects and samples of their poetry woven together by narrative. Through the narrative he revealed why some programs failed and others succeeded. Vallance (Note 1) portrayed her evaluation of materials about the Great Plains through posters. Usually, though, evaluations tend to be written descriptions, interpretations, and appraisals of outcomes, materials, or the program in use (e.g., Davis & Greenstein, 1969; McCutcheon, 1978; Vallance, 1977; McCutcheon, Note 2). There is no reason why a display could not present samples of students' products and a slide tape illustrating the teaching, accompanied by a guide to assist the viewer through the collections much as a museum catalog helps us through an exhibition. A museum catalog provides background information, links certain elements for us, and helps us interpret them. Such a catalog could accompany an evaluation display. A display arranged for program developers, revisers, or decision makers might be more graphic and lead to a deeper understanding than a written document alone because a display would require active participation by the viewers. Displays of different programs might enable viewers to make comparisons among them. These comparisons might assist developers, revisers, and decision makers working on particular programs. A display, however, is impractical in some situations because it is not easily transportable.

Qualifications of the evaluator. Given the foregoing discussion about evaluation, what sorts of skills and knowledge should a person doing qualitative evaluation possess?

Clearly, if the evaluator is to be called upon to collect evidence and make judgments—to observe and reflect—it is crucial for him or her to have a great deal of knowledge about elementary schools, law-related programs, and the law. This knowledge forms the frame of reference from which information is sorted out about classrooms; it forms the intellectual context of interpretations and appraisals. A wide range of knowledge of the history of education and ideas from sociology, psychology, anthropology, philosophy, law, and current local and national events are useful in providing bases for interpretation. In addition, this information acts as a ground against which observations can be compared to help an observer perceive what is significant or unique about the program, the setting, the materials, or the outcomes. In everyday life, we constantly compare this thing or event against those previously experienced. One way of understanding our new experiences is through this continuous comparison. An evaluator is better equipped to make these comparisons if he/she has had considerable experience providing a broad base of knowledge for use in perceiving differences among, interpreting, and appraising the programs.

Accompanying this need for knowledge is a need for sensitivity to the phenomena being studied—classrooms, children, educational materials, concepts from law and the humanities, and so forth. Communication skills are also needed, as is the ability to develop rapport with children and adults.

But more important, a questioning, fact-finding, and judging approach to evaluation must be understood. It is necessary for evaluators to adopt an inquiring attitude, posing questions such as: What is the character of these materials? Of this program? What are children likely to learn from it? What is going on? Then they must consider how answers to particularly relevant questions can be gathered and documented, described, interpreted, and appraised. An understanding of ways to make the approach disciplined is also necessary. Doing this sort of work calls for a certain amount of cognitive flexibility, as it requires a researcher to observe closely the situation at hand, then to step back and think, "What have we here?" as the interpretation and appraisal are considered. This problem-solving approach of observing and reflecting in a scholarly way is not foreign to human endeavors. Rather, it seems to be a natural part of our day-to-day life (see, e.g., Dewey, 1910). For this reason it is feasible for many evaluators to learn these processes of disciplined inquiry.

What we can and can't expect. As a result of a qualitative evaluation, educators are furnished with information. This information can be of varied types, can focus on different aspects of the situation, and can be communicated in various ways. We can expect, then, information that can help practitioners in a particular context deal with course development, revision, and decision making. The information can be expected to be specific to a particular context, to reflect the frame of reference of the evaluator, and to focus mostly on qualitative dimensions. We cannot expect norm-referenced information to be generated. For this reason it appears to be more difficult to compare qualitative information about several programs. Patterns can be noted among the programs, however, and on this basis comparisons can be made among qualitative evaluations. Bailey's overview of many programs of the European Architectural Heritage Year (1976) permits us to see the ways in which the degree of collaboration among schools, colleges of education, civic societies, and the media affected the success or failure of those programs. Three continuing needs were cited as a result of his documentation: "the need for integrating more closely work on the built environment with other elements in the curriculum; the need for further teacher education; and the great need for a wealth of resource material and for the knowledge of how to acquire and use it." Bailey went on to say: "Underlying all of these needs is the desirability of securing enduring public support for cooperative effect and for devising machinery able to give encouragement and information and to facilitate intercommunication" (1976, p. 23).

As we can see, evaluative studies can be compared qualitatively. In other words, patterns and qualities of one setting can be related to those elsewhere, thereby presenting a picture of a national or statewide educational movement. Qualitatively evaluating several law-related elementary school programs would enable us to examine what they have in common. What were the aims of different programs? Their materials? Student outcomes? What seemed to work in some contexts, but not in others, and why? A general evaluation of this sort would help local practitioners know what was happening elsewhere and to what end. On this basis, they could make informed decisions to facilitate course development, revision, and decision making in their own localities. Perhaps some programs developed elsewhere could be adopted and adapted to suit particular needs.

Many educators have charged that qualitative evaluations are overly subjective. That is, the studies reflect the evaluator more than they do the course or the classroom in which they are done. They need not do so, however, and this is one reason for emphasizing a disciplined approach. Providing evidence and revealing the line of reasoning behind one's reflections have been discussed as two principles of disciplined qualitative inquiry. An evaluation might be undertaken by a team who would discuss their interpretations and appraisals as a group. In this way, the shared meanings might be emphasized over the individual ones, resulting in a more objective study. However, a trade-off of this group approach would be the loss of the unique frame of reference of each evaluator. Salient interpretations may emerge through an individual's frame of reference that might be lost in the group process. Knowing the evaluator's frame of reference before hiring him or her is crucial.

Summary

In this paper several types of qualitative evaluations have been discussed, and processes common to many of them have been described. The paper is intended to serve as an overview of the approach and of ways it could bear upon law-related elementary school programs. Further readings (selected, for example, from the References) and participation in workshops and courses are advised for those intrigued with the idea.

The approach is aimed at providing information to help us conduct curriculum development, revision, and decision making in an informed, understanding way. What John Dewey said of excellent teachers applies to programs as well: "The successes of such individuals tend to be born and to die with them: beneficial consequences extend only to those pupils who have personal contact with such gifted teachers...the only way we can prevent such waste in the future is by methods which enable us to make an *analysis* of what the gifted teacher does" (1929, pp. 10–11). Let us hope that through careful qualitative evaluations we will be able to preserve the educational excellence of certain law-related elementary school programs.

REFERENCES

Bailey, K. V. *Education and heritage.* London: Heritage Education Group, 1976.

Davis, R., & Greenstein, R. Jennifer. *New York State Mathematics Teachers Journal,* 1969, 19, 94–103.

Dewey, J. *How we think.* Boston: Heath, 1910.

Dewey, J. *The sources of a science of education.* New York: Liveright, 1929.

Easley, J. A. The natural sciences and educational

research. In H. Broudy, R. Ennis, & L. Krimmerman (Eds.), *Philosophy of education research*. New York: Wiley, 1973.

Eisner, E. *The educational imagination*. New York: Macmillan, 1979.

Geertz, C. *The interpretation of cultures*. New York: Basic, 1973.

Hamilton, D. *Curriculum evaluation*. London: Open Books, 1976.

McCutcheon, G. Of solar systems, responsibilities and basics. In G. Willis (Ed.), *Qualitative evaluation*. Berkeley: McCutchan, 1978.

McCutcheon, G. Educational criticism: Methods and application. *Journal of Curriculum Theorizing*, 1979. 1 (2), 5–25.

Morris, E. F. Developing law-related studies. In S. E. Davison (Ed.), *Reflections on law-related education*. Chicago: American Bar Association, 1973.

Parlett, M., & Hamilton, D. Evaluation as illumination. In D. Tawney (Ed.), *Curriculum evaluation today*. London: Macmillan, 1976.

Scriven, M. Goal-free evaluation. In E. R. House (Ed.), *School evaluation: The politics and process*. Berkeley: McCutchan, 1973.

Stake, R. E. The countenance of educational evaluation. *Teachers College Record*, 1967, 68, 523–540.

Stake, R. E. *Evaluating the arts in education*. Columbus, Ohio: Merrill, 1975.

Taylor, P. A., & Cowley, D. M. *Readings in curriculum evaluation*. Dubuque, Iowa: Brown, 1972.

Vallance, E. The landscape of the Great Plains experience. *Curriculum Inquiry*, 1977, 7, 87–105.

REFERENCE NOTES

1. Vallance, E. Aesthetic criticism as portrayal. Paper presented at the annual meeting of the American Educational Research Association, Toronto, 1978.

2. McCutcheon, G. On the interpretation of classroom observations. Paper presented at the annual meeting of the American Educational Research Association, Toronto, 1978.

Another view . . .

Improving Law-related Elementary School Courses through Qualitative Evaluation

Gary Wehlage

While qualitative approaches are particularly important in evaluating programs in law and humanities, they possess features of which the educator should be fully aware. Without sensitivity to these attributes, an otherwise positive approach might turn into a negative experience. This paper expands upon Gail McCutcheon's initial article by pointing out those critical questions which should be kept in mind. Of particular importance is the issue of ethical guidelines which the qualitative evaluator may need to develop or have at hand prior to undertaking assessment.

Within the education profession there has recently appeared a movement toward the development of new conceptions of evaluation. This redirection in thinking about evaluation is based on doubts about the adequacy of conventional quantitative methodology to give useful information about educational programs. The best examples of alternatives to conventional evaluation designs are found in *Beyond the Numbers Game* (Hamilton et al., 1977) and *Qualitative Evaluation* (Willis,

1978). In addition, there is the work of anthropologist Harry Wolcott (1973, 1977). Strictly speaking Wolcott does not offer evaluations of schooling, but as exemplars of ethnography his writing has been important in shaping the alternative approach to research and evaluation which has now taken root within the education profession. Certainly the suggestions offered by Gail McCutcheon in her paper are squarely within this emerging paradigm.

In addressing the community of educators concerned with creating an evaluation approach adequate for the developing law-related curricula in elementary schools, McCutcheon has performed an important service by pointing out the limitations and inadequacies of conventional quantitative approaches to evaluation. The conven-

Gary Wehlage is Associate Professor of Curriculum and Instruction at the University of Wisconsin, Madison. He has written on research and evaluation methodology, conducted evaluations of school reform programs, and is currently engaged in an evaluation of Individually Guided Education.

tional wisdom is that statistical analysis of numerical data provides the most valid, powerful, and objective descriptions of educational programs and their effects on children. McCutcheon's paper points out, however, that the conventional approach offers a view of schooling that tends to hide the actual process of educating children, even though precise numerical "output" data are offered as effects of a program. The conventional approach tends to confine our picture of teaching and learning, as opposed to expanding our conception of what occurs in the process of schooling.

The McCutcheon paper asks educators involved with law-related programs to redirect their attention toward a study of the classroom in action—to curriculum in use. This is an important message for all educators because it can bring to the surface dimensions of schooling which conventional evaluation has overlooked in the past.

One of the things the paper does is to develop an expanded notion of student outcomes. Far from ignoring student outcomes, qualitative evaluators can include in the portrayal of a program such data as examples of written work; tape recordings of events or discussions; photographs of student presentations, plays, and artwork; as well as scores from tests. It is essential that this broader concept of achievement be used by both teachers and evaluators in assessing the effect of a curriculum. Good qualitative evaluation will not only present different kinds of achievement by students, but will also show it occurring in a range of contexts.

Much as I approve of the message contained in McCutcheon's paper, I do wish to quarrel with her on some points. First, the section which defines qualitative evaluation is not as helpful as it might be. There is a certain mystical circularity in defining the aim of this approach by saying it is a search for the nature, character, and essence of a program. In fact, there are several different versions of qualitative evaluation being practiced (as she points out), and each of these aims at something different, even though each rejects the use of statistical analysis as the basis of its approach. To tell those unfamiliar with qualitative evaluation that the essence of their curriculum will be described is not likely to be clarifying.

A second reservation I have concerns the usefulness of the distinction between description and interpretation in the section on "Principles and Processes." It may be misleading to claim that description is different from interpretation. The implication is that one could ask a qualitative evaluator to describe a curriculum but not engage in any interpretation. There is a well-articulated line of argument in the philosophy of history, for example, which points out that description of

events necessarily also involves interpretation. To describe requires one to be selective at several levels. In describing the events of a classroom, one must include some things at the expense of leaving others out. To describe is to choose categories which label things, people, actions, and events. The simple labeling of one person in the room as "the teacher" is an interpretive act.

Or, to offer a more complex example, consider the problem of what to call the events, utterances, and behaviors occurring during a 40-minute period in a classroom. The teacher and the children might call the period "reading," but what if they spend most of the time each day doing work sheets which call for the pupils to underline the correct word to complete a sentence? Is this reading? Some may choose to call it reading because they share the label used by the participants. Others may choose to call it literally "doing work sheets," or "completing sentences." No matter what words are chosen, the evaluator is engaging in the *selection* of devices which compress, focus, and interpret the happenings of the classroom.

The importance of this lack of distinction between description and interpretation is in making consumers of qualitative evaluation fully aware of what they are buying. If educators are under the impression that they can buy description without interpretation, they will almost certainly be disappointed. The assumption that description will somehow present an "objective" truth about a program while interpretation will offer a "subjective" distortion of reality is something the qualitative evaluator must guard against. In part, this assumption is a legacy from an inaccurate understanding of the dominant quantitative model, which sees science producing data which is somehow objectively uninterpreted. Neither quantitative nor qualitative evaluators can avoid the act of interpretation in making judgments about what information to collect, how to collect it, and what form to use in conveying the information which, to the best of their knowledge, is an accurate statement about people and events.

It is clear that the paper is written for those who would like to understand enough about qualitative evaluation so they can consider the use of this approach in their own programs. It may be, however, that some foray into the field of phenomenology is necessary to make clear what the term "social meaning" implies, since this is one kind of information which McCutcheon sees a qualitative evaluator conveying. What is the importance of information provided in statements about the social meaning people give to events? How does an evaluator arrive at statements about social meaning? I hope consumers of qualitative evaluation will have some understanding that interpretation of social meaning is likely to present information not traditionally found in evaluations.

My major criticism of the paper concerns problems surrounding the implications of "appraisal." This term implies that some kind of value judgment and criteria are employed to make evaluative statements about curricula and teachers. The appraisal dimension, whether it is presented openly or is implicit in certain statements, is the most sensitive characteristic of qualitative evaluation. Those familiar with the work of Sharp and Green (1975) in England may be aware that their writing, which is a form of qualitative evaluation of "open education" in a working-class school, created an uproar among some school people there. Some saw the findings and their presentation as a violation of ethical standards. The reports from England indicate that those wishing to study schools from a qualitative stance are viewed with a wary eye. It is apparent that qualitative evaluators are in need of a set of ethical guidelines for conducting their research.

Ethical Issues in Qualitative Evaluation

Let me outline briefly what I see as several problems of an ethical nature which may arise in the course of qualitative evaluations. The first issue concerns who should define the parameters and ground rules for evaluation. If a curriculum, such as law-related education, is to be studied in school contexts, who determines where the evaluator is allowed to go with his or her questions and probes? Should the sponsor of the curriculum have the right to restrict the evaluator by defining the range of questions asked? Or should those doing the teaching have some right to determine who and what is evaluated? The essential question here is what, if any, restraints should be placed on an evaluator in defining the scope and boundaries of a qualitative evaluation? Has the evaluator been issued a general fishing license in which all species in the pond are fair game? These questions are central because it is important from an ethical point of view for all parties to know in advance what the risks might be for participating in an evaluation.

This ethical issue becomes salient because the strength of qualitative evaluation is in the opportunity to see curricula in use. Potentially this allows the evaluator to distinguish between intended and unintended uses; it also allows for the discovery of intended and unintended effects. The unique power of qualitative methodology (as opposed to conventional quantitative techniques) is in discovering the hidden curriculum. The discovery of the hidden, unintended, unexpected, and undesirable is also what makes the qualitative model controversial and even feared. Evaluation

is already a stressful concept to many people, and qualitative approaches may increase the political and emotional stress placed on individuals.

Since I am one who engages in qualitative evaluation, my personal position is that I should be given relatively free reign regarding the parameters of my work. This, of course, is simple self-interest speaking, although it is defensible in terms of maximizing the professional knowledge which might be gained from my work. However, I also believe it is necessary for me to spell out in advance the possibilities of negative findings in areas which may not be explicit concerns of a curriculum. All of this ethical concern can be likened to our consumer protection laws; these are based on the premise that people ought to be guaranteed some truth in advertising, packaging, and labeling of contents. Certainly evaluators should be willing to meet such standards.

It can be argued that these ethical considerations apply to any evaluation, but they seem to be especially important for the qualitative investigator. Quantitative data are gathered and manipulated in ways which make the evaluation seem impersonal. There is anonymity in numbers. There is frequently no obvious connection between aggregate test scores, for example, and individual teachers and students. The very form in which quantitative data appear—correlate coefficients and analysis of variance—provides an insulating quality.

On the other hand, participant observation data necessarily appear as much more personal. While participant observation and interview studies ordinarily attempt to mask the names and identities of persons, insiders (who often have much to gain or lose personally) can frequently identify individuals because of familiarity with events. If the evaluation is accurate in reconstructing events, points of view, and controversies which developed, it is impossible to protect individuals from identification. To the extent that people locate themselves in a qualitative study, heightened anxiety and interpersonal conflicts may result. Indirectly the qualitative evaluator is responsible for these developments.

In presenting an account of a curriculum in use, for example, an evaluation may argue that in some cases student work in a class does not reflect deep understanding of democratic rights and responsibilities. Statements might include evaluation judgments that "discussions were not skillfully handled," and that "topics were not presented in an interesting or relevant way." Another scenario might describe a classroom which is studying democracy but is run by a teacher in an authoritarian manner. The evaluator could conclude that this apparent inconsistency is destructive to any deep understanding of democracy.

I cite these examples as a way to point out the problem of ethical relationships with clients and subjects. How does one establish the right to search for negative evidence regarding the personal performance of teachers conducting classrooms? What, if any, agreements have been established about the use of data which reflect on the competence, intelligence, and judgment of individuals? Presumably there should be some concept of informed consent operating in qualitative evaluation settings.

In addition to the problem of establishing specific ethical relationships, there is a more general problem of informing clients about one's professional point of view. Let me be specific by giving an example from my own experience. Several years ago I was involved in an evaluation of the Teacher Corps training program. This was a program which placed teacher interns in low-income schools to upgrade the quality of education for minorities and the poor. My own professional experience had led me to conclude that it would be misguided to train new teachers in the very schools that were, by Teacher Corps standards, already failing to educate low-income and minority children. Because I (and several of my colleagues) quite consciously held this belief, I felt an ethical obligation to express it in our investigation of the program's effectiveness. It would have been at the very least naive for us to pretend this bias did not exist, or would not influence us, even though we were trying to provide an honest assessment of the Teacher Corps program. What actually happened was that an awareness of the bias and its subsequent confession served to create an explicit hypothesis which became an important focus of the evaluation.

The general point I wish to make here is that neophytes in the field of qualitative evaluation should be aware of the strain this methodology may place on their relationships with clients and subjects. It is essential to spend some time clarifying expectations, interests, and groundwork before any intervention into the professional lives of people. The more personalized the evaluation, the more critical are these relationships. One should establish a set of ethical standards because, of course, it is the right thing to do morally. It is also an important pragmatic consideration if one wishes to continue as a qualitative evaluator.

REFERENCES

Hamilton, D., et al. *Beyond the numbers game: A reader in educational evaluation.* Berkeley: McCutchan, 1977.

Sharp, R., & Green, D. *Education and social control: A study in progressive primary education.* Boston: Routledge & Kegan Paul, 1975.

Willis, G. (Ed.). *Qualitative evaluation: Concepts and cases in curriculum criticism.* Berkeley: McCutchan, 1978.

Wolcott, H. *The man in the principal's office: An ethnography.* New York: Holt, Rinehart & Winston, 1973.

Wolcott, H. *Teachers versus technocrats: An educational innovation in anthropological perspective.* Eugene, Ore: Center for Educational Policy and Management, 1977.

Bringing It Together

Serendipitous or unintended learning is sometimes not only the most interesting but, as in this instance, some of the most important to emerge. The lessons of these papers, combined with our experiences since the invitational symposium launching the elementary education project, lead us to conclusions which, though unexpected, are important and provocative.

One of the most significant conclusions is that before issues specific to evaluation can be effectively explored, larger issues concerning educational goals must be addressed. More specifically, careful articulation of whatever a program is up to must precede any evaluation design. In the case of law and humanities in the elementary school, this a priori challenge has seemed, at times, trying. However, it has forced explicit identification of not only what law and humanities curricula might be but how these curricula might differ from other areas of the educational program. Evaluation forced us to do up front what all too often is an afterthought: specification of goals from both formal and informal perspectives.

When we recognize that evaluation facilitates this crucial process, a second conclusion flows logically from the first: evaluation should be an integral part of the curriculum/program development process. It should commence at the initial stages of planning and continue throughout the project's lifetime. As with the law and humanities curriculum, evaluation should be a part of—never an "add-on" to—the heart of the educational process.

Perhaps the greatest lesson gleaned from these papers and experiences with the elementary education project is an expanded vision of what evaluation is and can be in relation to the educational process in general. To be of real significance, evaluation should not be perceived in conventional or limited-usage terms. A great deal can and should be asked of it! Each of the papers in this section took evaluation well beyond "terminal" rating of a given curriculum or program. In one way or another, the evaluation process should be viewed as another important vehicle for collecting vital data about the ongoing program. In other words, evaluation can be looked to for program improvement, not just final grading.

Expanded visions of what evaluation can do for program improvement require that we look more closely at the evaluator than ever before. As content reflects frame of reference and point of view, so, too, does the evaluator. Before design or specific evaluator is determined, a range of persons should be met and talked with. These persons should be pressed to articulate their own understanding of the effort at hand. A careful record should be made of the questions asked by the evaluator during the initial interviews. The breadth of perspective at the initial stage is likely to reflect degree of breadth later in the evaluation process.

A final conclusion, and one closely associated with all the foregoing, is that just as specific curriculum strategies should speak to the needs of their users, there should also be a close fit between evaluation and its context—between evaluation and curricular program goals and the individuals developing those goals. Evaluation may have unique properties, but it shares one overriding similarity with the rest of education—that is, it cannot be effectively developed and implemented in a vacuum.

The sum of these papers and our own experiences since this project's inception suggest, then, that the potential of effective evaluation is yet to be reached. Used well, it can stretch, refine, and enrich educational efforts. This potential, alone, appears to be worth adjusting our sights and expectations.

Looking
Ahead

Questions and Hopes: A Synthesis and Vision

David Schimmel

This author took on a very difficult assignment and carried it off with aplomb. He was asked to extract the essential ideas or themes from both the papers and the symposium proceedings and to develop a synthesizing statement offering guidelines for development. Rather than restating what has been said, the author points out three critical questions, focusing on content, methods, and criteria, for which no consensus emerged. In addition to noting these questions, David Schimmel draws on his own extensive background and experience in law-related education to identify critical needs. This assessment of needs, which is couched in the positive form of "hopes for the future," indicates four basic areas requiring attention. Specifically, Schimmel hopes for long-range rather than short-range planning by project staffs, the development of elementary materials suitable to the realities of the elementary school context, a stronger commitment to and utilization of evaluation as an integral part of development, and, finally, serious attention to the impact of the "hidden curriculum" and the broad range of adults, other than teachers, who in fact teach our children. Critical needs and worthwhile hopes. We hope so, too.

When plans for this conference were being formulated, I naively agreed to try to synthesize the various conference papers and summarize the areas of agreement. Then Lynda Falkenstein called and asked how my synthesis was coming along. Having just finished reading about two dozen papers and finding very little agreement, I asked, first, whether it was too late to find another synthesizer, and, alternatively, whether it was too late to select another topic.

Since the program already had been sent to the printers, I agreed to continue my search for some unity in this diversity. Therefore, I went back over the papers and discovered that the agreement which existed could be summarized in one unsurprising sentence: All the specialists—whether their focus was language arts, governance, values, media, ethnic studies, problem solving, or community resources—agreed that their specialty is important to law, is relevant to the humanities, and should be incorporated into the elementary curriculum. But they seemed to agree on little else.

In view of this minimal presymposium consensus, it has been good to discover that during the symposium an impressive amount of agreement

David Schimmel is a lawyer and Professor of Education at the University of Massachusetts at Amherst. He is director of the School of Education's Program in Legal Literacy and is coauthor (with Louis Fischer) of *The Civil Rights of Teachers, The Civil Rights of Students,* and *The Rights of Parents.*

has emerged out of the debates and in the reports of our five sections. Lest I imply too broad a consensus, I want to focus on three important questions about which no agreement has emerged and then share four hopes for the future of our law and humanities projects. My purpose is to encourage staffs of various projects to continue to consider these questions and hopes after they leave this symposium and begin to plan their own programs.

The Questions

1. *What legal content and methods are appropriate for a law and humanities elementary curriculum?* All conference participants recognized that such a curriculum must be adapted to the interests and competencies of younger children. But there was no agreement on specifics. In fact the entire range of content and methods that are being used in secondary schools were recommended as appropriate for the elementary curriculum. Among the methods suggested were: case studies, mock trials, role playing, simulations, field trips, community speakers, value clarification exercises, the discussion of school rules, and the use of moral dilemmas. Content suggestions ranged from focusing on basic concepts such as authority, fairness, equality, and property to discussing the role of the "players" in the justice system—lawyers, policemen, judges, and probation officers. Others recommended

dealing with the reasons for rules in the classroom, the school, and the community, or focusing on how students should respond to an unjust rule or law.

This panorama of possible methods and content raises these questions: Is it educationally sound to try to adapt all of these approaches to the elementary grades? Are some approaches better than others? Are any not appropriate?

How should we determine what is or is not appropriate? Should we rely on learning theorists or child development experts? Should we base our decision on teacher preference? Student interest? Public pressure? Administrative support? All of the above? Or should some of these factors be weighed more heavily than others?

It is not important that we agree on the answers. What matters is that we systematically think through these questions before launching our programs. By consciously answering these questions, we will be better able to evaluate our efforts and help others understand the path we choose.

2. *What humanities content is appropriate for a law and humanities curriculum?* Many papers and conference participants did not confront this issue. Among those who did, there was a difference in opinion. Some believe that we should try to incorporate all humanities subjects into our projects. Others propose a more limited goal. Since much of the humanities (such as art, music, history, and literature) is already part of most elementary programs, these participants argue that we should focus on those dimensions that are not: namely, law and the humanistic values upon which rules and laws are based, plus the ethical conflicts involved in legal disputes.

Whichever position we support, these questions remain: Is there some humanities content that should be incorporated into every law and humanities curriculum? Is there some that should not? And what role, if any, should "professional humanists" play in answering these questions.?

Should we be concerned with humanizing the style of teaching as well as the content? If so, what must we do to make our teaching methods more humane? Should we "personalize" education to meet individual student needs? Or should we "individualize" education by developing techniques that enable students to learn at their own pace?

How we resolve these issues of content and method will basically shape the quality and impact of our programs.

3. *Are there any goals, standards, or criteria we can use to determine priorities or questions of quality?* Again I sense a split of opinion. Some feel that it is too early to confront this issue; they believe that if you push these questions too hard, they will lead to more conflict and divisiveness

than insight, that it is better to encourage a wide variety of creative approaches and see what works.

Other disagree. They feel that it is important to confront these questions now; that we can and should learn from the experience of the past—by avoiding prior mistakes and building on proven success; that if we do not try to reach consensus on standards and priorities now, it will be almost impossible to do so after project staff become involved in and defensive of whatever approach they have developed and implemented.

One possible compromise is for each local project to identify clearly their own goals, priorities, and standards before they begin, but not to seek any national consensus in advance. But I doubt that we would get a consensus on this either.

We now turn from questions to hopes, from issues that divide us to four ideas that we might build on together.

Hopes for the Future

1. *Long-term visions and plans.* Many projects in our field are supported by annual appropriations or short-term grants. As a result, good people spend a disproportionate amount of their time focusing on issues of survival. It is hard to worry about and plan for the consequences of a program for the next generation when we do not know whether the program will be in existence during the following year. And even when a project is securely funded for several years, it is easy to focus on current crises and daily administrivia. The urgent always seems to take priority over the important.

For these reasons, I believe it is critically important for the staff in all law and humanities programs to develop a long-range vision or plan of what they would like their project to accomplish in 10 years or by the year 2000. For futurists, 10–25 years is not the long term; but for people in our field, it is. It is sometimes hard for action-oriented, programmatic educators to be bothered with this sort of planning or to take it seriously. But our goals for the future shape our actions today and tomorrow. Therefore, I hope that each project's plans will confront questions such as: What specific knowledge, skills, and behaviors do we want to teach? Given limited time, what are our priorities? What difference do we want to make in the lives of children and their parents? In the lives of teachers, staff, and administrators? If our program is successful, how will it change the climate of the school? How will it help schools become more just institutions? How will it improve the life in our community? And, of course, how will our weekly classroom activities bring about these changes?

By developing a vision of the future that is linked with the present, we may have a better chance not only of getting the next grant but also of influencing the next generation.

2. *Curricular materials.* By the end of the 1980s, I hope to see at least as wide a range of law and humanities materials for elementary grades as now exists for secondary schools. But I also hope there will be two important additions:

■ At least four or five carefully developed and widely tested comprehensive, integrated, and sequential K–12 curricula available for classroom use.

■ Many more non-social-studies materials that link law with the standard curriculum in reading, English, history, home economics, and science. I am not suggesting that we abandon our efforts to integrate law into social studies. These efforts are critical, but they are not adequate.

One example of a promising project is Don Bragaw's suggestion of a law and humanities concordance. Such a concordance could be developed for the basal reader series of each major publisher to help elementary language arts teachers identify law and humanities materials in the texts they are now using. Similarly, a concordance could be prepared for school librarians identifying law and humanities materials in children's literature. Or a reference book could be developed for history teachers which builds on the legal issues currently mentioned but not developed in each of the standard history texts. Our movement now appeals largely to innovators, leaders, and risk takers. These developments will make it easier for cautious teachers to infuse law gradually into the traditional curriculum with little risk or controversy.

3. *Evaluation.* During the next decade, I hope that all law and humanities projects will be evaluated—systematically, openly, and early. While evaluation has not been a stranger to law-related education, I would like to see evaluators and the evaluation process viewed differently in the future.

In the past, evaluators typically were consulted after the planning process was completed; sometimes they were not consulted until a project was nearly over. In addition, evaluators usually asked tough, challenging questions about goals, methods, and materials. Because it then seemed too late to change things, project staff often reacted to these questions defensively, and many began to view the evaluator as a threatening and potentially dangerous adversary. This could result in a sense of intense frustration for both the evaluator and the project staff. Hence, I hope that in the future evaluators will be viewed not as enemies but as allies; that they will be consulted at the beginning of the planning process and viewed as important and helpful members of the project staff; and that they will be recognized as experts who can assist in designing the project as well as assessing its impact and suggesting improvements.

A second problem has been the way project staff have treated evaluation data. Frequently anything but overwhelmingly positive results have been guarded as "top secret." Even if the data were 60% or 70% positive, staff worried about the disclosure of mixed results on the theory that "anything negative can be used against us." As a result, little systematic data or objective analysis is now available to new projects about the successes and failures of the past. Therefore, I hope that in the future evaluation results will be viewed, first, as *helpful* information to be used to improve the curriculum during the life of the project and, second, as *public* information to be shared and exchanged with other professionals in the field. I also hope we can find ways to make this sharing seem less risky and more clearly in our mutual self-interest.

4. *The "hidden" curriculum.* During the 1980s I hope there will be widespread recognition that the hidden or informal law and humanities curriculum plays as central a role as our formal or explicit curriculum. Many conference papers have pointed out the significance of the hidden curriculum. They have written about how the school teaches by the way rules are developed and enforced, by the modeling behavior of teachers and staff, and by the total climate of the classroom and the school community.

Dobbins and Taylor, for example, suggest that we "carefully study the operation of the schools to determine whether...the message of the institution through its very operation is teaching lessons in conflict with the explicit curriculum of the school." "What," they ask, "will students learn about due process taught as subject matter but not practiced as a characteristic of the school environment?" Or what will students learn when they are urged to respect authority and obey school rules by someone who has violated their constitutional rights? The answer, I fear, is that they will learn to be cynical about rules and authority and perhaps about our law and humanities curriculum as well.

Many participants in this symposium have said that the hidden curriculum is as important as or more important than the formal curriculum. If we mean this, then shouldn't we act in ways that reflect this conviction? Shouldn't we expect all projects to deal directly with the hidden curriculum and explain how they plan to confront it? Shouldn't we expect projects to teach about how law applies to students in school just as they teach about how law functions in the community? In future conferences shouldn't we spend equal time discussing the development of programs and materials for the teachers of the hidden curriculum?

Who are these teachers? At least three groups have been mentioned.

- *All school staff and educational administrators* (from members of the school board to principals and their secretaries), who establish rules, policies, and procedures and sometimes act as judges.
- *All counselors and teachers,* who propose, interpret, and implement school regulations and establish their own norms and procedures for dealing with students.
- *All parents,* whose attitudes, comments, and actions can support or undermine what we teach in school.

I hope that before long we will have begun to design in-service curriculum materials and methods for each of these groups. This is not to say that the formal curriculum is unimportant; rather, it is to argue that it is not sufficient—that equal attention should be paid to the hidden curriculum and those who teach it, and that schools should try to become operating models of the law and humanities principles they teach.

My purpose in sharing these questions and hopes is to encourage you to develop your own vision of what a comprehensive law and humanities curriculum should be and what we need to do to translate our visions into reality. As we leave this conference, perhaps we should organize an open conspiracy of educators who are willing to confront tough and important questions, to plan for the future, to infiltrate our materials into the total curriculum, to evaluate our efforts openly, and to design strategies for the hidden as well as the formal curriculum. If we begin to address this agenda during the coming years, a future conference might be able to invite all the citizens of the school community to join our constructive conspiracy. By building an effective partnership among parents, administrators, students, and educators, we can practice what we teach about law and humanities in the elementary schools of our country.

Perspectives on Law and Humanities Education

Interviews by Mabel C. McKinney-Browning

In the sixties and seventies the trend in curricula developed for racial and ethnic minorities was to provide separate curricula to respond to the needs of these special groups. This trend was understandable and practical, and may, indeed, be the only way to ensure immediately that these issues of concern are addressed. However, if this approach has been less than wholly successful, the reason may be a failure to institutionalize multicultural, multiethnic, pluralistic issues and concerns in developing curricula, thus affecting the substance, organization, and methodology adapted by school districts and textbook writers in programs across the country.

The purpose of bringing to potential curriculum designers and practitioners of elementary law-related education an assessment of the considerations of importance to ethnic and racial minority communities is to affect future curriculum decisions about content, methods, and strategies.

In January and February 1980, I interviewed six members of racial and/or ethnic minority groups. Like most adults, they were concerned to some degree with the education of the future generation. However, they were also concerned with the environment and circumstances in which that education might take place. Each interview is a personal reflection of the experiences, interests, and expertise of the individual who participated in it. As I look at each interview separately, I am impressed by the uniqueness of each perspective. As I view them collectively, however, I am surprised by their similarities. For the most part, the issues of concern are the same, while the direction of that concern reflects differences in social and educational background. We may conclude from these interviews that the life experience of minority group members in the United States reflects both similarity and cultural or ethnic uniqueness, and further, in agreement with actor James Earl Jones, that "one's ethnic identity [is] part of one's existence."

The initial purpose of these interviews was not to seek a definition of the concept of law and humanities; rather, it was to try to converge the individual experiences of the people I interviewed with the common or collective experience of the social institution of law and the legal system. Out of this convergence grew several shared concerns:

1. That law-related education programs emphasize individual rights and responsibilities.
2. That law-related education programs reflect recognition of the varying experiences of minority communities with regard to social institutions and their representatives.
3. That law-related education programs teach not acceptance of the law, but critical analysis of the law as it affects individual lives and communities.
4. That law-related education reflect a concern for humane values in the law, not simply social control.
5. That law-related education teach individuals to deal within the system, to be part of the decision-making process, and to become active participants in determining their destinies in this society.

Readers should view this list of concerns as a starting point for understanding law-related education from minority perspectives. These interviews seek to expand the scope of the substance of law-related education programs to include minority concerns. To some extent, the interviews go beyond this goal by providing suggestions about approach and methodology. Finally, these interviews suggest that an examination of the law through the humanities provides a humane and historical context for a subject and a social institution that has frequently been questioned as to its ability to be truly just and humane for all people.

Interview with James A. Banks

[EDITORS' NOTE: James A. Banks is Professor of Education, University of Washington, Seattle. He is Vice-President of the National Council for the Social Studies and a Kellogg Fellow. He is the author of numerous articles and several books, including *Teaching Strategies for the Social Studies, Teaching Strategies for Ethnic Studies,* and *Multiethnic Education: Theory and Practice.*]

What is your sense of the nature of the future world in which today's children will be adults?

BANKS: I think that in some ways it's going to be very different from the world that we're living in today. I think it's going to be a world of enormous scarcity, a world with a lower standard of living, and a world where Americans will have to deal directly with Third World peoples. This means that Americans will have to learn to deal with differences, which historically we've not done very well.

We're going to have to start using fewer of the world's resources. We have been consuming a disproportionate share of the world's resources. That cannot continue. We're living in a shrinking, interdependent, global society.

The future is going to bring about many changes. For example, people are going to be living longer. We really don't have many effective roles for senior citizens now. We isolate them rather than making them an integral part of society. Jules Henry pointed this out some years ago in his book *Culture against Man.* These are some of the major changes that we're going to see in the future world.

What do you think are some critical elements of the current curriculum that we're going to have to improve now, in order to prepare children for that future world?

BANKS: I think one of the major things we're going to have to do is to help students understand that they are citizens of a global society. That will be very difficult to do because most people—not only in this nation but in other nations also—are very nationalistic. I think we're going to have to help children learn to deal with differences, such as social class, racial, and ethnic differences. Our curriculum remains primarily Anglo-centric and, to a great extent, male-centric. Also, I think the curriculum is going to have to help students

---

Mabel McKinney-Browning is Assistant Staff Director of the Special Committee on Youth Education for Citizenship and Assistant Coordinator of YEFC's elementary law and humanities project. She has been an elementary classroom teacher and supervisor in the Chicago public schools. Prior to joining the YEFC staff, she was Assistant Professor of Education, University of Illinois at Chicago Circle.

---

develop cross-cultural competencies—the ability, skills, and knowledge needed to function in a range of cultures and nations, not only within this nation but in other nations as well. For example, the cultural literacy of our students is causing many educators alarm. The report of the President's Commission on Foreign Language and International Studies talks about the limited cultural literacy of our citizenry and states that this is a serious problem in a modern global society. Breaking down ethnic and cultural boundaries helps students develop the attitudes, skills, and abilities needed to function in a global society. I also think we have to deal with the question of how to prepare students, especially dominant-ethnic-group students, to share power. I don't think we can continue to have a society where power is controlled primarily by one ethnic group. I think we're going to see attempts by powerless ethnic groups such as blacks, Mexican-Americans, and others to become more included in the structure of society. What kind of education will help people learn how to share power? I think this is going to be a difficult question to answer. So sharing power, developing more cultural and ethnic literacy, and learning how to revise the curriculum to reflect the diversity within our nation are some of the crucial issues that confront educators.

To what extent do you think the curriculum is currently responding to these issues?

BANKS: Oh, hardly at all. I think that there have been sporadic reform efforts such as multicultural education and nonsexist education, but these reforms affect the total curriculum in most schools very little.

I recently read in a newspaper report that the National Urban League has concluded that there is a movement back to conservatism in the nation, and that the pace of progress that blacks experienced in the 1960s has been considerably slowed. What effect will this state of the "union" have on the education of black children?

BANKS: I think that there is no doubt a swing toward what its advocates call neoconservatism. Of course, I don't know what's new about it except that it's more blatant. It is now legitimate to be conservative. I think it's important to understand first of all that neoconservatism is a reaction to the liberalism of the sixties. I think this movement, in part, is an orchestrated attempt to undercut the legitimacy of the libertarian philosophy and reforms of the sixties. Head Start, the neoconservatives are now saying, didn't work; integration, they are saying, is hopeless. The latest in this litany of neoconservative publications and writings is a new book by Arthur R. Jensen, called *Bias in Mental Testing.* I think that it is not coincidental that Jensen resurfaces in 1980, saying or implying again that blacks are genetically inferior to whites.

Now what is the implication of all this, and how is it going to affect the education of black students? I think unquestionably that it's going to have a very dispiriting effect. Teachers who are teaching black students will read Jensen and view him as an authority. This kind of academic legitimacy for what I think of as an essentially racist doctrine is going to have a negative effect on those of us who are trying to work for educational reform and equality. Already in my own ethnic studies classes students are asking me if Jensen is really accurate. First of all, I think he raises an irrelevant question. Regardless of a child's intellectual ability, the school should create programs to educate that child to the maximum of his or her ability. How much intelligence he has is to me not a significant question. I think the real purpose of a doctrine like Jensenism is to legitimize racial oppression and the powerlessness of blacks. I'm very concerned about the rise of so-called neoconservatism and the rise of Jensenism, because I see these ideologies as reinforcing the status quo—class, ethnic, and racial stratification. I think that we ought to vigorously refute these kinds of racist and antiequalitarian ideologies.

What concepts, attitudes, and values do you think the informal curriculum in school can teach?

BANKS: I think that schools teach a lot of values, concepts, and attitudes that reinforce the existing social class, ethnic, and racial stratifications in society. For example, I think the school teaches control. It teaches a lot of rigidity—line up, open the book, do what the teacher says. An opposing ideology would be a questioning stance—to question the status quo, to reform the status quo. Clearly you need order in the school, but as I look at the public schools I'm not very sanguine about the kind of structures that I see being taught.

A lot of attitudes are being taught that reinforce, support, and perpetuate the capitalistic class stratification in our society. As I view them, public schools rarely teach students to be sensitive critics of society and sensitive to reform of society; rather, schools teach them how to fit in. If all you teach students to do is to fit in, how do you develop reformers? How do you teach people to close the gaps between the ideals in our society and reality? Our nation has beautiful ideals—liberty, equality, justice. Of course, when they were first articulated by our Founding Fathers, they were meant to apply to white males with property, but through the years we've expanded their definitions. We've expanded the number of people included, and that has been continuing. The schools, I think, teach mythical versions of

our society's realities. The student often gets the impression from the curriculum, both the latent and the manifest curriculum, that this is a totally open society, that it is a classless society, and that anyone can become president if he or she wants to. The real role of the school ought to be to help students develop the attitudes, skills, and abilities needed to become reflective social activists.

What do you think children are learning about fairness and equality in school today?

BANKS: I think they're learning some ideals without always learning the complexities of the realities. I think they're learning a lot of stereotypes about what is fairness and what is justice. Larry Metcalf states that the toughest choices in life are not between good and bad, but rather between two equal goods. Hence a really tough choice is not justice as opposed to injustice, but one person's justice as opposed to another person's justice. I think students ought to learn about the complexities of these concepts and try to deal with the fact that justice and equality are sometimes inherently contradictory and in a real situation need some kind of balance.

Often schools teach the ideal. Students ought to know it. But to what extent is the ideal implemented in different communities, such as various ethnic communities? The school has an obligation to teach about realities, especially those realities that are particular to ethnic communities and that may be different from the experiences of the majority community.

What do you see as strengths of the law-related education movement?

BANKS: It can help ethnic students know what their rights and responsibilities are. I think it can help students see the positive aspects of police officers and help them understand what the officers do. Police officers also need to be helped to understand the ethnic experience. I think there's much need, and maybe this is beyond the scope of law-related education, for in-service training of police officers to deal with race relations. I think that, as long as we have mutual misunderstandings between ethnic youths and police officers, we're likely to see conflicts between these groups. Case-study approaches and having black youth meet and interact with police officers might be effective conflict-resolution strategies. This might help reduce some of the mutual suspicions and hostilities that I think are very real.

I am concerned that in law-focused education there be some recognition that some laws are unjust. Laws are often created by the oppressor for those who are oppressed. If the oppressed merely obey the laws, they will stay oppressed. I think this fact ought to be taught in law-focused education.

What weaknesses do you see in the law-related education movement?

BANKS: I have been a silent critic of law-related courses. I've been very concerned with what I've read in law education literature that gave me the feeling that students were to read the law and obey it, without going the next step further to see whether that law is consistent with humane values and whether that law will have to be changed. I think both are needed. Obviously, you can't do things that are against the law without getting punished if you get caught. However, laws should be obeyed until they can be changed. Law should be consistent with a society's idealized goals and values. I'm very sensitive to this point. I think we have to be very careful to help children understand that laws can be changed if they violate human dignity, equality, and other American creed values. Laws, it seems to me, should reflect humane values. We should obey them when they do, but when they don't we should work to get them changed. That's the aspect of law-focused education that has made me a bit uneasy, what I interpret as a nonreflective acceptance and obedience of the law. There is a lot of emphasis on the responsibilities of children in law-focused education and less emphasis, in the few materials I have seen, on social criticism and change in the social order.

What do you think needs to be included in the subject matter of law-related education in order to make it better able to contribute to developing competent citizens in any segment of society?

BANKS: I think that quite frequently many people simply don't know their rights. I think that students need to know how they can go about finding out what their rights are. How do you use legal services? How do you find out what your rights are? What are the legal institutions available for use by people who don't have a lot of money to hire a fancy lawyer. For example, how do you really use small claims court? A lot of people are not sure how to use many of these vehicles in society. How do we go about using these agencies so they will benefit our community and help satisfy our own individual needs and interests? I think that's one of the things that needs to permeate the curriculum.

We also need to help students understand the need for law within a social system. You can't have a society without laws. Chaos would result. I think we need to help students develop commitment to community. In the seventies, we saw a waning of commitment to community norms and values. People often felt, "If I want to smoke pot in the middle of the classroom, I can do it." I don't think that society can exist and prosper without some kind of norms. Laws do become a part of

shared community values. So I think we need to help students understand that they have individual rights and responsibilities, but also that they live in a community and have an obligation to help that community prosper and grow and meet the needs of all the people within it.

Do you perceive Kohlberg's moral stages as universally applicable?

BANKS: I'm not at all sure that any stage theory is as sequential and linear as the author states. But I think it's a useful conceptualization for looking at the child's socialization and learning of values.

What is the relationship between law-related education and moral/value education?

BANKS: I don't really know enough about law-focused education to say, but they ought to be related. Law-focused education ought to help students understand how laws are expressions of values in a society, and that the ultimate goal of law should be to enable a society to come closer and closer to what Kohlberg calls universalistic humane values. The ultimate goal of the law should be to assure that a society is just. So I see law-focused education and moral education as integrally tied together.

Do you think law-related education is a program that should be for the black community?

BANKS: If it's conceptualized the way I think it ought to be, yes. If it's dealing with law as a means for expanding justice and equality, and if it's dealing with making law a vehicle for human rights, yes. If it becomes a tool to teach people to fit in to the status quo, no.

How do you feel about a subject area that has been largely conceptualized with limited input from the black community?

BANKS: I would be very concerned about it being exported to the black community without change because I think black students would resent anyone who came to their schools and communities who appeared to be only a defender of the law. If that were the image of law-related education, I think it would turn a lot of black people off, especially black males. Law-focused education has to be approached very sensitively in the black community. I would encourage the law-focused education establishment to look, to explore, and to expand its research to see what kinds of actions can be taken in the black community and to do them sensitively.

How can teacher training programs be geared to minimize the influence of teachers' biases on their classroom performance?

BANKS: As a matter of fact, working with my own area of multiethnic education I have found this to be the greatest problem. People in workshops often ask me, What is the greatest barrier to implementation of multicultural education?

Is it lack of materials? Is it lack of teacher planning time? Is it lack of community support? Having looked at all those barriers, I come back to the fact that the real issue is the attitude and perspectives of the teachers. I don't believe that any reform movement such as law-focused education, global education, or multicultural education is going to succeed unless the attitudes and perspectives of teachers are changed. Unless teachers get new conceptualizations of the nature of society, they're going to perpetuate their own encapsulated images of society. What is the answer? Obviously, it seems to me, we must try staff development, at both the preservice and in-service levels. I think that unless you have an effective staff development program for any of these educational innovations, they're not going to be successful. That's the key, not the materials.

What importance does the black community give to "good" citizenship?

BANKS: I think most blacks are more concerned with getting institutional structures to respond to what they perceive as their historical "good" citizenship. We've been very peaceful. We've played by the rules, and yet institutional structures have not always rewarded our good citizenship. Since we are such "good" citizens, how do we get society to honor, respect, and legitimize our citizenship? How do we get society to respond in terms of equality and opportunity to the good citizenship that we've had for over 300 years. I would guess, and I'm only one black out of over 22 million, that a more overriding concern is, How do we get institutional structures such as the law to respond to the good citizenship behavior that we already exemplify?

Interview with M. D. Taracido

[EDITORS' NOTE: M. D. Taracido is President and General Counsel for the Puerto Rican Legal Defense and Education Fund, Inc. (PRLDEF), a national civil rights organization whose objectives are to increase Puerto Rican and Hispanic representation in the legal profession and to secure fair and equal treatment for Puerto Ricans and other Hispanics in such areas as employment, voting rights, housing, and health. She is a member of the Board of Trustees of the Bank Street College, the New York State Advisory Committee to the United States Commission on Civil Rights, the Hispanic Advisory Committee to the United States Attorney General, and the New York State Bar Association Joint Task Force on the New York State Division of Human Rights, and Secretary of the Public Interest Law Section of the New York State Bar Association and the National Puerto Rican Coalition.]

Our children will be adults in a world somewhat different from ours. Can you predict what the world will be like for Puerto Rican children?

TARACIDO: Ours is a very complicated world with little room for people with no skills. Unfortunately, because many Puerto Ricans have been denied equal access to opportunity, they lack basic skills. This has led to feelings of alienation and frustration. To make matters worse, ours is a shrinking economy with fewer opportunities for all. This is happening at a time when education, in the traditional sense, is under question. Education has always been seen as the door to economic opportunity, but young people today cannot be sure this is necessarily true. For example, in the last few years fiscal crises and declining enrollments in the public school systems around the country have resulted in massive teacher layoffs. It is no wonder that our young people experience a sense of hopelessness. We have to remedy this. I think we have a responsibility as a society to determine what the job markets of the future will be and to provide training and educational programs that address those markets, so that our young can feel they have a future to look forward to.

What do you think law-related education can potentially do for the Puerto Rican community?

TARACIDO: I think the most important thing that such programs can do is to let people know what their rights are. One of the big problems Puerto Ricans (like other minorities) have is that they are not knowledgeable about their rights. Getting that kind of information is important. Obtaining it as early as possible is most helpful. Your proposal to conduct law-related education programs in schools will not only reach the students, but also, I hope, spill over to their parents. It is important for parents to know what their rights are and what their children's rights are. I think a lot of the problems minority students face today in education are based on the fact that minority parents do not know that they have a right to push for programs that address the needs of their children. Law-related education could serve an important function, if, indeed, it is the kind of law-related education that means something in the context of the lives of those children.

What do you think are some important things for Puerto Rican and other minority people to know about the law?

TARACIDO: Well, I think you should promote law-related educational programs that address such areas, among others, as consumer education, student rights, and education rights. For example, parents whose children are limited English speaking should know that they have a right under federal law to programs appropriate to the needs of those children. Parents of a handicapped child should know that they have rights under federal law with regard to that child.

There are occasions when the practices of an employer are discriminatory. Students should know what to do when confronted with such practices. They should know that they can file complaints with local and federal equal opportunity agencies to challenge the discriminatory practices.

Housing discrimination is another issue. Puerto Ricans in large part are a poor population. Many live in substandard housing and, not surprisingly, seek access to better housing. Too often, for no better reason than that they are Puerto Rican, they are denied access to better housing. Again, they should know they have a right to challenge those denials.

In short, I think that the subject matter of law-related education should be directed at the day-to-day concerns of the minority communities. Let them know the legal remedies available to them to correct inequities.

What are Puerto Rican students' perceptions of the law? How do they view it? What biases do they have toward the law?

TARACIDO: Do you mean, How do students feel about police officials? Are you asking about their views about the criminal and juvenile justice systems? If so, that would clearly be another focus. If you are going to address criminal and juvenile justice law as topics in law-related educational programs, again it should be with an eye toward a discussion of what rights one has.

Justice and responsibility are among the law-related education concepts taught in schools. Describe what those terms mean to you as a lawyer.

TARACIDO: As a civil rights lawyer, justice to me means opening up and furthering equal access to opportunities. Puerto Ricans and other minorities have had obstacles placed before them. If, indeed, you can break down these obstacles, then the effect will be a just system.

As a society, we have a responsibility to ensure equal access to opportunity. A sense of responsibility is fostered if people feel they have a stake in the system. If, however, you are alienated, angry, and frustrated because of feelings of deprivation, then you will have little reason to feel a responsibility to the world around you. If we can create an environment that allows the sense of accomplishment to flourish—by that I mean a society where everyone has an equal chance to succeed—then we will have a just system that will produce responsible and giving persons.

Do you see law-related education as coming into the schools and taking away from other

programs you consider more crucial to your community.

TARACIDO: I think that any law-related subject could easily fit into the regular instructional programs of schools. For example, it could be part of a social studies class. At the high school level these courses could be electives that could be used to meet the requirements for graduation. If the educational program is one that addresses the needs of linguistic-minority children, the law-related subjects could be taught in the language of the children. As long as the law-related educational programs are integrated into the regular instructional program, there should be no objection to them.

Interview with Larry J. Johnson

[EDITORS' NOTE: Larry J. Johnson is a lawyer with the Center for Law and Education, Inc., in Cambridge, Massachusetts. He is a co-counsel in the Boston school desegregation case and consulting attorney to local legal services offices on educational issues. A former VISTA volunteer, he has worked in several educational programs for minority students. Mr. Johnson is a member of the American Bar Association and the Massachusetts Black Lawyers Association. He is also on the boards of several community organizations in the Boston area.]

What do you think will be the nature of the world that today's children will live in?

JOHNSON: The world is getting smaller, and relations between nations are changing. I don't think that the "nature" of the world is going through any kind of fundamental change. But the ability of people to perceive what's going on in other parts of the world, the development of technology in communication, is probably the primary determinant for changing the way people relate to one another.

The world that our children will grow up in will be a world where the neighborhood is, in fact, the world. The neighborhood will not stop at national boundaries. It may not even know national boundaries. I guess what I perceive as the nature of the world is characterized by the concept of greater unity. As someone said in discussing President Carter's State of the Union address, it was really a State of the World address. Basically, that is an admission of what has always been the case. In the future I think individuals are going to recognize that their individual condition is a function of the condition of the entire world. I hope education will respond to that. We are going to have to educate our children so that they can deal with the entire world.

What do you think about law-related education and what it can potentially do for black and other minority communities?

JOHNSON: Law-related education is very worthwhile for all communities, including the black community. The history of legal education in Europe was that it was part of history, part of civics, and part of philosophy. In America, legal education, primarily through Harvard University, became a graduate discipline and therefore was restricted to the few who could get to the graduate level. One of the main functions of our educational system is to make effective and responsible citizens of students. It probably makes sense and is consistent with that goal to educate students about the operations of the most pervasive feature of our governmental system, the legal system. So I welcome law-related education.

But I take as given that any change necessarily is costly to somebody. So to introduce law-related education, with a limited or declining budget for education, means that some other part of the system will pay that cost. It might be in terms of staffing. Since in the educational fields as in other fields blacks are the last hired, they may be the first fired. So the cost of introducing law-related education might be indirect—the loss of black staff members. The cost of introducing law-related education into the school system might be the loss of music, art, and other cultural programs in the schools.

In my view, the weakest part of the system bears such costs. Blacks pay for whatever change takes place. We may ultimately benefit, but in the first instance, we pay for change, and that's the bottom line based on relative power within the system.

Do you think the impact of law on black children is negative or positive?

JOHNSON: I believe, in a general way, the Machiavellian concept that law is the will of the ruling class. To the extent that blacks do not control the ruling class, laws do not represent our will as to what the reality is and how relationships function within that reality. Once a law becomes fixed, then the burden shifts. Then it becomes incumbent upon the black community to deal with the reality of the system and to cope within it or to change it. So for somebody to tell me that a law is bad makes no sense at all. A law is. How do you get around that law, or how do you change that law so you can do what you want to do? I think that's what we've got to be talking about—how to change or use a law in such a way that we do what we want to do.

What the notion of a "bad" law suggests is that the people who made it were not us. If we were making a law on that subject, we would not make it that way. To the extent that blacks are not represented in the decision making about laws, just as they are not represented in the decision making about other elements of the system that define and control our relationships, then I guess we are more adversely affected by and therefore more controlled by laws. As grave a reason for our possible adverse posture toward the law is our ignorance of law and consequent abuses of it. Ultimately law-related education can be beneficial to black communities because it can help deter those abuses. The more people are informed about laws, the less opportunity there is for laws to be misapplied.

What effect will greater awareness of the institution of law have on the black community?

JOHNSON: The benefit to blacks of being educated about the legal system is that they will be able to deal within the system. Since law is such a pervasive feature in our society, it's ridiculous to expect people to be able to navigate effectively in the society without knowing right and wrong ways of doing so. Also, I think that knowing how laws are made, how they are enforced, and how they are applied removes some of the mystique. In removing the mystique, we remove the fear and the sense of alienation, if not the alienation itself. Then law will become an instrument or tool rather than something to be feared.

What aspects of the law do you consider to be racist?

JOHNSON: I'm very existential. I think the level of racism that exists in the society at large exists in all strata of the society. So to the extent that there is racism in the drafting of a law, there is racism in the police force that accosts the black citizen on the street, there is racism in the probation office that handles the case and in the D.A.'s office representing the court, and there is racism at the level of the court. There is no way of getting out of it. Since it's all a part of the same system, it all partakes of the same level of racism that prevails in the society.

It's my belief that racism is basically the level of injustice that black people will endure. The level of the black community's willingness to endure injustice is reflected throughout the legal system—in making laws, in enforcing laws, in judges' rulings on laws. I think that, at this point, the level of critical racism throughout the legal system is very high. Law enforcement officers feel at liberty to violate the rights of black citizens. Judges feel at liberty to sentence black and white defendants disproportionately. Laws are being made that cut back the resources allocated to benefit the black community. Generally, we black Americans are at a low point of existence; therefore we're at a high point of racism throughout the judicial system.

What are important considerations in law-related education, or in education generally, of which the black community should be aware?

JOHNSON: Well, as I suggested before, the manner of instruction is more important than what is taught. What I think we need more than education in law is education in how to interact socially with other people. If we were properly socialized to the reality that exists out there, then, whatever the laws were, we could manipulate, use, or change them as we saw fit. Fundamentally, what blacks need most is a change of perception about our role in the world. I mean, what makes man *Homo sapiens* is that man can change his environment. Man does not have to accept his environment as given, and feel futile and frustrated in the face of it. For example, talking to a teacher in a school here in Boston, I asked her, "Why the bad conditions?" and she said, "Because the school is predominately black." No. That is not the answer. That says that because we're black, we are no longer change agents. What education needs to teach first, and particularly the black community, is a sense of self-worth and self-esteem and the ability to be change agents in our society.

I would like to have law taught in such a way that blacks recognize that law can be used as a body of knowledge, as a tool to change their environment, to do what they want to do. Blacks might consider the legal tool to be a more basic tool or skill to have than some other kind of tool, and therefore want to include it in their curriculum. Personally, I think that law, as a body of knowledge and therefore as a tool, is of such primacy in our society and our culture that it ought to be taught in schools. I just think the black community needs to understand the costs of such a decision. We need to decide for ourselves what those costs ought to be.

The concepts of justice and responsibility are frequently addressed by law-related education. Could you describe each of those terms as you view them legally, and as they are interpreted by the black community?

JOHNSON: Justice in our legal system is the notion that the right or fair result is obtained in a situation. The right result is often interpreted to mean the result that is prescribed by a set of laws, either written common law, or law as pronounced by a court, or law that is drawn up by an administrative body. So in the first instance justice is assumed to be obtained in our legal system if the applicable law is followed. The second instance of justice is consistent treatment within a given situation, even if there is no law to govern it. It is considered just if everybody is treated the same within a given set of facts or behaviors. I think justice, as it's legally applied, is grounded in compliance with outstanding laws and everyone being treated the same.

But I think that Justice, with a capital, is not simply compliance with a set of fixed laws or exact replication of result to everybody in the same situation. I think people recognize that everybody is different and no two fact patterns are ever exactly the same. By changing the actors, you change the experience they bring to the facts, and you change the outcome that ought to be reached. So the notion of justice that is sought by most of the lay public is that the right result ought to be sensitive not only to a body of law, to fixed precedent, or to what happens to other people in the same situation, but also to the particular needs and circumstances of the actors involved in the present situation. I think in those terms justice is not attained in our legal system. Our legal system and our whole social order are not willing to pay the costs of having the appropriate response to a given situation, rather than a more quantified or an objectifiable response.

Responsibility?

JOHNSON: Basically, our whole legal system is a systematic allocation of rights and responsibilities. That is, if I have a right to drive a car, I have the responsibility to drive in such a way as not to injure someone. Responsibility is the necessary condition of a right. All situations entail rights and responsibilities. All relationships have flowing within them a right and a responsibility—the right to take certain kinds of actions free from intervention, and the responsibility that checks or limits those rights. So maybe limitation is the best way to define responsibility. Responsibilities are the limitations to the rights we have in a relationship, and those limitations may either be self-imposed or externally imposed.

How is responsibility interpreted by the black community?

JOHNSON: That brings us back to the idea of blacks perceiving themselves, or not perceiving themselves, as active change agents. I think responsibility is most often interpreted by black and other minority groups as obedience. Generally, blacks perceive responsibility as an externally imposed limitation on them, which they are obliged, given their relative power in society, to be obedient to or, when possible, to circumvent. I think we seldom see responsibility as within our control.

How do you think law is perceived in black communities?

JOHNSON: Generally, law is an unknown to the black community; but to the extent that it is known, mostly it is welcomed. I think blacks, given their relative powerlessness in the society, find comfort and stability in the status quo of set laws that define for them their existence and their roles in society. I think it's a minority opinion within the black community that laws are to its detriment. But I think it might be a majority opinion that the ways laws are applied are to the detriment of the black community.

The black community is more conservative than the broader majority community. I think that is reflected in the way blacks respond to laws. I think they are more accepting. But that acceptance, of course, is grounded in their fear of retaliation for nonacceptance. So it might be a little coercive. The factor of coercion, the acceptance of legal reality, and the helplessness to do anything about it ought not to be forgotten. I think blacks have been trained to fear "anarchy" more than whites.

Are there areas of the law that you think would be critical in teaching black children about the law and the legal system?

JOHNSON: Process and relationships are more important than substance. I want to make clear that teaching the body of knowledge and calling it the law is useless because the law is constantly changing. Teaching students a body of law such as criminal law, or tort law, or property law isn't as important as teaching them how law responds to change, how powers align and realign, how you make a law, how you get legislation passed, etc. So the process of a society ordering its interpersonal behavior and the role of law in that society are what black students need to learn. They don't need to learn a body of laws that whoever is teaching them can change at any time.

Interview with Alice Blair

[EDITORS' NOTE: Alice Blair is District 13 Superintendent, Chicago Public Schools. She is a former teacher and has won the support of the community through her expert leadership as a school administrator. She is a member of the National Association of School Administrators, the National Association of Black School Educators, the National Association of Administrative Women, the Chicago Principals Association, and the Chicago District Superintendents Association, as well as numerous community organizations.]

Let's start by looking at the kind of individual you as a teacher are trying to create. I know that all teachers have some idea of the kind of child or adult they want to create through their teaching.

BLAIR: Well, as a superintendent in this district, I think that my primary responsibility is to make youngsters literate—to try to make 100% of them literate. In this school system and in most major urban areas, we fail to teach kids to read and write. I think if we do that, if we accomplish that, then all the other things will fall into place.

What do you think is the current status of citizenship programs in the public schools?

BLAIR: Well, I think that they're lagging. Certainly, though my goal is literacy, I think citizenship education fits in. Youngsters must understand the law. They must understand the government, which affects them because all things are political decisions. They need to understand those things if they're going to function in this society. I think we've moved away from civics and geography and history, all of which are necessary if these youngsters are to function well.

At this time, what percentage of the school program in your district do you think is devoted to citizenship training?

BLAIR: Social studies encompasses citizenship. The percentage in terms of emphasis on citizenship per se is not great.

Why do you think we need citizenship training, or do you think that we need it?

BLAIR: Certainly, at both the elementary and high school levels. As I said, unless children understand the government and the society, they can't function very well. They need to understand what it means to be a citizen in terms of voting and how it affects them, and I think if we had been doing our job, we'd have more 18-year-olds voting. Even though they have that opportunity available, they're not voting in any great percentage.

Given the state of education right now, especially in Chicago, people's attention is focused on all kinds of issues besides training for citizenship. Do you think that you would be able to get a lot of parent support for and involvement in a citizenship program?

BLAIR: My experience has led me to believe that if we have a program, whatever that program is, and we define how we want parents involved, in most cases they will become involved. In this district, we have tremendous community involvement, and I think we could have it for citizenship education if we defined that as one of our goals. I see no problem with involving parents.

Do you think law-related education would be useful in a school district where you are?

BLAIR: Yes, I do—for the same reasons that citizenship education is important and because I think that young people are aware of law without being taught in any packaged way what the law is and how it affects them. Certainly they have that kind of knowledge—in terms of street smarts dealing with police, brothers in juvenile court, and so forth—in this type of district.

Do you think that there are some special concerns that should be considered in developing law-related education programs for black students?

BLAIR: I don't personally think law-related education should be taught as a separate unit. I think that it ought to be incorporated into the social studies curriculum, so that it's all taught as a unit that falls into place where it should. In the same way I don't think black history ought to be taught as a separate unit. I think that it all will fall into place in teaching history and civics. It all ought to be part of the basic curriculum.

Are there issues that are distinctive to the black environment that are not dealt with if the curriculum focuses on or is derived from the white experience?

BLAIR: I think that certainly our youngsters perceive the law as punitive. They have to understand how the rules can be positive. If you talk law around here, you're talking police. You're talking about something that happens to them in their community. So they perceive the law as punitive, and it damn well may be, but they need to learn how they can change laws, how they can change the way the law affects them.

What qualities of citizenship or of a "good citizen" do you think might properly be addressed by law-related education for black students?

BLAIR: Voting. They must understand why they must vote. I think they can be great missionaries to their parents. People feel that they don't benefit from voting. We must get students to see the real need so that they can go home and say to their parents, who may be less sophisticated, that voting is important.

In your view, what is the importance of a voting public?

BLAIR: Well, in my opinion the importance of voting is choosing who is to be your alderman, who is to be your mayor. Who are the persons who should make decisions for you? Certainly, they ought to be persons who reflect what you believe are the right things for you and will benefit you and those with whom you live. So I think every decision—the school's decision whether to have milk in the school—is a political decision. Every decision that affects your life is a political decision. And teachers have to make that very clear.

So what we're asking children to become is more efficient decision makers?

BLAIR: That's just what you're training them to be anyway. I think that's the goal, the final goal of education, to make them decision makers.

What is your previous knowledge of law-related education?

BLAIR: A guidance counselor may come in and say that we have law-related education in the schools and that it's positive or negative. But I haven't read much about it or really been involved in it. When I came to this district, we had the lowest reading scores in the city, so my concentration has been on the improvement of reading. It would have been counterproductive for me to get involved in all the other curriculum issues at that time. I thought that reading was the one thing that I *had* to make an impact on.

At what level do you think teachers know about law-related education?

BLAIR: Probably the upper-grade teachers.

For the most part, then, elementary teachers have very little knowledge?

BLAIR: Up to seventh and eighth grade.

Why do you think that teachers have not, by and large, been introduced to law-related education?

BLAIR: It just isn't part of the curriculum. At the seventh and eighth grades we begin to introduce the Constitution, so teachers have to include knowledge of the law. But it has not been a part of the curriculum at the primary and intermediate levels, so teachers aren't aware of it. There have not been workshops, as far as I know, that have involved primary and intermediate teachers.

What concepts do you think law-related education should include?

BLAIR: Well, the law and you. How law affects you. Elementary youngsters are interested most in things in their immediate environment and how those things affect them personally. You could write programs around how law affects children and their families, just as the social studies books focus on children and their families. As students get into high school and college, they can move away from that immediacy to what happens in our society and in our world. But at the elementary level the way to approach law is in terms of how it affects children personally.

We've agreed that teachers, especially in elementary schools, don't really have much knowledge of law-related education. How might we go about reaching more teachers?

BLAIR: Much of our curriculum is mandated. Certainly proposals for new programs have to go to the curriculum development level in the Chicago schools and, if necessary, the state level. Since the social studies chairman at the board of education writes materials, then the best approach would be to go to that level and make sure law-related education is included at the primary, intermediate, and upper-grade levels.

To what extent do programs that are mandated from above get incorporated into the actual school program?

BLAIR: Well, many do now because they have a built-in accountability, with check sheets for teachers and so forth. So much is getting in now that may not have been taught before.

Is that happening in social studies in the schools?

BLAIR: No.

Interview with Gloria Emerson

[EDITORS' NOTE: Gloria Emerson is Director of the Native American Materials Development Center, a bilingual curriculum development project funded by the Office of Education. She is a Navajo of the Navajo Reservation of the Ship Rock Agency and has worked in the development of adapted science, social studies, and reading programs for Navajo students. Her most recent project is a high school text for Navajo students, *The Law of the People,* which is being developed through grants from Title IX Ethnic Heritage programs and the National Endowment for the Humanities. Ms. Emerson is a member of the Advisory Commission to the American Bar Association's Special Committee on Youth Education for Citizenship.]

Native American children will spend most of their adult lives in a world somewhat different from the one we live in. What do you feel will be the nature of that future world?

EMERSON: Well, I'm not very optimistic. Judging from past history, I expect Native Americans will continue to be discriminated against. In the past, there was discrimination because of conflicts over land and resources, and because our cultures were so different from the American mainstream. In the future, there will continue to be a grab for minerals, oil, gas, uranium, timber, land, water. This is especially true for those tribes who will fight to control their precious legacies.

I don't expect dramatic improvements for Indian people living in the cities. Poverty cannot be eradicated in a decade, and all the atrocities that breed on poverty will continue.

It might be my day for pessimism, but I believe there will be less consciousness raising, less questioning, more passivity, more acceptance of things as they exist, part of the powerlessness syndrome, or, perhaps, indifference, apathy. This will only change if there are significant changes in the attitudes of teachers and in curricula.

How would you suggest that Native American children best prepare themselves to function in what will probably be a more global experience than we have known before?

EMERSON: Through education, more political lobbying, more efforts to make the Indian Self-Determination Act passed by Congress work in Indian communities, where Indian people can make choices about their destinies. We also must always be suspicious of the white man's form of education, lest we pick up more elements that make societies decay.

It seems very possible that, with appropriate training, minority people in America could be selected for a special mission—to become emissaries from the United States to Third World countries. We possess a special empathy, and I think that we would be trusted and could do a great deal to counteract the "ugly American" image. There are many exciting ways that minority people in America, with authority from Congress

and the president, could interact with others on a global mission, helping make foreign policy decisions and perhaps even making multinational corporate policies more humane. Creating such a global mission involving minority Americans would, I believe, be a great act of patriotism on our part. Perhaps a country like Iran would be more willing to deal with the United States if there were foreign policy makers whom they could trust.

What social and political attitudes do Native American children develop as a result of living in American society that white children do not necessarily develop?

EMERSON: Perhaps a stronger and more zealous protection of language and culture, and recognition of the role of the American Indian in American history. I think that the Native American person is much more conscious of the shaping of American federal policies. The concept of sovereignty of tribes, which predates American government, is a concept that is viable and dynamic in many of the tribal governments. It shapes our political attitudes. I think that another attitude or perception that the Native American has is a closer sense of relationship with nature. That's really the idealistic point of view. I believe that Native Americans were early pioneers in ecology, concerned with preserving the ecosystem and recognizing the delicate relationship between man and nature.

Piaget's stages of cognitive development and Kohlberg's levels of moral development are quite frequently cited by law-related educators as the theoretical basis for making curriculum decisions. Do you feel that those two theories are applicable to the Native American student?

EMERSON: That's difficult to say. There has been very little significant research on the Native American's cognitive development. One cognitive study was done on the Navajo by a young woman from the University of New Mexico, but there are a lot of problems with her research because of the language barrier. Her findings, I believe, are suspect as a result. She had Navajo children perform Piagetian tasks and analyzed their cognitive processes during those tasks. Her findings suggest that there is no real difference between Native Americans and subjects tested in other countries of the world. Many Native American educators are very interested in Piaget and Kohlberg but are not willing to trust their theories fully.

Are there any developmental theories that we might better investigate for use in explaining cognitive and moral development in Native American children?

EMERSON: There is one research study on the Navajo reservation that relates to moral development. It's really too early to state that the study is authoritative. What is interesting about it is that it is being done by Navajo people themselves who are not educated according to Western pedagogical standards. They have been taught some Westernized methods of research, but they have done their own interviews in Navajo, very few of which have been transcribed for the Anglo educator. A lot of the statements that are surfacing are exciting. There are strong indications of a different structure of moral development. It's quite comprehensive and integrated information. I'm not familiar with any other related research.

Is it your sense, your personal belief, that cognitive development probably is parallel with Western cognitive development, but that moral development is not?

EMERSON: That would be a possibility, but I'm not really certain.

Are there differences in the way that American Indian children learn about the society generally that have implications for how they would learn about law, government, and politics?

EMERSON: Yes. In the traditional society, the teaching was done informally, in the intimacy of family and clan relationships. It emphasized familiar relationships so that we were imbued with strict code structures on how to deal with each other, controls, societal protection, etc. Much of this is decaying because of the Westernization process. I have not thought through, fully, how law-related education could be structured in terms of this intimacy within groups and subcultures.

In what way do adult role models, particularly teachers and school administrators, affect the social development of Native American children?

EMERSON: Their influence is very strong. That is not to say that it is positive all the time.

How do the biases of the instructor/teacher affect the learning of the student?

EMERSON: I think their biases and perceptions, their values, their mores, etc., have a very strong effect.

How can these biases be dealt with in teachers who are unaware of them?

EMERSON: Through teacher training. There are all sorts of models for teacher training which have to be examined.

What do you think law-related education will or potentially can do for Native American children?

EMERSON: I hope they will become more aware of the comparative nature of law. Many tribal societies have their own ideas and forms of law. That needs to be understood by both the non-Indian person and the Indian person. I think that is the primary area.

Justice, equality, responsibility, and privacy are among the more common law-related concepts taught in school. How might these terms be interpreted generally by the Native American community?

EMERSON: It's difficult to say. Again, it follows tribal lines. Each tribe has its own definitions of justice, and many of them are imparted through legends, myths, songs, prayer, etc. I think that applies to all the legal concepts you mentioned; I can't say specifically what those would be in each tribe.

How is law perceived by the Native American?

EMERSON: That is the topic of a 500-page text that we have developed called *The Law of the People,* and it's really difficult to put it into a nutshell for you.

Could you give me a few ideas about what is included?

EMERSON: Well, for one thing, the concept of ancient inherent sovereignty pervades all the law according to tribal government. Many tribes have patterned their governments on their own sovereignty concepts. That particular concept is a very dynamic one in the tribes. It is being protected to some extent by the Supreme Court. That is one area that would be of real interest to law-related education.

How do you think the American Indian perceives the justice or legal system as it exists in America?

EMERSON: I don't think I can do justice to that question. I can say that many of the tribal governments have established forms of a judicial system. Many of them have been faced with trying to come up with new definitions of law, codes, etc. Many of them also have a body of ancient, customary law, into which they have incorporated Anglo law. Many of the processes follow Anglo processes, procedures, etc. In some instances, there is a real clash of tribal custom and Anglo law within the reservation judicial system. In some cases there is a nice compatibility between the two forms of law, which makes it easier for the judges to make decisions, but in other cases it is very difficult.

When children are in elementary school, what do you think their relationship with the law is—their understanding of tribal law as well as the American judicial system?

EMERSON: Again, experiences will vary from reservation to urban area or city. I think that children in reservations, where tribal custom still prevails, are confronted with two sets of law—customary tribal law clashing with Anglo law. This hits them especially when they go off the reservation. For example, somebody going off the Navajo reservation, who is used to dealing with a different kind of system, might commit a crime, something that would not be a crime at home, and suddenly find himself in jail.

Will knowledge of law and how it functions in

American society necessarily increase the citizenship competency of Native Americans?

EMERSON: I definitely think so. They should know what due process is, for example. They should know what their rights are when they are arrested. I think such knowledge will arm them with survival information, so that they will not be victimized by malpractice and by people who take advantage of the consumer. Knowledge of the legal system will make Native Americans less apt to be victimized by bad practices in law.

Interview with Alvin Poussaint

[EDITORS' NOTE: Alvin Poussaint is Associate Professor of Psychiatry, Children's Hospital Medical Center, Boston, Massachusetts. He is coauthor with James P. Comer of the book *Black Childcare* and the nationally syndicated newspaper column "Getting Along." Dr. Poussaint is a member of the American Medical Association, a fellow of the American Psychiatric Association, and a member of the Board of Trustees of Operation Push.]

Black children are going to spend most of their adult lives in a world that will change economically, socially, and politically. What do you think will be the nature of that future world?

POUSSAINT: Well, I think the nature of the future world for black children will vary to some extent on the basis of class and educational factors. The world for the lower-income black child is going to be much more closed than the middle-class black child's. I think even an approach to understanding law and education will differ significantly along those lines because of the reality of the immediate future for a lot of poor black kids. There are all of the problems of the inner city—crime, early contacts with the law enforcement system, arrests. What reality provides will be different for a black child living in the inner city and a black child living in the suburbs.

I see continual racial problems for all black socioeconomic groups. So middle-class blacks will also have to understand something about the whole system, including the legal system. Their needs are a bit different from those of lower-income blacks, in that middle-class blacks have to know how to make maximum use of the legal system, how to make their way in it, as well as survival and protective measures. The racial problem and discrimination will not disappear any time soon.

How would you suggest that children prepare themselves to function in this environment?

POUSSAINT: As we look at the inner-city environment, it is not a question of how children prepare themselves but how parents and social institutions prepare the children and who should be involved in any process of education for them. I see the home, the schools, churches, and settlement houses all with a potential role in educating children about society, and specifically about the law and their relationship to it. In addition, we have to think about all the basic skills because this is the foundation for learning other things about the society.

My feeling is that frequently, in certain kinds of environments, kids do things that are, to them, essentially play, but that involve breaking the law. They don't perceive it that way, and they find themselves in trouble. For example, breaking into an abandoned building, even to play, is breaking the law. I don't think kids are always clear that by stealing they may land in jail. It is something that goes on in the neighborhood.

Children are influenced by the quality of any interchange. If they see adults on the street selling hot goods and no one bothers them or arrests them, the children may not be able to perceive that as an illegal activity that could result in punishment. If they get information that police officers are corrupt and take graft or bribes, again the conception of what's legal and illegal is totally confused. Children begin to see the whole society as functioning in that way. Life becomes a question of what you get away with rather than what you do.

The models of the law for many black inner-city children are contradictory and confusing, and those children have a real lack of information about the legal process. Young children have different ways of thinking about what police officers do. On the Wexsler IQ test there is the question, "What is the role of a policeman?" There is supposed to be a correct answer for which you get the highest points. If you take a kid from the inner city who sees police officers mostly beating up on people or involved in the periphery of criminal activity, his or her notion of the police officer's role will be very different from that of a kid who sees a police officer directing traffic for a party that his or her family is giving.

In any community, in the minds of children the police officers represent law, whatever that is. However you get to kids, somehow you're going to have to start from that point. The police officer is the person they see. They don't know what lawyers do. They're not quite sure what judges do. They don't know about bail or probation officers or any of those kinds of things, and, in particular, they don't know what their rights are. Law-related education, for them, means getting to know what their rights are and knowing what they can do and demand in terms of treatment.

How do you think children's perceptions of law and law-enforcement agents can be altered?

POUSSAINT: I think the answer to that depends

on whether you can alter perceptions police officers have about some children. The police department should be involved in institutions and in the community. I don't see why you can't get local district police personnel involved in talking at church meetings, to explain police officers' role and try to get a real sense of community participation. I think this can be done in the schools, too, not in an authoritarian way, but in a participatory way. I think that police precincts should be more open to people visiting, and should set up educational programs, as opposed to giving out lollypops. Perhaps then children would not see police officers as punitive. I think of the New York City program PAL [Police Athletic League], for example, which used to be very effective. I became friends with police officers in East Harlem that way. I think that police officers and others should educate teachers about the law, or put pressure on the system to include law in so-called civics courses. Civics courses help you memorize how many people there are in the House of Representatives and how many senators there are and that there's a mayor, but they don't say anything about the pragmatic things that are important in the everyday lives of these kids.

You see a need, then, for more practical information about law.

POUSSAINT: I don't mean just in terms of crime or crime prevention. People don't know anything about the law in regard to a lot of things they have to do. That's why they're such ready victims of people who want to exploit them for profit. They don't know what the law is about in an active way so that they can assert themselves in the environment. It's much more acceptable in our society, for a variety of reasons, for everyone to be concerned about health. It's vital, so churches and schools sponsor health days. But no one shows the same concern about maybe the next most vital area—the law. It's going to affect people's lives and determine their well-being—whether they will make it in society or will be in jail for 50 years. The public knows that health care is more than just administering to disease. Law is in the same situation. It is more than just getting a case into court.

In his symposium paper, Calvin Miller suggested that perhaps there is a difference in the social and political developmental process between black children and white children. Do you agree?

POUSSAINT: You see, you can't make any racial comparisons in this instance because I don't think social or political development has anything to do with race, except insofar as blacks have been discriminated against and have learned not to trust the system as much as whites. Again there are class elements to consider. Blacks see this system as very unfair if they don't have equal access to lawyers, for example. Half the time they can't get a lawyer. They're also treated more shoddily in social and political institutions because they do not have power. The way people talk to poor people, the common courtesies, is very different from the treatment extended to middle-class people when they deal with the law or the courts. Generally, the race issue affects all aspects of the person in one way or the other. I don't think there is anything intrinsic in race that affects social and political development, but how people prepare their children to adapt to this society may have a differential effect.

How can children be taught to realize that confrontation with authority is not a measure of "manliness"?

POUSSAINT: I think that one of the major psychological reasons for a lot of the killing in the black community is that everyone is trying to save face and protect their self-esteem. It's not the issue that's binding, but the feeling that everyone's messing over them. They'll kill for that, without thinking for a moment that they're saving face now but will have to be in jail for years. One of the things I feel, in relationship to law in its broader sense, is that black children have to learn how to deal with conflicts with other people without jeopardizing themselves. How do you help parents in the black community teach their children to walk away from a fight? A lot of parents just say, "Anyone mess with you, you get them." Who knows? You may make a kid feel guilty if he or she walks away from a fight. So you have to change values concerning conflict resolution. You have to teach the kids how not to become provoked beyond their level of control.

Sometimes teachers don't recognize that they have or display biases that provoke children. Teachers often don't realize that children are looking at the put-down in their body language, and not necessarily listening to what may be a legitimate complaint or important information.

POUSSAINT: It's very difficult to educate people about those kinds of things. In the sixties, and even now, when I'd say, "Well, that's a racist teacher," teachers felt that they were being slandered. Black people are so perceptive about racism that they can tell through body language that someone is racist; they can tell by facial expressions. Those kinds of subtleties are very, very hard to teach to white people because some of them feel that as long as they aren't using the word "nigger," they are not racists. This is why people are beginning to feel that black teachers, even if they were not as academically prepared, understood and didn't subject kids to those kinds of biases.